THE NETHERLANDS INDIES A

VERHANDELINGEN
VAN HET KONINKLIJK INSTITUUT
VOOR TAAL-, LAND- EN VOLKENKUNDE

254

KEES van DIJK

THE NETHERLANDS INDIES AND THE GREAT WAR 1914-1918

KITLV Press
Leiden
2007

Published by:
KITLV Press
Koninklijk Instituut voor Taal-, Land- en Volkenkunde
(Royal Netherlands Institute of Southeast Asian and Caribbean Studies)
P.O. Box 9515
2300 RA Leiden
The Netherlands
website: www.kitlv.nl
e-mail: kitlvpress@kitlv.nl

KITLV is an institute of the Royal Netherlands Academy of Arts and Sciences (KNAW)

Cover: Creja ontwerpen, Leiderdorp

ISBN 978 90 6718 308 6

© 2007 Koninklijk Instituut voor Taal-, Land- en Volkenkunde

No part of this publication may be reproduced or transmitted in any form or by any means, electronic or mechanical, including photocopy, recording, or any information storage and retrieval system, without permission from the copyright owner.

Printed in the Netherlands

Contents

Introduction

I	The colonial race	1
II	A new century, a new elan	19
III	Indiërs	45
IV	The threat from the north	73
V	The Dutch fleet	91
VI	August 1914	125
VII	Guarding strict neutrality	165
VIII	The European community in the Netherlands Indies	201
IX	Loyal subjects	231
X	A native militia	255
XI	The Turkish factor	287
XII	The German menace	317
XIII	The consequences of economic warfare	353
XIV	Adjusting to economic warfare	381
XV	The dangers of war and shipping	403
XVI	Gloomy prospects	427
XVII	Growing domestic unrest	453
XVIII	The end of Dutch international shipping and trade	487

XIX	Rice and sugar	515
XX	Restlessness	543
XXI	November 1918	579
XXII	Peace: Missed opportunities	613

Bibliography	631
General index	647
Index of geographical names	659
Index of personal names	669

Introduction

Topics of books often present themselves by chance. My dissertation about the Darul Islam rebellion in Indonesia was the result of research I had started for a book about Guided Democracy in Indonesia. Similarly, while trying to trace the origins of groups active in the Netherlands Indies in the 1920s which espoused a mixture of Communism and Islam, I became interested in the question of what had been the consequences of World War One for the Netherlands Indies. Initially I thought, as did almost everyone with whom I discussed the subject, that the war had virtually passed the colony by. Gradually I began to realize that this was not true and that the war had deeply affected the domestic political situation, had temporarily fundamentally changed the relationship between motherland and colony, and had had a great effect on the economic performance of the Netherlands Indies.

In this book, these political and economic developments in the Netherlands Indies between 1914 and 1918 and the domestic and international factors which influenced them are traced using Dutch- and Malay-language newspapers published in the Netherlands Indies, contemporary reports and books, and archival material. What I wanted to map out was simple: what developments in the colony were effectuated, stimulated, curbed or halted by a war which was being fought in faraway Europe. The questions I asked myself and the realities of the war fought implied that it was impossible to concentrate on domestic colonial politics. Much of what happened in the Netherlands Indies in those years and many of the perceptions people had about their current situation and future were related to the drastic changes in the economic circumstances war brought about in the Netherlands Indies. A mixture of what appeared to be pressing political, economic, and international issues defined the response of the Colonial Government and of the ordinary Dutch people in the colony to the nationalist movement.

The Great War broke out at a moment when Dutch people in the Netherlands Indies were having to come to terms with a society in which a modern nationalist movement was taking shape. All population groups – Indonesians, Chinese and Indo-Europeans – demanded social, economic and political emancipation and a new 'modern' stream of Islam, which stressed that Muslim society should attain an equal footing with that of the West made its appearance. Dutch people did not have much time to get used to these developments. Though such demands had not been completely absent in earlier years, the impression was that there was a sudden, unprecedented upsurge of nationalist feeling. The contemporary international constellation complicated the Dutch response. Though the international balance of power formed a guarantee of Dutch rule, there was a persistent lingering fear that one day a mightier nation might invade and seize the Netherlands Indies. In the years between 1900 and 1914, the threat posed by such an alien enemy had assumed a more concrete shape in the minds of Dutch people. The advance of Japan as a great power, since 1902 an ally of Great Britain, unnerved the Dutch public. Fear of what Japan might do only intensified during the war, providing some of the more radical Indonesian nationalist leaders with the ammunition to tease the Dutch. There was apprehension that Japan or another of the great powers could use several pretexts to act. One was that the Netherlands Indies was too weak to enforce its neutrality in wartime. Another was that the colonial administration neglected the interests of the Indonesian population. Remembering the demise of Spain as a Colonial Power in Asia, some Dutch people feared that the Netherlands might suffer a similar fate if it did nothing to improve the chances of Indonesian society. And what if the Netherlands were to actually find itself embroiled in the war?

In this context, Indonesians were more than colonial subjects. Their wellbeing or their contentment with their lot were now directly linked with the continuation of Dutch rule in the Archipelago. More was at stake than vague speculations about the spectre of a foreign power punishing the Netherlands for its misrule in the colony. Not ruling out a foreign invasion, and well-aware that the Dutch military position in the Netherlands Indies was weak, shortly after the outbreak of the war the colonial administration developed plans to involve Javanese conscripts in the defence of the colony. Talk of a 'native militia' acted as catalyst: it radicalized but also split the nationalist movement, with those not rejecting conscription outright demanding better education and more political rights. Their contention was that Indonesians would only be willing to participate in the defence of the Netherlands Indies if they were imbued with the feeling that they had a motherland to defend, and – but in the eyes of the Dutch administrators arguing the opposite amounted to sedition – that they would be worse off under another colonial overlord.

The debate was staged against the background of worsening economic conditions, rising prices, and, in the last years of the war especially the prospect of food shortages and an unruly, if not riotous, population. Throughout the war passenger and freight trade was strictly controlled by the Allied Powers. Part of the reason for this was that Great Britain and France, working out their measures in close concert, aimed at achieving the total economic isolation of Germany and Austria-Hungary. But there was yet another reason. British India, the Malay Peninsula and the Straits Settlements were the target of a twin conspiracy, both coordinated by Berlin. There was a Turco-German effort to incite a Holy War and subvert Allied rule in British and French colonies (and with respect to Russia directed at the Muslim population of the Caucasus and Central Asia). In tandem with this, a second plot evolved, an Indo-German conspiracy, in which Germany cooperated with Indian revolutionaries to ignite a revolt in British India. In their conspiracy the Netherlands Indies served as a kind of stepping stone, an intermediate station via which weapons bought in America and the Philippines, money, seditious pamphlets, and agents could be smuggled into India, Burma, and British Malaya. Consequently all ships entering and leaving the territorial waters in the Netherlands Indies were stopped and searched by the British Navy. Although the Dutch colonial authorities were unaware of the exact nature of the Indo-German conspiracy, they and the other Dutch people harboured their own fears. Because Germany was an ally of the Ottoman Empire, Muslims in the Netherlands Indies tended to be pro-German and anti-British, which led to the suspicion that one day Germany might try to seize power in the colony with the help of Muslim Indonesian accomplices.

Even though the prevailing mood in the Netherlands Indies in the first months of the war was one of gloom about the economic prospects, the colonial economy did rather well during the first years of the war. Export markets in Germany and Austria-Hungary fell away and exports to Holland suffered from a British quota system imposed to prevent re-export from Holland to Germany, but alternative markets were found, again in the United States and Japan. Similarly imports from Germany dwindled, but alternative sources of supply were found in the United States and Japan. The redirection of foreign trade coupled with problems encountered in the communications by mail and telegraph also allowed the commercial and estate community in the colony some independence from headquarters in Europe.

The change came in the closing months of 1916 when colonial foreign trade began to feel the consequences of Allied demands for ships and tonnage. Colonial products could no longer be shipped, and the import of rice stagnated. Now faced with the possibility of an acute shortage of food, the Governor General of the Netherlands Indies, J.P. van Limburg Stirum, seriously contemplated using the option of forcing sugar and tobacco estates to reserve one-quarter of their acreage for the production of rice. The situation seemed desperate. The collapse of the export sector was hurting Indonesian producers of colonial products and estates might have to dismiss their workforce, with all the consequent social unrest this would entail. Moderate nationalists seemed to have espoused radicalism, while socialist agitators had fanned discontent in the army and the navy. An increase in the burning of estate crops in the field and in sheds pointed to growing rural unrest. Famine would only lead to even greater instability.

Consultation with the Ministry of the Colonies in The Hague had become almost impossible. The mail and telegraph communications between the Netherlands Indies and Holland either hardly functioned or did not exist at all. Communication between the Ministry and the Governor General by mail could take weeks, if not months, to reach its destination, communication by telegram was also disrupted from time to time. Circumstances had of necessity provided the colony with some political independence. In his efforts to solve the crisis Van Limburg Stirum turned to the leaders of the nationalist movement. In 1918, in what came to be known as the 'November promises', a change in the relationship between motherland and colony and greater political participation of the leaders of the nationalist movement were held out as an inducement. The Colonial Government also pledged itself to look into working conditions and labour relations in the Netherlands Indies and draft labour legislation to protect the economically vulnerable. This all proved to be empty words. After the war had ended, and the spectre of a socialist revolution in Holland and large-scale unrest in the Netherlands Indies which the colonial authorities had considered a realistic possibility had passed, the promises degenerated into mere prospects which were not realized. No greater degree of economic or political independence of the Netherlands Indies was to be granted, while instead of closer cooperation with the nationalist movement a period of repression dawned.

All colonies in Asia experienced the political and economic effects of the war in Europe. Even the educational system had to adjust to changing circumstances. There is an enormous amount of literature about World War One and its warfare at sea and on land but little has been written about the consequences of the war in the colonies, except there when the colonies themselves became battlefields. One exception is Peter Hopkirk's *Like hidden fire; The plot to bring down the British empire,* but in it the emphasis is on 'the plot' itself, not on the political climate in which such a conspiracy could prosper; the rise of a nationalist movement and the upwelling of a new self-confidence in the Islamic community. He also pays scant attention to the impact of the Turco-German conspiracy in the Netherlands Indies. A colourful personality like E.F.E. Douwes Dekker, who played a role in the Indo-German plans, though admittedly a minor one, is not mentioned.

In literature about the Netherlands Indies, World War One is usually mentioned only incidentally; a few figures in a long series of statistical data or a few pages in a detailed study of domestic developments in the colony. The war is there, but at the same time it is absent. It is mentioned, but not elaborated upon. In a good overview of Indonesia's economic history,

Indonesië, by Palte and Tempelman, only one paragraph is devoted to World War One in which its is explained that it halted the robust economic expansion of the Netherlands Indies (which was not true initially). This formed one of the motivations to start this study (Palte and Tempelman 1978:31). In another detailed Dutch study of Indonesia's economic history, Burger's *Sociologisch-economische geschiedenis van Indonesia* (1975), World War One is mentioned only a very few times, and in around half of the cases merely serves as a time-marker, to indicate the end of a period before the war or the beginning of a trend which commenced after 1918.

Aspects of what happened in the Netherlands Indies during the Great War are dealt with by other authors, but part of this literature is in Dutch and Indonesian which makes it inaccessible to people who do not read these languages. The birth of the Indonesian nationalist movement, which also figures prominently in this book has been the subject of many studies. An undoubted classic is Robert Van Niel's *The emergence of the modern Indonesian elite*. It is a political history in which, by definition, the role of international economic developments which influenced domestic politics are mentioned only in passing and the Great War and its consequences are not dealt with as determiners on their own. He mentions that, in the course of the war, 'Dutch colonial relations became highly dependent upon the whims of the British Mistress of the Seas', but goes no further than stating that 'the pressures of war forced the British to curtail and restrict neutral shipping', not mentioning two important other reasons behind the Allied policy to control international sea traffic: the economic isolation of Germany and the role the Netherlands Indies was assigned in the Indo-German plans to subvert British rule in South Asia (Van Niel 1984:10). Similar remarks can be made about another important study: Akira Nagazumi's *Bangkitnya nasionalisme Indonesia* (1989). It concentrates on the formative years of the nationalist organization Boedi Oetomo, while the attention of members of Dutch community and their fears and disappointment with the turn taken by the nationalist movement is actually primarily concerned with another more radical organization, Sarekat Islam.

By concentrating on the Indonesian society, such studies do mean that insufficient light is shed on the discussions among Dutch individuals and policy makers about colonial and international events. Sometimes their opinions give only fleeting insights of the paternalistic view held by many Dutch people in the colony. In other instances, and World War One when the Dutch community in the Netherlands Indies desperately sought answers to what its members perceived as serious foreign and domestic threats, is one of these, they are highly relevant. One of the examples is the plan to recruit Javanese conscripts, which played a crucial role in the Dutch reaction to the nationalist movement and provided Indonesian leaders with a good argument to press for their demands. Van Niel and also Larson (1987), in his well-researched study of political developments in Surakarta between 1912 and 1942, focus on Indonesian opinions about raising a native militia. In yet another classic study about the Indonesian nationalist movement in which some of the characters discussed in this book also play a prominent role, Takashi Shiraishi's analysis (1990) of popular radicalism in Java between 1912 and 1926, the native militia plan is virtually not touched upon. When Shiraishi does mention it, support for a militia tends to be linked to the 'loyalist' nationalist organization, Boedi Oetomo. It does not emphasize that leaders of the more unruly Sarekat Islam also spoke out in favour of the idea and that the clash of opinions within Sarekat Islam was one of the main factors which contributed to the rift in this organization and upsurge in personal animosities among its leaders. Not discussing the reasons why the Dutch colonial administration wanted such an institution, and launched a campaign to drum up popular support for it tends to obscure the fact that the idea was born of the relief, or may be we should write because of the realization, that nationalists could be loyal and royalist colonial subjects and be very concerned with the hardship they were sure people in Holland were suffering after the outbreak of war. Moreover, Indonesian nationalists won extra room to manoeuvre, at the height of the militia campaign and also again later in the war, because the Colonial Government needed their cooperation to keep an alien enemy at bay and to maintain domestic law and order.

Zooming in on the four years of the Great War allows me to encompass within one study domestic and international political and economic developments, providing a broader background against which the militia discussion and other events evolved in the Netherlands Indies. It also illustrates how much politically and economically the Netherlands Indies was part of a 'globalized' world and how much the actual or dreaded consequences of war influenced the courses of action taken by Dutch administrators and by nationalist leaders.

Taking such an approach also means that the unselfish aspects of the so-called Ethical Policy, about which so much has been written and said, shifts into the background. Many of its Dutch proponents certainly were 'ethically' motivated. But taking into account perceived foreign threats during the First World War and in the years leading up to it, and the prospect of economic and political disaster in the later years of the war, allow no other conclusion than that many of the concessions and promises made were the expedient consequence of *Realpolitik*; a fact that was well understood by the leaders of the Indonesian nationalist movement. This topic has been taken up by Jan van Baal. Trying to explain Dutch 'ethical colonialism' and its altruistic aspects, he likens the Colonial State to a modern enterprise in which priority is given to the continuation of the company and not to the interests of its shareholders: profit is first and foremost used to ensure the company's preservation and expansion (Van Baal 1976:101-2). Another metaphor for the Netherlands Indies in the first two decades of the twentieth century is also possible: a company quoted on the stock exchange fearing a hostile take-over bid and to prevent this follows a course of action which nowadays is dubbed 'winning the hearts and the minds of the people', in an effort to remove what are perceived to be the causes of rebellions and terrorist movements.

Following this introduction, Chapters I, II, III, IV and V sketch the pre-war developments which influenced the political climate in the Netherlands Indies at the outbreak of the war: the international colonial race; the growing strength of the emancipation movement especially among Indonesians and Indo-Europeans; the rise of Japan as a contemporary superpower; and the discussions about the defence of the Netherlands Indies. Chapters VI to IX deal with the immediate response to the war by the colonial administration and members of European and non-European communities. Chapters X, XI and XII discuss two topics which throughout the war were perceived to be markers of identity and loyalty: the native militia and the role of Islam. In this section, the consequences of the war for the pilgrimage are explored. The following four chapters concentrate on the effects of the war on the colonial economy. Matters touched upon are the problems encountered in maintaining international trade and in keeping open communications between motherland and colony, a theme that will re-appear in Chapter XVIII. The radicalization of the nationalist movement, the role of leftist agitation, and the growing unrest among soldiers and sailors in the later years are discussed in Chapters XVII, XIX and XX. These chapters also deal with how the inhabitants of the Netherlands Indies reacted to deteriorating economic circumstances in that period and how the Colonial Government coped with the prospect that rice imports might fall away, inevitably leading to food shortages. The response of the colonial administration to a revolutionary fervour which reached an unprecedented intensity in the Netherlands Indies in 1918 and to the total collapse of the colonial economy which seemed irrevocable at that time are the subjects of Chapter XXI. The idea that the Netherlands Indies not only resembled a company quoted at the stock exchange fearing a hostile take-over but also one fighting labour unrest is hopefully conveyed in Chapter XXII in which some post-war developments of items discussed earlier are traced.

Introductions to books are not complete without expressing some gratitude. So many people helped me, it is impossible to thank them all. Two exceptions have to be made: the staff of the KITLV, which as always has been extremely helpful, and Rosemary Robson who edited my English.

CHAPTER I

The colonial race

I have drawn a coloured map of the various colonies which surround our Indian Archipelago, and when one sees those colours, one has to immediately admit that a draughtsman with his wits about him would easily be able to draft a striking picture of the risk we run. To the left, to the west, one descries the form of a snake, these are the English colonies, which lour threateningly from Singapore to Sumatra. On the other side is a gaping maw, the shape of Australia, which applies the Monroe Doctrine to New Guinea, in the vicinity like a hungry wolf Germany also lies in wait for us, and Japan, of which in former days nobody took any notice, turns out to have become a Big Power which can pose a real threat, while the greedy Yankee, who sticks at nothing, has already appeared in our near vicinity.[1]

It was a frightening world that the socialist H.H. van Kol unfolded in Dutch Parliament in November 1904. The message was clear: other powers were encroaching on the Netherlands Indies, and might not stop at its borders.

What was happening had started a number of decades earlier. Since the 1880s anxious Dutchmen had witnessed how mightier nations were carving up the world among themselves, and in doing so establishing themselves in regions which were uncomfortably close to the Netherlands Indies. The political and economic rivalries between the major European states had spread to parts of the world which up to that moment had been left untouched. At first this was mainly a competition between Great Britain, France, Germany, and Russia, though other states such as the United States and Italy then and before also figured in the scenarios constructed by Dutchmen about nations which wanted to establish settlements in the Dutch sphere of influence in Southeast Asia. By the end of the 1890s the two contemporary non-European Powers, the United States of America and Japan, had joined in.

Colonies, protectorates, and spheres of influence represented the status symbol of a modern self-assured nation. Colonial expansion was considered synonymous with the winning of overseas markets and economic growth. Even in Austria-Hungary people were caught up in the fever to occupy what

---

[1] *Handelingen Tweede Kamer* 1904-05:207.

in the European vocabulary of those days was termed 'empty' land: regions inhabited by what were called uncivilized or semi-civilized peoples, governed by their own chiefs and rulers. There was not only the 'scramble for Africa', but also a 'grab' for the Pacific and East Asia, and to a certain extent also for parts of the moribund Ottoman Empire. In some instances European governments had taken the initiative, fearful of the intentions of their competitors on the international scene. In other cases the lead had been taken by enterprising adventurers, overseas settlers, or commercial firms, turning to the motherland to protect their newly acquired wealth and concessions or to block the advance of others.

The 1870s had already brought home to the Dutch how helpless the Netherlands was when other nations were intent on territorial expansion, whether this concerned the Netherlands Indies or Holland in Europe itself. The Franco-Prussian War of 1870 had led to the first major scare in decades, in Holland and in the Netherlands Indies. An occupation of Holland might very well invite other powers to snatch at the Dutch colonial possessions, as had been the case in the days of Napoleon when British rule had replaced that of the Dutch. A few years later the 'Borneo Affair', the acquisition by British merchants of Sabah, sent an even clearer message to the Dutch that the Netherlands was in a very weak position if it were to become embroiled in a conflict over the boundaries of its colonial territory or sphere of influence with stronger adversaries.

Next came the occupation of the eastern part of New Guinea, the object of a mini colonial race between Germany and Great Britain. Initially the new German Empire had no colonial aspirations. The 1860s and 1870s had seen various German citizens who had pleaded for overseas possessions, including regions in the East Indies Archipelago which were not under Dutch control, but their protestations were ignored. Formosa and Indochina had been mentioned as were – in a series of article in the *Norddeutsche Allgemeine Zeitung* in February 1867 – Timor and the Philippines. The Fiji Islands, Samoa and, what did upset the Dutch, Sumatra and New Guinea also did not escape the eye of the champions of a German colonial venture. Such dreams of overseas German settlements were not yet shared by the governments of Prussia and the German Empire. Invariably Prince Otto von Bismarck turned down the plethora of petitions from German businessmen and consuls abroad asking for a German annexation of spots in the Pacific and elsewhere. Had he acceded to such suggestions Germany would have become the master of parts of Fiji and Samoa, taken possession of Hokkaido in Japan, driven the defeated French out of Indochina, and acquired a foothold in China. Germany would also have established itself in Borneo, Sumatra, and the Philippines, and would have administered colonies in Africa and Latin America.[2]

---

[2] For the early German plans, see, for instance, Gründer 1999:54-63.

Within ten years Bismarck changed his mind. In February 1884 he gave orders for the first German protectorate in Southwest Africa to be proclaimed. At various points along the coast the German flag was hoisted with due ceremony and a proclamation declaring the region a protectorate was read out. These ceremonies marked the beginning of an active German *Kolonialpolitik*. In the Pacific one of the spots German attention turned to was New Guinea, of which the western half belonged to the territory of the Netherlands Indies. In August 1884 Bismarck wrote to the Neu-Guinea Compagnie that its exploits would be given the same support and protection from the Empire as those in Southwest Africa (Von Koschitzky 1887-88, II:212). Part of the north of the island was declared a *Schutzgebiet*, a word invented by Bismarck (Gründer 1999:69).

In the Netherlands feelings were ambivalent. There was no ambition to extend the administration over East New Guinea, but the prospect of a new neighbour, which would not be long in announcing itself now that the world had been alerted to the impotence of Holland to prevent a British intrusion in Borneo, bristled with anxieties.[3] British politicians were also not pleased. Australians were adamant that the eastern, non-Dutch portion belonged to their sphere of influence. No other country should settle there. The British government tended to concur with this position, fearing that if it were not to, political complications with the Australian colonies would be the result. In London the British statesmen were not yet very used to having Germany as a new and, as it turned out, determined colonial rival. They had missed the hint that Germany was aspiring to a piece of the colonial cake.

Germany could not be stopped and an agreement over the division of East New Guinea was reached on 17 May 1885. Now, Emperor Wilhelm I could formally put the German territories in New Guinea and the New Britain Archipelago under protection of the Empire. Sovereignty over the region, which had already been christened Kaiser-Wilhelms-Land in March, was delegated to the Neu-Guinea Compagnie. On the same occasion the New Britain Archipelago was renamed the Bismarck Archipelago. At the end of November, New Ireland became Neu-Mecklenburg, New Britain Neu-Pommern and the Duke of York Islands the Neu-Lauenburg group. These names were chosen, the Dutch Ambassador in Berlin informed his government, because the most of the crew of the ships which sailed to these islands originated from these areas.[4]

As a Dutch newspaper had written in 1880 it be 'better to have colonial rivals as distant friends rather than as immediate neighbours'.[5] There was no escaping the fact that in the closing years of the nineteenth century such new

---

[3] *De Indische Gids* 1879, I:778-9.
[4] P.P. van der Hoeven to A.P.C. van Karnebeek, NA, Kol. Openbaar, Vb. 16-12-1885 8.
[5] *Algemeen Handelsblad*, cited in *De Indische Gids* 1880, II-2a:107.

neighbours were already gracing the scene in Borneo and New Guinea. In both cases some Dutch people could still see the bright side. Great Britain taking control in North Borneo would preclude adventurers from other nations, who were said to pose a much greater danger to Dutch rule – and Germans were the chief suspects – being able to colonize parts of North Borneo.[6] A similar argument was advanced with respect to New Guinea. There were some, and the Dutch Consul General in Melbourne was one of them, who argued that the German annexation had strengthened rather than weakened the Dutch position in West New Guinea. Neither Germany nor Great Britain would allow the other to take possession of the Dutch portion of the island.

Had Great Britain become the sole master of East New Guinea sooner or later serious problems might well have arisen to harass the Dutch. People who adduced these arguments thought that the German expansion in Africa and the Pacific had called a halt to what they considered the unbridled colonial appetite of Great Britain, to which the Netherlands Indies or part of it could possibly also fall victim. Such opinions were coupled with a certain malicious pleasure in seeing Germany outmanoeuvring Great Britain. This made it easier to accept the German colonial presence in the eastern portion of New Guinea. The appearance of Germany on the colonial stage had checked English ambitions also in the Netherlands Indies, and would, it was hoped, produce a new colonial balance in which Holland 'tranquil and calm' could still 'have pride of place'.[7]

The ideas among the wider public about the repercussions of the Anglo-German rivalry over the eastern portion of New Guinea resembled those entertained by the Dutch about the colony as a whole. These oscillated between fears that a mightier state, its pride wounded by developments elsewhere in the world, might look to territorial expansion in the Netherlands Indies to refurbish its image counterbalanced by the feeling that international rivalries formed a safeguard for the integrity of the Netherlands Indies.

International rivalry between the powers intensified at the close of the century. Berlin embarked on a new phase in German foreign policy in 1897: the *Weltpolitik*. Kaiser Wilhelm II enthusiastically took the lead in transforming the country from what had been essentially an inland continental power into a nation fired with the ambition to play a leading economic and political role on the international stage. The prestige of Germany and its emperor had to be enhanced. The German Empire should become a World Power and this should entail the acquisition of new overseas possessions. Among the regions upon which Wilhelm had set his eye were Portuguese Timor, the Sulu Archipelago,

---

[6] *De Indische Gids* 1882, I:28.
[7] *Tijdschrift voor Nederlandsch Indië* 1889, II:129.

one or more of the larger Philippine Islands, the Caroline Islands, and Samoa (Gründer 1999:190). Spurred by aspirations engendered by this 'world policy', the acquisition of overseas possessions and the enlargement of the German Navy, modestly launched under Bismarck, were now given a fresh stimulus.

With new rivals arriving on the scene in the late nineteenth century, and suspicious of adventurers trying to carve out their own kingdom, guarding the Dutch position in the East Indies acquired a new urgency. In the previous decades the Netherlands had already slowly but surely added territories to its East Indies possessions, expanding the region over which it exercised only de jure control. In reacting to the changing situation at the end of the nineteenth and the beginning of the twentieth century, the Netherlands contended itself with consolidating its hold over the East Indian Archipelago, bringing under direct control regions it had left untouched up to then. Parts of Sumatra and Celebes, often still virtually unexplored regions which hardly any European had yet traversed, were added to the colonial territory. In some instances a considerable military force had to be mustered. In others, the threat of force sufficed. Other expeditions were sent to the smaller islands of the Archipelago to gain the submission of the local rulers who still occupied an independent position. Underlining its intention naval vessels were ordered to remote corners of the Archipelago to show the rest of the world the extent of Dutch rule.

All this was first and foremost a move to forestall an incursion by other nations. Regions had to be brought under Dutch rule before anybody else could settle there and claim them as theirs. The Dutch administration – in The Hague as well as in Batavia – had no aspirations to look for new territories or exclusive zones of influence elsewhere in Asia. Even in the East Indies Archipelago policy was cautious. An expansion of Dutch rule in the Archipelago was an option not all could agree on. Some, Van Kol was one of them, argued in favour of the opposite tack: a contraction of colonial possessions. The Netherlands should concentrate on Java and Sumatra. Less seriously it was suggested the Netherlands Indies be made the first prize in an international lottery.[8] Upset by the difficulties the colonial army was experiencing in Aceh, the mood was far from bellicose. This seems to have been the prevailing feeling among the general public, though occasionally when military expeditions were being fitted out, the Netherlands went through its own spasms of jingoism. In Holland not many citizens seemed to be, and this greatly irritated their compatriots living in the Netherlands Indies, interested in what happened in the East or understood why military expeditions had to be mounted to conquer native states. The expansion of Dutch authority in

---

[8] *De Locomotief*, 24-8-1900.

the Archipelago was considered to be 'a burden or a motive for flaunting and showing off' (*Duitschers* 1885:42).

Among the Dutch in the Netherlands Indies who were well aware of the costs, financially and otherwise, of armed expeditions to subdue still independent regions in the Archipelago, the mood was also defensive rather than offensive. It was encroachments by others, not an enlargement of the empire, that first sprung to mind. But this, too, was a matter of interpretation. As Borneo had shown, the outside world might have different ideas about how far the exclusive zone of Dutch influence extended. Anxiety arose when European nations – especially Germany and Great Britain but Russia, France and Italy were also hovering on the brink of their consciousness – or their citizens contemplated or actually founded new settlements in regions not under direct Dutch control, but which might be considered outlying parts of the Archipelago.

People were even not completely sure either about the regions where Dutch control was apparently entrenched. Were these safe from outside intrusion? The appetite shown for the acquisition of new territory and the international power game between the larger states in the closing decades of the nineteenth century formed a source of many a bleak speculation about the future of Holland and its colonies. The negotiations between the World Powers of the day and the real or rumoured deals they made to enhance their own position baffled and alarmed many an outsider. In the Netherlands this manifested itself from time to time in the fear that the Netherlands Indies might well be one of the pawns in the international game; the price paid by one government to assure the cooperation of the other.

In 1900 anxiety mounted when an article which received much attention in the Dutch, Netherlands Indies, and British press appeared in a German newspaper. *The Times* even suggested that its contents had been inspired by the German government. The article, written by E. von Hartmann, a German 'philosopher', was a plea for a silent annexation of Holland by Germany. It contained a double threat: in the Far East the Netherlands would be unable to defend its colonial possessions against an attack by a Foreign Power; in Europe, Germany could easily disrupt the Dutch economy by imposing high import duties and by transferring the transit Rhine-trade to the Ems. Von Hartmann suggested that the Netherlands should do what the South German states had done some thirty years earlier. It should sign a defensive and offensive pact with the German Empire and enter into a customs union with it. Were it to comply, the Netherlands could hold on to the Netherlands Indies. As an extra bonus the colony would profit from an influx of German capital and manpower.[9] Von Hartmann was not the only one who contemplated such

---

[9] *De Locomotief*, 22-3-1900, 7-4-1900; *De Indische Gids* 1900, I:352-3.

a strategy. Around the same time the Dutch Envoy in Berlin reported that such views were shared by the architect of the new German Navy, Admiral Alfred von Tirpitz, and other senior German naval and army officers, and by leaders of the German business community (Kuitenbrouwer 1985:143).

An occupation of the Netherlands Indies continued to linger in the minds of those Germans, who aspired to a large colonial empire. The taking over of Portuguese colonies was what first came to mind but, as can be concluded from the words of the German Chancellor, Th. von Bethmann Hollweg in the early 1910s, a seizure of the Belgian Congo or the Netherlands Indies was not beyond the bounds of possibility (Berghahn 1993:132). Germany could well claim the Dutch colony as the price for a reconciliation with Great Britain, or, if France was in the picture, for a return of Alsace-Lorraine.

In the twentieth century, however, the greatest threat perceived by the Dutch did not come from a European Power. It came from Japan, which had made its entrance on the world stage as a major power after its war with China in 1894-1895. The victory of Japan established its reputation, inspiring fears and hopes in the rest of Asia. To Indonesians Japan was proof that an Asian nation could develop and become powerful. The Dutch, and they were not alone in this, began to express concern that Japan was ultimately set on acquiring the Netherlands Indies, or portions of it; an advance south for which Formosa, which Japan had gained from China, was an excellent stepping stone. The Philippines would follow; yet another step of Japan in its ineluctable march south en route to the Netherlands Indies, making for Borneo and Celebes. The speedy build-up of the Japanese fleet in the closing five years of the nineteenth century was observed with awe in the Netherlands Indies and in Holland. Japan's 'formidable Navy' with its 'fighting machines', the 'floating citadels', which had a far greater battle capacity than any of the ships of the Dutch Navy, inspired simultaneous admiration and anxiety.[10]

In the perception of the Dutch, Japanese jingoism now assumed a similar tone as that of the British.[11] When people in the Netherlands Indies spoke about a B.V., a *Buitenlandsche Vijand* (Alien Enemy) more often than not it began to denote Japan, and not a European Power. In the official correspondence between The Hague and Buitenzorg, Japan now also loomed as the potential enemy. Initially Japan was just a scribble in the margin of official records, whereas the text itself still referred to a European enemy. This, for instance, still queried with a question mark, was the case in 1903, when the reduction of the Indies Military Navy was discussed; that is the smaller flotilla ships with a low battle capacity permanently stationed in the East Indian

[10] *De Locomotief*, 6-1-1900, 8-3-1900.
[11] *De Locomotief*, 14-6-1898.

The unarmed idealist and the armed assailant. Onze Vloot propaganda. The Idealist: 'We should see the Indies not as a commercial but as an idealistic possession'. The other: 'Rightly so right. When he stays unsuff.'

waters and employed to impress native coastal states, and not the so-called auxiliary squadron, made up of better-armed, faster warships, which would be expected to grapple with a foreign enemy and, after a posting to the tropics for three years would return to Holland.[12]

The stepping-stone scenario was soon to be rendered outdated by actual developments. It was not Japan that took possession of the Philippines but the United States. It did not take long before the American victory was perceived first and foremost as a blessing. With the Americans entrenched in the Philippines the chance that Japan would turn south and occupy these islands tended to fade into the background, though a Japanese fleet could still always sail around the Archipelago. Spain, hampered by its weak colonial army and Navy, had been replaced by a nation with a strong military force. The Japanese government would think twice before engaging such a formidable foe in war. One of those who voiced this opinion was the correspondent of the Semarang newspaper *De Locomotief* in Japan. At the end of 1899 he concluded that the Japanese expansion into the Pacific was as good as cancelled out by the occupation of the Philippines and Hawai'i by Uncle Sam and that of Samoa and the Carolines by Germany. The Americans had raised a 'natural barrier between Japanese chauvinism and the Netherlands Indies pie'.[13] Later, when it had become plain that the United States planned to hold on to the former Spanish colonies, it initially became associated with all the wrongs of aggressive colonialism; and consequently was also seen as a potential threat to the Netherlands Indies. The United States had shown itself, the editor of *De Locomotief* now exclaimed, a true member of the Anglo-Saxon race, which because of its 'blood- and land-thirsty' nature was causing trouble in every corner of the world: 'While in Africa this has spilled rivers of blood to bring British civilization in the form of cotton fabrics, gin, and beer to the banks of the time-honoured Nile, Washington does not gainsay its descent and origin'. What the United States had done was unprecedented in history. Great Britain, 'even after its most fortunate war, has never been so voracious. Germany's annexation of Alsace and Lorraine is a child's plaything compared to it.' It would be best to have the Pacific Ocean and not just the Mindoro Sea between the United States and the Netherlands Indies.[14] Such voices remained an exception, though Roman Catholics sympathizing with Spain because of religious sentiments lashed out against the 'sharks of big capitalism' (Kuitenbrouwer 1985:147). People to the left of the political spectrum, no disciples of imperialism or the United States for that matter, were equally suspicious of American intentions, and would continue to be so. As far as Van Kol

---

[12] A.G. Ellis, Minister of Navy, to Idenburg, 25-9-1903, NA, Kol. Geheim, Vb. 7-12-1903 F19.
[13] *De Locomotief*, 6-1-1900.
[14] *De Locomotief*, 19-11-1898.

and other socialists were concerned the American danger remained a reality; the more so at those moments when politicians in the United States asserted themselves and warned the rest of the world that the United States fleet would react immediately wherever injustice was done to an American elsewhere in the world.[15] The relief with which others had greeted the American annexation of the Philippines did not last long. Within little more than fifteen years when Washington indicated that it wanted to prepare the Philippines for independence, a Japanese occupation of the Philippines again returned to haunt the Dutch in the Netherlands Indies.

Two international conflicts around the turn of the century influenced Dutch perceptions about the weak position the Netherlands was in even more. One was the Boer War, the other the Russo-Japanese War. In the shaping of Dutch notions about what the strife between the powers of the day might mean for the Netherlands and the Netherlands Indies, the significance of the Boer War cannot be underestimated. The fate of the Boer republics, the South African Republic (the Transvaal) and the Orange Free State, brought home to the Dutch, if this was not already been realized, that 'come what may power takes precedence over right'.[16] A small nation could not expect much benevolence from a mighty neighbour, whose politicians only had their own national interests at heart. Or, as a Member of Parliament phrased this, 'when one speaks of right and justice, they point at bayonet, sabre, rifle, and canon'.[17] In the minds of many Dutch people the Boer War unmasked the raw imperialism of the British Empire. They were convinced that Great Britain had truly become a nation of jingoists, intent on expanding its colonial possessions and spheres of influence.

The Boer War evoked strong commotions in the world. In the Netherlands anti-British public feelings ran even higher than in the rest of the non-British world.[18] The British Ambassador in The Hague, Sir Henry Howard, was to complain in retrospect in November 1900 that the previous year had been 'a trying time in regard to tact and temper'. He was looking forward to some 'rest and quiet'. A few weeks in Paris, London, and Germany away from 'this Boer atmosphere' would do him good.[19] In the Netherlands Indies the Dutch reacted in the same way as their compatriots in the motherland. All over Java and in cities and town in the outer provinces where Dutch civilians and sol-

---

[15] *Handelingen Tweede Kamer* 1904-05:207.
[16] *Handelingen Tweede Kamer* 1914-15:1728.
[17] *Handelingen Tweede Kamer* 1904-05:990.
[18] See Bossenbroek 1996 for a detailed analysis of the the relationship of the Netherlands with South Africa and reactions to the Boer War in the Netherlands.
[19] Howard to Lansdowne, 6-11-1900, PRO FO 800 136.

diers were stationed, fancy fairs, benefit concerts, and *soirées variées* were held to raise money. Collections were organized at races and on many other occasions; even on board the ships in the roadstead of Surabaya. In many places lists on which people who wanted to donate money could put their names circulated.

From time to time, the enthusiasm played tricks. Should there be anybody, though this is almost inconceivable, *De Locomotief* wrote, who supports the British jingo policy, then we suggest he not express his sympathies too loudly; especially not when there are cavalrymen around: 'undoubtedly they will make it clear to him in a somewhat hard-handed way, that in this case, though respecting everybody's personal conviction, their opinions differ from his'.[20] The streets did not become the scene of brawls between British jingoists and the Dutch Boer-lovers. It was in the *sociëteit*, the private club house, the centre of European amusement, where feelings occasionally ran high. In a number of such clubs, of which the Dutch as well as British and other Europeans were members, the playing – or the not-playing – of the Transvaal national anthem occasioned an upsurge of emotion.

Impressed by the reports about the fearless Boers and their initial military successes, young and old also started to impersonate the Boers. In *tableaux vivants* and at fancy-dress balls, popular forms of entertainment in those days among the European community, the Boer soldiers and their fortunes and misfortunes were brought to life. Some really acted it out: riding 'girded with a cartridge-belt, rifle slung over the shoulder, on horseback hill up and hill down', they 'played Boer', dreaming for a moment that they themselves were the brave warriors.[21] Others, who were inspired by reports about the way the Boers fought, prepared for a civilian defence of Java. They asked people who were interested in participating in a volunteer corps to register and to mention whether they owned a mount or not. Such initiatives were inspired by the fear that after Great Britain had been kicked out of South Africa, it might turn on the Netherlands Indies to compensate for the territories lost and recover the self-respect and prestige blemished by the Boer successes. It was feared that an additional reason Great Britain might have to act in such a way was the fierce anti-British sentiment in Holland and the Netherlands Indies. London might want to punish the Netherlands and the Dutch community in the Netherlands Indies for their pro-Boer sympathies. Such a doom scenario was occasioned not only by a bad consciousness. From time to time, such an act of revenge was indeed hinted at in the Straits Settlements.

The Boer War made it clear a government could painstakingly guard

---

[20] *De Locomotief*, 25-10-1899.
[21] *De Locomotief*, 10-2-1900.

neutrality in its official policy, but that it was not equally easy to assure that public opinion did not take sides. In The Hague one overriding concern was not to defy the British. The Netherlands could not afford to irritate London too much. People were convinced that the British as it were were waiting for any act by the Dutch that could be construed as a breach of neutrality to have an excuse to invade Java. It was argued that they would do so without a qualm, offended as they were by anti-British demonstrations and the Anglophobe articles in the Dutch press in Holland and in the Netherlands Indies. Anxiety was all the greater as these were days in which there was much talk of an impending war in Europe and Asia. Some of the Dutch in the Netherlands Indies were convinced that such a war could break out at any moment. A Russo-Japanese confrontation was likely to involve other powers as well, turning it into a *Groote Oorlog*. One Dutch author prophesied in 1900 that this Great War, an 'enormous struggle, which will stir the whole world', was probably only weeks and certainly not more than a few months away (X 1900:293). Another doom scenario was that Britain and France would soon be at war with one another and that for strategic reasons each of the two would attempt to occupy the Netherlands Indies; a circumstance in which people were afraid an officially declared neutrality would count for nothing.

The Boer War was a foretaste of some of the problems the Dutch were to encounter in a far greater magnitude during World War I. The British had no hesitation at all in searching ships sailing under neutral flags which they suspected to carry cargo or reinforcements destined for the enemy. Mail, including that sent to and from the foreign consuls, was also not immune; it could be intercepted, opened, held up, and censored. There was also a great to-do about the nationalization of the Dutch-owned railway company in Transvaal and the dismissal and expulsion of its Dutch personnel, who made up about half of the total number of employees. The company had incurred the wrath of the British among other reasons by having a Boer field-gun serviced and repaired in its workshops (Pakenham 1994:258). The nationalization made a deep impression. In years to come it was frequently cited to demonstrate what the fate of Dutch commerce would be should another nation drive the Netherlands out of the Netherlands Indies. Some of those who were dismissed because of the nationalization found employ with the railways in the Netherlands Indies. There appointment contributed to what was perhaps the first industrial strike by Indo-Europeans in the Netherlands Indies. The Indo-European employees were piqued by the fact that the Transvaal immigrants were given the better jobs, blocking their own prospects of promotion. Relations between the two groups were not improved by the habit of the South Africans of calling the Indo-Europeans 'brown Kaffirs' (Bosma 1995:93).

The Boer War also provided unequivocal evidence that Great Britain was the undisputed master of telegraph communication. Around 1900 communication techniques had reached the stage at which a wireless system was just developing. The submarine telegraph lines spanning the world were mostly British-owned. Great Britain could deny others access to the telegraph cables, or at the very least control the nature of the messages sent. At the height of the Boer War, London reserved the cable between Aden and Zanzibar for official communications, interfering with commercial intercourse between Portuguese East Africa and Germany among other disruptions.[22] Were the lines still open Great Britain could, as it did during the Boer War, demand that the telegrams were not to be sent in a language unintelligible to the British or in code. Control of the cable also meant control of the news about the war. Such experiences made people in Holland and the Netherlands Indies aware of how vulnerable the lines of communication between motherland and colony were. For private citizens and government officials alike it suddenly became a matter of great urgency to look for a telegraph connection that was not in British hands. This became a subject of a plethora of letters to the editor and articles in magazines and newspapers full of concern about the situation. So serious was the matter deemed, that suggestions were made for a public collection of money to finance an independent Dutch cable line. A 'Committee for the Promotion of Telegraphic Communication between the Netherlands Indies and the Motherland via Lines Independent of England' was also founded. Its secretary was J.J. le Roy, a lecturer at the Koninklijke Militaire Academie (KMA, Royal Military Academy). The government, the Dutch Minister of the Colonies well to the fore, turned to the Danes, the Germans, the French, and the Americans in order to give the Netherlands its lines independent of Great Britain.

As long as such a line did not exist, other precautions had to be taken to warn the Governor General in advance of the likelihood of war with Great Britain. At the end of 1900 a code was developed to be used even before a war had been declared, should important messages be no longer forwarded by wire from Singapore to the Netherlands Indies in a conflict with Great Britain. It was decided that telegrams alerting the colonial administration to an imminent war with Great Britain should be of such a nature that even when relations had deteriorated, they would still be allowed to be forwarded via the cable. The best way to accomplish this was to have the messages look as innocent as possible. 'Mother seriously ill, Corry' meant that strained relations with Great Britain were feared. From 'Mother worse', 'Mother precarious', and 'Mother hopeless' the messages reached their final stage in 'Mother dead'. Of course, 'Mother recovering' was among the possibilities. The following year codes were added for Germany (Willy), France (Marianne), the United States (Anna), Japan (Clara), and Portugal (Mina). Initially the telegrams had to be

---

[22] *De Locomotief*, 25-11-1899.

addressed to 'Paulus – Buitenzorg' or 'Mrs Van de Vijver – Batavia'. As the recipients of the message were real persons ('Mr so and so not' meant that the address could no longer be used), the addresses had to be altered a number of times; the final occasion being in August 1914.[23]

The authorities were successful in finding a partner for a non-British cable connection, though there had been some beads of sweat on brows when it leaked out in Java that The Hague was conducting negotiations with Berlin. Complication and 'counter-intrigues' were expected from the British side. It also took some effort to explain to 'Prussian' officials that 'loose-tongued' minor colonial civil servants (a complaint voiced more often by outsiders about the colonial administration) had been responsible for the leak.[24] An agreement to establish the Deutsch-Niederländische Telegraphengesellschaft was reached between the German and Dutch governments in July 1901. The company had a German and a Dutch director. The Dutch government welcomed the contract with great relief. It showed its gratitude by decorating the chairman of the board of Directors of the German counterpart, the Norddeutsche-Seekabelwerke. It took three years before the German-Dutch Telegraph Company became a fact. On 8 January 1905, the cable-vessel, the *Von Podbielski*, bought by the Dutch government left Nordenham to sail to the Netherlands Indies to lay the first stretch of the cable connection between Manado in North Celebes and Yap, from whence an onward connection led to Shanghai and Guam.

The theatre of war drew closer to the Netherlands Indies on 8 February 1904, when a surprise Japanese torpedo attack on the Russian Pacific fleet at Port Arthur signalled the outbreak of the Russo-Japanese War. The most daunting prospect of the conflict for the Dutch was that the Netherlands could well be implicated. Russian warships on their way from Europe to North Asia almost certainly would have to traverse the East Indies Archipelago, and no steam-propelled warship, however crammed the holds and decks were with coal, could sail the entire distance between Europe and North Asia without bunkering a number of times. Great Britain controlled its own network of coaling-stations stretching into the north of East Asia and was well provided for; France, with its Indochinese colony, maybe might, except when its ships were confronted with adverse weather conditions, be self sufficient in this respect; but Russia and Germany most definitely were not.

A novel argument for the active pursuit of a policy of colonial expansion presented itself. Foreign warships did not necessarily need a coaling-station

---

[23] Van Heutsz to Fock, 9-2-1906, Fock to Van Heutsz, 26-3-1906, NA, Kol. Geheim, Vb. 26-3-1906 V7.
[24] Dutch Envoy in Berlin to De Beaufort, 19-1-1901, NA, Kol. Geheim, Vb. 22-1-1901 V1.

in the Archipelago. A sheltered spot where coal could be transshipped from colliers and repairs could be made would do. It was also not out of the question that a Russian fleet, or for that matter a German one, would demand coal stockpiled in the harbours of the Netherlands Indies in excess of the amount allowed by international law. Under threat of force such a fleet might even try to 'lease' a coaling-station, copying the tactics the great powers had deployed in China, or alternatively occupy an island not yet brought under de facto Dutch control, not recognizing Dutch territorial rights, and the Dutch government was well aware of this ever since Berlin and London had disputed Spanish rule over the Sulu Archipelago in the early 1880s. Many of the islands which presented suitable conditions for bunkering were not well guarded by Dutch troops or ships, if indeed they already belonged to that part of the Archipelago where the Dutch exercised de facto control. In January 1905 when the Russian Baltic fleet was expected to arrive within a couple of weeks, the Governor General ordered frequent visits to islands west of Sumatra, where if resources stretched to it a military detachment should also be stationed. He feared that the Baltic fleet might anchor there using the pretext that the islands were not yet occupied by any European Power. The order was not so easily executed. As the Commander of the Navy pointed out, the island and bays in the region were many; not to speak of the other portions of the Archipelago through which the Baltic fleet, choosing a different route, could sail.

The Russo-Japanese War brought home a number of points: how difficult it was with a small fleet to guard the whole Archipelago against transgressions of neutrality; that foreign warships and other ships directed to Asia to provide them with coal and provisions could easily remain undetected (the Dutch fleet in the Netherlands Indies even completely missed the Russian Baltic fleet on its way from Europe to the Far East even when it sailed the Straits of Malacca); and how difficult it was to draft instructions to maintain neutrality which satisfied both sides in the war and covered all foreseen and unforeseen possibilities in allowing a belligerent fleet to bunker in territorial waters. Throughout the Russo-Japanese War, Batavia and The Hague spent a large amount of time in developing guidelines on how to prevent a Russian fleet fighting a naval battle with 'Dutch coal'. They and the general public worried about implications of providing Russian warships with coal, or limiting the amount of fuel with which they could be supplied according to international law. A Russian squadron might try to seize extra coal by force. It also could not be excluded that Japanese warships would try to attack Russian warships bunkering in the Netherlands Indies. Finding the right solution was a fiendishly difficult task and absorbed great swathes of attention during the Russo-Japanese War, leading to an almost endless stream of official correspondence, mutual irritation, and, as the stakes were high, on occasion to intense rows between Batavia and The Hague and in The Hague between the ministries most directly involved:

those of Foreign Affairs, of the Colonies, and of the Navy. The matter was the more serious because the Russo-Japanese War made The Hague for the first time the subject of intense bullying by one of the belligerents in an armed conflict. The Japanese government was intent on preventing the bunkering of the Russian warships on their voyage round the Cape of Good Hope to Asia and made no secret of this. On 5 November, the Japanese Ambassador called on the Dutch Minister of Foreign Affairs and submitted a strongly worded caution. It said that the Japanese government was

> convinced that if a neutral Power should permit the Baltic fleet, on its expedition, to enter into her territorial waters and to take in coal freely and without restriction at a spot where there is no danger of attack from the enemy [...] such territorial waters of a neutral Power would in effect, be converted into a base of hostile operations for the belligerent fleet, and her neutrality is seriously violated.[25]

This was followed on 21 December 1904 by a note which stated the Japanese position in no uncertain terms. It was set out unequivocally that for a Russian fleet, proceeding to the Far East, it was

> essential to the forward movement of the expedition and the development of its full fighting strength, that its scattered units should reunite at some point in the vicinity of [the] actual seat of war, in order to recoal, repair, and make final preparations and arrangements before advancing to meet the naval force of Japan.

Were the commander of the Baltic fleet to choose to use the territorial waters of the Netherlands Indies for these purposes, these would become 'veritable bases of warlike operations against Japan'. It was warned that, in that case, the Japanese government was left with 'no other course than to preserve to themselves the right to take, within the ports or waters so used, such measures of self-protection as the situation may demand'.[26] All ended well. In June 1905 the Minister of Foreign Affairs, R. Melvil van Lynden, informed Queen Wilhelmina that the previous evening at a dinner with the Japanese Ambassador, one of the guests, Prince Arisugawa, had made a 'lengthy communication'. Its purport was that the Japanese Emperor had instructed Prince Arisugawa to convey that he and his government had 'particularly appreciated the manner in which the Government of Your Majesty had guarded the upholding of neutrality, and were very grateful for the effective regulations and firm measures taken with regard to this by Your Majesty's Government'.[27]

Luckily for the Netherlands there were special conditions in the Netherlands

[25] Note Japanese government, 5-11-1901, NA, Kol. Geheim, Vb. 26-11-1904 E25.
[26] Mitsuhashi to Melvil van Lynden, 21-12-1904, NA, Kol. Geheim, Vb. 27-12-1904 X27.
[27] Melvil van Lynden to Wilhelmina, 21-6-1905, NA, Kol. Geheim, Vb. 1-8-1905 L18.

Indies which mitigated the threat of a foreign occupation or attack. For strategic or economic reasons the great powers might well cast an envious eye on the Netherlands Indies; for the same reasons they might leave it alone, aware that their rivals would never allow them to occupy the whole or part of the Archipelago and could react to any such move by employing military force.

The most important of these special features was the international nature of the Netherlands Indies. In 1872, the last barriers to an open-door policy had disappeared. Preferential import and export duties were abolished. The Netherlands Indies opened up to German, Austro-Hungarian, French, British and other foreign capital invested mostly in the export industries, banking, railways, inter-insular cargo shipping, gas and electricity, and in the plantation industry (Burger 1975, II:85). The open-door policy removed one of the excuses Foreign Powers could have used to mobilize their military might against weaker nations. Enforcing or maintaining an open door had been the cornerstone of British-China policy and within a few years was the public reason given by the Germans in their ostensible support for Moroccan independence, opposing an expansion of French influence. A liberal trade policy, a Dutch Minister of the Colonies had stressed in 1870, was the best defence against a foreign assault.[28]

The diverse origins of foreign investment were reflected in the composition of the European population in the Netherlands Indies. The Dutch formed the greater part, but people gathered there from all over Europe – most numerous among them the Germans, followed by Belgians, Britons, Swiss, and the French – remained clearly distinguishable. Their share was such that in official parlance the word Dutchman was ever hardly used, preference being given to the term European, which also, formally but not in actual social daily life, included the Indo-European population. Not only did foreign nationals come along with foreign money; for a long time the Dutch at home in Holland had not been very interested in a life in the East. Many employees on the plantations, missionaries, explorers and scholars originated from other European countries.

The same could be said about the colonial army. In 1900 still almost one-fifth of all Europeans serving in the army of the Netherlands Indies, some 3,000 soldiers, were foreigners. In 1904, at the time of the Russo-Japanese War, the number of foreign soldiers had dropped to 2,400, but proportionally their share had remained the same. At that time, fearing the consequences of the war for the Netherlands Indies, measures to facilitate the recruitment of foreigners for the colonial army were even deemed necessary.[29] Only in the years thereafter did the colonial army become less dependent on non-Dutch

---

[28] *De Locomotief*, 7-10-1870.
[29] Idenburg to J.W. Bergansius, 7-3-1904, NA, Kol. Geheim, Vb. 7-3-1904 D6.

soldiers. In 1916 their number had dropped to less than 800, or about 10 per cent of the European soldiers; a majority of them – 625 – being of German origin.[30]

Except for the common soldiers and the non-commissioned officers who were excluded from them, almost all of the European and American foreigners in the Indies had to live within the narrow confines of small European communities; its members depending on each other not only for business contacts but also for diversion and entertainment. This was an extra reason for caution in time of war, when intense feelings of nationalism which ineluctably accompanied the confrontations between the powers in the wider world were aroused. In view of the diverse composition of the European population, as early as 1870 not only were the usual proclamations with respect to neutrality issued in the Netherlands Indies. Explicitly referring to the many foreigners living in the Netherlands Indies the colonial administration made special appeals to the newspapers to maintain a strict neutrality in their reporting.

International competition came to the rescue of the Dutch. The Netherlands Indies was too rich a prize and the investments there of each of the main contestants in the European struggle for power, especially Germany and Great Britain (the French economic and financial interests were much less), too valuable for one of them to allow the other to invade and take possession of the Netherlands Indies. It was a comforting thought, cherished also by the Dutch government, that for economic and strategic reasons none of the powerful nations would allow a rival to gain control of the Netherlands Indies. As World War I drew closer, foreign economic investments by the countries of the Triple Alliance (Germany, Austria-Hungary and Italy) as well as of the Triple Entente (Great Britain, France and Russia) over the years had become of such importance, that the Dutch Minister of the Colonies, Th.B. Pleyte, hoped that should a European war break out this would safeguard the colony from an occupation by one of the belligerents. The stakes had become too high, and economic investments from contesting European Powers too great to let a rival power take control of the Netherlands Indies. An unequivocal open-door policy, Pleyte, stressed in Parliament as late as 1918, was one of the prerequisites which would allow the Netherlands to remain in the possession of its colony. It would, others argued, also be a reason to have the European Powers oppose a Japanese occupation of the Netherlands Indies (Teitler 1988:293).

[30] Zwitzer and Heshusius 1977:12-3; *Koloniaal verslag* 1901 and 1905: Bijlage A Tabel 3.

CHAPTER II

A new century, a new elan

In 1898 the sudden demise of Spain as a Colonial Power and the parallel that could be drawn with the position of the Netherlands as a weak European state with a large Asian colony does not appear to have worried many at the time. There was a feeling that what had happened to Spain could never happen to the Netherlands. Spain had mismanaged its colonies and had been confronted with wide-spread popular unrest. This was what had brought about the downfall; not the war with the United States. It was argued with a certain degree of persistence that the situation in the Netherlands Indies was different. In Java, remaining silent about the difficulties the Dutch experienced in other quarters of the Archipelago, a military observer had remarked at the time, 'we can trust the native population and their heads to be so devoted to us that even in times of war there is no fear of danger'.[1] Though his observation did not exactly ring true and not everybody was so confident about the pro-Dutch sentiments of the Javanese, 'Remember the Philippines' became a slogan of the critics of colonial policy warning Batavia and The Hague not to alienate the local population by their policies and instructions. People's loyalty, their contentment with colonial rule, was the key element to assure the continued presence of Holland in the Netherlands Indies, at least of equal importance to the strength of its colonial army and Navy, which had the task of repelling a foreign invasion (Egbert 1902:8; Visser 1913:6). It would also pre-empt any invasion of the colony under the pretext that the Dutch had ceded their right to rule because they had neglected the interests of the population.

To contemporary politicians and statesmen around the turn of the century, such reflections may well have been an incentive equally important as moral considerations to embark upon what is dubbed the Ethical Policy, defined by E.B. Locher-Scholten (1981:112, 176-218) as 'an active pursuit of the development of land and people of the Indian Archipelago, under Dutch rule and according to a Western model'. They stressed that the best way to assure the loyalty of the population was by demonstrating that Dutch rule was benevolent, and that the Dutch had the interests of the people at heart. It was to

---

[1] *De Locomotief*, 3-10-1898; Bootsma 1986:122, note 18.

Modern articles of clothing as trade mark of a Chinese firm in Kudus selling European and 'native cigars and cigarettes' (*Javasche Courant* 1914, Trade mark 7075).

remain Dutch government policy in the decades to come, resulting in an attitude towards Indonesian nationalism which many laymen thought was too lenient. In the Dutch parliament in February 1918 Th.B. Pleyte explained that one of the prerequisites for holding on to the Netherlands Indies as a Dutch colonial possession was an 'unselfish domestic policy' preparing the population for self-government.[2] This attitude was given substance by expanding educational opportunities, by launching various projects to improve welfare and prosperity, and by allowing a modest degree of political emancipation and a certain say in administering local affairs; though with respect to the last

---

2 *Handelingen Tweede Kamer* 1917-18:1502.

and the local Coucils which were instituted after 1905, it was in the first place the Europeans and the well-to-do of the other population groups who were allowed a say in the governing of local affairs.

Around 1900 life in the colony was changing drastically. These were years which must have been looked upon by many Dutch people in the Netherlands Indies as a period in which the old familiar society gave way to a new one. In contrast, up to the turn of the century when there had been almost no political activity at all, within a couple of years it seemed that throughout the length and the breadth of the colony people were demanding a radical overhaul of colonial society. These upheavals were not easy to ignore. The thoughts that were expressed, the demands that were made, the many meetings that were held, not to mention the turmoil and enthusiasm that was created by newly founded organizations left little doubt that something new was emerging. No population group was immune to changes. In 1913 the Dutch *Resident* of Surabaya noted that on all sides 'among the Natives, even among the Europeans and the Foreign Orientals a feeling of anxiety reigns'.[3] In the same year the Adviser for Native Affairs, G.A.J. Hazeu, stressed that because of the rapid modernization, the colonial administration had to come to terms with the fact that those who not so long before had been merely called the 'minor civil servants' or the 'small people' had started to realize they were human beings too and were demanding a decent treatment.[4] Everything happened so fast that for the Dutch members of the corps – and many of their compatriots – it was difficult to adjust to changing circumstances. Or, as Hazeu, commenting once more on internal developments, remarked in August 1916:

> They may find it difficult but the civil servants must familiarize themselves with the undeniable fact that within an unbelievably short span of time, the whole intellectual and political atmosphere here in this country has changed considerably; no harsh decisions to banish people will magically make the good(?), quiet days of the past return, nor can they stem the rising tide of modern political life, and all that pertains to it.[5]

By the second decade of the century, progress and development had become popular catchwords among the non-European inhabitants of the colony. *Kemadjoean* was what counted. It would bring a modern world in which these population groups would no longer be treated by the Europeans as inferior beings. Education, information, and political strife were the ways to achieve this aim. Periodicals were launched for the purpose of providing their readers with useful information. *Soeloeh Kemadjoean*, the Torch of Progress, or even

---

[3] *Sarekat Islam* 1975:296.
[4] G.A.J. Hazeu to A.W.F. Idenburg, 14-2-1913 (*Bescheiden 'Indische Partij'* 1913).
[5] Report Hazeu, 21-8-1916, NA, Kol. Openbaar, Vb. 22-11-1916 6.

more appropriately Progress Information, a periodical started in October 1913 with Oemar Said Tjokroaminoto as one of its editors, captured the spirit of this trend. Many other examples, including special magazines for women, can be added to the list.

Lying at the basis of the restlessness which characterized the first and the second decade of the twentieth century were racial distinctions. As in other colonies race was the principal criterion by which to set people apart. The white Europeans were the masters and claimed special rights and special treatment. According to the definition decreed in 1906, Europeans (the status of United States as a Colonial Power did not change usage) consisted of Dutch people and citizens from other European states and their legal or – in the case of a concubinage – legally recognized offspring. Others could apply for a status equal to that of Europeans. This was no trifling matter. An equal status with all the benefits that accrued to it adhered to a person even after death. As late as 1914, the reburial was being contemplated of a person from Ambon who had come down in the world and, distressed by financial misfortune, had lost his mind. A policy officer vaguely recollected that the poor man had been equalized during his life and a search for papers to prove this was begun. It was an important matter. If the hunch were true, the body had to be exhumed and reburied in a European cemetery.[6] The rest of the population was divided into two categories: Natives, the indigenous population of the Netherlands Indies, and Foreign Orientals, that is Arabs and other Asians, including the Chinese, but not the Japanese. The latter were legally Europeans. A ticklish problem was how Turkish citizens should be treated. They were Foreign Orientals, but the law was flawed by an embarrassing loophole. What should be done with Turks who claimed that they had been born on European soil, in the European part of the Ottoman Empire, for instance in Albania, from a Dutch perspective hardly a cradle of civilization?

A different set of legal rules for each of these three groups was in force. Penalties also differed. A European could be sentenced to imprisonment or to a term in a house of correction. For the same crime an Indonesian would be condemned to convict labour, either shackled or not. The inescapable impression created – not only by the different circumstances in which Europeans and non-Europeans had to serve their sentence, but also by the variations in these sentences pronounced by the judges – was that the law-giver was more lenient towards Europeans than towards the rest of the population. Such an assessment was certainly not unwarranted. In 1914, when the highest legal civil servant in the Netherlands Indies, the Director of the Department of Justice, had to contest the view that legislation was more severe towards Indonesians,

---

[6] *De Expres*, 10-4-1914.

he could only counter with some trivial exceptions. Europeans were, he wrote, threatened with more severe sentences in the bicycle ordinance for Madura and Rembang of 1911, the regulation for the ceding for public use of roads, squares, and the like in Semarang, the coconut decree of Padang, and the discipline and cleanliness decree of Batavia.[7]

From time to time senior Dutch colonial civil servants also complained that for similar crimes, and what they often had in mind was the publication of seditious or abusive press articles, Europeans were given a lighter penalty than Indonesians or were acquitted whereas Indonesians were punished. A moral aspect tinged the concern of the colonial authorities raised by such court rulings, but it had a practical side as well. Precisely the wish to avoid any impression of racial justice – though this was a term which infuriated the Dutch authorities when used in public – sometimes made the Attorney-General hesitant to bring charges against Indonesian journalists, leading to trials which invariably attracted plenty of public attention, knowing that a conviction only strengthened the idea that Indonesians were being punished for something for which Europeans might go scot-free.

In daily life the legal differences were accentuated by codes of dress. For centuries Dutchmen had reserved themselves the right to wear European attire. Since the early days of the Vereenigde Oostindische Compagnie (VOC, Dutch East Indies Company) it had been decreed that each population group should don its own national costume. By law it was forbidden to put on the apparel of another race or ethnic group. Javanese had to dress as Javanese, Bugis as Bugis, Arabs as Arabs, Chinese as Chinese and so on. Undisputedly this was often what the people concerned wanted, but breaches of the rule, except in specific instances, were unthinkable. Exceptions were granted only to members of the indigenous ruling elites and to Christians. Their assumption of Dutch apparel or items thereof was a clear sign that they had bridged some of the distance which set them apart from the foreign overlord.

Around 1900 the dress codes began to be enforced less vigorously, but had not yet been abandoned (see Van Dijk 1997). As late as 1904 the head of the Chinese community in Semarang requested and was granted permission for his wife to wear European 'national costume' in public.[8] He did this when already for a number of years there had been reports from various parts of the Archipelago that non-Europeans had begun to adopt Dutch dress and habits. One of the culprits for the change in outward appearance was the bicycle. To prevent Indonesians in Surabaya from being afflicted by sore feet, the Dutch *Resident* of that city generously allowed them to wear shoes when

---

[7] Report of the Director of Justice, 17-2-1914, NA, Kol. Openbaar, Vb. 15-6-1914 19.
[8] *De Locomotief,* 12-1-1904.

cycling. Significantly the Javanese Regent was opposed to this. He protested that the wearing of shoes by ordinary people was a violation of custom, and detrimental to the prestige of Europeans and that of Javanese civil servants.[9] Besides putting on shoes, people began to wear hats, long trousers, shirts, and ties, plus other items of cloth associated with the West. They also demanded the right to sit on chairs and no longer to have to squat on the floor when in the presence of Dutch or their own authorities, and had the nerve to address Dutch people in Dutch and not in the vernacular language, a serious breach of etiquette leading to reprimands and punishment.

What was frequently to be described by members of the Dutch civil service and of the indigenous elite in the decades to come as breaches of polite behaviour by Javanese and other people striving for emancipation had reared its head. On a less impertinent level, young Indonesians began to develop a predilection for Western music and dances. They played marches and other melodies, and danced waltzes and polkas at their meetings, a phenomenon still unheard of in the very first years of the twentieth century. They did so at a moment when a conservative public in Europe still frowned upon the tango, 'imitating those ridiculous twistings and contortions of the body of negresses and barbarians', as the Pope chose to describe the dance in 1914.[10]

The setting in which this all took place was also new. The first decade of the twentieth century saw the completion of Dutch territorial expansion. Areas which up to then had escaped colonial rule now came under Dutch control, giving the territory of the Netherlands Indies its final shape. The hesitancy displayed in earlier decades on the part of the Dutch government gave way to a deliberate policy of territorial aggrandizement. Fear that other Colonial Powers would gain a foothold in the Archipelago as they had done in Borneo and New Guinea was the major reason for such a step. National prestige was an equally important factor. The Colonial Powers felt they had a special task to perform. Expansion was proof of the supremacy of the West, and this was also in concert with prevailing moral standards. It was imperative that regions be brought under control so that the local population might share some of the blessings of civilization and to combat what was denounced as the abuses of despotic indigenous rule and non-Christian religions. Colonial aggrandizement was eventually presented by European politicians in the guise of a sacred mission.

The Netherlands Indies was not spared the Western convulsion to export the blessings of civilization. In 1904 a parliamentary commission concluded that '[t]hough the expansion of our authority should be eschewed as much

[9] *De Locomotief,* 9-6-1898, 19-11-1898.
[10] *De Expres,* 4-3-1914.

as possible circumstances often leave no choice but to go ahead, because the Netherlands cannot shirk the fulfilment of the moral obligations it has taken on itself as a colonial Power with respect to the native population'.[11] Feelings among Dutch politicians about what Locher-Scholten (1981:194-9) has dubbed 'ethical imperialism' were perhaps even stronger than elsewhere in Europe, as they were reinforced by a sensitivity to international public opinion about how the colony was run, and by the fact that in international politics the Netherlands was pretty insignificant. What Holland lacked in political power, it could compensate for in the moral field.

Opposition to colonial expansion came mainly from the left; from Van Kol and P.J. Troelstra and their political friends in the *Sociaal-Democratische Arbeiders Partij* (SDAP, Social Democratic Labour Party). Proponents of aggrandizement were not impressed by their critical observation that the reasons presented to justify Dutch military expeditions in the Archipelago could be used equally well by Germany to rationalize an occupation the Netherlands, were Berlin for reasons of national defence to deem such a step necessary. Their counterargument was that the two cases were completely different. Dutch expansion occurred within a clearly defined region which formed a political and ethnological unity, of which the boundaries were internationally accepted.[12] Likewise the argument that the British imperialist exploits were generally deplored in Holland, and that the subjugation of new territories put the Netherlands in the same class, did nothing to deter the advocates of Dutch expansion. By a show of force or at least wielding the threat of it, all remaining independent or semi-independent regions were brought under Dutch rule. When there were old contracts acknowledging Dutch sovereignty, these were exchanged for new ones which made the rulers who signed them, as was occasionally said by opponents of Dutch expansion, 'papier-maché monarchs'.[13]

The expansion of Dutch rule, geographically and administratively, and the concurrent economic penetration contributed to a change in the character of the Dutch community. For centuries a small group, around 1900 it began to grow rapidly. Among the new arrivals were many women, which was another new trend. In the past, it had been almost exclusively men who had left Europe for the Archipelago, now women joined them. Between 1900 and 1930 the population of females born in Europe but living in the Netherlands Indies grew from 4,000 to 26,000 (Van der Veur 2006:88). This influx of women inexorably affected the composition and outlook of the European elite. It became less Indonesian and much more Dutch. The presence of Dutch women meant it was no longer necessary and indeed even made it reprehensible, for

[11] *Handelingen Eerste Kamer* 1904-05:101.
[12] *Handelingen Tweede Kamer* 1904-05:281-2.
[13] *De Expres*, 13-3-1914.

Dutch males to take a woman from the local society as wife or concubine. Such women, who had given the European society a particularly local colour, were eventually denied access to the upper strata of colonial society.

The role of Dutch women as custodians of European manners was only partly responsible for the change in outlook of the colonial elite. The men now arriving from Holland to fill the growing number of jobs which required a certain level of education and special skills also contributed to the trend. Growing numbers in themselves already made it easier to preserve Dutch culture in the tropics. This trend was facilitated even more by the new type of person who now came to the colony. Engineers, technicians, and administrators made their appearance in increasing numbers. The nature of the Dutch civil service corps inevitably changed. Common people began to predominate. In 1913 a newspaper in Surabaya ventured the opinion that this was the reason why, in contrast to in the East Coast of Sumatra, an estate region, joining the civil militia was not popular in Java. Planters enjoyed drilling and shooting. They found it fun and socially agreeable, looking forward to the beer they would consume afterwards. In the larger cities in Java many of the Dutch community were office people who were not particularly fond of physical exercise.[14] This assessment did not ring completely true, (and to the beer, gin should be added), but it still serves to illustrate the changes that were taking place: a bureaucratization of society and the higher educational background of the Dutchmen who were coming to the colony. One of the consequences of the new situation was that the gap between the people and the Dutch civil servants had widened. In the same year a senior adviser to the Governor General noted that the new civil servants were not always gifted with the necessary 'knowledge, patience and tact' to maintain friendly relations with the population. The reverse was true. They reacted with contempt and ridicule to all kinds of 'Javanese idiosyncrasies'.[15] The motor car was another culprit. It had removed the necessity for civil servants on a tour the stay overnight in a village.[16]

The new considerations of status, the influx of people from Europe, and the plan to elevate the indigenous population made matters worse for a special class of people, whose social plight was somewhat veiled by the fact that race was not explicitly used as a legal criterion to distinguish them. They were the Indo-Europeans; legally classified as Europeans, but, if they did not already belong to the lower strata of society, socially often not accepted as members of the colonial elite. As people of mixed race they tended to be moved into a marginal position when the status criteria in the colonial elite changed emphasizing race and correct European standards of behaviour. Indo-Europeans

---

[14] *Nieuwe Soerabaja Courant,* cited in *De Locomotief,* 3-10-1913.
[15] *Adviezen* 1913:18.
[16] *Handelingen Tweede Kamer* 1918-19:2087.

could escape this, but only by behaving in a Western fashion. The same was true of some Indonesians. Adopting Western dress in the 1910s made them Europeans; and people, white Europeans included, were more polite and friendlier towards them than when under similar circumstances, they dressed according to the custom of their own ethnic group.

For many Indo-Europeans the stark choice was either to identify with the white society, and its European appearance, or to submerge in the local Indonesian society, no longer having any special status at all. The third alternative, holding on to their own culture, meant remaining a member of a group whose language, manners, and beliefs were looked down upon and ridiculed by white Dutch people; a fact which contributed to the putative hatred of the Dutch frequently attributed to Indo-Europeans.

Indo-Europeans as a group also missed out on the special attention the Dutch professed to pay Indonesians in their efforts to improve social and economic conditions of the latter. When policies were developed to educate the people, to better their economic position, or even to improve housing conditions, it was Indonesians and not Indo-Europeans (or Chinese and Arabs) whom the planners had in mind. What daunted the most was that not only was their culture marginalized, but that economically the Indo-Europeans, many of whom occupied lower-ranking clerical positions, were also downgraded. The opening up of educational opportunities to larger numbers of Indonesians threatened their economic position. Imperceptibly the Indo-Europeans began to lose out in the competition for the lower-ranking jobs as a growing number of Indonesians and Chinese qualified for these too and were prepared to work for a lower salary. As early as the end of the nineteenth century Indo-Europeans had wanted to reserve jobs in the modern sector for themselves, jealous of the Indonesians and Chinese who had entered the sector. A programme of the Social-Democrats in the Netherlands Indies in 1897 is most specific about the aspirations of the 'advanced', as they styled themselves. It was the social and economic position of the poor whites and Indo-Europeans which should be improved, the indigenous population had to play second fiddle to that dream. To 'combat the existence of a proletariat among the Indos', the programme called for 'fewer natives in the State Railways and the Postal and Telegraph Service, appointment of Eurasian girls as telegraph operators and ticket-sellers just as in Europe, replacement of native engine-drivers, chiefs at halts and so forth by Indos and Europeans, because the prosperity of the native lies in the cultivation of the Sawah'. Chinese also had to be banned from certain jobs – cashiers, an occupation which appeared to be one of the preserves of Chinese, had been mentioned as an example – to make way for Indo-Europeans (Tichelman 1985:111-2).

Their future as a group seemed to be at stake. To escape that fate farming was seen as one way out, but there was one major obstacle. For a number of decades ownership of land had by law been confined to indigenous Indonesians. The act had pre-empted complications which had made the political situation in Pacific Islands so explosive, but was clearly disadvantageous to Indo-Europeans whose Europeans status prevented them from owning land. To change this at least since 1897 Indo-Europeans had pleaded in vain they be accorded the right of landownership. A real impasse had been reached. E.F.E. Douwes Dekker, their most popular and radical political leader, called attention to the dilemma about acknowledging his offspring an Indo-European had put to him. Where he to do so they remained Europeans, if he did not they could buy land.[17]

Because of their background and lack of proper education, many Indo-Europeans did not qualify for higher administrative posts, for which an education in Holland was required. For positions where this did not count, Indo-Europeans were convinced that when filling them preference was given to persons fresh from Holland rather than to people from their own group with the same qualifications. It was an often-heard complaint that people from Europe were appointed to intermediate positions, which could equally well have been filled by Indo-Europeans.

To make prospects worse, new educational institutions established within the framework of emancipating the population were open to indigenous Indonesians only and not to Indo-Europeans. This was the case with the School tot Opleiding van Inlandsche Artsen (STOVIA, School for the Training of Native Doctors), and also loomed large in plans to establish a Law College (Van der Veur 2006:152). The educational discrimination was all the more vexatious as it happened in a period in which indigenous Indonesians and Chinese enthusiastically embraced Western schooling as the major vehicle of emancipation and for advancement in life.

It was among these Indo-Europeans, caught between Dutch and Indonesian society, that the first radical political movement in the Netherlands Indies found a response. Like all other such movements active before and after it, its leaders had to operate in a repressive climate. Legislation forbade all associations or meetings which had a political nature or formed a threat to public order. In formulating their demands Indo-Europeans stressed the one point that made them different from white Dutch people; the fact that they had been born in the Netherlands Indies and intended – or had no other choice than – to remain there.

A second group which made its mark at the beginning of the twentieth century was the Chinese; presenting indigenous Indonesians with another example of political agitation. After the Japanese had been granted European

[17]   *Nota Douwes Dekker* 1913:24; *Vervolg* 1913:92-3; Douwes Dekker 1912c:469-74.

status in 1899, the Chinese demanded the same right, even talking about a boycott of European firms discriminating against them.[18] Chinese had plenty of reasons to call for change. The majority of them was not held in high esteem by the white European community, and legislation curtailed their freedom of movement. Till 1910 Chinese (and Arabs) were not allowed to travel without special permission and had to live in special quarters in the major cities. To circumvent such rules, some Chinese converted to Islam (though the fact that this allowed them to marry Muslim girls also could have been a reason), and claimed native status. A few others acquired Japanese nationality; a move colonial authorities were sure was sanctioned, if not promoted, by the Japanese government as part of a scheme to increase the Japanese presence in the Archipelago in preparation of Japan's putative thrust southwards.[19]

The resentment aroused contributed to a re-orientation towards China and a renewed interest in Chinese culture. Instead of identifying with the Dutch, as some did, or remaining a more or less well-integrated, though in some respects clearly distinct, segment of local society, Chinese identity was now stressed. This was boasted by the short-lived drive for modernization which had manifested itself in China and the Straits Settlements in 1898, coupling a selective adaptation of Western ways with a return to traditional, age-old Confucian values, undiluted by heterodox accretions and adjustments which had been introduced in the course of centuries. The Chinese revival was reinforced by the arrival of new immigrants to work as labourers. They added a new element to the Chinese community, which for the greater part had previously been made up of families which had settled in the Netherlands Indies generations ago, and had taken over much of the language and many of the customs of the indigenous Indonesians in whose midst they lived.

The press also contributed to keeping the links with the country of origin alive. Besides the Chinese Malay newspapers and periodicals that were already being published, new ones appeared, with a few exceptions still written in Malay, which catered to the new interest in China and its culture and values. The editors and teachers who had come over from China to teach at the new Chinese schools were held responsible by the authorities for the spread of the Young China Movement all over the colony, and for the fresh worries the 'Chinese question' occasioned them.[20]

The fall of the Manchu dynasty in 1911 and the founding of the Chinese Republic in 1912 stirred up the Chinese community even more. Great enthusiasm, which took the colonial administration completely by surprise, and a

---

[18] *Pembrita Betawi,* 5-4-1903 refered to in Adam 1995:75.
[19] *De Expres,* 13-3-1914; Adviser Chinese Affairs to Director BB 7-11-1917, NA, Kol. Geheim, Mr. 298x/17.
[20] Adviser for Japanese and Chinese Affairs, 5-6-1913, NA, Kol. Openbaar, Vb. 30-8-1915 26.

Chinese patriotism. Chinese soldier with Chinese war flag. Trade mark of a Chinese firm in Batavia selling medicines. (*Javasche Courant* 1914, Trade mark 6693.)

Trade mark of a Chinese tea trader in Surabaya. The figure holds a Chinese trade flag in his right hand and a Chinese war flag in his left hand. (*Javasche Courant* 1916, Trade mark 8094.)

boost in self-confidence were the result. As in China, the symbols of modernity and progress which signified anti-Manchu feelings were embraced. The Chinese began to behave like Europeans. They reacted to the news of the Chinese Revolution by cutting off their pigtails and donning European clothes. In an attempt to calm down stories in the Straits press about large-scale unrest in the Netherlands Indies the Dutch Consul General in Singapore wrote that the Chinese 'endeavoured to imitate, with more and less success, European habits, such as dress, coiffure, calendar, and Sunday rest among other things'.[21] The Dutch could cope with this. More difficult to swallow was the new self-assurance the Chinese displayed. That some treated Europeans as their equals was an attitude, it was written with mild irony in *De Locomotief*, they would not have dared to show in the past when they still wore a pigtail, 'but, since they wear green, mundane socks, have become republican and just as religious Christians want to be called "Sir", this people stop at nothing'.[22] Judging from a contemporary report a modern way of life must have been embraced with great enthusiasm. *Pakean Europa*, European costumes, and shoes *model Europa* were in great demand.[23]

Restlessness manifested itself in various ways. In part this was provoked by the colonial authorities who banned the hoisting of the flag of the Chinese Republic. On 18 February 1912, on Chinese New Year, disturbances broke out in Batavia when the police enforced the ban and hauled down Republican flags. In Batavia the situation could be contained. In Surabaya it spun out of control, resulting in a tense atmosphere which lasted for more than a week. Protests against the refusal of the authorities to allow the hoisting of the Republican flag contributed to the tension in Surabaya, but it had all started with a ban by the municipal administration on letting off fireworks. The *Nieuwe Rotterdamsche Courant* deemed this a sensible decision. The roads between the city centre and the harbour all ran through the Chinese ward.[24] The newspaper also noted something disquieting. In Batavia and Surabaya the 'usually very quiet, hard-working Chinese element among the population' had taken 'a rebellious, here and there definitely hostile attitude towards the Dutch authority'.[25] The blame was put on the new immigrants; not the decent ones, but the lowest class among them, people who had nothing to lose. The prospect of an unruly Chinese community in the colony did not ease Dutch minds. The authority of their traditional allies in the Chinese community, the Chinese officers, seemed to be waning. The members of the established,

---

[21] Report Dutch Consul General in Singapore, September 1913, NA, BuZa, A-dos. 190, box 452.
[22] *De Locomotief*, 23-10-1913.
[23] *Nieuwe Rotterdamsche Courant*, 25-3-1912, quoting *Java-Bode*, 28-2-1912.
[24] *Nieuwe Rotterdamsche Courant*, 25-3-1912, 1-4-1912.
[25] *Nieuwe Rotterdamsche Courant*, 1-4-1912.

traditional Chinese elite had to face competition from newcomers and were attacked in newspapers in the Netherlands Indies and China for their reactionary behaviour and their involvement with colonial rule.

A new China was not a prospect to which the Dutch looked forward. China was a weak nation but the coming to power of the Republican government could herald different times. For some outside the Netherlands such a moment had already dawned. One journal, *The Islamic Fraternity*, writing about 'Dutch officials, to whom the oppression of the Javan people is as natural as breath to their nostrils', even reported that Peking had ordered cruisers to the Archipelago to punish the Dutch for the killing and maltreatment of Chinese, rumours which circulated in Java as well. *The Islamic Fraternity* added that the Dutch government had 'climbed down and humbly apologizing for the occurrence promised to compensate sufferers of Dutch outrage at Java' in suppressing the unrest in Batavia and Surabaya. It was an augury of more to come: 'The energetic action of the Republican government of China has inaugurated a new era of life, liberty and pursuit of happiness for the peoples of the East. The worm has turned at last, and the first nail is driven into the coffin of the European domination of Asia.'[26]

In the Netherlands and the Netherlands Indies, though still only occasionally, China made its initial appearance as a prospective foreign enemy. Such a possibility had already been predicted in 1904 by the then *Resident* of Batavia. Observing the mood in the Chinese community in his station he had pleaded for a positive response. Were this not forthcoming the moment China had recovered its strength a situation could emerge in which a section of the population in the Netherlands Indies would act as the allies of a foreign enemy, and become a 'domestic enemy to be reckoned with'.[27] In Holland in 1914 it was Van Kol who pleaded for the alleviation of the grievances held by the Chinese in the Netherlands Indies before the moment should arrive when China would have a powerful army and fleet.[28]

China came to be presented an example for Indonesian nationalists and others detesting Western colonialism of what a people's movement might accomplish. The radical daily *De Expres* wrote that Chinese revolution had proved that the Chinese people also no longer wanted to be a race of slaves.[29] The fear of Holland for China as the 'foreign enemy in a new cloak', was a theme which was repeatedly taken up in it. True to the conviction of its editors that striking fear into the heart of the Dutch people was the best way to frighten The Hague into concessions, this was sometimes accompanied by

[26] *The Islamic Fraternity*, May 1912; *Handelingen Eerste Kamer* 1913-14:241.
[27] Bakhuizen van den Brink to Rooseboom, 8-9-1904, NA, Kol. Geheim, Vb. 19-10-04 O22.
[28] *De Expres*, 14-1-1914.
[29] *De Expres*, 13-1-1914.

exclamations like 'Fear works; carry on Chinese Brothers [...]'.[30]

Unrest and unease had spread to the indigenous segment of the colonial society. In the vanguard of the early nationalist movement were indigenous Indonesians who had received Western secondary and higher education, but after graduation discovered that society was not ready for them. Their Western style of life was not accepted and the ideals of equality and democracy they had read about during their schooldays were far from put into practice in the colony. When they embarked on a government career, they discovered that jobs were still allocated according to the old standards in which deference to superiors was more important than educational background and that for years they would be stuck in positions lower than warranted by their schooling. Such people came from of a new class of young Indonesians who no longer felt in harmony with their social background. They were sons of members of the indigenous Indonesian bureaucracy, coloured by its strict hierarchy from the higher nobility down to the more humble officials, such as office clerks. In word and deed they rebelled against the strict rules and etiquette that governed these circles. They found a way out of their social confinement by joining the nationalist movement or pursuing a career in journalism; often combining the two.

The rise of nationalism among the Javanese and other ethnic groups of the Netherlands Indies was facilitated by the dissemination of Western notions of democracy and emancipation which became familiar to a growing number of Indonesians through an increased distribution of books, newspapers and magazines, and through the Western educational institutions which Indonesians had started to attend. Equally important was the introduction of a set of ideologies, which made it possible to phrase their aspirations in a new terminology and provided new standards by which to judge contemporary society. Construed and developed in the course of the nineteenth century in Europe and in the Middle East, such ideas acquired force in the Netherlands Indies somewhat later, in the years following the turn of the century. Europe furnished the ideals of Marxism and Socialism, and the Middle East the modernist tenets of Islam.

Islamic modernism stressed a revival of Islam. European expansion seemed at its peak. It had resulted in the colonization of much of the non-Western world and vast regions where the majority or a large part of the population consisted of Muslims had already been conquered. The Ottoman Empire had maintained its independence but was weak and had to accept European economic and political intervention. To close the gap with the West, the necessity of modern education was emphasized, as was a flexibility of thought.

---

[30]   *De Expres*, 13-1-1914, 17-1-1914.

This it was argued, Islam, which had once itself inspired a World Power, had gradually lost in the course of the centuries. Transforming the Islamic educational system by incorporating the teaching of secular subjects was part of the answer. Giving the Islamic community new strength by inviting Muslims not simply to follow the age-old established traditions but to try and find the correct interpretation which would make Islam compatible with modern times was equally important.

In a similar way to all other reformist concepts, the new ideas presented carried the seeds of profound social and religious controversies. The reformists in the Netherlands Indies not only were determined to combat Western superiority, they also tried to undermine the position of the religious leaders who adhered to the old ways. In this, they reserved much of their venom for such figures. Established practices were rejected on religious grounds and sometimes even ridiculed. Customs which did not originate in Islam, but had become generally accepted in the local community as an integral part of religion, were attacked with the same zeal.

The reformers could, and especially the more radical of them did so frequently, borrow from the vocabulary of the second novel ideology introduced in the Netherlands Indies, that of Socialism. The ideals propagated by Socialism, an egalitarian, democratic society cleansed of exploitation – and as it often was perceived also without the Dutch and taxes – were highly attractive.

Both Marxism and Islamic Reformism carried the appeal of offering an alternative to the capitalist West and the colonial system to which it had given birth. Having identified the evils of capitalism and colonialism, they traced out the way to end foreign domination and free Indonesians from their subordinate position. Even when people did not fully understand the finer points of Communism or Islamic Modernism, the two ideologies provided some impressive words to create a feeling of solidarity and to identify the enemy and those responsible for all the wrongs in society. Worthy of praise were either the poor, the people who suffered a miserable fate, and the oppressed, or the real or true Muslim, who by arriving at an understanding of the correct meaning of Islam had dissociated himself from a system which could be blamed for the continuation of colonialism. Appeals to uphold true Islam, *Islam sedjati*, were made to inspire people to take their fate into their own hands and resist Dutch domination. This went hand in hand with attacks on false Muslims (as opposed to the true ones), who would not relinquish ideas which had turned Islam into a religion of the weak and meek and who were held responsible for the passive acceptance of colonial rule. A true Muslim protested against injustice and exploitation; a false Muslim remained silent.

The hardship and suffering of the common people, of the little man – the *rakjat, wong tjilik*, or *Si Kromo* – had to be grappled. But, paradoxically, their poverty and the discrimination they suffered provided a basis for solidarity, a focus of identification. The 'oppressed' were the people who should be fought for; and to show that their champions were really touched by their wretched conditions *noms de plumes* such as Eternal Sufferer (*Eeuwige Lijder*), One Handicapped by Life (*Een Misdeelde*) or Wounded in Body and Soul, and significantly, also New Wearer of Suits (*Nieuwe Pakkendrager*) were used. At times such a champion chose to present himself in a deprecatory way; turning the negative into the positive. The oppressed were only half or quarter human; a very popular way to illustrate their fate. They were also the stupid ones, *Si Bodo*. *Domoor*, the Dutch word meaning idiot or fool also appeared as a pseudonym, as admittedly did *Si Tjinta-Bangsa*, Lover of My People. Only the clever ones, *Si Pintar*, had money and status. It was not just adopting a high moral tone, a denunciation of the materialism of the West. Like the clownish servants of the hero, who displayed genuine wisdom in the Javanese wayang play and in the end are the real winners, the stupid ones saw through the tricks and outward pretence, and knew what was amiss. It was the fool who had the superior intellect. Later, in a similar vein of irony, the Europeans were sarcastically denoted as the *bangsa sopan*, a tidy and civilized nation.

The growth of the printing industry, which made possible a vast increase in the publication of pamphlets, newspapers, and periodicals, acted as a catalyst. A plethora of articulate local newspapers emerged, reflecting the rebellious mood in sections of the Chinese, Indo-European and indigenous communities. It was a circumstance with which the Dutch had never had been confronted before. Neither the political organizations which were industriously being founded nor some of the newspapers and periodicals affiliated with them gave the Dutch much time to reflect. What was said and written did not gradually wax in tone. Within a short span of time, a few years only, they assumed a stand that many Dutch people considered to be seditious; a deliberate effort to gnaw at Dutch rule and to set the population against the white Dutch community and against the colonial administration.

Non-Dutch-language journals had been published since the 1850s, but these had never been a cause of much concern. By and large they had been harmless; copying news items from Dutch-language newspapers and providing information of use to Indonesians who wanted to improve their social and economic position within the framework of colonial society. After the turn of the century a political press took shape. Or, as it was phrased in the 1920s, only 'when the twentieth century with its social vehemence and intellectual progress had set in, when world traffic had also included these provinces in its gigantic network, inevitably that the press, elsewhere such a powerful weapon, emerged here as well' (Later 1923:58). This came as a bolt from the blue. In 1906 supervision of the press had been relaxed, ending a period in which it had been possible for the colonial administration to exercise preventive censorship. There were at that time a number of periodicals written in Malay or Javanese, but, prior to 1906, when collisions occurred between the press and the colonial administration it had mainly been Dutch-language media which had been the culprits.

This changed with the growth of political consciousness among the Indonesian, Chinese, and Indo-European population. The increase in the number of publications catering to these communities and in particular the change in tone had not been expected. What emerged apparently out of nowhere were what Dutch administrators called 'scurrilous rags', libelling and abusing Dutch officials and other people or social groups with whom the journalists of these papers did not agree. Among those expressing concern was the Minister of the Colonies in The Hague, J.H. de Waal Malefijt. In 1912 – at a time when the Adviser for Native Affairs, D.A. Rinkes, was still reassuring the Governor General that the nationalist press might make a noise, but did not pose a political threat – he stressed that the way in which Indonesian journalists were expressing themselves called for the reinstitution of the repressive powers previously wielded by the colonial administration. He maintained that it was intolerable that, as one of the civil servants of his department had said, 'the native press did not scruple to preach rebellion in overt or covert terms, yea even to incite murder'. Consequently, in June 1913, De Waal Malefijt urged Governor General A.W.F. Idenburg to prepare legal means which would allow the colonial administration to act against 'the overt preaching of rebellion against Dutch Authority, the outrageous way in which suspicion is fastened upon the best intentions of the government and the sowing of hatred and discord between the different races'. He considered it 'political suicide' to leave the matter in the hands of the judiciary with its 'ever-changing judgements'. The colonial administration should regain the special powers it had held prior to 1906. Courts, and this was an almost general mood prevailing among administrators in Java and The Hague, could not be relied upon to suppress dangerous agitation. Judges were too lenient, and the legal proof demanded in a court case against journalists accused of libel or sedition was not always easy to provide.

Only a few senior colonial civil servants did not join in the calls for wider powers to be given to the government. One was Rinkes. He denied that the Indonesian press was recrimatory, let alone inflammatory. There were exceptions, but these papers had only a small circulation; extra proof for Rinkes that their influence was easily overrated and that Indonesians were perfectly able to distinguish between good and bad, between responsible, well-edited newspapers and rags. Rinkes coupled his observation with a plea not to overreact and to continue to allow the press to function as an instrument of political control, essential in a society where the Dutch and indigenous civil servants held almost paramount authority. For the ordinary people, newspapers were almost the only place where they could complain about the behaviour of such officials without fear of immediate retaliation. Others were less sanguine. They lamented a situation in which it was impossible to act against 'cunning demagogues, who, because of [Western] education which is available in ever-widening circles have learned to recognize fairly big opportunities to slip through the net'.[31] Yet others deplored the fact that lawyers also played a role in this unsettling process by making journalists aware of the limitations of the law in taking action against the press.

Tension was almost unavoidable. Society was steeped in racial prejudice and stereotypes, while fear of competition for jobs and economic opportunities from people of another race was widespread. Indo-Europeans were concerned about the advancing status of Indonesians. On their part Indonesians viewed the Indo-Europeans as a group which blocked their access to the better-paid but still lower-ranking jobs, and also passionately guarded their exclusive rights of landownership, rejecting the granting of the right to own land to Indo-Europeans. Both groups saw Chinese as rivals.

Shortly before the founding of the first mass Islamic organization, Sarekat Islam, when Muslim traders in Surakarta reacted to the political and economic pressure exerted by the Chinese by a boycott of Chinese products. This reaction came as a complete surprise. Rinkes observed that such a show of solidarity and the use of 'the modern agitation technique of a boycott so much beyond the ken of daily round in old-fashioned Surakarta' by this 'narrow-minded, backward' community was remarked upon by many with 'some amazement'.[32]

Anti-Chinese feelings were not the only reason Muslims started to organize themselves. Others factors were also stirring. One was the opening up of Java to Christian missions. By allowing this, the Dutch government departed from its long-standing policy of discouraging missionary activities in Islamic regions in order to avoid social upheaval. The new course of events and the discussions in the Dutch parliament and press surrounding the change evoked a strong reaction among Muslims. Offence was taken at remarks passed by proponents of the opening up of Java to Christian mission that many if not most Javanese could hardly be called Muslims because non-Islamic beliefs and customs predominated their religious life. Insulted by the comments about the religious beliefs adhered to by their fellow Javanese and fearful that a Christian offensive was in the offing Islamic leaders launched their own drive. An atmosphere in which greater stress was laid on correct Islamic behaviour was the result.

[31]   Note Department II of the General Secretariat, 3-9-1913, NA, Kol. Openbaar, Vb. 17-12-1913 1.
[32]   D.A. Rinkes to Idenburg, 24-8-1912 (*Adviezen* 1913:1).

Inaugural meeting Sarekat Islam in Blitar 1914 (KITLV 3719)

Sarekat Islam became a popular trade mark. In this case used to sell bicycles
(*Oetoesan Hindia* 6-8-1914)

The new mood among Muslims was given concrete expression in 1912 in the founding of the Moehammadijah, a reformist organization, and of the Sarekat Islam. The Sarekat Islam, founded by Oemar Said Tjokroaminoto, described in *De Locomotief* as being one of 'the highly cultured natives', was the more political in nature of the two.[33] It could count on an enthusiast reception, first in Java and then in other parts of the Archipelago. An *Assistent-Resident* reported in July 1914 that the words Sarekat Islam had became a battle-cry.[34] There even was a brand of bicycle Sarekat Islam. A few years later people could buy Sarekat Islam watches.

In a very short span of time the organization grew into a mass movement with branches all over the Netherlands Indies. Muslims of all denominations joined, from those who did not pay much heed to the prescripts of Islam to the strictest adherents. Pertinently at meetings economic and social demands were at least as frequent as calls for a correct religious behaviour. Sometimes, as the newspaper *De Expres* noted, religious topics were not raised at all.[35] Nevertheless, an upsurge in religious life was perceptible. In May 1913 Rinkes observed that in dress, forms of greeting, and in dietary habits Muslim customs were being more widely espoused. The fashion of copying Western manners was no longer as pronounced as it had been a few years earlier.[36] All kinds of economic and political initiatives to improve the living conditions of Sarekat Islam members and above all to set up shops and cooperatives to compete with Chinese petty traders and shopkeepers were broached.

The emergence of the Sarekat Islam was also expressed in a strong feeling of belonging. Pressure was so compelling that people complained that they were obliged to take part in funeral processions of fellow members so frequently, they did not have enough time to run their daily business.[37]

Outsiders were not part of this. Their funeral processions were boycotted. Other traditional forms of mutual assistance, at planting time or when building a house for instance, were also withdrawn from them. Members of the same family landed up in opposite camps, ignoring each other's existence. Some divorces – which were frequent in Java – were blamed on Sarekat Islam.[38]

The Chinese were a prime target for such acts of solidarity. Just after the turn of the century Javanese newspapers had begun to identify the Chinese as an impediment to the development of the indigenous population. They had

[33] *De Locomotief,* 24-10-1913.
[34] Feith to *Resident* Batavia, 26-7-1914, NA, Kol. Openbaar, Vb. 9-3-1916 26.
[35] *De Expres,* 6-1-1914.
[36] Rinkes to Idenburg, 13-5-1913 (*Adviezen* 1913:35).
[37] Wegener to *Resident* Surabaya, 26-2-1914, NA, Kol. Openbaar, Vb. 7-11-1914 56.
[38] *Wedana* Bekasi to *Assistent-Resident* Meester Cornelis, 1-9-1914, NA, Kol. Openbaar, Vb. 9-3-1916 26.

hinted that were the government not to interfere, violence might be inevitable.[39] Resentment intensified after the Chinese Revolution. The way in which Chinese reacted to the fall of the Manchu dynasty irritated Javanese in the same way as it had done the Dutch. Their behaviour was described as haughty and rude. The Dutch Consul General in Singapore explained that the 'violent language' of the Chinese and the 'ostentatious way' in which many behaved 'caused many conflicts with their own more conservative countrymen, with the police, with the Arabs and especially with the natives'.[40] He noted that the arrogant behaviour of the Chinese had exasperated others, especially in Java. He was not alone in this assessment. Pleyte told the Dutch parliament that Javanese who had known the Chinese 'in baggy clothes, with a peculiar straw-hat, a long pigtail and bare feet', as a person who mixed cordially with the Javanese, spoke their language and settled in their villages, 'suddenly had to look up to the Chinese as a *toewan*, who although he had allowed him to address him by his name in the past, now demanded that he knelt in front of him'.[41] Reports from Java linked racial tension with the new found self-esteem of the Chinese. The Javanese Regent of Rembang wrote that since the establishment of the Chinese Republic, Chinese 'fancy themselves a great deal and look upon the Javanese as an inferior being, which has fostered a grudge among the latter against the Chinese'.[42] The Chinese under his administration bragged that within a few years they would replace the Dutch as masters of Java and rest of the Archipelago. In anticipation of this, 'the Javanese were going to have to show them all honour and obedience, which they are shortly going to be forced to do'.[43] In Surakarta, Chinese predicting that the new Chinese Republic would soon conquer the Netherlands Indies demanded more '*hormat*', more respect, and expressed the desire to be addressed as *Toewan*, Sir.[44] Hatred of the Chinese, according to the Dutch *Resident*, was intense in his district. Even a child of about eight, when asked what he wanted, had replied 'to kill all Chinese'.[45]

Watching such manifestations of anti-Chinese resentment, some Dutchmen could not hide their gloating. Rinkes considered the Sarekat Islam 'a nice (cold) shower for the Chinese, who have lain low for quite some time, but after their Republic had been founded, were again getting above themselves'.[46] Its

---

[39]   *De Locomotief,* 11-11-1913 referring to *Taman Sari,* October and November 1903 and *Bintang Hindia,* 1902 and 1903.
[40]   Memorandum Dutch Consul General in Singapore, NA, BuZa, A-dos. 190, box 452.
[41]   *Handelingen Tweede Kamer* 1913-14:215.
[42]   *Sarekat Islam* 1975:190.
[43]   *Sarekat Islam* 1975:232-3.
[44]   *Resident* Surakarta to Idenburg, 11-11-[1912] (*Sarekat Islam* 1975:328).
[45]   *Resident* Surakarta to Idenburg, 11-11-[1912] (*Sarekat Islam* 1975:331).
[46]   Rinkes to Moresco, 18-11-1913, NA, Kol. Openbaar, Vb. 13-5-1914 10.

function as *contre-poids*, counter-balance, to Chinese presumptions was one of the positive effects he saw in the founding of the Sarekat Islam.[47] A similar opinion was expressed by Pleyte when he defended his budget in parliament at the end of 1913. In his eyes, the 'awakening' of the Javanese served as a means to check arbitrary behaviour by indigenous Indonesian lower-ranking civil servants (he did not mention Dutch civil servants), and by those 'one considers the economic exploiters of the Javanese', singling out the Chinese petty traders as an example.[48]

The unrest occasioned by the founding of the Sarekat Islam, the demonstrations of anti-Chinese feelings, and the occasional brawl on estates where labourers under the influence of the religious revival demanded to have a day off on Islamic holidays, greatly upset the Dutch community. Idenburg reported to Pleyte that especially in East Java which was studded with sugar estates the mood was one of a 'highly nervous tension'.[49] Sugar companies began to consider arming their staff. One such company went as far as to publish a newspaper advertisement, asking for a military officer who could help it to take the necessary precautions to ward off an attack.[50] With Chinese and Dutchmen expecting the worst, the sale of firearms boomed. Fear of a day of reckoning spread fast. The Dutch started to speculate about the impending murder of Europeans in August 1913 during the Fasting Months. It was a major topic of conversation in the clubs. In Batavia people later spoke about the 'fearful' days.[51] There was even talk that the citizen's guard in town would be mobilized. European newspapers speculated about the prospect of a St Bartholomew's Night. The following year *De Expres* wrote that such 'journalistic feats' gave cause to think that the scare had been fanned by importers of revolver.[52] Yet even this newspaper, usually very sympathetic in its attitude to Muslims, showed some apprehension at the end of 1913 when three returning hajis had tried to smuggle in firearms.[53]

Tuban was the only place in which there were serious problems. Its *Assistent-Resident* earned himself the displeasure of his superiors. His chief accused him of cowardice because when faced with Sarekat Islam unrest, he had asked for troops. A plucky civil servant should first have tried to solve the problems by visiting the scene of the troubles, not by asking for military assistance. Nevertheless, much to his own chagrin the *Resident* had to send in sol-

---

[47] *Adviezen* 1913:42.
[48] *Handelingen Tweede Kamer* 1913-14:222.
[49] Idenburg to Th.B. Pleyte, 16-5-1913, NA, Kol. Openbaar, Vb. 16-5-1913 63.
[50] *Soerabaiasch Handelsblad*, 15-7-1913, cited in McVey 1965:7; Baars and Sneevliet 1991:110.
[51] *De Locomotief*, 29-11-1913.
[52] *De Expres*, 17-4-1914.
[53] *De Expres*, 2-1-1914.

diers. He justified his action by pointing out that he had only done so because European females in Tuban, fearful of a plot to murder all Europeans, had become terrified. He wrote to Idenburg that he could not cope with women. The idea that his refusal to send soldiers would keep 'a number of ladies in a continuous state of fear' had so burdened his conscience that he had changed his mind about not sending in troops.[54]

The commotion caused by the early activities of the Sarekat Islam did not escape the attention of the foreign press. In Australia, the Straits Settlements, and as far away as China, alarming reports appeared in the press about a break-down of law and order in Java. In Singapore, the Dutch Consul General reported that articles in the *Pinang Gazette* and *The Straits Times* which tried to demonstrate that Java was teeter on the brink of a revolution had upset those trading with Java.[55] An editorial in *The Straits Times*, basing itself on information from its 'well-informed and reliable correspondent, whose views receive ample corroboration from many sources in Singapore', predicted 'trouble of grave character' in the near future. It was claimed that because of 'drastic censorship of news' by the Dutch colonial authorities, the general public can glean but little of the innermost turmoil which is now tearing at the bowels of Dutch administration'. The sudden change had overwhelmed the correspondent. He saw 'signs which portend evil' everywhere:

> Insolence on the part of carriage drivers, domestic servants, and menials, hither unheard of is a common occurrence. Boycotts are the order of the day and some mysterious murders have occurred. [...] And it may be further mentioned [...] that there is no native in Java who does not wear his kris.[56]

In Australia, the Melbourne *Argus* (11-6-1913) drew the attention of its readers to the developments in Java with headlines like 'Fear of outrage' and 'Sinister conditions in Java'. Blaming the trouble on a 'secret society styled Sarekat Islam', its correspondent in Surabaya noted that it was a 'nervy' time and that there was 'not a firearm to be obtained for love or money'. Wrongly he added that Javanese troops had hurriedly been deployed to Sumatra and Ambona, and that 'purely Dutch soldiers' were concentrated in Java. In China, a newspaper reported that thousands of Chinese had asked and received permission to provide themselves with firearms, this because of actions by the natives who, it was claimed, harboured 'the greatest antipathy towards all foreigners', and had as their watchwords the extermination of the whitemen and the

---

[54] Gonggrijp to Idenburg, 21-8-1913 (*Sarekat Islam* 1975:203-9); *De Locomotief*, 19-11-1913, 5-12-1913.
[55] Consul General Singapore to Cort van der Linden, 15-9-1913, NA, BuZa, A-dos. 190, box 452.
[56] *The Straits Times*, 22-8-1913.

ousting of the Chinese.[57]

In reacting to the sudden expressions of political and social aspirations by almost all population groups in the Netherlands Indies, the colonial administration adopted a cautious attitude. Upholding law and order remained a key expression in the vocabulary of civil servants. Nevertheless, scope was created for political ideas to be circulated in writing and at public meetings. This was tolerated as long as this posed no immediate threat to law and order and to Dutch Power. As it was said in 1913 with respect to the Sarekat Islam: the 'Governor General desires that in its attitude towards the said association the Administration shows sympathy with the movement, of which the said association is a manifestation, [but] on the other hand shall closely and firmly guard against the violation of public law and order [...]'.[58]

Much depended on the mode of expression. Words thought to be too radical or blunt could lead to harassment by Dutch authorities and by the members of the indigenous administrative structure, and ultimately to arrest or censorship. Such repressive measures became more frequent in the course of years when the objective of changing society had become more outspoken and more widespread; when the 'accoutrements' to conceal its political nature, as it was concluded in 1920 by a commission to revise the legal system in the Netherlands Indies, had grown increasingly transparent over the years.[59]

The course decided upon at the top of the colonial bureaucracy, was not well received by the middle echelon, the civil servants in the field, or by the Dutch public. These Dutch *Residenten*, *Assistent-Residenten*, and district officers were more reserved and more reluctant to allow nationalist activities. Their attitude to the Sarekat Islam greatly disappointed Rinkes. In November 1913 he had called it a 'wonderful achievement', that, with the exception of some of the *Residenten*, the colonial civil servants had succeeded in winning the distrust of so many Indonesians within such a short span of time, about six months, because of the attitude most of them had taken towards the movement.[60] Four months later he observed that the Dutch colonial civil servants were 'in fact opposed to all native associations which are not very well "led", that is to say which do not unconditionally say yes and amen to everything that is expressed and judged from the side of the civil service, European or Native'.[61]

---

[57] Dutch Minister in Peking to Cort van der Linden, 15-9-1913, NA, BuZa, A-dos. 190, box 452.
[58] Secret circular letter of the 1st Government Secretary to the heads of regional administration in Java and Madoera, 11-10-1913, NA, Kol. Openbaar, Vb. 13-5-1914 10.
[59] Carpentier Alting 1920:291.
[60] Note Rinkes, November 1913, NA, Kol. Openbaar, Vb. 13-5-1914 10.
[61] Note Rinkes, 12-2-1914, NA, Kol. Openbaar, Vb. 13-5-1914 10.

A position similar to that of the Dutch civil servants was taken by members of the indigenous administration. In itself the new movement already presented a threat to their authority, as it was an expression of a new political system that was emerging. Many of them did not take kindly to the nationalist movement. When villagers got in trouble because of their membership of the Sarekat Islam, were maltreated or lost their jobs as village clerks and the like, it was usually at the instigation of these Indonesian administrators. Their actions often had the support of the members of the colonial administration, who considered such persons 'resolute officials', who were well able of putting the fear of God into people.[62] Conversely, congresses of the Sarekat Islam became gatherings during which such behaviour was reported and the antipathy to the native ruling strata and its bureaucracy could be expressed.

[62] Clignett to A.W.F. Idenburg, 14-6-1915, NA, Kol. Openbaar, Vb. 9-3-1916 26.

CHAPTER III

Indiërs

Some Indo-Europeans welcomed the awakening of Asian in general and Indonesian nationalism in particular. Most illustrious among those who tried to break out of the narrow confines of race was Ernest François Eugène Douwes Dekker, Nes to his friends, a second cousin of the Dutch author Multatuli, born in 1879 in Pasuruan in East Java of a Dutch father (a broker) and a mother of German-Javanese descent. The movement he begun was probably the most radical of all in the Netherlands Indies in the years before the Great War. His contemporary and friend D.M.G. Koch (1960:118) described Douwes Dekker as

> a remarkable man with an acute, lively mind, a strong desire for action tinged with romanticism, impressed with the intuitive certitude that what was true and good should be possible in the end [...] a man who felt himself an Indies D'Artagnan, called upon to fight against the sorrows of and wrongdoing against the poor and oppressed, born into a family where the tradition of Multatuli was vividly alive.

Van Kol, a socialist and not a friend, called him 'an agitator, but not an organizer by a long chalk'.[1] After his schooldays – he went to the Hoogere Burgerschool (HBS, Dutch secondary school) – Douwes Dekker had wanted to go to Holland to study engineering, but lack of money frustrated this ambition. Instead he found employment in the plantation industry. His strong sense of justice and the manner in which he vented his anger with the way the Indonesians were treated did not make him a model employee. His job on a sugar estate, his second (his first had been on a coffee plantation) he lost, according to his own account, after he had told the second-in-charge that he would throw him into the pulp machine (De Jong 1979:35). A misfit in colonial society Douwes Dekker did what other like-minded people also did and became a journalist.

Douwes Dekker was to become the main thorn in the side of colonial government. He was a great source of concern to Batavia not just because he

---

[1] *Handelingen* 1913-14, I:47.

turned the political movement of the Indo-Europeans in a radical direction, but especially because of his efforts to reach out to the Indonesian population. A movement confined to disgruntled Indo-Europeans was nothing new and the colonial administration could cope and rest easy with that. A campaign that transgressed the boundaries of this community and inspired Indonesians to speak out was potentially much more dangerous to law and order and was less easy to contain. For a time, Douwes Dekker's influence on the 'native movement' preoccupied the minds of the highest authorities in Batavia and in the other cities, especially in Java, where he and his associates pursued their activities. His ideas struck a favourable chord, and, what was more, Douwes Dekker indubitably possessed personal magnetism. Many Indonesians, young and old alike, found Douwes Dekker a pleasant person, who inspired feelings of sympathy and even affection.[2] He was also a good orator. Koch (1960:122) compared him to Soekarno when he recounts Douwes Dekker's power to capture an audience: 'He dominated a mass, which was relatively not large, but which he mesmerized'. Governor General Idenburg was similarly impressed. In August 1913, he wrote that 'from the *person* of Douwes Dekker emanates a significant influence especially on the younger, better-educated Native [...] by his personal appearance he exercises a kind of fascination on them from which they are unable to extricate themselves'.[3]

Douwes Dekker had been in contact with the Indonesian nationalist movement right from its inception. He was well acquainted with the students of the STOVIA among whom the movement took concrete shape. Douwes Dekker's house was nearby and STOVIA students frequently visited him to discuss social and political issues (Nagazumi 1989:56). One of them, Soewardi Soerjaningrat, who was to become a close comrade-in-arms, later recollected that Douwes Dekker's home became a club-house as well as a reading-room and library for STOVIA students (Setiabuddhi 1950:39). From close by and as a personal friend of some of the Indonesians involved, Douwes Dekker witnessed the founding of Boedi Oetomo (Noble Endeavour) in 1908, generally acknowledged as the first modern Indonesian organization and the starting point of the 'national awakening' (in this ignoring earlier Chinese initiatives).

There was talk that Douwes Dekker was to become the first editor-in-chief of a magazine to be published by Boedi Oetomo, but nothing came out of this, nor did he reach a position of any prominence within the organization (Nagazumi 1989:125-6). The discrepancy was too great. His ideas were too radical and those of the majority of the Boedi Oetomo members too moderate. As he wrote at the end of 1912, Boedi Oetomo degenerated, the idealism

[2] Rinkes to Idenburg, 16-1-1913 (*Bescheiden 'Indische Partij'* 1913).
[3] Idenburg to De Waal Malefijt, 25-8-1913, NA, Kol. Openbaar, Vb. 25-9-1913 56.

created 'was soon permeated by the spirit of officialdom. And, thereupon, the national idea deserted this inhospitable home. I myself had already foreseen this and commented on it before it happened' (Douwes Dekker 1912e:248).

In February 1910 Douwes Dekker accompanied by his wife and two children left Java for Europe. In Europe he travelled extensively. He visited the Netherlands, Belgium, Saxony, Prussia, Bavaria, and Switzerland, went to France, Spain, the Balearic Islands, Algiers, and Italy, and after a brief return to Holland, travelled to England and the Scandinavian countries. His tour brought Douwes Dekker into contact with the radical anti-colonial movement. In Paris he struck up friendship with Shyamaji Krishnavarma. Douwes Dekker was impressed. He wrote a special report about his meeting for the *Bataviaasch Nieuwsblad* and described Shyamaji Krishnavarma as 'the first Indian of note I had ever met'.[4] It was an acquaintanceship which made Douwes Dekker suspect in the eyes of the British authorities. Krishnavarma, editor of *The Indian Sociologist*, was among the first who – in 1901 – had called for *swadeshi*, an economic boycott of the British in India. He was considered a dangerous revolutionary and accused of having inspired Madan Lal Dhingra, who had murdered Sir Curzon Wyllie, Adjutant to the British Colonial Secretary in 1909. Shyamaji Krishnavarma struck Douwes Dekker as a 'political anarchist'. In January 1916, he recalled the conversation they had:

> He favoured individual acts of anarchy rather than the combined resistance of the masses. He said that individual acts of bombing people and so forth had a greater demoralizing effect on the Government than a revolution by the whole of the Indian nation was likely to have.[5]

Returning from his trip in June 1911, Douwes Dekker took up Residence in Bandung and embarked on a path that shocked the colonial establishment. As a former journalist he started two journals, intended 'for the education of the masses in democratic ideas'.[6] Within a year their contents would be closely monitored by the authorities. In September 1911, Douwes Dekker launched *Het Tijdschrift* (The Periodical), a bi-monthly. The following year a daily newspaper, *De Expres*, was published.

In *Het Tijdschrift* Douwes Dekker could disseminate his militant political views, calling for active opposition – and the evocation of fear – to fight the abuses of colonial society. National and international developments were closely followed, always championing the underdog and those whose rights and freedoms were being threatened or abused. The most outstanding feature of *Het Tijdschrift* was its international character. In this it was unique in the

---

[4] Statement Douwes Dekker, 24-1-1916, NA, Kol. Openbaar, Vb. 27-7-1916 25.
[5] Statement Douwes Dekker, 24-1-1916, NA, Kol. Openbaar, Vb. 27-7-1916 25.
[6] Statement Douwes Dekker, 24-1-1916, NA, Kol. Openbaar, Vb. 27-7-1916 25.

Netherlands Indies. Other periodicals were almost exclusively filled with articles by *Residents* of the Netherlands Indies. In launching his magazine Douwes Dekker made good use of his European trip. From its inception he could draw upon a score of international contributors with leftist, if not anarchist and libertine, opinions; and others with more esoteric ones. From Munich articles were sent in by Lydia Hertlein, who defended the right of motherhood for unmarried women in one of its first issues; while from Paris, 'the indomitable apostle of freedom', Shiyamaji Krishnavarma, argued that British rule in India was in the second of three phases of political despotism 'the final one of which inevitably ends with its being swept away'.[7] Other articles were by Sir Walter W. Strickland, contributor to *The Indian Sociologist*. Douwes Dekker introduced him as 'a scholar, naturalist, explorer [...] a brave champion of the rights of the natives in British colonies'.[8] From Paris there were also contributions by Mathilde Deromps and Edward Holten James. Mathilde Deromps had won the 'How can Egypt liberate itself efficaciously from the English yoke' award, a prize offered by the Young Egyptian League, with an essay on the 'Martyr Wardani' about the person who had been executed in 1910 for murdering an Egyptian minister.[9] Holten James regularly submitted revolutionary-tinged articles about Christianity; a subject also taken up by Jos van Veen from The Hague, 'a modernistic ex-curate' who 'has chosen poverty and privation above a well-manured life of hypocrisy.'[10] Nor should Har Dayal, a radical Indian nationalist, be forgotten.

In *Het Tijdschrift* these authors wrote about the violent crumbling of European rule in the non-Western world and did not repudiate political assassination as a weapon. In his own writings Douwes Dekker articulated the same thoughts. He stressed that, in view of legislation in Europe curtailing the rights of workers, he did not believe that a parliamentary system could bring about the society he wanted. On other occasions he hinted that violence might have to be used, adding that the revolutionary path he advocated did not necessarily imply that actual violence had to be resorted to. Among the many expressions that greatly disturbed the authorities was Douwes Dekker's claim in *Het Tijdschrift* in February 1913 that resistance to colonialism was a moral obligation. A colonial administration had to be defied. However friendly a face it might present, colonialism remained a system based on inequality of justice, in which those born as rulers would never yield their prerogatives. Of necessity it was a form of despotism, of tyranny. Listing the methods that could

---

[7] Krishnavarma 1911:107. The qualification is by Douwes Dekker: *Het Tijdschrift*, 1-12-1911, p. 216.
[8] *Het Tijdschrift*, 1-12-1911 p. 205.
[9] *Het Tijdschrift*, 1-9-1911, p. 216; Setiabuddhi 1950:62.
[10] *Het Tijdschrift*, 15-11-1911, p. 199.

be employed to combat it, here and in other articles Douwes Dekker freely used words such as demonstration, agitation, revolution, passive resistance, strike (singling out such important sectors as the postal, telegraph and railway services), boycott, and rebellion.[11] A fortnight later, referring to the American Revolution, he wrote about the indigenous population preparing itself 'to tear away with hostility from the mother country'.[12]

Douwes Dekker's were reminiscent of the words of socialist and anarchist agitators in Europe. He welcomed the Chinese Revolution during which 'the power of China's people expressed itself', and praised sabotage and syndicalism: 'The man of action now is fed up with reform. Reform, that is indeed socialism, has failed' (Douwes Dekker 1912a:411, 1912f:747). Another example was provided by what had happened in the Philippines. Douwes Dekker applauded the Emilio Aguinaldo rebellion and used it to draw comparisons with the situation in the Netherlands Indies. One of his central ideas was that concessions could only be won by evoking fear. He argued that in British India 'only after dynamite bombs had been thrown, people had been killed, buildings and institutions destroyed, did the oppressors realize that they had to make concessions in the end'.[13] He condoned a murderous assault on the life of the Russian Czar 'because each new so-called "attempt" must keep alive the stimulus of fear in persons who, by accident were born to the purple, yet because of character flaws do not belong on a throne'. He himself, Douwes Dekker continued, would reveal where people could find their 'political Browning-guns'. A month later, entitling his editorial 'Browning-guns' he elaborated on the theme, promising his followers 'to show them where they could find their political Browning-guns. [...] the maxims and the example of the great figures of human history. [...] whose words and thoughts are the crowbars to open the rusty doors of your armouries which have fallen shut.' (Douwes Dekker 1911a:165, 168, 1911b:242.) True to the revolutionary spirit that so attracted Douwes Dekker, in an effort to explain Jesus to the Javanese readers of *Het Tijdschrift*, he drew a parallel between 'a Roman province and a Dutch colony', and introduced Jesus as 'the bold apostle of freedom, the audacious preacher of independence, the glorious anarchist' (Douwes Dekker 1912b:437, 439). These were words which had not yet often sullied the ears of the colonial authorities.

Indonesians also contributed to *Het Tijdschrift* right from its inception. To the amazement of some Dutch people they did so in excellent Dutch. The Dutch even wondered whether 'some contributions to *Het Tijdschrift*, especially from Native contributors, had actually not mainly originated from the

---

[11] Editorial in *Het Tijdschrift*, 15-2-1913, cited in *Vervolg* 1913.
[12] *Het Tijdschrift*, 1-3-1913, cited in *Vervolg* 1913.
[13] *De Expres*, 1-3-1913, quoted in *Vervolg* 1913.

publisher'. Among the doubters was Rinkes. He did not rule out the possibility some contributors were completely fictitious.[14]

In November 1911, in 'a confession of faith' in *Het Tijdschrift* Douwes Dekker announced that he intended to found a party which 'embraces Dutchman and Native, and all political variations in between'. About a year later, in mid-September 1912 after it had been announced that a Indische Partij (Indies Party) had been founded a week earlier, a campaign was launched to publicize the new party. A 'propaganda deputation' headed by Douwes Dekker toured Java. From Bandung, Douwes Dekker's place of residence, they travelled to Yogyakarta, Surabaya, Malang, Madiun, Semarang, Pekalongan, Tegal, and Batavia. The trip was planned to pave the way for a merger of as many organizations as possible. When the realization dawned that the regulations of the associations Douwes Dekker had in mind – Boedi Oetomo and Sarekat Islam – did not allow for such a step, the goal was changed to close cooperation. At the Yogyakarta railway station, and this must have worried the colonial authorities, the deputation was welcomed by local Boedi Oetomo leaders; and during the interval in a public gathering in the evening of that same day, the deputation conferred with representatives of the Sarekat Islam. At the station they had also been greeted by Prince Notodirodjo, son of Paku Alam V, the ruler of one of the two Yogyakarta principalities, and chairman of Boedi Oetomo. Dutch sources claimed it was just a chance encounter. This may have been so, but at the end of the public gathering, the same Prince Notodirodjo thanked Douwes Dekker and the other speakers and wished them success – according to Douwes Dekker's own report – in their 'honest endeavour, as he chose to call it, to ensure the Indiër [...] of the rights to which he had already been entitled for so long'.[15]

Douwes Dekker had planned meticulously. Meetings during the propaganda tour had been well publicized in advance on handbills, bill-boards, and advertisements, and were reasonably well attended. Special invitations had been sent to persons the members of the deputation specifically wanted to meet. At railway stations brass bands turned out to welcome them. The climax came on 25 December 1912 in Bandung. In the ballroom of Maison Vogelpoel in the Bragaweg the Indische Partij was formally constituted. Deliberately, in violation of existing legislation, no permission had been asked to hold the meeting.[16] The establishment of the Indische Partij, the phraseology chosen, and these words stuck in the mind of the authorities, was 'a declaration of war by the tax-paying slaves to the tax-grabbing state of the home country'.[17] Black

[14] *Nota Douwes Dekker* 1913:19; Rinkes to Idenburg, 16-1-1913 (*Bescheiden 'Indische Partij'* 1913).
[15] *Het Tijdschrift*, 15-10-1912; *Vervolg* 1913:82.
[16] *Volksraad* 1918-19:248.
[17] Report of the audience granted to Douwes Dekker, Tjipto Mangoenkoesoemo and Van Ham on 13-3-1913 (*Bescheiden 'Indische Partij'* 1913).

was chosen as background-colour of the Indische Partij flag to symbolize the mourning for the bondage of the non-*totoks* in the colony.[18]

The gathering in Bandung was one manifestation of Indo-European bravado. The mood was definitely anti-Dutch and anti-*totok*. At the railway station 'thoroughbred' Europeans were ignored. When the trains arrived in the early evening carrying participants from outside the city, this raised a general cheer. The same happened when Douwes Dekker, who had come to the station to greet his friends, was chaired aloft. One and a half years later *De Expres* recollected that the whole station hall had resounded with loud shouts of joy.[19] The Dutch civil servant who had to report on the events said that at the station and at Maison Vogelpoel Indo-Europeans behaved as if they were in charge. He himself had fallen victim to this mood. In the Maison Vogelpoel the dinner he had ordered was grabbed from him by an Indo-European, who snapped that he was certainly more hungry.

Around nine o'clock in the evening Douwes Dekker escorted by his comrades in procession came from his house to the meeting hall. In front marched a military band, and torch-bearers lent drama to the parade. J.G. van Ham, a Boer officer who had settled in the Netherlands Indies, had arranged for a guard of honour of Boer soldiers on horseback. 'Sons of the land' only, including some Javanese, were admitted to the meeting, which was attended by about eight hundred people. *Totok*s were refused entry and intimidated. They were given a look of contempt, and some were deliberately run down.

Meant to be a party for all who did not belong to the European white segment of colonial society the Indische Partij called for the creation of what was designated an '*Indiërs* race'. Once this 'race' had been formed, and 'the Javanese no longer calls himself a JAVANESE, the Chinese a CHINESE, the European a EUROPEAN, but all call themselves INDIËR', it was explained in *De Expres* in April 1914, 'then all existing iniquities will automatically disappear'.[20] Unity was what was required and true to this credo members of the Indische Partij reached out to Islam and to the Chinese. Douwes Dekker stressed that the Chinese were not foreigners.[21] *De Expres* called it a mistake by 'our brothers' of the Sarekat Islam that they were obsessed by alleged Chinese hostility. Not the Chinese but others were the enemy of the Javanese people.[22] Christianity was treated with less indulgence. Douwes Dekker maintained that missionary activities were a political instrument devoid of any ethics, and consequently harmful and dangerous.[23] *De Expres* proudly wrote in 1914 that

---

[18] Rinkes to Idenburg, 16-1-1913 (*Bescheiden 'Indische Partij'* 1913).
[19] *De Expres*, 31-7-1914.
[20] *De Expres*, 17-4-1914.
[21] *De Expres*, 22-1-1914.
[22] *De Expres*, 11-2-1914.
[23] *De Expres*, 7-2-1914.

in one year the Indische Partij had succeeded in recruiting more Muslims as members then Christian mission had been able to convert in three centuries of colonial rule.[24]

True to his principles in establishing the Indische Partij Douwes Dekker, of whom it was assumed that he was inflicted with the Indo-European hatred of rule by Dutch people from Holland, sought out the cooperation of Indonesians. Some of them he had known since the founding days of Boedi Oetomo. By taking this step he tried to enlarge the group from which he could draw support for his revolutionary ideas; a prospect which really frightened the government. Idenburg suffered nightmares imagining what might happen were Douwes Dekker and his political friends to succeed in taking control of the Sarekat Islam and its mass following.[25] It was an unlikely prospect, but not completely unfounded. Douwes Dekker had succeeded in involving leaders of the early Indonesian nationalist movement in his plans. A few even became close comrades-in-arms.

At the end of 1912 and in early 1913 stock was taken. Dutch civil servants were asked to indicate how far Douwes Dekker's influence had penetrated their district. Almost all concluded that neither he nor his movement had been very successful in gaining support among the non-European population. It was observed that most Javanese who might be favourably disposed towards the Indische Partij had adopted a wait-and-see attitude. They flinched from Douwes Dekker's radicalism, and could not completely rid themselves of their suspicion of Indo-Europeans, many of whom were not prepared to treat them in a genuinely friendly fashion. An additional reason for distrust was the fact that the Indische Partij was in favour of granting Indo-Europeans the right of landownership; a point which was referred to with some frequency in newspapers affiliated with Boedi Oetomo and Sarekat Islam.[26] While all this may have been true, some civil servants pointed to some groups which were susceptible to his propaganda. In January 1913 the *Resident* of Bantam reported that Douwes Dekker exercised a 'fatal influence' on many native civil servants, who 'swallow all he says', while his articles, copied by the Malay newspapers, were not 'without their influence on Foreign Orientals and the more educated members of the Native population'.[27] This assessment seems to be corroborated by the other reports. Occasionally it was mentioned that Indonesian intellectuals and members of the Javanese bureaucracy had become members; motivated in some cases by the arrogance of the Chinese.

---

[24] *De Expres*, 15-1-1914.
[25] Idenburg to De Waal Malefijt, 25-8-1913, NA, Kol. Openbaar, Vb. 25-9-1913 56.
[26] Rinkes to Idenburg, 16-1-1913 (*Bescheiden 'Indische Partij'* 1913).
[27] Van Rinsum to Idenburg, 14-1-1913 (*Bescheiden 'Indische Partij'* 1913).

Of the Indonesians who joined the Indische Partij two stood out in particular. One was Tjipto Mangoenkoesoemo a native doctor. At the meeting at which the Indische Partij was constituted he was elected its Deputy Chairman. He also became editor of *De Expres*. Tjipto Mangoenkoesoemo had been born in 1886 in the village of Pacangakan in Jepara, on the north coast of Central Java. In 1911 he had distinguished himself during the outbreak of plague in East Java; a disease which in those days was still relatively new to the Netherlands Indies, where there had only been a few isolated cases up to that time. Tjipto Mangoenkoesoemo was the first to volunteer for service in the plague-stricken areas, where others physicians, also European ones, were hesitant to venture. For his services he was awarded a knighthood in the Order of Orange-Nassau, something he did not fail to mention in later years when he had became embroiled in conflicts with the colonial government. At moments when his relations with the authorities were at a low ebb, he threatened to return the decoration. He was, in the words of Koch (1960:146), somebody 'of great intelligence, with a lively mind and a strong sense of right and justice'.

Rinkes described Tjipto Mangoenkoesoemo as 'Mr. Douwes Dekker's big trump card'. Others also singled him out when they ventured to comment on the influence of the Indische Partij among the indigenous population.[28] The *Assistent-Resident* of Tangerang was sure that Tjipto Mangoenkoesoemo, not Douwes Dekker, was the reason why quite a large number of Indonesians who could understand Dutch read *Het Tijdschrift* and *De Expres*.[29] Initially Tjipto Mangoenkoesoemo was well regarded in colonial government circles and his contributions to *Het Tijdschrift* were praised for their moderation. Within a short span of time this attitude changed. Tjipto Mangoenkoesoemo's style was described as having been transformed into 'biting sarcasm'.[30] This contributed to making him notorious, as he himself described it, 'as the greatest revolutionary, who stalks the Indies' (Tjipto Mangoenkoesoemo 1915:2).

The other was a member of the higher, but impoverished, Javanese nobility: Raden Mas Soewardi Soerjaningrat. His father was a son of Paku Alam III. Soewardi had entered the STOVIA but had dropped out when he had to repeat a year and his study grant was stopped. Nevertheless, as a distinctive token of praise he had received a special certificate testifying to his excellent mastery of Dutch (Soeratman 1981-82:19). He had found employment in a chemist's shop in Yogyakarta, but was dismissed because he spent too much time writing for *De Expres* and other newspapers (Soebagijo 1981:63). Thereupon he became a proof reader for *De Expres* and chaired the local Sarekat Islam branch in Bandung.

---

[28] Rinkes to Idenburg, 16-1-1913 (*Bescheiden 'Indische Partij'* 1913).
[29] Vernet to Resident of Batavia, 7-1-1913 (*Nota Douwes Dekker* 1913, II:118).
[30] Darna Koesoema in *Weekblad voor Indië*, cited in *De Indische Gids* 1918, I:248.

Soewardi Soerjaningrat (l), E.F.E. Douwes Dekker (c) and Tjipto Mangoenkoesomo (r) in Java (Koch 1960)

As early as February 1913, the Governor General and his advisers began to think about whether action should be taken against Douwes Dekker. The utilization of extraordinary legal powers might also be appropriate to prevent what had been written in *Het Tijdschrift* and *De Expres* to appear in the Malay press.[31] Soon hesitation was thrown to the winds and action was taken against Douwes Dekker and his closest associates. It started innocently. At the end of

---

[31] De Graeff to the Council of the Indies, 20-2-1913, NA, Kol. Openbaar, Vb. 7-3-1913 35.

November 1913, it would be one hundred years since the Netherlands had been liberated from the Napoleonic occupation. This called for celebrations, likewise in the colony. It was not too long before it became known that in some places Indonesians had been persuaded (*perintah haloes*, a gentle order, was the term used to describe this method of suggestion) to contribute money for the celebrations. Alerted by this Batavia urged its civil servants to exercise the greatest circumspection in involving the population in the commemoration. Requests that they contribute financially could easily slip over in improper pressure, even abuse. Caution was essential 'because urging Natives to give contributions on a somewhat larger scale, would be calling on circles in which the meaning of the festivities might not be understood or at least not recognized as a cause for rejoicing'. They should not be presented with subscription lists and gifts should only be accepted from those persons who in the past had clearly testified that they desired 'to identify as much as possible with the Dutch Nation and who therefore will participate in a Dutch national festivity completely out of their own free will'.[32]

The exercise of celebrating the Netherlands regaining its independence from the French was a little bit awkward in a colony and might not exactly be a reason for rejoicing for the non-Dutch residents. The colonial administrators realized this and were not alone in doing so, not even in the European community. As might have been expected strong opposition was voiced by the leaders of the Indische Partij. Douwes Dekker announced that he would oppose the plans to celebrate the anniversary with 'vigilance and ridicule'.[33] Tjipto Mangoenkoesoemo chose another course. In July 1913 he founded a Native Committee for the Commemoration of the Netherlands Centenary of Freedom; generally known as the Native Committee or, in Malay the Comité Boemi Poetra (in a brochure by Douwes Dekker and friends correctly translated not as 'natives' but as 'sons of the soil'). The main objective was to plead for a change in the composition of the Koloniale Raad, the Colonial Council, a quasi-representative advisory body that The Hague had announced the previous year to be established in the Netherlands Indies. It should have more Indonesians among its members than initially envisaged, and the majority of these Indonesians should not, as the government intended, be recruited from the 'notables'. Tjipto Mangoenkoesoemo explained later that another motive behind the formation of the committee had been the collection of money among Javanese in Malang by the *patih*, the Deputy Regent.[34]

Tjipto Mangoenkoesoemo and Soewardi wanted to use the centenary to

---

[32] Circular 1st Government Secretary, 6-8-1913, NA, Kol. Openbaar, Vb. 17-10-1913 61; Idenburg to Pleyte, 30-8-1915, NA, Kol. Geheim, Vb. 14-10-1915 P12.
[33] *De Expres*, 26-2-1913, cited in *Vervolg* 1913.
[34] Memorie van verdediging van Tjipto Mangoenkoesoemo, NA, Kol. Openbaar, Vb. 25-9-1913 56; Douwes Dekker et al. 1913b:11.

SOERAT EDERAN No. 1.
DJIKA SAJA NEDERLANDER,...

OLEH

R. M. SOEWARDI SOERJANINGRAT.

DI KELOEARKAN OLEH

Comité Boemipoetra goena merajakan Pesta Seratoes Tahoen Keradjaän Belanda.

DI BANDOENG.

VLUGSCHRIFT No. 1.
ALS IK EENS NEDERLANDER WAS,...

DOOR

R. M. SOEWARDI SOERJANINGRAT.

UITGAVE VAN HET

Inlandsch Comité tot Herdenking van Neerlands Honderdjarige Vrijheid.

GEVESTIGD TE BANDOENG.

van de Eerste Bandoengsche Publiciteit Maatschappij.

The Malay and Dutch version of If I were a Dutchman'...

draw public attention to the undemocratic nature of the colonial system and to press for political reform. They intended to send a telegram of congratulations to Queen Wilhelmina. It should contain more than just platitudes. The senders would ask for the removal of the restriction on the right of free assembly and intended to emphasize that the Colonial Council should be constituted as soon as possible and be a truly representative and democratic forum. Before they could send the telegram the authorities had already intervened. The reason for Batavia to act was a brochure published by the Committee, ridiculing the celebrations, *Als ik eens Nederlander was...* (If I were a Dutchman...).

The pamphlet sent shockwaves through Dutch circles. In Holland C.Th. van Deventer, the founding father of the Ethical Policy, considered it an affront. He said in parliament that the pamphlet totally disregarded the civilization with which the Netherlands was imbuing its colony.[35] In the Netherlands Indies the pamphlet became the excuse for the colonial authorities to act against the top of the Indische Partij. The problem was not the pamphlet as such, Idenburg was to reveal in 1919 speaking of Soewardi, it was 'his whole mentality', which had prompted him to decide to act.[36]

In Java copies were confiscated by the police. This, of course, whetted everyone's appetite to read the pamphlet. Two weeks after its publication, the chairman and secretary of the committee, Tjipto Mangoenkoesoemo and Soewardi, were arrested. No risks were taken. Paranoia had taken root. The *Resident* of the Preanger, T.J. Janssen, under whose authority Bandung fell, was convinced that Tjipto Mangoenkoesoemo could count upon considerable support among the followers of the Indische Partij. Hence, he feared a 'mad coup' by the Indische Partij. Between thirty and forty soldiers were sent to the houses of Tjipto Mangoenkoesoemo and Soewardi. Other troops and policemen patrolled the city. Government offices and houses of civil servants were guarded. The two other members of the committee were also apprehended. One was the novelist Abdoel Moeis, editor of the newspaper *Kaoem Moeda* (The Young Ones) and publisher and editor of the paper *Hindia Serikat* (The United Indies). The other was the editor-in-chief of *Kaoem Moeda* Wignjadisastra. After twenty-four hours detention both were set free again. On his release Wignjadisastra promised to refrain from seditious writings in future, and to report only on abuses, after first investigating whether they had indeed taken place or not. Abdoel Moeis decided to halt the publication of *Hindia Serikat* for the time being.

The arrests were made even before Idenburg had ordered them. Janssen had acted of his own accord to prevent the movement, which he believed was still confined to a few 'hot-headed persons', from spreading. There had been

---

[35] *Handelingen Tweede Kamer* 1913-14:119.
[36] *Handelingen Tweede Kamer* 1918-19:2082.

no legal basis to justify Janssen's decision, but Idenburg, stressing the necessity to take into custody persons who formed a threat to the maintenance of law and order, condoned it. He also took up a suggestion by Janssen to apprehend Douwes Dekker. When Douwes Dekker praised Soewardi and Tjipto Mangoenkoesoemo as heroes and victims of the good cause in *De Expres* Idenburg set in motion the procedure to have Douwes Dekker banned from Java. It was a course of action some had already been suggesting for months. His advisers, Rinkes and Hazeu, had been against it. They feared opposition in Holland and were sure that banishment could well afford Douwes Dekker a 'martyr's crown'.[37]

What made the situation all the more serious in the eyes of the colonial government was that the pamphlet had also been published in Malay. They would never have been arrested the public prosecutor told Soewardi in jail, had there not been a Malay version (Douwes Dekker, Tjipto Mangoenkoesoemo and Soewardi Soerjaningrat 1913a). Idenburg deemed the whole affair so urgent that he called an emergency meeting of his advisers, the Coucil of the Indies, on 31 August 1913. At this meeting Idenburg asked the Coucil for its support in 'crippling the movement'. He also took the opportunity to point out an important change that had taken place during the previous six months. All kinds of seditious opinions were now being aired in Malay. Idenburg stressed that the import of this should not be underrated. In August, in a fifteen-page-long letter in which he explained his steps to the Minister of the Colonies in The Hague, he once again touched upon this matter. To underline the seriousness of the affair, he pointed to the plans of the Indische Partij to start a Malay edition of *De Expres*, which would therefore be written 'in the language in which the Native middle class throughout the whole of the Netherlands Indies can be reached'.[38]

The prospect of *De Expres* in Malay made Idenburg and other colonial administrators even more doubtful about whether the legislation provided the government with sufficient clout to prevent and curb the dangers that might arise from what was called a 'tendentiously edited periodical press, publishing its products in Eastern languages'.[39] The impotence of Batavia was put forward as one of the arguments for tightening the press regulations and returning the colonial administration some of the powers it had ceded less than a decade before. Idenburg explained to the Minister of the Colonies

---

[37] Idenburg to De Waal Malefijt, 25-8-1913, Rinkes to Idenburg, 16-1-1913, Hazeu to Idenburg, 14-2-1913, NA, Kol. Openbaar, Vb. 25-9-1913 56, *Bescheiden 'Indische Partij'* 1913.
[38] Minutes of the extraordinary meeting of the Council of the Indies, 31-7-1913, Idenburg to De Waal Malefijt, 25-8-1913, NA, Kol. Openbaar, Vb. 25-9-1913 56.
[39] Idenburg to Pleyte, 22-2-1915, 1st Government Secretary to Rinkes, 28-5-1913, NA, Kol. Openbaar, Vb. 17-9-1915 46.

that he had refrained from bringing the leaders of the Indische Partij to court because criminal law was riddled with loopholes, and judges on the whole tended to act in contradistinction to the interests of the colonial administration, instead of cooperating with it.[40] His legal advisers had also pointed out to him that the sentences a judge might pass on Tjipto Mangoenkoesoemo and Soewardi would probably be trifling and would not deter them from continuing their activities. The Council of the Indies shared this view.

The fact that shortly before their arrests Tjipto Mangoenkoesoemo and Soewardi, indignant at the way in which Dutch-language newspapers had reported the activities of their Committee, had published letters to the editor in *De Expres* entitled respectively 'Power and terror' and 'All for one and one for all' was seen as additional proof that they were determined to proceed with their campaign. Neither had eschewed bold words. Tjipto Mangoenkoesoemo had written about the thrill of provoking the government, forcing it to strain every nerve. Soewardi's article had ended with the words, *Rawé-rawé rantas malang malang poetoeng*; 'it will be slashed to shreds, obstacles will be broken down', a phrase which would be developed into a popular slogan in the nationalist movement.[41]

In a sense the Committee had accomplished what it set out to do. In their explanatory memorandum issued in their defence, which they had written while in jail, Tjipto Mangoenkoesoemo and Soewardi both explained that the intention of the committee had been to stir up as much outrage as possible in the European community: the more, the merrier. This was the only way to elicit a reaction from the Dutch public and parliament. Both claimed that it had never been their intention to mobilize the masses. Had any news ever reached the colonial authorities about disturbances caused by their activities? To prevent disorder, the pamphlet had deliberately not been written in Javanese or common Malay, but in literary Malay which limited its readership to educated people.[42]

Whatever Tjipto Mangoenkoesoemo, Soewardi, and Douwes Dekker might write or state in their defence, all was to no avail. Idenburg had made up his mind and was intent on safeguarding the Indonesian population against any further incursions by the three. He used the extraordinary powers vested in him to ban *Residents* of the Netherlands Indies to another part of the Archipelago. All three were interrogated as was required, but only as a for-

---

[40] Idenburg to De Waal Malefijt, 25-8-1913, NA, Kol. Openbaar, Vb. 25-9-1913 56.
[41] Minutes extraordinary meeting of the Council of the Indies, 31-7-1913, Memorie van verdediging van Soewardi Soerjaningrat, NA, Kol. Openbaar, Vb. 25-9-1913 56.
[42] Memorie van verdediging van Tjipto Mangoenkoesoemo, Memorie van verdediging van Soewardi Soerjaningrat, Proces-verbaal interrogation Abdoel Moeis, 13-8-1913, NA, Kol. Openbaar, Vb. 25-9-1913 56.

mality to comply with the law. On 18 August 1913 Tjipto Mangoenkoesoemo was assigned the island of Banda as his place of residence; Soewardi that of Bangka. Douwes Dekker was banned to Kupang in Timor. Douwes Dekker's efforts to 'reach the native population in particular young native intellectuals' carried great weight in the justification of this decision.[43] All three decided, as was the right of people sentenced in this way, to ask to be allowed to go and live in Europe. Idenburg granted the request. His purpose had been to render the three harmless, and was not set on a punitive expedition or revenge.[44]

The affair left a bitter aftertaste. In Batavia and The Hague there was a conviction that Idenburg could have intervened earlier and that he would not have been forced to take such draconian measures had the colonial government held wider powers. Realization also dawned that existing regulations only covered printed matter. Other forms of incitement by 'embittered extremists who had come to see the creation of discontent in their environment as a sacred vocation' had to be taken into account as well. This included public speeches, theatrical performances, and hand-written documents; also mentioned in the official correspondence about the issue was 'a loud conversation in a full club house' and even a chance remark ejaculated in anger or frustration.[45]

Another question discussed by the authorities was how to tighten up control of associations. Organizations could be refused formal legal recognition by the Governor General, but that was all. This did not automatically spell dissolution. Members could ignore the decision and continue to pursue their activities. Action against them had to be left to the courts, with all the reservations the colonial administration had about such a course of action. Copying British legislation in the Straits Settlements was considered, but rejected. European public opinion would not accept it. In contrast to legislation in the Straits Settlements, government control of organizations should remain the exception, not the rule. Unlike the Straits Settlements, there were many European associations in the Netherlands Indies, including labour associations, which because of their aims had a militant character. All these – the Coucil of the Indies also mentioned reading circles and evenings for cards – would be covered by a Singapore-like legislation. Any legislation should also allow for supervision over Chinese organizations, nationalist associations like the Sarekat Islam, and occasionally even some European ones; but hundreds of European associations should remain untouched by it.[46]

A similar dilemma was posed by the action the colonial administration took

[43] Decision Idenburg, 18-8-1913, NA, Kol. Openbaar, Vb. 25-9-1913 56.
[44] Idenburg to De Waal Malefijt, 25-8-1913, NA, Kol. Openbaar, Vb. 25-9-1913 56
[45] Note section II General Secretary, 3-9-1913, Note section A1 BuZa, 28-11-1913, NA, Kol. Openbaar, Vb. 17-12-1913 1.
[46] Cordes to Idenburg, 26-3-1913, Council of the Indies, 7-7-1914, NA, Kol. Openbaar, Vb. 14-6-1915 31.

against the Indische Partij. The Indische Partij was transformed into a banned organization. In the eyes of Idenburg and his advisers, it had taken on the guise of a political party. This was against the law in the Netherlands Indies. Members of the Indische Partij had made themselves liable to punishment. Meetings and torchlight processions or other parades had to be prevented, if necessary by employing force.[47] Strictly speaking acting against the Indische Partij meant the authorities also had to act against the Boedi Oetomo and the Sarekat Islam if political issues were raised at their meetings, and also, as the Coucil of the Indies had pointed out, against the Association for Women's Suffrage.[48] The solution found was to explain that what been the deciding factor in the case of the Indische Partij was the threat it posed to public order.

Having acquired the stigma of a subversive organization, the Indische Partij dissolved itself in April 1913. Memories were more difficult to erase. In 1914 calling cards, writing paper and the like in the colours of the Indische Partij were still advertised in *De Expres*. Its activities were continued by Insulinde, which had its headquarters in Semarang. Van Ham, the Boer leader and up to then secretary of the Indische Partij, became its chairman. He and other Insulinde leaders were put under police surveillance. 6 September, the day the Indische Partij had been founded, and by chance also the day the three exiles had sailed for Holland, was proclaimed I.P. Day by Insulinde.

The resolute action of the colonial authorities bore fruit. It had frightened off many members of the Indische Partij from joining Insulinde. This did not discourage *De Expres*. Heartening its readers it reminded them that the SDAP, by now well-represented in Dutch parliament, had been founded by twelve people. The newspaper itself experienced a drop in subscriptions and consequently faced severe financial difficulties. It was – for the time being – only rescued by money from the Tado Fund (Tot aan de Onafhankelijkheid, Till Independence) established by the Indische Partij. Yet, the paper stressed, the core remained as determined as ever.

To the hard-core members the three exiles assumed a saint-like aura. In April 1914, when Insulinde held its Patriots Days, three chairs behind the committee table remained unoccupied. 'The respective spirits will be invited to occupy the empty seats', *De Expres* wrote in advance.[49] The meeting itself was an enjoyable event with a *pasar malam* held in the garden. A telegram sent by the exiles 'Hold high the banner' created a furore. People testified to their devotion to them.[50] Dédéism, named after DD, defined in *De Expres* as this 'entirely independent building of thought, this political sociological system'

---

[47] 1st Government Secretary to Director of Justice, 1-4-1913, NA, Kol. Openbaar, Vb. 14-6-1915 31.
[48] Advice Council of the Indies, 3-3-1913, NA, Kol. Openbaar, Vb. 7-3-1913 35.
[49] *De Expres*, 28-2-1914.
[50] *De Expres*, 16-4-1914.

became the ideology of Insulinde.

The controversial festivities to commemorate independence from the French were organized with a somewhat tempered zeal all over the colony. There were countless early morning parades by military bands, not always appreciated by people who wanted to sleep in on these public holidays; prayer meetings in churches; and musical performances, dawn concerts and singing by schoolchildren and orphans. *Matinées musicales,* and film showings; *kermesses d'été,* and *pasar malam* fairs also featured prominently in the celebrations.

In spite of the misgivings expressed about the active involvement of non-Europeans in the festivities, ordinary people flocked *en masse* to enjoy the spectacles and assiduously attended the entertainment especially arranged for them: popular games; gamelan and *wajang wong* performances and other traditional dance parties. Occasionally, it was even observed that Chinese and Javanese had gone to even greater lengths to decorate their houses or hang out flags than had the Europeans. Natives and Chinese, and on a rare occasion also Arabs, participated in parades, which were often organized separately for the different population groups. Of these, too, it was sometimes remarked that much more effort was put into them than into the European parades.

In Kupang in Timor one of the main feasts was an *electrische dubbeltjes visserij,* electric dime fishery, in which people had to try to recover a coin from an electrically wired aquarium. It was reported that at first the natives thought it an easy game to get some extra money. This was a miscalculation: 'Kaja ajerblanda [strong sparkling water] said one who quickly withdrew his hand from the water. *Tadjam* [sharp] said his neighbour. And both went to throw hoop-la rings at a packet of tobacco, a knife, or a skein of coloured wool'.[51] Near Medan one of the programme items was 'cycling for Easterners'. In Semarang a 'surprising combination', a mixed public of 'Thomas Atkins and Kromo together with fathers and sisters and orphans from the Christian institutions, schoolchildren and high school pupils, as well as the barracks flowers' filled the theatre to watch what was mainly a demonstration of gymnastics and military skill.[52] The grand finale was impressive: the enactment of an attack on a column of marching soldiers by Acehnese. After the assault had been beaten off, children in orange, white, and blue suits formed a pyramid, with the Maid of Holland on top; all with Bengali illuminations providing a background, their smoke bothering the choir of Protestant orphan girls who adorned the scene with patriotic songs.

Javanese civil servants had their own special festivities, usually in the house of the Regent. In Semarang they were regaled with a *tajuban,* a traditional dance party with paid female dancers. Local leaders of nationalist organizations did not sit by passively. In Medan a deputation of the Sarekat Islam

---

[51] *De Locomotief,* 9-12-1913.
[52] *De Locomotief,* 19-11-1913.

marched along in an historico-allegorical procession that paraded through the town alongside floats of the wealthy estate companies. In Rembang a crowd of Sarekat Islam members – *De Locomotief* estimated that at least a few thousand took part, carrying Dutch flags and Orange pennants – visited the *Resident*. At the Residency statements were read praising educational policy, freedom of religion, and legal security. The *Resident* reported that in view of these accomplishments, Sarekat Islam members could not but join in the cheering: 'They had not failed to notice how many millions are spent to elevate the native'. This finished the procession went on to the Dutch social club where a fancy dress ball had just started. After performing a number of dances and shouting 'Long live the Netherlands – long live the SI – hurray! – hurray!' they left again.[53] In Semarang the Sarekat Islam held a special prayer session in the main mosque asking for God's blessings for the welfare of the Netherlands and its royal house. It was followed by a *selamatan*, a communal religious meal, 'for members and other natives.'[54] Similar prayer sessions were held in Purworejo and Surabaya. In the latter city the Sarekat Islam newspaper *Oetoesan Hindia* had even called upon its readers to come to the mosque to pray to celebrate Dutch independence.

Some performances were a perfect enactment of how life in a tranquil, contented colonial society should be. In Cirebon, after parading through town in sarong and a white coat, with an orange or red, white, and blue sash, their heads bedecked with a straw hat, schoolchildren paid their respects to the portrait of Queen Wilhelmina by kneeling down and making a *sembah*. Thereupon they sang a 'native song'. The correspondent of *De Locomotief* called it 'truly a gripping demonstration of homage'.[55] In Tegal the festivities were opened by the *controleur*. His three cheers for the House of Orange and the Netherlands was met with such a passionate response from the Europeans present that the 'subsequent glass of champagne brought a welcome refreshment to the dry throat'. This over and done with, a deputation of the Sarekat Islam appeared 'on fiery horses, dressed in splendid uniforms, with black moustaches glued on, and bedecked with medals'. After the Deputy Chairman had been offered a glass of lemonade, homage was paid to Dutch rule.[56]

In Ambarawa festivities started with a *selamatan* in the *kewedanaan*, the house of the Javanese district chief, where 'the *priyayi* ate and the many Europeans drank'. Next day the *controleur* delivered a speech in the city square. Natives and Chinese had assembled in front of the podium, Europeans had taken

---

[53] *De Locomotief*, 29-11-1913; Gonggrijp to Idenburg, 27-11-1913, NA, Kol. Openbaar, Vb. 23-1-1914 15.
[54] *De Locomotief*, 13-11-1913, 19-11-1913, 21-11-1913.
[55] *De Locomotief*, 19-11-1913, 22-11-1913.
[56] *De Locomotief*, 25-11-1913.

refuge in the cool of the gallery of the lieutenant-colonel's house. All cheered the *controleur's* exposition, speaking first in Dutch and than in Javanese, about what the Netherlands had done in the past one hundred years for its colony. In the evening people again went to the *kewedanaan*. There, a Dutchmen wrote to *De Locomotief* 'a beauty treated us to her rhythmic *tandak* movements, and the host to whisky and soda'.[57] The Europeans left before midnight. The Javanese continued to watch the dances; the civil servants inside the *kewedanaan*, the commoners outside it.

The person who reported to *De Locomotief* on the celebrations in Ambarawa could not hide his pleasure at the demonstration of native devotion to the Dutch crown. It formed a good opportunity for him to lash out against those who had expressed doubts regarding the loyalty of the Indonesian population: 'Let them talk, those who dare to claim that the native would not share our sentiment about our independence because in the past few days in Ambarawa it became apparent that he harbours sentiments for the House of Orange, although of course less than we do'.[58] It must have been a great relief – and letters by Dutch civil servants reporting to Idenburg on the festivities testified to this – after the spectre of a St Bartholomew's Night in August, barely three months before to observe that Indonesians – and the equally troublesome Chinese and Arabs – had joined in the festivities in great numbers.

Opposition by Indonesians and Indo-Europeans had been drowned in the manifestations of their fellow-countrymen who had joined in the parades and other festivities. From Surabaya it was reported that an Indonesian 'trouble-maker' had tried to persuade the local population to boycott the festivities. A girl from Semarang, she was only fourteen, wrote to Tjipto Mangoenkoesoemo that she and many of her fellow-girl pupils at the Middelbaar Uitgebreid Lager Onderwijs (MULO, Dutch lower secondary school) considered the anniversary a *totok* celebration in which they should not take part. She had also observed how members of the Indische Partij drove around in a car, with two orange flags and two flags of the Indische Partij, the latter boldly raised higher than the former, deliberately driving through Bojong, the quarter where many *totoks* lived. Elsewhere it appears to have been mostly Indonesian students at Western type educational institutions who had declined to participate. In Batavia students of the STOVIA, greatly to the annoyance of their director, had refused to attend in the feast organized by their school. The same had happened at the Opleidingsschool voor Inlandsche Ambtenaren (OSVIA, Training College for Native Civil Servants) in Bandung, Magelang, and Madiun. One of the reasons for the refusal of the OSVIA students in Madiun was that they considered the popular games too childish and below the dignity of people

---

[57] *De Locomotief*, 27-11-1913.
[58] *De Locomotief*, 27-11-1913.

who belonged, as many of them did, to the nobility.[59]

Such outbursts of protest remained an exception. At the end of November Idenburg could wire Queen Wilhelmina that all population groups 'by and large had celebrated the centennial feasts with great cheerfulness and with gratitude had commemorated what the Netherlands Indies owes to the Orange Dynasty'. The reply was equally high-spirited. Communicating her gratitude, the Queen expressed her hope that 'God would ever seek to strengthen the bond between the mother country and the Indies; that the one may benefit the other'.[60] Nevertheless, in August 1915 when Idenburg suggested celebrating in August the following year the centennial of the transfer of Java by the British to the Dutch on an at least equal scale, the response was far from positive. The Coucil of the Indies pointed out that celebrations in 1913 had not been characterized by sincere enthusiasm, and feared renewed Indo-European protests.[61]

The 'three exiles', as they were known, had witnessed nothing of this. They had arrived in Holland on 2 October. With the financial support of the Tado Fund they and their families began a new life. All three took up residence in The Hague. On their arrival their they were welcomed at the railway station by a small crowd of about fifty people, who greeted them singing the march of the Indische Partij; the Indies national anthem, as it was sometimes known. In the Netherlands they attended meetings, gave lectures to a variety of organizations and political parties, including the socialist ones. Occasionally, when he addressed such meetings Soewardi bedecked his head with a fez. On one such occasion a former colonial civil servant at one such occasions complemented the 'native speakers' on their excellent Dutch. From the public gallery, where special seats were reserved for them, they followed the discussions in parliament about their banishment in November.[62]

Tjipto Mangoenkoesoemo enrolled as a medical student at the University of Amsterdam. 'Higher education for a barbarian. My friend!', he wrote to *De Expres*, 'it felt so strange to take a seat in the lecture-room among the students, the flower of the Dutch youth'. Observing Indonesian students attending lectures filled him with pride. It was proof that 'the Indiër is not as stupid as he is commonly depicted'.[63] Besides resuming his medical studies, Tjipto Mangoenkoesoemo intended to carry on as a journalist. He explained that he refused to let down those who had contributed to the Tado Fund. He and Douwes Dekker were both mentioned as 'editors in the Netherlands' in the colophon of *De Expres*.

---

[59]   *De Indiër* 1-7:12, 14-5.
[60]   *De Locomotief*, 24-11-1913.
[61]   Idenburg to Pleyte, 30-8-1915, NA, Kol. Geheim, Vb. 14-10-1915 P12.
[62]   *De Locomotief*, 19-11-1913.
[63]   *De Expres*, 2-3-1914.

The three exiles in Holland. Sitting from left to right, Tjipto Mangoenkoesoemo, E.F.E. Douwes Dekker and Soewardi Soerjaningrat. (KITLV 3725.)

Shortly after his arrival Tjipto Mangoenkoesoemo also became editor of *De Indiër*, a 'weekly devoted to spiritual and material life in the Indies and East Asia', published in The Hague. He shared the editorship with Frans Berding, a friend of Douwes Dekker. *De Indiër* strove after an international network resembling that of *Het Tijdschrift*. In *De Expres* it was said that its editors

> were amongst other activities in close contact with the Committee Pro India in Zurich, (its members included Douwes Dekker's old friends Walter Strickland and Shiyamaji Krishnavarma), with Egyptian nationalists, who have their circle in Geneva, with patriots from British India, with the Islamic brotherhoods in Europe,

and it seeks constantly to widen its contacts with all who express the general resurgence of all Eastern peoples.[64]

Occasionally *De Indiër* did indeed contain the veiled references of *Het Tijdschrift* to a revolution – always explaining to the readers that the editors had a revolution of ideas in mind and not physical violence. Among its contributors was Mathilde Deromps, now testifying to her admiration for Madan Lal Dhingra, the 'killer of tyrants'. On the eve of World War I *De Indiër* refused to condemn Gavrilo Princip and his assassination of Archduke Franz Ferdinand.

Soewardi entered a training college for teachers. So did his wife, whom he had married the day before he left for Holland. *De Expres* informed its readers that after her return to Java she wanted to 'be useful to the education of our girls'.[65] Soewardi also continued to be active as journalist, contributing to newspapers and periodicals in Holland and the Netherlands Indies. Later on he became the Director of the Indonesisch Persbureau (annex Brochurehandel), the Indonesian Press Agency (annex publisher of brochures), of which either on purpose or by chance the abbreviation was IP. In setting up this press agency, Soewardi did not just want to serve the aims of the Indische Partij. He believed that by providing the Dutch public with more information about the Netherlands Indies Dutch politicians would gradually come around and become more sympathetic to the nationalist cause and would take the interest of the colony and its inhabitants closer to their hearts. Hence, the Indonesisch Persbureau was not only intended to become a link between the Dutch press in Holland and the native press in the Netherlands Indies. It wanted to use whatever channel available to inform the Dutch about the Netherlands Indies. Organizing meetings and lectures was a priority, and cheap brochures, 'Indonesische brochures', were to be published. Planned was also a series of 'Indische monografieën' dealing with current topics, written by 'an Indiër or a Chinese'. When the subject dealt with required this the opinions of a 'competent Dutchman' would also be given, 'in the form of either an ordinary essay or an interview'.[66] Among the first brochures were publications about the Indische Partij and the banishment of its three leaders.

Douwes Dekker set out to write a 'political handbook', a 'scholarly work about the historical evolution of the Netherlands Indies'. *De Expres* revealed that a rich friend had rented a study for him, 'an empty room, 3rd floor in a suburb'. It was furnished with 'two night tables, a chair, a gas heater and a lamp'. *De Expres* kept the address a secret, explaining that Douwes Dekker did not want to be disturbed while working on his book. The newspaper conclud-

---

[64]   *De Expres*, 11-5-1914.
[65]   *De Expres*, 2-2-1914.
[66]   Statutes Indonesisch Persbureau.

ed somewhat sadly that 'our hermit therefore will also not have much time to correspond'.[67] Douwes Dekker's wife followed a course in German and English commercial correspondence. It was hoped that this would later enable her to support the family, which would then no longer be completely dependent on the Tado Fund. Cogently Douwes Dekker used his time in Holland to expand his relations with foreign socialists and agitators. At the end of 1913 he travelled to Germany where among the persons he met were Karl Kautsky and Heinrich Cunow. Around the same time he was invited to France to discuss plans to call together an annual Asian congress with Krishnavarma and others. Lack of money prevented him from accepting the invitation.

None of the three was happy in Holland. After he had tried in vain to turn public opinion in Holland in his favour, Douwes Dekker, as he was to confess later, was to move to Switzerland to join in June 1914. He took up residence first in Versoix near Geneva and then in Zurich, where he was to study political economy. In 1950 in a book published in his praise it was said that he had done so 'to train in the fermenting of rebellion' (Setiabuddhi 1950:100). Soewardi, one his Dutch political friends confessed, experienced all 'the miseries of an Easterner with limited means in a strange, cold, indifferent country' (Fromberg 1918:16-7). He himself wrote in January 1917 that his exile and caring for his family had tired him mentally.[68] Soewardi even had been among the few persons who had the courage to abuse a high civil servant at the Colonial Office. Th.B. Pleyte described Soewardi's behaviour as a 'deviant outburst'.[69] It occurred in February 1917 when forced by his straightened financial circumstances, he had decided to send his pregnant wife and child back to Java. The person in question had refused him access to Pleyte when Soewardi paid a surprise visit to the Ministry of the Colonies. He had brought his wife and child along so that they could bid Pleyte farewell. He also wanted to know whether he himself would be allowed to leave Holland on the next mail boat. The civil servant in question had pointed out that an appointment had to be made to see the minister. As Soewardi wrote to him the following day, he had treated him as 'a mischievous boy', giving him a lesson 'in polite manners with some unchristian curses'.[70] Soewardi had responded in kind.

The person who suffered most from his stay in Holland was Tjipto Mangoenkoesoemo. Early in July 1914, Soewardi sent Pleyte a letter. Tjipto Mangoenkoesoemo was critically ill and might not have long to live. Pleyte was asked to show compassion and allow Tjipto Mangoenkoesoemo to return to Java. Nobody, except a few colonial die-hards, had felt comfortable with the

---

[67] *De Expres*, 23-2-1914.
[68] Soewardi to Abendanon, 16-1-1917, NA, Kol. Geheim, Vb. 6-6-1917 A8.
[69] Pleyte to Van Limburg Stirum, 6-6-1917, NA, Kol. Geheim, Vb. 6-6-1917 A8.
[70] Soewardi to Bakhuis, 21-2-1917, NA, Kol. Geheim, Vb. 6-6-1917 A8.

banishments. Even Idenburg felt some remorse. In his letter to The Hague of August 1913 explaining his decisions to ban the three, he had expressed the hope that in the not too distant future he could revoke his decision to ban Tjipto Mangoenkoesoemo and Soewardi from Java.[71] Of the three banishments that of Tjipto Mangoenkoesoemo had probably been taken with the greatest reluctance, that of Douwes Dekker with the most pleasure. In spite of what he did and was to do, Tjipto Mangoenkoesoemo could still count on the sympathy of senior colonial officials. Being one of the Javanese who caused the Dutch authorities the most headaches, and not renowned for his sedate behaviour, he still remained a person who was viewed sympathetically. As late as August 1916 the Acting Adviser for Native Affairs, Hazeu, wrote that Tjipto Mangoenkoesoemo had a far higher character than most of the leaders of the nationalist movement. He was almost universally admired by Indonesians for his honesty, unselfishness, and the sacrifices he made to help others.[72]

Pleyte, who had become the new Minister of the Colonies less than two weeks before Idenburg had signed the order to banish the three Indische Partij leaders, was also not unfavourably disposed. He was less in favour of repressive measures to curb somewhat excessive expressions of nationalism than his predecessor, De Waal Malefijt. Yet, loss of face had to be avoided. The image of the colonial administration had to be preserved. The feeling was that to reverse a decision of the Governor General within weeks 'would seriously weaken the respect for the decisions of that Government'.[73]

During the debate on the colonial budget in parliament Pleyte had already hinted that where a possibility to offer itself to show clemency he would seize the opportunity. Soewardi's letter seemed to present an elegant solution. Pleyte received more detailed information from the Amsterdam physician, Professor C. Winkler. What he learned was alarming. Tjipto Mangoenkoesoemo was partially paralysed and Winkler did not rule out that if his illness progressed Tjipto Mangoenkoesoemo days were numbered. Chances of recovery were slight. The only hope was to allow Tjipto Mangoenkoesoemo to return to Java, where, Winkler stressed, he would pose no threat at all to law and order. His energy was exhausted. Were Tjipto Mangoenkoesoemo to die in exile in the Netherlands, Winkler ended his letter, the political significance would be much greater 'though I do not understand how such a poor soul – because such name he now deserves – has [ever] been dangerous'. Immediately Pleyte sent a wire to Idenburg, suggesting the decision to banish Tjipto Mangoenkoesoemo to be revoked. In view of the urgency of the matter he

---

[71] Idenburg to Pleyte, 25-8-1913, NA, Kol. Openbaar, Vb. 25-9-1913 56.
[72] Hazeu to Idenburg, 21-8-1916, NA, Kol. Openbaar, Vb. 22-11-1916 6.
[73] *Handelingen* 1913-14:37.

asked for a reply by telegram.[74]

After consulting the Coucil of the Indies, Idenburg wired back within a few days that he consented, providing that Tjipto Mangoenkoesoemo submitted a formal request to him. Pleyte summoned Soewardi to his office, and explained that he as Minister of the Colonies would support such an appeal to Idenburg. The two also discussed who was to pay for the passage. Tjipto Mangoenkoesoemo was too poor to do so. Pleyte's solution was to treat Tjipto Mangoenkoesoemo as an 'indigent' and have the state bear the cost of the cheapest fare. He also pointed out, but this could hardly have been a serious alternative in view of Tjipto Mangoenkoesoemo's health, that the latter could always earn a free passage on a freighter by signing on as the ship's doctor.[75]

When Tjipto Mangoenkoesoemo heard about this conversation he reacted indignantly. In an angry letter he told Pleyte what he could do with his suggestion. Correspondence with Java would take months. He was not sure that his health allowed such a delay. Calling Pleyte's attention to the fact that a Dutch physician travelling to Java to combat the plague had been offered a first class passage Tjipto Mangoenkoesoemo wrote that ruined and ill as he was – for both of which he blamed the Dutch government and the decision to exile him – he probably had no other alternative than to accept the offer. On arrival in Batavia he was prepared to be sent to Banda – the place of exile assigned to him in August – 'if the vengefulness of His Excellency the Governor General has not yet been stilled after all the sorrow and misery experienced by me'. Piqued he announced his intention to return his knighthood in the Order of Orange Nassau. The offer of a third class fare had ashamed him. It seemed he had become unworthy of the distinction. Revealing that he was to make his letter and Pleyte's reply public, Tjipto Mangoenkoesoemo ended his letter by asking Pleyte to mention a date on which he could personally hand back his knighthood.[76]

In spite of the letter's 'highly unseemly tone [...] only partly to be excused by his overstrained situation', Pleyte once more summoned Soewardi to his office.[77] Soewardi had to convey to Tjipto Mangoenkoesoemo that the colonial office would mediate and that correspondence with Java was to be conducted by wire. Returning home – they both lived in the same house in The Hague – Soewardi succeeded in calming Tjipto Mangoenkoesoemo down. The same day Tjipto Mangoenkoesoemo wrote two letters. One to Idenburg in which he asked to be allowed to return to Java as soon as possible; and one to Pleyte in which he offered his apologies for his earlier letter, blaming his 'overstrained

---

[74] Soewardi to Pleyte, 3-7-1914, Winkler to Pleyte, 11-7-1914, Pleyte to Idenburg, 13-7-1914, NA, Kol. Geheim, Vb. 14-7-1914 B13.
[75] Note Pleyte, 20-7-1914, Pleyte to Idenburg, 28-7-1914, NA, Kol. Geheim, Vb. 24-7-1914-X13; Vb. 28-7-1914 E14.
[76] Tjipto to Pleyte, 20-7-1914, NA, Kol. Geheim, Vb. 24-7-1914 X13.
[77] Pleyte to Idenburg, 28-7-1914, NA, Kol. Geheim, Vb. 28-7-1914 E14.

situation' for its wording.[78] On 27 July Idenburg revoked the banishment. On 22 August 1914 Tjipto Mangoenkoesoemo left for Java. 'Forgotten are all those dark days spent here in these low countries, days of misery and want', he wrote in his farewell to the readers of *De Indiër*, announcing that in Java he would again take part in the 'renaissance' of his fellow-countryman.[79]

---

[78] Tjipto to Idenburg, 23-7-1914, Tjipto to Pleyte, 23-7-1914, NA, Kol. Geheim, Vb. 24-7-1914 X13.
[79] *De Indiër* 1-43.

CHAPTER IV

The threat from the north

Non-Europeans, and some Europeans shared their accolade, had hailed Japan as the herald of Asia's awakening and as an example of an Eastern nation which had forced the European states to treat it as an equal since it defeated China in 1895. Japan's conflict with Russia put it in an even more prominent position in the discussions about the future of Asia. Just before the outbreak of the Russo-Japanese War gloomy predictions had circulated in- and outside the Netherlands about what a Japanese victory would mean for the Netherlands Indies. The correspondent of *Schlesische Zeitung* in The Hague observed that since Japan had made immense advances in the intellectual and material spheres, 'It is an indisputable article of faith in the Dutch Archipelago that the bold state eager to spread its wings, caught up in the urges of its force to expand, has designs on the annexation of parts of the Dutch colonial possession'.[1] Other contemporary newspapers, among them the Cairo newspaper, *Al-Liwa*, surmised that a Japanese victory would signal the end of Dutch colonial rule in Southeast Asia. It argued of all the European nations it was the Netherlands which had the most reason to fear the outcome of the war. Japan had outgrown its population. North Asia was not the only direction in which it sought to expand its dominion, Southeast Asia was also in its sight. Formosa was presented as the bridgehead to the Netherlands Indies, whose immense richness in natural resources was no secret in Japan. The *Schwäbische Merkur* in Stuttgart was convinced that the war was the catalyst to decide who would be master of the Pacific. It would be crucial in determining whether Japan would be content with what it had, or whether 'unlimited hegemony' in the Pacific would be its lot. In the latter case the *Schwäbische Merkur* foresaw that in the latter case the slogan 'Asia for the Asians which is already resounding more openly from Tokyo into the world' would sooner or later pose a real threat to the European possessions in East Asia. All these European colonies were well defended, except for one:

---

[1]   *Schlesische Zeitung*, 18-2-1904.

the Netherlands Indies.² An Italian newspaper also noted that Japan lusted after parts of the Netherlands Indies. Though usually when this subject came up, Borneo and Celebes sprang most readily to people's lips, in this case it was Java which was supposed to be the cynosure of Japan's ambitions. The newspaper claimed that the location of Java and its natural resources would be sufficient to make Japan independent of the Western Powers.³ In the Netherlands itself, the Prime Minister, A. Kuijper, went as far as to imagine a combined horde of Chinese and Japanese attacking Europe. During a visit to Brussels he expressed the fear that three hundred million people might launch themselves into the Old World.⁴ In the Netherlands Indies, people were more realistic about an immediate Chinese threat. What they feared was not China but Japan, since the signing the Anglo-Japanese Treaty in 1902 an ally of Great Britain. The new power constellation in the Far East disquieted the Dutch who feared that London might condone a Japanese advance south, though others argued exactly the opposite, postulating that the treaty had made such a move less likely (Kuitenbrouwer 1985:147). The prospects of a war between Russia and Japan alarmed the pessimists, whose faith in the support of London in keeping the colony intact had steadily lessened because of the Boer War, and, farther back in history, the annexation of North Borneo. If Japan won the war, *De Locomotief*, wrote in February 1904, its ambitions will be limitless. This was the explanation offered why its editor wholeheartedly wished Japan would suffer a good thrashing.⁵

After Japan had defeated Russia, a country which many in the rest of the world had considered to be militarily far superior to it, Japanese aggression came to feature even more prominently in the aspirations and the haunted fantasies of people in Asia. The sheer fact that Japan, an Eastern nation, had successfully waged war on a Western World Power greatly impressed Asians and Europeans alike, the latter maybe even more than the former. Nowhere was this stronger the case than in the Netherlands Indies where the Dutch were often prey to a vague foreboding that a more powerful rival would one day oust them. Some, as the newspaper the *Algemeen Handelsblad* in Holland did not hesitate to do, castigated the British for having betrayed Europe and European interests by signing the Anglo-Japanese Treaty. Hag-ridden by its fear and hatred of Russia Great Britain was accused of having created a much more formidable rival. It had allowed Japan to become the paramount power in the Pacific. Inexorably the consequences would soon be felt: 'In Asia, in its India, impoverished and depopulated by the plague, England will notice what

[2] *Schwäbischer Merkur,* 18-2-1904.
[3] *De Indische Gids* 1906:1905.
[4] *De Locomotief,* 20-2-1904.
[5] *De Locomotief,* 13-2-1904.

the triumph of the yellow race over a great, Christian, white nation means. England will perceive in China and everywhere else how cheap labour and unrestrained power will enable the Japanese to bar European products from the market.'[6]

The Japanese victory also made a great impression in Indonesian society. Significantly, even in remote villages in Java colour pictures depicting the Japanese victory appeared (Thijs 1965:17-8). The vernacular newspapers discussed the event and its consequences at length (Adam 1995:130-1, 155). One of these, the Chinese-Malay *Kabar Perniagaan* (Trade News), concluded that Japan had become the strongest power in Asia (Adam 1995:136). In Singapore, Japan was praised as 'the first successful champion of the Asiatic race to have arisen since the Tartar invasion of Russia, at any rate since, in the eighteenth and nineteenth century, Holland, Russia, France and Great Britain had conquered and controlled all that in Asia was worth having, except Japan.'[7]

Religious sentiments were not left untouched. Rumour abounded in the international Muslim world that the Japanese considered changing their religion (Watson Andaya 1977:138-9). That this indeed would become a reality was not ruled out. In 1906 in a letter to the editor of a Singapore publication, it was argued that under no circumstances should Christianity become the national religion of Japan. A Christian Japan would only add to the misery of the people in Asia as Christianity foreshadowed the spread of prostitution, addiction to drink, and the waste of luxury. Muslims prepared themselves to win over Japan for Islam. Some went to Japan to preach. The famous university of Al-Azhar in Egypt declared it was prepared to accept students from Japan. In the Netherlands Indies Muslims also speculated about an Islamic Japan, a supposition which remained alive till World War Two (Thijs 1965:19).

Japan formed a source of inspiration to those in Asia and Africa who detested European hegemony. In Asians eye's Japan had shown what could be accomplished when people were prepared to make sacrifices and cast off old habits. Reflecting on the ideal of modernization and progress which educated Indonesians cherished at that time as the way to achieve emancipation, in 1903 a Malay newspaper compared the fate of the Javanese and the Japanese. It observed that the Javanese were far inferior to many other races in the world, which had not been the case three hundred years earlier. The reason presented for this decline was that the Javanese had kept to their traditional customs and had refused to adapt to modern life. With the Japanese it was a very different story. They had suddenly won so much esteem because they had discarded

---

[6] *Algemeen Handelsblad,* 1-6-1905 cited in *De Indische Gids* 1905:1098.
[7] Dutch Consul General in Calcutta to Van Tets van Goudriaan, 22-1-1907, NA, BuZa, A-dos. 190, box 450.

customs which were no longer consonant with the age.[8] Others seized the opportunity to present Japan as an example to illustrate what a good education system could accomplish. An article published in 1908 in the influential reformist Islamic newspaper *al-Imam* (The Leader) observed that the establishment of good schools had allowed Japan to outshine the European nations and had made its victory over such a mighty European Power as Russia possible (Laffan 2006:19). Another conclusion some Indonesians drew was that education had transformed Japan from the 'warlike nation' it had been into the 'centre of arts and science, of trade and industry in Asia'.[9]

Japan had become a prototype of what could be accomplished. The country had made it clear that 'superiority was no absolute monopoly of the Westerners', that 'physical or intellectual development was not a monopoly of the white race'.[10] As a new power Japan assumed the same function European nations and the United States had long held for the Asian states which had endured the onslaught of imperialism. As early as 1896 Japan was one of the countries to which the Filipino rebels of Emilio Aguinaldo had looked to for moral and military support. In the years before World War One, people in Aceh, Bali, Pontianak, and West Sumatra, convinced that Japan would certainly defeat the Netherlands in a military confrontation, if it was not already preparing for an invasion of the Netherlands Indies, turned to Tokyo, or at least this was what was rumoured, for assistance in their struggle against Dutch rule, and asked for intervention and the sending of warships.[11] In Java there were also Muslims, though it is impossible to reconstruct with any exactitude how many, who would welcome a Japanese invasion. At the time of the Russo-Japanese War the saying attributed to the Prophet Muhammad that Muslims should follow black banners (the flags of jihad) which came from the East was recalled in Batavia to intimate that Muslims should support a Japanese invasion of Java. Such speculations meant that the colour black was suspect in the eyes of Dutch administrators for at least a decade to come.[12] To others, who did not aim to oust the Dutch immediately, the accomplishments of Japan presented a pattern to be followed on the road to emancipation. Even in a journal published in the Middle East, the hope was expressed that the Javanese would learn from the Japanese show of strength.[13] As Tjipto Mangoenkoesoemo

---

[8] *Bintang Hindia*, 3-4-1903, cited in *De Locomotief*, 11-11-1903.
[9] *Volksraad* 1918:137.
[10] *De Expres*, 16-4-1914; speech by Soeropati at the annual congress of Insulinde, 11-4-1914 (*De Indiër* 1914:86).
[11] De Waal Malefijt to De Marees van Swinderen, 18-12-1908, Spakler to Van Heutsz, 27-4-1908, 19-2-1909, Dutch Vice Consul in Singapore to Idenburg, 20-3-1913, NA, BuZa, A-dos. 190, box 450, 452 and NA, Kol. Openbaar, Vb. 17-5-1913 17; Watson Andaya 1977:135-8; Ricklefs 1981:138.
[12] *Bescheiden 'Indische Partij'* 1913:158.
[13] *Liwa*, cited in Snouck Hurgronje to Idenburg 12-11-1904, NA, BuZa, A-dos. 190, box 450.

would state shortly before the outbreak of the World War One: 'You feel an awakening which in recent years has dominated the Eastern people, the development started with Japan, it has announced itself to China, the Philippines, among the British Indians, and finally also among the Javanese'.[14]

Aware of the threat of pro-Japanese feelings in the Netherlands Indies, the Dutch colonial authorities viewed Japanese visiting the Archipelago or settling in one of its islands with the utmost suspicion, especially when the region they happened to choose lay outside Java. They were convinced that these Japanese harboured ulterior motives and were planning to contact the domestic enemies of Dutch rule to conspire to produce a reason to wrest such regions from the control of the Dutch. Japanese traders suspected of trying to win over Indonesian leaders were arrested and their entry to the Netherlands Indies was barred. Celebes, where part of the local elite still had not come to grips to the recent advances made by the incursions of Dutch rule was considered especially susceptible to Japanese blandishments. Individual Japanese, among them officers on warships which visited the island in 1913, were believed to be trying to foster good relations with disgruntled noblemen. Such noblemen were suspected of having turned to the Japanese Consul in Batavia, or of plotting with Japanese who happened to be visiting Celebes. In the second half of 1915, one of its spies told the colonial government that a Japanese, clad in traditional Makassarese costume with a red sarong, a white coat, and a red velvet cap, had asked such noblemen for a written statement. According to this story, they had to list their grievances against Dutch rule and ask for help from the Japanese emperor.[15] A second area where the situation was delicate was the Riau Archipelago. The Dutch were sure that the Japanese were trying to win over supporters of the former Sultan who had been deposed by the Dutch. Even the fact that Japanese were trying to conclude trading arrangements with such people was seen as a subversive act. It was argued that the Japanese surreptitiously aimed to create the impression that the signatories still were the legal local heads of the population.[16]

Chinese inhabitants of the Netherlands Indies formed an exception to shower of the admiration for Japan. Japan's victory over Russia evoked mixed feelings among many of them. Indubitably also to them Japan presented an example of what an Asian nation could accomplish (Adam 1995:155). Nevertheless they were well aware that Japan aimed to expand its influence in China. All these apprehensions were overshadowed by the fact that in 1895 Japan had established yet another invidious reputation, for cruelty. People

---

[14] *De Expres*, 16-5-1914.
[15] Extract Gowa report J. Coenen, Idenburg to Pleyte, 17-10-1914, governor Celebes to Idenburg, 11-10-1915, NA, Kol., Geheim, Vb. 8-1-1915 R, Vb. 16-12-1915 X14.
[16] Report about meeting with Japanese Envoy, 4-6-1917, NA, Kol., Geheim, Mr. 1917/120x.

recollected that Japanese troops were notorious for their cruel treatment of the civilian population of the regions its army had invaded. This meant that there was at least one other group in the Netherlands Indies which looked askance at the Japanese victory over Russia and its possible consequences with as much apprehension as the Dutch. Newspapers observed that Chinese were more interested in the course of the war than were the rest of the population, and greeted news of Russian successes in the early days of the war with delight, cheering any news of Japanese set-backs.[17]

When Japan emerged victorious from the two wars the country fought around the turn of the century, it was difficult to accept that in a short span of time its army and Navy had been transformed into a formidable war machine. To resolve the conundrum of the Japanese achievement an explanation was constructed which became part and parcel of the popular image of the Japanese among Westerners. Japan's military performance in northern Asia was firmly believed to be the result of a well-organized network of military spies whose formation had been instrumental in the Japanese successes on the battlefields. It was maintained that spies who lived a humble life abroad had provided information which had been invaluable to the advance of Japanese troops. As early as 1903 a British Captain claimed that the 'whole East is sown with its spies', when he reported on his visit to China just after the Boxer Rebellion. To illustrate his statement he mentioned the march on Peking: 'When the legation was threatened, Japanese who had been working at inferior trades in Peking came in and revealed themselves as military officers who for months or years had been acquainting themselves with the plans, methods, and the strength of China' (Casserly 1903:49). Others made a similar observation. One of them was the German explorer and naturalist Albert Tafel, who had himself traversed Tibet disguised as a merchant around the same time. He wrote that Japanese spies were stationed all over Tibet, passing themselves off as merchants, teachers, or Buddhist monks and so forth.[18]

A fear of Japanese spies would re-emerge in full force on the eve of the outbreak of World War One, when, as contemporaries dubbed this, the 'East Asiatic danger' posed by the 'warlike island empire' was seen as an even more realistic, if not major, threat. The enemy to be prepared for was Japan. After the Boer War Great Britain was still represented as another candidate which might attack the Netherlands but was no longer frequently mentioned as such. The change in emphasis did not pass unnoticed:

[17] *De Locomotief,* 13-2-1904, 15-2-1904, 20-2-1904.
[18] *De Indische Gids* 1906, II:1905.

Engelsch heette toen de boeman	In those days the English were the bogey-man
waarmee men ons naar bed toe jaagt	With threats of whom we are sent to bed
Verwisselt is het nu met Japan	Now this has been replaced by Japan
't Gaat zoals 't die heer'n behaagt	Everything goes the way that pleases those gentlemen.[19]

Japan captured the imagination of the Dutch in two ways. Nobody could deny it had become an industrialized nation within a relatively short period of time. It was thought that the Dutch could learn from this how to set about promoting the indigenous industrial development in Java. Consequently, and such plans had already been toyed with since the beginning of the century by the successive Ministers of the Colonies, somebody was dispatched to Japan by The Hague in 1914 to study whether the economic policy of the Japanese government held elements which could be applied in the Netherlands Indies. The person who was assigned to the task in May 1914 was Van Kol. Van Kol who at that moment was already in Japan accepted. The assignment fitted his ideals like a glove. As he put it himself, for years he had devoted the best of his energies to the promotion of a large native industry. At the outbreak of World War One he returned to Holland, but was allowed a second trip to Japan in March 1915 to conclude his research. Van Kol (1916:35) was sure that Java could and should follow the example set by Japan:

> And *referring to Java?* Why would Java pass through an evolution different from so many other, yea most, countries on earth? Will there as well – where the similarity with Japan is really striking in numerous respects – similar causes not have similar consequences? Will earlier or later the unrelenting necessity not force the government to take a similar road to prevent further impoverishment, even famines?

For some other socialists imbued with their particular belief about how society should evolve from one stage to another, the Japanese experience held out other hopes. Soon colonial society might change in a direction favourable to their cause. In a very short time Japan had made the transition from 'an agrarian, feudal caste society' to one where proletarian life blossomed.[20]

The other side of the coin was that Japan was seen as a mighty warlike nation, preparing for territorial expansion. In 1913 in a report about the economic and political expansion of Japan a civil servant of the Ministry of the Colonies, Ch.J.I.M. Welter, concluded that every Japanese in the Netherlands Indies was a spy. He made much of the suspicious way in which Japanese

---

[19] *De Expres*, 14-5-1914.
[20] Minutes constituent meeting ISDV (Tichelman 1985:188).

Japanese admiral as trade mark of a Japanese firm exporting textile to the Netherlands Indies (*Javasche Courant*, Trade mark 7131)

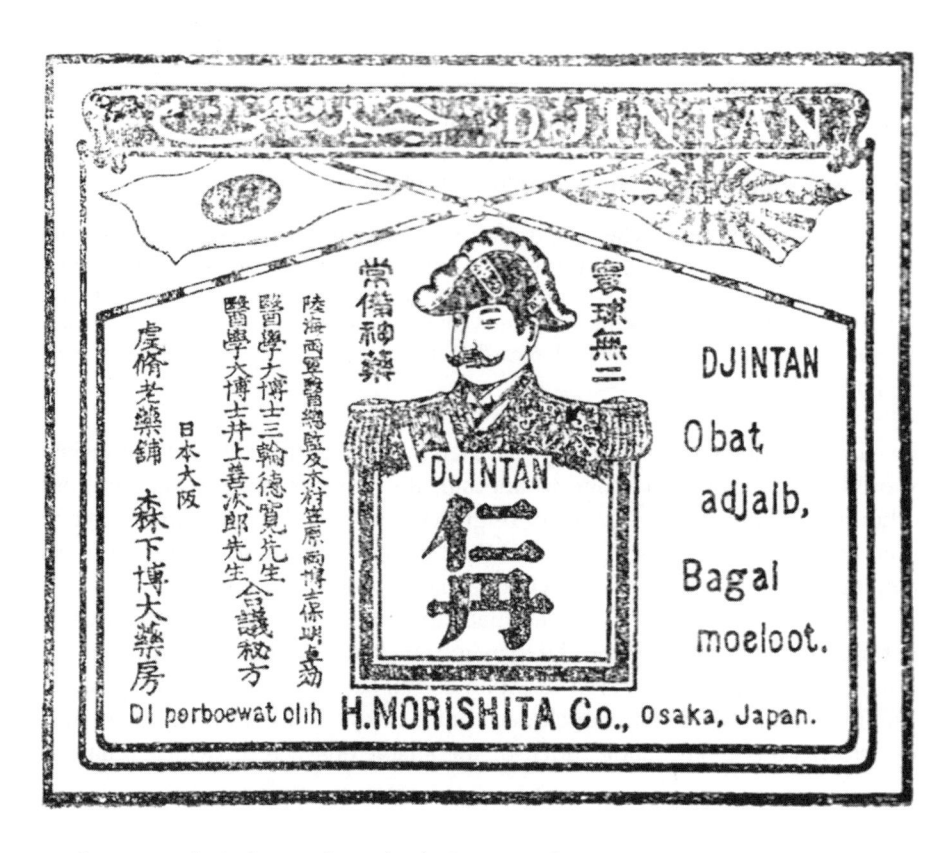

Japanese admiral as trademark of a Japanese firm exporting medicines to the Netherlands Indies (*Javasche Courant* 1914, Trade mark 7182)

officers who had visited the Archipelago in the previous years had behaved. By now Idenburg's advisers on the Coucil of the Indies had also concluded that Japan formed a threat.[21] The following year in the Dutch newspaper *De Telegraaf* Henri Borel, a Dutch expert on China, called attention to the activities of the India-Japanese League, an organization founded to promote Japanese trade in British India, which had expanded its activities to other parts of the world, including the Netherlands Indies in 1911.[22] Alluding to the presence of Japanese spies abroad, he warned that it was sufficiently well known 'that in the last ten and more years of the history of the Far East "trade" has been a cloak under which the secret Eastern policy lurks and simultaneously beavers away at its most intimate plans, its most hopeful dreams'.[23] He also referred to the stories which circulated about the Japanese military as excellent spy-masters. Indubitably the so-called spyphobia might at times take an exaggerated form, nevertheless,

> the Japanese Generals and admirals disguised as barber's assistant or house servants who at the time 'were stationed' in Vladivostok and Port Arthur, are still too fresh in the mind, to find the supposition that among the bosses of the small, insignificant Japanese shops in our colonies, sporadically somewhere or other certainly also colonels and naval commodores will be found, groundless.[24]

The Japanese, a colonial official was to state in a letter to the Governor General early 1915, were born spies (Mulders 1987:123).

The suspicion had grown in the minds of people in the Netherlands Indies that influential groups in Japan contemplated a drive southwards to satisfy Japan's hunger for territorial expansion. On the eve of World War One questions were asked in Dutch parliament about a power – not mentioned by name – where the occupation of the Netherlands Indies was openly propagated, and which had stationed a great many spies in the colony.[25] As in the previous decade, Europeans were convinced that Japan lusted after the European colonies in Southeast Asia, of which the Netherlands Indies was the weakest example, and consequently the most vulnerable to an attack. For some this particular danger posed by Japan would evaporate after the opening of the Panama Canal. More than it had been in the past the United States was seen as a protective force, if not a potential naval ally. This idea was based on the growing animosity between Japan and the United States, in 1913 leading to

---

[21] Advice Council of the Indies, 16-1-1914, NA, Kol. Geheim, Vb. 7-10-1914 V20; Verboom 1987:64; Van Gestel 1987:92-7.
[22] *De Expres*, 11-4-1911.
[23] *De Indische Gids* 1914, I:725.
[24] *De Indische Gids* 1914, I:725.
[25] *Handelingen Tweede Kamer* 1913-14:1395.

a clash over the treatment of Japanese immigrants in the United States and over Japanese support for Mexico. The opening of the Panama Canal would give American warships easier access to the Pacific. This, coupled with the growing strength of the fleets of Australia and New Zealand, would put a stop to Japanese arrogance and any dreams it might foster of conquering the Netherlands Indies. It was cautiously hoped that the new international power relations in the Pacific that were in the making made the possibility of a Japanese invasion less likely.

Others took the opposite standpoint. In their opinion the Panama Canal would only increase the likelihood that the neutrality of the Netherlands Indies would have to be guarded. Rather than being simplified international relations in the Pacific would only become more complicated. Such people saw the Japanese-American animosity as only one of the many contemporary international conflicts which might well escalate into a major war. Japanese economic and military achievements fuelled to the belief, already manifest at the turn of the century, that it was the Pacific as a region of economic growth and potential where an armed conflict between the great powers was most likely to erupt. 'The biggest source of anxiety for world diplomacy lies in the Far, and no longer in the Near East', Karl Haushofer, a Major on the Bavarian General Staff who had lived in Japan from 1908 till 1910, explained in a book about Japan, at the very moment that the Balkan Wars had broken out (Haushofer 1913:285). Economic rivalry and military build-up were bound to increase after the opening of the Panama Canal. The implicit conclusion was that Japan would almost certainly be among the belligerents in an imminent great war. Some of the possibilities raised at that time postulated that Japan might well act were the neutrality of the Netherlands Indies not meticulously guarded in an international armed conflict.

The implication was that in the event of Japan's participation in any such war once again the Netherlands Indies was presented as a stake in the international diplomatic game. Right from the outbreak of the war – in an effort to fan anti-British feelings abroad newspapers in Germany reported this to be a fact – it was speculated that in return for Japan's participation London would promise it a free hand in the Archipelago or at least in parts of it; though others argued that British investments in Sumatra were too large to permit London to leave that island to the clutches of Japan.[26] Another scenario was reported from Japan by J.C. Pabst, Major on the General Staff of the Colonial Army, a person whose opinions were highly valued by Batavia. Berlin was supposed to have offered parts of the Netherlands Indies to Tokyo in efforts commenced shortly

---

[26] *De Locomotief*, 8-11-1914; *De Indische Gids* 1914, II:1660-3.

after the outbreak of the war to detach Japan from the allies.[27] Such speculations would re-emerge from time to time; right up to the closing months of the war. In July 1918 when *Iswestia* revealed that in February 1915 Moscow had been prepared to allow Japan to seize parts of the Netherlands Indies (Borneo, Java, and Celebes were mentioned in the German press) in return for a more active Japanese participation in the war in Europe, people again discussed the possibility that this still might happen even though Russia had withdrawn from the war. Amid the furore, among the persons who stressed that Japan had no intention to invade the Netherlands Indies was Van Kol, acclaimed as a Japan specialist. He argued that the Dutch open door policy left Japan nothing to gain from invading the Netherlands Indies. The story was also denied by the allies, including the Japanese government. For some this offered little consolation. Had not British politicians lied about the British military links with France in the months before the war?[28]

Suspicion of Japan was strengthened by the fact that in the pre-war years Japanese had begun, albeit still in very modest fashion, to make their economic presence in the Archipelago felt. The colonial race in the Pacific had shown that peaceful penetration could well be a prelude to military intervention. Japanese immigrants, though their numbers were still small, became a source of concern, as were Japanese investments.[29] In both cases ulterior motives were suspected. Consequently, a 'strong increase' in the number of Japanese taking up residence in the Netherlands Indies was anxiously observed. People speculated that the influx might well accelerate in future because Hawai'i and the Philippines had now been closed to Japanese immigrants and Washington was considering a ban on immigration from Asia.

An additional danger apprehensively perceived was that were Japanese immigrants to feel threatened or discriminated against they might well turn to their home country for military assistance. Japan could, as other nations had done in other parts of the world, use real or imagined maltreatment of its citizens in the Netherlands Indies as an excuse for an invasion. Even when the Japanese did nothing wrong people were not sure that there was no danger looming. In July 1914, writing about Japanese settlers in Kuala Lumpur, *De Locomotief* remarked that law-abiding, diligent Japanese tended to make people forget that Japan was one of the most imperialistically oriented nations in the world, and that such immigrants, easily and for the most trivial reason, could turn to their government to ask it to intervene were they find

---

[27] Pabst to dep. VII General Staff, 5-1-1915, NA, Kol. Geheim, Vb. 30-3-1915 Y5.
[28] *De Indische Gids* 1918, II:1129-30; *Koloniale Studiën* 1918, II:524-5.
[29] At the end of 1914, there were 843 male and 286 female Japanese living in Java. In the rest of the Netherlands Indies 1,816 male and 1,078 female Japanese had settled, NA, Kol. Geheim, Vb. 22-9-1915 W11.

fault with their treatment in their host country.[30] Indicative of such feelings of fear that the great powers might use any excuse to invade was an editorial in *De Locomotief* in July 1916. Its editor wrote that it was generally expected that would the Philippines indeed be granted self-rule riots would erupt which would give Japan the excuse to invade.[31]

There was a prevalent *Japannervrees*, Japanophobia, or 'Japanitis' as the press chose to dub this. Criticism of colonial conditions in the Japanese press stoked apprehension. Such articles were perceived to be in a similar vein to the arguments adduced by European nations to justify their own colonial expansion, namely as an excuse to act in order to redress wrong and abuses. Fear went hand in hand with disdain. The Japanese community was held in low esteem. In the eyes of the Dutch apart from the occasional trader and shopkeeper, it consisted mostly of peddlers (of whom some travelled around selling medicine throughout the length and breadth of the Archipelago, whom the Dutch suspected were not much interested in their trade immediately incurring the suspicion that they were spies), whores, and brothel-keepers.[32] The occasional trader and shopkeeper could also not count on much sympathy. Writing about such people on the East Coast of Sumatra and in Singapore in 1916 it was observed that a Japanese was 'not thought to be a pleasant human being'.[33] At best, when it was opportune to write something nice about Japan, the country was blamed for allowing persons who did not know how to behave to come to the Netherlands Indies. The *Soerabaiasch Handelsblad* stated in 1917 that the Japanese lacked 'civilized pioneers', persons who obeyed the laws of the Netherlands Indies, who were able to adjust themselves to the local customs, and had learned to act sociably.[34] Another author suggested that articles in the European press in the colony attacking the activities of the Japanese in the Netherlands Indies did no harm. Even in Japan, those who travelled to the Netherlands Indies were considered 'outlaws' and people 'who lived on the fringe of civilization.' Criticizing the behaviour of such fellow-countrymen did not offend the 'really civilized Japanese'.[35] Nevertheless, such a position did raise doubts. There was a suspicion that as nobody was allowed to leave Japan without the express permission of the government, Japanese emigration was deliberately directed by Tokyo.[36]

The colonial government also had its misgivings. It feared that Japanese

---

[30] *De Locomotief*, 10-7-1914.
[31] *De Locomotief*, 10-7-1916.
[32] *Koloniaal Tijdschrift* 1917, I:96; Van Gestel 1987:97-100.
[33] *De Locomotief*, 2-3-1916.
[34] *Soerabaiasch Handelsblad*, cited in *De Indische Gids* 1918, I:738.
[35] *De Indische Gids* 1918, I:513-6.
[36] Remarks about Ernst Grünfeld's *Die japanische Auswanderung*, 1913, NA, Kol. Geheim, Vb. 22-7-1914 O13.

spies were mapping strategic mountain passes and roadsteads to facilitate an invasion, and that representatives of the Japanese government had tried to befriend disgruntled rulers and former rulers in the Archipelago. In October 1914 J. Loudon, the Dutch Minister of Foreign Affairs, informed the Dutch Envoy in Tokyo that sometimes action against Japanese citizens had to be taken. He stated this at a moment when the involvement of the Netherlands in the war and a subsequent attack by Japan on the Netherlands Indies seemed a likely scenario.[37] Anticipating complaints by the Japanese government, he provided the Envoy with a list of examples of the behaviour of Japanese nationals in the Netherlands Indies, who the colonial authorities suspected of having specific aims in mind detrimental to Dutch interests. Loudon urged his Envoy to present the data to the Japanese government 'in a friendly way'. Were this handled delicately enough, then Tokyo might understand why in some cases the colonial authorities had deemed arrests and deportations of Japanese necessary.[38]

One of the reasons for Loudon's action was that Batavia had become convinced that Japanese investors were angling to acquire land at militarily strategic spots. It was feared that their principal motive was not economic gain which would have been the case with other foreign investors, but that they were motivated by military considerations. They wanted to take hold of tracts of land with little economic value but harbouring great strategic importance located along the coast of the Minahasa in northern Sulawesi, in the Riau Archipelago, and along the mountain passes near Padang and its port on the West Coast of Sumatra, the gateways to the interior of the island.[39]

Such suspicions put Batavia and The Hague in a awkward position. Even before 1914 Batavia had pleaded that Sulawesi be closed to 'undesirable elements from Japan'. The Hague for obvious reasons – and fearful of how Japan would react – could not allow this sort of discrimination of Japanese subjects.[40] It could only agree to secret measures to be taken by Batavia to prevent Japanese acquiring long-term leases on land wherever they wanted in the Archipelago. To make it impossible that such places could be used to assist the operation of a foreign fleet in the territorial waters of the Netherlands Indies (the sailing of the Russian Baltic fleet to Asia had hammered home the importance of protected places close to shore to coal), in October 1912 regional civil servants were urged in by Batavia to be on the alert for foreigners anxious to acquire agricultural concessions in coastal regions or in areas along rivers

---

[37] Loudon to Van Asbeck, 14-10-1914, NA, Kol. Geheim, Vb. 18-8-1915 J11.
[38] Loudon to Van Asbeck, 14-10-1914, NA, Kol. Geheim, Vb. 18-8-1915 J11.
[39] Van Asbeck to Idenburg, 18-5-1915, Idenburg to Van Asbeck, 23-6-1915, NA, Kol. Geheim, Vb. 5-8-1915 A11.
[40] Idenburg to Pleyte, 6-3-1914, NA, Kol. Geheim, Vb. 7-10-1914 V20.

which were navigable by sea-going vessels. Before allowing any such deals to be struck the opinion of the Commanders of the ColonialArmy and Navy had to be sought. Initially the Japanese were not mentioned by name, but it was clear to everybody that for 'foreigners' Japanese should be read. If there was still any lingering doubt, this was removed by a second circular issued by Batavia in February 1913. It explained to civil servants outside Java that such advice always had to be asked if the request for a concession came from the Japanese, or from somebody of whom it could be assumed that he acted in their name. A year later, in March 1914, the civil servants were ordered to keep a constant (but discreet) watch over concessions already granted. They had to alert Batavia immediately if there was any suspicion that military instead of commercial and industrial aims were being pursued.[41]

These 'top secret' directives were issued with some trepidation. As in the case of the immigration of Japanese labourers, a formal ban could not be proclaimed. This would be in violation of the officially pledged open door policy; and especially in times of international tension could become a political liability were Tokyo ever to be resolved to redress the discrimination of the Japanese the instructions implied. The latter seemed a likely prospect. The directives issued on how to deal with Japanese investments in land had fortified Dutch civil servants in their opinion that Japanese were potential enemies. A series of Japanese complaints had been the result. In turn these had made the policy makers in the Netherlands Indies fear that anti-Dutch sentiments could take hold in Japan. The civil servants, of course, had to investigate 'Japanese machinations', but they had to do so with prudence and tact to avoid the Japanese who were suspected of ulterior motives taking offence.[42] It was glaringly obvious a different approach was necessary, but to those who had to develop new guidelines it was not altogether clear what form it should take. One solution proposed was to try to attract non-Japanese capital, in this way limiting the opportunities for the Japanese to invest.[43]

Besides the investors believed to be seeking out strategic spots deliberately there was also the spectre of Japanese spies and agents contacting local rulers outside Java as a first step to establishing protectorates in the Archipelago to think about. How to keep track of Japanese spies and potential saboteurs formed a major problem. At the time of the Russo-Japanese War and the sailing of the Baltic fleet, Idenburg had turned for help to the main Dutch ship-

[41] Circular Kindermann, 6-3-1914, Kindermann to Governor Celebes, 2-10-1915, Idenburg to Pleyte, 26-10-1915, note department C1 Colonial Office, NA, Kol. Geheim, Vb. 7-10-1914 V20, 16-12-1915 X14, 5-1-1916 L1.
[42] Kindermann to Governor Celebes, 2-10-1915, NA, Kol. Geheim, Vb. 16-12-1915 X14.
[43] Idenburg to Pleyte, 26-10-1915, note Department C1 Colonial Office, NA, Kol. Geheim, Vb. 5-1-1916 L1.

ping lines plying Asian waters, the steam-shipping companies Nederland and Rotterdamsche Lloyd, and the Java-China-Japan Line. Captains of their mail-boats were asked to notify the colonial administration if among the foreign passengers on board there were people whom they suspected of being a spy. They had to look out for 'passengers of a foreign nationality, of whom one knows or suspect that they are officers'.[44] All three lines promised to cooperate.

The request had not produced any results. The involvement of captains of the mail-boats proved a failure and captains of Japanese vessels could hardly be expected to cooperate. A more efficient solution had to be found. With Japanese particularly in mind in 1911 the Commander of the Colonial Army, G.C.E. van Daalen, pleaded for the establishment of an intelligence service (Verboom 1987:64). Two years later he urged for stricter immigration rules. For the time being Van Daalen's suggestions were not headed. The colonial administration wanted to abide by immigration rules which were 'as strict as possible for Chinese, Arabs and the like, who used to come to here as paupers and to live off and enrich themselves at the expense of the Native population', but for others, including Japanese, were as liberal as they could be.[45] To promote this policy all foreigners were charged a twenty-five guilder fee when they entered the Netherlands Indies.

From time to time between 1914 and 1918 anxiety about a Japanese invasion would lead to waves of intensified apprehension. In the second half of 1914, the prospect of Japanese espionage emerged to haunt the authorities and the public alike in full force.[46] The mood was such that Idenburg's secretary, A.C.D de Graeff, concluded in September 1914 that some policemen tended to see a spy in every Japanese.[47] Japanese who had the misfortune to travel with detailed maps in their possession, or who were spotted near strategic sites such as fortifications and ports ran the risk of being arrested, especially if they were bold enough to take pictures. One of the persons to whom this happened was a representative of the South Manchuria Railway Company who had come to Java to study the coal market. Arrested in September 1914 for taking pictures in Tanjung Priok he was detained in a police cell for a couple of hours, during which to his great consternation he had not been allowed to have a meal. To make matters worse a police mug shot was taken of him. A protest by the Japanese Consul, S. Ukita, was in order. The Consul complained that 'for an innocent man the idea of being photographed by the police is tantamount to an insult'. Ukita admitted that under the present circumstances it

---

[44] Idenburg to Van Heutsz, 30-1-1905, NA, Kol. Geheim, Vb. 30-1-1905 K3.
[45] Van Daalen to Idenburg, 5-11-1913, 14-2-1914, Cordes to Idenburg, 19-5-1914, Idenburg to Pleyte, 4-12-1915, NA, Kol. Geheim, Vb. 23-2-1916 W2.
[46] Van Asbeck to Loudon, 20-6-1916, NA, Kol. Geheim, Vb. 30-8-1916 A10.
[47] De Graeff to Attorney-General, 25-9-1914, NA, Kol. Geheim, Vb. 18-11-1914 C23.

had not been very wise to take photos of a harbour, but 'Japanese tourists visiting these colonies and going around with their camera to take photographs of open places should not be subject to any suspicion and enjoy the same what Dutch certainly have, in spite of it being times of war, to go about with a camera in Japan'. Idenburg concluded that in the case of this Japanese 'with a certain social position', Ukita had a point. In future police officers should act with 'moderation' in their dealings with Japanese. In September 1914 De Graeff wrote on Idenburg's instructions that in no case should Japanese when arrested be treated 'as vagabonds or criminals'.[48]

Distrust of Japanese intentions continued to plague the colonial administration and the Dutch public throughout the war. There were fears that Japanese spies were busily engaged in Sabang and other important ports. In Padang suspicion was aroused because there were five to six Japanese shops in such a small town and that each had a large staff, which changed every so many months, and consisted, so the description ran, of disciplined young men.[49] In Surabaya the editor of the *Soerabaiasch Handelsblad* called attention to the many Japanese bars which were frequented by sailors of the Colonial Navy.[50] In the same city a Japanese 'vendor of sweets and biscuits' was taken for a 'disguised Major on the Japanese General Staff' as he was selling his wares near one of the coastal batteries in January 1916. *De Locomotief* reported on the case under the headline 'The Japanese Spying Farce'.[51]

The first instruction of September 1914 setting out how to treat Japanese after their arrest seems to have been generally disregarded. In early 1917 new guidelines were issued. Again police officers were asked not to be overhasty in arresting Japanese and to treat Japanese suspects politely, addressing them as 'sir'. The suggestion provoked the scorn of the newspaper the *Sumatra Post*, which under the headline *Toean Yap* vehemently attacked the attitude that had inspired the instruction: 'that submissiveness, that fear of conflicts, that fear of the strong neighbour, in short Dutch diplomacy which has already sunk so low that it orders government employees to address recalcitrant individuals [...] with *toean*'. The *Sumatra Post* observed that Japanese all over the Archipelago acted arrogantly, and in view of this the circular was another example of the 'ridiculous compromises' which were compelled by 'anxious times for small nations'. The colonial administration should not yield to Japanese pressure.[52] Some Chinese, but for a completely different reason, were also irritated by Dutch kid gloves approach to the Japanese. In 1918 in Medan the newspaper

---

[48] Ukita to Kindermann, 15-9-1914, Ukita to Idenburg, 18-9-1914, decision Idenburg, 25-9-1914, De Graeff to Attorney-General, 25-9-1914, NA, Kol. Geheim, Vb. 18-11-1914 C23.
[49] NA, Kol. Geheim, Vb. 5-8-15 A11.
[50] *Soerabaiasch Handelsblad*, cited in *De Indische Gids* 1916, I:786.
[51] *De Locomotief*, 26-1-1916.
[52] *Sumatra Post*, cited in *De Indische Gids* 1917, I:674.

Andalas observed that Chinese were usually dealt with rudely by the Dutch, and Japanese, whatever their social standing was, never. The newspaper presented an explanation for this: the Dutch feared the Japanese jujitsu.[53]

The scaremongering about Japanese spies and agents was characteristic of the suspicions about Tokyo's malicious intentions. In 1915 the fear that Japan might act induced retired Officers of the Colonial Army and Navy to found a union, Bendor, to safeguard their pensions, which might be threatened were the Netherlands Indies to be lost. For the same reason former colonial civil servants living in Holland followed their example. In the latter case the initiative was taken in The Hague by a former *Resident* of Madura, F. Fokkens. In an article published in a number of newspapers, in June 1915 he appealed to civil servants and widows of civil servants to unite in view of 'a great danger' that threatened them (Fokkens 1916:3). He warned them that in the past nobody had given a thought to the possibility of the loss of the Netherlands Indies, convinced that the rivalry between the major powers would prevent this. The war had shown that such a guarantee counted for nothing. Were the colony to be conquered by an enemy, it was by no means certain that the Dutch state would be obliged to pay the former colonial civil servants their pensions, as this expenditure was drawn from the colonial and not the national budget. He received a great many positive responses and one month later the Bond van Indische Ambtenaren, the Union of Indies Civil Servants (later to become Pension Union of Indies Civil Servants), was established. It started modestly with about three hundred members. Admittedly the appeal had not been greeted with acclaim by everybody. At least one newspaper, the *Nieuwe Courant*, refused to publish the appeal, considering Fokkens's assessment that the Netherlands could well lose its colony in Asia defeatist.[54]

---

[53] *Andalas*, cited in *De Locomotief*, 4-6-1918.
[54] *Nieuwe Courant*, cited in *De Indische Gids* 1916, I:467.

CHAPTER V

The Dutch fleet

Each time international tension mounted, whether in Europe or in Asia, discussions flared up about the strength of the army and the Navy and their potential role in repelling an invasion. At one end of the spectrum stood those who argued that the Navy would never be able to defeat an enemy fleet and that the land forces would have to be relied on for the defence of the Netherlands Indies. Carried to the extreme, the consequences of this view were that the Navy only needed one or two larger vessels to show the Dutch flag abroad and to impress the natives. No money should be expended on building large well-armoured and heavily armed ships (Boeka 1903:15). Others advocated precisely the opposite. Because the Netherlands could never fit out an army large enough to drive back an invader, not even were all the forces to be concentrated in Java, all available means should be earmarked for the build-up of the fleet.[1] Generally, whether it was in 1870, 1900, 1904 or 1914, such discussions tended to assume a fatalistic, pessimistic, and at times hysterical tone.[2] The debate centred on weaknesses and not on strengths.

Civilians did not put much faith in either the colonial army or the Navy. Both failed rather dismally to impress. The fleet the Dutch maintained in Netherland Indies waters was not exactly best suited to a demonstration of might. Its ships were outdated and small. Many of its sailors suffered from venereal diseases. In the Netherlands Indies about half of the crew members was affected. Nine per cent had contracted syphilis.[3] Naval command tried to remedy the situation, but without avail. One of the rather naive measures taken had been to forbid shore leave in the evening. It did not work. The opposite was in fact observed: a significant increase.

The social gap that separated the ordinary crewmen from the established society was great. A telling example of this was what happened during the visit of the warship *Friesland* to Padang in 1904. Unquestionably her arrival cheered up life in the city. The 'Music, Drama and Gymnastic Society of

---

[1] *Indische Gids* 1900, I:641.
[2] For a thorough analysis of colonial defense policy between 1892 and 1920, see Teitler 1988.
[3] *Handelingen Eerste Kamer* 1913-14:365.

the Petty Officers and Ratings' put on a performance in the local club, De Eendracht. The audience was entertained with a comedy, 'My lieutenant', and comical sketches, the customary fare on such occasions in those days. The sailors made a good impression, not least because they showed a 'decent and helpful attitude' and had seen to it that 'nobody, that is to say at least not the women, had to sit beside the sailors of lower rank'.[4]

Similar remarks can be made about the army. In 1904 *De Locomotief* concluded that it was 'ill-trained and exhausted by the daily fight against the internal enemy, partly unshod and improperly armed'.[5] Around the same time the same newspaper maintained that the army would not be able to accomplish much against a foreign enemy.[6] The army about which *De Locomotief* was writing consisted of European and indigenous soldiers. Neither group inspired the general public with much confidence. Many of the European soldiers had been enticed by the bounty they received on enlisting, had signed up to try to escape poverty, or were on the run from the law. Soldiers were considered riff-raff and consequently treated as such. The European soldiers hovered on the fringes of the European colonial society. Even in the eyes of the Indonesian population, soldiers were inferior to other Europeans. As a newspaper noted around the turn of the century every Dutchman was a sir, a *toean*, to the natives. The exception was the soldiers, who were simply called *soldadoe*, soldiers.[7]

Indonesian soldiers, two thirds of them Javanese, did not fare much better in the public opinion of the European community. A note from the Department of the Colonies in 1906 observed that such soldiers came from the bottommost layers of society.[8] Except at the times when their service was needed, all the prejudices the white European community cherished about the Indonesian population and its various ethnic groups resurfaced in full force when their performance in battle was discussed. On the eve of the Russo-Japanese War *De Locomotief* wrote on a number of occasions that many native soldiers came from races devoid of military qualities, imbued with no or little martial spirit. The Javanese were useless in battle. They could not take on even an 'inferior' internal enemy on their own and when going into battle against such opponents had to be accompanied by European soldiers.[9] Native soldiers were dressed in European uniforms, but this did not make them good soldiers in European eyes. The fact that they went barefoot, as did the majority of the

[4] *De Locomotief,* 22-3-1904.
[5] *De Locomotief,* 5-1-1904, 23-1-1904.
[6] *De Locomotief,* 27-2-1904.
[7] *De Locomotief,* 8-2-1904.
[8] Note Department C, NA, Kol. Geheim, Vb. 13-7-1906 Q15.
[9] *De Locomotief,* 5-1-1904, 23-1-1904.

population, made them even less soldierly figures in the eyes of many whitemen. Presumably shoes made the good soldier. When the matter of Dutch troops joining the expeditionary force in China had come up, it was argued that nothing was wrong with sending Indonesian troops, as long as they were Ambonese soldiers – who wore shoes – who were sent, and not others who still went barefoot.[10]

As late as 1913 *De Locomotief* wrote that the European, Ambonese and Manadonese soldiers could make good soldiers under the capable guidance of the Dutch officers. The Javanese were a different story. Most of them lacked the required physical and intellectual endowments. Even so, there was a gleam of hope. Till recently, *De Locomotief* continued, the Javanese had lacked the requisite physical and mental training in their youth, but times were changing. In 'our peculiar days' the emergence of a nationalist movement had also manifested itself in an increased care of their bodies among the Javanese.[11] The colonial army, it was also argued at that time in the Dutch senate, could not be expanded simply by recruiting more soldiers from among the local population; that would be detrimental to its fighting capability.[12] That same year military experts had also decided that, for fighting a foreign enemy or for action in regions in the Archipelago home to warlike populations, half of the troops, no more, should consist of native soldiers, not more.[13] Despite such stereotypes, hesitantly the idea dawned that Indonesian soldiers were in fact not inferior to their European brothers-in-arms. In Parliament L.F. Duymaer van Twist pointed out that there were 'many good elements among the natives'. In the artillery corps they could hold their own with Europeans. What they lacked in physical strength, they made up by 'thought, calmness, and caution'.[14]

The struggle for hegemony in the Asia-Pacific region in the early twentieth century in which Japan, Great Britain, Russia, the United States, and Germany were the main contestants put the strengthening of the Dutch Navy high on the agenda. The danger of the threat of war was considered to loom largest in the colony, not in Europe. It had been argued as early as 1904 that the warships needed there should be more up-to-date than those in Holland itself. For the defence of the North Sea coast warships of the existing types, cast-offs so it were, would suffice.[15] Ten years later the Minister of the Navy, J.J. Rambonnet, explained in Parliament that in Europe the main task of the Dutch fleet was to assist the army in guarding neutrality. The strategic location

---

[10] *De Locomotief,* 20-7-1900.
[11] *De Locomotief,* 20-10-1913, 1-11-1913.
[12] *Handelingen Eerste Kamer* 1913-14:65.
[13] *Rapport* 1913:92.
[14] *Handelingen Tweede Kamer* 1913-14:1339.
[15] *Handelingen Tweede Kamer* 1904-05:662-3.

of the homeland coupled with the rivalry between Great Britain and Germany made it unlikely that the Netherlands would become a party in a conflict in Europe. In the Netherlands Indies the threats of war were greater. In contrast to Holland, where the army formed an essential part of the defence strategy, in the Netherlands Indies it was the Navy that would have to bear the brunt of resisting foreign aggression.[16]

As elsewhere in the world on the eve of World War One, in the Netherlands voices pleading for a strong defence force became more vocal, especially when the Netherlands Indies was concerned. The question of whether the days of Dutch rule there without such a force were not numbered was hotly debated at home as well as in the colony. Many alarmist scenarios were presented. Fear intensified at the time of the Balkan Wars, when especially *De Expres* manifested what Rinkes called 'evident nervousness'.[17] Believing that the great powers were eventually to be dragged willy-nilly into the conflict, the newspaper urged 'the comrades' to organize and prepare for the moment that Java would have to face an aggressor. The appeal was an indication that the leaders of the Indische Partij seized upon the contemporary international tension as yet another opportunity to show that they were good patriots. At the meeting at Maison Vogelpoel, the situation was used to argue that the fear shown by the authorities, a fear which some Indo-European were sure was justified, of arming the *Indiërs* was short-sighted. Had the Balkan Wars exploded into a European conflict, there could have been a very good chance that Japan would have used the occasion to invade the Netherlands Indies. Without arms the Indiërs would have been forced to stand idly by as the Dutch flag was lowered.[18]

Pessimists expected war, not lasting peace. H.C.C. Clockener Brousson, a former lieutenant in the colonial army, who had earned himself some fame as a journalist, claimed the efforts to prevent a major war would be unavailing. The Peace Palace, inaugurated in The Hague in 1913 and optimistically described in *De Locomotief* as the 'most modern of all international institutions', was no more than an additional sight in that city:

Vredesbonden, stomme honden!	Peace Bonds, stupid fools!
Dat weerhoudt geen wereldmacht.	Do nothing to restrain World Powers
Maar een vloot naar zee gezonden,	But to launch a fleet,
Stomme honden!	Stupid fools!
Dat beduidt voor Indië: 'Kracht'.[19]	For the Indies that means 'Power'.

---

[16] *Handelingen Eerste Kamer* 1913-14:428, *Handelingen Tweede Kamer* 1913-14:1366.
[17] Rinkes to Idenburg, 16-1-1913 (*Bescheiden 'Indische Partij'* 1913:158).
[18] Extract minutes constituent meeting Indische Partij, 15-12-1912, NA, Kol. Openbaar, Vb. 7-3-1913 35.
[19] *De Indiër* 1-2:18; *De Locomotief*, 3-10-1913.

As in 1900 for some, and probably for more people than at the turn of the century, the big powers seemed to be teetering on the threshold of a major war. In 1913 when the Dutch Parliament discussed the banishment of the three Indische Partij leaders, for instance, *one of its* members suggested that the debate had already dragged on for much too long. Instead of inconsequent blathering, issues of real importance should be raised. One of these was the defence of the Netherlands: 'One day there will be fighting, perhaps even very soon', he exclaimed to add punch to his words.[20]

It was an open secret that the Dutch fleet which had to guard the Netherlands Indies, which since 1905 was known as the Dutch Squadron in the East Indies, falling under the jurisdiction of the Ministry of the Navy in The Hague (and not as the colonial army did under that of the colonies), did not count for much. During the Russo-Japanese War *De Locomotief* had to admit that, reading the many complaints in Dutch newspapers and magazines about the condition of Dutch warships and the state of the Navy, made people dispirited.[21] As a consequence of the scare raised by the Russo-Japanese War, a new plan had been drawn up in 1906 to bring naval defence up-to-date. It opted for a fleet depending on fast, but small torpedo-boats. The plan had been presented almost at the very moment that Great Britain launched its first dreadnought. There had been no follow-up. In fact the size of warships had only grown bigger, and they were armed with increasingly heavy guns. All over the world countries were building and ordering dreadnoughts. The Dutch fleet had none of these new, large battleships. The defence of the Archipelago was entrusted to a number of destroyers, a few ironclads, and armoured plated battleships. The most pessimistic evaluation was that maybe one of these ships still preserved some battle-worthiness.[22] An alarmist pamphlet claimed in 1914 that the combined firing power of the Dutch battleships was inferior to that of one single modern dreadnought of which class Great Britain, Germany, and Japan had many in their navies.[23] Politicians tended to agree. Idenburg considered the fleet to be 'nothing but a heap of rust', while naval command dismissed the Dutch fleet as a *quantité négligeable*.[24] Rambonnet, himself a former naval officer, had to admit that the Dutch fleet did not amount to much, and in expressing this view he did not differ much from his predecessors, who almost without exception had stressed this point in an attempt to boost the Navy budget.[25]

---

[20] *Handelingen Tweede Kamer* 1913-14:47.
[21] *De Locomotief,* 18-2-1904.
[22] *Handelingen Tweede Kamer* 1913-14:1355.
[23] *Neerlands ondergang*1914:6.
[24] *Handelingen Tweede Kamer* 1913-14:1339; Bijl de Vroe 1980:56.
[25] *Handelingen Eerste Kamer* 1913-14:418.

Socialist agitation, in the pre-war years much better organized and effective in the Navy than in the army, gave the authorities additional cause for concern. For those on the right side of the political spectrum, the 'undermining class struggle', as it was sometimes dubbed, had resulted in what some regarded as a 'red fleet'. The Bond van Minder Marine-Personeel, the Union of Lower-Ranking Naval Personnel, had won considerable support among sailors. Its periodical, *Het Anker,* The Anchor, was widely read. In spite of efforts by some of the naval officers to check their crews' mail in order to confiscate the magazine, this situation had prevailed since the beginning of the century. Such was the worry of the naval authorities about the influence of socialist propaganda, that in March 1914 when sailors stationed at the naval base in Surabaya were invited by the association Concordia to attend the full dress-rehearsal of a play, their commander forbade them to march as a group from the union building to the theatre. Such a procession was seen as a violation of the ban on sailors participating in demonstrations. When the sailors – one hundred and seventy-five in all – disregarded the ban and did indeed march as a group to the theatre, they were kept under close guard by an armed patrol.[26]

From time to time senior officers, among them the Commander of the Navy in the Netherlands Indies, called for stern action to be taken against the union and its activists. In doing so they could count on the support of Rambonnet, a convinced enemy of *Het Anker* and all the magazine stood for. *De Expres* described him as 'the god of war of the Dutch fleet, the fierce opponent of the red spectre on board ships'.[27] Rambonnet stated in parliament, speaking he claimed from personal experience, that on the whole individuals sailors were a cooperative sort of people. It was only the 'powerful collective suggestion, the belief in the class struggle', and collective psychological phenomena such as 'loss of individual observation, individual responsibility and individual critical judgement' that made them susceptible to 'inflated words and extremist feelings'.[28] Such an observation did not go down well with representatives of the Dutch socialist party, who in turn pointed out the contribution of the Union of Lower-Ranking Naval Personnel to combating of moral abuses in the Navy, including rampant alcoholism.

Crewing was a major problem. The Navy was troubled by a shortage of sailors; not of officers, of whom there were too many, but among the ratings. The dearth had forced the Minister of the Navy to reduce the auxiliary squadron to five ships. A tour of duty in the tropics was considered to be an unhealthy one for the European sailors – a reason why the Dutch naval minister welcomed visits by Dutch warships to cooler regions such as China and

[26] *De Expres,* 11-3-1914.
[27] *De Expres,* 17-6-1914.
[28] *Handelingen Tweede Kamer* 1913-14:1373.

Japan – to which a crew which had just returned home should not be submitted again too soon. Recruitment decreased over the years and in 1913 only one hundred and fifty boys volunteered to enter the service and become a sailor. Animo to sign on was not great. One major reason for this was that a sailor had to serve a period of three years at a stretch in Asia. Another argument presented to explain why people – and according to some especially boys and parents from devout Christian families – were put off was the rough, immoral life of a seaman liberally dosed with booze and sex, notably when on duty in the colony, where, as Rambonnet chose to put it in 1912, sailors were forced to observe an unnatural abstinence.

Forced to deal with a shortage of crew, in March 1913 an experiment was launched to recruit Indonesians, who up to then had served only in very minor positions as batmen to naval officers and the like, to become what were dubbed 'war sailors' in the auxiliary fleet. Even when properly trained these first Indonesian sailors were considered inferior to their Dutch colleagues. Consequently – Pleyte was to stress that this was only a temporary measure – they received less pay. The experiment held out the extra advantage that, if it were successful, Indonesians could take the place of some of the European sailors, who considered their long tour of duty in the colony an 'inevitable disaster'.[29]

Opinions about the prospects of recruiting Indonesian sailors were mixed. The staunchest advocates of the plan were to be found in circles close to the Indische Partij. Clockener Brousson argued that there were various ethnic groups from whom good sailors could be recruited. They would not be inferior to those who served in the Japanese Navy, and certainly would show themselves more committed to defending the Netherlands Indies, which was their homeland, than Dutch 'hirelings'.[30]

As when under similar circumstances Indonesians had entered a field of employment previously closed to them, it was hard for some of the Dutch to admit that Indonesians could qualify. Reliability, honesty, discipline – and in this instance also sexual abstinence – were traits reserved for the own race. Officers argued that the Indonesians were too indolent, lacked resolution and failed to remain calm in tense circumstances so essential to 'the modern fighting sailor'. Moreover, they did not have the necessary energy. A Dutch sailor could do three times as much work.[31] Actual facts refuted such observations. In parliament Pleyte stressed that indigenous Indonesians would make excel-

---

[29] *Handelingen Tweede Kamer* 1913-14:2254.
[30] *De Indiër* 1-2:18.
[31] *Handelingen Tweede Kamer* 1913-14:2554-5; Idenburg to Pleyte, 17-3-1914, NA, Kol. Geheim, Vb. 1-12-1914 Q23.

lent gunners. In target practice they outperformed Dutch sailors.[32]

Agitation and moral conduct also played a role in the evaluation of the experiment to train Indonesian sailors. Some feared that mixing with the Dutch crew could infest the Indonesian sailors with the 'erroneous spirit' of socialism, which could have pernicious consequences for maintenance of the authority of Dutch rule in the colony.[33] Others raised the bogey sexual habits. This discussion was triggered off by an interview in a Dutch newspaper with an officer in the Colonial Navy, who had suggested that serving as a sailor would be a healthy occupation for people from North Celebes. Referring to a statement by the local Dutch *Resident*, he claimed that early and frequent sexual intercourse coupled with bad food – sago was their staple – had resulted in heart diseases, and had made 80 per cent of the young men in the Minahasa unfit for service in the army. The isolated life on board a warship and the healthy food served by the Navy could redress this.[34] Next day he disclaimed his words, but others took up the issue of native sexual habits. In parliament was remarked that it was a well-known fact that the ethnic groups from which the government intended to recruit the indigenous Indonesian sailors had sexual intercourse at a very young age. Agreeing with the efforts to change this by recruiting Indonesians for the Navy, he cautioned that isolation on board ships should not last too long. Otherwise 'other sexual usages which are perhaps even worse' might be the result.[35] He was sure that continence would be unbearable to natives. As proof he cited the newspaper, the *Java-Bode* (Java Messenger), in which this was mentioned as one of the reasons it would probably be impossible to recruit Indonesians into the Navy in great numbers. In the army sex formed less of a problem. Women accompanied their husbands to their stations. This was impossible in the Navy and might put many Indonesians off. Without ample shore leave and without an effort on the part of the government to promote marriage, the number of sufferers of venereal diseases might only increase in the Navy if Indonesian sailors were to be enlisted. When the Minister of the Colonies chose to ignore these remarks, the same member of parliament raised the issue again. This time he became more explicit. He pointed out the danger that because of a long spell on board 'the sexual urge, which exists in these boys, will lead in a wrong direction and [that] it would be much worse were they to seek satisfaction for this need in an abnormal way than if they did so for that matter in a natural way albeit out of wedlock'.[36] This time Pleyte did react. He said that there had never been

[32] *Handelingen Tweede Kamer* 1913-14:2561.
[33] *Handelingen Tweede Kamer* 1913-14:2455.
[34] *Handelingen Tweede Kamer* 1913-14:2556.
[35] *Handelingen Tweede Kamer* 1913-14:2556.
[36] *Handelingen Tweede Kamer* 1913-14:2562.

reports from the merchant fleet and the Indies Military Navy that Indonesians sailors had a 'worse' sexual life than Dutchmen. Nor was there any reason to assume that Indonesians in particular indulged in abnormal sexual relations when forced to serve abroad for some time.[37]

Rambonnet saw the training of Indonesian sailors as a realistic way to relieve the shortage of Dutch crew. However, it would not ease the pressure on scarce manpower resources. For a moment a 'Militia-Navy' conscription for the Navy for a period of two years was toyed with in Holland. Rambonnet was not in favour and wanted to make a 'final effort' to achieve a viable volunteer Navy.[38]

The army was also assailed by problems. Like the Navy it had to cope with problems of enlisting new recruits in Europe, which one Dutch newspaper declared was a clear sign of growing prosperity in Holland.[39] There was also a shortage of officers. To make matters worse, the salary of an officer had not kept pace with that of Dutch civilians employed in the colony, who had profited from the economic boom the Netherlands Indies experienced in the pre-war years. This some feared, but others denied this assertion instantly, could adversely affect the motivation of the officer corps.

Fears and doom-laden prophesies about an imminent war with Japan triggered off a renewed debate about the security of the Netherlands Indies in which opposing views raged about the best way to defend the Archipelago. Again it was widely argued that the contentment of the population formed an important prerequisite if the Dutch were to remain in power. Even the suggestion that part of the colony be sold re-emerged. In *De Groene Amsterdammer*, it was hinted that the Netherlands should do so before it was too late. The Netherlands could never win a confrontation with Japan. The most propitious move it could make would be to offer the islands most difficult to defend to Great Britain, Germany, the United States, or Australia, only holding on to Java and Sumatra. This would decrease the likelihood of a conflict with Japan, might even earn the Netherlands a new mighty friend, and would enable the Dutch to concentrate their efforts on the two islands which really constituted the heartland of the colonial possessions.[40]

Anticipating a foreign threat, in June 1912 the Dutch government appointed a special state commission to investigate what steps should be taken to improve the defence of the Netherlands Indies. As *De Locomotief* chose to phrase this the task of the state commission was to study how to defend the colony in spite of

[37] *Handelingen Tweede Kamer* 1913-14:2562.
[38] *Handelingen Eerste Kamer* 1913-14:364, 390.
[39] *Het Vaderland*, cited in *De Locomotief*, 25-11-1914.
[40] *De Groene Amsterdammer*, cited in *De Expres*, 22-6-1914.

lack of manpower and of money. Unconvinced the newspaper concluded that this was an absurd mandate.[41]

The state commission published its report in August 1913. In it it sketched a gloomy picture of international relations in the Pacific. It was pointed out that in recent years the region had undergone major changes. Germany had become an established Colonial Power in Asia, the United States of America had acquired the Philippines and had built naval bases in Manila and on Guam in Micronesia, and Japan had emerged as a major power. Beginning to find its feet Australia had experienced a period of economic growth, while China had also entered a new phase in its existence. Additional complications would arise from the opening of the Panama Canal. All these factors taken together had created a new international constellation which posed a much greater danger to the colony than it had ever experienced before. The likelihood that the Netherlands Indies would become involved in a war either directly or through a violation of its neutrality grew more likely the more 'the Asian Powers in the East and the Colonizing Western States approached one another'.[42] If until recently the only danger had come from complications brought about by a war taking place far away from the colony, in the future the possibility of an armed confrontation fought in or near the Archipelago could no longer be excluded.[43] In the opinion of the Commission, the possibility of potential involvement in a war was still heightened even more by the development of international law, which bristled with strict rules defining the obligations of neutrals. Belligerents would take offence at a lax attitude and would not hesitate to declare war if neutrality was not zealously guarded. This danger was all the more serious as it was 'not an unlikely supposition that the relations between the Powers in the East could lead to wars, in which the lines of operation of the Powers involved, may, yes indeed sometimes have to, run through the Indies Archipelago.'[44]

The conclusion was that the only adequate means to defend its neutrality would be for the Netherlands Indies to remain a scrupulous neutral bystander in any armed conflict in the Pacific. Other nations fighting a war would think twice before involving the Netherlands, if a confrontation with the Dutch Navy would almost certainly result in serious damage to their own fleet, weakening its fighting value in an engagement with the main enemy. In the view of the state commission not taking the precaution of improving the colonial defence amounted to 'a reckless, irresponsible frivolity'.[45] To demonstrate what was at

[41] *De Locomotief*, 10-10-1913.
[42] *Rapport* 1913:6.
[43] *Rapport* 1913:15.
[44] *Rapport* 1913:16.
[45] *Rapport* 1913:7.

stake the Commission – and its assessment provoked a heated debate – drew attention to the consequences of the loss of Java and the other islands of the Archipelago. The Netherlands, which internationally was still held in high esteem precisely because of its vast colonial empire, would sink to the level of one of the least significant European states. For the Dutch economy losing the Netherlands Indies would be nothing less than a national disaster. The population of the Netherlands Indies would also undergo great hardship. The state commission did not elaborate on this, but the observation tallied with the conviction, also shared by many on the left, that the Indonesian population benefited from Dutch rule and from the efforts made to develop the colony, and that other nations would act less benevolently.

In short, the colony needed to be defended strongly enough to ensure that 'for any nation, however powerful it might be, the assault on our territory or the violation of our neutrality [would be] an undertaking of a serious nature'.[46] This had an additional advantage. The state of the Dutch means of defence was to be a factor of consideration for other nations in deciding whether or not to come to the assistance if the Netherlands Indies were attacked. The state commission left no doubts about how such a condition should be realized. What was needed was an artillery fleet, not a fleet, as was still being suggested in 1906, which derived its strength from torpedo boats.

The ideal would be to have a Navy with nine large battleships, each costing about twenty-five million guilders, forming the core; preferably they should at least be of the same speed and armed with the same heavy guns as the dreadnoughts the British, the Germans, and the Japanese were building. The first dreadnought had to come into service in 1917. Four such warships should be ready at all times to engage an enemy in colonial waters. This implied that a fifth reserve dreadnought also had to be stationed there as well. The period of major overhaul which battleships had to undergo every four of five years, tying them to port for a considerable length of time, should be taken into account. The other four battleships should be stationed in European waters. Five vessels in the Netherlands Indies was less than the number of battleships of the big powers, but, the state commission argued, such nations would never throw the full weight of their complete fleet against the Netherlands Indies. The battleships should be stationed in European waters after having served in the tropics for twelve years. It was calculated that they could still be used in Europe for another eight years.

The total extra annual cost of building the battleships plus a number of smaller warships was calculated at a little over twenty million guilders. The members of the state commission could not agree on how to divide these costs between the homeland and the colony. A minority was in favour of an

[46] *Rapport* 1913:10.

equal division. The majority wanted to have the lion's share to devolve onto the shoulders of the colony. They argued that this way the colony and the homeland would share in equal parts in the total annual expenditure of the Navy in the colony. The homeland should finance 5.35 million guilders; the colony 8.75 million guilders. The rest of the money had to come from cuts in army expenditure. *De Locomotief* wrote that such figures made people 'boggle at the thought'.[47]

In its report the state commission devoted a special paragraph to the recruitment of personnel. To man the battleships would require a large increase in the number of ratings. The Commission was optimistic about the prospect of training Indonesians. It foresaw one problem. Following the advice of the Commander of the Colonial Navy the commission pleaded for a segregation of Indonesian and European personnel wherever possible. Were this not to be done, Indonesian sailors would perform less well. European sailors even when they were lower in rank, would look down on them. Conversely, Indonesians sailors 'with a certain kind of awe looked up to the usually heavier built Dutch sailor, the representative of the ruling white race' and would be afraid to give orders.[48] Even were a considerable number of Indonesians to enlist in the Navy the state commission considered it very unlikely that enough European crew members could be enlisted on a voluntary base for the fleet it envisaged. An extra 2,800 men were needed for the lower ranks. This made the establishment of a naval militia unavoidable.

There was one dissenting voice: A. van Gijn, the chief accountant of the Ministry of Finance. He refused to underwrite the report. In a note to Queen Wilhelmina, which was added to the report as an appendix, he explained why. Van Gijn accused the advocates of an artillery fleet of having forced their opinion on the other members of the state commission. The recommendations envisaged a utopian situation. They were based on a comparison between what the Netherlands could muster in the future and the 1913 strength of the fleets of the big powers, which would only grow in size, firing power, and speed in the years to come. Were the Netherlands not to acquire yet larger and more expensive dreadnoughts in the future the Dutch fleet would soon be relegated to the second rank.

The recommendations were made at a time when extra expenditure on the army in homeland had to be considered because of alarming developments in Europe. Members of parliament protested that although the defence budget increased year after year this had not produced an army and Navy which could perform their tasks as they should. One of the most vocal of these

---

[47] *De Locomotief*, 17-12-1913.
[48] *Rapport* 1913:51.

opponents was Van Kol. He called upon people to remember that since the close of the nineteenth century, it had invariably been the same. The government indicated the limited fighting capacity of the Navy to ask for money for new ships. After these warships had been built they almost were immediately declared to be obsolete by contemporary standards. Van Kol calculated that between 1904 and 1913 seventy million guilders had been spent on a fleet which was considered to be of little or no value in 1913.[49] He said – as at the time of the sailing of the Baltic fleet some civil servants of the Ministry for the Colonies had argued along the same lines – that the Netherlands would do better with a weak fleet than a strong one. Nobody would have protested during the Russo-Japanese War had the Russian fleet entered Sabang. Were the Dutch cockle-boats to be replaced by more impressive battleships the reaction might be different. With a strong fleet it would be impossible not to join battle, though still without any chance of winning.[50] Opponents of the fleet plans also pointed out that it was sheer madness to try and join in the race with the big naval powers to acquire ever larger and better-armed warships. In their view the best guarantee against foreign aggression remained the competition between the great powers which would never allow a rival to occupy Holland or the Netherlands Indies. If none of them came to the assistance when the home country or the colony were attacked, as some of the most pessimistic voices croaked, a large fleet would make no difference.

Naturally, army circles were appalled by the fact that the state commission did not show much faith in the colonial army as a potential deterrent. The commission had teetered on the verge of wanting to do away with the colonial army. It had suggested reducing its budget by 6 million guilders. The function of the army in the Netherlands Indies should – apart from a limited role in coastal defence and in the destruction of railways and telegraph lines in the event of an invasion – be confined to three main tasks. It should concentrate on fighting any internal enemy, that is suppressing local unrest, and in this respect the state commission praised its performance in Aceh; on defending the seat of the government; and on protecting a number of fleet stations and the main naval basis.

The state commission had based its recommendation on the conviction that any eventual battle for the Netherlands Indies would be one for the control of the seas. Once an enemy commanded these waters even a large, well-equipped army would not be able to accomplish much. At most, it could temporarily retain a hold on some of the islands of the Archipelago. Were Java to be cut off from the outside world the island would certainly fall into enemy hands

[49] *Handelingen Eerste Kamer* 1913-14:418.
[50] *Handelingen Eerste Kamer* 1913-14:419; note Ministry of the Colonies, 13-12-1904, NA, Kol. Geheim, Vb. 21-12-1904 J27.

sooner or later. In the cold light of the day, Java lacked the natural resources both to keep its economy running and for a prolonged resistance. Relying on the army, half of its strength made up of 'elements (*natives*) of presumably less fighting value than those of which the enemy army consisted', to defend Java was utopian 'self-deception'.[51]

The commission also pointed out that though Java might still be 'politically the most important and economically most developed' island of the Archipelago, other regions, especially Sumatra, were gaining quickly in economic significance. The days in which a defence of the colony could concentrate on Java were past. Other regions had become economically too important. To abandon them would be to forfeit abundant sources of prosperity, and would be a blow to national prestige.[52] All this called for a dominant role of the Navy, which could be directed quickly to areas all over the Archipelago.

The army officers did not accept it was a foregone conclusion that Java had lost its paramount importance and that in contrast to the past, defence strategies should no longer be concentrated on its defence. They also refused to acquiesce in the observation that an army could not defend the island. In their view a strong fleet was fine, but a strong army was an even more important asset. They maintained that it was a folly to assume that a Dutch fleet could command all the seas and straits of the Archipelago. In a battle with the Japanese Navy the Dutch fleet would be destroyed within hours. An army would be able to prevent the occupation of Java for weeks, enough time, maybe, for international relations to turn to the advantage of the Netherlands.[53] The Navy should concentrate on guarding neutrality and on inflicting heavy losses on an enemy fleet.

Shocked out of their complacency some officers went on a lecture tour. Others wrote articles, or published books and pamphlets. One of them was Colonel W.R. de Greve, a member of the General Staff and a future Commander-in-Chief of the colonial army. He was convinced it was Java on which the Dutch Colonial Power was founded. If there was the slightest chance that the Navy would be weaker than an approaching enemy fleet – and he and others were sure that would be the case were a big power such as Japan to be the aggressor – the defence of Java by the army should have priority. To have the Navy defend an Archipelago – and De Greve resorted to the words of Napoleon to stress his point – against a stronger foe who commanded the sea was foolish. It was not beyond the bounds of possibility that the Navy might experience the same fate as that of the Russian fleet locked in without any chance of escape at Port Arthur. In De Greve's view it was even worse

---

[51] *Rapport* 1913:19, 24, 31.
[52] *Rapport* 1913:17, 23.
[53] Van Daalen to Idenburg, 26-11-1913, NA, Kol. Geheim, Vb. 1-12-1914 Q23.

that the plans of the commission called for a period in which the Netherlands Indies would be especially vulnerable. Army strength would have to be cut down years before the Dutch Navy had its five dreadnoughts. There was yet another very good reason why the army should not be reduced in strength. Were the plans of the state commission ever to become reality, the army would cease to be strong enough to suppress a large-scale uprising in Java. Five years earlier it had taken three and a half battalions to put down a rebellion in West Sumatra, in a region with little over one million inhabitants. What about Java with its population of thirty million people? Would the eight battalions the state commission suggested suffice if these were confronted with a rebellious movement in the island?[54]

De Greve's arguments, which attracted wide attention, elicited a reaction from the Navy. Its Commander in the Netherlands Indies, Vice Admiral F. Pinke, stressed the economic development outside Java. Moreover, it was not only money that mattered. 'The question is whether or not even before a shot has been fired, even before a hand has reached out towards our property, we are willing to accept that part of this property will be taken away from us for good while we have to look on passively.' Pinke castigated the plan of concentrating the defence on one island, Java, and maybe also on part of Sumatra as 'an open declaration of impotence'. It might also solve nothing. Another island handed over to the enemy could well serve as a convenient bridgehead for an invasion of Java.[55] Pinke was not very complimentary about the competence of the army to fence off an invasion. The result would only be 'some prolonging of a hopeless resistance'. The state commission had been right. The only task to be assigned to the colonial army was to assist the Navy. Its strength could be reduced considerably without much harm.[56]

Pinke's argument won the support of the most senior colonial civil servant, the Secretary General. He postulated that should an enemy occupy any part of the Archipelago outside Java, it might well be that at a peace conference, the whole or a portion of it would have to be ceded to that enemy. The situation that would then arise would be of a mighty state not well disposed to the Netherlands having a foothold in the Archipelago. This would compel even much greater defence expenditures if it was desired that Java remained Dutch. Pessimistically he was convinced it would be to no avail. Java would inevitably fall. Poverty and anarchy would prevail within a given period were Java to be sealed off by the enemy. This would signal the end of Dutch colonial rule in Asia.[57]

[54] De Greve 1913:8-17.
[55] Pinke to Idenburg, NA, Kol. Geheim, Vb. 30-6-1914 O11.
[56] Idenburg to Pleyte, 17-3-1914, NA, Kol. Geheim, Vb. 1-12-1914 Q23.
[57] Note General Secretariat, NA, Kol. Geheim, Vb. 23-7-1914 S13.

Major General J.P. Michielsen, who as a member of the state commission, had agreed with its opinions and who recently had been appointed Commander-in-Chief of the colonial army, also came to the defence of the army. In May 1914 he wrote to Idenburg that he would never have been in favour of the Commission's recommendations had he at that time been able to forecast such developments as had manifested themselves in the Sarekat Islam.[58] His predecessor, Van Daalen, expressed a similar view. Were widespread unrest in Java, organized by Sarekat Islam to be orchestrated it would be impossible for the army to be prepared on all fronts. Were the unrest to spread to Sumatra, the situation could well become perilous.[59]

The army could count on the support of Idenburg and the Coucil of the Indies. Idenburg wanted both: a strong army and a strong fleet. In his eyes a strong fleet was essential, not least because Japan might not have Java in mind as a target for expansion. Looking for regions in which to settle its surplus population it might prey on islands with a low population density, Celebes for instance. To thwart any such intention a strong fleet was essential. At the same time Idenburg was prepared to consider a significant reduction in the colonial army only where it was certain that a fleet could put to sea which could successfully defend the colony against an invasion under all circumstances. It should never come to pass that when the Dutch Navy had been defeated Java, the seat of the colonial government, would fall into the enemy's hands without any fierce resistance being offered, whatever the prospect of the outcome of such a battle would be. Consequently, as money was scarce, the strength of the army should at least remain as it was. This did not obviate the fact that extra money had to be allocated to improve the Navy. Idenburg even pleaded for seven, not five, battleships. He suggested that without too many additional costs this could be accomplished by adjusting the proposals for the Dutch fleet in European waters. Instead of the four large battleships proposed by the state commission, three smaller ones could suffice at home. Were the colony not to get its seven dreadnoughts, willy-nilly the colonial army needed urgent expansion, and thus extra money.

The debate about the comparative advantages of a naval or army defence, made even more abstrusely by many unknown parameters, especially for the laymen who joined in and indeed not only for them, was complicated by technological developments. Landmines, or mine grenades as they were called at the time of their introduction, submarines, and aeroplanes had made their appearance. Submarines and airplanes meant that warships, as Van Kol chose

---

[58] Idenburg to Pleyte, 17-3-1914, Michielsen to Idenburg, 27-5-1914, NA, Kol. Geheim, Vb. 23-7-1914 S13, Vb.1-12-1914 Q23.
[59] Van Daalen to Idenburg, 26-11-1913, NA, Kol. Geheim, Vb. 1-12-1914 Q23.

to phrase this, could be attacked from above and from below.[60]

Submarines had already been a topic of discussion for some time. In 1906, at the request of the Governor General, one of his advisers had written a report in which he argued that since the Netherlands could never keep pace with the larger powers in building large battleships, the best defence of the Archipelago with its many straits and narrow passages lay in its recourse to naval guerrilla warfare. Submarines and torpedo-boat destroyers should be preferred above battleships. No enemy would dare to contemplate a *coup de main* if it was known that submarines armed with torpedoes could appear on the scene any moment, 'approaching invisibly, the periscope two feet above the water'.[61] The then Commander of the Navy in the Netherlands Indies, clearly no advocate of submarines, did not agree. He stressed that the German and French navies had submarines but that almost nothing reliable was known about their tactical value as a defensive weapon.[62]

By 1913 the deployment of submarines had become accepted practice, though Pinke still tended to look at them askance. In his eyes it was mastery of the seas that counted.[63] The state commission also entertained doubts. Its report stated that submarines were too slow and could not remain invisible all the time. They would only be of use for local defence.[64] Another impediment was that they had still not yet been perfected. At the end of 1913 the first submarine for the Colonial Navy was scheduled to be transported to Java on a dry dock. The transport had to be delayed. During a trial run in the North Sea, it turned out that its engines generated to much heat. Even in the cool European climate the temperature on board had become unbearable. A second cooling-machine had to be installed before the voyage could be made.[65]

Opinions varied about the employment of an air force even more. The Minister of War was clearly impressed by the possibilities. He was convinced military aircraft was of even greater importance to a small nation than to the larger ones. On the ground an enemy army of sufficient strength usually succeeded in preventing a sound reconnaissance by an army patrol. Such a task was much more efficaciously performed by an aeroplane. It could move around freely, and could pass an enemy 'to the right, to the left, above, and below'.[66] *De Expres* also thought an air force held a particular attraction. Smaller countries like the Netherlands would be ruined for eternity were they

---

[60] *Handelingen Eerste Kamer* 1913-14:418.
[61] Nota over de verdediging te water van Nederlandsch-Indië, NA, Kol. Geheim, Vb. 5-5-1906 F10.
[62] Note commander Navy, NA, Kol. Geheim, Vb. 4-8-1906 C17.
[63] Pinke to Idenburg, NA, Kol. Geheim, Vb. 30-6-1914 O11.
[64] *Rapport* 1913:39.
[65] *De Locomotief*, 18-12-1913.
[66] *Handelingen Tweede Kamer* 1913-14:1191.

to strive to realize their dreadnought dreams. When money had to be earmarked for the defence of the Archipelago, it could better be used for building up an air force. Pointing out the differences in flying an aircraft in a cool and in a hot climate, *De Expres* suggested that a fighting plane should be developed suitable for use in the tropics. This could make an Netherlands Indies air force superior to those of Great Britain, France, and Japan.[67] Others doubted the use of aircraft in warfare, even in reconnaissance missions, as 'the first thing one does in the army is to take cover under every tree, hedge or bush, etc.'. A small country like the Netherlands, faced with a large expenditure on its army and Navy, and confronted with novelties such as submarines, could not afford a military air force on top of this.[68]

The Dutch government opted for a more modest course than that suggested by the state commission: four instead of five battleships in the colony, but bigger ones and more heavily armed. The fleet in Europe could do without such battleships. Idenburg who wanted seven dreadnoughts, could not agree. In vain he implored The Hague not to cancel the fifth reserve battleship.

In October 1913 news spread that the government was contemplating ordering the first dreadnought. It was to be financed by a loan to be borne by the Netherlands Indies. A new topic of debate now raged. Who had to pay and who profited most from the colony remaining under Dutch rule? And, if the Netherlands Indies were to provide a significant contribution would this mean a serious setback to efforts to develop native society, or would the exploitation of its natural resources provide enough financial capacity to bear the financial burden? Even in Holland the suggestion of having the colony pay raised a few eyebrows. In his note rejecting the recommendations of the state commission, Van Gijn had already postulated that were money to be earmarked for the economic and social development of the Indonesian population to be withdrawn from the colonial budget in favour of the army and the Navy, the result would be a precarious situation, in which no large fleet would be able to assuage the feelings of insecurity which might upset the colony.[69] Others also feared unrest in the Netherlands Indies. Van Kol believed having the Netherlands Indies finance the dreadnoughts meant an insurmountable obstacle for the stated intention of the Dutch government to promote people's welfare in the colony, and therefore potentially dangerous.[70] As a good socialist, he suggested that it had to be the Dutch business community which drew

[67] *De Expres*, 7-3-1914.
[68] *Handelingen Tweede Kamer* 1913-14:1192.
[69] Van Gijn to Wilhelmina, pp. 15-6 (*Rapport* 1913).
[70] *Handelingen Eerste Kamer* 1913-14:420.

hefty profits from the colony that should foot the bill.[71]

Political adversaries deployed counter arguments. The colonial budget was a huge one, growing each year by fifteen million guilders, and would soon equal to that of Japan. Another argument they put forward was that it would only benefit the local population if they remained under Dutch rule and could profit from the Dutch policy designed to improve their spiritual and material well-being.[72] Such self-glorification, which was shared by many, was not without critics. In Holland *De Groene Amsterdammer* called it a gross presumption to proclaim that Dutch rule was the most desirable and that this made it fair to have the Dutch subjects in the colony pay heavily for this prerogative. In the Netherlands Indies *De Locomotief* agreed. The 'maritime cheer squad' had to realize that there was not much reason for the native population to contribute willingly to the strengthening of colonial defence. Undeniably, money was being spent for their benefit, but still only a very small percentage of Indonesians went to school. Health care was poor, as well as legal security and so forth and so on.[73] In another issue *De Locomotief* ventured to suggest that were the Netherlands Indies to have to pay for the Dutch fleet, the Sarekat Islam would exploit this in its propaganda among the Javanese and others who were bowed down by many pressing needs, and who were not the least bit interested in the talk about a foreign enemy.[74]

As the latter words indicate, the suggestion did not go down well in the colony with those who were staunch supporters of the Ethical Policy. They stressed that the fleet plans should not proceed to the detriment of the money spent to develop native society, nor should it result in an increase in direct and indirect taxes for the European or other population groups. Unrest might be one of the results; presenting the additional danger, as De Greve and others had also pointed out, that internal turmoil would present an excuse for jealous powers to interfere. It would be better to use the money to build schools or to improve medical care. Opposition was also strong in the circles of the former Indische Partij, well known for their distinct dislike of anything that came from Holland and their fierce anti-*totok* sentiments. Within a few days commenting on the 'criminal fleet dream', *De Expres* stated that the *Indiërs* would not mind a bit were the shares of Dutch imperialists to go to the dogs, and carried headlines such as 'The Indies as Object of Exploitation'.[75] One of the contributors to *De Indiër* wrote that in the Netherlands Indies people 'do

---

71   *Handelingen Eerste Kamer* 1913-14:35.
72   *Handelingen Eerste Kamer* 1913-14:363.
73   *De Locomotief*, 1-7-1914.
74   *De Locomotief*, 28-11-1913.
75   *De Expres*, 13-1-1914, 7-2-1914.

Already 350 Dutch ships pass the Suez Canal each year. Onze Vloot Propaganda. The Bedouin: 'What a mighty merchant fleet that must be. Daily I see ships with the red-white-blue flag in the Channel.' (*Neerland's ondergang* 1914.)

not ask for iron-clads, they ask for schools!'[76]

The Dutch government – maybe the idea had been copied from Germany where to avoid a political confrontation over the Navy budget a parliamentary debate had been postponed – refused to discuss the report of the state commission during the budgetary debate in parliament that took place and the end of 1913 and in early 1914. In her queen's speech Wilhelmina had explained that

---

[76] *De Indiër* 1-2:17.

the government did not consider it to be in the interest of the state to provide any further information. First, and this would take time, the Governor General in Batavia had to be consulted by a special Envoy. The subject was too important to be settled by correspondence.

Fortified by the report of the state commission, the proponents of a strong fleet launched a campaign to impress upon the Dutch population the dangers which lay ahead in the near future and what the consequences would be were another nation to grab the Netherlands Indies. Instrumental in this was the association Onze Vloot (Our Fleet) which had been founded in May 1906. Like its counterpart in Germany, the Flottenverein founded at the instigation of Krupp, and with similar drives in Great Britain and France as additional examples, Onze Vloot aimed at mobilizing public opinion in favour of a build-up of the Navy. By organizing lectures all over the Netherlands, its members spread the message that a powerful fleet was a prerequisite for the defence the Netherlands Indies. In the first years of its existence, the activities of Onze Vloot had not really caught much public attention. This changed after the publication of the report of the state commission. Its recommendations were what the members of Onze Vloot had been waiting for. The call for a large fleet appealed to them as did the glorification of Dutch might and the emphasis on the esteem in which Holland was still held all over the world, exactly because of the Netherlands Indies.

Onze Vloot could count on the support of a score of influential public figures. Members of the executive committee, many of them former naval officers or senior civil servants, included H. Colijn and former Governor General C.H.A. van der Wijck. At the close of 1913 the association claimed a membership of over seven thousand. It also boasted that its activities had been well received by Dutch people living abroad. Nevertheless, Onze Vloot remained largely an affair of the Dutch in Holland. It had to be admitted that in the Netherlands Indies there was still only one branch at that time, in Balikpapan of all places.[77] In Surabaya a branch for East Java was set up in July 1914. It appealed to people from other parts of the Archipelago to join as long no branch existed yet as in their own place of residence.[78] It would be November 1916 before the adjutant to Idenburg, C.L.M. Bijl de Vroe, founded a branch in Batavia. Months passed before it was granted corporate personality in March 1917. Its chairman became A. van der Boon. In 1917 the Perserikatan Minahasa (Minahasa Union) became a member of the branch.[79]

In October 1913 Onze Vloot published its first pamphlet in support of the report of the state commission. It sketched the disastrous consequences of the

---

[77] Circular by Onze Vloot, cited in *De Expres*, 20-2-1914.
[78] Letter to the editor, in *De Locomotief*, 3-7-1914.
[79] Bijl de Vroe 1980:101; *De Locomotief*, 14-3-1917.

loss of the Netherlands Indies for the home country. An alarming title was chosen: *'s Lands welvaart in gevaar!* (The country's prosperity in danger!), ' A serious word to the Dutch people'. The author was W.A. van Aken; former naval officer; and first secretary and treasurer of Onze Vloot. The state commission had clearly touched a patriotic chord. It was exclaimed that at last people, and important ones at that, had the courage to state publicly that 'the Netherlands is not a small nation [...] that the Netherlands with its colonies [...] is a great Power [...] that we are not small and powerless'.[80] It issued a serious plea that were the circumstances in and around the Pacific Ocean to remain as they were, or perhaps worsen, the Netherlands would have to make great financial sacrifices for the defence of its colony. Should the Netherlands not do so, overwhelming national poverty would be the result and the Netherlands would lose much of its international status. Danger loomed. Ten years earlier had the Russian-Baltic fleet forced its way into colonial territorial waters, an act the Dutch fleet would have been unable to prevent, the Japanese certainly would have jumped at the opportunity: 'The Netherlands Indies lay and lies open to them!'[81]

In a similar vein to the ideas expressed by the state commission, Onze Vloot protagonists stressed that a strong fleet in the Netherlands Indies would certainly be valued by friendly powers as a contribution to maintaining the status quo in the Far East. Another pamphlet put out by Onze Vloot stated that a strong fleet in the Netherlands Indies could join with the navies of the United States and Australia to counter an attempt by Japan to become the master of the Pacific. 'Or do you think that they alone will protect us, with their ships, their lives, and their money?' [82] Were the colony to be attacked, Van Aken stated at a meeting in Haarlem, the United States and Australia would certainly come to the assistance of the Netherlands, providing that the Netherlands had a strong fleet.[83] Others did not believe in such a scenario. The *Nieuwe Soerabaia Courant* called it an illusion to think that the United States would enter into a confrontation with Japan because of the Dutch colonies. Were Australia to come to its assistance, this meant that Great Britain would become involved as well, but this country was Japan's ally.[84]

Representatives of Onze Vloot had to admit that its first pamphlet was greeted with much criticism.[85] Even those, like the editors of the *Nieuwe Rotterdamsche Courant* who were in favour of a stronger defence castigated its

---

[80] *'s Lands welvaart* 1913:2-3.
[81] *'s Lands welvaart* 1913:9.
[82] *Neerland's ondergang* 1914:6.
[83] *De Locomotief,* 17-12-1913.
[84] *Nieuwe Soerabaia Courant,* cited in *De Locomotief,* 22-12-1913.
[85] *Neerland's ondergang* 1914:3.

one-sided emphasis on the economic benefits to Holland of the Netherlands Indies, not touching upon the equally important task of developing the colony for its own sake.[86] Another newspaper in Holland, *De Telegraaf*, wrote that it was not right and proper to suggest that if the recommendations of the state commission were not followed, sooner or later the Netherlands would lose its colonies. This amounted to scaremongering and one-sided and unworthy propaganda.[87]

In the Netherlands Indies newspapers expressed similar opinions. *De Expres*, exulted by the admission by Onze Vloot that were the Netherlands to lose its colonies, the country would be reduced to being one of the least significant nations in the world, qualified the wording of the pamphlet as 'manly language!'[88] *De Locomotief* wrote about 'the hyper-nationalists of Onze Vloot' – one of the other qualifications used by the newspaper was 'hadjis of Dutch nationalism' – and disparaged the 'savage pamphlet' and 'fleet fever rash'.[89] On another occasion *De Locomotief* wrote that it was not in accordance with modern notions of colonial policy to stress the benefits of the colony to the home country.[90] In Surabaya the *Nieuw Soerabajasch-Handelsblad* commented that the conclusions of the state commission and the support given to them by Onze Vloot alluded to 'Tom Thumb and the seven-league boots'. It was folly to aim at taking on the big powers. People who pleaded for such a course had lost all sense of proportion.

In holding out the economic consequences of losing the Netherlands Indies, *'s Lands welvaart in gevaar* had refuted the opinion that the colony was only of importance to a small group of capitalists and only in general terms. Another pamphlet published shortly afterwards, written by C.G.S. Sandberg, a geologist from Haarlem, set out to demonstrate this in more detail. The cover showed an emaciated, bent, naked man, leaning on a crutch. It depicted 'the limping and begging Mercury [...] the image of our future, if the Netherlands does not do its duty [...]. The quick winged-god of trade degenerated into a poor devil [...]'; or maybe *De Indiër* suggested 'the emaciated beggar, one can come across in famine-stricken regions (Blora) in Java'.[91] The title Sandberg used, and he had given the lectures he delivered the same motto, was even more alarmist and captured the public imagination: *Indië verloren, rampspoed geboren* (The Indies lost, a catastrophe born).

The pamphlet was one long, extensive enumeration of professions and

---

[86] *De Indiër* 1-15:169.
[87] *De Telegraaf,* cited in *De Locomotief,* 17-11-1913.
[88] *De Expres,* 20-2-1914.
[89] *De Locomotief,* 17-12-1913.
[90] *De Locomotief,* 27-7-1914.
[91] *De Indiër* 1-26:10.

The Indies lost, a catastrophe born (Onze Vloot publication 1914)

trades in Holland which directly and indirectly, completely or in part, depended on colonial trade. Attention was drawn to the many Dutch people employed in the Dutch shipbuilding industry; to those who found a job in the production and transport of the goods needed to build ships; and to the labourers in the Dutch export industry. Turning to what was needed to fit out ships sailing to the Far-East sailors, beer brewers, vegetable- and fruit farmers, cattle breeders, pastry cooks and biscuit manufacturers were not forgotten, to say nothing of manufacturers of beds and carpets and glassblowers. All these people lived in Holland, and had to be housed, fed and dressed, and their children went to school. This meant customers for grocers, bakers, butchers, shoemakers, tailors, doctors, carpenters and so on; in short it is easy to get the impression from Sandberg's words, almost the whole Dutch population – he himself spoke of the largest part – benefited from the trade with the Netherlands Indies.

This was not the end of the story. Dutch manpower was also active in the colony and the Netherlands Indies formed a market for Dutch equipment. Machines made in Holland were used when cargo was loaded and unloaded in the ports of Java and the other islands, in the construction of harbour works, and in dredging works. Dutch staff supervised such activities. In the transport sector in the Netherlands Indies most engineers and other European personnel in the railway companies were Dutch. At least so it had been: 'The State, which in the first place is called to serve the interests of the [Dutch] people and race, for some time and for pernicious reasons of economy engages foreigners in various branches of the service, *who do not even have to naturalize themselves!'* (Sandberg 1914:9). Were the colony to be lost orders for the Dutch industry from the Netherlands Indies would dry up. Sandberg stressed that the Transvaal had proved this. The event had formed a clear warning that had the Netherlands to part with its colony, Dutch commerce and industry in the Netherlands Indies would be replaced by that of the new Colonial Power. Whether a country professed to adhere to an open door policy or not was irrelevant. Its government would always give priority to its own industry and commerce.

Two steps were said to be essential to avert such a calamity. One was aimed at defusing the dangers posed by an internal enemy; the other at those emanating from an external one. To deal with the first Sandberg suggested that Christian missionary activities in regions not yet converted to Islam, which he claimed formed the largest portion of the Archipelago had to be stepped up. Any further advance by Islam could only be to the detriment of Dutch rule. The second threat had to be countered by a strong army and Navy. The Netherlands should not gamble on rivalries between the powers,

Netherlands's ruin can and must be prevented (Onze Vloot publication 1914)

or put any faith in their guarantees of territorial integrity. Recent developments had proved that such promises were empty promises: 'Remember the Transvaal, Libya, Morocco, Turkey, Cuba, Persia etc., etc. ad infinitum' (Sandberg 1914:22). It would not be difficult for the big powers to conjure up a pretext to adopt an aggressive policy, couched in ethical terms such as the bringing of civilization, or putting an end to misgovernment.

A third pamphlet was written by C.W. de Visser, a former Captain in the Dutch Navy: *De verdediging van Ned.-Indië tegen het Oost-Aziatische gevaar* (The defence of the Netherlands Indies against the East Asian danger). His aim was to make Dutch people aware of the perils in store and of the threat posed by Japan and sometime in the future by China. To demonstrate that he was not just conjuring up a spectre, De Visser called attention to the fact that often, as was supposed to have happened in 1912, when Japanese warships called at ports in the Netherlands Indies, on the days natives and Foreign Orientals were invited on board, large signs were displayed with the Malay text: 'These ships are conquered on the Europeans [that is the Russians]' (De Visser 1913:8). And, to underline the reality of the threat even more, he related the story of a Japanese naval officer, who, during a visit to schools in Makassar and Manado, had told the Indonesian pupils that within fifteen years Celebes would be theirs. De Visser suggested that the Netherlands would be on its own in fending off a Japanese threat. Europe would not intervene if Japan were, for instance, to seize mineral-rich Bangka Island as such an action would not hurt the direct interests of the 'big money world'. How little Europe could do had been proved by the Balkan Wars and the Italian conquest of Tripolitania in North Africa during the Italo-Turkish War of 1911-1912 (De Visser 1913:10).

By early 1914 the Onze Vloot campaign had gained real momentum. In Holland provincial newspapers received articles about the importance of the Netherlands Indies to Holland, which they could publish free of charge, from a press agency in Amsterdam, the Nederlandsch Correspondentiebureau voor Dagbladen (Dutch Correspondence Bureau for Newspapers) headed by Jac. Rinze. *De Expres*, always prepared to make use of the poetic vein of its editors and contributors wrote:

Kom Rinze geef jij nu de stoot	Come on Rinze set the ball rolling
We moeten hebben een sterke vloot	We should have a strong fleet
Roep het uit in alle talen	Proclaim it loud in every tongue
Indië zal 't wel betalen.[92]	The Indies will pay for it.

Just in case Sandberg and De Visser had not yet have been plainly spoken

---

[92] *De Expres*, 5-5-1914.

„Indië verloren — Rampspoed geboren."

The Indies lost, a catastrophe born. Onze Vloot Propaganda. 23,000 unemployed return from the Indies. There they join a still more enormous number of victims of the loss of our colonies. (*Neerland's ondergang* 1914.)

enough Onze Vloot published yet another pamphlet in May 1914: *Neerland's ondergang kan en moet voorkomen worden* (The Netherlands's ruin can and must be prevented). Its aim was to demonstrate to the critics of *'s Lands welvaart in gevaar* that Holland really was in danger of losing its overseas possessions. This time the cover displayed the Dutch Virgin sunk in despair – *De Expres* described her as 'a well-rounded damsel'[93] – while a vulture in the sky carried away a human figure representing the Netherlands Indies. The role of the bogeyman was assigned to Japan. The readers were reminded of Japan's victory over Russia. It was recalled that this was the first time 'the yellow Asian' had defeated 'the old rulers of the civilized West'.[94] China, 'our largest Asian neighbour, the enormous Chinese empire, the young Republic', was also not forgotten in the warning about a coming struggle between East and West. For the moment China was still preoccupied with domestic affairs. But what would happen when the Chinese government had put its house in order? Were there not 600,000 Chinese living in the Netherlands Indies?[95]

In this brochure Onze Vloot also did its best to highlight the economic significance of the Archipelago to the Dutch economy. People should not think that after the Netherlands Indies had been occupied by another country, the existing economic ties could be salvaged. In the first place governments took care of their own industrial and commercial community, even when they paid lip-service to an open door policy. The history of the Boer Republic had proved this, as had developments in 'the Philippines, Cuba, etc.'.[96]

To lend additional strength to the argument the last twenty pages, about half of the total pamphlet, were filled with letters to Onze Vloot stressing the vital importance of the Netherlands Indies to the Dutch economy. They came from such correspondents as the Chambers of Commerce of Rotterdam and Amsterdam, of Enschede and Oldenzaal (pointing out the consequences for their textile industry), of Wageningen (telling how many students of the Academy for Agriculture, Horticulture, and Forestry found employment in the Netherlands Indies), of Kaatsheuvel (pleased, *De Expres* commented sarcastically, that more and more Indonesians were wearing shoes), of Vlissingen (Flusing) (signed by J. van Raalte, President of the important shipbuilding yard De Schelde); and of Haarlem (with its production of railway and tram carriages).[97] In addition letters penned by key figures in the Dutch economy were included. Most illustrious of them was G. Vissering, President of the Nederlandsche Bank, the Dutch Central Bank, and former President of the

---

[93] *De Expres*, 4-7-1914.
[94] *Neerland's ondergang* 1914:4-5.
[95] *Neerland's ondergang* 1914:5.
[96] *Neerland's ondergang* 1914:15.
[97] *De Expres*, 6-7-1914.

Javasche Bank. Among the letters was also one from J.B. van Heutsz, who was an avowed proponent of strengthening the army and Navy. Van Heutsz was sure the colony would be more than happy to bear the costs of a well-equipped and well-manned fleet and a strong army. 'Thunderously' the colony would cry out that only a powerful fleet and army guaranteed its 'continued existence in the present manner under the Dutch flag.'[98] Neither for the European nor for the native population would this pose too heavy a financial burden. The soil of the Netherlands Indies held treasures far more valuable than the money needed to pay for the interest and redemption of the loan which would be required to finance the improvement of the armed forces.

Such pamphlets provided opponents of Onze Vloot with ample ammunition to strike back. They used the pamphlets to argue that Holland had to finance the expansion of the Dutch fleet. Had not the propagandists of Onze Vloot convincingly stressed the economic importance of the Netherlands Indies to the homeland? Opponents also remained convinced that the whole campaign was purely intended to safeguard the interests of the well-to-do. The socialist leader Troelstra translated O.V., the letter monogram of *Onze Vloot*, as *Ons Voordeel*, Our Benefit. *Het Volk*, The People, the socialist newspaper, drew attention to the fact that 'the cry of the bourgeoisie' was a conscious drive to have the Navy budget raised considerably. It was quick to point out that this was happening at a time when there was no money to expand the compulsory schooling of working-class children by one additional year. Pointing a finger at the extra direct and indirect taxes the Javanese population would have to pay, *Het Volk* concluded that the 'sense of justice of the Dutch bourgeoisie' demanded that the Javanese also had 'to sacrifice his farthing to preserve Dutch capitalists from the loss of the much-loved billion which is their hope, their prop, and their pride'. It was 'extortion to have the security premium for Dutch fire power paid by the Javanese'.[99] Other socialists cautioned against the whipping up of militarist and nationalist passions, recalling the British mood during the Boer War (and remaining silent about that of the Dutch at that time). Protests were directed to the fact that dangerous and false arguments were used in the campaign conducted by Onze Vloot and its supporters. It was not Holland which would benefit from the retention of the Netherlands Indies, this privilege would be reserved for the business community alone.

> The investor feels the palpitations of his Indies stocks heart. The factory owner, the shipping company entrepreneur, the mining developer wants to maintain his privilege over others, wants to secure a market. And in this way, gradually, much

---

[98] *Neerland's ondergang* 1914:22.
[99] *Het Volk*, 31-1-1914, cited in *De Expres*, 5-3-1914.

to the benefit of the conservative-militaristic elements in our country a fervent breeding ground is prepared for imperialist swagger, because of which it is difficult to see matters in their correct framework and right perspective.[100]

After Wilhelmina, in her Queen's Speech in September 1913, had announced that the Dutch government seriously considered strengthening the fleet, the report began to circulate that commercial circles – following examples abroad, most noticeably in Turkey and Germany – would appeal to the Dutch population to collect money for a battleship after parliament had approved the expenditure on the first dreadnought. The driving force behind the initiative was C.J.K. van Aalst, President Director of the Rotterdamsche Lloyd and President of the Nederlandsche Handel-Maatschappij (NHM). Before the year was out, Van Aalst and other key representatives of the Dutch business community contacted the government. They said they were prepared to contribute 120,000 guilders to the building of a second dreadnought. The stated reason for their offer was the consequences for their colonial interests of the 'desire for expansion', which they claimed was manifesting itself in Japan and China.[101] The offer was gratefully accepted by the government.

In the Netherlands Indies *De Locomotief* and other newspapers were quick to demonstrate that Van Aalst and his commercial friends annually made enormous profits from the colony.[102] Most vocal probably was *De Expres*. Holding out the example of Germany, where the fleet had become a matter of national pride, doubts were expressed in *De Expres* about whether the millions of Dutch people would indeed raise the money needed for the construction of a dreadnought; implying that many in Holland did not care in the least about the Netherlands Indies.[103] Its editors were also somewhat bewildered by the sudden campaign which was mounted to impress upon the Dutch population that it might not be long before the Netherlands Indies was lost. What special information had Van Aalst and his protagonists to back up their alarmist views?[104] What *De Expres* wrote annoyed Batavia. In May 1914 Idenburg instructed the Attorney-General to investigate whether a prosecution of the newspaper was in order.[105]

All this talk about armament and the threat of war did not fail to bypass Indonesian society. In July 1914 when the local Sarekat Islam of Semarang was recognized by Batavia this called for a big celebration. A parade through

---

[100] *De Expres*, 3-4-1914.
[101] Note Pleyte and Rambonnet prepared for the Council of Ministers, November 1913, NA, Kol. Geheim, Vb. 1-12-1914 Q23.
[102] *De Locomotief*, 12-12-1913.
[103] *De Expres*, 25-2-1914.
[104] *De Expres*, 12-12-1913.
[105] Monsanto to Idenburg, 23-5-1914, NA, Kol. Openbaar, Vb. 17-9-1915 46.

town formed the highlight. Modernity and war were conspicuously present. Floats not only displayed freighters complete with smoke coming out off their funnels, but also guns (some with cannonballs dangling from their muzzles), dreadnoughts and aeroplanes[106].

In The Hague the government took its time deciding. At the end of the parliamentary year it had still not submitted its plan for the defence of the Netherlands Indies. It was not that the government did not consider the matter urgent. Though Pleyte did not believe that the Netherlands would be embroiled in a European war, he did not preclude an armed conflict with Japan intent on occupying less densely populated parts of the Archipelago such as Celebes. He rated the chance of a Japanese invasion of Java low. It would prove too costly for Japan. The likelihood would decline even more steeply were the Netherlands to have a strong fleet patrolling colonial waters.[107] In parliament as well as in his correspondence with Idenburg Pleyte stressed that every effort was being made to draft a proposal. In June 1914 he stated in parliament that not a day had passed in the nine months he had been Minister of the Colonies without people working on it.[108] One of the bottlenecks, and certainly not the easiest one to solve, was how the fleet plan should be financed, and how the financial burden should be divided between the home country and the colony. Pleyte wrote to Idenburg that this 'continuously, – yes, I may say: in some periods daily – occupied the thoughts of the Government'.[109]

To find a solution required close consultation between the Ministers of the Navy, of the Colonies, and of Finance. Van Aalst, representing the business community, was also involved in the deliberations. In Batavia Idenburg was kept informed by Pleyte through official as well as private letters. Pleyte and Van Aalst agreed with the opponents of the fleet plans that the population of the Netherlands Indies had to be sheltered as much as possible from the financial consequences. They wanted to prevent a situation in which income generated by the colony would have to be used for the fleet to the detriment of the 'welfare policy' and the care of the native population. It was admitted that the population was already heavily taxed. Its burden of taxation should not be increased yet further.[110] Pleyte himself was convinced that sparing the indigenous population was also important since they had begun to organize themselves. They demanded their lot to be improved and would certainly

---

[106] *De Locomotief*, 24-7-1914.
[107] Minutes meeting Pleyte and Van Aalst on 7-7-1914, NA, Kol. Geheim, Vb. 19-8-1914 S16.
[108] Reaction Pleyte to Note, NA, Kol. 18-2-1913, Pleyte to Idenburg, 29-6-1914, NA, Kol. Openbaar, Vb. 28-3-1914 47, Vb. 29-6-1914; *Handelingen Tweede Kamer* 1913-14:2489.
[109] Pleyte to Idenburg, 29-6-1914, NA, Kol. Geheim, Vb. 29-6-1914 L11.
[110] Kropveld, 15-5-1914, NA, Kol. Geheim, Vb. 29-6-1914 L11.

protest about a higher cost of living or a reduction of their wages.[111] He wanted the expansion of the fleet to be financed by those who could afford it best. In the Netherlands Indies the money should be produced by those companies active in the colony. Private individuals should not be affected. Initially Pleyte had considered a special wealth tax in the home country and a capital tax in the colony. The stumbling block was that in this way a new kind of taxation would be introduced into the Netherlands Indies. Pleyte feared that the drafting of the necessary legislation could well result in an unacceptable delay.

After consultation with a deputation from the business community, the government assigned Th.A. de Meester and D.G.J.H. Kropveld, a former public prosecutor in Surabaya who acted on behalf of the Van Aalst group, the task of drawing up a plan of how to finance the proposed fleet. Among the extra taxes proposed in the Netherlands Indies by them were an increase in export duties and in the freight tax for the shipping and private rail- and tramway companies. Van Aalst and Pleyte could live with the suggestion. Pleyte was sure that additional freight duties should not to be shifted onto the population; especially not as the transport companies had suggested the tax themselves. He also did not object to an extra export tax on estate products such as coffee, tea, rubber, tobacco, and sugar, and on oil. Copra, a 'native product' was another matter. Here the additional tax proposed by De Meester and Kropveld could well be passed on to local small producers. Pleyte's objections annoyed Van Aalst and his business associates. They refused to come up with alternative suggestions about how to cover the 1.5 million guilders an extra copra export tax would yield. Van Aalst informed Pleyte that to their regret they could not offer any proposals for raising such a large sum.[112] Pleyte's solution was to propose to raise the export tax on the other export products.

A bill concerning the income and expenditure for improving the fleet was completed in the middle of July 1914. It called for larger battleships than those initially planned for, of course costing more: three million guilders extra per ship. Idenburg was given till 10 August to comment. The outbreak of World War One intervened. As he wired to Pleyte, Idenburg correctly presumed that the tabling of the bill would be postponed till the consequences of the new international circumstances could be assessed.[113] Van Aalst and his associates did not have to part with the money they had pledged for the building of a second dreadnought. At the outbreak of the war the Navy bill was withdrawn. Large battleships had to be built abroad and war made it

---

[111] Pleyte to Idenburg, 29-6-1914, NA, Kol. Geheim, Vb. 29-6-1914 L11.
[112] Van Aalst to Pleyte, 26-6-1914, NA, Kol. Geheim, Vb. 9-6-1914 L11.
[113] Idenburg to Pleyte, NA, Kol. Geheim, Vb. 10-8-1914 N15.

impossible for the Dutch government to buy one (Beunders 1984:41). No Navy Act was promulgated during World War One. In November 1921 a new Navy Bill was brought before Parliament. In October 1923 it was turned down by a narrow margin of fifty votes against and forty-nine in favour (Beunders 1984:87,198).

CHAPTER VI

August 1914

Shortly before the outbreak of hostilities in Europe, at least three newspapers in the Netherlands Indies, the *Java-Bode*, *De Locomotief*, and the *Preanger-bode*, reported that a Japanese fleet had entered Wijnkoopsbaai on the south coast of West Java. The source of the news was a telegram from Cibadak addressed to the Governor General, in which it was stated that fifteen Japanese warships had been sighted in the bay. The *Assistent-Resident* of Sukabumi was instructed to investigate. He sent a telegram to a government official stationed on the coast. The reply was that nothing was known about any Japanese fleet. After headquarters in Batavia had contacted him, the local agent of the Koninklijke Paketvaart Maatschappij (KPM, Royal Packet Company) shipping company in Pelabuhan Ratu submitted a similar report. Army and naval command had also been alerted. General De Greve, by now chief-of-staff of the colonial army, personally travelled to Pelabuhan Ratu by car to check. There were no Japanese warships in sight. All had fallen victim to a practical joke. Someone had wanted to deceive the telegraph clerk in Cibadak and had succeeded with a vengeance. Without giving the matter a second thought he had transmitted the telegram with its alarming news.[1]

The reaction elicited by the telegram is a minor example of the anxiety that had gripped people all over the world. The dying days of July 1914 were pregnant with rumours and speculations about what was going to happen. The gloom that was building up only grew even more sombre after Vienna's ultimatum had expired and war was declared on Serbia on 28 July 1914. The Netherlands succeeded in remaining neutral, but inevitably could not escape the economic and financial consequences of the war. A severe crisis was in the making. It was to affect almost all sectors of the Dutch economy. Shipping, trade, fisheries, agriculture, and industry, none escaped repercussions at the outbreak of war. Anxiety was stirred up to greater heights because a shortage of wheat, and hence of bread threatened. Holland was dependent on imports for the bulk of its wheat. Available stock would suffice for two or three weeks.

---

[1] *De Locomotief*, 28-7-1914, 31-7-1914.

The new harvest at the end of September would provide only enough wheat for domestic consumption for about two months. Good pre-war bread became but a memory. The Dutch had to eat 'war bread', made of one-quarter of wheat flour to three-quarters bran. To guard against a food-shortage export bans, including one on wheat, were instituted. Fuel also threatened to become scarce. To prevent a forcing-up of prices, burgomasters were given the authority to confiscate stocks of food and fuel.

One reason for the threat of scarcities was the fact that Great Britain and France aimed to create a complete economic blockade of Germany and Austria. British warships operated off Dover and off the north coast of Scotland, blocking the entrances to the North Sea. South of Dover, the French Navy patrolled the seas. Neutral merchantmen were arrested and directed to French and British ports. The stopping of neutral merchantmen in a search for contraband had been a point of concern and deliberations for years. During the Russo-Japanese War searches on the high sea of neutral merchantmen by Russian warships had caused great dismay in British commercial circles. At that time London had refused to call for a change in the international rules on contraband. The British government had felt uneasy about the searching of British ships, but had not protested. The prime minister, A.J. Balfour, had explained why. He said that

> [W]e can not be sure that the time will not come when our role will be changed; and that we shall be the belligerents, and when that time comes it will indeed be unfortunate if we had by our own action at the present moment forfeited any of the privileges which belong to a belligerent and which we might at such a time ourselves desire to exercise.[2]

Impressed by the damage to the trade and shipping, the liberal government of his successor, Sir Henry Campbell-Bannerman, had adopted a different position in 1907 at the time of the Second Peace Conference in The Hague. Cautious, preferring other states which would arouse less opposition from Germany and other powers, to take the initiative, the Foreign Secretary, Sir Edward Grey, had prepared proposals for the abolition of the concept of contraband – and when this proved impossible, for the restriction of goods belligerents could forbid their enemies to be supplied with by neutrals. Initially he had even pleaded for the immunity of enemy private property carried as cargo in ships captured or searched at sea. The Peace Conference ended in a great disappointment for the British delegation and for Grey personally. Apart from a well-intentioned resolution about the urgent necessity to cut defence spending, plans for a naval conference, to be held in London, were the only

---

[2] *The Times*, 29-10-1904.

concrete result. 'The whole conference', one of the British delegates, E. Crowe, reported, 'practically united against us on every question of naval warfare, except as regard our proposal to abolish contraband, which was accepted by a majority but which that majority subsequently declined to stick to'.[3] The subsequent Sea War Conference in London did not abolish contraband, also not the so-called conditional contraband; not weapons, but goods which could be used by an enemy army and Navy, such as foodstuffs, garments, and even hay for horses. It drafted a definition, listing products which were to be considered contraband, but at the outbreak of World War One the governments concerned had not yet ratified the London Declaration.

In August 1914, it was blatantly obvious that London had forfeited any reservations it might have entertained about interfering with neutral shipping. The Triple Entente Powers published lists of absolute and conditional contraband, of goods which in order to prevent them ending up in Germany or Austria, they would not allow to be shipped to neutral ports, or if so only in limited quantities. In the latter case guarantees were demanded that such imports would not ultimately end up in Germany or Austria. On the lists were items like foodstuffs, forage and grains suitable for feeding animals, clothes, fabrics for clothing, boots and shoes, suitable for use in war, and gold, silver, and money. After the outbreak of war London forced ships on their way to Rotterdam or Amsterdam with wheat and other contraband goods as their cargoes to return to Great Britain. Other ships which carried such goods from other countries of origin were arrested, thereby adding to the gloomy food prospects in Holland. *The Times* defended the Allied policy writing that Great Britain did not want to make bread more expensive in Holland, if only it were possible for the supply to Germany to be cut in other ways.[4] Similarly imports of cotton for the textile industry in the eastern part of Holland of cotton were cut by the British, indirectly affecting the batik industry of Java, which had become dependent on Dutch cloth. After a couple of weeks when it had become evident to London that all these products were to be used exclusively for Dutch consumption, imports were allowed, albeit in lesser quantities than before.

As Dutch foreign trade included the transit of German merchandise, London also called a halt to some exports from Holland. The British government justified this policy by pointing out that it could not be ascertained whether cargo had originated from Holland or from Germany. Among the products which suffered were sugar and beet sugar. British imports of sugar from the Netherlands Indies in Great Britain were still allowed, providing that

---

[3] Crow to Tyrrell, 11-10-1907, PRO FO 800 69.
[4] *The Times*, 9-10-1914.

the ships transporting the sugar sailed directly to a British port without first calling at a Dutch one.

Paris pursued a similar policy. The Netherlands, as one French Senator remarked, should be economically neutral as well.[5] In the eyes of some Dutch people France was even more stringent than Great Britain. The delays in French ports were lengthier, more cargo was considered contraband, and unloading took more time. The Dutch suspected that the reason for the French pestering could only be that its government was influenced by the French press which had contained among other incorrect reports one about German troops marching through the south of Limburg. As the former editor of *De Locomotief*, P. Brooshooft, put it, the French press was motivated by 'ignorance and an innate suspicion'.[6] A few weeks later he observed that British, French, and British Indian newspapers showed 'a suspicious interest' in the way in which Holland observed its duties as a neutral country.[7] Some, among them the *Times of India* and the *Daily Mail*, called for a blockade of the Netherlands, when it remained a source of imports of food and other essential products for Germany.

With international trading virtually grinding to a standstill, mass unemployment threatened in Holland. Consequently, great apprehension was voiced about the growing number of jobless and the many people who might no longer be able to buy essential foodstuffs or, having no money to pay their rent, would be evicted from their houses. To help out the many families threatened with economic ruin, Queen Wilhelmina took the initiative for the setting up of a Netherlands Koninklijk Nationaal Hulp Comité (Royal National Relief Committee). She herself became honorary chairperson. The committee, which also aimed to provide assistance to companies which had run into trouble because of the war, was constituted on 10 August during a solemn gathering in the Trêveszaal in The Hague. Newspapers did not fail to mention that when the Queen addressed the meeting she could not hide her emotion, speaking at times in a tremulous voice.[8]

Impressed by the grim prospects for Europe and the consequences the war might well have for the Netherlands, expressions of official public joy on festive days were cancelled. Celebrations planned for the birthday of the Queen Mother were called off. Flags were not flown on public buildings on that day. The same decision was taken with regard to 31 August, Queen's Birthday. Austerity was the catchword and would remain so till the end of the war. At the Queen's own request celebrations were postponed till the war had ended.

---

[5] *De Locomotief*, 7-10-1914.
[6] *De Locomotief*, 22-10-1914.
[7] *De Locomotief*, 9-10-1914.
[8] *De Locomotief*, 22-9-1914.

This was a moment many people in the Netherlands and elsewhere in the world believed – or hoped – would not be far off. Hopes were pinned on the fact that the high costs of modern war technology would impede a prolonged war. Before this goal had been reached and peace had been concluded, public life should be sober.

In the Netherlands Indies Idenburg decided not to cancel the customary audiences held by Dutch civil servants on Queen's Day to which representatives of all population groups were invited, but in view of the grave situation to cancel the customary balls which were planned in many cities. In December he confided to his adjutant that dancing was not proper given the circumstances (Bijl de Vroe 1980:46). He was forced to change his decision. Instructions from The Hague were explicit: 'Her majesty emphatically requests (to) cancel audience and avoid everything drawing attention to birthday'.[9] In Batavia the customary audience at Idenburg's palace was called off. Idenburg also did not present any honours either to native Indonesians and foreign orientals in the colony as was the custom. Civil servants were not even given a full day off. To ease the pain, their chiefs were given the discretion to determine how long and during what hours their subordinates had to work on Queen's Day.

The Hague's decision upset the calculations of those in the Netherlands Indies who intended to turn Queen's Day into a day on which to testify to their loyalty to the Queen and to the Dutch state. One of the persons most eager to do so was the Sultan of Yogyakarta. He could not be dissuaded from offering his congratulations on Queen's Birthday in person to the *Resident*, saddling the latter, who had to follow instructions not to celebrate Queen's Birthday in any way, with a bit of a problem. All the *Residents* could accomplish was when he visited the Residency in the morning of 31 August that the 'old ruler' as he called him – the sultan was about eighty years of age – did not wear his full-dress uniform of an army Major-General, but came in undress. His two sons who accompanied him were similarly clad in the undress uniforms of lieutenant-colonels.[10]

If the truth be told, people did not feel like celebrating. In the Netherlands and elsewhere in Europe governments decided that it was not proper to organize festivities when soldiers were killing each other at the front. Even dancing was discouraged. In Holland the atmosphere was such that a visitor from the Netherlands Indies, who had looked forward to his stay in his fatherland and had arrived there during the first days of the war, almost immediately decided to return to Java as quickly as possible. He wrote home that '[e]verywhere there was gloom, poverty began to manifest itself everywhere, merrymaking

---

[9]   Pleyte to Idenburg, 24-8-1914, NA, Kol. Geheim, Vb. 25-8-1914 Y16.
[10] *Resident* Yogyakarta to Idenburg, 3-9-1914, NA, Kol. Geheim, Vb. 30-12-1914 K25.

was absolutely out of the question, theatres, concerts, fairs did not go on'.[11] In the Netherlands Indies the mood was much the same. Concerts and theatrical performances, even by such a famous Dutch actor as Eduard Verkade, who only a few days earlier had still attracted full houses, were suddenly much less busy. Fancy fairs were cancelled because of the 'sad circumstances'. In the north of Sumatra, as an extra gesture of sensitivity, the local authorities asked directors of cinemas not to show war films. The Javanese elite joined in this effort to avoid excessive festivities. In Yogyakarta the installation of a new crown prince was celebrated with less lustre than was customary.

The grave consequences of the war – initially still qualified as a European war – for the country's economy coupled with the tense international situation compelled the Dutch Senate and Parliament to shorten their recess. Both convened on 3 August to discuss the political and economic situation that had been thrust upon them and the measures to be taken to deal with the situation. Foreign affairs formed no part of the debate. The Dutch government refused to say anything about such matters. The Prime Minister, P.W.A. Cort van der Linden, explained that his government was afraid that any word incautious about that subject could expose the Netherlands to the 'gravest danger'.[12] Urgent decisions had to be taken. Cort van der Linden asked the members of the Lower House to complete their discussion of the emergency measures suggested by his government concerning the armed forces and the economy within one day.[13] Ranks were closed. All proposals put forward by the government were accepted unanimously. Troelstra, stressing that if there was one government in Europe which was innocent of 'the terrible crime' it was that of the Netherlands, joined in the call for unity. He announced that his party would continue its socialist propaganda against militarism and capitalism with redoubled vigour after the war. At the end of the month, Troelstra could also proudly point out the exemplary behaviour of the crew of the 'red fleet', and at the decision of the Bond van Minder Marine-Personeel to abandon any agitation for the time being.[14] He was probably not aware that in Surabaya the chairman of the union had gone further and had urged the members of his union to forget that they were socialists. Had the socialists at home not inveighed so loudly against the strengthening of the fleet, the Navy would have had bigger and better ships. This mistake should not be repeated. In future the colour to be fought for should not be red, but Red, White, and Blue, the national colours. His audience greeted these words with cheers.[15]

---

[11] *De Locomotief,* 5-10-1914.
[12] *Handelingen Eerste Kamer* 1913-14:2589.
[13] *Handelingen Tweede Kamer* 1913-14:585.
[14] *De Locomotief,* 5-10-1914.
[15] *Soerabaiasch Nieuwsblad,* cited in *De Locomotief,* 17-8-1914.

Decisive measures were all the more necessary because in the Netherlands and elsewhere in Europe people had panicked when war broke out. The financial world, already reacting nervously as international tension mounted, came under severe pressure. It was observed a few weeks later in a Dutch periodical that it was difficult to find words to describe the consternation elicited by the political reports following Vienna's ultimatum (Van Nierop 1914:348). In Amsterdam, as in other European stock markets, share prices plummeted. Traders who had borrowed money on shares as security feared financial ruin and forced the exchange to close on 28 July. The closure became effective the following day. This had not even happened in 1870 at the outbreak of the Franco-Prussian War. The exchanges in London, Paris, and Berlin closed on 31 July.

In Holland commercial and savings banks were confronted with runs on their buildings by customers who wanted to close their accounts. At the Rijkspostspaarbank, the State Postal Savings Bank, a sum amounting to over one million Dutch guilders was withdrawn on 30 July. The following two days the figure rose to two-and-a half, and almost five million guilders respectively (Van Nierop 1914:362-3). Banks reacted by refusing withdrawal of deposits, except when it could be established that the money was to be used for urgent purposes. To back them the government extended the period within which a bank had to honour a request for payment of deposits from two weeks to six months; allowing for intermediate withdrawals of at most 25 guilders per week. People also tried *en masse* to change paper currency for silver coins. Armed with chairs, mattresses, and cushions they queued in the evening to make sure that they were served the following morning (Vissering 1920:235). Generally speaking, the public was hesitant to accept bank notes. Some feared immediate depreciation and sold their paper currency at a price lower than its face value. Coins were hoarded. People refused to part with their coins and small change was not given, which undermined the faith in paper money even more. Shopkeepers refused to act as an 'exchange bureau' for customers trying to get rid of their banknotes. To cope with a situation in which many members of the public had lost their confidence in financial institutions, the Dutch government prohibited the export of gold on 3 August. As an additional measure the Central Bank was allowed to extend its uncovered circulation from two-and-a-half to five times its gold and silver reserves. To keep money transactions at a reasonable level, the state and even municipalities were forced to print *zilverbonnen*, 'silver paper money' to replace the coins of small denomination (Treub 1920:135-9).

Besides the flight in coins, another major problem which had to be solved was that of credit and loans. Some feared that they would not be able to cash in outstanding loans. Others wondered whether they would still be able to pay their debts or receive the credit they needed to pursue their business. The

C.J.K. van Aalst, President NHM (*Gedenkboek* 1924: between pages 90 and 91)

possibility of a moratorium on the payment of debts, endorsed by a number of Chambers of Commerce, was considered. It was rejected by the government on the grounds that such a measure would be counterproductive and would only add to the panic. Great Britain and France did introduce a moratorium, Germany did not.

Leading bankers acquiesced in the stand taken by the government. They wired the Minister of Agriculture, Industry, and Trade, M.W.F. Treub, that a moratorium was 'a highly precarious leap in the dark'. It would upset the whole credit system, lead to enormous disasters especially for the Netherlands Indies, and would damage the reputation of the Netherlands for a long time to come.[16] The major Dutch banks had worked out their own solution. They formed a syndicate to come to the rescue of companies engaged in industry and trade that had run into trouble. Van Aalst had been the key figure in bringing this about, and most of the negotiations to establish such a syndicate took place at the offices of the Nederlandsche Handel-Maatschappij (NHM, Netherlands Trade Company). The syndicate had to help out bona fide companies with sound security, which had ran into trouble because of the exceptional circumstances and needed credit to avoid bankruptcy. Its establishment caused some confusion. An advertisement had to be published in the Dutch papers to assure the public that it would be incorrect to conclude that the consortium came to the rescue of the stock and money markets, and of wholesale business only. Small businesses or private persons were equally eligible for help. By September it had already turned out that applications for financial assistance were not as numerous as initially expected; and that the financial consequences of war in the Netherlands were less catastrophic than had been feared in the inevitable confusion during the first days of the war. Although rather an anti-climax, Treub concluded that the syndicate had done a good and useful job. It had restored confidence that credit was still available.[17] Ten years later the NHM was ready to acknowledge the praise it considered its due. In a commemorative volume of the company it was suggested that most of the financial measures taken by the government at the outbreak of World War One had been at the suggestion of Van Aalst and other bankers, whom, the government indeed had pledged, it would consult at all times before concrete measures were taken.[18]

When the war was discussed in the Dutch Parliament it seemed as if the Netherlands Indies did not exist. Attention focused on the situation in Holland. The colony was only alluded to in passing as an additional argument to reject a moratorium on debts. The Dutch possessions in the West Indies did not rate

---

[16] *Handelingen Tweede Kamer* 1913-14:2593.
[17] *Handelingen Eerste Kamer* 1913-14:593; Treub 1920:145.
[18] *Gedenkboek* 1924:94.

a single mention. In a sense it was not at all necessary that the Netherlands Indies should have featured in parliamentary debate in The Hague. The colony was much better prepared to cope with the immediate consequences of war on economic life than was the mother country. With the constant fear of a Japanese attack contingency plans had been drawn up years before. In this respect Germany and the Netherlands Indies formed an exception. Nowhere else in the world had governments prepared the economic and financial measures which needed to be taken in the event of war. Consequently, the Javasche Bank knew precisely what to do at the end of July 1914 (Vissering 1920:251).

The disregard the Dutch Parliament showed for the fate of the Netherlands Indies in July and August was shared by the general public in Holland. This attitude contrasted sharply with the concern expressed in the Netherlands Indies about developments in Europe. A.J. Lievegoed wrote a lengthy article in *De Locomotief* at the end of August in which he complained about the lack of interest in Holland in the way the colony might be affected by the war. He observed that people in Holland were more concerned about Poland and Finland, about the German possessions in China and Samoa, and about the fate of the Czechs, Albanians, and stranded American tourists in Europe, than about the Netherlands Indies. In Holland people knew all there was to know about the armies and fleets of the belligerents, but were ignorant of the strength of the Dutch naval squadron that had to defend Java.[19] There were exceptions to this rule. One Dutch weekly raised the question of whether measures had been taken to declare the Netherlands Indies independent the moment the Netherlands should become involved in the war. Such a proposition was grist to the mill of the emerging nationalist movement in Java. 'Unbelievable!', was the comment in *Oetoesan Hindia*. Such an eventuality would raise the status of the Javanese in the national and in the international context, and would mean that the fate of the Netherlands Indies would not be decided in the North Sea but in the Java Sea.[20]

The Netherlands Indies had plenty to complain. War came at a moment when the economic boom it had experienced since the turn of the century had seemed to have stagnated for more than a year. In August 1914 it seemed as if the consequences of the war would be as grave in the colonies as in Holland, perhaps even more serious. Merchant vessels, and not only those flying the flag of a belligerent, remained in port. In retrospect the term 'general panic' was used to describe the atmosphere prevailing in shipping circles during the first days of the war (Voogd 1924:63). Captains and owners of Dutch ships refused to take them to sea before a proclamation of neutrality had been pub-

[19] *De Locomotief,* 10-10-1914.
[20] *Oetoesan Hindia,* 16-10-1914.

lished in the *Javasche Courant*. This did not happen till 4 August. Neutral merchant ships which sailed before and after that date risked being stopped and searched at sea. German and British warships carried out this task in Asia, but most problems arose in European waters. Dutch ships sailing from North and South America to Holland, or from Holland to the Netherlands Indies experienced a similar fate. It was no exception for such ships to be stopped five to six times, perhaps more in the first days of the war. One Dutch ship was even forced to call in at Bizerta, Malta, Marseilles, Gibraltar, Cherbourg, Le Hâvre, Dover, and London (Voogd 1924:63).

Another problem facing Dutch trade in those confused early days of the war was that German merchantmen were taken as prizes by Allied warships. Some had Dutch cargo on board. To deal with this problem a Committee for Seized Exports was formed in the Netherlands in October 1914. In the Netherlands Indies instructions on how to reclaim such goods before prize-courts were published in the *Javasche Courant* around the same time. The information consisted of notices on procedure issued by the British authorities in the Straits Settlements. Part of the Dutch cargo confiscated would be returned, but settlements were far from satisfactory. Over 850 Dutch companies which disagreed with the decision of the prize courts in Allied countries and in Germany and Austria, which later in the war also had to decide on questions about whether their warships and submarines had rightfully destroyed neutral freighters, turned to the Dutch government for help in November 1916. They urged that an international court of appeal be instituted.

Passengers cancelled their journeys. Mercantile houses in the Netherlands Indies, among them the NHM, unsure of what the fate of their cargo would be, had already decided before 28 July not to ship their merchandise. This reaction was consonant with the trends generally prevailing in trading at that time. Unsure of how prices would react – some predicted a rise, others a fall – the dominant mood was one of wait-and-see and to put off buying and selling for the time being. After the war had broken out insurance companies refused to insure cargo against the risks of war.

Apprehension grew when exporters learned from the civil servants in Batavia and from newspaper reports about the confiscation of colonial products on board ships which had been forced to enter French and British ports. Their prompt reaction was to unload such cargo before ships set sail. Pleyte informed his colleague in Foreign Affairs that this had caused 'great consternation' in the shipping companies concerned.[21] These companies, of which the Rotterdamsche Lloyd and Stoomvaart Maatschappij Nederland were the two most important, immediately noted a sharp fall in the cargo offered. August

---

[21] Pleyte to Loudon, 11-9-1914, NA, Kol. Geheim, Vb. 11-9-1914 M18.

Sultan Hamengkubuwono VII of Yogyakarta in his uniform of a General in the Netherlands Indies army, circa 1910 (KITLV 4027)

1914 was a disastrous month for the export of colonial products. Compared with July the export of coffee dropped drastically from 2,303,000 kg to 400,000 kg, that of copra from 7,162,000 to 1,727,000 kg, and that of sugar from 233,331,000 kg to 126,541,000 kg. The tobacco export experienced a decline from 1,725,000 to 394,000 kg and that of tea from 2,634,000 to 1,538,000 kg. The rubber export in August 1914 amounted to 137,000 kg instead of 418,000 kg in the previous month.[22]

The postal service between Asia and Europe was another victim. The German trade and mail service to and from the Netherlands Indies came to a halt after German steamers in Asian waters were either seized by the enemy or did not venture to leave port. With the exception of mail from Medan and from the Dutch sub-post offices in Singapore and Penang, the sending of post by British mail was suspended after 8 August. This was done partly at the request of the British government of the Straits Settlements, which wanted to relieve the burden of the censorship offices in Singapore and Penang. The French mail service was no longer used after 12 September.[23] It did not form a realistic alternative as war had disrupted the overland rail link between Marseilles and Holland. The Dutch mail service was the only possibility that remained, but ran into serious delays because of an initial hesitance to sail and the stopping and searching of liners in the North Sea and in ports. In order not to delay the postal service unnecessary from August till the end of 1914 mail for Holland was forwarded from Gravesend to Flushing with steamers from the shipping company Zeeland. Sending mail to Germany and the other Continental Powers from the Netherlands Indies and vice versa became increasingly difficult. Letters and parcels destined for Germany on Dutch steamers had to be unloaded in Genoa. When they were taken along to British and French ports they were subject to the Allied measures to isolate the Continental Powers. Such shipments ran the risk of being confiscated. After the Ottoman Empire entered the war, mail for Turkey, including letters addressed to the Dutch Consul in Jeddah and to Indonesian Muslims in Mecca, also had to be redirected from French and British ports to Genoa, causing considerable delays. This route was even disrupted before May 1915, when Italy joined the Allied Powers. When relationship between Italy and the Continental Powers soured the Ottoman government seized Italian mail at Jeddah in March 1915. Thereafter, mail still could be sent, but there was no way to avoid the mail restrictions introduced by the allies.

All this circuitous mail did not mean that communication between the German community in the Netherlands Indies and Germany was completely

---

[22] *De Locomotief,* 17-10-1914.
[23] Information of the Department of Agriculture, Industry and Trade, cited in *De Locomotief,* 29-7-1916.

disrupted during the war. The British censor was keen to intercept money, cheques, and merchandise – even in small quantities, mindful of the saying many a mickle makes a muckle – and German war propaganda, which also came to mean German newspapers and magazines in which according to the Allied a distorted picture was given of what happened at the fronts. Letters could still be sent to and from the Netherlands Indies, and German newspapers still reached the Netherlands Indies; though not by British mail. Letters with a suspect content were confiscated when neutral ships were searched but the remainder was allowed through. To circumvent seizure of German mail that was carried on neutral ships by the Allied Powers, codes were developed by the German government to keep open the communication with countrymen in Asia, Africa, and the Americas, essential for trade and for the conduct of war. Nevertheless, the chance was high that such mail would be seized, soon eliciting no more than a formal protest by the Dutch Captains and The Hague.[24] According to the Acting German Consul General in Batavia about 90 per cent was 'lost'.[25] There were other ways of having messages reach their destination. Sometimes Dutch people were prepared to act as a courier. Another method – until discovered – was to use the telegraph connection between the Netherlands Indies and Japan which was less scrupulously monitored by the censor, using a special code. Important German diplomatic and commercial correspondence sent by sea mail to addresses in neutral countries occasionally also escaped the attention of the British censor, especially when the message was in code or written in invisible ink. Such letters from Germany or from the Netherlands Indies were sent to an address in Holland or in some other neutral country. From there they were forwarded to their real destination. German Envoys, including the Acting Consul General in Batavia, also transposed commercial messages into a special secret code; investing them with a cloak of innocence. The reverse also happened. German diplomats sought the cooperation of German companies to disguise official correspondence. In the Netherlands Indies a central role in this respect was played by the important Hamburg-based estate company and trading house of Behn, Meyer and Company, which had had branches all over Southeast Asia before the war and acted as agent for the German shipping lines.[26]

For more than a month no mail from the colony, including the reports regularly sent by the colonial administration to Ministry of the Colonies, reached

---

[24] *De Locomotief,* 22-2-1916.
[25] Interrogation Th. Helfferich, 3-8-1917 and Windels, 11-8-1917, NA, Kol. Geheim, Vb. 10-1-1918 S1.
[26] At the beginning of 1917 the sending of German mail to and from the United States, and from there to and from the Netherlands Indies, by submarine was briefly contemplated. Senders who wanted to make use of this service had to write the word *Tauchbootbrief* on the envelope.

Holland. In the middle of September the last written reports that had been received by the Ministry of the Colonies at the Plein in The Hague were dated one and a half month previous.[27] The Netherlands Indies likewise received no post from Europe. The first mail from Holland, with Dutch newspapers carrying detailed information about what was happening in Holland and the rest of Europe, reached Java on 11 September.[28]

To make matters worse, the telegraph links between the two parts of the empire also broke down. Telegrams could not be sent nor reach their destination. In 1914 use of a German cable turned out to be a serious liability. German cables were vulnerable to British attacks. At the end of July, Le Roy had alerted the Ministry of the Colonies to the fact that special precautions had to be taken to protect that part of the cable to Yap that ran through the Archipelago. He pointed out that German warships guarded the cable at Shanghai and at Yap. A Dutch warship should patrol the waters near Manado.[29] Idenburg, informed of this by The Hague, refused to send a warship to Celebes to guard the cable and the station at Manado against an attack. He was afraid of the consequence of splitting the 'a naval force already too weak'.[30]

What Idenburg did, and this step initially amazed Pleyte, who inquired the reason by wire, was to replace the German staff of the Manado station with Dutchmen.[31] A few days later, on 4 August, after Great Britain had entered the war, a similar measure was taken with respect to British staff at the telegraph stations of the Eastern Extension Australasia and China Telegraph Company in the Netherlands Indies. The Coucil of the Indies had advised this be done in order to honour the rules about the way a neutral country should treat belligerents impartially. As an additional precaution, military officers were stationed at the offices to censor foreign telegraphic communications. As with so many of the measures the colonial government took to guard neutrality, ignorance of how things went in real life anticipated serious flaws. Dutch officials did replace the telegraph operators, but not the other British members of the staff. As two copies of a telegram were filed for administrative purposes, these Britons, as became clear in February 1916, forwarded the text of telegrams from abroad which the censors had refused to pass on to the addressees.

In his letter in which Le Roy had alerted Pleyte, the former had stressed the importance of the German cable for uninterrupted communication between The Hague and the colony at a time of international crisis. Despite their precautions it was precisely this telegraph link between Europe and Asia

---

[27] Pleyte to Loudon, 11-9-1914, NA, Kol. Geheim, Vb. 11-9-1914 M18.
[28] *De Locomotief,* 11-9-1914.
[29] Le Roy to Bakhuis, 31-7-1914, NA, Kol. Geheim, Vb. 1-8-1914 O14.
[30] Idenburg to Pleyte, 3-8-1914, NA, Kol. Geheim, Vb. 4-8-1914 Z14bis.
[31] Pleyte to Idenburg, 3-8-1914, NA, Kol. Geheim, Vb. 4-8-1914 Z14bis.

Governor General A.W.P. Idenburg (Van Gent, Penard and Rinkes 1923: Photo 259)

which broke down first. On August 8 the installation on Yap, a major link in the German communications system in the Pacific, was destroyed by well-directed fire from British cruisers; this had been announced to his colleague in Manado by the German telegraphist with the words 'Adieu Kamarad dort kommen die Engländer', but within a fortnight the Germans succeeded in building an improvised station.[32] For a brief period the shelling of Yap also put an end to the telegraph link between Java and Tokyo. The Netherlands Indies had once again became largely dependent on 'British lines', and the censorship Great Britain had imposed on telegraphic communications at home and in her colonies and protectorates immediately after it had entered the war. This dependence was an additional reason for apprehension in those first uncertain days of the war. The Dutch in the Netherlands Indies were sure that Great Britain would not inform Batavia were the Dutch government to choose to join the German side. London would not allow the Netherlands Indies to prepare for an attack. Were British armed forces to strike, they would do so without warning.[33] To intensify the sense of isolation, the French line between Pontianak and Saigon had broken down too, and could not be used.

For the time being telegrams had to be sent via Eastern Extension, which only accepted properly addressed messages with a French and English text.[34] London also demanded that telegrams bore the full name of the sender and the addressee. Pleyte personally instructed his staff that telegrams had to be addressed to 'Governor General, Batavia'.[35] If coded messages in cipher had to be sent, this should be done via the Dutch Envoy in Washington, using the connection via Guam and Yap to Manado. Dutch trade was also hit by the measure. Trading companies used to conduct much of their telegraph correspondence in code. Departing from this custom meant that wires were much lengthier, and hence more expensive, and that the companies had to part with an established way of identifying products.

Trade and communication were not the only matters to suffer from the war. Passengers, often fairly strapped for cash, suddenly found themselves stranded in foreign ports when the ships on which they sailed, in most cases German vessels, were unable to continue their voyage. Ships of neutral countries offered the only opportunity for them to continue their travels; and some captains showed enough compassion not to ask the full fare. Tourists who wanted to return home as quickly as possible were likewise looking for sea transportation on ships flying a neutral flag, for instance Dutch ships calling

---

[32] Teitler 1984:31; Holtappel to Pop, 24-8-1914, NA, Kol. Geheim, Vb. 18-12-1914 P24.
[33] M. 1922:844.
[34] Sending telegrams to Curaçao was even more difficult. The line was disrupted at Santo Domingo, and from there the telegrams had to be transported by ship to Puerto Rico.
[35] Note Pleyte, NA, Kol. Geheim, Vb. 6-8-1914 D15.

at Genoa and Marseilles. In Genoa hundreds of tourists on holiday in Italy and Switzerland tried to take passage on Dutch liners. Some of them offered large sums of money far in excess of the ordinary fare. Instructed to do so by the owners, Dutch Captains usually accepted only Dutch people. Conditions on board were crowded; the more so as Dutch passengers from the Netherlands Indies, who in normal times would have preferred a leisurely trip overland for the last leg of their journey, decided to remain on board. Extra bunks had to be placed in the cabins, forcing the passengers to accept 'billeting'. Smoking salons and lounges were converted into dormitories. On at least one such ship, meals were rationed. In anticipation that, as indeed did happen, the ship would be stopped and forced to sail to a British or French port, less copious diners were served. To make room for over one hundred additional Dutch tourists on another Dutch passenger ship cooks, stewards, and Javanese servants had to vacate their cabins and move to the quarters usually reserved for soldiers and to the forecastle. She, too, was stopped a number of times. When it finally became clear that she was to be allowed to continue her journey to Holland, the passengers broke into the Dutch national anthem. On rare occasions such additional passengers complained. A Dutchman who had boarded a Dutch ship at Marseilles considered the third-class cabin below the dignity of him and his daughter. Later he sued the captain for endangering the lives of his passengers by sailing too fast in foggy weather in an attempt to reach a Dutch port as soon as possible. He lost his case.

The fate of German and Austrian passengers was even more hazardous. At the most the Dutch had to share a cabin, or if they were forced to disembark in a French city, had some difficulty in explaining that they were not Germans, and that the language they spoke was Dutch. When Germans or Austrians managed to board a Dutch ship, they and the German members of the crew were usually arrested if the ship on which they sailed was searched in Asian and European waters. They remained interned for the duration of the war. Only clergymen and elderly persons were allowed to continue their journey. For those Germans who had made their living in the Netherlands Indies and were arrested, a life lay in store for which an existence as a member of a colonial elite had not prepared them. One, probably a planter from Sumatra, complained in a letter published in *De Locomotief* about the way the prisoners were treated in a camp in Colombo. The washing facilities were dreadful, they had to do the dishes themselves, and had to cook their own meals. The camp beds on which the prisoners were expected to sleep were not provided with mosquito nets; and, because brushes and polish had not been handed out, they could not clean their shoes.[36]

---

[36] *De Locomotief*, 9-9-1914.

Occasionally Germans serving in the Dutch colonial army were among those arrested. After protests by the captain of the ship, by their superior officer, or by the Dutch Envoy they were usually released again. Sometimes merely having a German name sufficed to arrested. As Dutch nationals who had visited Germany could also run into trouble the Ministry of the Colonies came to demand from civil servants and army officers who had been on leave in Holland, that if they had been in Germany that they travel home with a new passport.

In the Netherlands Indies a few days elapsed before the news of the war sank. On 1 August *De Locomotief* still reported that the outbreak of the war had been received calmly by the population. People were aware of the seriousness of the tidings, but Europe was too far away for them to become emotionally involved. The newspaper added that the war did not seem to make the least impression on the natives or the Chinese. The *Indische Financier* dated the same day also carried a reassuring message. Discussing the panic on the financial markets in Europe it pointed out that, although there were close links between the exchanges in Batavia and in Amsterdam, there was no reason to fear the worst. Europe was far away, and most investors in the colony had put their money into estates in Java and Sumatra. Contrary to what really was to happen, it wrote that the estates were not threatened by the war in Europe. The conclusion drawn was that the intrinsic value of shareholdings and bonds was not at risk.[37] To this *De Locomotief* added equally encouragingly that it was not difficult to imagine why there were runs on banks in Holland, but that the situation in the Netherlands Indies was completely different. Holland was close to the theatre of war; the Netherlands Indies formed 'a closed circulation area, which as such is completely outside the war'.[38] The newspaper begged its readers not to withdraw money from the banks. Banks needed their supply of precious metals. Anyway: 'Large amounts of money in your own house is not safe and should unrest occur the plundering of private houses is more likely, in any case easier, than an attack on the safes of the banks'.[39]

It was one of the many appeals in the colony aimed to avert a panic in early August. Observing that people were on edge Idenburg had a special instruction sent to the Dutch *Residents*. Should circumstances require this, they had to assure the population that there was 'not the slightest reason for the tension and anxiety' which could be 'observed here and there', and that the economic situation did not warrant 'excessive concern' either.[40] In *De Locomotief*

---

[37] *Indische Financier,* cited in *De Locomotief,* 4-8-1914.
[38] *De Locomotief,* 4-8-1914.
[39] *De Locomotief,* 4-8-1914.
[40] Idenburg to Pleyte, 13-8-1914, NA, Kol. Geheim, Vb. 18-9-1914 I19.

of 1 August it was noted that 'calm judgement in facing a dark present and grim possibilities is a great strength'.[41] Six days later a reader who observed a pervading atmosphere of 'extraordinary nervousness' appealed to his fellow-Europeans to act normally. They should not forget that Europeans had a task to fulfil in the colony. Millions of natives looked up to them: 'Our calm gives them composure. If we do lose our calm than the people who expect guidance from us will lose their heads and turn to excesses.'[42] The author of these words was not the only one who held this opinion. White Dutch people should set the example. If they did not panic, the population would not either.

Such suggestions fell on deaf ears. The same economic consequences elicited by the news the war had had in the motherland could be observed. Prices rose, the volume of exports and imports declined, food shortages threatened, the supply of credit virtually dried up, and there was a run on gold and silver reserves. Shipping, including inter-island traffic, and the estate industry were especially affected, as were export firms all over the Archipelago. On estates and in harbours the prospect of mass unemployment loomed. Local indigenous producers of export products, rubber, tea, copra, maize, cassava, and beans and peas, and forest products, also suffered. Exports virtually ground to a standstill and prices dropped steeply.

The financial world reacted accordingly. Though there had already been a drop in prices in July the initial hope had been that the exchange in Batavia could stay open. The panic that held sway in Europe had to be avoided, and it had to be said, as it was stated in a report by the Javasche Bank, the stock-exchange in Batavia was of little significance.[43] The Netherlands Indies proved less self-contained than people had argued. The exchange had to be closed. Many wanted to sell their shares.

The commercial credit system, an essential element in the business networks, where it was common practice for export firms to advance loans to Arab and Chinese middlemen who in their turn provided credit to their local supplier, came under pressure. European firms set the example. In Batavia it was the NHM which was among the first to renege. The NHM refused to honour letters of credit or to provide credit to companies which were its customers. Such suppliants were referred to the Javasche Bank.[44] Other European firms demanded cash payments and their Chinese and Arab customers soon followed suit, or ran into difficulties because they had no cash to pay for new purchases or to meet outstanding financial obligations. All this led to the gloomy prediction that many private companies, even banks, would not survive the financial cri-

---

[41] *De Locomotief*, 1-8-1914.
[42] *De Locomotief*, 7-8-1914.
[43] *Feiten* 1916:42.
[44] Secret note President Javasche Bank, 11-8-1914, NA, Kol. Geheim, Vb. 18-9-1914 H19.

sis that seemed the inevitable accompaniment to the outbreak of the war and would soon be bankrupt. Some suggested a moratorium, a suspension on collecting debts and other financial obligations. As in Holland this never eventuated. The Javasche Bank intervened by extending its activities to the provision of credit, including those against the pledge of loans or mortgages, and other forms of transfers and the borrowing of money. Not to hurt commerce unnecessarily, the bank advisedly decided not to increase its interest rate.

In such grave circumstances The Hague deemed it necessary that Idenburg, whose term in office was to end in December, should remain in office. On 4 August he was sent a wire via the German and Eastern lines first in Dutch, and to be sure that it indeed reached its destination, repeated the next day via the second line in English. Idenburg was informed that 'with high approval' (the Queen) the appointment of a successor had been postponed 'unlimitedly' and that mindful of the current situation Pleyte trusted that he, Idenburg, would not object.[45]

The economic crisis with which Idenburg and his staff had to cope was acute. Business slowed down. A fall in foreign trade and production, whether brought about by the contraband policy of the Allied Powers or the hesitation about sailing, would exert a negative effect on the income of the state, which could well lose a significant portion of its customs and tax revenues. In the first nine months of 1914 these earned 1.5 million guilders less than during the same period the previous year; almost all of which had to be attributed to the decline of international trade as a consequence of the war.[46] As in the mother country where the Minister of Finance had called for the 'highly essential thrift', the colonial administration had to economize. Were the estate sector to collapse, much of the national income would dry up. At the end of August when the situation had already improved somewhat *De Locomotief* gloomily predicted that in such circumstances the Netherlands Indies was forced to rely for its finance 'on the fragile fiscal capacity of the native population, on the sixty million or more, which the land rent, the salt, the opium, and the pawnshop services yield together'.[47] Consequently public projects were postponed and salary increases promised to European and Javanese civil servants were cancelled. In September, Idenburg also called for a cut back of expenses for tours of duty. Civil servants should travel on duty only when strictly necessary. Idenburg insisted that they had to limit the use of motor cars, and where possible should travel overland instead of booking a sea passage.

---

[45] Pleyte to Idenburg, 4-8-1914, 5-8-1914, NA, Kol. Geheim, Vb. 5-8-1914 B14, Vb. 6-8-1914 D15.
[46] *De Locomotief,* 1-12-1914, citing *Korte berichten* published by the Department of Agriculture, Industry, and Trade.
[47] *De Locomotief,* 29-8-1914.

The office of the Javasche Bank in Batavia (Van Gent, Penard and Rinkes 1923: Photo 207)

In The Hague Pleyte went further. A national budget was presented to Parliament in September. It was somewhat of a farce. The departments had prepared its drafts before war had begun. The Constitution demanded that a budget be submitted but this had to be done at a time when nobody had had any inkling about the financial consequences of the war. Even the government admitted that it was little more than a gesture.[48] Still it already had one immediate consequence for the colony. One of the decisions Pleyte took was to scrap any rises, how small these might be, in expenditure on personnel from the draft budget. An exception was only made for a few very specific groups such as native schoolteachers and the sub-district heads. To solve the acute problem of the shortage of liquid assets induced by the war, the Ministry of the Colonies also contemplated speeding up and extending plans developed in 1913 to attract private capital for such government enterprises and services as the people's credit banks, forestry, and the government railways and postal service. To raise additional money the 'first Indies loan', which had already been discussed before the outbreak of the war, was floated. It was intended not to add money to the budget but to pay off the floating debt of the Netherlands Indies in Holland. Subscription was opened in March 1915. Within weeks the loan was oversubscribed in the Netherlands Indies. A reason to be proud. The

---

[48] *De Locomotief,* 31-10-1914.

loan was as much an investment opportunity as a chance to kindle colonial patriotism. People wondered whether the loan would have similar results in Holland (which it did). Mention was made of large contributions by members of the Javanese nobility and by affluent Chinese, who as their rich compatriots in the Straits Settlements were pillars of colonial society. The staff of the General Secretariat (the Governor-General's office) also subscribed a modest amount of money.[49]

The reaction of the European community to news of the war exacerbated the situation. People's anxiety mounted by the day. All over the Archipelago people phoned newspapers editors, civil servants, and other supposedly well-informed persons to check the many rumours which were circulating and to find out what was happening in the colony and in Europe. It was reported that in Semarang the *Resident's* phone rang almost incessantly.[50] Such was the increased demand for calls that during the whole of August trunk lines had to be opened to the public for two extra hours in the evening.

Almost all cities of any significance saw runs on the bank. Even in far-away Gorontalo in North Celebes panic struck. The indigenous population were also not unscathed. A remark by a Chinese that it would not be long before Dutch banknotes would no longer be legal tender acted as 'a spark in a barrel of gunpowder'. Almost all coins were withdrawn from circulation.[51] It was the same everywhere. Paper currency was distrusted. Occasionally people inquired whether bank notes could still be cashed. Many preferred coins. Consequently an extra supply of silver money had to be sent to banks. The export of gold and silver was prohibited.

Anticipating a financial crisis, as early as 1 August Pleyte had asked the Queen to allow Idenburg to change the backing of bank notes, current accounts and balance to coins or coin material of the Javasche Bank. Using this power Idenburg lowered the ratio from two-fifths to one-fifth. This offered the possibility to increase the amount of paper money in circulation to deal with a situation in which there was a mounting demand for cash payments, just at a time people were withdrawing large amounts of silver coins from the bank without having any intention of spending the money in the near future. As an additional security and aware that 'gold [was] nowhere obtainable', special contracts were concluded with the mining companies in the Netherlands Indies by the Javasche Bank which gave the bank preferential rights to buy gold.[52] In an attempt to decrease the distrust in paper currency, banknotes of the Javasche Bank were formally declared legal tender. To combat the hoard-

---

[49] *De Locomotief*, 13-3-1915, 16-3-1915, 18-3-1915.
[50] *De Locomotief*, 5-8-1914.
[51] *De Locomotief*, 15-9-1914.
[52] Report Javasche Bank cited in *Feiten* 1916:44.

ing of coins the Dutch *Residents* were instructed by Idenburg to act as rigorously as possible against anybody who undermined trust in banknotes and by doing so stimulated the withdrawal of coins from circulation.

Initially the measures were ineffective. People in all the population groups continued to flock to banks to change their notes for coins. Occasionally the police had to be called in to calm people down. In Semarang, the local branch of the Javasche Bank was overrun by customers. After it had opened its doors those waiting outside 'dashed in and the whole day it continued to be a continuous flood of people desiring silver. At certain moments the agitation among those still waiting was such that quarrels and small scuffles occurred, to which Europeans were also not immune.'[53] Tram and railway companies demanded the exact money in coins for fares. They refused to accept payment with large notes which would have required change in coins. The tram and railway companies were perfectly within their rights to do so, and it may have been their contribution to decreasing the exchange of notes for coins, but Europeans castigated such behaviour as setting a bad example to the non-European population. It inexorably stimulated the distrust in paper currency of the indigenous Indonesians who for years had been in the habit of treating railway stations as a convenient place to change banknotes for coins. At at least one station the result had been that the Chinese shopkeepers living nearby refused to accept paper currency.

The Batavia head-office of the NHM was partly blamed for the panic. It refused to pay out silver coins to anybody, not even to long-standing customers who needed the money to pay their employees' wages. As a consequence the Javasche Bank had to help out the shipping company, the KPM, and a number of estate companies which had an account with the NHM but were refused silver coins. Another large company, which also needed money to pay its employees, the Nederlandsch-Indische Gas-Maatschappij (Netherlands Indies Gas Company), was only provided with coins by the NHM after it threatened to close its account. The NHM had prepared for an emergency such as that which occurred in August 1914. Since 1912 it had built up large stock of coins. The Director of the NHM, A.F. Marmelstein, did his best to keep this so-called war-cash box intact. Expecting a run on his bank, in vain he tried to persuade the Javasche Bank to give his company three million guilders in silver coins. He even called on the mediation of Idenburg. The President of the Javasche Bank and Idenburg refused to comply. They could not permit such a substantial decrease in the stock of the Javasche Bank, exactly at a moment when that bank needed all the gold and silver it had to pay out to the public and to endorse its banknotes. Marmelstein was given to understand that for

---

[53] *De Locomotief,* 8-8-1914.

the sum for which he asked the Javasche Bank could bring into circulation an amount of banknotes five times higher. The most Marmelstein was prepared to commit himself to, and he considered it a 'fair deal', was that the NHM would not withdraw cash from the local branches of the Javasche Bank as long as its own stock remained intact.

Even Pleyte could not persuade the NHM to change its policy. Pleyte had 'instantly' phoned the NHM main office to summon Van Aalst to his Ministry when Idenburg had informed him about the company's attitude on 8 August. The result had been disappointing. Van Aalst was not available, and his deputy, A.H. Muller, was not very eager to send instructions to Batavia rapping Marmelstein over the knuckles. When instructions were finally sent, they did not exude the spirit Pleyte had expected. They merely told Marmelstein to lend the colonial government every assistance without prejudicing the interests of the NHM.[54] Pleyte concluded that the conduct of the NHM had been questionable. Idenburg shared this opinion. He wired Pleyte a few days later that the company was 'only alive to its own interests'.[55] This was neatly phrased. According to a secret note drawn up by the President of the Javasche Bank – at the request of Pleyte the words were not included in the version of the report to be shown to the management or Van Aalst – the attitude of the NHM in Batavia at the outbreak of the war had been one of 'irrational fear, egoism carried to the extreme, and complete indifference to the interests of society and the rights and interests of its clients'.[56]

The stubbornness of the NHM meant that in Surabaya and Semarang especially, the NHM withdrew large amounts from branches of the Javasche Bank. To add to the irritation, the manager of the NHM office in Surabaya refused to participate in a meeting of the *Resident*, local banks, and rich Chinese and Arabs to discuss combating the hoarding of silver. He remarked arrogantly that his company was sound enough and had coins enough. It did not have to call on help from Chinese and Arabs.[57]

The monetary policy of the NHM became the talk of the town. It fortified the general public in their belief that banknotes had lost their value. This meant that to all intents and purposes Marmelstein could have made himself liable to the rigorous action Idenburg had demanded *Residents* take against people fuelling distrust in banknotes. Marmelstein was indeed punished, but was too important a person to suffer serious repercussions. Angered by the policy of the NHM, which as it was stressed a number of times in official

---

[54] Marmelstein to Idenburg, 10-8-1914, NA, Kol. Geheim, Vb. 18-9-1914 L19.
[55] Idenburg to Pleyte, 11-8-1914, Pleyte to Idenburg, 18-9-1914, NA, Kol. Geheim, Vb. 11-8-1914 R15, Vb. 18-9-1914 H19.
[56] Secret note President Javasche Bank, 11-8-1914, NA, Kol. Geheim, Vb. 18-9-1914 H19.
[57] Secret note President Javasche Bank, 11-8-1914, NA, Kol. Geheim, Vb. 18-9-1914 H19.

correspondence only considered its own interests and not those of the state, Idenburg sent a wire to The Hague on 5 August. In it he withdrew his suggestion that Marmelstein be awarded a royal decoration on Queen's Birthday. In retrospect the President of the Javasche Bank would later complain that because of the lamentable conduct of the NHM, the public had been robbed of its senses. Between 4 and 8 August the bank had literally been stormed by people wanting to change their paper currency for coins.[58] In total the various offices of the Javasche Bank had been forced to pay out twelve million guilders to people who came to hand in their banknotes.[59]

Apart from changing banknotes, many people went to the bank to empty their accounts. Most of them were Europeans, Chinese, and Arabs. The indigenous population still did not make much use of the services of banks. In Surabaya 48,000 guilders was withdrawn from the Savings Bank in one day. Under normal circumstances the bank paid out 7,000 guilders per day. On the same day, the branch of the Javasche Bank in Surabaya had to pay out 80,000 guilders. The demand for ready money was such that in Semarang the board of the local Savings Bank put an announcement in the newspapers informing the public that the bank would resort to its statutory right to institute a three month period between requests for withdrawals and the actual pay-out. The bank explained that it could cope with the many requests for restitution, but that it had to act in anticipation of even more withdrawals. It could not do otherwise. Most of its money was invested in solid mortgages, which if suddenly realized would place the debtors in grave trouble, and in shares, which could not be sold at a time when the exchange was closed.[60] To help out its employees, who could well find themselves suddenly without cash money because of the decision of the Savings Bank the Internationale Crediet- en Handelsvereeniging Rotterdam (Internatio, International Credit and Trading Association Rotterdam) decided to pay moderate advances, with savings-bank books as a pledge. The Semarangsche Hulpspaarbank (Semarang Savings Bank) also announced that in order to help out small savers and to combat usury, it would pay out small advances in this way.

Simultaneously, and in this respect Europeans also led the way, all over the colony people began to hoard. In many cities carriages packed with bags of rice, tins of petroleum, dried milk, and tinned food bought by passengers who were often female Europeans became a frequent sight. From Kupang in Dutch Timor an extraordinary demand for evaporated milk was reported.[61] The panic which gripped citizens in a number of regions was augmented by

---

[58] Secret note President Javasche Bank, 11-8-1914, NA, Kol. Geheim, Vb. 18-9-1914 H19.
[59] *Koloniaal verslag* 1915:165-6.
[60] *Oetoesan Hindia;* 5-8-1914, *De Locomotief,* 6-8-1914.
[61] *De Locomotief,* 28-9-1914.

emergency purchases made by the government, army and Navy. The commander of the Navy, Pinke, ordered the purchase of rice, sugar, coffee and flour for a period of six months (Teitler 1986:13). The commander of the army, Michielsen, ordered the regional army supply officers in Java to lay in a stock of rice, tinned milk, dried fish, butter, and flour, also, but people were not aware of this at first, to be used for distribution among the population should this become necessary. Later Navy beans, sugar, and sago were added to the list.[62] As a precaution, in order to be able to act if food shortages were to occur in certain parts of the Archipelago were imports of rice to dry up, this was followed on 8 August by an instruction to the army's quarter-master general to stock extra food supplies. He was given the extra responsibility transporting food to regions which might potentially suffer a food shortage. He was provided with two special advances for this purpose; one of one and a half million guilders; the other of over three million guilders.

Though runs on shops had already started talk of the massive purchases by the authorities added to the atmosphere of alarm. In Yogyakarta staff from the nearby estates were alerted by phone to come to the city and stock provisions. It was recollected a few days later that it seemed as if a famine was imminent.[63] The run on the shops in Yogyakarta had commenced after reports began to circulate that the army was buying up the whole supply of milk, butter, and chocolate in the city. Indeed, so much butter was bought by the army that some of it had to be sold again after a few days. Large-scale purchases by the army also contributed to the panic elsewhere. In Batavia people feared that in little more than a week there would no longer be any bread in the shops. In Surabaya the army was blamed for the rising price of bread. In Semarang leading trading firms blamed the panic in the city on the army and its sudden and seemingly unlimited purchases. The result had been a sharp rise of prices in the city, and especially so in the interior.[64] From Salatiga it was reported that after the army had started to make large purchases 'almost everybody went a little crazy' and that shops were 'as it were plundered whatever the price'.[65] What was being referred to in all these reports were essential commodities. Many shops faced a drop in sales because customers unsure of what the future would bring were hesitant to part with their money.

Bleak financial prospects – newspapers reported that the colonial administration contemplated lowering the salaries of its civil servants, according to some rumours as much as by half – and a rocketing demand for some

---

[62] Verslag omtrent de belangrijkste militaire maatregelen sinds 31 Juli j.l. getroffen, NA, Kol. Geheim, Vb. 18-1-1915 P.
[63] *De Locomotief,* 8-8-1914.
[64] *De Locomotief,* 5-8-1914, 11-8-1914, 19-3-1915.
[65] *De Locomotief,* 24-8-1914.

commodities meant that shops refused credit. Up to that moment buying on credit had been an accepted practice and some owners of shops, as happened in Batavia, used the opportunity to force their clients to settle outstanding bills. They refused to sell any more commodities before debts were paid. Even a newspaper like *De Locomotief* joined in. As of 6 August *De Locomotief* demanded cash for subscriptions and advertisements. Some welcomed this new, unusual situation as a blessing in disguise. Credit, the buying with, as it was called, *bonnetjes*, on account, had been widespread. In the opinion of its critics this credit system in the wholesale and retail trade had turned into an unhealthy habit. There were too many outstanding debts and people spent much more than they could afford.[66] They expressed the hope that the sudden demand for cash payments would provide an opportunity to scotch this evil once and for all. It did not come to this. After about two weeks the old practice of buying on credit was resumed.

Expecting a disruption in supply and confronted with the sudden demand shopkeepers, importers, and wholesale traders raised the prices of food-stuffs, drinks, and textiles. European traders, in their own words, 'adjusted prices to the demand'. *De Locomotief* reported from Bandung that consumer prices skyrocketed. The result had been 'great bitterness'.[67] In Semarang one firm doubled the price of flour within a day; another raised the price of a box of matches in six hours from eighty-five to two hundred guilders. Shopkeepers defended their decision by pointing out that Europeans were prepared to pay whatever was asked, even an increase of two hundred per cent.[68] Occasionally they went too far. In the West Javanese city of Sukabumi, a Chinese wholesale trader was forced to distribute a leaflet in which he apologized for the fact that he had increased his prices by 60 per cent. Fearing a boycott by his Chinese customers, he promised to make restitution of the money paid in excess. In Surakarta a shopkeeper decided to lower his prices by 25 per cent after angry customers had threatened that they would stop visiting his shop after the war.[69]

The situation was aggravated by the fact that imports stopped or were disrupted. Some products grew scarce almost immediately. One of these was beer from Europe, but as the editor of *De Locomotief* wrote, he had bought some Japanese Asahi beer and it had not tasted different.[70] Much more alarming was the prospect of a decline in the supply of rice. After a week the bans on rice exports abroad had been lifted, but much solace this had not given. The war came at a moment that the Archipelago was suffering from an extremely

[66] *De Locomotief*, 8-9-1914.
[67] *De Locomotief*, 5-8-1914.
[68] *De Locomotief*, 10-8-1914.
[69] *De Locomotief*, 7-8-1914, 26-8-1914.
[70] *De Locomotief*, 7-11-1914.

long drought and concomitantly poor harvests. Coupled with the prospect that because of the disruption of international shipping, rice imports might not be forthcoming for some time, the result was great trepidation. In Java though there were still large stocks of rice available, prices rose sharply almost everywhere; boosted by the fact that the colonial administration started to buy up rice in large quantities. It was reported that in doing so any price asked was unquestionably accepted.[71] One of the consequences of the rise in price was that pawnshops were inundated with indigenous customers who wanted money which they thought they needed to buy rice.

The situation outside Java was more critical. In South Borneo, one of the worst struck areas, the yield had been half of that of the previous year. In Ternate the harvest had been 'very disappointing'; while from South Celebes it was reported that because of a bad harvest rice shortages threatened.[72] The estate and mining regions of Sumatra formed an especially weak spot. These were threatened with the prospect of a sudden shortage of rice – and a sharp increase in its price – as French Indochina, Siam, and Burma had instituted export bans and international shipping any way had come to a standstill. In the north of Sumatra the price of an one hundred kilogram bag of Siam rice tripled from ten to thirty guilders.[73] Europeans were sure that the labour force on the estates would certainly rise when there was no longer rice to feed them.[74] In Jambi, Lampung, and the Riau Archipelago people also feared food riots. In the Riau Archipelago, on the island of Pulau Tujuh, this fear was realized. Great anxiety among the population was also reported from Billiton. Rumours were rife that Chinese miners, who expected a shortage of rice, intended to plunder the small town of Tanjungpandan.

On the East Coast of Sumatra, where about two hundred thousand estate workers had to be fed, the Dutch *Resident* summoned a meeting with planters and the managers of shipping agencies and import houses to discuss the food situation. The region was almost completely dependent for its supply of rice on imports from abroad. Afraid that worse was to come, the meeting decided to try and buy 120,000 bags of rice in Rangoon and Siam, a supply sufficient to feed the labour force and the 'free natives in the cities' for three months. When necessary the purchases had to go ahead against any price asked, a very popular phrase at that time. Managers promised to start planting *ketela*, sweet potatoes, and other secondary crops, like maize and soya bean, on their estates as a substitute staple. Soon this was to give rise to a new anxiety. The large-scale, sudden planting of secondary crops could well lead to diseases, which

---

[71] *De Locomotief,* 17-8-1914.
[72] *Koloniaal verslag* 1915:31-2, 35-6, 41-2.
[73] *Feiten* 1916:82.
[74] *De Locomotief,* 30-5-1916.

might also affect the main crop, tobacco. In Bangka an appeal was made to the indigenous Indonesians and Chinese to prepare extra fields for the growing of food crops. The situation on the island appeared so alarming that anxious to feed the many miners, the colonial administration was prepared to pay for rice bought by private firms in Rangoon, even accepting the risk that because of acts of war the cargo could be lost at sea.[75] It was one of the rare instances in which colonial and home governments were prepared to offer insurance against the risk of war.

On 4 August Batavia banned the export of rice. Ships destined for Europe which had already loaded rice had to discharge their cargo. An export ban of important secondary crops, like cassava, maize, peas and beans, followed three days later. Special measures were taken for Bali and Lombok. Rice exports from these islands to other parts of the Archipelago were forbidden. Simultaneously Dutch civil servants took action to fix the price of rice. Hoarding was threatened with the confiscation of stock. As an additional threat, the Attorney-General sent a circular to the newspapers ostensibly asking the help of the editors to warn the public that the criminal code covered punishment for spreading unsubstantiated rumours intended to influence the level of prices. He did not fail to mention that the press regulation allowed action to be taken against the deliberate spreading of incorrect reports. The publication of false rumours in newspapers, even when an editor did not know that these were not true, was liable to punishment.[76] The warning was to no avail. Newspapers continued to report about rising prices and a panicking public.

In the efforts to calm the public down yet another circular, quoted extensively in the press, was sent to Dutch regional civil servants. It said that the supply of food was still amply sufficient, that prices could be kept under control, and that the circulation of money would remain normal providing that coins were not withdrawn. The circular stressed that the colonial administration fully comprehended what was going on and had taken the necessary action to curb the panic.[77]

Feeding their work force was not the only problem faced by the estates. Dutch- and foreign-owned plantations had to deal with an acute shortage of cash. No money could be wired or sent to them to pay the labour force or to meet other financial obligations. In normal times production was financed by advances from banks which would be repaid from the sale of the estate products, but in this precarious time this source of money threatened to dry up. Private banks – and again the NHM has to be mentioned unfavourably – could

---

[75] *Javasche Courant*, 4-9-1914.
[76] *De Locomotief*, 6-8-1914.
[77] *De Locomotief*, 13-8-1914.

The office of the NHM in Batavia (*Gedenkboek* 1924: between pages 56 and 57)

not or would not help out. The result was that many estate companies had almost no money in hand; a situation made all the more pressing because the Islamic fasting month was approaching and labourers expected their customary advance. One company in Deli had only sixty guilders in cash.[78] Railway companies, themselves feeling the consequences of the drop in economic activity, were also not always helpful. In Sumatra the Deli Spoorweg Maatschappij, the Deli Railway Company, demanded cash payments for its services. It also asked the estates to pay outstanding bills within three days. The company justified its request by pointing out that it needed money urgently to pay its own staff. As an indication of the financial problems in which the Deli Railway Company found itself it announced that it could not, as was normal practice, advance a month pay to its Muslim personnel to pay for their extra expenses at the end of the fasting month. Owing to circumstances, this would be halved.[79]

European estate managers feared trouble with the Indonesian labour force if wages were not paid in full. Occasionally disputes over pay did indeed lead to disturbances. In the middle of August a British estate in Sukabumi had to call in troops to restore order.[80] Some estates in dire need of cash decided to sell all the stock they had with all the consequences this would have for prices. In other cases, one of the regions where this happened was Malang, estates had used the money that remained to buy foodstuffs for their European

[78] *De Locomotief,* 29-10-1914.
[79] *De Locomotief,* 17-8-1914, 18-8-1914.
[80] *Oetoesan Hindia,* 15-8-1914.

staff and indigenous labour force and had to stop production temporarily.[81] Sometimes estates instructed the owners of small shops on their land to sell their merchandise for pre-war prices; promising compensation if this meant that they had to sell at a loss.

Informed of such predicaments, Pleyte urged Idenburg to help the estates in any way possible. The Javasche Bank should give advances to Dutch- and foreign-owned estates with produce as a security. It was a superfluous request. Fearing a 'general debâcle' – a production stop, massive unemployment among the labour force, and in the wake of this 'all kinds of riots and disturbances in the interior' resulting in a even larger panic among the public – the Javasche Bank had already acted in the direction suggested by Pleyte.[82] As early as 2 August the Javasche Bank promised financial assistance to estates which were in financial hot waters because of the war. Among these were estates in Sumatra for which the branch of the NHM in Medan had refused to buy bills of exchange. As other private banks also refused to accept bills of exchange, in the third quarter of 1914, the Javasche Bank had an extra volume of business in this sector of monetary trade of 20 million guilders.[83] By fits and starts, other banks followed the example of the Javasche Bank, partly prompted to do so by the fact that import firms unable to transfer their money to Europe had built up large deposits.

The feeling among the general public, which was well aware of the problems confronting the estate sector, was that many estates in Java and Sumatra, and certainly those which were foreign owned, should stop production. Predictions were rife that labour would have to be fired on a massive scale, which might well result in unrest among the native population. In a society riddled with rumours, even holidays allowed to estate workers to celebrate the end of the fasting month were initially believed to be lay-offs caused by the difficult situation in which estates found themselves.[84] Under normal circumstances the Dutch did not worry much about such temporary periods of high unemployment. They were convinced that native society could cope. Excess labourers returned to the countryside where they were fed by their fellow-villagers. This time it was a different story. Lay-offs would be accompanied by a rise in prices of basic food-stuffs. People expressed the fear that were it to become impossible for a large section of the population to buy food in sufficient quantities, this would create a situation in which the people would be susceptible to agitation. It was stressed a number of times in *De Locomotief* that estates should refrain from dismissing their labour force at a time when prices

---

[81] *De Locomotief*, 7-8-1914.
[82] Report Javasche Bank, cited in *Feiten* 1916:43.
[83] Report Javasche Bank, cited in *Feiten* 1916:46.
[84] *De Locomotief*, 21-8-1914.

escalated sharply. Keeping workers on meant an extra financial burden, but the estate managers should have a larger and more important interest at heart: domestic peace. Under no circumstances should the colonial army, which might be needed to defend Java against a foreign enemy, need to be deployed to quell local unrest.[85]

Bristling with similar fears the colonial administration also took precautions. Large public works had to be slowed down if possible, except for projects which might be useful to combat unemployment. If mass dismissals became a reality, the execution of labour-intensive projects had be speeded up. Indigenous Indonesians who had become redundant could again do work which in recent years had been taken over by machines. Wherever possible the new jobless should – as some indeed would in early August – be engaged 'against a moderate daily wage' in the digging of irrigation canals, the construction and repair of roads, and on harbour works, where dredging could be done manually.[86]

It transpired that the reality was not to be as fraught as initially feared. Within a week the immediate crisis had passed. Idenburg and the President of the Javasche Bank won great acclaim. In retrospect one German businessman, Emil Helfferich (1921:10), wrote that their unique cooperation and determination had done much to calm emotions down. Newspapers began to report about the ebbing away of the 'great nervousness' of the first few days. The runs on the banks diminished. A reverse process set in. People *en masse* deposited in the banks the silver coins they had withdrawn a few days earlier. Helfferich attributed this in part to the policy of the Javasche Bank. He relates how, with what he calls 'a good understanding of the psyche of the Chinese', at banks names of Chinese and the amount they withdrew were written down conspicuously. Helfferich explains that Chinese did not like to have their name written down, just as Arabs were averse to having their picture taken. Consequently they returned their money as soon as possible and asked that their names be struck off (Helfferich 1921:10). No special regulation to relieve the Javasche Bank of its obligation to exchange paper currency for coins had to be issued, and no extra paper money had to be put into circulation. Visits to concerts and theatres were resumed. Later horse races, the highlight of social life in many cities, were once again part of the social calendar. Contrary to the more gloomy expectations, they were as usual attended by large crowds. The telegraph links with Europe were restored. After days of anxiety and no opportunity to send or receive messages, people flocked to the telegraph offices to contact relatives and business associates abroad. At the busiest offices a

[85] *De Locomotief,* 5-8-1914, 6-8-1914.
[86] *De Locomotief,* 24-8-1914.

Governor General J.P. van Limburg Stirum at the horse races in Bandung, 1917
(KITLV 50645)

night service had to be instituted.

The measures taken by the colonial administration to contain the rice price had been successful. The restoration of the shipping links with Singapore and other Asian ports also helped quell anxiety. As no prolonged food crisis eventuated, in September the colonial government found itself burdened with a stock of rice – 20,000 tons – it had bought for a price higher than that at which it could sell it. State companies were instructed to buy the rice they needed from this stock. Reassured, the government lifted the export ban on cassava, and beans and peas on 1 September, that on maize on 10 October.

Across the board prices dropped. Nevertheless, at the end of August it was reported from Batavia that loaves of bread had become 'a little bit smaller and somewhat more expensive'. The bread price was indicative of what was happening. Compared to pre-war standards, the cost of living rose, while the purchasing power in all population groups declined. Indigenous Indonesians left the cities, where life had become more expensive, for the countryside. Other city dwellers who had been able to afford some luxury in the past, adjusted their menus. Chicken replaced beef, coconut oil was used instead of butter, more local vegetables and fruits were eaten. The positive effect was that this stimulated the rural economy; the negative effect was that such products were growing more expensive in the villages.[87]

Some found themselves in real trouble. Among them were those who had been fired, or had been forced to accept a drop in wages, or had seen their income dwindle in other ways. The principal victims were people in the estate and trading sector. Other sufferers were missionaries. Apart from the fact that money could not be transferred to them from Europe, donations dried up. Less income forced missionary societies to stop the posting of new missionaries in the colony for the time being. The stipend of missionaries already in the field in the Netherlands Indies was drastically reduced, in some instances even halved. The two measures were interrelated. The boards in Holland feared that were their number still allowed to increase missionaries would impose upon themselves and their families 'much hardship, which will bound later on their health'.[88]

Europeans became thrifty. The panic shopping of the first days of the war was replaced by a tendency to buy only the bare necessities, postponing the purchase of clothes, household goods and the like. Owners of shops, hotels, and restaurants frequented by Europeans felt the consequences and had to dismiss personnel or lower their salaries. Some hotels had to close. Tourists cancelled their trips to the Netherlands Indies. Others who had arrived returned home as fast as they could. Luxury commodities could not be sold. In October the rent for space in warehouses in Surabaya was doubled. They were full of cars and other goods importers could not sell.

In the estate sector a massive lay-off never eventuated. The following year the official report of the Minister of the Colonies to parliament would state in a veiled way that business on the East Coast of Sumatra 'here and there to a greater or less degree' was reduced, but that nowhere had production been stopped.[89] Nevertheless, unemployment grew. Because of the initial consequences for international trade, coolies in ports found themselves without work and income, or were forced to offer their services for much lower pay; sometimes, as was reported from Gorontalo, they asked only one-third of their normal wage.[90] Estates dismissed labour and staff. In the larger cities in Java groups of unemployed Javanese strolling idly became a familiar sight. Many had travelled home from the estates in Sumatra, which had also stopped recruiting labourers in Java. The situation in Sumatra was not better. Some of the labourers who had become redundant were employed in the construction of railways. In North Sumatra preference for this sort of work seems to

---

[87] *Preanger-bode*, cited in *De Locomotief*, 30-1-1915.
[88] *De Standaard*, cited in *De Locomotief*, 5-10-1914.
[89] *Koloniaal verslag* 1915:21-2.
[90] *De Locomotief*, 15-9-1914.

One of the houses with single walls and roof tiles built within the framework of combating the plague. It has single walls and roof tills (Van Loon 1919).

have been given to Chinese, who were considered a greater threat to law and order than the indigenous Indonesians.[91] Recruitment of coolies in China was stopped. At the end of November, this was followed by the repatriation of coolies. The government bore part of the cost. It paid 25 guilders per person for about three hundred unemployed Chinese whom the *Resident* of the east coast described as 'bad elements' constantly on the prowl. The measure contributed to the maintenance of law and order, but not completely. The *Resident* of the East Coast of Sumatra reported there were still many unemployed at his post, some of whom refused to take a job because of the low wages offered.[92] The local Dutch community continued to worry about a 'plague of coolies who wander about', fearing that the government did not have the money to send them all back to China.[93] To combat theft and other 'vices', the private police forces of the local Sultans were assigned to ordinary police duties.[94] At least

[91] *Koloniaal verslag* 1915:21-2.
[92] Van der Plas to Idenburg, 18-1-1915, NA, Kol. Geheim, Mr. 1915/26x.
[93] *De Locomotief*, 1-12-1914, citing the *Sumatra Post*.
[94] *De Locomotief*, 16-12-1914.

as late as January 1915, on the East Coast of Sumatra large groups of jobless Chinese, roaming around footloose and fancy-free, were arrested and repatriated by the colonial authorities. In some cities of Java Chinese without visible means of support were also sent back to China at public expense.

In the construction industry labour was hit by the decision of the colonial government to continue only those works which were strictly necessary or could serve as relief projects. It was reported that construction industry had almost ground to a halt.[95] One exception to this rule were the plague regions. As it was stated in the *Encyclopaedie van Nederlandsch-Indië* the principal aim of the government scheme to combat the plague was to 'increase the distance between the plague-infected rat(s) and people to such an extent that the chance of infection of the latter is reduced'.[96] In practice this meant an improvement of housing. Hollow bamboo was replaced by wood or stone, was sealed off, or filled with cement; thus creating extra employment and a continued high demand for products such as roof tiles.

Civil servants suffered as well. Their pay was frozen. Pleyte considered a raise in the salary of Dutch colonial civil servants in 1915. In spite of the growing unemployment in Holland, it remained difficult to attract qualified, well-educated Dutchmen for employment in the colonial civil service. Higher pay would change this. Reluctantly Pleyte later withdrew his proposal. He had to bow to the argument advanced by Idenburg and his advisers that a rise in pay was politically imprudent. Discontent could well be the result if people were to realize that in such economically difficult times they had to pay extra tax to improve salaries of civil servants.[97] The decision did not go down well with those in government pay. This was one of the reasons army officers in the Netherlands Indies formed their own association. They argued that many officers and their families had to live in poverty, while on the whole the economic situation in the Netherlands Indies was not yet so bad that a rise in salary was out of the question.[98]

The crisis had passed but had disquieted many. In Amsterdam, representatives of the major Dutch estate companies met on 17 August to draw up guidelines in case telegraph communication with the colony should break down again. Not sure how Great Britain would act many thought that such a moment could well not be far off. Once again Van Aalst had taken the initiative. The meeting decided that in four cities located in the heart of the main estate regions – Batavia, Semarang, Surabaya, and Medan – local committees

---

[95] *De Locomotief*, 4-12-1914, citing *Korte Berichten* issued by the Department of Agriculture, Industry, and Trade.
[96] De Raadt1919:392.
[97] Idenburg to Pleyte, 9-10-1915, 13-10-1915, NA, Kol. Geheim, Vb. 18-2-1916 O2.
[98] *De Locomotief*, 28-1-1916.

should be founded. They should determine how to proceed in such an event. The committees were charged with the task of pleading the interests of the plantations with the colonial administration and were responsible for advising individual estate managers on what to do. It was stressed that they had to perform their task without taking nationality into account. Once it was decided, a deputation visited the Secretary General of the Ministry of the Colonies to ask his mediation in having the decision published in the *Javasche Courant*; the best way to ensure that estate managers all over the Netherlands Indies were informed.

The very same day a wire was sent to Java. Idenburg was not overjoyed. He feared that exactly at a moment that panic had subsided its publication would upset people. A report in the *Javasche Courant* about the meeting should not contain any reference to a new break-down in telegraphic communication. Idenburg stressed in a wire in English to Pleyte that business was again 'calmly going on'. Any mention of such a possibility would 'disturb again seriously (the) calm state of mind (of) commercial people and other inhabitants'.[99]

The Governor General did not have much choice. Newspapers in Holland had published the decision. The colonial press would certainly cite these reports when copies reached the Netherlands Indies (which *De Locomotief* did on 1 October). The message Idenburg disliked the most, that about a breakdown in telegraphic communication, could not be omitted. Pleyte made this clear. It formed the quintessence of what the estate companies wanted to convey; it was the moment the committees had to start working. Idenburg had to consent. At the suggestion of Pleyte, the note was added that the Minister of the Colonies considered the initiative of the companies in Holland 'a measure of extreme precaution'. As an additional reassurance, the gazette observed that, though a new disruption in telegraphic communication between motherland and colony could never be ruled out completely, the Governor General did consider it highly unlikely that it would happen again. Idenburg also zealously guarded his own authority. He made it plain to the estate companies that in the event of a new crisis it was he who would take the decisions, and not some local committee.

For sugar producers and traders, the war proved a blessing. The sugar industry had been on the brink of collapse. In previous years the sugar estates in the Netherlands Indies had lost much of their share of the European market. Selling-prices had been low. Most of the sugar consumed in Great Britain had come from Germany and Austria-Hungary, and from sugar-beet fields in France which were now laid waste because of the war. Confronted with the drying up of these sources of supply, London placed huge orders in the

---

[99] Idenburg to Pleyte, 18-8-1914, 19-8-1914, NA, Kol. Geheim, Vb. 20-8-1914 V16.

Netherlands Indies. As early as the beginning of September Idenburg could report with satisfaction to Pleyte that the sugar sales to England had yielded enormous profits.[100]

All in all, the Ministry of the Colonies showed itself pleased with the way Batavia had coped with the crisis. There was also praise for the Javasche Bank, which had spent large amounts of money to meet the demand for cash not only from the business community, but also from the colonial government, which had been forced to undertake a large expenditure to back up neutrality.

There was less acclaim for the ban on the export of rice, which had been suggested by the Ministry itself. The main reason for this was probably that, contrary to the financial measures taken, the decision to ban the export of rice had met with fierce disapproval, even in the colonial press. The colonial authorities were accused of having failed to realize that 'natives' and people in Europe ate rice of a different quality. The export variety, the so-called table-rice, was 'much too good for the general population and for feeding coolies on Bangka' (Mees 1915:463). A lobby was started by rice dealers in Holland who had already paid for the rice which was not allowed to be exported and had become 'very upset'.[101] The traders succeeded in convincing Pleyte that only a small quantity was at stake, which could easily be substituted by rice of a cheaper variety from Burma. A telegram was sent to Idenburg asking him to lift the ban. Idenburg consented. Rice exporters were allowed to ship rice to Europe on the condition that they first imported an equal amount of Rangoon or Saigon rice 'fit for the consumption of the natives'. The rice had to be of such a quality that it was indeed to the taste of the Javanese.[102] This decision immediately posed a new problem. Exporters in Java, who had expected the ban to last, had already sold part of the quantity they had committed themselves to sending to Holland and other countries in Europe on the local market. They now feared – and their representatives in Holland did not fail to impress upon Pleyte the disastrous consequences – that their European buyers would demand delivery of the originally contracted quantities, which would be impossible for them to honour. Pleyte wavered, suddenly in favour of maintaining the export ban. Idenburg's reply was reassuring. It concerned only a few exporters, on whom pity should not be wasted as they had made big profits.[103]

The Ministry of the Colonies was extremely unhappy with the NHM. It was disappointed by the lack of cooperation received in the efforts made

---

[100] Idenburg to Pleyte, 9-9-1914, NA, Kol. Geheim, Vb. 16-9-1914 A19.
[101] Pleyte to Idenburg, 15-8-1914, NA, Kol. Geheim, Vb. 17-8-1914 Hbis.
[102] *De Locomotief,* 12-9-1914.
[103] Idenburg to Pleyte, 25-9-1914, NA, Kol. Geheim, Vb. 25-9-1914 B20.

to ward off a financial crisis, and by the company's refusal to pay out coins and to provide credit; decisions which a wider public the Netherlands Indies held against Van Aalst and the NHM till well after war had ended (Helfferich 1918:479). The NHM was also held responsible for the ban on the export of gold and silver. Initially the Javasche Bank had deemed such a step unnecessary. The bank had been confident that, in view of the war, nobody in the Netherlands Indies intended to export gold or silver. Only after the Javasche Bank had learned that the NHM had shipped gold to Singapore, had its management advised Idenburg to set up an export ban.[104]

Marmelstein did not understand what he had done wrong. He wrote to Idenburg that 'in these difficult days' the NHM had done all it could to help the government. He added that he would be pleased to learn why Idenburg had complained to The Hague.[105] Van Aalst reacted in a similar vein. In the middle of October he sent a letter to Idenburg. He took all the blame. Marmelstein had acted on his instructions. Blame may not be the right word. Van Aalst was the saviour of the nation. He reminded Idenburg that 'in those tense days' when the Dutch economy 'ran the serious danger of becoming disastrously disrupted' he had frequently – 'without exaggeration we may say day and night' – been consulted about the economic policy to be followed. Because of the measures taken and of the consortium that had been formed under his leadership, danger had been averted. The Netherlands Indies had been spared those anxious days. Nobody in the colony had ever known how critical the situation had been, and what disaster could have struck there, had no resolute action been taken by the NHM in Holland.[106] Idenburg was not impressed. He asked his Secretary General to write a brief reply. He, Idenburg, had read Van Aalst's letter with interest, and wanted to let the matter rest. Dragging it up would only disturb the relationship between the NHM and the Javasche Bank.[107]

---

[104] Report Javasche Bank, cited in *Feiten* 1916:44-5.
[105] Marmelstein to Idenburg, 10-8-1914, NA, Kol. Geheim, Vb. 18-9-1914 H19.
[106] Van Aalst to Idenburg, 15-10-1914, NA, Kol. Openbaar, Vb. 25-1-1915-.
[107] Idenburg to Pleyte, 31-10-1915, Kindermann to Van Aalst, 16-12-1914, NA, Kol. Openbaar, Vb. 25-1-1915.

CHAPTER VII

Guarding strict neutrality

Rear Admiral F. Pinke and Lieutenant General J.P. Michielsen met on 29 July after a telegram had been sent to Idenburg from The Hague to alert him to the fact that a breakdown of peace in Europe was very likely in the evening of the previous day. They did not seem to be in particularly worried. Suddenly they were confident that the Dutch fleet in the Netherlands Indies could cope. They based their optimism upon the consideration that at the outbreak of a war the European naval squadrons in the Far East would be fully occupied with protecting their own colonial possessions and their own shipping. Busy elsewhere, the fleets lacked the strength to launch an invasion of the Netherlands Indies. A raid by a limited number of enemy warships could not be ruled out but Pinke and Michielsen judged the Dutch colonial army and Navy strong enough to deal with such a contingency. The situation would not be so propitious were Japan to seize upon a European conflict to launch a war of conquest against the Netherlands Indies. A Japanese attack would pose a real threat, but was not considered very likely. Pinke and Michielsen did not yet see any indication that Tokyo contemplated such an act of war. With these considerations in mind, the two commanders gave priority to the guarding of neutrality and not to the repulse of an enemy attack.

Judging the danger of a breach of neutrality to be greatest in the western part of the Archipelago, it was decided to concentrate the Dutch squadron at Tanjung Priok and not at its Surabaya base. The core of the fleet should remain at anchor there, ready to act in concert. Only under extraordinary circumstances, and Idenburg was following Pinke's advice when he refused to send a warship to Manado to guard the German telegraph cable, should the squadron be divided up. From Tanjung Priok the warships could easily reach any putatively potential trouble spots where neutrality might be threatened. As a precaution, as soon as possible smaller warships should steam to Sabang, Emmahaven in Padang, and the port of Makassar, all protected harbours with stocks of coal. Were neutrality to be violated these warships could 'pending further action by the Dutch squadron add at least some immediate force to a protest to be lodged'.[1] Special attention was also paid to the island of Tarakan on the northern part of the coast of East Borneo with its important oil installations. Yet another smaller warship had to be sent to Pontianak to assist in suppressing disturbances in West Borneo; disturbances some people in those rumour-ridden days were sure had been provoked by a foreign country to lure Dutch troops away from Java (Idenburg and De Graeff 1920:370).

After the outbreak of the war, the Dutch naval squadron had to call off manoeuvres east of Java and was ordered to Tanjung Priok as planned. Crew and officers had already been informed about the Vienna ultimatum. This made little impression on them. They assumed that the news had been sent as a wireless message to them to add a touch of realism to the exercise. The manoeuvres had been continued without a second thought, but exactly at the moment when the 'enemy', that was Dutch destroyers acting as such, was sighted by the battleships, the order was received to terminate the exercise and to proceed to Surabaya, where coal and victuals were to be taken in, after which the vessels sailed to Tanjung Priok (M. 1922:843-4). In Tanjung Priok the warships were fitted out for real battle. All unessential wooden objects and other inflammable materials, including books and even chicken coops, on board were removed (Bauduin 1920:16). The hulls, which had been painted white again to suit the tropical climate after the Russo-Japanese War, were repainted grey.

Now that a European war had become a reality some of Pinke's confidence ebbed. He no longer deemed it safe to have his fleet remain moored in Tanjung Priok.[2] A captain of a merchantman, and Pinke's thoughts turned especially towards Germans, might suddenly try to do something were news, whether true or not, to reach him that the Netherlands had joined the war. He could decide to scuttle his ship to block the exit of the harbour, or force a collision with one of the Dutch warships, causing considerable damage. A more compelling reason for Pinke to change his mind was that at anchor in the roadstead of Tanjung Priok, a Dutch squadron was vulnerable to a surprise torpedo attack. Consequently the warships sought shelter in Banten Bay. It was hoped that they could remain there for the time being, undetected by a potential enemy. A flotilla ship was entrusted with guarding Tanjung Priok. Within a week the fleet was moved again. First it was ordered to sail to the Karimun Jawa Islands, north of Semarang. Thereupon, so as to hide the fleet from a chance sighting by merchantmen plying the Java Sea, the squadron moved to the Kangean Islands east of Madura.

---

[1]   Resumé van het besprokene tussen den Legercommandant en den Commandant der Zeemacht op 29 Juli 1914, NA, Kol. Geheim, Vb. 14-9-1914 T18.
[2]   For a detailed account of ship movements and Pinke's opinions and decisions, see Teitler 1986.

Unlike what happened in Holland no mobilization order for the army was issued. This might have provoked Japan. A general panic should also be avoided. Instead, Idenburg allowed Michielsen to take all those measures which would otherwise have been set in motion after mobilization had been declared, instructing him to avoid attracting unnecessary public attention. The army staff seems to have thought of everything. The private tram- and railway companies were reminded of their obligation to obey orders issued by the civil and military authorities if troops had to be transported or rails had to be destroyed to render tram- and railway useless. Should war become a reality, officers and former officers of the army would take over from civilians as stationmasters. A special uniform was designed for such military stationmasters. No detail was overlooked. A directive about the amount of food soldiers were entitled to during mobilization carefully differentiated between Europeans, Africans, and Ambonese on the one hand, and natives and convicts on the other. Bread and butter was the prerogative of the first group. The order assiduously noted that fresh pork and smoked bacon did not form part of the natives' meal.[3] Nor were horses forgotten. Dutch civil servants were asked to issue instructions to their staff for the requisitioning of grass by the army. In October Michielsen and his staff introduced identification tags which soldiers had to wear in battle, made of drill and inscribed with washable ink. An older type did exist, but most soldiers had forgotten about this. Detailed plans were also drawn up for the evacuation of the government offices in Batavia to Bandung if an enemy fleet appeared off the coast of Java. This was deemed an important precaution. Batavia was a weak spot in the Dutch defences. Obviously the city was vulnerable to bombardment from the sea, and it was extremely exposed to an attack by land. It was almost impossible to defend in fact.

Preparations were also made to order units from other islands to Java. Such a relocation of troops would not fully solve Michielsen's problem, exacerbated by the fact that five companies from Java were pinned down in Aceh and in Borneo to suppress local unrest. Unable to deploy the number of troops he deemed necessary Michielsen urged that some of these companies be sent back to Java. He was immediately rapped over the knuckles. He was given to understand that Idenburg was convinced that the military commander in Borneo was wise and well-informed enough not to withhold soldiers he did not need from Java; whilst Aceh was the last region from which troops could be withdrawn.[4]

Adding to Michielsen's problems was the fact that the colonial army

---

[3] *Javasche Courant*, 14-8-1914.
[4] Michielsen to Idenburg, 2-9-1914, Kindermann to Michielsen, 17-9-1914, NA, Kol. Geheim, Vb. 18-1-1915 P.

was still chronically undermanned. There was a shortage of three thousand European men, or one-quarter of its organic strength, and of over seventeen hundred indigenous Indonesian soldiers. The financial incentives to encourage people to enlist were improved to promote fresh recruitment of both groups of soldiers. A few years later, it was claimed that this step had only resulted in an influx of 'undesirable elements' among both groups.[5] In conformity with prevailing views about which ethnic groups made excellent soldiers, special attention was paid to the enlistment of Ambonese and Manadonese recruits. In North Celebes the *nagari* heads were promised an extra ten guilders for each villager who enlisted.[6] The campaign was successful, at least with regard to numbers. In the middle of October, fifteen hundred new Indonesian recruits had enlisted. Needless to say the army was not prepared for the influx. Barracks became overcrowded and galleries and officers' messes had to be converted into sleeping places. The training time allotted to these new soldiers was shortened to about half of what it would have been under normal circumstances.

Among Europeans the campaign was not as propitious. Because sea communication with Europe was disrupted, the drive had to be confined to the Netherlands Indies. In the middle of October the shortage of European soldiers had risen by another one hundred.[7] The number of non-commissioned officers was also inadequate. In order to cope the European corporals and soldiers of the school for warrant officers were promoted and sent to join the troops in the field. Rules being rules, even a soldier who had been admitted to a hospital and still confined to his bed was promoted to corporal.[8] Faced with this shortage of troops, Michielsen decided to leave the guarding of railways, bridges, and tunnels, to be protected against sabotage by 'malevolents from the population (that is agents of the enemy)', to auxiliary forces like the citizen's militia, the armed police, and the native corpses.[9] Members of the citizen's militia were given the opportunity to report for actual military service.

Issues dealing with concrete acts of warfare now emerged to exacerbate the troubles of the colonial authorities. As during the Russo-Japanese War, it soon became clear that a proclamation of neutrality could not cover all eventualities. The proclamations issued in 1914 forbade the entry into territorial waters of warships of belligerents and vessels which could be equated with these;

---

[5] *Soerabaiasch Handelsblad,* cited in *De Indische Gids* 1917, II:1248.
[6] Michielsen to Idenburg, 8-8-1914, NA, Kol. Geheim, Vb. 18-1-1915 P.
[7] Verslag betreffende de belangrijkste militaire maatregelen sinds 31 Juli j.l. getroffen, NA, Kol. Geheim, Vb. 18-1-1915 P; *De Locomotief,* 28-12-1914.
[8] *Preanger-bode,* cited in *De Locomotief,* 22-10-1914.
[9] Michielsen to Idenburg, 6-8-1914, Idenburg to Pleyte, 13-8-1914, NA, Kol. Geheim, Vb. 18-9-1914 I19, Vb. 18-1-1915 P.

stating that if such ships disobeyed they would not be allowed to leave again before the war had ended. A number of exceptions were made. Entering a port or roadstead to take in provisions and fuel was allowed, providing that the warships left again within twenty-four hours. Provisions should not exceed the normal amount aboard in peace-time. The amount of fuel provided should only be enough to allow the vessel to reach the nearest port in the home country. Fuel and provisions were not to be sold without the permission of the authorities. Warships which entered ports and roadsteads because of damage or seeking shelter from bad weather could anchor as long as it took to make basic repairs without adding to their fighting capability or till the weather improved.[10] A third exception was made for vessels of war used exclusively for religious, scientific, or humanitarian purposes. As had been done at the outbreak of the Russo-Japanese War, sea captains, shipowners, and natives were warned of the dangers of running a blockade, and of the shipping of contraband and military dispatches. It was advised that those who disregarded the warning could not count on the protection of or intervention by the Dutch government.

One of the problems which arose almost immediately was that of the nearest home port. Pinke, and in his wake Idenburg and Pleyte, were of the opinion that for British warships calling in at ports in the Netherlands Indies the nearest port in their own country was one in the British colonies and dominions in Southeast Asia. They refrained from mentioning that this in almost all instances meant Singapore. The British Consul General in Batavia, T.F. Carlisle, did not agree. He made a subtle distinction. For warships of 'the British Navy proper' the nearest home port meant a port in Great Britain; for those of the Indian Navy a port in British India, and for warships of the Australian Navy, Thursday Island.[11]

More essential was the matter of auxiliary warships; merchantmen and ocean liners transformed into warships. The proclamation of neutrality spoke of warships and vessels equated with warships. It was a vague definition which left room for interpretation. In 1907, during the Second Peace Conference in The Hague, the British Foreign Secretary, Sir Edward Grey, had still considered the definition of auxiliary warships to be 'not of vital importance'.[12] London clearly thought differently in 1914. On 9 August the British chargé d'affaires in The Hague explained to the Dutch Minister of Foreign Affairs, J. Loudon, that British merchantmen were only armed for the purpose of putting up a defence when attacked and that this was valid under international law.

---

[10] Later during the war a similar stipulation was issued with regard to enemy merchantmen seized by belligerents.
[11] Idenburg to Pleyte, 14-9-1914, NA, Kol. Geheim, Vb. 14-9-1914 U18.
[12] Grey to Fry, 30-7-1907, PRO FO 800 69.

They could not be converted into men-of-war on the high seas. Consequently the British government would not allow such ships to be interned after a stay exceeding the twenty-four hours allowed for the taking in of fuel and provisions; or that its captains would be forced to remove the guns before proceeding to sea. The chargé d'affaires explained that German merchant vessels were a different matter. These could be converted into warships. Such ships should be interned 'in the absence of any binding assurance that the latter should not be converted so, an assurance for which the neutral government must assume all responsibility'.[13] Two days later the Dutch government was presented with a number of indications which provided reasonable grounds for the suspicion that a German merchant vessel would be converted into a warship once she had left territorial waters. Among the items listed were 'any signs of shipping ammunition, concealing arms and ammunition on board, mounting guns, taking in an unnecessary large quantity of coal, and especially painting ship a warlike colour or refusing to take passengers on board if the vessel is fitted for passenger accommodation'. Expressing 'the confident hope' that if the Dutch government had not already issued the necessary instructions, it 'would do so immediately', the chargé d'affaires revealed that he had notified British consular officials in Holland to report all suspect cases to the British legation.[14] In Batavia Carlisle sent similar directions to the British consuls in Netherlands Indies ports. He asked them to report to him when German merchant ships did anything to arouse suspicion and to contact the local authorities at once if they suspected that merchantmen would be likely to be transformed into auxiliary warships in the near future.

The Dutch government reacted to the British demonstrations almost instantly. Instructions went out that merchantmen which on the grounds of construction, equipment, or crew showed evident signs that they were to be used as a cruiser or mine-layer had to be treated as warships if they carried guns or mines on board.[15] This left the problem, one which was to result in the first diplomatic row with London, of how to act in the case of merchantmen carrying weapons for defensive purposes. The British government had argued that these ships should not be treated as warships. Some Dutch politicians and civil servants agreed. Pleyte feared that if they were considered warships and appropriate action was taken, such an act could well close Dutch ports to almost all merchant vessels of the belligerents, with all the consequences this posed for the import of products of which shortages threatened in the early days of war. A civil servant noted that, quite apart from this, it would

---

[13] British Chargé d'Affaires to Loudon, 9-8-1914, NA, Kol. Geheim, Vb. 14-8-1914 D16.
[14] British Chargé d'Affaires to Loudon, 11-8-1914, NA, Kol. Geheim, Vb. 14-8-1914 D16.
[15] Loudon to Pleyte, 12-8-1914, NA, Kol. Geheim, Vb. 14-8-1914 D16.

Mountain battery (Van Gent, Penard en Rinkes 1923: Photo 240)

be unwise to resort to a policy which would hurt Great Britain especially.[16] Nevertheless, to the annoyance of London this was exactly what the Dutch government was to do. All merchantmen with arms on board were treated as warships by the Dutch. The Dutch naval Minister Rambonnet confided to the British Naval Attaché that although he himself could differentiate between an auxiliary cruiser and a merchantman defensively armed, 'the people might not [be able to]'.[17] He added that if the original instructions about how to treat armed merchantmen as warships were changed, the German Navy and the Dutch people, who have been 'somewhat afraid of a violation of their territory by England', might accuse the Dutch government of no longer being strictly neutral.[18]

In the Netherlands Indies another topic took precedence. As during the Russo-Japanese War, most attention was paid to the bunkering of warships of the belligerents. To prevent any illegal fuelling and provisioning of warships of the belligerents by merchantmen, special measures were deemed necessary. In Sabang the entire stock of coal was bought by the Navy and transferred to the naval base in Surabaya. In November the three month period within

[16] See NA, Kol. Geheim, Vb. 14-8-1914 D16.
[17] Chilton to Grey, 10-8-1914, *State Papers* 1914:336.
[18] Chilton to Grey, 10-8-1914, *State Papers* 1914:336.

The *Koningin Regentes* is made ready for battle. All flammable and loose objects are removed from board. (M. 1922:842.)

which no coal was to be provided to a warship that had bunkered previously became the subject of discussion. Realizing that the war was already three months old and in order to prevent the Netherlands Indies becoming a base of war operations, The Hague suddenly decided that before a second ration of fuel could be allowed, the captains of warships had to mention on paper the ports they had called during this period. The consent of Idenburg before coal could be supplied was a second requirement. Pinke made no secret of the fact that he considered these new directions from The Hague impracticable. One problem was that consulting the Governor General might take most if not all of the twenty-four hours a warship was allowed in port and in roadsteads for bunkering. A telegraph network covering the whole Archipelago was still non-existent, and the opening hours of its stations were restricted. More importantly what The Hague wanted was potentially very dangerous. Naval officers would certainly refuse to reveal where their warships had been. The consequence could well be that the Dutch authorities had no other choice than to intern ship and crew. Pinke was sure that such a course of action would elicit a hostile response. Pointing out to Idenburg that the first warships of the belligerents which might be subjected to the new rule were two French torpedo-boat destroyers, he sketched how, after their internment, the complete combined fleet of the Allied in Asia might descend on the Netherlands Indies to demand the release of the two destroyers. The prospect was reason enough for Idenburg to disregard the directives from The Hague.[19] However, relations between Pinke and Rambonnet had incurred heavy damage.

As during both the Boer War and the Russo-Japanese War, government and press held different opinions about what the newspapers could report and write about. The colonial administration was adamant that the position of the Dutch forces should not be revealed by the press. At Michielsen's suggestion a special issue of the *Javasche Courant* appeared on 5 August forbidding the reporting on movements of the troops and ships of the colonial army and Navy. Journalists considered the ban an absurdity. It was far too generally worded. Reports about a Dutch warship anchored in a roadstead, about troops sent to regions outside Java to suppress local resistance, about military parades and about many other events which had little or nothing to do with the Dutch effort to guard neutrality might become punishable. What journalists had feared became a reality. An editor of the *Soerabaiasch Handelsblad* was sentenced to two weeks' imprisonment for reporting about soldiers sent to Borneo, and about a ship which had left the port of Surabaya, which turned out to be a warship.

Other court cases were more directly related to the Dutch effort to guard neutrality. E. van Ghert, editor of the *Nieuwe Soerabaia Courant*, was brought to trial for a report in August about the running in of a German merchantman by two Dutch warships at Surabaya in December 1914. He was sentenced to a fine of one guilder; the minimum penalty, and one-tenth of what the public prosecutor had demanded. Circumvention of the rules was acted upon as well. One of the persons who was to learn this lesson was H. Tersteeg of the *Soerabaiasch Handelsblad*. In July 1916 his newspaper carried a report of the sailing of Dutch warships, but names had been replaced with dots. It did not help. Tersteeg was prosecuted. When the court acquitted him, the public prosecutor appealed. The appeal was a clear attempt to scare journalists in the Netherlands Indies who, the public prosecution was sure, wanted to place themselves above the law. Not the irresponsible press should decide what could be published and what not, but a responsible government (Van Geuns 1918:212). The High Court sentenced Tersteeg to one month's imprisonment

---

[19] Pinke to Idenburg, 4-12-1914, Idenburg to Pleyte, 9-12-1914, NA, Kol. Geheim, Vb. 18-1-1915 N1.

in 1917. Two months had been demanded. A recommendation for mercy was rejected by the Governor General.[20] A journalists' monthly wrote about a 'deeply unjust punishment'. Tersteeg's colleague, M. van Geuns, fully agreed. He called the verdict a 'shocking action against Indies journalists' (Van Geuns 1918:211). He also wondered what harm had been done by the report. The army and Navy in the Netherlands Indies amounted to nothing, and with so many Japanese spies around, Tokyo would be informed anyhow about the position of Dutch warships.

Idenburg, Pinke, and Pleyte thought differently. They considered such contested press reports an affront, a serious threat to Dutch neutrality, and took them to heart personally. Pinke was sure that from what Tersteeg had written, the movements of the whole fleet could be deduced.[21] At times Idenburg would become enraged by what newspapers wrote. In April 1915 when the *Java-Bode* copied a report from the Dutch newspaper *De Telegraaf* that two German submarines had sailed into the Scheldt, he reacted furiously. In private he called the editor a traitor to his country. Such a person should not be imprisoned for one or two days. He should be flogged with the cat (Bijl de Vroe 1980:52).

Reports about the movements of Dutch warships were not the only matter worrying Batavia. After three written appeals to newspaper editors to refrain from reporting which could cast doubts on Dutch neutrality abroad had proved to be in vain, Batavia once again issued a special edition of the *Javasche Courant* on 10 September. Well aware that the belligerents did not want their own press to report on movements of troops and ships, Batavia forbade the publication of reports on the movements of warships of belligerents in the Archipelago. The regulation proclaimed during the Russo-Japanese War about deliberately endangering neutrality was revived. A prison sentence for Europeans and forced labour on the chain-gang for members of the other population groups for between five and ten years was threatened.

As had been the case with the ban on writing about the movements of Dutch warships prosecutions followed. Van Geuns of the *Soerabaiasch Handelsblad* was prosecuted in October 1914. His newspaper had published the incorrect report that a German raider, the *Emden*, which had been disturbing shipping in the seas between the Malay Peninsula and India, had entered the port of Sabang, and that two British warships were patrolling in the vicinity. Van Geuns defended the report by pointing out that information about the movements of the *Emden* was vital to colonial exports, especially East Java sugar. Informing the public about the whereabouts of the *Emden* was of far

---

[20] *Indisch Tijdschrift van het Recht* 1917:445-54; Van Heekeren 1918:200.
[21] *De Locomotief*, 7-12-1914.

greater importance than keeping to a stupid ban issued by the authorities. *De Locomotief* commented that evidently Van Geuns valued sugar interests more than national ones.[22] Van Geuns was sentenced to three months' imprisonment. For technical reasons, the High Court declared the verdict invalid. Batavia withdrew the ban on newspaper reporting of movements of belligerent warships at the end of May 1915. Van Geuns claimed that his lawsuit had been instrumental in bringing this about (Van Geuns 1918:211). The ban on the disclosure of movements of Dutch troops and warships in the Archipelago remained in force.

On hearing the news of the war, nationalist feelings among Germans, Britons, and the French ran high, the men – at least this was the impression created – were anxious to obey the orders of their consuls to leave as soon as possible for their homelands or nearby colonies to enlist in the army. Many tried to book passages on Dutch ships which raised the question of whether Germans, Frenchmen, and Britons eligible for military service were contraband. It was not deemed unlikely that the ships on which they took passage would be confiscated by the belligerents.[23]

On board ships calling at Netherlands Indies ports and carrying migrants for Australia emotions also ran high. On one of these, the *Roon*, moored in Cilacap in Java, fights broke out between British and German passengers. The Germans put the blame on the drunken British. They claimed that it had been only the third-class British passengers, members of the lower working-class, who had created problems. Relations between Germans and Britons in the second class, all civilized people, had remained good. The British passengers claimed that after news of the war had reached the *Roon*, the Germans had treated them as they pleased, that is 'as dogs'.[24]

On 10 August, Idenburg obliquely alluded to such patriotic feelings by appealing to foreign nationals, who, as it was put, enjoyed the hospitality of the Netherlands Indies, to collaborate in the strict observance of Dutch neutrality. Everybody, irrespective of nationality, had to refrain from acts which held the danger of making the territory of the Netherlands a base for conducting hostilities. Idenburg's appeal did not go unheeded. In Medan the board of the local German Union asked its members not to demonstrate their patriotic feelings in public. The Germans were living in a foreign, hospitable country and 'in a time at which national sensitivity comes so sharply to the fore, we, the guests, should do everything we can by behaving tactfully and by respecting and sparing the patriotic feelings of other nations, whichever they may be,

---

[22] *De Locomotief*, 9-12-1914.
[23] *De Locomotief*, 17-8-1914.
[24] *De Locomotief*, 14-8-1914, 15-8-1914, 19-8-1914.

to preserve our good name'.[25] Such appeals were to no avail. Disregarding the occasional voice of constraint, the Germans, old residents and new arrivals alike, throughout the war testified to their nationalist feelings. In Balikpapan in Borneo, for instance, in the local club of which a German was the chairman, pictures were exhibited of British and French prisoners-of-war guarded by German soldiers in 1916. The exhibition also enraged the local Dutch community, of whom the majority was anti-German. Pleyte wrote to Wilhelmina in 1918 that all the time the Germans were bearing witness to their 'common emotion and their devotion to king and fatherland'.[26] Frenchmen and Britons did not act much differently. All such foreign nationals zealously kept track of what their enemies were doing. The Dutch authorities were caught in the crossfire. An incident in Surabaya in April 1916 illustrates this nicely. A British protest about the sale of portraits of the Kaiser and the Sultan of Turkey in a shop in the Arab quarter prompted the police to confiscate them. The owner of the shop turned for help to the German Consul in the city. After his formal complaint, the portraits were returned to the shop.[27]

As during the Boer War with passion running high national anthems became a way to vent patriotic feelings. Germans embraced this method, as did French and British nationals. In Semarang the Dutch and French national anthems were sung at the railway station when the French male citizens of the city, six in total, obeyed the order of their consulate to report for military service and left for Batavia on the first leg of their journey home. On their arrival in Batavia, they were met by the French Consul, H. Fliche, and his wife. Fliche, dressed in a 'grand uniform' held a French flag in his hand, on which were written the words *Vive la France, aux braves coeurs*. His wife, presenting the six men with a rose and a tri-colour cockade, broke into 'La Marseillaise'. It was greeted with cheers of *Vive La France*, and 'May God protect the French army'.[28] The Turks quickly got in on the act. In Cirebon, two women, a mother and daughter, in a small Turkish opera company dressed as Turkish officers waved the Turkish flag and sang martial songs.[29]

The Dutchmen joined in enthusiastically, singing the national anthem of whatever country they favoured, which was usually not Germany. The editor of *De Locomotief* stressed that such behaviour was not fitting. In a colonial society in which people from various nationalities lived together restraint should be shown. Alluding to the 'national decency' of the Dutch he pleaded that Germans be treated courteously, especially as they had formed a merito-

---

[25] *Sumatra Post*, cited in *De Locomotief*, 25-8-1914.
[26] Pleyte to Wilhelmina, 10-8-1918, NA, Kol. Geheim, Vb. 10-8-1918 K7.
[27] *Oetoesan Hindia*, 4-4-1916.
[28] *De Locomotief*, 17-8-1914.
[29] *De Locomotief*, 9-12-1914.

rious segment of colonial society for years. An 'international balance' had to be maintained. It was commendable that the Dutch sang patriotic songs, but to honour Dutch neutrality they should refrain from singing foreign national anthems: 'Provoking international demonstrations was a national satisfaction of the lowest sort'.[30] Even the singing of the Dutch national anthem did not pass undisputed. In early August – and rumours that the Netherlands and Germany were at war may have been a reason for this – German guests in a restaurant in Surabaya tried in vain to prevent the Dutch national anthem being played by the band. When the other guests stood up and sang the anthem at the top of their voices the Germans left the restaurant.[31]

Though they could well face the dangers of war on their journey home French, British, and Belgian nationals usually succeeded in reaching their homelands and the battlefields. In view of the strict British and French naval control of the sea lanes to Europe, this was less easy, if not almost impossible, for Germans and Austrians acting with equal patriotic zeal. Realizing that taking passage on a neutral steamer bound for Europe or for Kiaochow, to where part of the German reservists were ordered, held the very prospect that if French or British warships stopped such ship, they were to be interned, most Germans accepted the fact that they were stuck in the Netherlands Indies. Soon those who had not left were joined by compatriots from abroad who had succeeded in escaping to the Netherlands Indies, or were forced to evacuate to that region. They came from Singapore and the Malay Peninsula, from Colombo and French Indochina, and from Hong Kong. Even a number of native policemen from German Papua New Guinea, their uniform consisting of a cap and a loincloth, fled to Hollandia. The colonial administration did not consider they belonged to the armed forces. It was decided to treat them like Belgian refugees in Holland. After they had been disarmed they were not interned as a neutral state was compelled to do with regular soldiers.[32]

To this influx of Germans living in South and Southeast Asia were added the crews and passengers of German ships, which could not sail on from ports in the Netherlands Indies; in total there were about fifty vessels. Among their passengers were also European emigrants on their way to Australia. Idenburg gave such third class passengers short shrift, stigmatizing them as 'undesirables' to be got rid of as soon as possible. This was easier said than done as Australia refused to admit any of German and Austrian nationality.[33] Emigrants on board ships arriving in Tanjung Priok were accommodated on

---

[30] *De Locomotief*, 12-8-1914.
[31] *Oetoesan Hindia*, 8-8-1914.
[32] Michielsen to Idenburg, 3-1-1915, 1st Government Secretary to Palmer, 5-1-1915, NA, Kol. Openbaar, Vb. 9-12-1918 66.
[33] Idenburg to Pleyte, 13-8-1914, NA, Kol. Openbaar, Vb. 14-8-1914 28.

Onrust, a nearby island which the colonial government felt highly suited to isolating and detaining undesirable elements. Some of those who travelled on ships which chanced to enter another port were more fortunate. The British emigrants on the *Roon* were moved to Semarang, where because of the Colonial Exhibition which had just been opened houses converted in makeshift hotels had remained empty. As a consequence of the war, the number of visitors was far fewer than expected.

The arriving Germans and Austrians were all victims of British naval superiority in Asia. In the first days of the war, the Netherlands Indies became a sanctuary for German and Austrian merchantmen which had fled French ports in Asia or had decided to avoid them. The influx became greater still when captains of German ships were ordered by their companies to leave British ports shortly before Great Britain entered the war. Ships fled to Sabang and the other ports in Sumatra, to the Riau Archipelago, to the harbours on the north coast of Java, and to Makassar. Ambon found itself experiencing a sudden influx of foreign merchantmen. At one particular moment twelve steamers from various countries lay anchored in Ambon Bay; a sight the inhabitants could not remember ever having seen before. For them the presence of so many foreigners meant an exiting interlude in the usually 'somewhat monotonous and prosaic life'.[34] Once in the Netherlands Indies the German and Austrian ships could not leave. Their captains and owners were not prepared to risk an encounter with British warships. The mail these German ships carried formed an additional problem. One of the steamers, the *Kleist*, was the very last ship of the German mail service. Other German merchantmen also carried mail. The Dutch authorities took it upon themselves to forward this mail to Europe, which was no easy task. Problems were not encountered with the mail carried by the *Roon*, which had to be sent on to Australia.

Many of the Germans in the Netherlands Indies, whether residents or recent arrivals, travelled to Batavia to contact the German Consulate General. Not all were satisfied with their reception. One of them noted in disgust that the declaration of war had caused the staff of the consulate to lose their heads completely. They had forgotten to lock the cupboard containing secret documents and codes, enabling a spy from the British consulate to copy a list with the names of the German reservists. He also complained that they did not know how to deal with their compatriots who came to the consulate for advice and help. Reservists did not receive any support. In fact, they were treated incorrectly and were fobbed off with inadequate advice. Some had told him that the German Deputy Consul General, E. Windels, who had to hold the fort as the Consul was on leave in Berlin and could not return to his post because

---

[34] *De Locomotief*, 29-9-1914.

of the war, had at times been extremely brusque and discourteous. One of the reasons for such intense disappointment was that the staff of the consulate considered the chance slight that the more adventurous Germans who presented them with all kinds of wild plans to reach Germany would succeed in their efforts. No money was provided for Germans who wanted to head for China or dreamt, as some indeed did, of chartering a sailing cutter, as some indeed did, to head for the German possessions in East Africa or the Arabian Peninsula.[35]

Some Germans did succeed in reaching Europe or China using false identity papers, but most Germans were trapped in the Netherlands Indies for the duration of the war. Only on very rare occasions, serious mental illness is an example, was the Dutch government prepared to consider mediation in the repatriation of Germans. Sailors were housed in sailors' homes founded by the German community, or had to stay on board for the remainder of the war. Some of the German residents who failed to leave the Netherlands Indies took up their old jobs again. Others suddenly found themselves unemployed. They joined the growing number of Germans in the colony who were without any income. It was a diverse group: Germans who had fled from British and French possessions in Asia; passengers and crews of German ships taking refuge in the Netherlands Indies; Germans, who at the outbreak of the war had been fired by British, French, and Belgian estates or firms, though initially this did not seem to have been done on a massive scale; and – a problem the authorities in Holland also had to cope with – wives and children left behind without adequate financial support by husbands who had left to report for military service in their fatherland.

For the stranded Germans life became difficult over time. They were assailed by boredom and restlessness as time went by. Within months there were also the first reports of crew members who caught malaria and other tropical diseases, or committed suicide. Throughout World War One the names and exploits of such Germans, their brawls and efforts to earn some extra money, occasionally popped up in newspapers and contemporary documents. Some of the sailors tried to find work ashore. In exceptional cases crew members had to be arrested by the Dutch authorities when they ignored their captain's order to return to their ship, refused orders to do work on board, or had resorted to begging when their financial resources had dried up. Some accepted any job offered or tried to earn a living by giving singing lessons and the like. It was probably the crew of the *Roon* who were responsible for a change on the entertainment scene in Semarang. In October 1914 *De Locomotief* reported that Europeans, stewards of a large ship that lay idle in Cilacap, had

---

[35] See NA, Kol. Openbaar, Vb. 9-12-1918 63.

made their appearance as waiters in a restaurant at the Colonial Exhibition in Semarang.[36] The colonial authorities sometimes made full use of the difficult position where such people found themselves in. In March 1916 eight cooks of the *Kleist* made themselves useful in Padang by preparing the elaborate welcome dinner for the new Governor General, J.P. van Limburg Stirum, when he set foot on colonial soil for the first time on his way from Europe to Java. Others played the music which accompanied the musical greeting of Dutch and Indonesian schoolchildren. They must have been adept musicians. The Dutch schoolchildren sang the Dutch national anthem-to-be, the 'Wilhelmus'; the Indonesian schoolchildren local songs, which the person who sent a report on the event to *De Locomotief* noted 'lent a certain sacred atmosphere because of the peculiar rhythm' to the tribute.[37]

In the course of time, the situation of the sailors grew more precarious. They received their pay, or at least part of it, but as the war dragged on and prices rose they could not make ends meet. In August 1918 about fifty members of crew of the *Roon* had to be detained after they had run amok when they had been informed that their pay was to be cut. At the end of December of the same year, the railway company generously decided to transport the Christmas presents sent to them free of charge. The maintenance of the German freighters themselves were largely neglected during their protracted stay in the ports of the Netherlands Indies. When Abdoel Moeis, visited Sabang in January 1917 he was struck by the poor condition of these ships. He noted that they were extremely filthy and that the sides were overgrown with barnacles.[38]

In the middle of August, when the initial fear that the Netherlands might be dragged in the war had abated somewhat, Pinke decided on a less defensive and more active naval policy. The squadron was split up. One ironclad, the *Tromp*, and two torpedo-boat destroyers were ordered to the eastern part of the Archipelago, to the Moluccas and surrounding waters. The other three ironclads – *De Zeven Provinciën*, the *Koningin Regentes*, and the *Hertog Hendrik* – ironclads escorted by four destroyers were detailed to cruise the seas around Bali and Lombok. The brief given to the commanders was to look out for foreign warships and to assure that these did not violate the colony's neutrality.[39]

Soon it turned out that a more pressing problem was at hand. In the middle of August, a British protest was received concerning the sailing of a number

---

[36] *De Locomotief*, 17-10-1914.
[37] Bijl de Vroe 1980:88; *De Locomotief*, 18-3-1916.
[38] *Neratja*, 29-11-1917.
[39] Pinke to Idenburg, 19-8-1914, NA, Kol. Geheim, Vb. 1-4-1915 A6.

The warship the *Koningin Regentes* (KITLV 34113)

of German merchantmen; which, as Pinke wrote in his diary 'displayed what seemed to us a disturbing but generally admirable activity' (Teitler 1986:40). One, the *Offenbach*, had left the port of Surabaya with its decks piles high with coal. The British Consul in Batavia was convinced that she had sailed out to provision German warships. His suspicion was fortified by the sailing of two other German merchantmen which also carried coal as deck cargo. These had left the port of Makassar around the same time. Batavia reacted immediately. The export of coal and durable foodstuffs was rigorously rationed. Ships leaving ports in the Netherlands Indies were only allowed to carry coal and provisions deemed sufficient for the voyage to the next port.[40] The decree was poorly formulated and soon had to be amended. Its wording implied that the decree was also in force for ships sailing from one port in the Netherlands Indies to another, or if sailing to another Dutch port in the Archipelago, first called at Singapore or Malacca. It had to be explained that the prohibition concerned only genuine export.[41] To be on the safe side Pleyte sent a confidential letter to De Scheepsagentuur in Amsterdam and Internatio in Rotterdam the following month. In order to prevent 'problems', both firms were asked not to sell coal in the Netherlands Indies before the colonial authorities, if possible the Governor General himself, had had the opportunity to 'judge whether

[40] *Javasche Courant*, 13-8-1914.
[41] *De Locomotief*, 26-8-1914.

the sale is desirable from a political point of view'; and to inform their agents accordingly. Both did so.[42]

The incident put Idenburg in a somewhat awkward position. His staff had completely forgotten about secret instructions about how to deal with the shipping of coal which had been issued to the local Dutch civil servants. According to these rules which were issued to prevent colonial territorial waters to being transformed into an operations base for one of the belligerents local authorities should prevent the sailing of merchantmen if there was a reasonable suspicion that they intended to provision a warship of the belligerents with fuel, munitions, and weapons. Unless their captains agreed to unload such cargo, passing ships were only allowed in territorial waters for a period of twenty-four hours. Ignorant of these instructions, in his reply to the British Consul Idenburg put forward various reasons to show that the colonial authorities had done nothing wrong, even when it was true that the merchantmen in question had planned to supply German warships with coal. It was pointed out that the 1907 treaty concluding the The Hague Peace Conference about the rights and obligations of neutral states did not require a neutral government to prevent the supply of belligerent warships by a third party outside territorial waters. At this moment the whole situation still appeared innocent to Idenburg. There were no reasonable grounds to assume that the *Offenbach* was going to serve as an auxiliary cruiser, the stowing of coal as deck cargo was not unusual, and no provisioning of German warships had taken place in colonial territorial waters.[43]

At the end of August the *Tromp* sighted the *Offenbach* near Jampea, south of Celebes. It now dawned on the authorities that she probably was not such an innocent vessel as Batavia had thought and, but the realization only slowly grew, that she might be involved in a scheme to provision German warships cruising Southeast Asian waters harrying Allied merchantmen. As Batavia would soon realize Germany had prepared well, involving consuls, businessmen and other Germans living in Southeast Asia in the plans to supply German raiders with coal and victuals.

There were at that moment two such German raiders prowling the waters in the vicinity of the Netherlands Indies: the gunboat the *Geier*, which at the outbreak of the war had been on her way to the German part of New Guinea, and the cruiser the *Emden*, which had crossed the Archipelago on her way from the Pacific to the Indian Ocean after the outbreak of the war. The *Geier* – which had stopped and searched a Dutch merchantman, the *Houtman*, in the waters between Makassar and Surabaya on 5 August – was a nuisance, but no more than that. The *Emden* created a real uproar. Pursued by British, French,

---

[42] Pleyte to De Scheepsagentuur, 7-9-1914, Pleyte to Idenburg, 7-9-1914, Scheepsagentuur to Pleyte, 9-9-1914, NA, Kol. Geheim, Vb. 7-9-1914 B18, Vb. 7-9-1914 D18, Vb. 11-9-1914 N18.
[43] Idenburg to Pleyte, 18-8-1914, NA, Kol. Geheim, Vb. 2-10-1914 P20.

The German raider the *Emden*

Russian, Japanese, and Australian warships, on her own she sank about twenty Allied vessels, including a French torpedo boat and Russian cruiser, which were sunk when the *Emden* raided the port of Penang. Her exploits were an additional reason why the colonial government attached such importance to the ban on writing about movements of foreign troops and ships in the Archipelago. The operations of the *Emden* in the Bay of Bengal, the Andaman Sea, and along the Malay coast led to panic in British India, Ceylon, and the Malay Peninsula, where people had been unaccustomed to the idea that one day they might be confronted with an attack by a foreign enemy. In October in Singapore a member of the Legislative Council of the Straits Settlements would state during one of its meetings about Penang, an island actually raided by the *Emden*, that it was completely without military protection, because 'I am here' (*Proceedings* 1915:B77). British merchantmen in the Straits Settlements and Colombo did not dare to put to sea, which also meant that the British mail was disrupted. At a certain moment forty-two Allied ships had taken shelter in Colombo for fear of an encounter with the *Emden*. The threat posed by the *Emden* also put a temporary halt to trade between the Netherlands Indies and the British and French colonies. Owners in the Netherlands Indies kept their ships, which were supposed to sail to these Allied destinations in port. It was reported somewhat exaggeratedly that trade in Surabaya grounded to a halt (Van Geuns 1918:211).

To continue their exploits the *Emden* and *Geier* needed fuel and provisions. In the first days of the war rumours that German warships had actually been furnished with coal in the Netherlands Indies were especially rife in the British communities of Batavia and Surabaya. The British Consul General, Carlisle, reported every scrap of information about such provisioning he received from his compatriots and consuls to British naval intelligence in Singapore. To the annoyance of the Dutch authorities Carlisle did not make much effort to check the veracity of the reports which reached him, nor did he put much faith in Dutch assurances that the information he received was incorrect. Pinke was especially annoyed by this as it concerned 'the good name' of the ships under his command. Even worse was that Batavia was sure that Carlisle's unsubstantiated reports contributed to the anti-Dutch mood which was beginning to form in French and British possessions in Southeast Asia and in the Allied communities in Japan and China. In all these places people were sure that the Dutch in the Netherlands Indies were assisting the German war efforts.[44]

Public opinion in Allied colonies was turning against the Netherlands, if not becoming downright hostile. In Saigon and Singapore people demanded a ban on all exports to the Netherlands Indies, including that of rice. In Saigon the mood was so fraught that a Dutch employee of one of the largest French companies in the city had been fired. Anti-German riots a month before, when houses and offices of Germans had been attacked by mobs, which had also smashed everything in the International Club to smithereens, were still fresh in people's minds and it was feared that the company might become the target of such violence if it employed Dutchmen. In Singapore the Dutch Consul General noted that among Chinese and indigenous middlemen especially anti-Dutch feelings had been manifest. Dutch trade and shipping had felt the consequences. The strong anti-Dutch sentiments had been fanned by newspaper reports that the naval authorities in Singapore were convinced that the *Emden* and *Geier* were not only allowed refuge in the territorial waters of the Netherlands Indies, but were actually provided there with coal and victuals. The news that the Dutch government had denied warships of belligerents access to the Scheldt, thereby not allowing British or French ships to reach Antwerp, provided extra fuel for the anti-Dutch mood. Rumours in Singapore, Saigon, Rangoon, and Calcutta claimed that relations between the Netherlands and Great Britain were on the brink of being severed. In an effort to turn the tide, the Dutch Consul General in Singapore elicited a denial from the Singapore administration. In the statement issued on 14 September, the governor of Singapore stated that on the authority of the British Colonial Secretary he could assert with confidence that the relations between the

---

[44] Pinke to Jerram, 29-9-1914, NA, Kol. Geheim, Vb. 19-3-1915 G5.

Netherlands and Great Britain were 'most cordial'.[45] The statement of the governor of Singapore was considered important enough to be published in the *Javasche Courant*.[46]

In Java, where newspapers had carried reports about the manifestations of anti-Dutch feelings in the rest of Southeast Asia, Pinke, reasonably sure of himself that his fleet had succeeded in preventing any bunkering of German raiders, used the Batavian newspaper *Bataviaasch Handelsblad* to deny empathically that any violation of neutrality had been committed in the territorial waters of the Netherlands Indies.[47] Idenburg, afraid that the import of rice might stagnate, also acted. Hearing about the developments in Saigon, he wasted no time in asking for the mediation of The Hague. The Ministry of Foreign Affairs had to assure the French authorities that neutrality was most strictly observed in the Netherlands Indies. To the satisfaction of the Dutch authorities Paris reacted without delay. The Governor General in Hanoi was asked for information about the anti-Dutch mood in his colony. He was also instructed to take all measures to prevent anti-Dutch demonstrations. In The Hague the French Ambassador assured the Dutch Ministry of Foreign Affairs that the colonial administration in Saigon did not nurture an anti-Dutch disposition. Nevertheless he had to admit that the Indo-Chinese press was hostile.[48] Dutch journalists in the Netherlands Indies seized upon the anti-Dutch mood outside the colony to take their revenge. To demonstrate precisely that the colonial fleet was not lax in guarding neutrality, newspapers should be allowed to report on the movement of Dutch warships.[49]

The rumours about the Dutch allowing the *Emden* and *Geier* to take refuge in territorial waters were untrue but the efforts to furnish the two German raiders with coal and provisions was a real issue. The matter was all the more pressing as the British Navy kept a close watch on the German merchantmen anchored in the ports, roadsteads, and bays of the Netherlands Indies. Occasionally British warships entered territorial waters to find out what these German freighters were up to. Would the naval authorities act in accordance with the proclamation of neutrality if they had to order the arrest of British warships operating in territorial waters and have them laid up till the end of

---

[45] Sparkler to Idenburg, 5-9-1914, Röst to Sparkler, 15-9-1914, NA, Kol. Geheim, Vb. 17-11-1914 A23.
[46] Protesters damaged the Dutch consulate in Durban in May 1915. The British government was prepared to compensate the damage but only as 'an act of grace' and a token of friendship. The Dutch government, taking the position that it was entitled to the money, refused to accept the British offer.
[47] Teitler 1986:58; *Bataviaasch Handelsblad*, cited in *De Locomotief*, 11-9-1914.
[48] Idenburg to Pleyte, 6-9-1914, Pleyte to Idenburg, 11-9-1914, NA, Kol. Geheim, Vb. 7-9-1914 A18, Vb. 17-9-1914 F19.
[49] *Bataviaasch Nieuwsblad*, cited in *De Locomotief*, 5-12-1914.

war? Pinke thought such a policy was unfeasible, which proved how impractical and unrealistic the proclamation in fact was.[50] Occasionally Dutch warships were ordered to leave port or, when such ships were not available, smaller vessels were sent to sea to warn captains of such warships, mostly British vessels, that they had entered territorial waters. In most cases the colonial authorities were informed about transgression only afterwards. All the Dutch could do in such instances was to lodge formal protests. Even this was often not feasible. Many reports of foreign warships entering territorial waters made by civil servants and local people, not the best naval observers and at times given to exaggeration, were too inconclusive to act upon them.

Preventing the bunkering of German warships in the territorial waters of the Netherlands Indies posed a gigantic problem. As Pinke confided to Vice Admiral Sir Thomas Henry Martyn Jerram, the commander of the British fleet in East Asia at the end of September, 'the total coastline of all the islands has a length nearly that of the equatorial circumference of the earth and that perhaps [a] thousand and more anchorages are found along this coastline'.[51] Some of these places lay in isolated outposts. For instance, a Dutch civil servant on his way to one of the islands near Madura, sighted a large ship, of which he could not make out the nationality. After he had found out that an armed launch had steamed to shore, he reported the incident by mail to his chief in Sumenep, pleading the urgency of having a telegraph connection at his post. Without a telegraph it might take a week, and even longer, before a message could be sent if a foreign warship violated neutrality. He added between brackets that one single, lonely European civil servant even if he by chance happened to be present could not prevent such a transgression.[52]

In his letter to Jerram Pinke had also written that he had not had a day's rest since the outbreak of the war. This may have been true but the real chase to keep watch over German merchantmen began at the end of August. After the *Offenbach* had been discovered near Jampea, the *Emden* had been sighted in the vicinity by the *Tromp*, and the *Geier* reportedly had also been spotted there. As one of the crew members of the *Koningin Regentes* said it was the beginning of 'the steaming back and forth on the trail of the various colliers of the *Emden*'. It was a 'tedious and boring time' (M. 1922:844). The Dutch warships were sent from pillar to post, sailing to and fro in search of coalers. Initially, the entire Dutch squadron sailed to Celebes. When it was reported that the *Emden* had bunkered in waters off the northwest coast of Sumatra and that British warships had been sighted nearby, the Dutch warships were ordered

---

[50] Pinke to Idenburg, 27-1-1915, NA, Kol. Geheim, Vb. 19-3-1915 G5.
[51] Pinke to Jerram, 29-9-1914, NA, Kol. Geheim, Vb. 19-3-1915 G5.
[52] Van der Plas to *Assistent-Resident* Sumenep, 29-12-1914, NA, Kol. Geheim, Vb. 19-3-1915 G5.

hence early the following month. Only the *Tromp* remained in the eastern part of the Archipelago, where she was to have a busy time. On 8 September, the *Tromp* arrested two German steamers of the Deutsch-Australische Dampfschiff Gesellschaft, and an American ship, the *Rio Päsig*, in a bay north of Seram. One of the German ships was the *Linden*. On an earlier occasion she had already been ordered out of territorial waters because of her cargo of coal. Encountered in territorial waters for the second time, her cargo was confiscated. The *Linden* was taken to Ambon. Presented with the choice of unloading her coal or leaving Dutch territory on the condition that re-entering it meant an embargo, the captain of the second German vessel, the *Ulm*, also loaded with coal, opted for the first alternative. The *Rio Päsig* left. She was later captured by the British. Having escorted the German ships to Ambon, the *Tromp* immediately had to sail on to Halmahera, to assist in suppressing an uprising, only to be ordered on again to Lombok, this time her quarry being a merchantman carrying no flag.[53]

In the west the scene of action was Telok Dalem Bay on the island of Simalur, or Simeulue in Acehnese. Three German merchantmen were moored off Simalur. One of them was the *Markomannia*, a steamer of the Hamburg-Amerika Linie. It was no secret that she accompanied the *Emden* on her exploits as a coaler and supply ship. Just outside territorial waters the *Markomannia* was transhipping coal from a Greek freighter, the *Pontoporos*, which had been taken as a prize by the *Emden*. The two other German ships were freighters, the *Choising*, which just before the start of the war had fled from Singapore and after sailing to Tanjung Priok had left that port with Lourenço Marques as her stated destination, but in fact had been ordered to supply the *Emden* with coal; and the *Hörde* of the Hamburg-Amerika Linie.

The *Markomannia* and *Choising* remained outside territorial waters but not so the *Hörde*. She had sought the protection of the bay, where she had first been sighted by a local Dutch civil servant on 19 September. He had ordered her captain to leave, but four days later the *Hörde* was sighted still within territorial waters by a Dutch torpedo boat destroyer. Asked why the *Hörde* had not left, her captain replied that she had run into engine trouble. Later he explained that he had made no hurry to repair the damage because he had not wanted to have his crew work day and night and exhaust themselves in the tropical heat. *De Zeven Provinciën* arrived the following day. The circumstances were highly suspicious. The *Hörde* was on her way from Manila to Guam, and though her captain maintained that he had changed direction for fear of an encounter with British warships, she was far too far off course for this (and on the wrong side of Sumatra to boot). Besides a cargo of cigars and copra, her holds contained

---

[53] Pinke to Idenburg, 23-9-1914, NA, Kol. Geheim, Vb. 1-4-1915 A6.

A captured enemy coal-ship escorted by the *Koningin Regentes* (M. 1922:844)

5,000 tons of coal for which no bill of loading could be presented. Suspicion was also raised by the fact that the fourth officer, Captain-Lieutenant Erwin von Möller, took charge of the conversation with the Dutch naval officers who inspected the ship and her cargo. It was surmised, and rightfully so, that he was a German naval officer, who because of his rank was the real commander of the ship. At the outbreak of the war Möller, a tall man with an English appearance, as Idenburg would later describe him in a telegram to Pleyte, had commanded a river gunboat in China. Thereupon he had travelled to Manila, where he had boarded the *Hörde* at the last moment and had been assigned the captain's cabin. On Pinke's instructions the *Hörde* was given some respite to repair the engine. After the extra time had elapsed the captain was ordered to sail to Padang or Sabang to unload the coal. Should he choose to refuse, his ship would no longer be allowed to enter territorial waters.

On reaching Sabang the captain of the *Hörde* refused to unload his coal, asking for extra supplies instead to be able to sail to Dar-es-Salaam. The request was denied. Permission to depart was also withheld. The captain was left with no other choice but to sell his load of coal to the Sabang Company. The fact that the *Hörde* was not allowed to put to sea landed Möller in a difficult position. He, as it was to clearly emerge, had an important assignment and he made every effort he could to leave Sabang on board another German ship. He conferred with German captains in port and asked them to give their word of honour not to disclose what had been discussed. He succeeded in persuading the captains of two merchantmen, the *Gernis* and the *Preussen*, to try to sail out. The captain of the *Gernis* was determined to steam to the Bay of Bengal to supply the *Emden* with provisions, a voyage, he estimated, which would take him sixteen days. Unable to buy enough flour in Sabang and finding no salt meat at all on the island, he collected foodstuffs from the other German steamers in the bay. Möller was smuggled on board the *Gernis* disguised as a stoker. After the *Gernis* was refused permission to leave, Möller, by now wanted for questioning by the authorities, gave himself up. As he did not want to cause a stir in his stoker's uniform he waited till it was dark to do so. Möller was arrested.[54] Later he was interned on the mainland, where he was housed comfortably in the Aceh Hotel in Kutaraja.

In Sabang the Captains of the *Hörde*, R.O Hensen, of the *Gernis*, J. Henken, of the *Preussen*, H.H.V.F.A. Lübcke, and others were interrogated. They played their cards pretty close to their chests. Lübcke suffered an attack of acute amnesia about the meetings on board of the German merchantmen at Sabang. Judging from the words of the chief engineer of the *Hörde* dinners on board of that ship must have been dull affairs. He had never exchanged a word with

---

[54] Minutes interrogation Von Möller on 6-10-1914, NA, Kol. Geheim, Vb. 15-12-1914 K24.

Möller.[55] Möller himself was incommunicado. He refused to speak about his time in Manila and the route of the *Hörde*. Such information related to the movement of the German warships. Möller denied that he had taken over command of the *Hörde* and called himself the 'intellectual leader' on board. All he would reveal was that his intention had been to direct the *Hörde* to rendez-vous with German warships.[56] Hensen admitted that he had been ordered by the agent of the Hamburg-Amerika Linie to steam to a particular spot in the Indian Ocean. The orders had come from Möller himself and from the estate company and trading house of Behn, Meyer and Company. In the ship's log the place was identified by the ciphers 12384. Hensen refused to say where this was and whether this might be Telok Dalem Bay, of which he had noted down in the ship's papers 'end of journey'. He said that to do otherwise would be treason against the state.[57] Only Henken was more talkative. From him the Dutch authorities got an inkling about the German plans to use German steamers sailing the Archipelago to supply German raiders with fuel and provisions. Steamers of the Norddeutscher Lloyd and Hamburg-Amerika Linie had already been instructed to assist such German warships before the outbreak of the war. Their captains had been provided with a secret code for making contact.[58]

A bone of contention emerged in those first months of the war other than preventing the fuelling of German warships. Soon the Dutch authorities were confronted with British protests about radio contact made by German merchantmen which had taken refuge in the Netherlands Indies and by radio stations on shore with German warships plying Southeast Asian waters. At the start of the war Batavia had taken its precautions. It had informed the consuls of the belligerents that international law forbade wireless communication in territorial waters by and with belligerent warships and that the colonial authorities were determined to enforce this rule. Initially nobody in the Navy – and Pinke claimed in his diary because of the enormous pressure at that time – had thought of the fact that German merchantmen moored in territorial waters would be able to contact German warships by radio (Teitler 1986:20). On 8 August, after such communications had indeed taken place the captains of German merchantmen which had taken refuge in the Netherlands Indies were told that they were not allowed to use their radios. Three days later the radios were sealed. No radio parts were removed, nor were antennas

---

[55] Minutes interrogation Bock on 1-10-1914, NA, Kol. Geheim, Vb. 15-12-1914 K24.
[56] Minutes interrogation Möller on 5-10-1914, NA, Kol. Geheim, Vb. 15-12-1914 K24.
[57] Minutes interrogation Hensen on 1-, 2-10-1914, NA, Kol. Geheim, Vb. 15-12-1914 K24.
[58] Record of the interrogation of Captain J. Henken on 3-10-1914, NA, Kol. Geheim, Vb. 15-12-1914 K24.

taken down or sealed. Pinke considered the first measure too complicated to be feasible as not enough experts were available to accomplish this task; the second useless as running a simple wire up the mast would suffice to receive messages (Teitler 1986:21-3).

From the second half of September, The Hague and Batavia were inundated by protests about communications from radio stations in the Netherlands Indies. Great Britain had discovered that the Germans had set up a system of wireless communication to keep in touch with their raiders and warships and suspected that radio stations in the Netherlands Indies were involved (Shennan 2000:78-9). In The Hague the British Envoy transmitted complaints on behalf of the British Foreign Secretary, Grey. In Batavia the Consul General lodged protests on behalf of the Straits government and Jerram. Some of these concerned the radio station at Sabang, about which in a rather insinuating fashion was occasionally added in the British press that (as all four radio stations in the Netherlands Indies) it had been built by Telefunken. Others spoke about radio messages to and from German steamers in the ports of Cilacap, Sabang, and Makassar. The Riau Archipelago was another focus of the attention for the British authorities. They were convinced that the region harboured German spies who had to keep in contact with German warships and merchantmen. At the end of August one of the islands, Bulan, was visited by three British officers from Singapore. They told the secretary of a local estate that they had sailed to the island for a picnic. Their actual behaviour aroused suspicion. The officers showed great interest in the hill tops and inquired after the nationality of the estate manager. On hearing this the Dutch *Resident* was not a little shocked, the more so as he had just received information, mentioning Bulan by name, that the British authorities in Singapore were on the look out for Germans in the Archipelago, who were in radio contact with German warships. He was sure that there were no spies among the few Germans who lived under his authority, but nevertheless promised Idenburg that he would do his utmost to prevent espionage.[59]

Not everybody, not even in the Dutch Navy in the Netherlands Indies, fully understood the potentials and limitations of radio communication. The British admiralty in East Asia seems to have been equally uninformed about its possibilities. The British Consul in Batavia maintained on the end of September that at three occasions the Sabang radio station had attempted to have British merchantmen reveal their position by asking for their speed and course.[60] A few days later the British Envoy in The Hague, Sir Alan Johnstone, informed Loudon on 1 October that the station was constantly jamming Calcutta

---

[59] Coeven to Resident Riau, 9-9-1914, Resident Riau to Idenburg, 9-9-1914, NA, Kol. Openbaar, Vb. 9-12-1918 39.
[60] Carlisle to Idenburg, 26-9-1914, NA, Kol. Geheim, Vb. 18-11-1914 D23.

and other radio stations in India. Three days later a second letter followed. Repeating the accusation, Johnstone claimed that Sabang appeared to be assisting German cruisers and that the stations P.F.A. and P.F.S. were working together. It was assumed that P.F.S. was located in Rotterdam; from where with the contemporary technology it would have been impossible to send messages to a region as far away as Southeast Asia.

It was not difficult to gainsay some of the complaints. A civil servant at the Ministry of the Colonies scribbled in the margin that the British admiral in Asia, from whom the complaints originated, had acted in 'nervous haste'. There was as yet no wireless station in Rotterdam. P.F.A. and P.F.S. were the call signals of two Dutch merchantmen of the Rotterdamsche Lloyd. Every government and Navy official could have easily found this out. Lists of such call names were widely available. The allegation that the Sabang station passed on information to German warships could likewise be refuted. Steamers which wanted to transmit a message via the Sabang station were asked to mention their position and speed. This was standard practice, allowed by international radio conventions.

The jamming of the Calcutta radio station was a genuine cause for complaint. The reason was frequent and lengthy communications between the Sabang station and Dutch warships. The squadron at that time was cruising the waters off Simalur. For one reason or another, experts did not know why, communication in that area was difficult. Transmission required full capacity. After Pleyte had asked Idenburg to 'mitigate' the inconvenience caused by the Sabang radio station, the latter urged the station to limit its communication with ships which sought contact.[61]

A week later Johnstone presented a new protest. It concerned a complaint by the naval authorities in Australia about a radio station at Situbondo (built the British hasted to point out by Telefunken). Civil servants quickly realized that the town of Situbondo, a small city with a wireless station in the eastern corner of Java, was meant. Pleyte asked Idenburg to investigate. Idenburg replied that the complaint was 'absolutely unfounded'. On the day in question there had been no contact between the radio station and foreign vessels.[62]

The *Roon*, moored in Cilacap, also aroused suspicion. At the request of the British, the ship was searched a number of times to ascertain that she could not be equipped as an auxiliary vessel and to check that her radio had been sealed. In view of the British protests about radio messages sent from the

---

[61] Johnstone to Loudon, 1-10-1914, 4-10-1914, 5-10-1914, Pleyte to Idenburg, 7-10-1914, Idenburg to Pleyte, 8-10-1914, Von Faber to Idenburg, 16-10-1914, NA, Kol. Geheim, Vb. 7-10-1914 U20, Vb. 8-10-1914 X20, Vb. 18-12-1914 24.
[62] Johnstone to Loudon, 13-10-1914, Idenburg to Pleyte, 27-10-1914, NA, Kol. Geheim, Vb. 15-10-1914 J21, Vb. 28-10-1914 A22.

vessel the army had also erected a field radio station nearby. Nightly rounds by the harbour master and the police kept the *Roon* under strict surveillance. Nevertheless, it cannot be ruled out that some Dutch people were aware that transmissions did take place, but for one or another reason they did not want to report this to the proper authorities. A sailor on the *Roon* who had fallen out with her captain claimed this was the case. It must have aroused at least some suspicion that each time a message was sent all the lights on the ship had to be turned off.[63]

Pinke was positive that all possible precautions had been taken, but the British continued to complain about radio messages sent from the *Roon* to the *Emden* and *Geier*. A wireless operator in Australia was sure that he had intercepted such messages and had recognized the distinctive tone of its radio operator. Johnstone wrote in one of his protests that such messages probably conveyed intelligence about British shipping. He pointed out that this implied that the wireless apparatus on the *Roon* had not been dismantled. This was a 'failure to fulfil duties of neutrality'. An immediate inquiry was demanded. Loudon complied.[64] In a wire to Idenburg Pleyte indicated that the matter was of a serious nature.[65] This time Idenburg displayed some annoyance. Pinke had already conveyed him his displeasure over the rash way in which the British naval authorities had drawn the conclusion that German merchantmen violated the ban on radio contact. He had stressed that not much importance should be attached to British complaints as long as they were not substantiated by facts. Believing Pinke, Idenburg informed Pleyte that the colonial authorities had done all they could. They needed more than just vague accusations. What was more, the two German raiders were nowhere near Java. The *Emden* was in the Bay of Bengal, the *Geier* in Honolulu.[66]

Idenburg and Pinke should not have been so confident. The local authorities, unfamiliar with the working of wireless installations, had blundered. The first concrete information indicating that German merchant vessels and warships were indeed in radio contact emerged at the end of September. It involved the steamers the *Luneberg* and the *Stollberg* which were moored in Makassar. A British complaint that their radios were being used greatly irritated the Dutch authorities. They were convinced that they had done all they could to prevent this. The complaint was used to criticize Carlisle's behaviour and to express irritation about the violation of territorial waters by British warships, whose crews at times disembarked on isolated islands for a swim

---

[63] Statement sailor Roon to the British Consul General, NA, Kol. Geheim, Vb. 27-1-1915 G2.
[64] Johnstone to Loudon, 28-10-1914, NA, Kol. Geheim, Vb. 30-10-1914 E22.
[65] Pleyte to Idenburg, 30-10-1914, NA, Kol. Geheim, Vb. 30-10-1914 E22.
[66] Pinke to Idenburg, 23-10-1914, Idenburg to Pleyte, 31-10-1914, NA, Kol. Geheim, Vb. 2-11-1914 J22, Vb. 19-12-1914 U24.

and other forms of recreation. It was not a formal protest, but took the form of a letter to Jerram from Pinke (who, fed up with the many complaints by Carlisle based on 'false rumours' and 'foolish but at the same time also dangerous gossip', refused to communicate by mail with the British Consul General) (Teitler 1986:74). In the letter it was also pointed out that up to that moment no German warship had entered the territorial waters of the Netherlands Indies. In reply Jerram gave the assurance that he and Carlisle had no doubts about the intentions of Batavia to maintain a strict neutrality. He wrote to Pinke that he had only drawn attention to the two steamers in Makassar 'with the objective of assisting you by showing where leakings existed'.[67]

As had become standard routine, after a British complaint had been received a new investigation of the ships in question was ordered. In some instances it was the second, third, or fourth time. This time the inspection did not rule out the possibility that the accusation was well founded, though that this was still considered to be very unlikely. The conclusion was that the way in which the radio installation had been rendered useless was not foolproof. One of the flaws was that the aerials had not been removed. The eventuality that the ships had a second radio on board could also not be precluded. With this in mind Pinke ordered the removal of the aerials of all German merchantmen in Netherlands Indies waters. Pertinently this instruction was only in force for merchantmen. Warships – at least Allied ones – were excluded. Pinke was indignant when he heard that the captain of a British man-of-war in Makassar had been asked to lower her antenna at the end of 1915. He complained to Idenburg that it had been agreed that a promise of a captain of a warship not to use his radio sufficed.[68]

Another result of the investigation in Makassar was that Pinke launched a serious attempt to thwart more old-fashioned ways of communication at the end of October. It had been discovered that the captain of the *Stollberg* kept carrier pigeons. He had explained that this was a hobby of his. Pinke pondered over this piece of information for some time. Finally he decided to ask the regional authorities to report to him whether there were pigeons on board of German ships in their post. He did so, though, as he himself confessed, he found it hard to imagine, how these birds were to be used.[69] Later, in January 1915, a German watchmaker was arrested for possessing pigeons, allegedly intended for another German steamer in port.[70]

Among the ports where Pinke's instruction was obeyed was Tanjung Priok. On one of the ships anchored there, the *Freiberg*, seven pigeons were

---

[67] Jerram to Pinke, 6-10-1914, NA, Kol. Geheim, Vb. 19-3-1915 G5.
[68] Pinke to Idenburg, 1-12-1915, NA, Kol. Openbaar, Vb. 9-12-1918 70.
[69] Pinke to De Graeff, 29-10-1914, NA, Kol. Geheim, Vb. 18-12-1914 V24.
[70] *De Locomotief*, 25-1-1915.

discovered: five adults and two squabs. The captain explained that he had bought a number of pigeons in Antwerp. In the course of time they had multiplied. The authorities were unrelenting. The Resident of Batavia, H. Rijfsnijder, ordered the harbour master, E.A. Kuchlin, to point out to the captain that in his own interest it would be best to kill the birds or have them removed from his ship. Kuchlin complied, but could find only five pigeons. He was sure that two adults had flown to another German ship, the *Hagen*. There it was that Kuchlin duly went. He saw two birds and asked her Captain, A. Wilm, to return them to the *Freiberg*. Wilm was only prepared to part with one of the pigeons. He said that he himself owned the other pigeon. Thereupon Wilm was given to understand that it would be better for him to kill his pet. He did not take kindly to this. His reply that the British were certainly behind the search was taken by Kuchlin as an insult. Oversensitive, as more of his contemporary Europeans were where it concerned his personal honour, Kuchlin considered the accusation serious enough to contemplate a court case. Indignantly he announced that he would be back in a few days' time to ascertain what had happened to the pigeons. When he returned both German captains was absent. Kuchlin could only find the two squabs in their cage. Of the five older ones of the *Freiberg* and the one of the *Hagen* there was not a trace.

An incident was born. Annoyed by the frequent investigations of German ships, the German Deputy Consul in Batavia made the pigeons the centrepiece of a complaint. By doing so the fate of the birds was also brought to the attention of the civil servants of the Ministry of the Colonies in The Hague. The Deputy Consul protested that no investigation should take place on board a German merchantman in Tanjung Priok without him being informed beforehand. A special agreement from 1905 gave him this right. At that time the colonial authorities had promised not to conduct a police investigation aboard German ships without alerting the consulate first. Idenburg did not agree. The circumstances of the day and the duty of the colonial government to ensure that ships of the belligerents respected Dutch neutrality demanded immediate, prompt action. He argued that the promise of 1905 had just been a polite gesture and could not be upheld. Usually there was no time to wait for a representative of the consulate to arrive on the scene.[71]

More discomforting news about German radio traffic was to follow. At the end of October the radio station in Sabang throughout the night intercepted several coded messages. They bore the mark of a telegraphist on the *Emden*. An investigation was launched. On the *Scandia*, the first ship visited, nothing suspicious was found, but suddenly one of her sloops was spied heading for the

---

[71] See NA, Kol. Vb. 9-12-1918 39.

Preussen, where people were hurrying back and forth on the deck. Inspection of the *Preussen* revealed a receiver hidden under the cushion in the cabin of the telegraphist and an aerial concealed along the inside of the rope-ladder to the top of the main mast and not visible from the shore. Neither receiver nor aerial had been there when the *Preussen*, a vessel of the Hamburg-Amerika Linie, had arrived in Sabang on 3 August. At that time she had not carried an aerial. At the end of September, after the investigation of the *Luneberg* when all aerials of the German ships in Sabang had been lowered and sealed, she still had not carried one. The governor of Aceh reported to Idenburg that the receiver had been built with material on board and had been cleverly concealed. As a punishment the captain, an officer of the German Navy, and the radio operator were moved to Medan to be prosecuted for violation of the rules proclaimed to guard Dutch neutrality. They were not placed under arrest as the possibility that they would be able to escape was considered to be nil. Initially the court in Medan acquitted them. The court did not consider the sending of messages aimed at facilitating an act of war, an enemy activity which violated Dutch neutrality. They were sentenced to one year's imprisonment by the High Court in Batavia in 1916, and subsequently were moved from Medan to Semarang to serve their time. The *Preussen* was confiscated.

In November, after repeated British complaints about the *Roon* (and the German steamers *Lübeck* and *Sydney* moored in the same port), Pinke finally decided to send a real wireless expert to Cilacap. The report was devastating. The sealing of the radios had been clumsily done. The equipment could still be used without breaking the seals. The receivers were also still intact. The hoisting of a copper wire in the halyards was all that was needed to receive a wireless message. The discovery made it very probable that the *Roon* and *Lübeck* had used their radios. Idenburg confided to Pleyte that he was very disappointed because he had been convinced that the dismantling of the wireless installations had been effective. He concluded that it was best to remain silent about the findings. In Holland Pleyte and Loudon agreed. They believed there was every reason to do so. The British Envoy in The Hague had conveyed the satisfaction of the British Admiralty with the measures taken in Cilacap. Pinke expostulated that he had clean hands and that regional civil servants were responsible. He wrote to Idenburg that sealing had to be done by experienced people but there were not enough experts in the Navy to serve the whole Archipelago. The *Assistent-Resident* of Cilacap was made the scapegoat. He was reprimanded for the extraordinarily careless way in which the seals aboard the two German ships had been affixed and the previous inspections had been conducted.[72] Idenburg now was resolute. The sealing of radio equip-

---

[72] See NA, Kol. Geheim, Vb. 12-1-1915 T, Vb. 27-1-1915 G2.

ment was not enough. Vital parts had to be removed. Orders to do so were sent out in December.[73]

The German ships kept the Dutch naval squadron fully occupied in the closing months of 1914. In the middle of October the crew of a Dutch warship witnessed the sinking of the *Markomannia* and the taking of the *Pontoporos* by the British light cruiser, the HMS *Yarmouth*. The event excited them to such an extent that when the telegraphist reported the incident he forgot to use the secret code. A protest from the Japanese Consul that Dutch warships radioed information about the movement of British and Japanese warships in plain language inexorably followed.[74]

Relief came when the *Emden* was sunk near the Cocos Islands by the Australian cruiser transporting Australian troops, the HMAS *Sydney*, on 9 November. Her exploits had inspired fear but had also drawn admiration. *De Locomotief* wrote of the *Emden* as the Flying German. For the Malay inhabitants of Colombo she had become the *Kapal Setan*, Devil Ship, a term also used in the Malay press in the Netherlands Indies, in which her activities had been covered as intensely as in the European newspapers. The *Emden* had also impressed Rambonnet, the Dutch naval Minister. In January 1915, when he contemplated what kind of cruisers the Dutch Navy needed, he thought in particular about a vessel of the *Emden*-type, which he was convinced had proven its worth.[75]

The *Emden* was sunk after she had put a fifty-man-strong landing party ashore commanded by Captain Lieutenant Hellmuth von Mücke, which cut two of the three cables of the British telegraph station on the Cocos Islands and blew up the transmitting mast. The landing party managed to escape in an old ramshackle 97 ton three-masted sailing schooner, the *Ayesha*, which lay moored in the harbour. After having been at sea for sixteen days, the *Ayesha* made a brief visit to Emmahaven at the end of the month. She flew the German war banner and pennon at her mast-head. The Dutch authorities refused to grant the *Ayesha* recognition as a German warship. They considered the schooner a prize. Von Mücke protested, his flying of the war banner had been deliberate. He demanded water, food, fuel, and canvas. Von Mücke also wanted sea charts, clothing, soap, tooth- and hair-brushes. His crew had not brushed their teeth for three weeks and had had one comb to share. The Dutch, considering the *Ayesha* a prize refused to allow these latter goods on board, only providing her with whatever was required to make the *Ayesha* seaworthy. Sarcastically Von Mücke wrote later that the authorities had probably been of the opinion

---

[73] De Graeff to Pinke, 30-11-1914, circular instruction Kindermann, 10-12-1914, NA, Kol. Geheim, Vb. 27-1-1915 G2.
[74] Pinke to De Graeff, 29-10-1914, NA, Kol. Geheim, Vb. 18-12-1914 V24.
[75] Rambonnet to Pleyte, 7-1-1915, NA, Kol. Geheim, Vb. 8-1-1915 Q1.

that soap, tooth- and hair-brushes would have added to the fighting capability of the *Ayesha* (Mücke 1916:46-9). The arrival of the *Ayesha* was an excellent opportunity for a boost to German morale. The crew was welcomed by the German Consul. Sailors on the German steamers anchored in port, among them the *Kleist* and *Choising* (which had been forced to sail to Emmahaven after a fire had broken out on board), cheered loudly. Cigars, cigarettes, wine, clothing, and German magazines were thrown on board.

When the *Ayesha* put to sea again on 28 November her sailors sang 'Die Wacht am Rhein and Deutschland', 'Deutschland über alles'.[76] The British Navy was waiting, but the *Ayesha* succeeded in escaping the attention of the *Empress of Japan*, a converted Canadian Pacific liner, which especially had been directed to these waters to intercept her. In her search for the *Ayesha* the *Empress of Japan* accidentally entered territorial waters. The Dutch government duly protested. After drifting for about three weeks off the coast of Sumatra, the *Ayesha* was joined by the *Choising*, which had left Emmahaven two weeks after her. On board of the *Choising*, the *Ayesha* crew continued their journey via the Red Sea and Turkey back to Germany. On their return all the members of the *Ayesha* were awarded a silver cross.

Instead of the *Ayesha*, the *Empress of Japan* took one of the two British colliers which had been captured by the *Emden*, the *Exford*. Her Captain, Julius Lauterbach, the prize-officer of the *Emden*, was sure that his ship had been taken within Dutch territorial waters (Lauterbach 1918:12). He and his men were sent to the Tangling Barracks, where the crew of the *Markomannia* were already detained. They were housed in the Emden House. Lauterbach himself, being the highest-ranking German officer in the camp, was accommodated in a small house of his own. On arrival Lauterbach and his men were greeted with a 'powerful hurrah' and 'Deutschland, Deutschland über alles' (Lauterbach 1918:15; Harper and Miller 1984:18).

With the knocking out of action of the *Emden*, the risk of violations of neutrality in the waters around North Sumatra had grown less. One ship was left to patrol there.[77] The crisis was over before the year had ended. The British under-secretary for Foreign Affairs concluded in a letter to Viceroy of India, Lord Charles Hardinge, that the German Navy had 'practically disappeared from the Pacific'.[78] Pinke noted with relief in March 1915 that with the sinking of the *Emden* an end had come the plethora of rumours about German warships steaming around the Archipelago, or at least that the Allied Forces 'would no longer believe them unquestionly, as they had done all too often in the past'.[79]

---

[76] *De Locomotief*, 3-12-1914.
[77] Pinke to Idenburg, 17-2-1915, NA, Kol. Geheim, Vb. 1-4-1915 A6.
[78] Nicholson to Hardinge, 6-1-1915, PRO FO 800 377.
[79] Pinke to Idenburg, 25-3-1915, NA, Kol. Geheim, Vb. 5-5-1915 P7.

Despite the passing of immediate danger, throughout the war the Dutch naval squadron was kept on full alert. Neutrality had to be protected. This pressure was so palpable that in August 1916, when one of the rare periods occurred in which all ships were free to hold joint manoeuvres, this was considered so important that the Muslim crews were only given a few hours off to celebrate the end of the Fasting Month.[80] The possibility that forces of the belligerents might still forcibly attempt to take coal or oil was a possibility that could not be ignored. Now there was a turning away from the bombastic language so prevalent at the time of the Russo-Japanese War. Idenburg was still of the opinion that Sabang and other coaling stations had to be defended. His successor, J.P. van Limburg Stirum, took a slightly different view. Shortly after his inauguration in March 1916, he made it plain that in his opinion fighting superior forces was a hopeless task. What was important was to find a minimal defence that would still convince the outside world that real resistance had been offered without sacrificing too many lives.[81]

The forty-two moored German merchantman (plus the two Austrian ones) with a total tonnage of over two hundred thousand tons also continued to bother the colonial authorities, Pinke, and The Hague periodically. Behn, Meyer and Company wanted guarantees for the safety of the German ships, and in November 1915 wanted to move the *Roon* from Cilacap to Tanjung Priok, where she would be better protected against raids by Allied warships. Pinke was adamant that in such an instance no guarantees should be given that the merchantmen could count on the protection of a Dutch warship sailing as escort. Such an escort was occasionally given in Europe to protect Allied or German merchantmen, by the Dutch Navy as well, but Pinke did not want to become committed by such precedents. He was prepared to send warships along, but did not want to promise this in advance. In his opinion a general guarantee that the German merchantmen were safe in colonial territorial waters had to suffice. The colonial Navy was much too small and the Archipelago much too large to be able to guarantee formally that neutrality could be backed up everywhere by the presence of one or more Dutch warships. Imagine, he wrote in September 1916, what would happen if German raiders were to appear again, and all the British merchantmen sailing in the Netherlands Indies were to ask for protection by a Dutch warship.[82]

---

[80] *De Locomotief*, 17-11-1917.
[81] Erdbrink to Commander of the Army, 13-9-1916, NA, Kol. Geheim, Vb. 10-1-1918 R1.
[82] Pinke to Van Limburg Stirum, 6-9-1916, NA, Kol. Openbaar, Vb. 9-12-1918 73.

CHAPTER VIII

The European community in the Netherlands Indies

In the very first days of the war one of the fears that arose to haunt the Dutch in the Netherlands Indies was that the Netherlands would not succeed in its efforts to remain neutral. To serve a nervous public, Dutch-language newspapers were full of war telegrams about the situation on the battlefields and the mood in Europe. Maps showing the movements of the armies were published (later in the war also about the Balkans) and special Sunday editions and bulletins appeared. Telegrams, maps, and Sunday editions would remain a prominent feature of the newspapers for the duration of the war. The latest news telegrams from Europe were posted outside newspaper offices. In Medan, an American Methodist missionary, the Reverend Ward (who was to die in battle in France in 1918) did the same. He published war reports in English and Chinese on two blackboards in front of the American-Chinese school of which he was the head. Ward, a man who according to a local newspaper 'has repeatedly shown that he had more militaristic and political than religious blood in his veins' soon had to stop doing so. The way in which he reported developments in Borneo did not please the authorities: 'Chinese revolution in Borneo; two towns captured; 100 men advancing to take Pontianak'.[1]

Presenting reliable, trustworthy news at that time was difficult. Newspapers from Holland were unavailable, while Great Britain controlled cable traffic. The latter fact meant that most war telegrams which reached the Netherlands Indies were of Allied origin or had to pass the gaze of the British censor. In Bandung one Dutch citizen, already annoyed by the anti-German public opinion that was gaining ground, became so upset by what he called the poisoning by Allied 'lie and soup telegrams' that he started a one-man campaign against the local *Preanger-bode*. He must have been a choleric person. The *Preanger-bode* belonged to that category of newspaper which served as a source of German reports for other newspapers in the Netherlands Indies, while other

---

[1] *De Sumatra Post*, cited in *De Locomotief*, 11-8-1914.

newspapers also did their best to obtain German news telegrams (which could only reach the Netherlands Indies via the telegraph link to San Francisco and Guam). Using the pen-name Paul, he began by venting his opinion in a rival Bandung newspaper. This channel was closed to him when one of its shareholders considered what he wrote too biased in favour of Germany and feared a drop in advertisements and readers. Not taken aback, 'Paul' continued his crusade and started his own bulletin, *Oorlogs-commentaar* (War Comment). It was distributed as far away as Probolinggo in East Java. People who did not like his stance took revenge. They brought out a fake issue, of which the contents enraged Germans.[2]

Other people did not trust the war telegrams either or were carried away by incorrect reports. Rumours about ultimatums and demands by Berlin, Paris, and London abounded as did speculations about how the motherland and consequently also to the Netherlands Indies would fare. When the news that Germany had invaded Belgium had not yet reached the Netherlands Indies, people in Java ventured to speculate that were Germany not to respect the neutrality of Belgium Holland might be invaded as well.[3] One of the scenarios put about during the first tumultuous days averred that all depended on how London would react. Were Great Britain to remain neutral, the Netherlands would also succeed in doing so. In such a situation the Netherlands Indies would probably be spared an invasion. Others predicted that were Great Britain to join the war, which it did on 4 August, the Netherlands would still not be attacked. Such people assumed that the Netherlands was of little or no strategic importance to the belligerents. Great Britain which had a small army would think twice before invading Holland, where a 150,000 strong army, it was proudly written, awaited the aggressor.[4] *De Locomotief* wrote that 'It seems to be our national good fortune that in this war the Netherlands turns out not to be strategically remunerative for any of the parties'.[5] This assessment was not altogether true. The northern tip of Holland had strategic value as a point from where to obstruct and observe the sailing of a German fleet into the North Sea. For some British statesmen and officers, W.S. Churchill among them, this was reason enough to consider an occupation of one of the Frisian Islands, Ameland (Halpern 1994:101). In the south lay the river the Scheldt. Running from the North Sea to Antwerp through Dutch territory, the Scheldt formed a main cause of concern for people in Holland and the Netherlands Indies. The river could well involve Holland in the war as it might be used by Great Britain and France to send food, troops, and war materials into Belgium.

[2] *De Locomotief*, 22-10-1914, 26-11-1914, 15-1-1915.
[3] *De Locomotief*, 4-8-1914.
[4] *De Locomotief*, 4-8-1914.
[5] *De Locomotief*, 10-8-1914.

After 16 August its strategic importance actually grew, and along with this the pessimistic forecasts flew thick and fast, when the Belgian government evacuated to Antwerp, and German troops besieged the city.

Besides the possibility of Holland being invaded, another prospect which continued to haunt some Dutch people, especially it appears in Holland, was that Great Britain would strike at the Netherlands Indies. Alluding to such fears among the Dutch general public, Johnstone wrote to Grey in February 1915 that an 'excellent effect would be produced to have some member of the Cabinet to make an official announcement that Great Britain disclaimed the idea of touching the Dutch colonies'.[6] Grey complied. He gave a speech about the right of small countries to write their own destinies. Other British politicians, well aware of the mood in the Netherlands, contemplated using the integrity of the Netherlands Indies as a kind of bonus to lure The Hague onto the side of the Allied Powers. Again Churchill was one of the party. Expecting that Germany would attack Holland in the spring of 1915, he contemplated offering the Dutch an Anglo-Japanese guarantee that the Netherlands Indies were not to be invaded as one of the incentives to have the Netherlands join the war on the Allied side.[7]

Equally disquieting for the government and the general public was the Anglo-French economic blockade of Germany. There was a general unease about the isolation of the colony which the war might bring. It was a situation for which the colony was unprepared. Until the outbreak of the war the Netherlands Indies had, as a prominent German Resident in Batavia, Emil Helfferich, chose to phrase this this, been 'mothered' from Holland (Helfferich 1921:9). All decisions of any importance, whether political or commercial, had been taken in Holland. There were also more specific worries. London and Paris might not hesitate to apply force to end Dutch trade with Germany. The German government from its part might well take similar action were it felt pressed by the Allied obstruction of the transportation of corn and wheat to Holland. Dutch export to Germany terminated. *De Locomotief* commented anxiously in September that closure of the borders with Germany would amount to a declaration of war.[8] In this respect export bans imposed by the Dutch government directly after the outbreak of the war because of domestic scarcity were seen as a blessing in disguise. From various sides it was pointed out with some relief that German protests could be countered by explaining that such measures had not been taken to hurt German interests, while the bans simultaneously decreased the chance that Great Britain and France would consider Dutch territory a leak in the economic isolation imposed on Germany. In the

---

[6] Johnstone to Grey, 19-2-1915, PRO FO 800 69.
[7] Johnstone to Grey, 21-4-1915, PRO FO 800 69.
[8] *De Locomotief*, 16-9-1914.

same spirit it was suggested that colonial exports to Holland should be limited to sufficiently cover Dutch domestic demand. It was hoped that such a course of action would not give Berlin much reason to protest. London and Paris would also be satisfied.

Reports about the German army invading Limburg, about British troops occupying Flushing, and about the Netherlands having declared war on Germany – newspapers in the Netherlands Indies brought the news in bold type – fuelled the apprehension. The initial successes of the German army in Belgium and the landing of British troops in France came as a solace. Such events decreased the likelihood that German troops would march through Holland or that a British force was to sail up the river Scheldt. Relief was dampened again after the fall of Antwerp in October 1914, when it was immediately speculated in the Singapore press that the German Navy would use Antwerp, and the Scheldt, as a base for its submarine attacks on ships in the North Sea.[9]

The impression created in the Netherlands Indies by the news telegrams from Europe and the many rumours which circulated was that the position of the Netherlands in Europe was becoming more precarious by the day. It was written in *De Locomotief* of 8 August that reports from Europe were received daily about a violation of Dutch neutrality or at the very least a threat to it. *De Locomotief* claimed it was virtually certain that Dutch territory would be touched by the war. Many, if not everybody, in the Netherlands Indies expected war. The tension, the commander of the Dutch fleet in the Netherlands Indies, F. Bauduin (1920:8) wrote, had become 'unbearable', adding that, to most of the crew it was a matter of indifference to what foreign nation the warships belonged which would sink their ships, but be destroyed the Dutch squadron would, as its fighting power was 'absolutely nil' (Bauduin 1920:10). What, for instance, was to happen if the German army had to withdraw from Belgium, or a German fleet was pushed towards the Dutch coast by the British Navy? But, *De Locomotief* continued in an effort not to upset its readers even more, it should not lose sight of the fact that violations of neutrality and the efforts to prevent them did not yet constitute acts of war. The exploits of the German raiders added to the panic in the Dutch community. Coupled with rumours about the Netherlands being in war with Germany news about the *Geier* made some Dutch people living in coastal areas even prepare for a flight by car into the interior (Bauduin 1920:11).

Pessimism in the Netherlands Indies assumed such proportions that on 7 August Idenburg wired, still forced to use English, The Hague to ask permission to 'put [the] minds [of the] inhabitants at ease' by publishing the state-

---

[9] *De Locomotief*, 25-11-1914.

ment that Dutch neutrality was not threatened.[10] After Pleyte had responded the following day that he saw no reason for any anxiety, a special issue of the *Javasche Courant* was published on 10 August. It contained a statement by the Governor General, soon to be copied by the rest of the press, that word had been received from the Dutch government that the belligerents respected Dutch neutrality. Such a reassurance served its purpose. It diminished the anxiety of the people, who showed less inclination to hoard food and coins. In Gorontalo in Celebes, for instance, even though in that distant place the news must have been received some days later, the report that the Netherlands had succeeded in remaining neutral 'performed within a few hours'.[11] Idenburg himself was not reassured. Until well into 1915 he remained convinced that the Netherlands would not succeed in keeping out of the war (Bijl de Vroe 1980:44).

Even though anxiety was somewhat appeased, there was still Japan, or what two Dutch colonial civil servants publicly called the 'Yellow Robbers'.[12] In the first days of the war Dutch people in the Netherlands Indies became increasingly apprehensive about Japan's designs. Reports that Japan had confirmed that it was to honour its treaty obligations with Great Britain, and news about a Japanese squadron sailing, resulted in many scares in the Netherlands Indies. At the beginning of August 1914 Idenburg and his two chief military advisors, Pinke and Michielsen, did not rule out an invasion by Japan, though they did not consider such a possibility highly likely. This agreed with the information that reached them from Japan. In the first days of the war the Dutch Envoy in Tokyo, D. van Asbeck, informed Idenburg, and through him the government in The Hague, a number of times that, only were the Netherlands to take the side of Germany, might a Japanese attack on the colony become a reality.[13] It did not take long before war with Japan appeared a realistic prospect. On 10 August Van Asbeck sent a cipher to Java, to be forwarded by wire to The Hague, that the Japanese authorities had confidentially informed him that Japan considered Dutch resistance to a landing of British troops along the Scheldt an unfriendly act against Great Britain. He had been given to understand that Japan might retaliate by acting against the Netherlands Indies. On reading the telegram Idenburg, Pinke, and Michielsen contemplated a mobilization order. After weighing up the pros and cons they decided against such a move. In view of the way the population had reacted to the outbreak of the war they realized that mobilization could well result in 'great anxiety and unrest with all precarious consequences that went with

---

[10] Idenburg to Pleyte, 7-8-1914, NA, Kol. Geheim, Vb. 10-8-1914 N15.
[11] *De Locomotief*, 15-9-1914.
[12] *Sin Po*, cited in *De Locomotief*, 1-11-1917.
[13] Van Asbeck to Idenburg, 7-8-1914, 9-8-1914, NA, Kol. Geheim, Vb. 31-12-1914 T15.

it'.[14] Another cogent reason for them not to issue the order was the prospect that such a step might elicit questions from the Japanese government, to which Batavia could not give a satisfactory answer. The three came to the conclusion that the moment to decide on mobilization should be delayed till concrete information had reached them that Tokyo was fitting out an expeditionary force.

The following day the issue came up again. The telegraph station on Yap had been damaged by a British bombardment and there was a possibility that telegrams from Tokyo would no longer be forthcoming, a fear which proved unfounded. The colonial government felt cut off from the rest of the world. Idenburg and his staff did not preclude the fact that they would be deprived of essential information. The bombardment of the telegraph station on Yap also meant that the measures Idenburg had ordered at the outbreak of the war to be prepared for a Japanese invasion also seemed to have been vitiated. Idenburg had instructed the military Envoy in Tokyo, the Envoy in Peking, and the consuls in Shanghai and Manila to report to him every scrap of information that might indicate a Japanese move against the Netherlands Indies. It proved an idle instruction which did not ease anxiety. In Japan, where, Pinke claimed, 'miraculous results had been achieved by stealth and deceit', the absence of a naval expert was felt to be a great disadvantage, while no news from the consular agents elsewhere in Asia did not mean that people could breathe more easily.[15]

Once more it was decided not to mobilize, but to send a new telegram to Pleyte to ask him once again whether he still stood by his assurance of 8 August. The telegram was sent on 12 August. At last able to use the secret code developed at the beginning of the century, Pleyte could set the Governor General's mind at rest: Idenburg should 'not be uneasy about Corry and Willy'.[16] The message was the sign to slow down the military preparations, and to stop – on 17 August – the emergency purchases of food by the army.

Fears of Japanese intent lingered on as the war progressed, with German propaganda trying to highlight the dangers Japan siding with the Allied Powers posed to the Netherlands Indies. In February 1916 all this reached a climax when the contents became known of an article published in Japanese newspapers by Yosaburo Takekoshi, a former member of parliament, and founder of an Association for the Penetration of the Pacific entitled: 'The first

---

[14] Conferentie van Z.E. den Gouverneur-General met de Commandanten van Zee- en Landmacht, 11-8-1914 and 12-8-1914, NA, Kol. Geheim, Vb. 18-1-1915 P.
[15] Pinke to Idenburg, 1-11-1915, Idenburg to Pleyte, 24-12-1915, NA, Kol. Geheim, Vb. 8-3-1916 P3.
[16] Pleyte to Idenburg, 13-8-1914, NA, Kol. Geheim, Vb. 14-8-1914 A16.

step to our new naval policy'.[17] Even before the war Yosaburo Takekoshi had shown himself to be a proponent of a Japanese drive south and of the leading role Japan should play in the emancipation of the peoples of Asia. Yosaburo Takekoshi had visited the Netherlands Indies before the war and a correspondent of *De Locomotief* in Medan was sure that at the root of Takekoshi's fierce anti-Dutch attitude was the 'extremely unpleasant treatment' of Takekoshi during his trip to Java, when Dutch civil servants had first agreed to but then had prevented a meeting between Takekoshi and the Sunan of Surakarta.[18]

In his 1916 article, the idea of a Japanese conquest of at least part of the Archipelago was propagated in no uncertain terms. Yosaburo Takekoshi began his article by recalling the complaints made by European statesmen about the burden of the civilization missions the European states had taken on. Observing that Japan had assimilated Western civilization he wrote that Japan was prepared to help relieve the Europeans of this burden. The first step to be taken along this road was to free the Malay population which was living in miserable conditions under Dutch rule. Stating that at the outbreak of the World War German warships in search of Allied merchantmen had been supplied with coal in the Archipelago (which was not true, but had nevertheless been rumoured all over Asia), and recalling the complications about the bunkering of warships during the Russo-Japanese War, Yosaburo Takekoshi postulated that it did not necessarily have to form a danger to Japan were it to have a strong power nearby. What, however, always did present a threat was to have a weak nation in the vicinity which could not uphold its neutrality. The conclusion was that Japan should at least occupy Java and Sumatra, which would give it control over the Sunda Straits.

Yosaburo Takekoshi's article also fanned fears in another way. He not only called for an occupation of Java and Sumatra, but went further and suggested that, copying the practice of the Dutch, the Japanese government should conclude treaties with rebellious ethnic groups in the Archipelago, transforming their territory into a protectorate.[19] His views were supposed to have influenced many Japanese and were hotly debated in the press both in the Netherlands and the Netherlands Indies.[20] The following year *De Locomotief* recalled that Yosaburo Takekoshi's article had created an extraordinary commotion in the Dutch community in the colony.[21] Another factor at play was that some Japanese were sure that the German influence in the Netherlands

---

[17] A translation of Yosaburo Takekoshi's articles was published in the *Algemeen Handelsblad*, 24-2-1916. The translation was copied by *De Indische Gids* 1916:448-52.
[18] *De Locomotief*, 18-11-1916.
[19] *De Indische Gids*, 1916, I:449-52, 613; Van der Weijden 1916:8-9.
[20] *De Locomotief*, 25-8-1916.
[21] *De Locomotief*, 5-12-1917.

was great, presenting the fact that the husband of Queen Wilhelmina, Prince Hendrik, was a German as evidence. It was argued that, because of this, the Netherlands could well end up in the German camp, which would turn the Netherlands Indies into a German base in Asia. Japan which had driven the Germans from China and other parts of the Pacific could never allow this. One of the suggestions to prevent such a development from becoming a reality was that Japan should buy the Netherlands Indies.[22] Such discussions in Japan were followed with apprehension. The editors of the Chinese-Malay newspaper *Warna Warta* commented in November 1916 that they knew of no country which was so fearful as the Dutch. Were a Japanese warship to appear at Tanjung Priok, the government would certainly be afflicted by diarrhoea.[23]

In 1914 it was not before the end of August that people began to breath more easily. At that time *De Locomotief* wrote that it was becoming increasingly likely that the Netherlands could manage to stay out of the war. The reason the newspaper presented was feeble, and was still inspired by a misconception about the strength of the Dutch army: the nearer the moment to a decisive battle came, the more the small Dutch army was to become a factor of importance, which the belligerents could not afford to make their enemy.[24]

After the initial fright had ebbed somewhat the European Dutch community turned its energy towards the defence of the colony. Estate managers put their trucks and motor cars (complete with their drivers) at the disposal of the colonial army. Inspired by a combination of bravura and patriotism, coupled with a fear for domestic disturbances, the Dutch in their clubs and other meeting places began to discuss the establishment of a volunteer corps, for which the colonial government should provide the arms.

In early 1914 the growing concern about international developments had already triggered off the first plans to create such bodies. In Batavia this had even resulted in some commotion when a number of members of the Indische Partij had won places on the board of the newly constituted corps.[25] After the outbreak of the war, more people began to contemplate the establishment of volunteer corps. To some such an enterprise was nonsense. They said they understood that able-bodied men who had to look on idly in the colony while Holland might be attacked might want to actualize their feelings of patriotism, but pointed out that such persons could easily do so by temporarily signing up to the colonial army. This would be enough proof of the fact that such per-

---

[22] *China Press*, 9-8-1916, cited in *De Locomotief*, 30-8-1916.
[23] *Warna Warta*, cited in *Koloniaal Tijdschrift* 1917:251.
[24] *De Locomotief*, 24-8-1914.
[25] *De Expres*, 12-1-1914.

sons were prepared to die for their motherland.[26]

These voices of restraint were few and far between. Meetings were held all over Java and in the major European settlements in the other islands, nurturing patriotic feelings. In Lembang all adult European male inhabitants, thirty in total, left no doubt about their desire to join a newly established volunteer corps. The *Preanger-bode* remarked that it was to be 'small but strong'. Most of its prospective members were Boers who had taken refuge in Java and had experience of warfare in South Africa.[27] It would probably not be safe to say the same about the corps envisaged in Buitenzorg. In this city the initiative had come from civil servants employed at the General Secretariat and the other government offices located in the city, who wanted to do their bit in securing Dutch rule in the colony during those dangerous days. Women enlisted in the corps as well, not to fight should the need arise, but to serve as nurses with ambulances and in hospitals. In Bandung, Sukabumi and other cities the Red Cross organized ambulance classes and other courses to prepare women for their allotted task. There was one problem. Bandages were in short supply. In Holland an export ban had been issued on bandages and medicines. The Dutch government had done so without thinking about the Netherlands Indies, the *Nieuwe Rotterdamsche Courant* wrote in 1916.[28] Exports were resumed after the minister of the colonies had intervened.

Some of the initiatives taken were directed towards assisting the army in times of crisis either as their sole or as their major aim. Among these was a motor club envisaged in Surabaya. The club was supposed to function as a 'relay service'. Members had to carry messages for the army. The Vrijwillige Automobiel Korps (Voluntary Automobile Corps) had the same objective. It was limited to Dutch nationals who owned a car with at least four seats, which could be driven at least at a speed of 40 km/h, and had no difficulty in ascending a gradient of one in twelve. Four seats were required because a registration of private cars already begun by the army before the war had demonstrated that the army was not interested in cars with only two seats. Other corps were unquestionably established in anticipation of unrest among the population. In Bandung and in Malang, and probably also in some other cities, the organizations founded were Ordebonden (Leagues of Law and Order). This was certainly the case in North Sumatra, where Europeans feared that they would all be killed.[29]

In the establishment of volunteer corps and law and order leagues, much time and effort was poured into the drafting of rules and the designing of

---

[26] *De Locomotief*, 8-8-1914.
[27] *Preangerbode*, cited in *De Locomotief*, 10-8-1914.
[28] *Nieuwe Rotterdamsche Courant*, cited in *De Locomotief*, 13-9-1916.
[29] *De Locomotief*, 30-5-1916.

uniforms. In Sukabumi – where the inaugural meeting was opened by the *Assistent-Resident* with the cry 'Long live the Queen, Long live the Motherland, Long live the Colonies' – the choice was for a uniform resembling that of the colonial army. The main difference was that the volunteers were to have a turned-down collar instead of a stand-up one, and were to wear a bamboo hat. In Malang and Buitenzorg prospective volunteers were more exuberant. In Malang they decided to don a bamboo hat with an orange cockade as their distinguishing mark. Their colleagues in Buitenzorg wanted to adorn their bamboo hat with a carmine red ribbon.

Local Dutch civil servants looked with favour upon such initiatives taken by the Dutch European community. Batavia was rather dubious, especially when the corps envisaged were supposed to lead a semi-independent existence, thereby dodging full army control. One of the reasons for concern was that people who wanted to create volunteer corps still cherished a romantic recollection of the Boer War. Army headquarters had a different view. It was now argued that lack of both discipline and military training had been the cause of the downfall of the Boers.[30] One of the victims of the restraint shown by the authorities was the League of Law and Order in Bandung. Almost three hundred men had registered. Seventy-six of them were members of the Union of Non-Commissioned Officers. The League of Law and Order had to be disbanded within a month, even though the *Resident* had welcomed its establishment. He had gone so far as to vow to take personal responsibility to see that the weapons requested from the government would be used only in a 'proper way'. His superiors thought differently. On the advice of Michielsen, a request for recognition was turned down. A new effort was made to establish a body that tailored to the set conditions but the initial gusto had evaporated. Only thirty people enlisted. None of the initiators of the original plan was among them. They were only prepared to join if they received the rank they themselves had assumed in the League of Law and Order. The sarcastic comment was that it would have made the League look like the Venezuelan army.[31]

Other volunteer corpses, including those in Buitenzorg, Sukabumi, Padang, and Medan were recognized, as was the new one in Bandung. They received financial support from Batavia to help contribute to the training of their members. Officers were allowed to buy pistols and sabres at a discount. A small number of bullets was provided for free for training purposes. Such corps were not large. The one in Sukabumi had 150 members. That in Medan consisted of about 200 members.

The animo to form armed volunteer corps faded away in the middle of

---

[30] *Java-Bode*, cited in *De Indische Gids* 1914, II:1733.
[31] *De Locomotief*, 26-11-1914.

September, when it transpired that the Netherlands had still not become involved in the war and no native disturbances of any significance had erupted. Calls to found them grew far less and existing corps in the course of time became invisible. There was no money to maintain uniforms and arms and some corpses had difficulty in actually getting their members participate in exercises. Those which did survive turned exercises into pleasant social outings. Brass bands accompanied members on marches through towns, before the members assembled in the local club, where afterwards they had pea soup. The meetings of the Medan corps was described as 'a nasi goreng and cask beer gathering of friends' in May 1916.[32] It was considered absolutely incapable of suppression any unrest in the region.

Energies now turned to campaigns to help the *noodlijdenden*, the destitute, in Holland, of whom it had become clear from the news telegrams there were many. The general opinion was that living conditions in Holland had become extremely difficult. A letter to the editor in *De Locomotief* in early August, at a time when reports about conditions in Holland were still scarce, spoke about a 'general panic' and about everybody, including those who lived far away from the theatre of war being forced 'to fight for self-preservation, namely to ensure they did not die because of lack of foodstuffs, of which the prices have now risen extravagantly'.[33] Within weeks even more alarmist stories began to circulate. These warranted a new request for information by Idenburg in order to put the minds of the population in the colony at rest. On 24 August, referring to newspaper reports about the scarcity of foodstuffs and the mass unemployment in Holland, he wired Pleyte and ask for a reliable picture of the situation. Using the information he received, Idenburg had an announcement published in the *Javasche Courant*. It announced that the minister of the colonies had wired him that the financial and economic problems created by the war were diminishing, but that because of a lack of raw materials and export prohibitions unemployment was growing.

At this moment the first initiatives had already been taken to collect money for the destitute in Holland and for the 'thousands upon thousands in the country and especially in the big cities without work'.[34] To help such people *De Locomotief*, the first to do so, issued an appeal, suggesting that people in the Netherlands Indies should follow the example of railway employees in Holland, who set aside a small portion of their wages to assist the poor. The contributions had to be sent to *De Locomotief*, mentioning 'For the Netherlands'. In September when the first Dutch newspapers with reports about the situation in Holland reached the colony, the campaign was intensified. One circular

---

[32] *De Locomotief*, 30-5-1916.
[33] *De Locomotief*, 6-8-1914.
[34] *De Locomotief*, 25-8-1914.

letter claimed that conditions in the motherland were far worse than had been imagined. It was believed that unemployment and mobilization had taken a high toll. Some must even have thought that the reservists called up for military service did not receive any pay at all, or if they did no more than a trifle:

> And then we ask ourselves what do the women and children have to live on? – and who takes care of the old, and the infirm, in short of all whose breadwinners watch over our independence, and because of this cannot provide for their relatives? And this is only the beginning, how long will it last? Do not forget: the winter is almost here. Compared with this silent want, this inglorious suffering of hunger and cold, we in the Indies do sit in Abraham's lap.[35]

Later, when the childrens festival of Sinterklaas was approaching, this was used as an extra occasion to appeal to give generously. In the misery that had gripped Holland, the children's parties there would certainly be less festive than in the colony.

A fever to do something for the destitute in Holland seemed to grip the Dutch community. Money-boxes were placed in shops, restaurants and clubs, and even at the pavilion 'The woman' at the Colonial Exhibition. Apart from this, a great many activities were organized which had as an additional bonus that the boredom of everyday life was alleviated a little. In Cirebon, and this city was no exception, there was, as one of the inhabitants described this, a 'ground swell' of initiatives. People, 'even the most shy and modest artists' were busy rehearsing Dutch country dances, planning a soccer match, or preparing for cabaret, theatre, and music performances. Cirebon which had appeared moribund seemed to have come to life. Its inhabitants rejoiced in the quarrels between the various committees which were planning similar events.[36]

Many responded favourably to the appeals all over the Netherlands Indies to help the destitute in Holland. In Yogyakarta the civil militia parted with eight thousand guilders. In Batavia the proceeds of the annual horse-races were reserved for the cause. In Semarang a painter, Th.B. van Lelyveld, offered two of his paintings as a prize in a special lottery. In the same city, the proceeds of an aeroplane-merry-go-round were also earmarked for the poor in Holland, while a standholder at the Colonial Exhibition had an advertisement published in the newspapers promising that when a customer bought a certain number of cigars, he would put aside one-tenth of the money received to help people in Holland. In Surabaya one-fifth of the proceeds of the film 'Room no. 30', a piquant picture, people then thought, after a story by the French *vaude-*

---

[35] Circular letter, cited in *De Locomotief*, 15-9-1914.
[36] *De Locomotief*, 11-11-1914, 17-11-1914.

ville author Georges Feydeau, was set aside.

Soldiers were not left behind. In Semarang European soldiers in the garrison issued an appeal to their comrades. They stated that 'though our income is not large, and our pay is small we can (and let us all do so) set aside a trifle for the many families which have seen their breadwinners leave to fulfil their duty to their Motherland'.[37] In Surabaya the Navy organized a special day of which the proceeds went to the destitute in Holland. On the cultural side visitors were entertained by music of the sailors' pluckband 'Stella Bella di Soerabaja' (Stella Bella in Surabaya) and by Ambonese soldiers performing Alfurese dances. For the more military inclined there were models of German howitzers to be admired and they could attend a machine-gun demonstration. Theatre groups of soldiers or non-commissioned officers, such as De Vriendenkring, Circle of Friends, in Magelang, and Aceh in Banda Aceh, held special performances. In Salatiga the association of European non-commissioned officers Ons Belang, Our Interest, asked their members to surrender one day's pay.

Collections pure and simple were not forgotten. In Buitenzorg women went from door to door 'to ask people, albeit without any pressure' to part with a monthly donation.[38] Among those who promised them a 'liberal monthly contribution' were Michielsen and Idenburg. Idenburg committed one percent of his salary. In Semarang the example of the Buitenzorg ladies failed to strike a chord. It was reasoned that it was much hotter there and walking around for any length of time might demand too much of women. It would be better to ask employees of trading firms to do the hard work. Because of the war they had time enough to spare. Even so, and this was much applauded by a journalist from *De Locomotief*, women in Semarang did raise money. They did so not by going from door to door, but by collecting money at outdoor cafés and similar venues.

Clothes were also collected. The Salvation Army did so, and in Java a Mrs Ter Horst-den Boer put an appeal in newspapers asking for used wearing apparel and underclothing. She was convinced that many Europeans could easily spare some clothes. On arrival in the colony most had brought along clothing too warm to wear in a tropical climate. A *naai-commissie*, sewing committee, in Utrecht reacted with pleasure when a shipment of three crates reached them. 'Overcoats, men's and boys' clothes, children's shoes, precisely everything that was needed most' had been sent. Unemployed seamstresses had been engaged to transform old and new clothes into 'practical articles of dress which will be distributed among destitute families'.[39]

---

[37] *De Locomotief*, 2-9-1914.
[38] *De Locomotief*, 15-9-1914.
[39] *De Locomotief*, 19-2-1915.

Civilians in the Netherlands Indies organized fancy fairs, soirées variées, concerts, and cabarets. Sometimes professional artists were the main attraction, like the negro singer and dancer Jumbo in Semarang, but more often than not civil servants and other dilettantes did the lion's share. Soccer matches, sometimes with teams of European civil servants taking part, tombolas, bazaars, and children's parties and shows, all with the same aim, completed the picture.

Outside Java people were busily involved in similar activities. In Celebes the *Makassaarsche Courant* issued an appeal for prizes for a lottery. In Medan a cinema parted with its proceeds on Queen's Birthday. The Association for Women's Suffrage in the same city organized a collection in the plantation belt. Within a few days 5,000 guilders had been collected; a sum which took *De Locomotief* weeks to collect. In the weeks to come the Ladies' Committee, as it was referred to, remained among the most successful in raising money. In Medan, the Deli Automobile Club, in an act of almost perfect neutrality, also donated a hundred guilders each to the Red Cross in Holland, Belgium, Germany, France, and Great Britain.

In the middle of September, after news about the relief committee established in The Hague at the instigation of Queen Wilhelmina had reached Java, the scattered initiatives were coordinated. In Batavia the Centrale Comité voor Hulpverschaffing (Central Committee for Relief) was constituted. Chaired by J.B. van der Houven van Oordt, Deputy Chairman of the Coucil of the Indies, it counted Michielsen and Pinke among its members. Idenburg assumed the office of honorary chairman. As the committee was intended to be a national one, symbolizing the unity of all the inhabitants of Netherlands Indies irrespective of race, a Javanese and a Chinese also sat on the board. Simultaneously Dutch civil servants were asked to support similar initiatives at their posts. The response was great. Local committees were founded all over the Archipelago. In Java, following the example set by the central committee, Javanese and Chinese notables became involved. The former were usually represented by the Regent or the head of a district, and sometimes also by the most important religious functionary of a regency, the head *penghulu*. In Yogyakarta the Prime Minister, Ario Adipati Pangeran Danoeredjo, and the Captain of the Chinese, Yap Hong Sing, sat on the local committee. In Surabaya the Regent, R.T.A. Niti Adiningrat, and the Major of the Chinese, Han Tjiong King, were among the members. The same happened with the special women's committees which were formed. Members of their boards included the wife of the Regent and the wife of the head of the local Chinese community.

Occasionally Arabs also found their way onto the committees. In Surabaya it was their Captain, Syech Ahmad bin Abdoellah Bobsaid, who joined. He energetically set about his task, calling together meetings in the local Arab club, Al Arabijjah, where those attending, about a hundred persons, were presented with a subscription list they could sign if they wanted to contribute. Arabs and Chinese also organized separate drives for money to help the poor in Holland. Sometimes the results of the fund-raising among Foreign Orientals were impressive. In Semarang the Chinese Major titular donated 10,000 guilders. Nevertheless, it is questionable whether all Chinese donated as generously as they might have done. Explaining the poor results of a collection in Cirebon a Chinese trader in the town pointed out that the Chinese (and the Arabs) could have afforded much more, but that they were discouraged from doing so by the discrimination to which they were still subjected. The correspondent of the *De Locomotief* added that this view mirrored that of the 'educated section of the Chinese community'.[40] In Yogyakarta in early October at a meeting of Arabs and people from Bengal, 12,125 guilders was collected. An equally large sum – 13,500 guilders – was raised by the Armenian community in Surabaya. In Surabaya another joint Arab-Bengali drive resulted in 23,310 guilders.

Such sums were much larger than the proceeds of many of the European initiatives. These usually generated a few hundred guilders at most. Some Dutch people gave generously, and in this respect the plantation belt in Sumatra stood out, but contrary to what the many initiatives taken might have suggested, Dutch people on the whole were not overly generous. Newspaper editors and correspondents who reported about what happened in their cities, and in doing so were also inspired by a certain scorn of the rich, often pointed out that contributions usually came from the less well-to-do and that rich people were very reluctant to part with their money. One of the reasons for the disappointing results was that the Dutch in the colony feared bad times ahead and were determined to hold on to their money. They were reluctant to pay the higher entrance fees for special theatrical performances and other events, or stayed home because they did not consider the cause important enough to brave the heavy rains, which were also to ruin bazaars and other open-air events.

The destitute in Holland remained a major focus for charity, but it was not long before additional causes thrust themselves to the fore. Newspaper reports and telegrams about the German advance in Belgium and about the many Belgian refugees who fled to Holland made people increasingly aware of how stricken by the war Belgium was. Belgium Committees were constituted, and collections and charitable performances organized for the Belgian Red Cross, for financing an auto-ambulance, for widows and orphans of Belgian soldiers, for destitute Belgian infants (this organization had its headquarters in Holland and a branch in Batavia) or more specific for the destitute Flemish population.

[40]   *De Locomotief*, 25-2-1915.

Italian patriotism in the Netherlands Indies. Trade mark (7998) of an Italian export company. (*Javasche Courant* 1916.)

Sometimes the Belgian consuls took the lead. Among their initiatives was the sale of lace made by Belgian war widows in the larger cities of Java. There were even anonymous gifts to allow Belgians in the Netherlands Indies to travel home. In early December Yogyakarta was the scene of *Belgen-dagen* (Belgians Days). Women wearing a cockade of the Belgian national colours made a collection. Many took part, and for some among the general public this proved too much. It was reported that at the club old men playing cards 'cursed the war more than ever before'.[41] The proceeds of the Yogyakarta *Belgen-dagen* were modest: 500 guilders. The idea of sending an ambulance to the battlefields in Europe was contemplated. With this purpose in mind, in Batavia an Insulinde Red Cross was founded. The effort did not bear fruit. The charity network was far-flung and events were even organized by a Netherlands Indies Relief

---

[41] *De Locomotief,* 9-12-1914.

Committee for the Destitute on Curaçao, an island where the consequences of the war were far worse than in the Netherlands Indies. In Batavia the proceeds of the Pasar Gambir Fair of 1915 went to this cause.

Such noble intentions were thwarted by chauvinism. Not all Dutchmen were in favour of collecting money for Holland. The objectors argued that it should not be forgotten that the colony had also suffered from the economic effects of the war. There might come a moment that people would regret money having been sent to Europe, as large sums would be needed to support a growing number of unemployed and needy in the Netherlands Indies itself. The colonial economy should in no way be weakened by transmitting money to Holland.[42] Others came up with a compromise, suggesting that part of the money should go to Holland and an equal or lesser amount should be set aside to be used should an emergency arise in the Netherlands Indies. To accommodate such voices, at its inception the Central Committee for Relief had already stated that were the colony to suffer in the same way as Holland was doing the money collected was to be used in the Netherlands Indies; not precluding that some of the money would go to the people in the colony who experienced financial problems because of the war. In some cities two subscription lists circulated; one to give money to the destitute in Holland; the other to give money to the recently unemployed in the colony. To cater for all and everybody's wishes, it was even suggested having three different collecting boxes placed at main roads (to be removed at night): one for Europeans in Holland; one for Europeans in the Netherlands Indies; and one for natives.[43]

Other Dutch people only wanted to give money to help their poor compatriots, or accused the Belgians collecting money of thinking about their fellow-countrymen only. Consequently, in Surabaya it was initially decided that people were to be given the choice to decide themselves for whom they wanted to give a donation in a door-to-door collection: the poor in Holland; the destitute in the colony, or the Belgians. Later, yet another solution was found. Money was collected for 'destitute Dutch people and Belgian refugees in Holland'. The destitute Dutchmen in Belgium, on whom a committee in Brussels had taken pity formed a special category. Money for them was also collected in the Netherlands Indies.

In total in the remaining months of 1914 almost 400,000 guilders was raised for the destitute in Holland. In March 1916 the amount had reached 900,000 guilders. By that time indigenous Indonesians, Chinese, and Europeans were again enthusiastically organizing charity functions for victims of natural disasters in Java and in Holland. Severe flooding in Java in early 1916 increased the pressure to transform committees established to help the destitute in Holland

[42] *Bataviaasch Nieuwsblad,* cited in *De Locomotief,* 31-8-1914.
[43] *Oetoesan Hindia,* 27-10-1914.

into general committees which could spend part of the money collected in the Netherlands Indies. The Curaçao Relief Committee was disbanded in July 1916.

As had been the case during the Boer War and the Russo-Japanese War, the attitude of the public and of the press was one of the main concerns of authorities in Holland and in the Netherlands Indies. Films, plays, and music came under close scrutiny by the central and regional colonial authorities in their drive to be assured that foreign nationals were not offended or did not became agitated. The commander of the army banned the playing of 'It is a long way to Tipperary' by army music corpses in March 1915. In Batavia the local censor forbade war films and newsreels showing marching soldiers and members of the European royal houses. A film about Napoleon was also off limits. The fact that such restrictions were not completely ridiculous was shown in January 1915 when Germans in Bandung took offence at a film they considered an insult to their Kaiser.[44] The ban may also have been inspired by the fear of fights in cinemas between over-excited Europeans of different nationalities. The showing of newsreels was allowed at restricted viewings with only congenial nationalities in the auditorium, occasions often used for fund-raising. One such event, in the Palace Cinema in Batavia in March 1915 to raise money for Red Cross societies of the Allied showed that such fears were not unfounded. *De Locomotief* wrote about a' singing and whistling demonstration' against Germany. It was one of the moments seized upon by Dutch people who were not caught up in the anti-German mood in the colony to testify to their more moderate opinions. What in their opinion had made the event the more repugnant was that the Deputy Chairman of the Council of the Indies, the commander of the colonial army and other senior Dutch civil and military authorities had been invited by the Belgian Consul and had been forced to witness the manifestation of Allied patriotism. *De Locomotief* called the event one of those incidents which touched the seamy side of our neutrality.[45] In Batavia uniforms were also forbidden on stage.

Films, plays, and music were a minor irritant. Much more attention was paid to newspapers. One of the major fears of the authorities was that a vocal press or a press in which ship and troop movements were reported would result in problems for the Netherlands in its relations with the great powers of the day. One difference was that since 1906, when the 'Regulations on printed matters in the Netherlands Indies' dating from 1856 had been changed, the power of the authorities to intervene had markedly decreased. The colonial government no longer had the power to punish authors of articles which

---

[44] *De Locomotief,* 8-1-1915, 15-1-1915.
[45] *De Locomotief,* 13-3-1915, 18-3-1915.

were considered to be politically dangerous, or to take special action against publishers who had made such publications possible. As in Holland, the authorities could only bring a lawsuit and had become fully dependent on the considerations of the civil court.

The reforms of 1906 had been a gesture to placate the European public in the Netherlands Indies and to satisfy the liberal disposition of the Parliament in The Hague. The new legislation initially benefited most and above all the Dutch-language press. There were Chinese and native newspapers at that time, but in general they were well behaved and did not pose the colonial administration many problems. Within a year this changed. An increasingly bold native, Chinese and Indo-European press gave the colonial authorities cause to regret the new freedoms which had been created. There was much lamentation among government officials in the Netherlands Indies about politicians in The Hague, who were unfamiliar with conditions in the colony and did not realize that the natives needed a strong hand. These ill-advised people had, as the Council of the Indies put it in 1913, 'in an ill-starred moment' removed the provisions which had allowed the government to act against an unruly press.[46]

Before August 1914 the presence of the native press had become the principal argument wielded by those in favour of reintroducing some form of administrative justice; the more so after Idenburg, unable to put an end to the publications of the Indische Party, and seeing no other possibility to stem the flow of its agitation, had decided to banish its leaders. It was only after the war had started that the exploits of Dutch-language newspapers were mentioned by the colonial government and the regional civil servants as a major reason to look for more effective instruments to keep the press in check. A press that refrained from offending belligerent nations and did not hold any news that could endanger Dutch neutrality was what the government rather optimistically had in mind. The journalists of the Dutch-language newspapers wanted something else. Informing their readers about the course of the war and expressing prevailing feelings in society, was their aspiration.

The two goals did not tally. As late as May 1917, the British Ambassador in The Hague noted that the Dutch authorities did everything they could to prevent the papers stirring up the people, who he believed were 'strongly anti-Hun'. He observed that the Dutch government 'always lives in terror lest some incident should occur which would carry the population off their feet'.[47] A similar fear had the colonial authorities in its grip. To cope, at the outbreak of the war Batavia and The Hague had not confined themselves to general warnings about the risk the nation ran if 'excessive sympathy' was shown for

---

[46] Advice of the Council of the Indies of 8-11-1913, NA, Kol. Openbaar, Vb. 17-9-1915 46.
[47] Townley to Cecil, 30-5-1917, PRO FO 800 195.

one or other of the belligerents. They also had tried to keep journalists who disregarded such appeals in check.

In the Netherlands Indies the Secretary General of the colonial administration in the middle of August sent a circular to the newspapers in which he outlined the special role the press should play in upholding neutrality. He wrote that though the Governor General realized that it was 'completely unnecessary' to do so, Idenburg had nevertheless requested him to inform the press that he trusted that journalists would be willing to observe 'great objectivity' in writing about the war.[48] A section of the press was not impressed. They doubted whether the restraint editors were asked to show mattered much. World Powers intent on declaring war on the Netherlands did not need any excuse. Nevertheless, some editors-in-chief vowed to cooperate. One of them was J.E. Stokvis of *De Locomotief*. Using the occasion to lash out at colleagues who thought differently, and who by chance he did not happen to like, Stokvis pointed out that deliberately insulting a belligerent was despicable. It was not justified by exalted references to the freedom of the press, as resorted by some of his fellow-editors. At all times 'journalistic licentiousness' posed a danger. This was all the more true with the war now in full swing. On another occasion, Stokvis argued that if the powers were ill-disposed towards the Netherlands and they could not take issue with the correct attitude of the Dutch government, they would use a critical or insulting press as their excuse to act. It was the duty of the press to support the government in guarding neutrality and avoid everything that could give a potential aggressor a cause for complaint. This was all the more a necessity 'in a country where the international contacts are many and the irritability runs high'. The press should show restraint and caution at a time in which its influence could potentially be greater, but also more fatal.[49]

It proved to be extremely difficult to persuade the press in Holland and the Dutch-language press in the Netherlands Indies to refrain from publishing articles which offended nationals of the belligerent nations. Almost from the outbreak of the war the German Acting Consul-General, Windels, protested about articles and cartoons which depicted Germany as the aggressor. As in Holland, many Dutch people in the Netherlands Indies blamed Germany for the war. The invasion of Belgium and the horror stories about the conduct of German troops in Belgium had greatly contributed to this attitude (see also Elout 1920). A 'pure-blooded Dutchman' wrote on a postcard in September to the German Consul that all good Dutchmen hated Krauts.[50] The German Consul received more letters of this ilk. After he lodged a protest, the police

---

[48] *De Locomotief*, 14-8-1914.
[49] *De Locomotief*, 17-10-1914, 5-12-1914.
[50] Windels to De Graeff, 29-9-1914, NA, Kol. Geheim, Vb. 18-12-1914 P24.

were instructed to try to identify the sender. In one case, but there may have been more such instances, a copy of an anonymous letter, with the contested passages rendered illegible, was distributed. A reward of one hundred guilders was offered.[51]

The anti-German mood did not mean that the Dutch had suddenly become pro-British. The Boer War was still fresh in people's memories. In the Netherlands Indies, probably the same could be said as Louis Raemaeckers of *De Telegraaf* told a journalist on the *Morning Post* about public opinion in Holland: German defeats were greeted with the 'Marseillaise' and not with 'Rule Britannia'.[52] According to a reader of De Locomotief, the fact that many blamed Germany was occasioned by the same 'sense of justice that the Dutch had felt when trampled on by the English-Transvaal War' and who had been deeply shocked in August 1914 by the perfidity of the German nation against Belgium.[53]

The Dutch colonial press which in times of peace could not be said to have been a model of moderation mirrored these sentiments. Using strong words Dutch-language newspapers in the Netherlands Indies attacked the Kaiser and the crimes supposedly committed by the German army. Their particular 'tropical style' contributed to the popularity of their newspapers, but for the senior Dutch administrators who had to cope with the consequences it was not easy to come to terms with this. In November 1916 the Attorney-General was to postulate that editors of the more important Dutch-language newspapers were 'so busy that in the hot climates where they execute their profession, after a shorter or a somewhat longer period, they became virtual neurotics'.[54]

Of the largest newspapers, the *Het Nieuws van den Dag voor Nederlandsch-Indië* (The News of the Day of the Netherlands Indies), the *Bataviaasch Nieuwsblad* of Karel Zaalberg, and the *Soerabaiasch Handelsblad* of Van Geuns and G.J. Boon followed an anti-German course. B.J.O. Schrieke was to qualify them as 'rabidly Allied'.[55] Throughout the war *Het Nieuws van den Dag* remained one of the newspapers which most disturbed the colonial administration with its vehemently anti-German tone. Its editor in 1914, Karel Wijbrands, made no secret of his hatred of Germans. He wrote that 'he would like to strangle a German after every dessert, and would like to hear his death-rattle' (Baars and Sneevliet 1991:60). His successor in 1915, W.K.S. van Haastert, likewise well-known for the derogatory way in which he wrote about Indonesians, also left no stone unturned to lash out against Germans. In the view of the authorities,

---

[51] *De Locomotief,* 16-3-1915.
[52] *De Locomotief,* 14-1-1916.
[53] *De Locomotief,* 9-11-1914.
[54] Attorney-General to Van Limburg Stirum, 27-11-1916, NA, Kol. Openbaar, Vb. 14-6-1919 26
[55] Note Schrieke 30-4-1917, NA, Kol. Openbaar, Vb. 14-2-1918 38.

Het Nieuws van den Dag used the 'most offensive qualifications' and bore witness to a 'pitiful one-sidedness'.[56] Only the *Bataviaasch Handelsblad* followed a pro-German editorial policy. Among its contributors, writing under a pseudonym, was Emil Helfferich (Helfferich 1948:276). The British retaliated. After some time the *Bataviaasch Handelsblad* was denied access to Reuter's telegrams (Bosma 1995:169). In Semarang *De Locomotief* tried to strike up a moderate, balanced tone. From the outbreak of the war and true to his convictions, its editor-in-chief, Stokvis, did his utmost to remain impartial. In explaining his position he made a distinction, and in this he was not the only one, between the German people, who were to be admired for their cultural and economic achievements, and the Prussians. It was the latter who had to be feared, and who made a German victory a danger to Holland and the Netherlands Indies. A defeat of Germany was equally to be deplored as this would mean the ruin of German culture.[57]

Stubbornly Stokvis refused to condemn the Germans as the only nation capable of extreme violence in a war, even when in the first months of the war the facts seemed to prove him wrong. His efforts only enraged some of his readers. A French reader – *un ami* – took offence at his observation that it would be better to wait and see how the French and British soldiers behaved in enemy territory before coming to the conclusion that 'war plunder' was an exclusively German disposition. *Un ami* wrote that the French had not murdered women, children, old people, and priests when Algerians and Tunisians had fired on their troops. They also had not reacted in such a way in the Crimea, Syria, or Indochina, nor in Morocco where boiling oil had been poured on French troops. A Dutch military man agreed with Stokvis. In doing so he provided some insight into how the Dutch army behaved. He claimed that it was standard practice in the Dutch colonial army after it had encircled a house or a fortification of 'subversives' to riddle it with bullets when a warning to come out into the open was not obeyed, not bothering whether women and children might still be in the house. He stressed that such behaviour was part and parcel of the entourage of war. The difference with what had transpired in Belgium was that there the incidents had happened after an enemy place had already been taken.[58] Other readers took offence at Stokvis's reaction to the First Battle of Ypres in October and November 1914. German shelling was widely blamed for the destruction of incomparable historical monuments in the city. Stokvis, refusing to promote the idea that 'plundering of old cities was an exclusively German undertaking' in *De Locomotief*, reacted by pointing out that Allied troops had done the same at Dixmude. A discussion followed whether Dixmude was 'a beautiful old city'

---

[56] Monsanto to Van Limburg Stirum, 15-1-1917, NA, Kol. Geheim, Mr. 1917/16x.
[57] *De Locomotief*, 19-9-1914, 29-10-1914.
[58] *De Locomotief*, 9-11-1914, 11-11-1914, 13-11-1914, 14-11-1914.

or a simple village devoid of any monuments, and about what had occasioned the initial damage to the town, an Allied or a German bombardment.[59] The anti-German newspapers also did not take kindly to the editorial policy of *De Locomotief*. *Het Nieuws van den Dag* accused *De Locomotief* of having yielded to German influence and indirectly – this was the conclusion Stokvis drew from the fact that *Het Nieuws van den Dag* had deliberately mentioned the first names of the journalists of *De Locomotief* – of being Jewish.[60]

In a sense the Germans who had already taken up residence in the Netherlands Indies before the outbreak of the war felt trapped. In 1916 the *Hamburger Nachrichten* published a letter from a German trader in Surabaya. He wrote that because of anti-German sentiments among the Dutch in the Netherlands Indies, many Germans intended to leave the colony once the war was over.[61] Confronted with an anti-German public opinion and a generally hostile Dutch-language press, the German community launched its own periodical *Die Deutsche Wacht, Niederländisch-Indische Monatschrift für Kolonialpolitik, Volkswirtschaft und Völkerrecht*. The first issue appeared on 17 January 1915, the birthday of the Kaiser. Its publisher was a bulwark of German patriotism which had been founded on the same day, the Deutscher Bund in Niederländisch-Indien, and was granted recognition as a legal organization by the colonial government two month later. President of the Deutscher Bund was Theodor Victor Zimmermann. Deputy President was Emil Helfferich. At the end of the year 873 Germans had joined the Deutscher Bund. Twelve hundred people had subscribed to *Die Deutsche Wacht*.[62]

Finding a printer for *Die Deutsche Wacht* had not been an easy job. Dutch printing houses did not want to have anything to do with the German initiative. Finally the Dutch company G. Kolff and Co. declared it was prepared to take on the job (Mohr 1948:274-5). In the articles in it much of the blame for the war was put on the unfair British reaction to Germany's rise in the world as a political and economic power. To justify the publication of *Die Deutsche Wacht*, it was explained that before the war no need had ever been felt for such a special publication. Germans and Austrians had been quite happy with the Dutch newspapers. With public opinion turning against Germany and Austria-Hungary, the situation had changed. The Germanic voice had to be heard. Nevertheless, it gave a reassurance that in appreciation of the hospitality enjoyed by the German community in the Netherlands Indies, *Die Deutsche Wacht* would show restraint.

Die Deutsche Wacht was not the only German initiative to propagate the

---

[59] *De Locomotief*, 21-1-1915, 23-1-1915.
[60] *Het Nieuws van den Dag*, 8-8-1916, cited in *De Locomotief*, 11-8-1916.
[61] *De Locomotief*, 26-6-1916.
[62] *De Locomotief*, 17-5-1916.

German point of view. Around the same time it was launched, the first issue of *Oorlogsberichten uit Duitsche Bladen* (War Reports from German Papers) appeared in Surabaya. Its editor was W. Müller. Not surprisingly *De Locomotief*, referring to the biased reporting on the war in the Netherlands Indies, welcomed its publication.[63] However, such initiatives did not mean that the European community had been devoid of information highlighting the position of the Central Powers. After the first mail from Holland had reached the colony, reports could be copied from German and Austrian newspapers. Another source was the German news agency Wolff (which reached Java by mail, meaning that the Wolff war telegrams were at times published with a delay of two months) and the *Ostasiatische Lloyd*, published in Shanghai. In Surabaya Van Geuns had been succeeding in obtaining 'German telegrams' from Shanghai since the beginning of September. He claimed that this cost the *Soerabaiasch Handelsblad* between 1,300 and 1,400 guilders per month. In view of this Van Geuns accepted financial assistance from the German consulate in that city. Later *De Locomotief* suggested that he had been bought by the Germans. Van Geuns persisted in claiming that he had concluded a purely business deal which had not influenced the editorial policy of the *Soerabaiasch Handelsblad*.[64]

The position taken by many of the Dutch-language newspapers also bothered Idenburg. He was repeatedly confronted with protests from the German mission, while *Residents* received complaints by the local German consuls. Idenburg feared that an anti-German press could well endanger neutrality. It did not take him long to find out that there was little that the colonial authorities could do. In Holland and the Netherlands Indies charges were brought against journalists and authors on the grounds of their anti-German writings. Usually acquittal followed or at most a very light sentence, even when the public prosecution had demanded one year's imprisonment. In the Netherlands Indies Idenburg could try to have journalists convicted for a violation of the articles in the Penal Code which made the dissemination of hatred punishable by law. Among the offences listed, these so-called *haatzaai* articles covered the generation and stimulation of feelings of hostility, hatred, or contempt 'between different groups of the population of Dutch subjects or *Residents* of the Netherlands Indies'. This formula had been deliberately chosen in the belief that by speaking about groups the article would cover conflicts between the numerous distinct groups which made up colonial society.

In May 1915 the High Court of the Netherlands Indies dashed these hopes completely. The court interpreted the word groups in such a way that it did

---

[63] *De Locomotief*, 28-1-1915.
[64] *De Locomotief*, 1-2-1915, 4-2-1915.

not refer to the many groups, distinguishable by religion, ethnic origin or what ever other criterion used, but to the three formal legal categories that made up colonial society: Europeans, Foreign Orientals and natives. Significantly the High Court had ruled in this way not in a case that concerned an article in the press that could have upset the relations between Dutchmen, Indo-Europeans, Chinese, or natives, for which the *haatzaai* articles had been devised, but in dealing with one which was imbued with an insulting, anti-German tone. The High Court overturned a decision of the Court of Justice of Batavia of January 1915, which had sentenced the editor of *Het Nieuws van den Dag*, G. van Loon, to eight days' imprisonment for publishing an article in November the previous year. In it Van Loon had compared the treatment of German and Austrian women and children by the British authorities in the Straits Settlements to the fate of the civil population of Louvain, who after occupying German troops had been fired at on 25 August and transported to Germany to work there as labourers: 'They were left no choice by the modern Huns. Are the English not aware that there still exists something like an eye for an eye, a tooth for a tooth. If yes, why not practise this maxim at the present time?' The Batavian court had passed the sentence because in its opinion the article had aroused or promoted feelings of hatred and animosity between Belgians, Germans, Austrians, and Britons residing in the Netherlands Indies. The High Court argued that under the term 'groups' could only be understood groups that existed legally at the time of the proclamation of the *haatzaai* articles. It was of the opinion that the public prosecution had – taking the chance circumstances in force at the time of the prosecution as a starting point – given a wrong and arbitrary explanation of the term groups.[65]

The ruling of the High Court put the colonial administration in an awkward position. Before May 1915 it had succeeded in having newspapers moderate their tone by threatening them with legal action. This approach could no longer be used. Newspapers were now free to lash out in an increasingly aggressive tine against Germany. Batavia had lost the legal means to act against such articles. This was made patently obvious when the German consulate drew attention to an article published in *Het Nieuws van den Dag* at the end of October 1915, in which the Germans were called 'riff-raff [...] excommunicated by the whole of the civilized world because of the massacres at Louvain, at Dinant etc. [...]. [B]eing accessory to the butchering of the Armenian population', their hands dripping 'with the blood of innocent murdered victims!'[66] Windels protested that the newspaper had heaped the 'worst possible insults on the German people'.[67] He requested the matter be

---

[65] See for the decision of the High Court, *Indisch Tijdschrift van het Recht* 1915:643-53.
[66] *Het Nieuws van den Dag*, 27-10-1915.
[67] Windels to Hulshoff Pol, 29-10-1915, NA, Kol. Openbaar, Vb. 13-4-1916 26.

prosecuted. Reluctantly the Attorney-General had to conclude that the ruling of the High Court had made it highly unlikely that a court case would have any success.[68] Windels was not pleased. In 1916 a number of times he sent a letter of complaint to the colonial administration deploring the 'increasingly more offensive inflammatory press attacks' on Germany in the Netherlands Indies. Windels could not believe that the *haatzaai* articles were unusable. What was written in the newspapers was of such a nature that it created distrust of law-abiding Germans in the Netherlands Indies.[69] Anew Van Limburg Stirum and his advisers considered what action they should take. Once more they decided against legal steps.

Idenburg felt fairly sure that he was faced with a very serious problem. In his view abusive anti-German articles might well become a matter of life and death of the nation. Windels was not the only one to have protested. From Vienna Idenburg had learned that the Austrian government was far from pleased with reports about the war in the Netherlands Indies. Anxiously Idenburg wrote to Pleyte in January 1916 that newspaper articles could endanger the existence of the state. Governments were held responsible for what they permitted the press to write.[70] His successor, Van Limburg Stirum (count John I, as he came to be called), soon to be alternately praised and reviled for his self-willed resolution, shared Idenburg's concern. In view of the anti-German articles in the colonial press and mentioning *Het Nieuws van den Dag* specifically by name, in one of his first letters as Governor General he pleaded with Pleyte for an amendment to the *haatzaai* articles and for the penalization of offensive writings and cartoons.[71] The Attorney-General agreed. Convinced that the anti-German tone of some of the Dutch-language newspapers could jeopardize relations between the Netherlands and Germany, he suggested – admittedly an unruly native press was also lurking at the back of his mind – a special system with a press Coucil and a number of warnings before banning a publication for a certain period of time or forbidding an editor to write.

Van Limburg Stirum saw a complex of factors at work. The anti-German articles, the attacks on government policy, the propensity of the Dutch to write with contempt about the other population groups, and that of nationalist journalists to write articles which were considered to incite hatred against the colonial government and the Dutch, all formed good reason for him to be in favour of specific legal means to curb the press. In Holland, where the government was confronted with a similar impotence to act upon anti-German statements, it was decided not to amend the Penal Code. Van Limburg Stirum wanted to

---

[68] André de la Porte to Idenburg, 9-11-1915, NA, Kol. Openbaar, Vb. 13-4-1916 26.
[69] Windels to 1st Government Secretary, 29-7-1916, NA, Kol. Geheim, Mr. 1917/16x.
[70] Idenburg to Pleyte, 20-1-1916, NA, Kol. Openbaar, Vb. 13-4-1916 26.
[71] Van Limburg Stirum to Pleyte, 18-4-1916, NA, Kol. Openbaar, Vb. 1-8-1916 15.

persist. In the Netherlands Indies, specific circumstances had to be taken into account. The main difference between motherland and the colony was that in the Netherlands Indies Dutch authority was superimposed on what in those days were still called alien races. Maintenance of law and order over a heterogeneous population demanded 'a more severe orderliness' and permitted 'a restriction on the greater freedom of the individual than in the mother country'.[72] Insults directed towards people belonging to another group, including citizens of another power, were intolerable. In contrast to his predecessor, Van Limburg Stirum did not stress Dutch neutrality or the need not to offend the belligerents. His main reasons for being so concerned were public order and the interests of the state.

As a consequence of the position taken by Van Limburg Stirum, his legal advisers found themselves fully occupied with the problem. Part of the discussion about the *haatzaai* articles, but not the main focus, revolved around the question of whether terms like *Boches*, Huns, and barbarians, could and should be considered slander. An extension of this was whether it would in any way be possible to act against articles in which Germans, or for that matter Britons, were imputed to be infested with all kind of moral faults because of the way German or British soldiers behaved in Europe, but to which the author in order to avoid prosecution immediately added the rider that such a qualification did not refer to Germans or Britons Resident in the Netherlands Indies.[73] In The Hague Pleyte also turned his full attention to finding a foolproof phrase. His solution was to threaten anybody who publicly expressed feelings of hostility, hatred, and contempt with punishment. This was the right and proper way to deal with the Dutch journalists who insulted natives and, conversely, with people like Soewardi and Tjipto Mangoenkoesoemo. Pleyte was sure that the formula could also be used to take action against journalists who used words which elicited formal protests from Envoys.[74]

The *haatzaai* articles were not reformulated. Finding the right formula and solving differences of opinion took more time than the Great War was to last. Because of the failure of the *haatzaai* articles a prosecution no longer formed the main goal for all. At the beginning of 1917 the then Attorney-General, H.V. Monsanto, pleaded against this. Law suits should not be initiated. The press in the Netherlands Indies should remain free in its evaluation of the war in Europe, irrespective of the words its representatives chose. Monsanto stressed this included gibes and the use of derogatory names for Germans, which could so often be read in *Het Nieuws van den Dag*. Prosecuting the newspaper

---

[72] Van Limburg Stirum to Pleyte, 18-4-1916, NA, Kol. Openbaar, Vb. 1-8-1916 15.
[73] Note Attorney-General to Van Limburg Stirum, 27-11-1916, NA, Kol. Openbaar, Vb. 14-6-1919 26.
[74] Note Pleyte, 5-4-1916, NA, Kol. Openbaar, Vb. 13-4-1916 26.

for such language would be to accord too much honour to the editor.[75]

Nevertheless, Idenburg, Van Limburg Stirum, and Pleyte did not stand idly by while the Dutch-language press insulted Germans and vehemently attacked the measures the colonial government took to avoid the impression that one or another of the belligerents had received a preferential treatment. In January 1915, a report sent from Japan by Pabst to army headquarters in Batavia prompted Idenburg and Pleyte to decide to try to exert influence on the Malay and Dutch-language press in the Netherlands Indies. Pabst had called attention to rumours circulating in Tokyo that, in an effort to lure Japan away from the Allied camp, Berlin had promised it part of the Netherlands Indies. Alluding to this, Pabst suggested that in order to show the outside world the absurdity of such a German offer, it should be made widely known that the population of the Netherlands Indies did not desire another overlord and certainly not a Japanese one. When the realization dawned abroad that the inhabitants of the colony were prepared to underline their pro-Dutch sentiments with deeds, it would be understood that it would be difficult to honour such a German promise.

Pabst's report impressed Idenburg and Pleyte. It induced them to accelerate existing plans to start a secret press offensive aimed at improving the image of the Netherlands Indies abroad. An additional reason to make such a move was that a bad press abroad, especially in Japan, could turn into a public campaign for the occupation of the Netherlands Indies. Cuba was a case in point. The Dutch also saw proof of their fears in what had happened in South Africa. In 1918 the former Senator P.J.J.S.M. van der Does de Willebois argued that the British assault had been preceded by a campaign in the British press – according to De Waal Malefijt almost completely groundless – against the suppression of the natives in the Boer republics.[76]

In The Hague and assuring himself of financial support by the Departments of Foreign Affairs and Agriculture, Industry, and Trade, Pleyte, on the advice of Idenburg, called in the help of H.J. Kiewiet de Jonge, a Resident of Dordrecht. Kiewiet de Jonge was chairman of the Algemeen Nederlandsch Verbond voor de Bestrijding van Onjuiste Beoordelingen en Berichten in de Buitenlandsche Pers (General Netherlands League to Counter Incorrect Judgements and Reports in the Foreign Press). During the Boer War, the League had set up a press office. The Dutch government had already enlisted the help of the office in 1906 during a military expedition against Bali and had continued to do so if and when the occasion arose. The plan was that through this agency, newspapers in the Netherlands Indies and the foreign press could be influenced and be provided with articles and information, concealing that its source was the Dutch government. It took some time before concrete steps were taken.

---

[75] Monsanto to Van Limburg Stirum, 15-1-1917, NA, Kol. Geheim, Mr. 1917/16x.
[76] *Handelingen Eerste Kamer* 1917-18:560.

In August 1916 Rinkes's leave in Holland was used to develop a strategy. A former employee of the Dutch diplomatic agency in Cairo, N. Spijkman, was sent to Batavia – ostensibly as a tourist, though this was a disguise he dropped almost immediately after arrival – to accomplish what Spijkman himself called 'great political intentions'.[77] To keep his contacts with his employees secret, Spijkman addressed his first telegrams about his work in Java to his mother; asking her to convey his messages to 'Dordrecht', that is Kiewiet de Jonge. In its wires to Java the Ministry for the Colonies likewise used the alias to transmit Kiewiet de Jonge's directions.

Shortly after his arrival, Spijkman found employment with the Nederlandsch-Indisch Pers Agentschap (NIPA, Netherlands Indies Press Agency). He became its manager in April 1917, after another editor, D.W. Berretty, had left to found his own news agency, the Algemeen Nieuws en Telegraaf Agentschap (ANETA, General News and Telegraph Agency). Though Spijkman launched himself energetically on the task, most of his activities came to naught. One of the reasons for this was that ANETA was much more successful than NIPA. Spijkman blamed his failure on the fact that Berretty was an Indo-European, which give him easier access to the colonial administration and the Dutch-language newspapers. Spijkman even tried to convince his superiors that ANETA formed a political threat and should never be allowed to monopolize the news service about Holland in the Netherlands Indies and vice versa. He stressed that as an agent of Reuter's and as an 'Indo-organization', ANETA represented a hazard, as this made the news agency biased in favour of the British viewpoint and towards the political aspirations of the Indo-European community to become independent of Holland.

Spijkman was likewise unsuccessful in helping Batavia in changing the way in which the Dutch-language newspapers wrote about Germans and Germany or about the action taken by the authorities to uphold Dutch neutrality. Spijkman was to state a number of times in his reports that the manner in which newspapers commented on the latter matter was anti-national and characterized by 'infamous slander and reproaches'.[78] In 1917 when Van Limburg Stirum summoned him to ask for advice about how to change this, Spijkman had to admit that he could do nothing, fearing the temper of the newspaper journalists and the way they fought out their differences of opinion.

---

[77] Report Spijkman no. 1, NA, Kol. Geheim, Vb. 27-9-1918 H9.
[78] Report Spijkman 1-2-1917 - 15-4-1917, NA, Kol. Geheim, Vb. 27-9-1918 H9.

CHAPTER IX

Loyal subjects

On 14 August 1914 the *Resident* of Batavia sent a letter to the leaders of the Sarekat Islam under his authority. In view of the war in Europe and its repercussions for the colonial economy H. Rijfsnijder deemed a word of caution necessary. If there was ever a moment to realize the objectives of the Sarekat Islam, goals which Rijfsnijder hastened to stress were highly valued by the colonial administration, it now was the time to do it. The harvest in his territory had been good and food would still be available for months, but wisdom was required. A shortage of food – the 'most terrible of all disasters' – might eventuate were irresponsible waste of food not prevented. The age-old tradition among Muslims of selling off their remaining stock of food to raise the money necessary to celebrate the end of the Fasting Month with joy and lustre bode an additional reason for prudence. Rijfsnijder explained that nobody should be disturbed in this jollity, but that in contrast to previous years people should practise drastic retrenchments. They should spend as little as possible on celebrating this important day in the life of Muslims. In view of this Rijfsnijder impressed upon his correspondents that it is 'your task, no your duty' to explain 'seriously and with all your powers of persuasion' that troubled times lay ahead. Members of the Sarekat Islam had to be made aware that they had to cut their coat to suit their cloth; and that secondary crops had to be planted.[1] Other Dutch residents, all cognizant of the fact that the end of the Fasting Month was approaching, made similar appeals for thrift. At times they also pointed out the detrimental consequences runs on the bank had on small traders and on the estates which had to pay their workforce.

Within days, as one Dutchman in West Java described the situation, Indonesians were gripped by a *perang* (war) fever.[2] They were eager to learn where Hungary and Italy were located (Germany, Great Britain, France, and Russia were more familiar), and what sea mines, fights between fighter planes, and wireless telecommunication meant. In the cities, Indonesians who were

---

[1] Rijfsnijder to Djajadiningrat and others, 14-8-1914, NA, Kol. Openbaar, Vb. 9-3-1916 26.
[2] *De Locomotief,* 17-11-1914.

well-versed in Dutch translated the telegrams posted in front of the offices of Dutch-language newspapers for their fellow-countrymen. Elsewhere in the cities and in the countryside people crowded around literate Indonesians, who, as was the common practice also in the days of peace, read out aloud reports in the Malay press, which covered the war as intensely as the Dutch-language newspapers did. Malay newspapers partly copied their reports from Dutch-language newspapers and informed their readers in detail about speeches delivered in the European capitals, about the reactions in the Middle East and in the British and French colonies, and about the developments on the war fronts. Like the European population, in the first weeks of the war Indonesians began to speculate about the possibility that Holland would be dragged into the war and the consequences this would have for the colony. Some were sure that such a war had already started. In North Celebes it was rumoured that the Japanese had occupied Batavia. In Java anxiety augmented when the Malay newspapers published the false report that the Netherlands and Germany were at war.

Witnessing from close by how nervously the European community reacted to the news from Europe, trends set by Europeans such as hoarding and distrust of paper currency were copied. The People's Credit Banks which were run by the government came under pressure from customers who wanted to withdraw their savings or who, afraid that dire times were on the way, asked for credit. In order to cope the managements of local branches were instructed not to pay back deposits before the end of the term of notice had expired and not to provide new loans should they suspect that the money would be used to buy food.[3] In a sense indigenous Indonesians were worse off than Europeans. Unaccustomed as they were to visiting a bank, some fell victim to persons who convinced them that paper money was no longer legal tender and offered them less for their bank notes than the nominal value. They might get nine guilders in coins for a note of ten. Others, disquieted by the steep increase in prices, made great financial sacrifices in order to hoard food. Many were also forced to borrow money. The shops they used to patronize had stopped providing credit. Higher costs of living, the prospect that commodities such as rice, salt (imported from Egypt), batik textiles (dependent on the import of cloth from Holland and chemical dyes from Germany), sugar, and matches – an item frequently mentioned in Dutch-language as well as Malay newspapers – could soon become too expensive to buy added to the unease. Disquiet was fortified even more by rumours about massive lay-offs, a possibility which was also discussed in the Malay press. Superstition played a role as well. In Bali some were sure that they had seen a star with a tail, a bad omen.

---

[3] Circular of the Adviser for the People's Credit System (*Feiten* 1916:52).

Indonesian social and political leaders did their best to reassure the population and to prevent a panic. Tjokroaminoto was one of them. In an effort to stop all kinds of 'nonsense' from spreading, at a number of meetings he explained that the battlefields were far away – twenty-eight days at least –, that the Netherlands was not a party to the war, and that there were no indications that this was to change.[4] When the rumour that the Netherlands was already at war took hold, *Oetoesan Hindia*, of which Tjokroaminoto was editor-in-chief, cautioned its readers to trust only official communiqués.[5] *Oetoesan Hindia* also printed the soothing announcements published by the colonial government intimating that there was no reason whatsoever to fear that the Netherlands would become involved in the war or that the delay in shipping meant that a famine was imminent. The measures taken by the colonial government to assure the domestic supply of rice and to restore faith in paper money were explained at length. One of the points *Oetoesan Hindia* made was that Indonesians, in contrast to Europeans, did not need imported foodstuffs. They could live on a simple meal of rice and salt. So, there was no reason to worry. The government had seen to it that there was enough rice for the population, and Egyptian salt could surely soon be replaced by salt from Madura, which, it was added, anyway, had the added advantage of being cheaper.[6] The request by the authorities to the press that it should not write about the belligerents in negative terms was duly noted. It was actually seized upon to point out the special mission of *Oetoesan Hindia*. The war in Europe was not the newspaper's concern. What was important was to underline its negative consequences for the Javanese, such as the prospect of mass lay-offs and rising prices. *Oetoesan Hindia* warned that expensive times lay ahead. Members of the Sarekat Islam and other Muslims should organize their finances with care. They should be thrifty.[7]

Individual members of the Sarekat Islam took up the plea for thrift. They presented this as one of the indications of progress. Many Sarekat Islam branches held special meetings to discuss the rocketing prices of foodstuffs and to advise their members on how to act in those difficult days. Occasionally, and this was a real novelty, women were specifically invited to attend such Sarekat Islam meetings. After all it was they who did the shopping. People were urged not to indulge in unnecessary expenditure to celebrate the end of the Fasting Month. They should refrain from spending money on fireworks and expensive clothes.[8] The appeals seem to have been successful. Either from free will or by

---

[4] *Oetoesan Hindia*, 23-9-1914.
[5] *Oetoesan Hindia*, 18-8-1914.
[6] *Oetoesan Hindia*, 18-8-1914.
[7] *Oetoesan Hindia*, 4-8-1914, 15-8-1914.
[8] *Oetoesan Hindia*, 29-8-1914.

necessity, in various places the end of the Fasting Month was celebrated more soberly than before. There were fewer fireworks than usual. During meetings members aired their complaints and worries about the high level of prices. In Semarang one of them even ventured the opinion that the moment might be nigh when he would have to steal and rob to procure rice for his family. A suggestion that the branch should buy rice and distribute it among its members was rejected by the chairman. The logistics seemed insurmountable. It would be better to ask the *Resident* to fix prices. Additional meetings were organized in the city to impress upon members that paper currency had not lost its value, and that they should not exchange notes for coins at a loss.

The disruption in international trade, rising prices, and the prospect of mass unemployment encouraged speculations among the European community about large-scale unrest when Indonesians were to become impoverished in great numbers or no longer be able to afford the high prices of basic commodities. Indonesians could also run in trouble in yet another way. Tempted by high prices, they might sell all the rice they had and then be forced sometime later when prices had gone up still further to buy rice themselves. Aware of this possibility, within days after the outbreak of the war Dutch civil servants impressed on the people living in their territories the need to hold onto a stock of rice for their own consumption in the months ahead. Other warnings were also issued. The *Resident* of Semarang in a meeting with European trading firms and Chinese shopkeepers pointed to the consequences of deliberately forcing up prices. This was a dangerous game. The native population and others in straightened circumstances might end up in a situation in which they found themselves tempted to appropriate food by force. Riots and rows with Chinese could well lie in store.[9]

Some Europeans remained optimistic. In a report from West Java to *De Locomotief* it was adducted that the crisis caused by the European war did not affect natives in the least. They were used to times of hardship and would continue to till the soil as they always had done. Javanese peasants did not need any money, nor did they consume expensive foodstuffs or sweets such as milk, butter, chocolate, and tinned food. Villagers would react to rising prices in their traditional way: 'They first eat rice once a day, thereafter once every two days supplementing it with cassava, sweet potatoes, or maize, then they do not eat rice at all – before they resort to wantonness [...]'.[10]

Opinions like this were rare. As the words of the *Resident* of Semarang indicate, anxiety about how the population would react was coupled with the fear that the relationship between the natives and Chinese would deteriorate.

---

[9]   *De Locomotief*, 10-8-1914.
[10] *De Locomotief*, 12-8-1914.

In the early days of war, some Chinese even feared an uprising among the indigenous population (Idenburg en De Graeff 1920:370). Though the anti-Chinese riots which had been so frequent in the previous years had abated, incidents might easily re-erupt. Javanese and other groups could blame Chinese shopkeepers, who controlled much of the retail trade, and intermediate traders for the rise in the cost of living. This was indeed what happened. People began to suspect that the argument that prices had risen because of the war was a pretext and had nothing to do with the truth. In Java solidarity among the Javanese was stressed as a means to cope with the difficult times. It was essential to consider the plight of fellow-Javanese, not that of other 'nations'.[11] From Situbondo a correspondent of *Oetoesan Hindia* noted that the cooperative shops which had been established before the war (and which were often far from being a success story) had not raised their prices. He noted that such behaviour was in sharp contrast to the practice in Chinese-owned shops. In other reports in *Oetoesan Hindia* about how expensive life had become, it was also suggested that this was caused by articles sold in Chinese shops. Sometimes it was stated that the rising price of rice was certainly a deliberate ploy of the rich, the leeches, to hurt the poor, that is the Sarekat Islam supporters. What other reason could there be? In Southeast Asia there was no war, which meant that rice could be shipped to Java from Siam without any problem. The authorities had to intervene and put an end to the rising prices. If not it would be impossible to maintain public order.[12]

If Indonesians grew export crops, they could and would blame Chinese for the falling prices they received or for the loss of marketing opportunities. In Cirebon, for instance, a centre of the production of beans and peas, Chinese wholesalers awaited the coming harvest in the middle of August with trepidation. Export had been prohibited, but were Chinese middlemen to refuse to buy beans and peas from the Sundanese producers, or, as it was hinted in *Oetoesan Hindia*, were to pay a ridiculously low price, this might be interpreted by the local population as extra proof that the Chinese were scheming to bring about their economic ruin.[13]

Plagued by worries which had arisen in the past couple of years by the activities of the Sarekat Islam, and to a lesser extent by those of the Indische Partij, the Dutch themselves did not feel safe either. The establishment of Law and Order Leagues was one outward and visible sign of their apprehension. Rumours about an impending uprising was another. The Dutch asked Javanese and other Indonesians they knew how they thought the population would react were the Netherlands to become involved in the war. *Oetoesan*

---

[11] *Oetoesan Hindia*, 13-8-1914.
[12] *Oetoesan Hindia*, 5-8-1914, 6-8-1914, 11-8-1914, 19-8-1914, 12-8-1914.
[13] *De Locomotief*, 15-8-1914; *Oetoesan Hindia*, 17-8-1914.

G.A.J. Hazeu (KITLV 3953)

Hindia concluded that such behaviour was evidence not of some sudden upswelling of anxiety but of deeply rooted fears.[14] The Fasting Month exacerbated such worries. Europeans nurtured the idea that this was the period in which Muslims could become especially restless and in which malcontent dissatisfied with Dutch rule might more easily resort to violence than at other times of the year. It was predicted that there was a good chance riots could erupt around 25 August when the end of the fasting was celebrated; partly because at that moment Muslims would realize that they could not afford to buy as much food and clothing as they had been accustomed to do in the past. The worst affected regions might well be those with many estates. In Java and in Sumatra such worries were reason enough to be increasingly alert, and this also applied to the authorities.

Keeping pace with this apprehension, particular attention was paid to the Chinese and Malay newspapers. Michielsen, unaware that Idenburg already had taken such a step, asked the Director of Education and Religious Affairs, G.A.J. Hazeu, to have 'teachers of native languages' investigate whether undesirable opinions were being expressed in the non-European press.[15] Hazeu

[14] *Oetoesan Hindia*, 7-11-1914.
[15] Idenburg to Pleyte, 6-8-1914, Verslag omtrent de belangrijkste militaire maatregelen sinds 31 Juli j.l. getroffen, NA, Kol. Geheim, Vb. 12-9-1914 P18, 18-1-1915 P.

was able to re-assure him. Reports were 'of a moderate and calm nature'. No indications had been found of a 'less favourable disposition' towards Dutch rule.[16] On the contrary, it soon became clear that editors testified to their loyalty in 'often touching ways' (Van der Weijden 1916:28). Hazeu's assessment was only partly right. News about the war had not improved the image of the West. Nationalist newspapers and periodicals posed the rhetorical question whether the war being fought in Europe was a manifestation of the much acclaimed Christian civilization. The conclusion of such articles was that the West had lost any right to treat Muslims and other Indonesians as inferior beings or as barbarians. Europeans were also well aware that the war had not added to the prestige of the West in Asia.

Michielsen and others should not have worried about the initial reactions at the outbreak of the war. Contrary to the trepidation expressed by Europeans, Indonesians did not seem to have considered the tension in the world as a portent to rise up in rebellion. The prospect that another nation might take over the position of the Dutch was not overlooked, was even perhaps expected but no plans were made to exploit the situation to cast off the Dutch yoke. Educated Indonesians fostered no illusions about the outcome of an armed conflict between the Netherlands and the contemporary powers. They knew that the Dutch stood no chance. If anyone wanted to maintain Dutch rule, praying that the Netherlands was to stay out of a war was the only option open to them. *Oetoesan Hindia* commented that it was a law of nature that the weaker is devoured by the stronger, and that the stupid is swallowed up by the clever.[17] The usurpation of a Dutch colonial overlord by one power or another does not seem to have appealed to many at the time. It was even reported from Java that Javanese told their fellow-countrymen stories about how badly the indigenous population was treated in British colonies. It was said that no non-Europeans, not even the rich ones, were allowed to own their own houses there.[18]

Though names were seldom mentioned in the press and in speeches, the Indonesians also thought Japan was the most likely aggressor. The editors of *Oetoesan Hindia* could understand Tokyo's motives for desiring territorial expansion, because Japan was said to be unhappy with the fact that part of Asia was occupied by Europeans. They put Japan's motives on a par with the intention of the Allied to chase Turkey out of the European continent. Later, in 1916, the article by Yosaburo Takekoshi was quoted in detail in *Oetoesan Hindia*, complete with remarks about how rotten Dutch rule was, but mainly

---

[16] Verslag omtrent de belangrijkste militaire maatregelen sinds 31 Juli j.l. getroffen, NA, Kol. Geheim, Vb. 18-1-1915 P.
[17] *Oetoesan Hindia*, 9-5-1916.
[18] *De Locomotief*, 22-8-1914.

as an appeal to the Dutch authorities to realize how great the threat was. *Oetoesan Hindia* explained that for a variety of reasons there was no love lost for the Japanese. Japanese were Buddhists, were apparently not looking for ties of friendship with the autochthonous population, were condemned by the Chinese, and were at war with Germany and Turkey.[19] The following year, in October 1917, a brawl with some Japanese was the occasion for the same newspaper to remark that such people were already behaving as if they had become the foreign oppressor. A few days later it was observed that especially outside Java, the Japanese behaved objectionably.[20]

In the eyes of the leaders of the nationalist movement, those of Boedi Oetomo first and foremost, it would be best to have everything remain as it was. They and others were disquieted by the news which had reached the Netherlands Indies about the fate suffered by the populations in European countries which had been invaded; first Belgium and later in the war, Serbia. A new foreign ruler would be a change for the worse. One of the arguments advanced for this was that the huge amount of money which had already been spent to teach Dutch to Javanese, the language through which Javanese could gain access to modern science, would be wasted. Were the Netherlands to be replaced, the Javanese would have to learn a new language to communicate with the new ruler. In that instance all the efforts and money poured into learning Dutch would have been wasted. Such comments would seem to indicate that the Ethical Policy the Dutch government had embarked upon since the turn of the century had made its mark. In 1915 Boedi Oetomo leaders toured Java to convince the people not to consider the Dutch their enemy. They suggested to their audiences that, after a rule of three centuries, the Dutch might be expected to be familiar with the needs of the Javanese. Not all that was longed for had been reached, but a start had been made. Reforms took time. Some of the leaders of the Sarekat Islam expressed similar views. Much was still to be improved, and here were plenty of government measures which should be undone, but the colonial government had their support. They often turned to the point that strong language might have been used in the past to criticize colonial conditions, but that reforms had to be achieved by peaceful means. Evolution not revolution was what they had in mind.

In line with this position, in the weeks after the outbreak of the war *Oetoesan Hindia* carried a number of statements in which loyalty and the duty to defend Dutch rule was stressed. In the middle of August, in a statement printed in larger type, the editors sang the praise of Idenburg, lauding him as the person who had seen to it that the bond between the Dutch Kingdom

---

[19] *Oetoesan Hindia*, 9-5-1916.
[20] *Oetoesan Hindia*, 9-10-1917.

and the population of the Netherlands Indies had grown stronger. Thanks to his policy feelings of loyalty and affection had been implanted in the hearts of the Javanese. The upshot was that to assure the safety of the fatherland the Javanese were prepared to 'attack a sea of problems, to climb a high mountain, to enter a sea of fire' to assist the Dutch, who 'for three hundred years had guided and protected' them.[21]

The pro-Dutch feelings were also displayed in a plethora of spontaneous manifestations. There could have been even more, had local Dutch authorities in some cases not refused permission to hold meetings to testify to native loyalty to Dutch rule. In the Moluccas, but this was a partly Christian region, students in confirmation classes vowed that, as the Acting-*Resident* chose to put it, they were prepared to go to Holland to 'give their lives for the protection of QUEEN and Motherland'.[22] In the same region, in a circular letter the Ambonsch Studie-Fonds (Ambonese Study Foundation) begged the Ambonese in the colony, soldiers and civilians, to be prepared to 'fight for a free and independent Netherlands'. Appealing to 'the attachment to the country which we have to thank for our development, our prosperity', it was recounted how for centuries Ambonese 'had fought under the Dutch tricolour'.[23]

In Java, the island where nationalist sentiments had been most obvious in the previous years, many spoke out in support of Dutch rule. In Bandung, Sundanese civil servants vowed to stay at their posts whatever might happen. They would do all they could to calm down their compatriots and prevent unrest. In Magelang, Javanese civil servants publicly testified to their loyalty to Dutch rule. To remove all doubts about the loyalty of the Javanese bureaucracy, if there were any, those present at a meeting of the Regentsunion (Regents' Union) in Semarang in November gave testimony of their support. They assured the Dutch Queen that 'under all circumstances [the] native population, [...] grateful for Her Majesty's beneficent reign, [...] shall remain loyal and cooperative in maintaining Netherlands Rule over these colonies'. The initiative for the statement had come from the chairman of the meeting, Pangeran Ario Adiningrat, Regent of Demak. When he explained that it was important in these times that the Dutch government be presented with some token bearing witness to the fact that the population desired to remain loyal to Dutch rule and were willing to support it in those difficult times, everybody present agreed.[24]

The most important leaders of the Sarekat Islam and Boedi Oetomo were not to be outdone. Early in August *Oetoesan Hindia* carried an article by Mas Ngahebi Dwidjosewojo, teacher of Javanese at the Teachers' Training College

[21] *Oetoesan Hindia*, 14-8-1914.
[22] Boer to Idenburg, 15-6-1915, NA, Kol. Geheim, Vb. 5-8-1915 Z10.
[23] *De Locomotief*, 17-9-1914.
[24] Idenburg to Pleyte, NA, Kol. Geheim, Vb. 25-11-1914 N23.

Celebrating the Queen's birthday at a 'native school' (Van Gent, Penard and Rinkes 1923:Photo 60)

in Yogyakarta, and a prominent member of Boedi Oetomo. In it, Dwidjosewojo presented his views about the best way to maintain domestic peace. After stating that he was convinced that the Dutch would remain in control of Java and would not lose the island to Germany, Great Britain, or Japan, Dwidjosewojo called for the unity of all inhabitants of Java, of whatever race. He stressed that it was everybody's duty to follow government instructions, as these were inspired by no other aim than the desire to protect the welfare of the people: 'Though it is our right to condemn wrongful regulations, it behaves us now to be careful with this right and all the more so do we have to be careful in airing our criticism'. Rice traders in particular should follow the directions of the government. If they were determined only to pursue huge profits and the war was to drag on, turmoil would be the outcome. Dwidjosewojo feared that the rising price of rice, together with growing unemployment and cuts in wages, would encourage social unrest: 'There will be no war, but disorder manifesting itself in many thefts, assaults, robberies, and such like'.[25]

Sarekat Islam leaders reacted in the same vein. If anything they wanted to

[25] *Oetoesan Hindia*, 13-8-1914.

help. In Surakarta the President of the local board sent a letter to the Dutch *Resident* explaining that in those 'difficult days' the Sarekat Islam wanted to testify to its loyalty to Dutch rule. He asked what assistance its members could give. The answer was disappointing. The *Resident* wrote back that the Netherlands was neutral and that consequently no help was yet required.[26] In Blitar, after having been informed about the cancellation of festivities on Queen's Birthday, the Sarekat Islam branch organized a mass prayer session on that very day. Thousands attended the ceremony on the *alun-alun* where the principal Islamic leader of the region said a prayer in which he asked for God's blessing 'in these dark days' on the Netherlands and Queen Wilhelmina.[27] The meeting concluded with a large *slametan*, a communal meal, where rice, sambal, and chicken was served on 400 large plates.

The government could also count on the loyalty of the representatives of the Chinese community. In their effort to reach a normalization of prices, civil servants had received the support of the Chinese business community, equally anxious to restore normal economic conditions. In Semarang it was a Chinese trader who had initiated the fall in the rice price by offering a large quantity of rice for a moderate price. Elsewhere leading Chinese traders had done their best to restore public faith in paper currency. They pledged that whenever possible they would conduct financial transactions in banknotes and not in coins. At various places, for instance in the area of the West Coast of Sumatra and in Batavia, Chinese formally testified to their loyalty to Dutch rule. When Idenburg visited Magelang in November, the Chinese quarter in town was awash with Dutch flags and those of the Chinese Republic.[28]

With the Sino-Japanese War still firmly in mind and in reaction to the bullying of China by Japan, the Chinese if anything were giving vent to their anti-Japanese sentiments, and in extension of this to an anti-Allied disposition. Though the Dutch often singled out the Chinese-Malay press as producing the most unruly and inflammatory newspapers, these came out in support of Dutch rule. *Djawa Tengah* explained to its readers that they had to support the government if the Netherlands Indies were attacked. In 1916 *Warna Warta* wrote that the Chinese were in no doubt that they would be worse off if Dutch rule was replaced by that of another power. At the same time both newspapers pleaded for a change in colonial policy. *Djawa Tengah* pointed to the legal discrimination of the Chinese and natives in contrast to the European status of the Japanese. Assistance in a Dutch war effort by Chinese and indigenous Indonesians would be more readily forthcoming if Batavia really were to take the interests of these population groups to heart. *Warna Warta* reminded people

[26] *De Locomotief*, 21-10-1914.
[27] *De Locomotief*, 9-9-1914.
[28] *Koloniaal verslag* 1915:13-4; *Oetoesan Hindia*, 29-8-1914; *De Locomotief*, 13-11-1914.

of the Chinese who had been killed in recent years by the government.[29]

In November 1914 after Japanese troops had landed on the German-held Shantung Peninsula, pamphlets written in Chinese started to circulate. They called for a boycott of Japanese products, of which Chinese shops were the main distributors. Initially the government and others, and this may have been wishful thinking by people afraid to offend Japan, reported that on the whole the effect of the appeal was negligible. Anti-Japanese sentiments grew when Tokyo delivered a note to China – the Twenty-One Demands – aimed to bring China fully within the Japanese sphere of influence, in January 1915. Brandishing the threat of an invasion, it called for the recognition of Japan's hold on the port of Ch'ing-tao and Manchuria; and demanded that China turn to Japan for loans as well as military and financial advisers. News of the Japanese note caused a wave of nationalist feeling among the Chinese in the Netherlands Indies. Rich Chinese subscribed to bonds issued by the Chinese government. They and their less affluent countrymen could also contribute to collections. Some of these were made by children from Chinese schools. Apart from such financial support, there were also appeals to return to China to fight for the fatherland.

Because of irritation caused by the Twenty-One Demands, the boycott took a more uncompromising form. Shopkeepers were visited at home to urge them to stop selling Japanese goods. Sometimes these pleas were backed up by verbal threats or anonymous letters. When advertisements for Japanese products were displayed on shop fronts these were smeared with tar and dirt. The houses of the shopkeepers received similar treatment. The colonial government was not pleased with such an upsurge in Chinese sentiments. It started a police investigation to find out who were the driving force behind the hostile actions. It, and in this it was joined by a wider section of the Dutch community, feared that the boycott might upset the relationship with Japan. After a complaint by the Japanese Consul Batavia also sent one of its civil servants on a tour through Java to calm people down. He explained that China and Japan had come to an understanding and begged that the Chinese, as guests in the Netherlands Indies, should not put their host in an awkward position. In Medan a writ for libel was taken out against a newspaper, *Sumatra News*, because it had written about the 'guileful and savage Japanese people' who looked down upon the Chinese. Three people were convicted to two months' imprisonment.[30]

Even the people associated with the Indische Partij proclaimed their loyalty. At the time of the Onze Vloot agitation, the editors of *De Expres* had already been quick to stress that the Netherlands Indies should be defended

---

[29] *Djawa-Tengah*, cited in *De Locomotief*, 17-2-1915, *Warna Warta*, cited in *De Locomotief*, 28-3-1916.
[30] *Indisch Tijdschrift van het Recht* 1916:435-44.

IX Loyal subjects

and administered by people living there. On one occasion the newspaper had written that 30 million inhabitants of Java were certainly capable of raising an army strong enough to defend the island.[31] *De Expres* had also not opposed an 'Indies fleet', a fleet of which the strength had been decided upon by the people of the Netherlands Indies, in a colonial parliament. The Navy they had had in mind was one that tallied with the ideal of becoming independent of Holland, of the Indië los van Holland campaign. What had been rejected was 'a Dutch fleet built with Indies money' which would, it was true, be employed to defend the Netherlands Indies, but which did so only in the interests of people in Holland and not of those in the colony.[32]

At the outbreak of the war such ideals resurfaced. In *De Indiër* an Indonesian, Soemataram, lamented the fact Indonesians 'can't handle a sabre, and can't shoot'. This was the upshot of a stupid Dutch mistake. Because they had been afraid that Indonesians would use these weapons against their own master, Indonesians now could not come to the assistance of the government in defending the colony against 'a land-hungry neighbour or a blood-thirsty and rapacious European country'.[33] The best defence of the Netherlands Indies, or rather Java, which was the area foremost in the minds of many people, was to entrust this to the people who lived there. It could not – and this point was also stressed by others – be left to 'mercenaries', to Dutchmen and other Europeans. Such soldiers would have to fight in an alien country and in alien surroundings. They would lack the determination to defend the Netherlands Indies which would inspire local inhabitants, defending their homeland.

Douwes Dekker himself, to whom as he would write to Pleyte, it was 'a tormenting thought to have to remain idle while I know that my country is in danger', rushed from Switzerland to The Hague to offer his help in defending Java against an aggressor.[34] On 19 August he sent Pleyte a wire from Geneva. He was unshakeable in his belief that not dreadnoughts, but the arming of the people, was the answer to prevent, as he expressed this, the Japanese exploiting the Javanese in the way the Dutch had done in the nineteenth century. To underline his opinion Douwes Dekker postulated that an army composed of committed men, familiar with the countryside had been the main reason the Boer Republics had been able to resist the superior forces of the British for such a long time.[35] After a month when he still had received no reply – the telegram never reached Pleyte – Douwes Dekker travelled to The Hague to present his plan to the Minister of the Colonies in person. Venturing that more countries

[31] *De Expres*, 10-3-1914.
[32] *De Expres*, 25-2-1914.
[33] *De Indiër* 1-43:205.
[34] Douwes Dekker to Pleyte, 22-9-1914, NA, Kol. Geheim, Vb. 23-9-1914 F19.
[35] *De Indiër* 1-52:245-7.

might become involved in the war and stressing that the defence of the motherland was a citizen's right and not merely his duty, Douwes Dekker suggested that he could bring his personal influence to bear to establish a volunteer corps of 'many thousands of Indiërs'.[36] Pleyte turned the offer down. Perhaps rather undiplomatically, on 22 September, he fobbed Douwes Dekker off saying he was not in favour of arming a population, of whom most were still at a low level of development. The real reason for the refusal was that Pleyte could do without the assistance of a 'hot-headed' Douwes Dekker, a person 'who can only find peace in a position which is linked to the war'. Pleyte was sure that Douwes Dekker's only motive for his offer to establish a volunteer corps had been to seek publicity to further his own plans for the colony.[37]

Apart from the manifestations of solidarity, the appeals to collect money for Holland were also taken up outside the white European community. *De Locomotief* had calculated that though most Javanese could not give very much the proceeds of such actions could be enormous. If each of the 6 million households were to give two and a half cents, they could still raise 150,000 guilders.[38] The question was, and the happenings at the time of the celebrations of Dutch independence were still fresh in people's mind, how should money be collected among the Indonesians. Any impression of coercion should be scrupulously avoided. *De Locomotief* suggested that the solution was easy. Moneyboxes could be placed at strategic places outside the villages. Crossroads frequented by the population would be a convenient place to do so. Were boxes to be placed in the villages, villagers might feel obliged to donate. The authorities were also sensitive to the problem. When they learned that police officers in Yogyakarta had started a collection among the Javanese inhabitants, they ordered them a few days later to return the money to the people.

It was not only the Indonesian and Chinese notables who sat on the central and regional Committees for Relief who were active in the collection of money. Others also joined in. At a Boedi Oetomo meeting in Semarang one of those present, praising the colonial government for the support it gave to 'our efforts to progress and to become humans', suggested that Boedi Oetomo should try to organize native support for the unemployed in Holland.[39] The Regent of Jepara had yet another argument why Javanese should collect money for the poor in Holland. Each time there had been a natural disaster in the Netherlands Indies, Dutch people had been ready to give money to help. Now it was the turn of the natives to dip into their purse; or, as he stated at a meeting of the Semarang committee: 'Where the elder brother acts in this way,

---

[36] Douwes Dekker to Pleyte, 19-8-1914, NA, Kol. Geheim, Vb. 23-9-1919 F19.
[37] Note Pleyte, NA, Kol. Geheim, Vb. 23-9-1914 F19.
[38] *De Locomotief*, 28-9-1914.
[39] *De Locomotief*, 14-9-1914.

the younger brother should not be left behind now that the Netherlands is in distress'.[40] He admitted that appeals to donate money might be interpreted by the ordinary Javanese as a touch of gentle coercion, but did not mind. When the objective was so good such conduct was tolerable.

Occasionally Sarekat Islam stalls were put up at fancy fairs organized by the Dutch community to raise money for the poor in Holland. In other places *wajang orang* performances were staged. In Magelang students of the OSVIA put on a Stamboel performance. It was a big disappointment. Only thirty people attended.

On Saparua, one of the islands in the Moluccas, 2,500 guilders were collected to be sent to Queen Wilhelmina to help the poor in Holland. These native Christians, their Dutch minister wrote, 'distinguish themselves to a particular extent by their loyalty to the Dutch Government and by their love for Her Majesty the QUEEN and Her House'.[41] He attributed this loyalty to the influence of the Gospel of Christ that had stimulated their notions of solidarity with their fellow-Christians in Holland at a time when distress was mounting there. In Java the Regentenbond reserved 3,000 guilders for the destitute in Holland as a token of allegiance.

Such loyalty and enthusiasm was not universal. The initiatives to collect relief money for Holland irritated some. Though one of the stated aims was that people in the colony should not be excluded from help, not everybody was entirely convinced that this would indeed be the case. Dissatisfaction was especially great among the Indo-Europeans, who once again detected proof they were being discriminated against. Voices of discontent could also be heard from among the Javanese. It was Javanese labour which had made possible the profits which permitted the transmission of money to Holland. It would only be just if part of the money collected were to go to the poor in Java, for instance to the wives and children of those who had died of the plague. In Surabaya, reminding the local relief committee of its pledge that money was also being collected for destitute Indonesians, seventeen foremen who had been fired after the outbreak of the war applied for financial assistance. In the same city rich pilgrims, probably Arabs, offered the Sarekat Islam a considerable amount of money – it is a pleasure, a correspondent of *De Locomotief* wrote, finally to be able to say something praiseworthy about these people – to assist Javanese who had suffered from the economic consequences of the war. Their money did not have to be used immediately. Families were taking care of the newly unemployed.[42] The local Sarekat Islam also tried to help. It made preparations for an investigation into the number of indigenous people who

---

[40] *De Locomotief*, 28-9-1914.
[41] Wesseldijk to Boer, 14-6-1915, NA, Kol. Geheim, Vb. 5-8-1915 Z10.
[42] *De Locomotief*, 14-11-1914, 16-11-1914.

D.A. Rinkes

had become unemployed and contacted a schoolteacher to assist in establishing a special organization to help them.[43]

One obvious cause for Muslims to collect for was the Red Crescent. Shortly after Turkey had become involved in the war, *Oetoesan Hindia* wrote that what Muslims should do was to give charitable aid, which the Red Crescent was more than willing to accept. The newspaper said that this was in accordance with the neutral stand adopted by the Dutch government.[44] The initiatives to raise money for the Red Crescent, which at times received the overt support of German and Austrian consuls, were various. In Surabaya, in a gesture of criticism of the drive for Holland, a number of Arabs, British Indians, and indigenous Indonesians took the initiative to collect money for the destitute

[43] *De Locomotief*, 7-12-1914.
[44] *Oetoesan Hindia*, 17-11-1914.

in Turkey. To this end a map of Europe with the topographic names in Latin and Arabic script was sold. The map was prominently advertised in *Oetoesan Hindia*. In the advertisement it was pointed out that on the map people could look up where the battle-sites in Europe were located. As an extra attraction to tempt people to buy the map it was claimed that the map was the first one of Europe using Arab script printed in the Netherlands Indies. Part of the proceeds went to the Red Crescent. In Bandung, in February 1916, the proceeds of a cinema show with newsreels about the war went partly to the Red Crescent, partly to the German and Austrian Red Cross, and partly to destitute Javanese and Chinese inhabitants of the city.[45] The following month the Malay-Chinese newspaper, *Sin Po*, organized a viewing of newsreels in Batavia to raise money for the Red Crescent. The collections for the Red Crescent were quite successful. At the end of 1917 over 23,000 guilders had been collected. Even in Dutch New Guinea, at that time hardly a place with a large concentration of Muslims, sly traders, it was reported, sold articles for the Red Crescent.[46]

Chinese also organized special drives to raise money for the poor in Holland. The heads of the Chinese quarters went around to collect money, while the political elite, the Chinese officers, targeted the wealthy segment of the Chinese community. Various Chinese associations organized performances. A Chinese theatre in Pekalongan gave a special show for the needy in Holland. This was repeated in Semarang where people could attend a Malay play performed by a Chinese theatre group. In Yogyakarta a Chinese opera was staged to raise money for the Belgian refugees who had fled to Holland. In Pangkalan Brandan in North Sumatra the proceeds – 900 guilders – of a soccer game between two Chinese teams went to the poor in Holland.

Yet another way in which sections of the indigenous population testified to their support of Dutch rule was by offering their services in the defence of the colony. Steps were taken to establish indigenous volunteer corpses, in Malay initially translated as *tentara merdika* or free army, just as neutrality sometimes was rendered as *kemerdikaän*, freedom. For those who wanted to join an additional incentive was, as it was for Douwes Dekker and his political associates, that in this way they could show that they were ordinary citizens no different from the white Dutch community, perfectly capable of doing their bit if the country were in danger. They were people whose voices should be taken into account.

The first suggestion that such a corps be established came up in Magelang.

---

[45] *Oetoesan Hindia*, 5-2-1916; Rinkes to Idenburg, 9-7-1915, NA, Kol. Openbaar, Vb. 23-9-1915 19.
[46] G. Simon, Neuzeitliche Strömungen im niederländisch-indischen Islam, cited in *Koloniaal Tijdschrift* 1917, I:702.

The topic was raised after Europeans in the town had discussed the possibility of forming their own local corps on 8 August. On 9 August the Javanese – among them, according to a report in *Oetoesan Hindia*, many former soldiers, civil servants, devout Muslims, and members of the Boedi Oetomo and Sarekat Islam – called their own meeting, chaired by the Regent. The meeting decided that everybody who was 'sound in wind and limb' should enlist in a volunteer corps and assist the 'Company', that is the government, when danger threatened. Women did not have to stay behind. The Regent suggested that women could make themselves useful by forming an association of their own to take care of the provisions for their husbands who had joined the corps. This decided, the Regent explained that the next step to be taken was to ask the government to supply thousand rifles. Soldiers should instruct the volunteers how to use these and how to march. His words were greeted with a roar of applause. The Dutch *Resident* was less enthusiastic. He did his utmost to temper the excitement when the Regent informed him about what had been decided. It made no sense to hand out umbrellas before the rain had started. Matters were not yet serious enough to justify the establishment of a volunteer corps. What was more, it might be impossible for the government to provide the rifles requested. The regular army might need all the fire-arms available. Plans had to be changed. Instead of a volunteer corps, a shooting club was founded. 'Europeans, native civil servants and chiefs, as well as other prominent and well-to-do natives' could join.[47]

Similar initiatives were taken in Sidoarjo, where the local chairman of the Sarekat Islam suggested the establishment of a volunteer corps consisting of Sarekat Islam members, in Buitenzorg, in Kedu, and in Bandung. In Bandung it was a physician, Haminsar, who in conjunction with Soetan Muhammad Zain, Abdoel Moeis, and Wignjadisastra (the latter two former members of Tjipto Mangoenkoesoemo's Comité Boemi Poetra) appealed to the Javanese in the city to form a special native ambulance corps, open to both men and women. He himself would become its president. The name chosen for the organization Djaja-baja, the title of Javanese village police officials, indicates that the aims went further than just offering medical services. Envisaged was an *ordebond*, which had to prevent disturbances not by the use of force, but by persuasion. Members saw it as their task to remove unnecessary concern from and not present wrong information to, as a Dutch newspaper phrased this, the 'simple people'.[48] For some this was not enough. At one of the meetings in Bandung where the scheme was discussed, an Indonesian – he was described as a native who had left government service because he could not cooperate

---

[47] *Oetoesan Hindia*, 14-8-1914; *De Locomotief*, 12-1-1915.
[48] *Preanger-bode*, 18-8-1914, cited in *De Locomotief*, 18-8-1914.

with his old-fashioned chief – raised the question of why the Indonesians in the ambulance corps were not fitted out with arms.[49] As many of his compatriots were likewise to argue, he wondered whether the natives were not trusted by Batavia to defend their own motherland.

In the estate belt of East Sumatra, the request to constitute an armed corps to maintain law and order and to fight a foreign enemy came from the Sarekat Islam. As in Magelang the Dutch *Resident* tried to dissuade the initiators from continuing with their plans. An additional reason for his reluctance may have been that one of the advisors of the Sarekat Islam branch, an Arab, had urged that the permission of the Turkish sultan should first be asked. The *Resident* told the initiators that before they proceeded any further, they had to prove that people really were prepared to join. It would have been better if he had held his tongue. At the end of August a well-attended meeting took place in the Oranje cinema in Medan. The chairman of the local Sarekat Islam, Mohamed Saleh, delivered a glowing speech in which he suggested that though the immediate danger seemed to have passed, nothing was ever certain. Japan had entered the war, and the Netherlands could still be dragged into it. Ending his speech with 'Long live the Netherlands and its colony!', he asked his audience to join him in this declaration and to sign a form promising to honour the obligations enjoined upon those entering a volunteer corps. Loud and lengthy applause, mixed with cheers 'Long live the Netherlands' greeted his words.[50]

In the western part of Sumatra, in Fort de Cock, it was Maharaja Soetan Casajangan Soripada, who called a meeting of Indonesian heads, civil servants, and 'well-to-do citizens' in the club Madjoe (Progress) at the end of August. Casajangan had lived in Holland and had acquired a certain fame by founding organizations such as the Het Eeuwige Juliana Instituut voor de Eenheid en Vooruitgang van Grooter Nederland (The Eternal Juliana Institute for the Unity and Progress of the Greater Netherlands). The theme of his speech not unnaturally tied in with this. Prosperity in the Archipelago could be attributed to 'Father Government', and the interests of the population were closely linked to those of the government. He asked himself how the people could protect their own interests and those of the government if they had no weapons. As happened elsewhere, his suggestion that a corps of volunteers be formed was greeted with great enthusiasm by the audience. Four days later a formal request signed by eighty people was presented to the *Assistent-Resident*. The next day a party was organized, attended by the *Assistent-Resident* to 'seal

---

[49] *De Locomotief*, 22-8-1914.
[50] *Sumatra Post*, cited in *De Locomotief*, 7-9-1914; Note Schrieke 30-4-1917, NA, Kol. Openbaar, Vb. 14-2-1918 38.

the affection and loyalty of the natives to the Government'.[51] In Makassar 'Christian natives' rallied to form a volunteer corps. In Medan a missionary wanted to recruit among the Christian Chinese.

The top leaders of the nationalist movement were more cautious. Boedi Oetomo convened a meeting of branch leaders to decide in which way loyalty and devotion to Dutch rule could best be expressed. Leaders of other organizations were also invited to attend. The meeting, which took place in the Stadstuin (City Garden) of Semarang on 13 September, did not produce the result the board had intended. Between three and six hundred people attended (the lowest estimate coming from *Oetoesan Hindia*, the highest from *De Locomotief*).[52] The debate centred on what concrete support could be given to the government if the Netherlands Indies were to be attacked. Dwidjosewojo explained what was at stake. The drive for colonies in the past few decades had not left him unimpressed. He pointed out that in the 1910s more countries were actively engaged in acquiring colonies than ever before. This meant that were the Netherlands to become involved in the war, a new foreign overlord would be likely to take over rule in Java. The Dutch army and Navy certainly did not have the wherewithal to repel an invasion. Dwidjosewojo wondered whether a new colonial ruler would mean an improvement in the fate of the Javanese. Since the turn of the century, the colonial government had begun to take the welfare of the population to heart, irrespective of the race to which they belonged. Citing examples of such new efforts, Dwidjosewojo mentioned the schools established by the colonial government. The schools were of 'great assistance to the progress of the natives [as they meant] the opening of the door which leads to progress'. Were the Netherlands to continue on this path, 'real progress' would certainly be the result. The Javanese would become the equal of other peoples. Were another nation to take the place of the Netherlands, the future would be jeopardized. A new master could treat his new possession with less consideration and act in the spirit of the late but not lamented Vereenigde Oostindische Compagnie.

Dwidjosewojo fervently argued that this meant that it was the duty of the Javanese to defend their island against outside aggression. But how? Though Javanese had known how to wage war and how to use weapons less than 100 years ago, they had lost this skill. Donating money was a possibility, but: 'Generally speaking, we have no money, we are poor, so in that way we also cannot help; so far we have made other races rich by our labour'. These words were greeted with loud applause. In the weeks to come Tjokroaminoto and others would also reiterate these two points. Colonialism had paid to Javanese expertise in waging war. Colonialism had also made them poor. In

---

[51] *De Locomotief*, 9-9-1914.
[52] *De Locomotief*, 14-9-1914; *Oetoesan Hindia*, 15-9-1914.

Semarang, Dwidjosewojo concluded that what remained to be done was what the Javanese had always done. They could contribute their bodies and the labour of their hands and feet. They could act as transport workers or join an ambulance. This was what they could offer the Dutch government and army in times of war.[53]

Dwidjosewojo had been cheered, but critical voices were also raised at the Boedi Oetomo meeting. Not everybody agreed with the Dwidjosewojo's eagerness to rush to the assistance of a Dutch war effort. Some of those present used the occasion to plead for political reforms. One of them, Raden Soemarsono, called a declaration of loyalty out of order. The pledge could only be given by leaders who really represented the people, in other words by an elected parliament. Another who took the floor was Raden Soedjono, chairman of the Sarekat Islam in Semarang. He also made it clear that in his opinion the initiative taken by Boedi Oetomo was superfluous and beside the point. With some sarcasm Raden Soedjono pointed out that what Dwidjosewojo had suggested was no different from the so-called *gugur gunung* services, a special corvée the government was entitled to ask from the population if an emergency or disaster threatened. In the past the Javanese had always complied with such a demand and they would offer their labour again were they ordered to do so. The whole crux of the matter was not how to help the Dutch, but how to shield Javanese society from the consequences of the war. Plans should be developed to prevent the population suffering. Money could be saved, stocks of rice built up, or the area under cultivation expanded.

Soedjono's words triggered off a lively discussion in which Tjokroaminoto also participated. Speaking, as he stressed, as a private person because he had not been able to consult the other members of his board, Tjokroaminoto ruled out assistance to the Dutch army. Retribution for such help from an invader would be severe. Civilians who did help might experience the same fate as the population of Louvain. If Indonesians were intent on improving their military skills, they could always become a soldier. There were other ways to help the Dutch. Indonesians could refuse to act as transport workers for the enemy. They should also decline to act as spies for an invader, even if large sums of money were promised as a reward. Above all, God had allowed the war and people should pray to Him that the Netherlands would not become a party to the war. As other nationalists, Tjokroaminoto used the occasion to stress that the natives were not skilled in using arms. He turned this observation into a plea to the government to take measures to redress this and expand the possibilities open to Indonesians to undertake military training. He also underlined, and his words were greeted with much applause, that under the

[53] *De Locomotief,* 14-9-1914; *Oetoesan Hindia,* 15-9-1914, 23-9-1914.

present circumstances the colonial authorities should do something to earn the cooperation of the indigenous population. Batavia should be more receptive to the suggestions advanced by the Sarekat Islam, Boedi Oetomo and other organizations. Unity of all the population groups would be what counted in a confrontation with a foreign enemy. Confronted with such dissident voices, the leaders of Boedi Oetomo gave in. They concluded that the meeting could not come to any decision.

The opposition to the proposals of the Boedi Oetomo board were indicative of the mood of many supporters of the nationalist movement. In the early days of the war opposition like it did not receive the attention it should have, as such opinions were overshadowed by the many demonstrations of loyalty and the pledges to assist the colonial authorities in maintaining law and order. Even in Aceh, local leaders stated that they were prepared to fight for Holland wherever they should be sent. In view of all this, Idenburg had been able to wire Pleyte a few days before the City Garden meeting took place that the political conditions were good and that the natives 'without exception [were] very loyal'.[54] This observation ended up a fortnight later in the Queen's speech. She stated that the attitude of the native population left nothing to be desired. Various speakers in Parliament used the occasion to praise the loyalty of the natives. One of them, Van Deventer, suggested that when peace returned the Indonesians should be rewarded for their stance by allowing them to have a share in the administration of the colony. It goes without saying that this was with a rider stating that all depended on their cultural and intellectual development. *Oetoesan Hindia* was pleased. It reacted by writing that the Dutch had finally begun to understand. The promise was a good sign.[55]

Manifestations of loyalty in themselves already served Dutch defence. In an attempt to show the outside world how pro-Dutch the local population was – Pabst had convinced Idenburg that this was necessary – in early 1915 Rinkes and the *Residents* of the Moluccas and the Minahasa were asked to list all manifestations of loyalty since the outbreak of the war. Rinkes was given additional instructions to try to influence the native press. The following year the campaign was stepped up after the arrival of Spijkman, who offered articles entitled 'The Dutch voice' free of charge to *Kaoem Moeda*, *Sinar Djawa*, *Oetoesan Hindia*, and other Malay newspapers.

Support for the Dutch did not abate. In an 'atmosphere of robbery and murder on a large scale', as one Indonesian sketched the situation in a Dutch-language newspaper in Batavia, the Dutch were still needed to protect and

---

[54] *Atjeh-Nieuwsblad*, cited in *Oetoesan Hindia*, 19-9-1914; Idenburg to Pleyte, 9-9-1914, NA, Kol. Geheim, Vb. 16-9-1914 A19.
[55] *Oetoesan Hindia*, 7-11-1914.

guide the population on its path to independence.[56] It was a fairly generally expressed opinion. To become the object of war would be no pleasure; it would bring great misery.[57] In reaction to the uproar Yosaburo Takekoshi's article had created *Oetoesan Hindia* wrote in 1916 that 'we may expect nothing good if a Foreign Power should come bursting in and brandishes the torch of war in our motherland, violates our daughters, exterminates our cattle, destroys our properties, and sacrifices everything to its own interest, which, moreover, is absolutely not ours'. There was only one slogan: 'Orange for ever. Long live the Queen.'[58] At other moments love for the Dutch tricolour was stressed. In September 1916 a representative of the central board of the Sarekat Islam reminded his audience that people should not forget that were Dutch rule to be threatened, the population would also find themselves into a tight corner.[59] Nevertheless, in spite of such opinions which fell reassuringly on Dutch ears, gradually as the war progressed, less accommodating voices could be heard. The catalyst was developed by the Dutch administration to involve Indonesians in the defence of the colony. Reacting to the plans, Indonesians were quick to point out that much was still amiss in colonial society, and that concessions by the colonial administration were called for before such a native militia could be considered.

---

[56] *De Indische Gids* 1915, II:1300-2.
[57] *Oetoesan Hindia*, 5-2-1916, 6-2-1916.
[58] *Oetoesan Hindia*, cited in *De Locomotief*, 15-3-1916.
[59] *De Indische Gids* 1916, II:1684.

CHAPTER X

A native militia

At various meetings the calls to assist in the defence of the colony highlighted not so much the question of native volunteer corpses, but that of the establishment of a militia (the contemporary term for an army of conscripts). The campaign to establish a native militia came to be known as the Indië Weerbaar (Resistant Indies) movement. It was propagated in the colony with an intensity comparable to that of the Onze Vloot campaign in Holland.

Conscription had been toyed with for decades. The first suggestions for a European militia dated from the 1880s, when a militia had been advanced as an alternative to the existing citizen militias (a sort of voluntary police force). A native militia was first discussed in 1907. Between 1907 and 1914 the issue was raised from time to time. One of the persons to do so was P.C.C. Hansen. Under the pen-name of Boeka in 1909 he published an article, 'Indië Weerbaar', in *De Indische Gids* about a guerrilla war fought against a foreign invader by a Javanese voluntary militia, commanded by Javanese. One of the advantages Hansen saw was that members of such a militia were accustomed to the climate in Java. Japanese soldiers were not. In a sense it was a daring proposition. Hansen pleaded for rifle drills for the militia members. Apparently still harbouring lingering doubts about how far Javanese could be trusted, he cautioned that good care had to be taken to see that the number of rifles in circulation in Javanese society remained small (Boeka 1909).

Initially, the colonial authorities reacted pretty lukewarmly to suggestions about forming a native militia. Mounting international tension on the eve of the World War brought about a change in attitude. Batavia and The Hague came to see a native militia as a useful addition to the regular army. The many manifestations of loyalty formed yet another reason to consider the formation of such a force. That the military in the Netherlands Indies was in favour became clear in 1914 when a 'staff-officer', that is Major J. van der Weijden, indeed a member of the General Staff of the colonial army, wrote an article in the *Java-Bode* in support of a native militia. Van der Weijden tried to convince his readers that recent developments had proved that a native militia did not necessarily have to be a public danger. He explained that it would not create a force of 'enemy soldiers' as some feared. In his argument Van der Weijden disclosed that the authorities had gone far beyond concluding that conscription was possible. They had grown convinced that a militia would cement interracial solidarity: 'Standing side to side in the defence of the Archipelago against alien violence will strengthen the bond between Dutchmen and Natives'.[1] The manifestations of loyalty after the outbreak of the war had indubitably impressed Van der Weijden. On another occasion he wrote that these pledges 'from all circles and layers of Native society' had proved that the population would not turn against the Dutch were a foreign enemy to invade Java. The 'incorrigibly anxious' had been mistaken (Van der Weijden 1916:29).

Conscription – to be confined to Java and the Minahasa – emerged a hotly debated issue during World War One. The idea was for a militia of Europeans and Javanese, but not the Chinese. As the immediate pre-war years had shown as a group the Chinese were too restless. The Arabs were also excluded because they were distrusted for religious reasons and for the putative influence they might exert on the Muslim population. Conscription would open a reservoir of potential soldiers and would cost less than the recruitment of fresh professional soldiers. This, of course, was an important argument in its favour. Another plus point was the realization that new volunteers for the colonial army might not be forthcoming once the Netherlands Indies was actually at war (Van der Weijden 1916:21-2). Fringe benefits were deployed to convince doubters that a militia was a useful institution. One, and this was an argument advanced by Europeans and Javanese alike, was that military training would encourage discipline, neatness, and personal initiative among the Javanese. Bearing this in mind some went as far as to plead for compulsory gymnastics in the schools the Javanese children attended to prepare them for such military service.

Leaders of the Sarekat Islam and Boedi Oetomo were among those who argued that a militia was a good way to instill discipline and to improve the physical condition of the young people. Boedi Oetomo leaders expressed the hope that a militia would restore the military prowess the Javanese had once possessed in days long past. Military training might revive the *ksatria*, the warrior class, spirit of the past. Another argument frequently mentioned in favour was that the stature of the Javanese would be improved if they showed that they were prepared to make sacrifices for the defence of their country. Acceptance as trusted soldiers was presented as a way to bring the Javanese a step further on the road towards emancipation. Enhancing the role of the Javanese in the defence of the colony would, to borrow contemporary parlance, be one of the ways to ensure that the Javanese would become full human beings. This was considered so important that just after Austria-Hungary had

---

[1]   *Java-Bode,* cited in *De Indische Gids* 1914, II:1733.

declared war on Serbia, Boedi Oetomo announced that at a party meeting in August it would discuss the possibility of the establishment of a lower military school for natives.[2] It was argued that a military school would contribute to the emancipation of the Javanese, and would improve their standing in relation to the other population groups which made up colonial society. The voices of the Javanese leaders were not crying in the wilderness. Similar views were not unheard of in the Indo-European community, where Insulinde members from Surakarta had already spoken out in favour of a militia at the end of 1912. They stressed that conscription would be a good way to improve the lot of the poor Indo-Europeans, who were loafing around idly.[3]

Some of the questions raised about a native militia were of a technical nature. One, and this point had already been raised in 1909, was the absence of a register of births for the Javanese population. The absence of such a register made recruitment a complicated matter. One solution suggested was to call up Islamic boys a certain number of years after circumcision. Another possibility considered was to leave recruitment to the village heads. A more important reason to worry was that the absence of a register of births would allow young Javanese men (except for the educated ones, of whom it was easier to keep track) to dodge conscription or to desert melting away in the masses.

The main issues which the militia discussion raised were different. They centred on political and security implications. Defence had to be strengthened, but it might be dangerous to arm natives to accomplish this. Some Dutch people found this a real dilemma. One newspaper wrote that '[w]ithout the energetic support of a Native militia we will lose our colony to a *foreign* enemy and with that Native militia to an *internal* enemy'.[4] People who aired such an opinion were not very impressed by the manifestations of loyalty. They doubted whether the Javanese would actually rally to the assistance of the Dutch in a real crisis. To some the vows of loyalty were nothing but an insignificant gesture by a few intellectuals. They believed that the masses had no opinion at all. Others were distrustful of the intellectuals. In 1916 when the *Resident* of Kedu suggested that the students in the highest class of the OSVIA should receive training in markmanship, the Governor General seemed positively inclined. When he asked senior civil servants in the field of education for their opinion about such training of students of eighteen years and older – as had been introduced in some European countries – the answers were diverse. Some were in favour. Others advised against. They warned that it was exactly among these young Indonesians that the 'dissatisfied elements' were

---

[2] *De Locomotief,* 30-7-1914.
[3] *De Locomotief,* 13-6-1915, cited in *De Indische Gids* 1915, II:1467.
[4] *De Indische Gids* 1917, I:664.

to be found.[5] Experiments were started, but only on a small scale, and limited to young European men.

Those sympathetic to the emerging nationalist movement, among them senior advisers of Idenburg, showed more of an inclination to support plans for a native militia. They usually considered only the conscription of young men who belonged to the intellectual and social elite of Javanese society; though this selection criterion was often disregarded in the heated debates which followed. The editor of *De Locomotief*, who could also not agree with the blunt refusal of some *Residents* to discuss native volunteer corpses, suggesting that if the government trusted the nationalist movement it should not withhold the arms and military training they asked for from the population. There was no danger in doing so as long as the colonial government did not embark on a policy which alienated the population.

Many at the time considered Javanese to be poor military material. Because of the militia plans, a volte-face was required. The dreams some Dutch people in the Netherlands Indies and in Holland fostered about a people's army of Javanese resisting a foreign invasion were very wide of the mark of the widely held views about the soldierly qualities of the Javanese. Therefore it is not surprising that Major Van der Weijden commented in 1916 that a Javanese could make a good soldier. To underline his statement he recalled the fierce resistance which Diponogoro had mounted during the Java War in the 1820s. When Javanese realized that their existence was at stake, they would fight as bravely as the Japanese. Van der Weijden's conclusion was clear: 'The Javanese is not inferior, he is being made inferior by us' (Van der Weijden 1916:31).

The idea of a militia consisting of fierce Javanese provided the Dutch with new comfort and confidence. The editor of *De Locomotief* speculated about a defence mounted by millions of Indonesians. Blatantly conjuring up an image of savages, he posed that 'the people not bound by Western civilization nor by uncomprehended law of war [would] present the intruder with a defence which will appear to be an invincible obstacle for many of his operations'.[6] In Holland the newspaper *Algemeen Handelsblad* wrote that without arming the natives the colony would be lost. A militia would make the difference: 'When a fleet of submarines is on guard in our Indian waters, and this is backed up by an army of 3 million Javanese, with yet another several 100,000 Malays, Manadonese, Ambonese, Timorese, the evil lusts of whoever it is, will certainly be somewhat tempered'.[7]

Others remained unconvinced. The idea that the Javanese population was

---

[5] *De Locomotief*, 16-9-1916; Creutzberg to Van Limburg Stirum, 26-10-1917, NA, Kol. Openbaar, Vb. 14-6-1918 17.
[6] *De Locomotief*, 26-11-1914.
[7] *Algemeen Handelsblad*, cited in *De Indische Gids* 1916, I:611.

to be fitted out with arms filled them with horror. A reader of a Dutch newspaper in Holland who had lived in the Netherlands Indies wrote in a letter to the editor that natives were unsuited for the task of defending the colony, and that they would remain so in the near future. According to him, this was not the greatest weakness of the conscription plan: 'The brown brother [...] with the weapons in the hand is simply not to be trusted'. Needless to say, the author of these words was no advocate of political and social emancipation. Emancipation would only speed up the ruin of the Dutch. Life in the colony was already characterized by what he considered to be increasing recalcitrance, anti-social unmanageability, and a love of boyish protests. His conclusion was that the 'brown brother' hid his racial hatred with 'Eastern disingenuousness'. The better educated he was, the better he succeeded in hiding his true feelings.[8] In Java itself the *Nieuws van den Dag*, viewing any emancipation of Indonesians with mistrust if not with downright hostility, especially remained vehemently opposed throughout.

In the plans of Batavia and The Hague, a militia in Java should be confined to young men with a certain level of education. The main reason to opt for such an educational criterion was that military service had to be as short as possible. The feeling was that within such a period (initially eight-and-a-half months was proposed) simple farmers could not be turned into good soldiers, especially because they carried an extra handicap as they did not understand the language of instruction used in the army, Malay. Not so long before military experts had even argued that it would take up to six years to turn a native – that is a Javanese – into an 'employable combat soldier'.[9] Educated Javanese would cause fewer problems. They were said to be able to become good soldiers in the same relatively short span time as it took the lower classes in the Holland to achieve this (De Greve 1913:9). Moreover, the military would not be pleased if it had to cope with 'a great many stupid fellows'.[10] Some countered that such ideas left eligible for conscription only a category of Javanese, who, like the Dutch, as a group were too small, and had many civil servants among its members, people who could be ill-missed in their job.[11] Owners of sugar estates and tobacco factories also raised concerns. They feared the consequences for the colonial economy if young Javanese were withdrawn from the workforce because they had to enlist for military service.

To drum up support for a militia it was decided to launch a propaganda drive. Idenburg assigned Rinkes this special task in the spring of 1915. He was to propagate the idea of a militia through the native press and in public

---

[8] *De Maasbode*, cited in *De Indische Gids* 1917, I:789.
[9] *Rapport* 1913:94.
[10] *De Locomotief*, 26-11-1914.
[11] *Bataviaasch Handelsblad*, cited in *De Indische Gids* 1916, II:962.

lectures. Consequently, even the Commissie voor Volkslectuur, the Committee for the Spread of Popular Literature, became involved in the organization of lectures about the need for a native militia. Local Dutch and Javanese civil servants were likewise mobilized. What happened after this resembled the agitation that had surrounded the Onze Vloot propaganda. Japan was singled out as the main threat and Dutch-Japanese relations suffered as a consequence. In their eagerness to depict the seriousness of the danger posed by Japan, the Dutch expressed their opinions so bluntly that Tokyo took offence. Japanese aggression was frequently mentioned, and they were not choosy in their vocabulary, as the most important reason to improve the defences of the Netherlands Indies. The tone was so unbridled that some feared that if the Indië Weerbaar advocates did not take care to mince their words, the campaign would do more harm than good for the future of the Netherlands Indies.[12] One of the persons who expressed apprehension was the Dutch Envoy in Tokyo, D. van Asbeck. He inquired in The Hague whether nothing could be done to put an end to the offensive reports about Japan in the Dutch-language newspapers in the middle of 1916.

The Japanese Consul General of course protested. He was provided with an excellent opportunity to do so at the end of 1916 when a Japanese *Resident* of the Netherlands Indies, Yoroyoshi Minami, who had reacted in kind to Dutch bombast was prosecuted. Minami, editor for Japanese affairs of what in colonial jargon was called the Chinese-Malay newspaper *Pertimbangan*, had commented on the maltreatment of a Japanese citizen by the police in Semarang. In an article entitled 'Siapa lebih kedjam' (Who is more cruel), Minami (who did not speak Dutch) stigmatized campaigners of Indië Weerbaar as instigators who had been ordered by Batavia to blaze abroad that Japan had acted cruelly in Korea and Taiwan. Minami also noted that in Indië Weerbaar propagandists presented Japan as an expansionist and cruel nation while they remained silent about the fact that European Powers had robbed Asians of their independence with the sole aim of lining their own pockets. Minami had also intimated that in order to keep the natives stupid and so be able to continue the exploitation of the Netherlands Indies, the Dutch government did all it could to prevent the development of friendly relations between Japanese and Chinese. He had even accused the Dutch government of having stimulated the Chinese boycott of Japanese products for this very purpose.[13]

Within a week after the article had appeared in the *Pertimbangan* of 18 September, the colonial authorities opened an investigation. What had offended senior civil servants and other Dutchmen most was that Minami would

---

[12] *De Telegraaf*, cited in *De Indische Gids* 1917, II:935.
[13] *De Locomotief*, 28-9-1916; *Warna Warta*, cited in *Koloniaal Tijdschrift* 1917, I:112-3; *De Indische Gids* 1917, I:701.

have appeal to Indonesians, prompting them to organize and resist Dutch rule: 'The first thing you must do is to start a movement to make the whole of the Indies strong, not to repulse an attack by Japan, but only truly to gain freedom; one has to rise; at present the Netherlands cannot obtain weapons from abroad; always impress your freedom on future generations'.[14] During Minami's trial, part of the discussion focused on the word *bergerak* Minami had used. Soon, *pergerakan* was to become the general word to denote the nationalist movement. In 1916 Dutchmen were not sure what to make of such a word. Did *bergerak* mean *opstaan*, to stand up or to rise, in the sense of to rebel?[15] No Indonesian had rebelled against Dutch rule. This, the public prosecutor maintained was not because of Minami, but only to the 'indifference and high level of civilization and development and impartiality and so forth of the readers of the newspaper'.[16] The public prosecutor pulled out all the stops to show how spiteful Minami's article had been, and how it fitted in with the actions of the enemies of Dutch rule: Minami's words saying that many Japanese had died for the Chinese revolution; Takekoshi's anti-Dutch articles; and the praise in *Pertimbangan* by Darnakoesoemo of Douwes Dekker as a saviour who one day would return to rescue his people. He also did not fail to mention that Darnakoesoema was a former editor of *De Expres*. Minami himself denied that he had done anything wrong. He only admitted that his tone had been somewhat sharp. This he attributed to a severe attack of malaria fever when he had written the article and to the fact that he had fallen very ill when, not understanding the instructions, he had taken three quinine tablets three times, instead of three times one. The article had to be finished and Japanese were used to continue to work till they dropped down. Minami was sentenced to one year's imprisonment, half of what had been demanded. The court had found a very important mitigating circumstance: Minami was 'a half-hearted loudmouth and not much more than an instrument in the hands of others'.[17]

Malay and Chinese newspapers copied Minami's article. They also drew attention to the reaction of the Japanese Consul General, Matsumoto, who demanded that Minami should be expelled immediately and not after he had served his sentence. Another demand made by the Consul General was the prosecution of the radical protagonists of the Indië Weerbaar movement. Among them were the editors of those Dutch-language newspapers which were most outspoken in depicting the Japanese threat and hence were guilty of sowing hatred against Japan and the Japanese in the eyes of the Consul General. He warned that if no action were taken, the safety of Dutchmen in

[14] *Pertimbangan*, cited in *De Locomotief*, 28-9-1916.
[15] *De Locomotief*, 14-11-1916.
[16] *De Locomotief*, 16-11-1916.
[17] *De Locomotief*, 22-11-1916.

Japan might no longer be guaranteed. Batavia did not yield to Japanese pressure. No editors were prosecuted. Minami had to serve his sentence. After his release, Minami returned to Japan in October 1917. By then *Pertimbangan*, the 'Organ of all oppressed races', had already ceased to exist.

Accusations of *haatzaai* and subversion had led to the conviction of Minami, who banged the table demanding proof of the accusation during his trial. The Attorney-General and the judge may have been so eager to sentence him that his trial set a judicial precedent. For the first time it was deemed unnecessary to prove that the accused had consciously intended to sow hatred to find him guilty. The Director of Justice took the precedent as a sign that judges were alive to the dangers louring over law and order in the colony.[18] Indonesians and Chinese had other ideas. They seized upon the heavy sentence to present examples of Dutchmen who had insulted the feelings of non-Europeans and had got off scot-free.

Following in the footsteps of what had happened in the German community in the Netherlands Indies, the hostile press led to the foundation of a Japanese weekly. It was written in Malay and named *Tjahaja Selatan*, Southern Glow. The paper aimed to present a better image of Japan. *Tjahaja Selatan* wanted to counter what the editors described as the false reports and fallacious opinions about Japan which were published in the Netherlands Indies press. After some initial problems – all the Chinese contacted with a view to becoming editor-in-chief refused the offer – the first issue appeared in May 1916. Editor was Fukuda. The anti-Japanese Chinese-Malay newspaper *Sin Po* wrote that Fukuda had owned brothels in Singapore and that he was an alcoholic. *Sin Po* also claimed that the Bank of Taiwan had provided Fukuda with 1,200 guilders starting capital.[19] After thirty weeks *Tjahaja Selatan* went bankrupt.

Relations with Japan did not suffer alone. Another consequence of the pro-militia campaign was that domestic political discussions gained a new dimension. To many of the nationalist leaders who were aware of the weak position of the Netherlands Indies and the disquiet the war had caused among the Dutch, the militia debate provided an excellent opportunity to press for political and social reforms. They wanted better health care, an improvement in hygiene, and better education. With growing force it was stressed that the colonizers, the civil servants and the members of the business community, should change the way they treated the general population. *Oetoesan Hindia* in July 1917 wrote, for instance, that it depended on the attitude of European

---

[18] Note Director of Justice, 28-12-1916, NA, Kol. Openbaar, Vb. 14-6-1919 26.
[19] *De Locomotief*, 16-6-1916.

civil servants whether the Indonesian population would remain loyal to the Dutch, or would welcome another foreign ruler. When Europeans stopped acting in a superior way and started to treat natives as their equal, the Dutch did not have to fear that the 'Japanese peaceful penetration' would take serious root among the population.[20] In a similar vein and arguing that there was very little 'love' lost among the people for the colonial government, in September 1918 it was stated that Dutch civil servants should start to treat the population as their younger brothers and not as slaves. Dutch companies should stop acting in a way which caused only resentment.[21]

Indonesians stressed that equal duties implied equal rights. The implication was that support for a militia was coupled with demands for a representative body in the colony. Compulsory education would often be mentioned as a second concession the Dutch government had to make in return for a native militia. Had this been put into practice it would have proved a very expensive gesture. According to a contemporary estimate, it would cost between 100 and 150 million guilders; six to ten times the existing budget for education (Van Reigersberg Versluys 1917:18).

Most inclined to support a militia were the members of the central board of Boedi Oetomo, the organization from which supporters most of the draftees would have come were recruitment to be limited to young men with a certain level of education. Four of its members – among them Dwidjosewojo – went on a tour throughout Java to drum up support for a militia from local branches in June and July 1915. They wanted to explain to the population that the war in Europe had shown that 'peaceful citizens of a neutral state can be disturbed in their peace and tranquillity with wife and children by foreign intruders [and] how human rights are simply trodden on, in one word how over there the right of the strongest has asserted itself enormously'.[22]

The delegation did not win the popular support it had hoped for. It returned with a long list – twenty-six points in total – of objections and conditions advanced by Boedi Oetomo members and others who had attended the meetings they had addressed. Among these were pleas to end legal and social discrimination first, have conscription preceeded by the establishment of a representative body, and have compulsory education preceed conscription. People had also argued that the Javanese were already taxed to the limit. They could not shoulder yet another burden (which was countered by the argument that come what may the Javanese had to carry the financial costs of a war and

---

[20] *Oetoesan Hindia*, 11-7-1917, IPO 28/1917.
[21] *Neratja*, 18-9-1918.
[22] Hoofdpunten van de door de afgevaardigden v/h hoofdbestuur der Boedi Oetomo te houden voordrachten over de wenschelijkheid van de invoering van militieplicht onder de inlanders van Java en Madoera, NA, Kol. Openbaar, Vb. 13-5-1916 27.

that a militia was far less expensive than a large professional standing army). At meetings others had pointed out that conscription was in the interests of the rich and the government only, the poor had little to gain from it. Still others worried that pupils would not complete their education if finishing school meant that they ran the risk of being drafted. They had also met with disbelief. The government would never allow a militia. Its soldiers would certainly chase the Dutch away.[23]

The same was experienced by Abdoel Moeis when he toured West Java in August 1916 to get support for the Indië Weerbaar movement from the local Sarekat Islam branches. Opposition at the meetings he addressed was great. Nobody wanted to become a soldier, to be ordered to a battlefield. 'I stood almost alone, and was taunted and called a traitor to my country', he wrote in a report to the *Preanger-bode*.[24] People roared when he tried to explain to them how much they would suffer were another nation to take the place of the Dutch. Nevertheless, using all the powers of persuasion he had succeeded in having meetings speak out in favour of Indië Weerbaar.

Such reactions reflected the general mood. Members of the Boedi Oetomo accused their leaders of serving as instruments of Dutch rule (Radjiman 1917:148). If the truth be told Javanese had flocked to the meetings. They had done so partly to vent their opposition, and partly after some urging by members of the Javanese civil service to attend. A militia was not a prospect that appealed to the Javanese if it touched their own fate. When Batavia sounded out the opinion of the *Residents* and Regents in Java, the conclusion was that enthusiasm among the population was like a damp squid. The Director of the Civil Service feared that the mood among the educated Javanese was even less favourable.[25]

Javanese nationalist leaders used the militia campaign first and foremost as a political instrument. Their support for a militia was because they saw it as a means to enforce reforms. This was particularly clear in August 1915 during a conference of Boedi Oetomo in Bandung, where the militia was one of the main points on the agenda. Again strong reservations were the order of the day. Those present made no secret of their opinion that Boedi Oetomo, which had only a few thousand members at most, could not speak on behalf of the Javanese population, especially not when what it had to say concerned an issue which was to touch the lives of many. Only a representative body could reflect the opinion of the people. In line with this, a motion was carried which expressed support for conscription only conditionally. Stressing that it was

---

[23] Ringkasan pendapat lezing-lezing oetoesan hoofdbestuur B.O. tentang militie-plicht boeat boemi-poetra, NA, Kol. Openbaar, Vb. 13-5-1916 27.
[24] *Preanger-bode,* cited in *De Locomotief,* 8-9-1916.
[25] Tollenaar to Idenburg, 26-11-1915, NA, Kol. Openbaar, Vb. 13-5-1916 27.

essential that law and order remained undisturbed for the gradual advancement of the Javanese, and that the people be obliged to assist in this effort, the necessity of a native militia was acknowledged. In return, the colonial government should pay a price to gain the cooperation of the population. In view of the many objections and because of the uncertainty of what concrete form conscription would take, the population had to be consulted before any further steps were taken. This meant that a representative body should be created.[26] In the Dutch-language newspapers it was reported that the motion was received with thunderous applause.[27]

Reservations among members of the Sarekat Islam were even greater. Only a minority of the branches in Java – according to Abdoel Moeis only 20 out of 120 – were in favour.[28] Nevertheless, the central board decided to acquiesce in the plan. Using the opportunity to stress that the party's ultimate aim was independence under the protection of the Netherlands – an objective which might be threatened were the Archipelago to be occupied by another country – in August 1916 a resolution was drafted which called for reforms and a change in attitude on the part of the Dutch. It was observed that Dutch civil servants and other members of the European community were far from being paragons of the Ethical Policy. They continued to treat the population with contempt and disdain. Observing that 'the delusion of superiority of the Dutch' and the arbitrariness in the behaviour of both Dutch civil servants and private persons had caused displeasure and resentment among the population, the colonial government was urged to act to find ways to remove the causes of popular discontent. Only then could it be assured that if the Netherlands Indies were invaded 'the displeasure and resentment will not elicit resistance from the population, unwillingness to place their trust in the government, making the task of the state more difficult'. In conclusion it was stated that the ways to improve the defence of the colony was a matter to be decided on by a Parliament, elected by the people of the Netherlands Indies. Admitting that it would take time to form such a representative body, and that international developments might make the establishment of a militia a compelling necessity, it was asserted that conscription should at the very least be coupled with an improvement in the civil rights of the population. This was the only way the people would consider conscription 'a national duty' and would accept it without feelings of 'aversion and resentment'. The Sarekat Islam board presented compulsory military service as the lesser of two evils. Improving the defence of the Netherlands Indies indubitably would result in additional taxes. The native population, living 'in very miserable economic

---

[26] Motion Boedi Oetomo meeting, NA, Kol. Openbaar, Vb. 13-5-1916 27.
[27] *The Preanger-bode,* cited in the *De Indische Gids* 1915, II:1613.
[28] *De Locomotief,* 19-1-1917.

circumstances' could ill afford to bear such extra financial burdens.[29]

The fact that such critical voices were so openly and frequently expressed puzzled the editors of newspapers in Holland. Up to that moment they had received from the Netherlands Indies only reports about manifestations in support of Dutch rule in such troubled times, and had enthusiastically welcomed such tidings as an indication that the colony was ruled in a right and proper fashion. Was the resolution of Sarekat Islam a threat, as the *Nieuwe Rotterdamsche Courant* maintained, or, as *Het Vaderland* put it, a warning?[30] Another conclusion was that 'people over there' had deceived the Dutch in Holland by reporting only on proponents of a militia, ignoring the opposition to it.[31]

In their coupling of conscription with political reforms Indonesians presented the Dutch with a problem. There were those who agreed that political concessions had to be made in return for conscription. 'Remember the Philippines' was no longer heard as a slogan, but to some Dutch people, and Idenburg was among them, the Dutch should rule the colony in such a way that the population would realize that they would only be worse off were another country to replace Dutch overlordship.[32] Elaborating on the theme that it was the attitude of the people which in the last resort would determine whether the Netherlands could hold on to its colony, some Dutch people began to express their disappointment in fact that too little had been done to secure the loyalty of the Indonesians. The *Bataviaasch Nieuwsblad* wrote that had such a policy been followed, it would have rendered the cry 'Asia for the Asians' ineffective as a political slogan.[33] In *De Locomotief* it was initially argued that conscription should be restricted to the intellectuals and the urban well-to-do. If they aspired to full civil rights, this implied that they had to shoulder full civic duties.[34]

Others found the link between a militia and political reform less obvious. They pointed out that both the Javanese and the Dutch would suffer were the Japanese to take over. Or, as a report by a senior naval officer about the strengthening of the Dutch fleet stated, the Japanese had 'completely different views about the rights to which an oppressor is entitled than civilized Westerners are entertaining'.[35] In the eyes of these Dutch people, this observation made the demand for political concessions irrelevant. Some also grumbled about

---

[29] Motion Central Sarekat Islam, 29-8-1916, NA, Kol. Geheim, Vb. 15-11-1916 Q14.
[30] *De Indische Gids* 1917, I:490-5.
[31] *Koloniaal Tijdschrift* 1917:236-8.
[32] *Orgaan der Vereeniging 'Indië Weerbaar'* 1-3:13.
[33] *Bataviaasch Nieuwsblad*, cited in *De Indische Gids* 1916, I:608.
[34] *De Locomotief*, 15-9-1914.
[35] Note Tijdeman, NA, Kol. Geheim, Vb. 1-12-1914 Q23.

the lack of appreciation shown for their good intentions. Another reason put forward as grounds to refuse concessions in return for conscription was the economic and social development of the population the colonial government wanted to achieve. Had the aim of the Dutch presence still been the exploitation of the colony, as it had been before 1900, matters would have been different. Now that Javanese benefited from Dutch rule there was nothing wrong in having them have to serve their country (Van der Weijden 1916:24-5).

There was also some irritation. In expressing their opinion, some Javanese did not behave as servile people and did not hesitate to bring home their point in plain, unsubmissive language. Their initiative in daring to formulate demands in this way did not go down well in the European community. The journal of the Nederlandsch-Indische Officiers Vereeniging (Netherlands Indies Officers Association) asserted that when the indigenous population fully realized that the loss of the Netherlands Indies would be as great a disaster for them as for the Dutch, they would recognize that it was not becoming to ask first 'what do we get in return' before agreeing to a militia.[36] This lamentation was uttered in relation to what had happened during a debate organized by the Indische Krijgskundige Vereeniging (Indian Military Association) in the military club Concordia in Batavia in April 1916. Forty Indonesians had attended. On this occasion, at which General De Greve, pleading for a general conscription of Javanese, had conjured up a picture of 'farming soldiers or drilling farmers' much in the fashion of the later people's armies, four of them had given a talk.[37] One was Satiman, who described life in the military barracks as hell on earth and argued that much was demanded of the native population, while nothing was given in return. He was immediately put in his place by Captain W. Muurling. Muurling said that the distrust in the good intentions of the Dutch administration which such words implied was completely unfounded. Indonesians should be aware that the government had frequently shown that it acted in a fair and just way and would certainly continue to do so in the future. Satiman (and the other Indonesians who had addressed the meeting in a similar vein) should not forget that they were guests at the meeting. The journal of the Netherlands Indies Officers Association concluded that, in view of 'the sympathetic attitude of a large part of the native population in August and September 1914', what had been said at the meeting had come as a disappointment. The Indonesians who had taken the floor surely did not belong to the 'most enlightened members of Native society'.[38]

The Indië Weerbaar drive reached its climax in the summer of 1916. In July 1916 the Comité Indië Weerbaar was formed. H. s'Jacob, chairman of the

---

[36] *De Indische Gids* 1916, II:968.
[37] *De Indische Gids* 1916, I:774.
[38] *De Indische Gids* 1916, II:968.

Chamber of Commerce and Industry of Batavia, was appointed its President. Deputy Chairman was M.C. Koning, the manager of the KPM. The committee had two secretaries. One was H.G. Brandon. The other was W.V. Rhemrev, a retired Indo-European captain in the colonial army. Among the organizations supporting the committee were the Boedi Oetomo, Sarekat Islam, the Regentenbond, and Narpo Wandowo (Union of Princes). Insulinde refused to join. Elsewhere in Java committees were founded, on which Indonesians and Chinese, preferably the Regents and the heads of the Chinese community, also sat. At times, and how could it be otherwise, such committees organized fancy fairs, music and theatrical performances, and other events to raise money. Stirred up by the nationalist sentiments evoked by the campaign, and by the stress laid upon improving the defence of the colony, individuals also did their bit. In Semarang people who thought it unfair that money was being collected only for ambulances in Europe started a drive to finance a 'Red Cross car' for the colonial army. An Ambulance Committee Central Java was formed. The familiar scene was repeated. Once again ladies visited offices to collect money and a soirée was organized in the club. The Indische Lloyd promised free insurance for the ambulance. The *De Locomotief* also threw its weight behind the campaign and put inserts in its copies in an effort to convince people to donate money. In West Java three tea planters donated 1,800 guilders. The money was intended to be used to buy a machine-gun for the army.[39]

The committee certainly displayed a talent for organization. Its campaign was scheduled to reach its climax on 31 August 1916, Weerbaarheidsdag, Defence Day. In the days leading up to that date, mass gatherings were held in cities all over Java to explain an Indië Weerbaar motion. The resolution read that the war had pressed 'upon every nation the inexorable lesson that it had to be capable of organizing its own defence and if so needed [to be] ready to maintain its independence with its own forces and energy [...]'. Noting that the state of defence of the Netherlands Indies filled 'everybody who is revolted by the possibility of an eventual overpowering and all the fatal consequences thereof with feelings of the deepest disappointment and perturbation' the motion stressed the 'vital interest of enabling the Netherlands Indies to defend itself on land and sea speedily and thoroughly'.[40] In order not to lose the support of the central board of the Sarekat Islam, the term militia was not mentioned in the resolution.

Yet more meetings were held on Queen's Birthday to express formal support for the motion, and where Dutch people, but not only they, expressed patriotic feelings. On 31 August care was taken not to hold the meeting in the

---

[39] *De Locomotief,* 11-9-1916, 18-9-1916, 27-9-1916, 11-10-1916.
[40] s'Jacob to Wilhelmina, 2-9-1916, NA, Kol. Geheim, Vb. 9-9-1916 N1.

evening. It was a Thursday, and *malam djoemat*, the evening before Friday was an especially sacred time for many Muslims.

All meetings, on 31 August and before, were a patent manifestation of nationalist feelings. Dutch flags were displayed and red-white-blue Indië Weerbaar posters were pasted up all over towns. It was reported that the meetings were all well attended, and that more people had turned up than expected. In Semarang, former non-commissioned officers wearing their decorations and accompanied by a band marched through town on 31 August. In Bandung hundreds of Indonesians did the same. Members of the volunteer corps marched in the van. The parade ended at the *alun-alun*, where gymnastic displays put on by European soldiers and a drill by Ambonese soldiers, preceded the actual meeting. In Surabaya, where the driving force behind the Indië Weerbaar movement was S.J. Hirsch, the President of the influential Algemeen Syndicaat van Suikerfabrikanten (General Syndicate of Sugar Producers) that is the association of administrators of sugar estates, the meeting took a special form. In the four corners of the Municipal Gardens Europeans, Natives, Chinese, and Arabs assembled and each group was addressed by its own representative. For the Europeans the speaker was J.G. Boon of the *Soerabaiasch Handelsblad*. Thereupon the crowds walked to the music pavilion in the centre of the park where Hirsch read the resolution with a loud voice.

Everywhere in Java all seems to have gone as planned. In smaller cities like Sukabumi, Salatiga, Purworejo, and Purwakarta thousands of people attended. Nevertheless, imperfections could be spotted, indicating that among Dutch people enthusiasm was not as great as the reports would have us believe. In Surakarta the brother of the *sunan* attended a meeting on 27 August, as did many princes of the royal courts. The manifestation could be counted a success, but it also had all the hallmarks of a failure. Many Javanese, Chinese, and Arabs attended – reportedly 10,000 in total –, but only a few Dutch people were present. The chairman of the meeting spoke publicly about a disgrace.[41] In Makassar no meeting at all was held. Nobody wanted to organize it. The same had happened in Magelang, a garrison city.[42]

Outside Java Indië Weerbaar also won support. In Banjarmasin the drive resulted in the establishment of a European volunteer corps, 39 persons strong.[43] In Aceh a committee had drawn up a motion urging for measures witch would result in a Weerbaar Indië, a defensible Netherlands Indies, as soon as possible. It was reported with some pride that thanks to the telephone the text had been transmitted to Dutchmen all over Aceh in no less than two days. By phone people could also express their support to the motion. On 31

---

[41] *De Locomotief*, 27-8-1916, 28-8-1916.
[42] *De Locomotief*, 1-9-1916, 7-9-1916.
[43] *De Locomotief*, 4-9-1916.

August a few hundred people assembled in the Juliana Club in Banda Aceh, the capital, to express their support. All were Dutch. No Acehnese, Chinese, or Arabs were present. They had not been invited. The excuse was that the organizers of the meeting had been in such a hurry that they had forgotten to invite representatives of the non-European population. The Dutch people present were addressed by the Governor, Lieutenant General H.N.A. Swart, who quoting President Theodore Roosevelt, impressed upon his audience that no one who was not prepared to die for a holy cause was worth living. The national anthem resounded in the club.[44] The mistake of not inviting non-Dutch people was redeemed in October, when 500 people, Europeans, Chinese, and Indonesians, attended a meeting on 15 October at which an Indië Weerbaar committee was constituted in Banda Aceh. For those who did not understand Dutch, the Dutch speeches were translated by Mohamad Djam, adviser to the local Sarekat Islam, who took the opportunity to urge his fellow-Indonesians to join the new association. Indonesians should realize what the consequences would be, were the rule of the Dutch to be replaced by that of another power. Electing a board of which Mohamad Djam, a number of Acehnese, and a local Chinese were to be among the members, was no problem: 'The Governor, practical as always, suggested that he would suggest the persons for the board. Agreed was shouted as one voice.'[45]

In West Sumatra the call was taken up by those who wanted to defend traditional customs against any further Islamization of society. They harnessed Orange, loyalty to the Dutch Queen, and Indië Weerbaar to this struggle.[46] In East Sumatra where feelings of insecurity were especially acute and a drive had been started to induce European men to join volunteer corpses, support had a wider base. In Medan a meeting was organized by Je Maintiendrai on 31 August. Je Maintiendrai had been founded earlier the same month. Its inaugural meeting had been marred by an embarrassing incident. As someone from Medan wrote in a telegram to *De Locomotief* the *Assistent-Resident* had been unadroit 'clumsy' enough to invite a Japanese to attend because he wanted to remove the impression that it was an anti-Japanese manifestation. The Dutch people present decided otherwise and rejected the Japanese in question from the meeting.[47]

Chairman of Je Maintiendrai was H. Ketner, head administrator of the Hollandsch-Amerikaansche Plantage Maatschappij (Holland American Plantation Company) and one of the initiators. Among its board members was the chairman of the local Boedi Oetomo branch. The main aim of the associa-

---

[44] *De Locomotief,* 12-9-1916, 30-10-1916.
[45] *De Locomotief,* 30-10-1916.
[46] *Oetoesan Melajoe,* cited in *Koloniaal Tijdschrift* 191:106.
[47] *De Locomotief,* 3-8-1916.

tion was to provide the East Coast of Sumatra with a Weerbaarheids-vereeniging (Defence Association). True to the conviction of its founders that the East Coast of Sumatra was economically important enough not to be abandoned in the event of war, the Medan meeting passed a slightly different resolution. It called for the speedy establishment of a militia and for a strong defence not only of Java but also of the other islands of the Archipelago.[48] The resolution was received at the 31 August meeting amid loud cheering and the singing of the 'Wien Neêrlands bloed' '(He who has Dutch blood) the then Dutch national anthem.[49] Within months Je Maintiendrai would have 1,150 Dutch, 931 Indonesian, and 37 Chinese members, and 15,760 guilders in hand.[50]

As was the case with the Sarekat Islam and Boedi Oetomo in Java, the board members of Je Maintiendrai were more inclined to express support for a militia than were the rank and file. The latter displayed some radical tendencies. This became evident in September 1916 when a meeting to promote the aims of Je Maintiendrai was held in the Oranje Bioscoop in Medan. The chairmen of the local branches of the Boedi Oetomo and Sarekat Islam spoke out in support of Je Maintiendrai. The audience could not agree wholeheartedly. One of those present flatly appealed that any backing be refused, as long as the population was treated unfairly by the colonial administration. To substantiate his words he mentioned that the Indonesian members of the municipal Coucil were still appointed, and that roads in the Indonesian quarters of town were neglected, while those in European neighbourhoods were well kept.[51]

On 31 August 1916 the most important meeting of all took place in Deca Park in Batavia, opposite the palace of the Governor-General. The Indië Weerbaar leaders had looked forward to the meeting with some misgivings. They had realized that Indonesians had seized upon their movement to voice their own demands. Hence during a preparatory meeting the organizers had decided that it 'was self-evident that debates in which deviant opinions are defended' would not be tolerated.[52] Voices of protest might detract from what they had in mind and might even doom the meeting into a failure. It even made one of proponents of Indië Weerbaar, D. van Hinloopen Labberton, doubt whether it was wise to hold a public meeting. Whatever the manifestation was it was not a failure. If we may believe the Batavia correspondent of *De Locomotief* this could not be attributed to the efforts of s'Jacob, the chairman of the Indië Weerbaar committee. His opening speech, much too long and spoken in a soft,

---

[48] Ketner and Schadée to Van Limburg Stirum, 8-8-1916, Ketner and Schadée to Pleyte, 31-8-1916, NA, Kol. Geheim, Vb. 9-9-1916 N10, Vb. 23-11-1916 C15.
[49] *Orgaan der Vereeniging 'Indië Weerbaar'* 1-3:14.
[50] *De Locomotief,* 11-12-1916.
[51] *De Indische Gids* 1916:1684.
[52] *De Locomotief,* 26-7-1916.

The Decapark in Batavia (collection Kees van Dijk)

uninspired voice, had almost ruined the meeting. Almost nobody had been able to hear what he had said. That the thousands for whom s'Jacob's words had been inaudible had not rioted the correspondent attributed to the fact that they were natives.[53] What he believed had saved the day was the speech by Soetan Toemenggoeng, *assistent-wedana* of Senen. He had brightened up the mood conspicuously. Enthusiasm had reached a climax when 'the small, sympathetic native' waving the Dutch flag had cried out *'Hidoeplah SBM Koningin Wilhelmina!'*, Long Live HM Queen Wilhelmina.[54] s'Jacob had erred even more in the eyes of the Batavia *De Locomotief* correspondent. When the motion had come up, s'Jacobs had asked those who were against to leave. How could he have suggested this? In the crowd it was impossible to leave.[55]

Whatever his own performance s'Jacob afterwards proudly wired Queen Wilhelmina that dozens of native and Chinese societies – 43 to be exact – had sent representatives to the meeting.[56] He estimated that between 10,000 and 15,000 people had attended. *De Locomotief* was also impressed by the 'tremendous crowd'. It wrote that 10,000 people had been present, among

[53] *De Locomotief*, 4-9-1916.
[54] *De Locomotief*, 4-9-1916.
[55] *De Locomotief*, 4-9-1916.
[56] s'Jacob to Wilhelmina, 2-9-1916, NA, Kol. Geheim, Vb. 9-9-1916 N10.

them 'strikingly many ladies and natives'. The resolution had been accepted with 'thunderous applause'.[57] What had transpired at the Deca Park greatly impressed Van Limburg Stirum. In a lengthy wire to Pleyte, he called attention to a 'remarkable sign of evolution in native thought' and in the relationship 'between different classes and with us'. Van Limburg Stirum was convinced that the main reason why a militia received such massive support was that people realized that Dutch rule was the best guarantee for political and social development. Hence, he also wired that 'in native minds obtaining political rights and attaining higher social and political standing are intimately connected with a militia'.[58]

In The Hague the government published a statement. It was full of praise for the 'peculiar' meetings of 31 Augustus. It was explained to the full to the Dutch public that these should be seen as manifestations of the 'progressive development of native society and of the changes in the relationship between the different population groups as well as with the Motherland'.[59] Pleyte also had a message for Van Limburg Stirum, which he had to convey to s'Jacob and Ketner. It must have brought the Dutch community in the Netherlands Indies down to earth with a jolt. The 'extraordinary burdensome circumstances of the day' did not allow for more than modest steps to be taken to strengthen the defence of the Netherlands Indies.[60] The message was not exactly encouraging, which was indeed the reaction from somebody in Aceh, and he was not the only one to draw this conclusion.[61] Queen Wilhelmina praised the Indië Weerbaar campaign in her Queen's speech. She had the same sobering message.

The meeting in the Deca Park over, the Indië Weerbaar committee dissolved itself. Within months a new committee took its place. A committee to set up an association to promote the defence of the Netherlands Indies was founded in January 1917, again with the goal of achieving the participation of all population groups. The initiators were concerned not only with military defence of the colony but also with its economic resilience. Chairman was K.A.R. Bosscha, manager of an estate near Bandung and a member of the Indië Weerbaar committee in that city. Among the members were Rhemrev, Van der Boon, the chairman of the Batavia branch of Onze Vloot, E.H. Carpentier Alting, E.A. Zeilinga, W. Muurling, R.A.A. Achmad Djajadiningrat and J.A. Soselisa. The association was formally founded on 31 August 1917.

---

[57] *De Locomotief,* 31-8-1916.
[58] Van Limburg Stirum to Pleyte, 4-9-1916, NA, Kol. Geheim, Vb. 9-9-1916 N10.
[59] *De Locomotief,* 23-10-1916.
[60] *De Locomotief,* 23-10-1916.
[61] *De Locomotief,* 30-10-1916.

In between there was one matter that remained unresolved. Before 31 August Indonesian leaders who supported the movement had already made it clear that they wanted to send a delegation to Holland to plead the Indië Weerbaar cause. They saw a trip to Holland as a good tactic to have their voice and their demands heard there. s'Jacob, and probably Van Limburg Stirum, did not like it. s'Jacob's worst fear was that the visit of a deputation would spoil the intentions of his committee. When the idea had come up, he could only agree because he considered the task of his committee finished after the Deca meeting. If the nationalist leaders wanted a deputation to travel to Holland, so be it.[62] The matter was not solved so easily. After rumours had spread in Batavia about discord in the Indië Weerbaar committee, which to the chagrin of the press always met behind closed doors, its secretary, namely Brandon, explained in a letter to the newspapers in that city at the end of September that the committee had been dissolved but that it wanted to help to organize the trip for the deputation.[63] The secretary took great care to stress that the deputation and the Indië Weerbaar motion were two separate matters. It was also emphasized that sending a deputation to Holland was something the 'native associations' valued very much, and that 'most European groups' did not see the good of it. In spite of these words the committee more or less took over. It 'ordered' the delegation to present the motion to the Queen, the Minister of the Colonies, and the States General. It also suggested that the deputation, as it came to be called, would be chaired by D. van Hinloopen Labberton. *De Locomotief* wrote that the Deputation was the 'most expensive postman conceivable'.[64] A Chinese-Malay paper concluded that Van Hinloopen Labberton was going along as a *baboe*, as nanny.[65] Others used the same qualification. Van Hinloopen Labberton was 'an expensive sea baboe'.

A second *baboe* to be suggested by the committee was Idenburg. To see that everything went smoothly in Holland Idenburg was indeed asked to act as the delegation's mentor in Holland. This suggestion had the full support of Van Limburg Stirum. Idenburg's role as 'protector', as Van Limburg Stirum styled this, was essential. In Holland the deputation would need such a person, somebody who could give moral support and counsel. At all costs it should be avoided that the mission be a failure. That would only result in a 'new core of malcontents'.[66] Pleyte had to explain in Parliament that Idenburg's role should not be interpreted as an attempt to censor the delegation or to keep a check on what its members said and did.

---

[62] *De Locomotief,* 26-7-1916.
[63] *De Locomotief,* 29-9-1916.
[64] *De Locomotief,* 30-9-1916.
[65] *Djawa Tengah,* cited in *Koloniaal Tijdschrift* 1917:251, *De Indische Gids* 1916, I:747.
[66] Van Limburg Stirum to Pleyte, 11-9-1916, NA, Kol. Geheim, Vb. 15-11-1916 Q14.

Another reason for involving Idenburg was that Van Hinloopen Labberton, who had just become a teacher at the newly founded Bestuursschool, an institution intended for the further training of civil servants, was controversial. 'Labby' had been a contributor to *Het Tijdschrift* and stood out as teetotaller in a European society with a preponderance for heavy drinks. He was also a staunch supporter of the association ideal and a theosophist. Because of his views he had to live with the nickname 'the astral rabbit'. His conduct irritated people on both the left and to the right. Members of the Dutch community considered him a 'hyper-ethicist'. People of a leftist inclination held a somewhat different view and called him a theosophical imperialist. At the outbreak of the war Van Hinloopen Labberton had given talks about world peace. He soon changed his mind and became one the main protagonists of a militia. According to one of his critics, he had 'travelled over Java wearing a head-cloth and speaking high Javanese to win over the hearts of the Natives' (Semaoen 1918:86). He advocated conscription as an institution by which to educate the population and give the Javanese more self-confidence.[67] For Van Hinloopen Labberton a militia had become a matter of faith. As Muurling had done, he criticized the Javanese speakers at the meeting in Concordia for the bluntness with which they had demanded political reform. He was also among those Dutch people who were most outspoken in his denunciations of Japan, doing his best to picture as vividly as he could the cruel nature of Japanese rule in Korea and Formosa, depicting Japan as a ferocious animal.[68] Minami had even singled him out by name as the fiercest anti-Japanese orator in Indië Weerbaar.

Van Hinloopen Labberton could also not count on much sympathy from Van Limburg Stirum and his advisers. They did not rate his qualities highly. He could only be entrusted with simple tasks: arranging accommodation; organizing visits; financial management; and drawing up time schedules. s'Jacob explained in a telegram to the former Governor-General that Idenburg's role would be 'of value in preventing mismanagement and causes of disappointment'. Idenburg, as would become crystal clear was afraid of the political implications of the deputation's trip to Holland, and was not overjoyed by the offer. He accepted, but only on the condition that Van Hinloopen Labberton gave his consent and would take no initiatives during his stay in Holland without consulting him first. Van Hinloopen Labberton promised to do so.[69]

In the delegation the Boedi Oetomo was to be represented by Dwidjosewojo, the Sarekat Islam by Abdoel Moeis (a member of the Indië Weerbaar

---

[67] *Volksraad* 1918:535.
[68] *Warna Warta*, cited in *Koloniaal Tijdschrift* 1917:251.
[69] s'Jacob to Idenburg, 6-9-1916, Pleyte to Idenburg, 11-11-1916, Van Limburg Stirum to Pleyte, 7-12-1916, NA, Kol. Geheim, Vb. 5-9-1916 N10, Vb. 11-11-1916 M16.

committee in Bandung), the Regentenbond by Raden Temenggoeng Danoesoegondo, Regent of Magelang (who as the oldest member of the deputation would be presented in Holland with a royal decoration), and the Union of Princes by Pangeran Ario Koesoemodiningrat, the brother of the Sunan of Surakarta.

The aims of the deputation received the formal support of the colonial authorities. In his correspondence with the Ministry of the Colonies Van Limburg Stirum expressed the hope that by this 'extraordinary action from the native side', more attention would be paid in Holland to the complaints heard among the population about the absence of political participation, the lack of educational opportunities, and the legal insecurity of the indigenous population. He saw an additional advantage in the fact that a plea for stronger defence conveyed by natives could not fail to make an impression in Holland.[70] His view was shared by the management of the Javasche Bank. In the bank's report for 1916-1917 it was noted that

> the war urges that in the interests of the Netherlands in the colonies every attention is concentrated on the development of the population of the Netherlands Indies in a direction which satisfies the modest demands of the population as well as meeting the necessary demands for the retention of the colonies.[71]

In conclusion it was stated that such a policy could not but cement the unity among the various population groups.

Nevertheless, Batavia entertained doubts about the mission and refused to act in haste. The members of the deputation had wanted to leave on the first sailing opportunity; on the *Goentoer* on 13 September. Batavia delayed the departure of the deputation by several months. The Indië Weerbaar committee initially explained that the reason for the delay was lack of sailing opportunities and the need to prepare the visit to Holland with care.[72] The Minister of the Colonies had to be given time to consult with the Queen first.[73] In its letter to the newspapers it finally admitted that the delay had been at the request of Van Limburg Stirum. It was announced that the deputation would depart in January.[74] In retrospect, Abdoel Moeis considered the delay a blessing in disguise. At the time of the Indië Weerbaar drive H.O.S. Tjokroaminoto had been ill, and the party had been in too much disarray to counter the anti-Indië Weerbaar propaganda among its members, which Abdoel Moeis attributed

---

[70] Van Limburg Stirum to Pleyte, 11-9-1916, Pleyte to Wilhelmina, 15-11-1916, NA, Kol. Geheim, Vb. 15-11-1916 Q14.
[71] *De Indische Gids* 1917, II:1434.
[72] *De Locomotief,* 12-9-1916.
[73] *De Locomotief,* 8-9-1916.
[74] *De Locomotief,* 29-9-1916.

to outsiders. Since then the central board had succeeded in consolidating its influence. The result was that the number of branches which supported the sending of a deputation to Holland had swelled from 20 to 80.[75] Tjokroaminoto had indeed succeeded in winning branches over. He had addressed meeting, explaining that Indië Weerbaar formed part of the campaign for emancipation and that it was a duty of a nation to be able to defend itself. Popular as he was, his words carried weight.

Though initially the Indië Weerbaar committee rejected any such suggestions, stressing that it had 24,000 guilders at its disposal, a sum insufficient to pay for extra members, the deputation now had two additional members. One was Rhemrev, one of the two secretaries of the Indië Weerbaar committee, and the source of the discord among its members. Rhemrev had been added to the delegation after, on the initiative of one H.F. Neuman, a resident of Batavia, a number of 'Dutch' organizations, probably at the instigation of Rhemrev himself had pleaded for his inclusion as 'a Dutchman born here'; a qualification indicating how sensitive Indo-Europeans were about their position in society.[76] The campaign to include Rhemrev was supported by the *Nieuws van den Dag* and other Dutch-language newspapers. To put it mildly, Rhemrev was not a modest man. He was proud that he was a Companion 4th Class of the Military Order of William and presented himself as the 'Dutch representative' in the deputation. He even claimed that he had been the initiator of the Indië Weerbaar drive (Rhemrev 1917:1-2). His supporters, and Rhemrev himself, used the term during his stay in Holland, calling him the Father of Indië Weerbaar, or in Malay *Bapa I.W.*[77]

Rhemrev's joining the deputation radically changed its nature. It was no longer a deputation representing the native and nationalist segment of the population. His inclusion was also used in vain to try to get rid of Van Hinloopen Labberton, who whatever his faults might have been, was a staunch supporter of the gradual emancipation of the Indonesian population. It was argued that with Rhemrev on board it was no longer necessary for Van Hinloopen Labberton to go along. When this failed, another move, initiated by Neuman, was to plead for the inclusion of representatives from the Minahasa and the Moluccas, regions where Christianity had made its mark, and where the indigenous associations were much more moderate than in Java.

The second drive was partially successful. The second addition to the deputation was F. Laoh, an employee of the KPM and President of the Perserikatan Minahassa, an organization which claimed to have 12,000 members, some of them soldiers from North Celebes. The authorities had initially overlooked this

[75] *De Locomotief,* 19-1-1917.
[76] *De Locomotief,* 13-10-1916.
[77] *Neratja,* 24-11-1917.

union when the mass meeting in Batavia was planned. Though in September the Indië Weerbaar committee had indicated that other groups were welcome to join the deputation, and had revealed that such requests had been made by the Minahasan and Ambonese communities no representative from Ambon was included. People from the Moluccas were very disappointed. One newspaper wrote that the omission was a disgrace:

> Doesn't the Committee know that an enormous amount of Ambonese blood has been spilled for the Netherlands in battles in Aceh, Lombok and Jambi? Had it not been Ambonese who had captured the rulers of Bone and Gowa, and who had killed the Batak archrebel, Singa Mangaradja?[78]

On 3 January 1917, the members of the deputation boarded the *Sindoro* for the voyage to Holland. The gangplank was decorated with flags and flowers. Half the deck had been reserved to enable people to say goodbye. Abdoel Moeis had left his place of residence, Bandung, two days before. He had been seen off by hundreds of members of Sarekat Islam. To the accompaniment of music the crowd had marched from his house to the railway station. In Batavia he joined a dinner for the deputation hosted by s'Jacob, whom Abdoel Moeis described as 'the president and soul' of Indië Weerbaar. The first port of call was Padang, the city Abdoel Moeis had left eleven years before. The quay was thronged with people. The members of the deputation disembarked to attend a meeting where the aims of Indië Weerbaar were explained. Abdoel Moeis took the opportunity to see his family and friends. The *Sindoro* delayed her sailing by a few hours to allow him more time with them. A second call was made in Sabang. Here the members of the deputation were received in the Sabang Setia (Loyal Sabang) a club 'for all subjected nations'.[79]

During the long voyage the Indonesian members of the deputation experienced the harsh realities of what colonial relations in those days meant. Abdoel Moeis noted that the European passengers refused to sit at the same table as the natives. He himself was shunted by 90 per cent of the passengers. The reason was that he was not just a native but that he was seen as one of the leaders of a rebellion that had taken place in Jambi.[80]

The *Sindoro* sailed through the Red Sea and the Suez Canal. Having traversed the Mediterranean Sea, she sustained heavy damage near Gibraltar. During a storm she struck a rock and began to make water. All passengers were brought ashore. Rhemrev and some other members of the Deputation thought it safest to stay in Gibraltar till the *Sindoro* was repaired and could continue her voyage to Holland. The more adventurous, among them Van

---

[78] *Tjahaja Timoer*, cited in *Koloniaal Tijdschrift* 1917:816.
[79] *Neratja*, 29-11-1917.
[80] *Neratja*, 3-12-1917, 10-12-1917.

Hinloopen Labberton and Abdoel Moeis, decided to travel on overland via France, Switzerland, and Germany. It promised to be a hazardous journey. They would try to reach the Netherlands, it was reported from Madrid.[81] In fact, they arrived in Holland in the evening of 5 March, ahead of the other members of the Deputation. While in Switzerland Van Hinloopen Labberton and Abdoel Moeis addressed the Dutch community in Geneva. Abdoel Moeis, for whom it was the first occasion on which he addressed an audience in Dutch, used the opportunity to criticize the Chinese in the Netherlands Indies. He explained to his audience that the Sarekat Islam had been founded in reaction to the way in which Chinese middlemen exploited the small man. He made no bones about the fact of how arrogantly Chinese had begun to behave, caught up as they were in the thrill of the political developments in China'.[82] After his arrival in Holland, he touched upon this theme at various meetings. On one occasion he called attention to the fate of Javanese who had fallen victim to the pernicious practices of rice brokers (not mentioning that most of them were Chinese) who bought rice on speculation at a low price before the harvest from peasants who were pressed for money. Reports about Abdoel Moeis' speeches complemented by the assessment that he intended to set the Javanese against the Chinese reached the newspapers in the Netherlands Indies via the Dutch press. Confronted with such reports, Abdoel Moeis had to deny that he had tried to stir up the Javanese against the Chinese. He defended himself by stating that he had wanted to stand up for the oppressed people and had wanted to demonstrate that one of the aims of the Sarekat Islam was to have indigenous Indonesians enter the wholesale trade. His words did not suffice to stop a campaign against him in the Chinese-Malay press, which continued well into 1918.[83]

In Holland a cautious Idenburg had seen to it that the police kept the members of the delegation under surveillance. Names of people who visited them were noted down. Police supervision was somewhat relaxed when a socialist Member of Parliament, J.W. Albarda, protested. Pleyte tried to reassure him. Idenburg had only asked for help from the police to protect them from 'accidents in the street'.[84]

Almost at once Dwidjosewojo and Abdoel Moeis clashed with Idenburg. From the very beginning Idenburg had made it clear that he would not acquiesce in members of the deputation holding speeches or participating in political demonstrations before they had been received in audience by the Queen

[81] *De Locomotief,* 1-3-2002.
[82] *De Indische Gids* 1917, I:489-90.
[83] *Oetoesan Hindia,* 14-9-1917, 15-9-1917, 17-9-1917; *Neratja,* 9-11-1918, 25-2-1918, 6-3-1918, 7-3-1918; Tichelman 1985:641, 645.
[84] *De Locomotief,* 26-3-1917, 28-3-1917.

and by the Minister of the Colonies. Were they to do so he would withdraw as councellor of the Deputation and put an advertisement in Dutch newspapers explaining the reasons why he was no longer prepared to act as such. When true to their conviction and also in accordance with the brief Boedi Oetomo and Sarekat Islam had given them Dwidjosewojo and Abdoel Moeis ignored Idenburg's demand and in public spoke about the political concessions the Dutch would have to make for a militia a conflict was born. A meeting Idenburg had arranged with members of the Dutch States General and the Council of State in April was cancelled. Idenburg had hoped that the members of the delegation would have been able to give vent to their 'political heart' on this occasion. In return in the meantime they should not address political meetings. Abdoel Moeis and Dwidjosewojo had stated their conditions. They demanded that after the meeting with the members of the States-General they could report on what had been discussed in the periodicals of the Sarekat Islam and Boedi Oetomo. They said that this was an obligation to their parties they had to honour. Practically their resolve to honour their obligations meant the end of Idenburg's role as 'protector'. He refused to act 'as impresario or host at a public meeting'. A second reason for Idenburg's unwillingness to go ahead with the meeting was that Abdoel Moeis had addressed a gathering in the Zuid-Hollandsche Koffiehuis (South Holland Coffee House) before the deputation had been received in audience by the Queen. On hearing about Abdoel Moeis's speech, Idenburg had immediately sent a letter to the deputation in which he announced that he severed all ties with them. Rhemrev called the cancelling of the meeting with members of the States-General 'a punishment' for Abdoel Moeis's behaviour. He claimed that it was thanks to his efforts that Idenburg had not withdrawn his assistance completely, and that Idenburg had not informed the newspapers about the conflict.[85]

The deputation were received in audience by the Queen. At the meeting on 20 March her husband, Prince Hendrik, was also present. Idenburg had planned a nice ceremony. First, Pangeran Ario Koesoemodiningrat read the Javanese version of the Indië Weerbaar resolution. Thereupon Danoesoegondo read a Dutch translation. Finally, Van Hinloopen Labberton presented the text to the Queen. After the ceremony Koesoemodiningrat, Van Hinloopen Labberton and Idenburg were received privately by Queen Wilhelmina. Koesoemodiningrat expressed the loyalty of the Sunan. Van Hinloopen Labberton translated his words. Idenburg looked on. Later, the resolution was also presented to the Queen Mother, Emma, and to the chairmen of the Parliament and the Senate.

Relations with Van Aalst and other leading businessmen and industrial-

---

[85] *De Locomotief,* 22-11-1917; *Neratja,* 1-12-1917; *Koloniaal Tijdschrift* 1917:535.

ists were much better. They embraced the deputation. The members were received at the office of Van Aalst's NHM. One of the highlights in this respect was a diner hosted by Van Heutsz – who wanted a large submarine fleet supported by reconnaissance cruisers, a large army and a native militia[86] – in the Koningszaal of Artis. The dinner was attended by J.Th. Cremer, Idenburg, and a number of other politicians. The government was represented by Treub, not by Pleyte. It was a unique occasion: the very first 'political banquet' attended by Indonesians in Holland. Political (and not just witty) dinner speeches were held. Van Heutsz used the opportunity to expound his views about the relationship between motherland and colony and to plead for a strong military defence of the colony.[87] Another speaker, J.Th. Gerlings, prepared the Indonesian delegates for what they could expect in Holland. Wording the general mood of the Dutch establishment Gerlings explained that he (and he added that Van Deventer who had died in September 1915 would certainly have agreed with him, were he still alive) did not consider the Javanese mature enough for a real representative body with legislative power (Rhemrev 1917:10).

Members of the deputation also were invited to countless dinners and addressed meetings organized by a great variety of organizations: Onze Vloot, the SDAP, the Sociaal-Democratische Partij (SDP, Social Democratic Party, soon to become the Communist Party in Holland), the Indische Vereeniging, association of Indonesian students, the Indologen-Vereeniging, association of colonial civil servants and so on. They also went to the air base Soesterberg, where Abdoel Moeis, Rhemrev, and Van Hinloopen Labberton had their maiden flight, and attended military exercises and parades, where, one critic wrote, they were shown 'how far the European civilization is advanced in destruction and killing'.[88]

Idenburg's fading into the background provided Abdoel Moeis and Dwidjosewojo with ample opportunity to call attention to the political reforms the Boedi Oetomo and Sarekat Islam deemed necessary. What *De Locomotief* had feared in advance happened. In September *De Locomotief* had asked the deputation to state what its programme was before it left for Holland. It had written about 'gratitude' and 'a sense of decency' on the part of its members which would prevent that the Indië Weerbaar motion would not be made subordinate to political demands, but had not been sure.[89] Dwidjosewojo and Abdoel Moeis spoke frankly about the reforms which they felt were essential in the Netherlands Indies. They warned, as Abdoel Moeis did, that Holland

---

[86] *De Locomotief*, 12-3-1917.
[87] *Koloniaal Tijdschrift* 1917:643-6.
[88] *Weekblad voor Indië*, 19-8-1917, reproduced in Poeze 1986:115.
[89] *De Locomotief*, 30-9-1916.

would feel the consequences were the Dutch to dare to use an iron fist against a people in the process of awakening. Their speeches, probably contrary to what *De Locomotief* had expected, were received with benevolence. Sympathy, with exceptions of course, reigned.

It did not escape people's attention that Abdoel Moeis, who like Soewardi probably was convinced that providing the Dutch public with information about the colonial situation would eventually make Holland more responsive to the demands for political and economic emancipation in the colony, did not have much to say about the defence of the Netherlands Indies. His true theme was political change. This should not have come as a complete surprise. Abdoel Moeis's newspaper, *Kaoem Moeda*, had already sent a telegram to a Dutch Member of Parliament in May 1916 explaining what Indonesians wanted: 'We Javanese demand equal rights for strengthening our energy to defend India belief our demand will draw attention of *kamers* [Parliament] letter follows'.[90] Abdoel Moeis and Dwidjosewojo even impressed Soewardi, who himself was a confirmed opponent of Indië Weerbaar, and had first thought them to be toadies (Poeze 1986:115).

Laoh was determined not to be left behind. He drew attention to the discrimination experienced by Minahasans, pointing out that Minahasan soldiers received less pay than their European colleagues. Laoh told Pleyte and others that Minahasans would accept a militia only after statute labour had been abolished.[91]

The frankness of the Indonesian members of the deputation upset colonial die-hards, who had not kept abreast with the trend political developments had taken in the Netherlands Indies. It also worried members of the general public who could only think about Indonesians as 'slavish and docile'.[92] To such people who had read about the many pledges of loyalty, the words of the members of the deputation came as a shock. It was the first time that Indonesians publicly vented their disenchantment with colonial relations in Holland. They did not bother to mince their words and left no doubt that they had no intention at all of meekly complying with government wishes. Nevertheless, after he had returned to Java, Abdoel Moeis expressed his surprise about how 'calmly' the Dutch public had reacted to the 'harsh words' spoken by the members of the deputation.[93]

While demanding change, Dwidjosewojo and Abdoel Moeis took great pains to explain that for the moment they still considered Dutch rule the best, and that they were prepared to assist in upholding it. Not doing so – and

[90] *De Locomotief*, 9-5-1916.
[91] *De Indische Gids* 1917, I:806-7; *Handelingen Tweede Kamer* 1917-8:1485; Ratu Langie 1917.
[92] *Koloniaal Tijdschrift* 1917:1240.
[93] *Koloniaal verslag* 1917:536.

Independence – would only mean that another power would take over from the Dutch. As was becoming clear in the political debate in Java, this stance set the members of the deputation apart from the radical left in Holland and in the Netherlands Indies. When Abdoel Moeis and DwidjoSewojo, accompanied by Soewardi, attended a socialist May Day demonstration, they politely refused the invitation to join the ranks of the anti-militarist movement. The latter did not seem to understand that had DwidjoSewojo and Abdoel Moeis agreed, it would have removed one of their principal means of gaining concessions from the Dutch government. They probably also rattled their audience by saying that Indonesians were worse off than the proletariats in Europe. Indonesians were oppressed and subjugated at one and the same time.

The visit to Holland ended in discord. Rhemrev was to blame. He was the odd one out, a conservative. In 1919 Rhemrev would go on to found De Oranjebond van Orde (Orange Union of Law and Order) and in 1933 would become one of the leaders of the Nederlandsch-Indische Fascisten Organisatie (Netherlands Indies Fascists Organization). Matters were not helped by him making no secret of the fact that he did not consider a native militia an ineluctable element of the Indië Weerbaar movement. He stigmatized a native militia as an absurdity, a danger to the evolution of the colony and quoted the report of the State Commission of 1912 which had stressed that such an institution was utopian (Rhemrev 1917:10, 12). He also spoke in a derogatory way about the fighting capacity of the Javanese. All this led him to conclude there was no need at all to grant any political concessions. Rhemrev left no stone unturned to stress that his views were what the Indië Weerbaar aspired to. The movement aimed to achieve a strong defence of the colony, not at wresting political concessions from The Hague. The granting of political rights would not suddenly transmogrify 'minors' into adults. Rhemrev even accused the Indonesian members of the deputation of corrupting the aims of Indië Weerbaar. He could not deny that at a certain moment political rights would have to be granted to Indonesians, but as so many other contemporary Dutchmen he maintained that this was something far in the future, when Indonesians were ripe for it. As far as he was concerned the main reason the deputation had visited Holland was to win support in the motherland for a strong defence of the Netherlands Indies, and nothing else. Stressing that the Netherlands Indies was 'the mainstay of Dutch national prosperity', Rhemrev wanted promises and money from The Hague (Rhemrev 1917:6). The Netherlands should not withhold from the Netherlands Indies 'the sword it had already needed for such a long time for its own self-defence and not for imperialistic purposes' (Rhemrev 1917:8).

Rhemrev's views generated enormous tension among the members of the deputation. He especially clashed with Van Hinloopen Labberton and with Abdoel Moeis, the most outspoken member of the deputation (Drooglever

1980:109). During his time in Holland Rhemrev never let a chance slip by to belittle Van Hinloopen Labberton. He refused to recognize him as chairman of the deputation and revealed that former Governor General Van Heutsz and G. Vissering, the President of the Central Bank, rated Van Hinloopen Labberton's intellectual qualities low. Rhemrev even made a fool of Van Hinloopen Labberton in public. This happened during a meeting in The Hague of the Vereeniging ter Beoefening van de Krijgswetenschap (Association for the Study of Military Science). After Van Hinloopen Labberton and other members of the deputation had spoken, Rhemrev took the floor. He related how he had rebuked Van Hinloopen Labberton when the deputation had been received by the Queen. According to his story, which was denied by Van Hinloopen Labberton, while they were waiting for the Queen to make her appearance, Van Hinloopen Labberton had been seated in the second row. When Van Hinloopen Labberton had tried to take up a seat in the front row, Rhemrev had pulled on his jacket and had told him that he ought to be ashamed, and had ordered him back to his place in the second row. Rhemrev finished up his story by stating that Van Hinloopen Labberton had complied, pale with anger.[94]

The differences of opinion between Rhemrev and Abdoel Moeis were clear but how deep the antagonism was had been kept from the public but it could no longer remain secret when it came to a head after the deputation had boarded the *Rijndam* to return to Java via the United States. Most of the passengers of the *Rijndam* were colonial civil servants and army officers with their families. Surrounded by kindred spirits, Rhemrev abandoned all pretence of tact. He did not hide his profound dislike of Van Hinloopen Labberton, and shortly before the *Rijndam* reached San-Francisco insulted the Javanese members of the Deputation. During a lecture on board for which he had dressed, as he had also done in Holland, in army uniform complete with his decorations, he told his audience that the Javanese were too stupid to hold a rifle. Abdoel Moeis, who was in the audience, reacted furiously. He accused Rhemrev of trying to blacken the deputation's aim, adding that he regretted this all the more because Rhemrev 'likes to pass as a Westerner, but for seven-eighths has native blood in the veins'.[95]

After the deputation had returned in Java, Rhemrev was expelled from the movement. Disgusted by Rhemrev's words, Indonesian protagonists of a militia began to differentiate between a Van Hinloopen Labberton and a Rhemrev Indië Weerbaar movement. They praised Van Hinloopen Labberton as a friend of the Indonesians.[96] Rhemrev and Van Hinloopen Labberton

---

[94] *Neratja*, 29-11-1917.
[95] *Nieuwe Rotterdamsche Courant*, cited in *De Indische Gids* 1917, II:1335.
[96] *Neratja*, 24-11-1917.

continued to quarrel, not least in the press; one of the many personal feuds in colonial society. The row became so heated that Rhemrev sent two seconds to Van Hinloopen Labberton in November 1917 to challenge him to a duel with swords. Van Hinloopen Labberton responded by saying that he was prepared to take on the challenge, but only after a military honour Coucil had ruled that Rhemrev was an honourable person first. It was not done to fight duels with dishonourable persons. The duel never eventuated. Rhemrev took Van Hinloopen Labberton to court. He accused him of libel and of having called him 'dishonourable' in November 1918. Called as witnesses were s'Jacob, Dwidjosewojo, Abdoel Moeis, Laoh, and other leaders of the Indië Weerbaar movement.[97]

In the end, when it had become clear that conscription of Europeans was to precede that of the Javanese, the Europeans also spoke out against a militia. Even Je Maintiendrai protested. It founded a committee which was given the task of studying whether conscription would still be necessary if the existing volunteer corps were transformed into *weerbaarheidscorpsen*, fighting units. The protest was joined by the Deli Planters' Association.

Much of the opposition came from Indo-Europeans. They were afraid that the positions they would have to leave to do military service would have been taken over by others when they returned to civilian society and began to worry about the opportunities European conscription would provide for the advancement of Javanese in white-collar jobs. It was argued that if a person had diplomas military service posed no problems. It would be a different story for people 'who had started a career in trade or elsewhere fresh from the primary school'.[98] Fear of life in the barracks and the amoral connotation this held also haunted some. Conscripts would spend their pay on 'pleasures', and could never be completely protected from the atmosphere in the barracks of the colonial army. To do something about this, in November 1917 a meeting was organized by the Central Council of Roman Catholic Social Unions to discuss the 'moral well-being' of the drafted soldiers, who were all in 'the most dangerous phase of their developmental years'.[99]

The discussion about a native militia had one important result. A quasi-representative body was founded. The demands of the nationalist organizations may well have speeded this up. A representative body for the Netherlands Indies had been contemplated since at least 1893. That such a Coucil be given a really democratic nature had been one of the demands of the Comité Boemi Poetra. During the discussions about a militia, Pleyte had given the assurance

[97] *Neratja*, 16-11-1918.
[98] *De Locomotief*, 22-11-1917.
[99] *De Locomotief*, 27-11-1917.

that no conscription of Javanese would take effect before such a parliament had been created. A Volksraad (People's Council) was formed under the law passed in 1916 and inaugurated in Batavia in May 1918. It had thirty-six members, partly elected by the members of the local Coucils and partly appointed by the Governor General. Among them were well-known advocates of a militia like s'Jacob, Van Hinloopen Labberton, Pabst, Dwidjosewojo, Abdoel Moeis, and Laoh. Tjokroaminoto was also a member. The gesture proved futile. As the People's Council had merely an advisory function and had no deciding vote, opponents of a native militia continued to press for the establishment of a real parliament before conscription could be considered. Distrust of Dutch intentions had not evaporated. At the first session of the People's Council in June 1918, one of its members, Abdoel Rivai, said that he had heard people speculate about whether the People's Council would not again be abolished or its competence be reduced still further after the war had ended and the danger to the colony had passed.[100]

Before the People's Council was established, a European militia had already been instituted by an ordinance in March 1918. The event signified the beginning of the end of the age-old institution of the civil. The conscription of young European men started much to the dismay of a number of members of the People's Council, especially the Europeans and Indo-Europeans. They wondered whether the colonial government had not broken its promise about consulting the Coucil first about a militia, and why such a haste was thought necessary.

In July 1918, the first 665 European conscripts in Java were called up. They were sent to the 'cooler' garrisons in Buitenzorg, Malang, and Bandung. To the dismay of the professional European soldiers, the conscript soldiers were put up in separate quarters. Separated or not, they wore a uniform. This meant that they could personally experience how civilian colonial society discriminated against European soldiers. Conscripts were barred from access to coffeehouses and the like (Van Heekeren 1919b:142).

Some tried to evade military service by migrating to other islands. Estate companies sent their younger staff to Sumatra and recalled their older employees to Java. It was rumoured that this policy was also followed by some government offices.[101] Those who tried to evade conscription and were caught were sentenced to seven days' imprisonment, after which they still had to join the militia.

---

[100] *Volksraad* 1918:136.
[101] *Sumatra Post,* cited in *De Indische Gids* 1918, II:892.

CHAPTER XI

The Turkish factor

In 1914 relations between Istanbul and Berlin had been cordial for decades. German officers had acted as instructors in the Turkish army since 1883. They had assumed this role after France, defeated in the Franco-German War of 1870-1871, had been unable to honour a request from Istanbul to resume the training its army officers had provided up to 1870. Ties were strengthened even more after Germany embarked on her *Weltpolitik* in 1897. The Ottoman Empire became one of its targets, one of the places on the globe where the German Empire stepped up competition with the other powers, in particular with Great Britain.

Kaiser Wilhelm II did his bit to foster good relationships and lure Turkey into the German sphere of influence. He visited Turkey twice, in 1889 and 1898. During the 1898 visit every effort was made to cement relations with the Sultan, his ministers, and senior officials (Palmer 1993:190). The Kaiser did his utmost to praise Islam. To show his appreciation of the past exploits of Islam he visited the grave of Saladin and commissioned a marble tomb to be built to hold the mortal remains of this legendary hero of the Crusades. Wilhelm's visit paid off. He was called the 'Protector of Turkey', and was hailed as the 'personal and political friend of His Majesty Abdulhamid'.[1] Wilhelm II not only presented Turkey with a marvellous new tomb of Saladin; he gave Istanbul a fountain. When it was unveiled in 1901 Germany sent an impressive military and naval delegation to the city. The Kaiser himself sent the Sultan a flattering letter. He complimented him on the way he upheld 'the dignity of his throne and the prestige of Islam'.[2] W.F.H. von Weckherlin, the Dutch Envoy, reported that the festivities bore the 'character of a renewed big fraternization party'. The Envoy continued by reporting that on both sides the impression was given 'that Turkey had only one single unselfish friend in the world'.[3] It was

---

[1]   Van der Staal Piershil to De Beaufort, 23-10-1898, Von Weckherlin to De Beaufort, 23-12-1900, NA, BuZa, Politieke gezantschapsrapporten Istanbul.
[2]   PRO FO 800 143.
[3]   Von Weckherlin to De Beaufort, 28-1-1901, NA, BuZa, Politieke gezantschapsrapporten Istanbul.

not the only time that Von Weckherlin had drawn attention to the 'more than hearty disposition of the Sultan towards the German Emperor'.[4]

German industry, not least Krupp, profited. It appears the only intention not accomplished was Berlin's request to have Turkey part with an uninhabited island in the Red Sea to serve as a German coaling station. It was only a minor setback. During Wilhelm's tour the foundations were laid for a number of German projects which were inspired by a mixture of prospects or perhaps dreams of rich profits, feelings of national pride, and the pressure of international competition and mutual envy. They concerned the lines of communications which as objects of international rivalry were closely associated with the delineation of spheres of influence all over the world. The principal loser was Great Britain. There were two main German achievements. The first was the concession to build the Berlin to Baghdad Railway, linking the Mediterranean with Baghdad, and ultimately with the Persian Gulf, the 'most important undertaking of German "Weltpolitik" of all' (Gründer 1999:182). When completed, it would provide Germany with a direct railway line between Berlin and the Persian Gulf, threatening the British position in India and giving Germany an overland route to Asia as an alternative to British-controlled sea routes. The second was a telegraph cable line connecting Istanbul with Central Europe. There was also a third, minor German coup, which likewise undercut the British economic position. The Deutsche Levant Linie signed a contract with the Hamburg-Amerika Linie to start a regular service between Istanbul and New York in 1902. Four years later a shipping line between Germany and the Persian Gulf followed.

The consequence of these close relations had been the development of a strong pro-German and anti-British faction in the Turkish military and government. The presence of German military officers, described by the British Ambassador, Sir Gerald Lowther, as the backbone of German influence in Turkey, was instrumental in this. In the Turkish army officers had gained prominence who had been trained either in Turkey or in Germany by Germans. With a note of envy Lowther had to report back to London in 1909 that the Turkish government relied on the army, and that its officers 'looked towards and admired the military efficiency of the German army'.[5] In their campaign to win Turkish sympathy the Germans had made good use of a recently established paper in Istanbul, the *Osmanischer Lloyd*, to denigrate the British. The *Osmanischer Lloyd* let no opportunity slip to draw attention to articles in the British press critical of the new Turkish regime. Lowther described its contents as 'malicious and fabricated innuendos about British designs and

---

[4] Von Weckherlin to Van Lijnden, 23-9-1901, NA, BuZa, Politieke gezantschapsrapporten Istanbul.
[5] Lowther to Grey, 12-5-1909, PRO FO 800 79.

machinations, evidently intended to poison the native mind against us'.[6]

The crucial moment for Turkey to decide whether to stay neutral or to join the German side in war came on 10 August 1914. On that day two German warships, the battle cruiser the *Goeben* – described by a British naval historian as 'one of the Kaiser's newest, fastest, and most powerful warships' (Halpern 1994:223) – and the light cruiser the *Breslau* hotly pursued by British and French warships took refuge in the Dardanelles. The two of them made up the mediterranean division of the German Navy. Reuter's erroneously reported that both German warships had been interned and that their guns has been decommissioned. The news agency presented the news as a major victory for the British Navy. Reuter's claimed that the safety of shipping in that part of the world had been as good as assured.[7] This was rather wide off the mark. In Istanbul the government announced that the two ships had been bought by Turkey from Germany to compensate for two dreadnoughts which Turkey had ordered in Great Britain, but which London had commandeered after the outbreak of the war. The confiscation had been a serious blow to Turkey's national pride. The two dreadnoughts, the *Sultan Osman* and the *Reshadieh*, had become the object of a patriotic drive. To finance their purchase, the Turkish government had mounted a nation-wide campaign to collect private donations. Compared to it, the Onze Vloot drive in the Netherlands paled into insignificance. Civil servants, already hard hit by a delay in the payment of their salaries, parted with one month's pay, Abdulhamid was said to have pledged a large sum, and all over the country local committees were set up to urge people to contribute to the national cause. Foreign firms and their employees were not immune to what the new Dutch Envoy Van der Does de Willebois called extortion. They were 'most impudently' told how much to contribute.[8]

After they had sailed into Turkish waters the *Goeben* and *Breslau* were renamed. The Turkish flag was hoisted on both warships on 16 August. The crews entered Turkish naval service and donned Turkish uniforms, complete with a fez. At the end of October both ships took part in a surprise bombardment of Odessa and Sebastopol on the Black Sea coast. The Turkish Empire had entered the war. Three weeks later on 11 November Sultan Mehmed V proclaimed a holy war. There was not a shadow of a doubt left that religion obliged all Muslims in the world to side with Turkey and its two allies. To renege was a sin (Snouck Hurgronje 1915:121). Leaflets about the holy war were dropped over the battlefields in Europe by German aeroplanes.

---

[6]   Lowther to Grey, 12-5-1909, PRO FO 800 79.
[7]   *De Locomotief*, 12-8-1914.
[8]   Van der Does de Willebois to Loudon, 4-2-1914, 7-2-1914, NA, BuZa, Politieke gezantschapsrapporten Istanbul box 54.

Though neutral, the Netherlands did not escape being mentioned as a target in the holy war. A Universal Proclamation to All Peoples of Islam was published in November. Besides addressing itself to the subjects of the Triple Entente, the proclamation called upon the 40 million Muslims in the Netherlands Indies to free themselves from the colonial yoke, and to kill or chase away the semi-civilized Dutch.[9] The Dutch Envoy only got hold of an English pamphlet in May 1915 and protested. In June Turkish and Arab newspapers carried an article, 'Rectification of a mistake'. The rectification said that the mention of the Netherlands Indies had been an error, the result of a mistake and an oversight.

Prior appeals by the Ottoman Empire for international Muslim solidarity in its struggle against its foes, and the realization that Muslims elsewhere in the world looked up to the Sultan for protection and guidance, had given Europeans cause to fear Turkish subversion among their Muslim subjects. The Dutch could mention concrete examples of Ottoman prestige and its consequences. An Acehnese delegation had travelled to Istanbul in 1868 to offer Sultan Abdulaziz suzerainty over Aceh. In 1873, and again to the horror of the Dutch government, Abdulaziz considered mediation in the Acehnese-Dutch conflict.

After the accession to the throne of Sultan Abdulhamid II in 1876, the emphasis on the role of the Sultan as Caliph, as the spiritual leader of the Muslim world, assumed a more conspicuous form. During the Russo-Turkish War of 1877, Istanbul tried to arouse international feelings of Muslim solidarity in Russia and Afghanistan by declaring the conflict with Russia a holy war (Palmer 1992:150). The ill-fated outcome of this war for Turkey had led to the first apprehension in the Netherlands and in Great Britain of Turkish intentions in their colonies. Ottoman agitation might try to incite Muslim subjects in European colonies to avenge Turkey's defeat, which the European Powers were accused of allowing to happen.

Out of this remodelling of Ottoman policy and fuelled by the occasional alarmist rumours grew the fear for pan-Islamism, a concept that was much more a European than a Turkish invention. The term was a Western one, coined along the lines of pan-Slavism and pan-Germanism. Some Muslims even called pan-Islamism 'a mare's nest discovered by *The Times* correspondent at Vienna'.[10] In Germany, where the joining in union of the 'German Holy War' and the Islamic *Dschihad* needed some explaining, thoughts tended in the same direction (Galli 1915:5, 21). In retrospect, pan-Islamism has also

---

[9] Snouck Hurgronje to Loudon, 25-1-1915, 23-7-1915 (Gobée and Adriaanse 1957-65, II:1687-8, 1690-7).
[10] Evans 1987:21, citing Browne 1904.

been dismissed as a creation of the British India Office.[11] A similar role in presenting pan-Islamism as a daunting, realistic threat can be ascribed to the Dutch Ministry of the Colonies, especially to Christiaan Snouck Hurgronje, a renowned Dutch Islamologist, who in his capacity as Adviser for Native Affairs to the Governor General was the main architect of Dutch Islam policy around the turn of the century. In Snouck Hurgronje's opinion any manifestation of pan-Islamism, whether it took the form of anti-Dutch articles in the press in the Middle East, efforts to underline international Muslim solidarity, or attempts to promote an Islamic culture, contained a hint of danger to European Power in the Islamic world.

Snouck Hurgronje considered a resolute and unequivocal response essential to combat what he believed was the core of pan-Islamism: the guardianship of the Sultan of the Ottoman Empire of the Muslim world, even in regions where European nations ruled. He never tired of explaining that such a notion was a fallacy. The international Islamic community did not have a spiritual leader, a person whose position was comparable to that of the Pope. For years Snouck Hurgronje remained the most formidable proponent of alerting the world to the dangers of pan-Islamism. Admired as one of the world most famous and knowledgeable experts on Islam – a man who had stayed in Mecca and had published extensively on Islam in and outside the Netherlands Indies – he had the ears of both the Governors General and the Ministers of the Colonies. The Dutch Ministers of Foreign Affairs were less impressed by his drive. Their interests were different. Besides law and order in the colony, the nature of their office meant they had to take other considerations into account. As far as the Ministry of Foreign Affairs was concerned, fears of pan-Islamism and Turkish 'machinations' and 'intrigues' were exaggerated. Its civil servants could not understand why the study of a few Arab youngsters from Java in Istanbul on the suggestion of the Turkish Consul in Batavia, an issue which had led to a public outcry in the Netherlands around the turn of the century, was supposed to be of far greater danger to the established order in the Netherlands Indies than the tens of thousands of pilgrims who travelled to Mecca for the hajj each year.

Mutual irritation between the Ministry of the Colonies, envied because of its generous budget, and the Ministry of Foreign Affairs was the result. In May 1900, for instance, an aggravated Minister W.H. de Beaufort requested for the time being to be spared of the suggestions of Snouck Hurgronje about how to react to anti-Dutch newspaper articles in the Middle East. Cremer refused to comply with such 'a surprisingly formulated request in correspondence

---

[11] Niemeijer 1972:38, quoting Storrs 1937.

C. Snouck Hurgronje (KITLV 2510)

between colleagues'.¹² Snouck Hurgronje, who, as a contemporary wrote, was 'a very capable and a very irascible man', at times added fuel to the fire.¹³ He reacted with venom each time others seemed to question the dangers of pan-Islamism, or if they disregarded his advice in whatever other way. In 1905 when he was informed that an employee of the legation in Istanbul had spoken well about an Arab boy from Java who was studying in that city, Snouck Hurgronje dismissed the evaluation out of hand. The information was irrelevant. What counted was that such students were scions of some of the most pan-Islamic families in Java and were raised in an anti-Dutch spirit. He was sure that on their return they would propagate the political viewpoints taught to them. Snouck Hurgronje was not surprised that students from Java made a favourable impression. In Istanbul they had learned 'with Turkish dexterity to take advantage of the ignorance of the representatives of the Netherlands in Turkey of circumstances in the Netherlands Indies to dish up perfidious stories'.¹⁴

The ideas of pan-Islamism, whatever these may have been – it was a ubiquitous spectre just as nowadays Islamic fundamentalism is – should not be allowed to spread to the Netherlands Indies. Association with Western culture was the ultimate goal for the colony. Islamic culture was antithetical to this goal. Every indication that – in their daily life not in their religion – Muslims preferred Islamic or Eastern ways to Western ones was seen as a setback on the road to civilization and an indication of an anti-Dutch mentality. Schooling and clothing, with the fez to some acquiring an almost subversive image, became yardsticks by which to measure loyalty to the Dutch or the severity of the infection with pan-Islamic ideas. Charity fell into the same category. For people who themselves raised money so enthusiastically for the victims of the Boer War, collecting money for causes like the construction the Hejaz Railway between Damascus and Mecca, on which work had started in 1900, could only be a political statement. In Snouck Hurgronje's eyes the appeals to Muslims, including those outside the Ottoman Empire, to contribute generously were an inextricable part of a pan-Islamic plot. No better plan could have been envisaged to demonstrate the political unity of all Muslims without arousing conflicts with the Colonial Powers than the collecting of money for the Hejaz Railway.¹⁵ In the Egyptian paper *Al-Liwa* the Dutch efforts to hamper collections for the Hejaz Railway were contrasted with the collections made in the

---

12   De Beaufort to Cremer, 25-5-1900, Cremer to De Beaufort 2-6-1900, NA, BuZa A-dos. 190, box 450.
13   *De Indische Gids* 1900:236.
14   Van Bijlandt to Ellis, 17-4-1905, Note Snouck Hurgronje 12-6-1905, NA, BuZa A-dos. 190, box 451.
15   Snouck Hurgronje to unknown addressee, 12-11-1904, Snouck Hurgronje to Rooseboom, 28-7-1904, NA, BuZa A-dos. 190, box 450; Gobée and Adriaanse 1957-65, II:1572.

Netherlands Indies for the marriage of Queen Wilhelmina.[16]

Alleged pan-Islamic activities garnered plenty of the attention in Holland and the Netherlands Indies. Seeking religious education in Mecca was viewed with suspicion, enrolling at schools in Cairo, where the famous Islamic university Al-Azhar was located, was frowned upon, but going to Istanbul, the political centre of the Ottoman Empire was perhaps the worst crime a Muslim in the Netherlands Indies could commit. Such concerns were not confined to the Dutch. In Amsterdam a Sumatran from Palembang, Abdoel Rivai, who had come to Holland to continue his medical studies and would become a member of the People's Council in 1918, was also upset. In July 1900 he launched a bi-weekly, *Pewarta Wolanda*, the Netherlands Reporter. The aim of this Malay-language periodical, published in Amsterdam and distributed in the Netherlands Indies, was to 'try to decrease the influence of Turkey among many Mohammedans in the Indies'.[17] Intended to be distributed among Indonesian rulers, civil servants and the well-to-do classes, *Pewarta Wolanda* would do this in part by convincing parents to send their children to the Netherlands and not to Istanbul for their education.

The apparent support of the pan-Islamic ideal by the German Kaiser was also abhorrent to the Dutch. During his 1898 visit, Wilhelm II had flattered the Sultan by referring to his position as Caliph. In Damascus, at the end of his tour, he had stated that Abdulhamid II 'and the 300 million Muslims scattered across the globe who revere him as their Caliph, can rest assured that the German Emperor is, and will at all times, remain their friend' (Hopkirk 1994:23-4). It was a remark which alarmed those Dutch people who were haunted by the spectre of pan-Islamism. The Dutch newspaper the *Nieuwe Rotterdamsche Courant* singled out the Kaiser's words as the reason why an anti-Dutch press campaign had been resumed in the Ottoman Empire.[18]

Unsure of the loyalty of the Muslim population in the Archipelago, the concept of pan-Islamism held an especially threatening connotation for Dutch colonial administrators, Snouck Hurgronje first and foremost, and many among the general Dutch public were also alarmed. They suspected that pan-Islamism, propagated by the Sultan and his advisers at Istanbul, was geared to impress upon Muslims in the European colonies that the Sultan was the supreme authority whom they had to obey. This made the European nations governing such regions at the best vassals of the Sultan, and at worst the unlawful rulers. In Java and other regions firmly under Dutch control, the aim of pan-Islamic propaganda did not necessarily have to concern

---

[16] *Al-Liwa* 2-1-1901, cited in Rooseboom to Cremer, 5-2-1901, NA, Kol. Geheim, Vb. 7-3-1901 D5.
[17] *De Locomotief*, 12-7-1900.
[18] Cited in *De Locomotief*, 17-12-1898.

ousting the Dutch. As the *Nieuwe Rotterdamsche Courant* formulated it in 1898 the aim might be to force upon the Netherlands a contract stipulating that 'we Christians can remain in our possessions, but [have to] recognize the supreme authority of the Mohammedan Sovereign'.[19] Reassuringly the *Nieuwe Rotterdamsche Courant* noted that it was an illusion to expect that such an ideal would ever be realized. Nevertheless, pan-Islamism could produce a sea of troubles.

Elsewhere in the Archipelago, where rulers in desperation sent or tried to send deputations to Istanbul to ask the Sultan's help against the Dutch, pan-Islamism could fortify resistance against the advance of Dutch colonial rule. Those who feared pan-Islamism as an obstacle to a further Dutch expansion in the Archipelago saw the danger first and above all loom in Aceh. Other sultanates in Sumatra, Borneo, and Celebes were also considered to be vulnerable to pan-Islamic propaganda. Rumours about moral support and even military support from Istanbul could, and did, stimulate resistance to Dutch rule.

Around 1910 the fears had abated somewhat. Fewer incidents involving alleged pan-Islamic agitation were reported, maybe because Snouck Hurgronje had left the Netherlands Indies to return to Holland in 1906. His successor, G.A.J. Hazeu, did not consider himself an expert on Islamic affairs. He preferred to occupy his mind with other scholarly activities. The respite was short. The wars fought against non-Muslims at the beginning of the 1910s, in Libya against Italy in 1911, and in the Balkans in 1912 and 1913, gave rise to a new wave of international Islamic sympathy for the plight of the Ottoman Empire. In India, Muslims, vowing of their loyalty to the British Crown, protested against the position taken by London in the Balkan Wars, which they felt amounted to a war against the Balkan Muslims.[20] Others in India, who spoke more rashly, simply talked about wars between Muslims and Christians (Sareen 1995:8). In the Netherlands Indies a rise in pro-Turkish sympathy was observed at the time of the Turco-Italian War. Feelings intensified during the Balkan Wars, when Turkey had to gird itself against four Christian nations. The Young Turks in Istanbul deliberately raised the issue of Muslim solidarity and announced that they would collect money outside Turkey to strengthen the army and Navy.[21] They warned that not only the Ottoman Empire was threatened, but Islam itself was also in peril. Sympathy in the Netherlands Indies translated itself into concrete deeds. Portraits of the Sultan and his son decorated walls of houses. Donations were readily forthcoming. One of the organizations to which the money went was the Alhilal Alahmar (Red

---

[19] *Nieuwe Rotterdamsche Courant*, cited in *De Locomotief*, 7-11-1898.
[20] *De Expres*, 3-2-1914.
[21] Dutch Envoy in Istanbul to De Marees van Swinderen, 3-2-1913, NA, BuZa A-dos. 190, box 452.

Crescent) founded in Batavia at the end of 1912. Despite all this, D.A. Rinkes could reassure Idenburg. The donations had come mostly from Arabs and from natives in the coastal cities. A much smaller amount of money had been collected in the Netherlands Indies than in the Straits Settlements.[22]

The Balkan Wars were fought at a time when the founding of the Sarekat Islam and the large following the organization had attracted had again made Dutchmen wary of the power of Islam as a symbol of anti-Dutch propaganda. Agitation from abroad would only fuel such sentiments. To exacerbate such feelings, on the eve of the Great War rumours circulated of visits to the Netherlands Indies and other colonies in Asia by Turkish spies, allegedly former army officers, who were suspected of wanting to sound out the attitude of the local Muslims towards the Sultan.[23] In the Dutch Senate, Van Kol claimed that the Young Turks had spent millions on pan-Islamic propaganda. He was worried. In 1911 Van Kol had personally observed that nobody in the Dutch legation in Istanbul had the capacity to keep track of such activities.[24] In Parliament W.H. Bogaardt singled out the Turkish defeats in the Balkans as the main reason for the revival of pan-Islamism. He said this in an attempt to demonstrate that the revival of Islam in the Netherlands Indies had nothing to do with increased Christian missionary activities, which was argued by many who castigated Idenburg for what they called his Christianization policy.[25]

The entry of Turkey into the war on the side of Germany exacerbated such worries. Snouck Hurgronje, who had moved to Leiden in Holland and acted as adviser to the Ministry of the Colonies, was especially upset. The Universal Proclamation to All Peoples of Islam, or the Jihad Document, prompted him to resume his campaign against pan-Islamism with renewed vigour. His quarrels with the Dutch politicians and civil servants who did not follow his advice also acquired a new dimension. In a number of letters to the Ministry of the Colonies, he stressed that the pamphlet condoned the idea that a holy war was not only one waged by armies, but could also be pursued by gangs of robbers and take the form of individual assassination attempts.[26] The affair fortified Snouck Hurgronje in his conviction that the Dutch legation in Istanbul was staffed by nincompoops; an opinion he had uttered with a certain degree of regularity for more than fifteen years. The Dutch Envoy had laid hands on the proclama-

---

[22] Van der Does de Willebois to Marees van Swinderen, 3-2-1913, 6-3-1913, NA, Kol. Openbaar, Vb. 16-5-1913 29; Advice Rinkes, Vb. 13-5-1913 24.
[23] *De Locomotief*, 12-12-1913.
[24] *Handelingen Eerste Kamer* 1913-14:349.
[25] *Handelingen Tweede Kamer* 1913-14:86.
[26] Snouck Hurgronje to Pleyte, 23-7-1915, 22-10-1915, NA, Kol. Geheim, Vb. 6-8-1915 B11, Vb. 2-3-1915 L3.

tion much too late. Consequently the venomous message had circulated freely for months also, Snouck Hurgronje was sure, in the Netherlands Indies. What upset him even more was that the rectification had been formulated in such a way that the readers were given the impression that it was only because the Dutch government had recognized the Turkish Caliphate that the Netherlands Indies was excluded from the appeal to Muslims to rise up in rebellion against their colonial overlords.[27] Indignantly Snouck Hurgronje pointed out that in the Arab version of the rectification it was written that the Netherlands should not have been included among the targets for murder and robbery, because of its correct behaviour towards the Caliphate. There was only one interpretation: the Netherlands stood into a subordinate position to the Caliphate.[28] When it came to the crunch it did not matter much whether the Netherlands had been explicitly mentioned or not. Convinced that a holy war had been nothing more than a historical concept for many Muslims, Snouck Hurgronje blamed the pamphlet for the revival of medieval, fanatical incitement of religious hatred.[29] Irately he pursued his crusade. As late as 1917 he was still writing about the proclamation in a Dutch colonial scholarly journal (Snouck Hurgronje 1917).

So intense was his fear of pan-Islamism, Snouck Hurgronje urged for a ban on the pilgrimage in 1915. He pointed out that Muslims under Western rule were subjected to zealous preachings of an unprecedented intensity in Mecca. There was only one remedy. The pilgrimage should not be allowed to be resumed before the appeals for a holy war had stopped.[30] Prestige also played a part in Snouck Hurgronje's considerations. At the outbreak of the war the Turkish government had withdrawn the capitulations, the commercial treaties governing extraterritorial jurisdiction, on 1 October. Foreigners no longer enjoyed a special legal status and it was not out of the question that Muslims from the Netherlands Indies would witness the Dutch Consul in Jeddah being treated discourteously by the local authorities. Merely issuing a warning to Indonesian Muslims that the journey was hazardous and that time spent in the Hejaz would only lead to financial and other problems would be inefficacious. Muslims – and Snouck Hurgronje stressed that experience had proved him right – would disregard such a warning. They listened only to the Arabs and other persons who arranged their pilgrimage and who profited from it.

Pleyte and Idenburg refused to abandon a pilgrimage policy in which no obstacles were put on the way of Muslims in the Netherlands Indies who wanted to perform the hajj.[31] Batavia feared that such a prohibition would lead

---

[27] Snouck Hurgronje to Loudon, 25-9-1915 (Gobée and Adriaanse 1957-65, I:1351-4).
[28] Snouck Hurgronje to Pleyte, 23-7-1914, NA, Kol. Geheim, Vb. 6-8-1915 B11.
[29] Snouck Hurgronje to Pleyte, 2-3-1916, NA, Kol. Geheim, Vb. 2-3-1916 L3.
[30] Snouck Hurgronje to Pleyte, 23-7-1915, NA, Kol. Geheim, Vb. 6-8-1915 B11.
[31] Pleyte to Snouck Hurgronje, 6-8-1915, NA, Kol. Geheim, Vb. 6-8-1915 B11.

to discontent and be used by pan-Islamic propaganda. Snouck Hurgronje did not see why. He was sure that such a measure would be understood because the Dutch authorities had never made any effort to obstruct the hajj in the past; forgetting, or perhaps unaware, of the fact that the regulations issued in the past to regulate the voyage and to protect the pilgrims against financial misfortune and other troubles had been met with fierce criticism. Snouck Hurgronje was furious that his advice was not followed. A very serious argument of his had been treated disparagingly. It had been tossed aside heedlessly as if it had originated from an ignorant office clerk.[32]

Batavia did not issue a ban on the pilgrimage. Nor did the colonial authorities in British India, who had even more reason to fear Turkish and Islamic agitation. Nevertheless, as no pilgrim ships of Dutch or British companies sailed after the outbreak of the war the pilgrimage from the Netherlands Indies virtually came to a halt after 1914. Europeans saw an unintended advantage. Patterns of expenditure would change, mitigating somewhat the effect of the rising costs of living for the indigenous population in the Netherlands Indies.

To be on the safe side and to dissuade Muslims from trying to travel to the Middle East, the General Secretary issued a widely distributed notice in May 1915. The message was copied in both the Dutch-language and the vernacular press. To underline the advice to postpone a pilgrimage till after the war, Muslims were warned that rising prices and a depreciation in the currency of the Netherlands Indies had made a stay in the Arabian Peninsula much more expensive than it had been in the past. Muslims were also informed that all buoys and beacons had been removed from the harbour of Jeddah and that in view of this, Dutch shipping companies – the Nederland, Rotterdamsche Lloyd, and Oceaan – had stopped their service to Jeddah. Pilgrims could travel only with companies of which there was no guarantee that their ships would turn up at Jeddah in time for the return journey home. The fact that the Turkish government had withdrawn the capitulations was also brought to bear in the argument. The notice explained that, as a consequence, the Dutch consulate might not be able to offer the usual protection and assistance. All in all, sufficient reason for a 'serious warning' not to make one's way into 'danger and trouble'.[33] The Dutch who had become deadly scared of the new manifestations of Islamic zeal regarded the warning as not worth the paper it was written on. The *Nieuwe Rotterdamsche Courant*, – and some suspected Snouck Hurgronje of having written the article himself – pleaded for a ban in early 1916. It expressed the same fear of spiteful indoctrination that Snouck Hurgronje had adduced. The 'political consequences of the war for Islam'

---

[32] Snouck Hurgronje to Pleyte, 23-7-1915, NA, Kol. Geheim, Vb. 6-8-1915 B11.
[33] *Javasche Courant*, 7-5-1915.

should be of overriding importance in formulating a hajj policy, not the difficult living conditions in Mecca. Without guarantees that pilgrims from the Netherlands Indies would not be exposed to incitement against Dutch colonial rule the pilgrimage should be forbidden. The *Nieuwe Rotterdamsche Courant* also wrote that there was nothing wrong with such a temporary ban. It did not curtail the freedom of religion. A ban would only be regretted by persons who gained financially from the hajj.[34]

To dissuade prospective pilgrims even more, the readers of the notice of the General Secretary were reminded of the repatriations of the pilgrims in 1914. After Turkey had entered the war, 28,000 pilgrims and others who had wanted to return to the Netherlands Indies had to be repatriated under difficult circumstances. Despite all the uproar, most pilgrims had been able to take passage on Dutch ships and had left the port of Jeddah before the middle of November. After this manoeuvre had been accomplished, the Dutch Consul, J. Wolff, assumed that there would no longer be much for him to do. He had decided to leave for Holland. Though the Ministry of Foreign Affairs had not responded to his request to be allowed to go on leave – the communication between Jeddah and The Hague had already been cut for one and a half months – Wolff had decided take his annual leave without waiting for formal consent. He had assigned the administration of the consulate to the secretary-dragoman, had left enough money to pay the salaries of the staff for eight months (in gold, as the war had disrupted international finance), had taken the remaining money with him, and had embarked on the last Dutch pilgrim ship that left the port of Jeddah on 20 November 1914.

At that moment there were still about 1,600 pilgrims from the Netherlands Indies in Jeddah. They had made the outward journey from Penang or Singapore aboard ships sailing under British, Russian, Chinese, or Japanese flags, had a return ticket, but had been unable to find passage home. Not all the blame for this could be laid at the feet of the war. Under normal circumstances shipping companies sailing from the Straits Settlements had also failed in the past their obligation to offer pilgrims a return journey within weeks of the end of the hajj ceremonies. Because 'a very large number of pilgrims' had fallen victim to this, the Straits authorities were actually in the process of sharpening the sanctions against such companies. They had presented new legislation on this score as late as November 1914.[35]

Wolff painted a gloomy picture of what lay in store for the Muslims from the Netherlands Indies who had not been able to leave the Arabian Peninsula or did not want to do so:

---

[34] *Nieuwe Rotterdamsche Courant*, cited in *De Indische Gids* 1916, I:76 and *De Locomotief*, 3-2-1916.
[35] *Proceedings* 1915:B 83.

The fate awaiting those left behind is pitiable. Jeddah is cut off from the outside world, there is no longer any post and telegraph connection and the supply of foodstuffs, on which the Hejaz, which itself produces next to nothing is dependent, has stopped. [...] The pilgrims who at present are almost all without means are faced with hunger and misery and they should not count on the support and actual sympathy of the selfish native population.[36]

The fate of the remaining pilgrims had not been as bad as predicted. The Ministry of the Colonies was able to inform the Governor General that the remaining pilgrims had left for home at the end of December.

Early in 1915, all or at least most of the regular pilgrims had returned safely to the Netherlands Indies. Many of those who had failed to board the Dutch pilgrim ships in November 1914 had made their way to Singapore on board of merchantmen of the Ocean Steamship Line, which had taken on passengers irrespective of the company with which they had booked their return passage.[37] While they were home, thousands of other Indonesian Muslims who had taken up residence in the Hejaz for a prolonged period of time had remained behind. Most of them – it was estimated that their number amounted to about 3,000 – had settled there to study religion. Others either lived off a pension, had found a job related to the pilgrimage, or had found employment as traders or servants. For these people the hardship Wolff had predicted arrived with a vengeance. Many ran into financial trouble. For those whose earnings depended on the hajj, income dwindled when fresh pilgrims stayed away. 1914 had already been a bad year for them. The situation would only worsen. Financial support from relatives at home to help them through difficult times was no longer forthcoming. There was no way of sending money to the Middle East. If they still had Netherlands Indies currency, their money soon became almost worthless. Netherlands Indies currency was difficult to change. Even when this was still possible the value had depreciated by one-quarter in November, to become even more worthless as time progressed. The consequence was that many Muslims from the Netherlands Indies had little choice other than to resort to begging, to take on work as a coolie, or to sell their possessions, including their wardrobes and religious books. It was reported that people who had once been rich were forced to eat rice mixed with corn.[38]

To alleviate the fate of those Muslims who had stayed behind in the Arabian Peninsula and to facilitate their return a Comité Menoeloeng Hadji2 Bermoekim di Mekah (Committee to Help Hajjis Living in Mecca) was set up in Batavia. It consisted of five members, all of them prominent: R.A.A.

---

[36] Wolff to Idenburg, 18-11-1914, NA, Kol. Openbaar, Vb. 28-12-1914 40.
[37] *De Locomotief*, 18-3-1918.
[38] *Oetoesan Hindia*, 20-4-1916.

Achmad Djajadiningrat (Regent of Serang), H. Hassan Moestapa (chief *penghulu* in Bandung), R. Pengoeloe Tafsir Anom (chief *penghulu* in Surakarta), Tjokroaminoto, and Rinkes. As the colonial administration tried before it, in an attempt to dissuade Muslims from making the pilgrimage the Committee issued a circular letter alerting the Muslim population to the disturbed situation in the Hejaz. Muslims were warned that Mecca and Medina 'were not at all safe and tranquil, food was expensive, and sometimes was not available at all.'[39] It was also explained that many Indonesian Muslims living in Mecca had been forced to contract debts to pay for their keep. When new loans were unavailable, they had been forced to resort to begging. To help such persons the Committee offered its services as an intermediary between Muslims in the Netherlands Indies and their relatives in the Middle East. People could report to the Committee how much money they wanted to transfer and to whom. The Committee would undertake to see to it that the money reached its destination. Though he could not promise that the money sent to the Committee would reach Jeddah, Rinkes gave the assurance that the donors would not run the risk of losing their money because of acts of war.[40]

Because of the strenuous efforts of the colonial administration and of the local branches of the Sarekat Islam, the circular achieved a wide distribution all over the Netherlands Indies. Malay newspapers also published it. Many informed the Committee that they wanted to send money to the Hejaz. The problem which remained was how the Committee was to accomplish this task. A bill of exchange or a cheque was out of the question. The only option was to send the money to Jeddah by ship. Doing so, had the additional advantage that Muslims who wanted to return to the Netherlands Indies could board the ship for their return journey. The plan coincided with the intention of the colonial government, conscious of the fact that the living conditions of most of them had become intolerable, to evacuate as many of the Indonesian Muslims as possible from the Arabian Peninsula. In the summer of 1915 four Dutch ships, requisitioned for the purpose by the Dutch government, sailed to Jeddah. The shipping companies ran no financial risk. Batavia guaranteed them 100 guilders per passenger; an amount which, of course, later had to be repaid by the Indonesians after they had been repatriated for free. A cash sum of 100,000 guilders in English gold was taken along. Most of the money – 82,000 guilders – had been received by the Committee and was intended for specifically named persons in the Hejaz to allow them to buy daily necessities, to settle their debts, and if some money was still left to pay for their fare or part of it. The rest had come from other donations and should be used to help out

---

[39] Djamaah Djawa jang bermoekim di Mekah.
[40] Rinkes to Idenburg, 22-6-1915, NA, Kol. Openbaar, Vb. 23-9-1915 19.

those who most urgently needed financial assistance.[41]

Wolff was ordered to return to his post to arrange the repatriation. He was responsible for seeing that all went well in Jeddah. His task was not easy. He had to arrange that those who could not pay for their passage signed a declaration of debt. To spare him to have to write thousands of such declarations, forms were printed in Java and sent to Port Said, where Wolff was detailed to collect them. In Port Said he was also to receive a list of how much money had to be handed over to whom, plus the 100,000 guilders. The transfer of money had to take place in the greatest secrecy in Port Said. Were the British to find out, they would certainly confiscate the money. It was contraband destined for enemy citizens. London did not even allow monetary remittances to destitute Muslims from the Malay Peninsula living in Mecca.

All the efforts to collect money and the administrative fuss and bother it entailed were for nothing. Wolff had to take the cash back to Holland with him. In Java nobody had given the consequences of the sudden distribution of such a large amount of money among the Indonesian community in Jeddah a second thought. Nor had Wolff. On arrival in Jeddah he realized that handing over the money was too risky. Rinkes, as he himself had done, had thought that Wolff could hand out the money and still keep it secret that a shipment of gold coins had arrived. This proved impossible. When the moment of transfer had almost arrived Wolff feared that if people learned that he carried such a large amount of money with him, the repercussions could be dreadful. The first problem was the local authorities in Jeddah who because of the war either had only received half of their salary or sometimes nothing at all. If they were to find out they might well demand their share. The situation could become desperate were the inhabitants of Mecca to get wind of the shipment. They could well frustrate the repatriation. Hard hit by the drying up of the stream of pilgrims, they were highly disappointed that the four Dutch ships only came to fetch people and had no fresh pilgrims on board. Wolff did not rule out that, notwithstanding the miserable circumstances in which the Indonesian Muslims had to live the authorities in Mecca even would try to keep them there as a kind of security. They might try to hold the pilgrims hostage in an attempt to force the Dutch government to send fresh pilgrims and more money for those Muslims from the Netherlands Indies who still lived in Mecca.[42]

Wolff succeeded in convincing the Turkish authorities, (and judging from a letter to the Ministry of Foreign Affairs in The Hague this must have cost him a load of food and tobacco) that the ships were the last opportunity for the Indonesian Muslims to leave, that debts had to be suspended, and that

---

[41] Kindermann to Wolff, 29-6-1915, NA, Kol. Openbaar, Vb. 23-9-1915 19.
[42] Wolff to Idenburg, 3-8-1915, NA, Kol. Openbaar, Vb. 23-9-1915 19.

it would be best to allow the Muslims from the Netherlands Indies to return home and not to force them to remain till debts had been paid.[43] Four ships left Jeddah to transport 4,200 Muslims back to the Netherlands Indies in August 1915. It is likely that Muslims from the Malay Peninsula, who found themselves in the same dire straits as those from the Netherlands Indies were among the passengers. In Kedah the rumour went round that the only way for pilgrims from the Sultanate to return home was to pass themselves off as Dutch subjects.[44]

Less than one hundred of those repatriated had a return ticket. So many of the others did not have money to pay for the fare that Wolff decided that it was a hopeless task to ask them all to sign a declaration of debts. He wrote to Idenburg that registration should take place in the port of disembarkation.[45] Convinced that his mission was accomplished, Wolff closed the consulate. He went to Holland. The Indonesian staff joined the repatriated Muslims on their voyage to the Netherlands Indies.

About 2,000 Indonesians refused to leave. They were made to understand that they stayed on their own risk and that they could no longer count on help from the Dutch government. The same position was taken the following year when the British government complained about the many 'destitute Javanese pilgrims' in Mecca who had to be fed by an Egyptian relief foundation and by the Sharif of Mecca. The British government informed The Hague that these pilgrims claimed that they had not been given enough time to wind up their business affairs in 1915 before the Dutch ships left. Only a few, about one hundred, had succeeded in leaving. They had boarded a relief ship especially sent by an Indian Committee in Bombay. Of the others, many had become dependent on special eating-houses arranged for the poor where at dawn porridge and sometimes also some bread was doled out. London asked for a ship to be sent to take them home. The Hague initially refused to help. The British government was told that there had been a misunderstanding. Most of the Muslims were not Javanese but people from other parts of the Archipelago or children of pilgrims. It was a curious argument. Javanese pilgrim was a general term to denote pilgrims from all over the Netherlands Indies. Nevertheless, a British request could not be ignored. Reluctantly the Dutch authorities came to the conclusion that they had no other choice but to send two ships to Jeddah to repatriate the about 1,600 Indonesian Muslims still there, and also to pick up some of those who had made it to Bombay, but had been stranded there.[46] Because Wolff, by now promoted to Consul General in Jeddah, was

---

[43] Wolff to Loudon, 4-8-1915, NA, Kol. Openbaar, Vb. 23-9-1915 19.
[44] Adviser Kedah to Lee Warner, 13-3-1916, ANM HCO Kelantan 322/1916.
[45] Wolff to Idenburg, 3-8-1915, NA, Kol. Openbaar, Vb. 23-9-1915 19.
[46] *Koloniaal verslag* 1917:127-8.

'elsewhere' Rinkes, who happened to be on leave in Holland, was ordered to Jeddah. Money the Committee to help hajjis living in Mecca had still in hand was used to buy fabrics in the Netherlands Indies from which the pilgrims to be repatriated could make their own clothes during the trip home. The first ship left Jeddah on 22 December 1916, a second one on 2 January 1917. Each carried about 600 Muslims.[47] Part of those who returned made a sorry impression. According to a pitiful report in the *Soerabaiasch Handelsblad* 'they had lived on alms, on what often was tossed to them or what they found in the rubbish dumps of the holy city' during their three-year stay in Mecca. 'They went well-fed, strong, with ample clothing, and full of enthousiasm. They have returned much less in numbers, thin, their bodies dragged in rags and sorrow in their hearts.'[48] Nevertheless in one and the same breath it was observed that especially the women looked lively, and that many of them had children who were born in Mecca. As during the repatriation operation in 1915 Batavia stood surety for the fare of still one hundred guilders. When the authorities tried to collect the money, it turned out that, in Kediri at least many of those who had been repatriated Muslims had given a false address.[49]

Pan-Islamism raised greater concern in Great Britain, Russia, and France than it disturbed the Netherlands. The proclamation of a holy war was aimed in the first place at their Muslim subjects. For the Triple Entente Powers it was essential to deny that the war had anything to do with religion, and to give as much publicity as possible to Muslim leaders who testified to their loyalty to the Allied Powers. All three issued lengthy statements blaming German political machinations for the fact that Turkey had joined the war. In India, the British statement was issued and published in the *Gazette of India* and translated into the major languages spoken by Great Britain's Muslim subjects in India and Southeast Asia. Great pains were taken to highlight how great a role Germany had played in setting the Ottoman government and Muslims in Turkey and other countries against Great Britain. The story of the *Goeben* and *Breslau* was retold, but a discreet veil was drawn over the commandeering of the two Turkish dreadnoughts ordered in Great Britain. Acts of Turkish aggression against the British position in Egypt and of the attempts to ferment unrest among British Muslim subjects everywhere in the British Empire were exposed to the full light of the day. All this propaganda was geared to lead to the inevitable conclusion that German machinations were to blame for Turkey's participation in the war. The opportunity was seized to stress that no German act or word could ever change the loyalty of the 70 million Muslims

---

[47] *De Locomotief,* 6-1-1917, 8-1-1917.
[48] *De Locomotief,* 25-1-1917.
[49] *De Locomotief,* 19-2-1917.

in India, Africa, and the Malay States who lived under the protection of the most exalted banners of justice.[50] In this and other statements, the British government reiterated that 'His Majesty's most loyal Moslem subjects' could be sure that the war had nothing to do with religion and the holy places of Islam would not be attacked.[51]

Statements issued by the British government were supplemented by others from Islamic leaders and rulers in the colonies. A host of Indian rulers and organizations pledged their material and military support to the British cause in September. When Turkey entered the war a new cascade of statements poured in. In an attempt to dissuade waverers from taking the side of Germany and Turkey, pro-British manifestations and declarations by Muslims were given the full glory of publicity. Again these included statements by Indian rulers. The initiative for the new round of pro-British statements in India had come from the Aga Khan. In his own declaration, he expressed his 'deep sorrow' that the Turkish government had joined the side of Germany and 'acting under German orders is madly attempting to wage a most unprovoked war against such mighty sovereigns as the King Emperor and the Tsar of Russia'. The Aga Khan laid the full blame on Berlin and Vienna. Germany and Austria were depicted as the enemies of Islam. The war was not 'the true and free will of the Sultan but of German officers and other non-Moslems who have forced him to their bidding'. Austria had taken Bosnia. Germany 'has long been plotting to become the suzerain of Asia Minor and Mesopotamia'.[52]

Muslims in the Malay Peninsula, where with the exception of the Straits Settlements British rule was only decades old, also had to be convinced not to take the side of Germany and Turkey. There was a possibility that they might form a fertile target for German and Turkish agitation. The Malays were Muslims, and they had been joined by Indians who had migrated to the Peninsula in large numbers. The loyalty of the Chinese who were unequivocally anti-Japanese was another source of worry. Requests were sent to the colonial administrations in Colombo, Hong Kong, and India for circulars or pamphlets to be produced in the vernacular languages 'to prove the justice of the British cause in the present war' to Chinese and Indians living in the Malay Peninsula.[53] The statement of the Aga Khan was distributed among the Malay Muslims. The same was done with like-worded expressions that it was the 'bounden duty at this critical juncture to adhere firmly to their old and

---

[50] ANM HC 1723/14.
[51] Notification issued by the Government of India indicating the policy of His Majesty's Government in respect of the Holy Places (ANM SoS 37/1915).
[52] ANM HC 1723/14.
[53] Secretary to the High Commissioner to the Colonial Secretary of Colombo, 14-1-1915, ANM HCP 59/1915.

tried loyalty to the British government' or sentences with a similar purport.[54] The aim was first and foremost to ensure the loyalty of the Indians who lived in Malaya; in particular the 'Sikhs, Punjabis, Pathans and Tamils of the petty-trading and coolie classes'.[55]

To make certain of the loyalty of the indigenous Malay population, their rulers and the Sultan of Brunei were provided with the same information. The result was reassuring. The Malay rulers pledged their loyalty and that of their subjects. The Sultans of Perak and Selangor and the Yang di-Pertuan Besar of Negeri Sembilan signed a joint statement on 5 November 1914. They forbade their citizens 'to render any assistance whatever to Turkey' or 'to raise or be influenced by any agitation in favour of participation on the side of Turkey'.[56] The fourth ruler of the Federated Malay States, the Sultan of Pahang, was irate about the listing the names of the four rulers in the preamble. As was the custom, the order had been determined by the date the states had come under British protection. The Sultan of Pahang was mentioned third and concluded that the Sultan of Perak, whose name came first, had been put in a position of superiority over him.[57] Offended he issued his own statement. The Sultan observed that the Federated Malay States 'had never gained any advantage from the Turkish Government', and said he was sure that 'the inhabitants of this State of Pahang have felt and understood the abundant prosperity, happiness and freedom they have enjoyed since Pahang came under British Protection'.[58]

Among the rulers of the Unfederated States, the Sultan of Kelantan held a public service in which prayers were said for the success of the British army. The Sultans of Johore and Trengganu also expressed their loyalty to the British Crown. To prove his sincerity the Sultan of Kelantan put his personal army at the disposal of the British. In Singapore the British military Commander, Brigadier General Dudley Howard Ridout, turned to the most influential Muslim leader in the city, the head of the Arab community, to convince him of the evils of the Ottoman Empire and the vile role of Germany. His tactic seemed successful. The Arab in question abandoned his initial pro-Turkish stance (Othman 1997:5). A few months later, in March 1915, leaders of the Muslim community in Singapore also sent message of loyalty to the British King (Shennan 2000:77). As subsequent developments would show, such statements said nothing about the disposition of the larger Muslim community, and maybe also nothing of that of its signatories.

[54] Telegram of Viceroy of India to Secretary of State, ANM SoS 37/1915.
[55] Secretary to the High Commissioner to the Secretary to the Government of India, 14-1-1915, ANM HCO 59/1915.
[56] Proclamation, 5-11-1914, ANM HCO 1806a/1914.
[57] Under Secretary Federated Malay States to Secretary to the High Commissioner, 25-11-1914, ANM HCO 1806a/1914.
[58] Proclamation Sultan of Pahang, ANM HCO 1806a/1914.

The British extended their efforts to try to counter Turkish and German propaganda to the Netherlands Indies. One of the reasons prompting them to do so was that the Arab community in Southeast Asia was a highly international one, interknit by many business and family links between the Arabs who had settled in the region. The Consul General in Batavia made sure that British statements justifying the war with Turkey found their way into the Dutch-language press, from which they were copied by the Malay-language newspapers. In other press releases, he drew attention to the section of a speech King George V had delivered at the opening of Parliament in London in which the King had said that the war with Turkey had been forced upon Great Britain. The many statements by Muslim leaders and organisations in support of the British cause and denouncing the stand taken by Istanbul were not overlooked. Other releases drew attention to vows made by Muslims in Sierra Leone, and by the chief cadi of Cyprus, who had defended the war against Turkey and had hailed the fact that the island had been annexed by Great Britain.

Of course the German and Turkish consuls in the Netherlands Indies tried to gainsay these statements. They disqualified other British information as 'false reports' by the British consuls and by Reuter's. German propaganda was designed to create the impression that the statements of Indian rulers in favour of Great Britain had been forced upon them. As an illustration of the pressure exerted by the British, it was reported that the Aga Khan had been forced to board a ship sailing to Europe, and that his friends forcibly tried to prevent this.[59]

Judging from the reaction in the Javanese press, the British propaganda efforts were not very successful. In Dutch-language newspapers and in their own Malay-language newspapers Indonesians could read about Islamic leaders in Saudi Arabia and elsewhere who supported the Turkish holy war appeal. The information about the pro-British vows of Indian rulers was received with suspicion. At best, it was suggested that the rulers had been duped by Allied propaganda.

British propaganda even seems to have been counter-productive. In retrospect, in 1917 Schrieke concluded that Muslims in the Netherlands Indies had reacted with scorn when they learned about the statements of loyalty to British rule. The Islamic press almost without exception had considered it impossible that a real Muslim would fight against Germany or Turkey.[60] The Malay-language press indeed reacted to British propaganda with dismay. A poem in the Semarang Sarekat Islam newspaper *Sinar Djawa* declared that rulers who remained loyal to the British were egoists.[61] *Oetoesan Hindia* copied

---

[59] *Lokal Anzeiger*, cited in *De Locomotief*, 22-12-1914.
[60] Note Schrieke, 30-4-1917, NA, Kol. Openbaar, Vb. 14-2-1918 38.
[61] *De Locomotief*, 3-12-1914.

an article from *Le Petit Hindoestani* which stressed that true Muslims did not attach any value to what the Aga Khan did or said. The Aga Khan was not a Sunni Muslim like Muslims in the Netherlands Indies. He was the leader of a Shi'ite sect, who dressed as an Englishman, and with a chin shaven clean as a whistle, enjoyed the night life of London.[62] Reports in the press about Indian troops – and a number of elephants – who were on their way to the battlefields of Europe did not improve the British image either. In November 1914 the *Sumatra Post* in Medan received a letter from a reader. He wondered whether it was true that England had assured itself of the assistance of other nations with fine promises and money, and when this did not help by causing agitation. His sarcastic conclusion was: 'All possible tribes, regardless of from which part of the earth and from which race or rough hordes are armed by England and fight as English soldiers – if possible all wild animals from English colonies are brought to France and are set on the Germans – because England wages war for justice and civilization'.[63] Later, a pamphlet distributed among the Arab community in Batavia which drew attention to the joy of Muslims in Bosnia and Herzegovina over the liberation of Mecca from Turkish rule was greeted with a strong protest by *Oetoesan Hindia*. Readers were reminded that in the Netherlands Indies too a firm faith in the Caliph of Islam was essential.[64]

The denials of British reports by the Turkish Consul in Batavia were considered more trustworthy. *Oetoesan Hindia* wrote that they confirmed what had been suspected all along. The Turkish government had committed no wrongdoings. Turkey was supported by its genuine subjects and by genuine Muslims in the rest of the world. The British information about the support of Islamic leaders and about German and Turkish schemes to incite the Muslim population in British India and elsewhere to rebel were dismissed as being inspired by fear. The British press releases were put to use to draw attention to the repressive nature of British (and of French) rule. Perhaps in order not to sound too rebellious it was added that British rule was worse than Dutch rule. To illustrate this, a point was made of the fact that in the Netherlands Indies the government supported the indigenous population in its efforts to establish schools. Rebellions were not the fruit of inflammatory pamphlets, but were inspired by cruel suppression and by injustice. If the British government trusted its subjects in India, why did it have to undermine the esteem of Turkey.[65] Bomb attacks in India were presented as another indication that Great Britain could not count on the support of the population in its colonies.

[62] *Oetoesan Hindia*, 14-11-1914.
[63] *De Locomotief*, 24-11-1914.
[64] *Oetoesan Hindia*, cited in *Koloniaal Tijdschrift* 1917:391.
[65] *Oetoesan Hindia*, 5-11-1914, 10-11-1914, 16-11-1914.

On another occasion *Oetoesan Hindia* suggested that Great Britain had not entered the war to come to the assistance of Belgium. It had been prompted by far more selfish reasons.[66]

The anti-British propaganda produced by M.M. Rifat, an American citizen of Egyptian origin who was living in exile in Geneva, made a greater impression on Muslims in the Netherlands Indies. Rifat was editor-in-chief of the *Patrie Egyptienne*, which displayed the motto 'Egypt for the Egyptians and by the Egyptians'. Just after the outbreak of the war Rifat had addressed a letter to the German people. In it he expressed his sympathy and admiration for the German Emperor, the German army, and the German nation on behalf of the Muslim population of North Africa, Turkey, Persia, and India. The tenor of his writings was that while England kept India, Egypt, and other Oriental countries in political and economic servitude, while France murdered people in Morocco, and while Italy waged a war of extermination in Libya, the German and Austrian people had testified to their friendship for the peoples in the East. Rifat also postulated that Belgium had made the mistake of opposing Germany because its government had been misled by false promises and reports spread by the Triple Entente. After having made this observation, Rifat appealed to the Eastern nations to give Germany and Austria all the financial, moral, and armed support they could. A victory for Germany and Austria would be a victory of Asia and Africa over the pirates of the Triple Entente. In a second public letter which was addressed to the German Chancellor, Rifat listed the crimes committed by 'perfidious Albion'. In the name of freedom Great Britain had bombarded Alexandria in 1882, had violated the neutral status of the Suez Canal, had attacked the peaceful Somalis on the pretext of fighting the Mahdi, and had stimulated the carnage in the Balkans. It had also waged the Opium War on China, and in cahoots with the barbaric Russians had divided up Persia. In short, the history of the British Empire was one of 'gigantic intrigues, deceitful tragedies, treacheries, which had cost the lives of millions of innocent peoples'.[67] Statements like those made by Rifat did not pass unnoticed. In the Netherlands Indies they were seen as an indication of what people under colonial rule really thought.

The at times naive efforts by the British to stir up anti-German feelings among Muslims also failed. A British communiqué was published in London in early 1916. It was forwarded to the press by the British Consul General in Batavia. The communiqué drew attention to German documents which had been seized in German East Africa, in which plans were discussed to promote the breeding of pigs and to forbid teachers to perform Islamic religious func-

---

[66] *Oetoesan Hindia*, 15-10-1914.
[67] Au peuple allemand 1-9-1914; Rifat to Bethmann Hollweg, 17-9-1914 (*De Indiër* 1-50/51:233-4).

tions, such as acting as circumciser. *Oetoesan Hindia* published the report in full. The editors did not believe a word of it.[68] Attacks on Turkey in European-language newspapers elicited the same response. They were received with dismay. In 1917 the *Bataviaasch Nieuwsblad* called Enver Pasha 'The Great Murderer of the Armenians'. A Malay newspaper reacted by pointing out that the Commander-in-Chief in Europe and therefore the man responsible for the ill-fated military offences at the front, Field Marshal Sir Douglas Haig, did the same kind of work. He should be honoured with the same qualification.[69] Enver Pasha was a 'Turkish hero' to Muslims in the Netherlands Indies.[70]

As reactions indicate, Turkish participation in the war meant that Muslims in the Archipelago were generally pro-German and anti-British. This disposition was strengthened even more by the anti-German sentiments prevalent among the Dutch people living in the Netherlands Indies. The Dutch-language newspapers which were most despised for the abusive way they wrote about the indigenous population were also the most fiercely anti-German in tone.

Haunted by the pan-Islamic spectre the Dutch in the Netherlands Indies were not sure what the consequences of Turkey entering the war would be for law and order. With an undertone of relief, the Ministry of the Colonies concluded in its report to Parliament for 1915 that the influence had been nihil. There had been no stirrings of unrest.[71] This was not to say that there had been no trouble at all. Occasionally the war and what was dubbed pan-Islamism did function as an extra incentive to resist Dutch rule. Support from or for Turkey became an actual rallying cry in some regions. In the eastern part of Celebes, at that time still a troublesome island for the Dutch, a hajji who claimed to act on the instructions from Istanbul had called together villagers and had urged them to rise up in rebellion in November 1915. He foretold that Turkish rule would soon replace that of the Dutch.[72] In Jambi people awaited the arrival of a 'kapal Stambul', a Turkish warship, to help them in their rebellion against Dutch rule in October 1916. In Pasir, on the East Coast of Borneo, Muslims also counted on Turkish support to oust the Dutch.[73]

The vernacular Muslim press made no secret of on whose side it stood. Simultaneously editors and contributors usually stressed that they were loyal subjects of the Netherlands and would remain so. One of the most outspoken newspapers in this respect was *Kaoem Moeda*, of which Abdoel Moeis was

---

[68] *Oetoesan Hindia*, 13-4-1916.
[69] *Pantjaran Warta*, 10-7-1917, IPO 28/1917.
[70] *Oetoesan Hindia*, 20-4-1916.
[71] *Koloniaal verslag* 1916:17-8, 21-2.
[72] *Koloniaal verslag* 1916:32c.
[73] *Koloniaal verslag* 1917:xi; Note Schrieke, 30-4-1917, NA, Kol. Openbaar, Vb. 14-2-1918 38.

editor-in-chief. It was, to quote Rinkes, vehemently pro-Turkish.[74] Another Sarekat Islam newspaper, *Sinar Djawa*, held a poem written by 'Politicus' attacking Great Britain and Russia. Russia was the chief culprit:

> Russia is a very strong empire
> But stupid and very malicious
> The cause of all misfortune
> Which has now engulfed the world
>
> Because the Russians sided with Princip,
> A man with a dishonest heart
> Who killed two persons
> A youthful royal couple.

Such words went too far for Batavia. The poem was considered to be capable of inciting hatred between Christians and Muslims. Prosecution was considered. The editor of *Sinar Djawa* flew to the defence of Politicus. He was a Muslim, but not a very devout one. There had been no malicious intent. Politicus had written the poem because he had been deeply upset by stories about Muslims in Baku who had prayed for the defeat of Turkey. He thought it unthinkable that Muslims would desire the destruction of fellow-Muslims.[75]

One of the most radical Islamic periodicals of those days was *Medan Moeslimin*. In its first issue *Medan Moeslimin* used the Turkish war effort and the sacrifices this implied to impress upon its readers that the Muslims in the Netherlands Indies should show the same perseverance in their own struggle in which they were engaged. *Oetoesan Hindia* also strongly sympathized with the Turkish cause. In the opinion of its editors after the Ottoman Empire had entered the war it had become impossible for true Muslims to remain impartial bystanders to the slaughter in the faraway West. To reassure Dutch administration *Oetoesan Hindia* added that this did not mean that it would resort to acts which would endanger Dutch neutrality.[76] *Oetoesan Hindia* referred to Turkey as the Caliphate of the Muslims in the Netherlands Indies. It 'embodied Islam', the 'image of Islam', the only Islamic region in the world which had maintained its independence; all qualifications which could not but horrify those fearful of pan-Islamism.

From the very beginning *Oetoesan Hindia* and other Malay newspapers advised their readers not to fall victim to deceit. They were cautioned that many of the news telegrams which reached Java contained lies. They did not

---

[74] Report Rinkes, 6-7-1915, NA, Kol. Openbaar, Vb. 17-9-1915 46.
[75] *De Locomotief*, 3-12-1914, 4-3-1915. Gavrilo Princip was the murderer of Prince Franz Ferdinand and his wife.
[76] *Oetoesan Hindia*, cited in *De Indische Gids* 1915, I:243.

escape the attention of the British censor. War was not waged only on land and on sea, but also with the pen and the telegrams.[77] Readers were informed that one consequence was that at a time when in actual fact Germany had conquered half of Belgium, Allied telegrams mentioned only Allied victories.[78] To acquire a more balanced view readers should also take notice of the German telegrams from the Wolff News Agency. *Oetoesan Hindia* published these telegrams. It did not do so arbitrarily. It also did its best to supplement the Wolff telegrams with information gleaned from other sources. Among these were telegrams of the Lloyd Othman, which *Oetoesan Hindia* copied from newspapers in the Middle East. Another valued source for *Oetoesan Hindia* was *China Press*. Editors at times apologized that recent issues had not yet reached them.

Muslims in the Archipelago cheered Allied setbacks. Gallipoli provided the perfect occasion. A three-column article on the front page of *Oetoesan Hindia* explained that the defeat of the Allied forces showed one should not look down upon the community of God. Praise was due to the 'Islamic army' for its courage, to the German army for the assistance given, and to 'our Caliphate' for the way it had organized the Turkish army. The author of the article, who was not a member of the editorial staff of *Oetoesan Hindia*, lashed out against Reuter's and the reports Reuter's had published about the defeats of the Turkish army and the critical situation in Istanbul. Reuter's was 'the great liar', 'the transmitter of gossip', and 'a master at lying'. Shamelessly it only 'spread lies'. Decent newspapers should not publish the Reuter's nonsense (here the editors of *Oetoesan Hindia* who did copy the Reuter's telegrams added between brackets 'steady on, sir, steady on').[79]

Such feelings were shared by a significant portion of the Arab community in the Netherlands Indies. Their anti-British disposition was an additional source of worry to the colonial authorities. Because of the religious esteem in which the Arabs were held by the population, they had given cause for concern for decades. Again it had been Snouck Hurgronje who had stirred up the hornets' nest. He had held Arabs in the Netherlands Indies and their 'accomplices' in the Straits Settlements responsible for many of the contested press articles and the other forms of agitation, which he inevitably saw as part and parcel of a pan-Islamic scheme. Snouck Hurgronje suffered no illusions about why the Arab community was hostile to Dutch rule. One of the reasons he mentioned was that some Dutch civil servants were real *Araberfresser*. Another was that Arabs were classified as Foreign Orientals. As such, like the Chinese, they were obliged to live in a special quarters in a town, which were

---

[77] *Oetoesan Hindia*, 7-11-1914.
[78] *Oetoesan Hindia*, 10-9-1918, 16-11-1918.
[79] *Oetoesan Hindia*, 17-1-1916.

often located in the more unhealthy neighbourhoods. The 'equalization' of the Japanese had offended them as much as it had the Chinese.

Arabs were Ottoman subjects. In their subsequent struggle for emancipation, the Arabs had turned to the Turkish government for support. The colonial administration had a real problem here. In view of growing discontent, something had to be done to remove its causes and soothe-ruffled Arab feathers. Disgruntled Arabs might indeed teach the Muslim population 'reverence for the Lord of the Believers and awareness of their rights against a tyrannical Government of unbelievers', but such an outcome would be all the more dangerous

Angel and Turkish flag. Trade mark of a Chinese coffee trader in Palembang. (*Javasche Courant* 1916 Trade mark 7949.)

as a new Indonesian intelligentsia with a Western education was emerging and tended to be drawn to precisely those larger cities where the Arabs were living.[80]

In 1917 the colonial authorities were convinced that the pro-German disposition of Arabs, and their suspected role in augmenting pan-Islamic and anti-Dutch feelings were reason enough to instruct the local Dutch civil servants to gather information secretly about the political inclinations of the leaders of the Arab communities in their territories.[81] Internment the moment the Netherlands was forced to enter the war was also considered. In the opinion of the then Commander of the colonial army, De Greve, all Arab males between sixteen and sixty years of age should be locked away in camps without delay to maintain law and order among the natives if Germany were to become the enemy. Such a mood was easier said than done. There was one problem which made De Greve waver: the nationality of the Arabs. Most of them came from the Hadhramaut, present-day Yemen. Because of the developments in the Middle East by 1917 Batavia was uncertain about whether the Hadhramaut still formed part of the Ottoman Empire or had become a British protectorate. If the Arabs were British subjects and the Netherlands entered the war on

---

[80] *De Locomotief,* 7-11-1898; Snouck Hurgronje to Van der Wijck, 21-11-1897 (Gobée and Adriaanse 1957-65, II:1616).

[81] Circular 1st Government Secretary, 4-4-1917, NA, Kol. Geheim, Vb. 12-9-1917 H11.

The religious leader from Mekkah. Trade mark of a trading company in Batavia. (*Javasche Courant* Trade mark 6716.)

the side of Great Britain, they could hardly be interned, even though their pro-German sympathies were well known. Given the opposite scenario with Great Britain as the enemy and Arabs considered to be British nationals, internment would be unnecessary. In this eventuality the Dutch colonial army would have to protect the colony against the very real threat of a British invasion. Soldiers would have more important tasks to perform than guarding pro-German and thus harmless Arabs.[82] The Governor General refused to heed De Greve's suggestion. Under no circumstances would he allow mass internment of Arabs. He thought it sufficient that if war were to break out only those Arabs who posed a real danger should be imprisoned.

Belying such misgivings about the disposition of the Arab community, its leaders expressed support for the established colonial authorities. As they did in the Malay Peninsula, Arab leaders in the Netherlands Indies participated in the fundraising (even for the British Prince of Wales National Relief Fund). As among the Chinese, feelings were at the very least mixed. Arabs took the initiative to collect money for organizations like the Turkish Red Crescent. In view of the many actions for the destitute in Holland and for the Belgian Red Cross, such collections could hardly be forbidden. Nevertheless, the Dutch Minister of Foreign Affairs must have frowned somewhat when the Turkish Envoy in The Hague handed over 2,366 guilders for flood victims in Java in 1916. *Oetoesan Hindia* saw in the gesture a clear sign of the strengthening of the material and spiritual bond between the Netherlands and the Caliphate.[83]

Collections were allowed, but only on the condition that they did nothing to damage Dutch neutrality and that no money was given to the Turkish

---

[82] De Greve to Van Limburg Stirum, 1-3-1917, NA, Kol. Geheim, Vb. 12-9-1917 H11.
[83] *Oetoesan Hindia*, 6-4-1916, 11-4-1916.

state.[84] Rinkes was even present at one of the meetings organized by the Arab community to raise money for the Turkish Red Crescent in April 1915. After the Turkish Consul had invited him to take the floor, he had commended the cause. One of the unintended consequences of Rinkes's speech was that Indonesians Muslims began to send money to him. More importantly Dutch people were outraged. Their reaction showed that they had not been able to shake off the paranoia of the beginning of the century. Pan-Islamism and the Caliphate continued to haunt their thoughts. When what Rinkes had done became known the *Java-Bode* lamented: 'Where are the days of a Snouck Hurgronje and Hazeu?'[85] Arabs should only be allowed to collect among Arabs, not among the natives. Support for the dissemination of pan-Islamism in the

Trade mark of an Arab trader combining the symbols of the Sarekat Islam and of religion (*Javasche Courant* 1914. Trade mark 6790)

Netherlands Indies amounted to treason. The *Java-Bode* called it a disgrace that Rinkes had been present at such a dreadful meeting. Were the Netherlands to enter the war on the side of the Allies the country would reap the bitter fruits of Rinkes's 'careless talk'. Measures were taken against Alhilal Alahmar in December 1915. After an Arab newspaper published in Batavia had written that Alhilal Alahmar was determined to support the Turkish Empire in its struggle, the Attorney-General banned the organization on the grounds that its activities were in violation of Dutch neutrality.[86] In a special circular letter he once again stressed that there should be strict supervision to ensure collections were made only for humanitarian ends, not for political purposes.

There was more for the Dutch to be gloomy about. The following month at a mass meeting in Surabaya portraits of Queen Wilhelmina and the Turkish Sultan were displayed on the same level. This was an affront. To rub the insult

---

[84] Attorney-General to Idenburg, 27-10-1915, NA, Kol. Openbaar, Vb. 25-1-1916 44.
[85] *Java-Bode*, cited in *De Indische Gids* 1915, II:1291-6.
[86] *Opkomst* 1967:400, 439; Mandal 1997:5.

in, Tjokroaminoto had been delighted. He had the audacity to call Wilhelmina the temporal ruler and the Sultan the Caliph. Again the *Java-Bode* protested. The government should eliminate any doubts among Muslims that there was only one ruler in the Netherlands Indies. Batavia had to do its utmost to suppress an upsurge of pan-Islamic sentiments. No sanctions were taken against Tjokroaminoto. Rinkes only gave him a 'very serious lecture'. Flags also entered the picture. At times there was confusion about the Sarekat Islam flag. With its crescent and star, the symbols of Islam, the Sarekat Islam flag resembled that of Turkey. The close resemblance resulted in a temporary ban by the authorities on flying the Sarekat Islam flag in 1917. Members of the Sarekat Islam were at a loss to understand why.[87]

[87] *Oetoesan Hindia*, 26-9-1917, IPO 39/1917.

CHAPTER XII

The German menace

During the Russo-Japanese War, the Netherlands Indies had run the risk of becoming a base of operations for one of the belligerents. The same happened, albeit somewhat differently, in the initial years of the Great War. Berlin did all it could to exploit its alliance with Turkey. One of the results was the combined effort of the German government and Indian revolutionaries to subvert colonial rule in the British colonies and protectorates. The scheme had its origin in San Francisco with the Ghadr (Mutiny) movement. The Ghadr movement had been founded in 1913 by an Indian exile, Har Dayal, a twenty-three-year-old former Oxford student. Its name recalled the Indian Mutiny of 1857 and explained the aims of the movement. Members fanned out over the world from the United States to accomplish what Ghadr stood for. Before the war, Indian refugees in San Francisco had already put out feelers to find out whether Berlin was prepared to support an insurrection in British India with weapons and money once war between Germany and Great Britain had been declared. The initiative had come from Har Dayal. Berlin responded positively. Both the Kaiser and General H.J.L. von Moltke, the chief of the German General Staff at the beginning of the war, had no difficulty imagining what could be accomplished by inciting Muslims in India and the Near East to rise up against Great Britain once Great Britain and Germany were at war (Ferguson 2001:213). In Chicago, Los Angeles, Washington, New York and other American cities, German diplomats, other German citizens, and people of German descent started to cooperate with Indians to plan an uprising in the British colonies.

Soon after the first contacts had been made Har Dayal was arrested by the American authorities. He broke bail and fled to Switzerland, then the refuge of all kinds of agitators from all over the world (Hopkirk 1994:48-50). Geneva was the home of the Club of Egyptian Patriots, a group of anti-British Egyptians meeting once a week in the house of Rifat. Others were active in Zurich. Here a group styling itself Pro India, which had chosen 'India without the English, India for the Hindus' as its motto, had been founded in 1912. Its members included E.F.E. Douwes Dekker's old acquaintances Walter Strickland and Shiyamaji Krishnavarma. Pro India published a magazine under the same name.

The idea of hurting Great Britain, France, and Russia by instigating unrest among their Muslim and Hindu subjects gained new momentum after July 1914. The scheme was enthusiastically supported by the Kaiser and Von Moltke. No time was lost effectuating a plan. The combined force of anti-colonial propaganda, calls for a holy war, feelings of religious solidarity, and agitation by agents recruited by the Germano-Indian conspiracy was a powerful factor in undermining British rule. After Turkey had entered the war it assumed even greater proportions. Coupled with rumours about Allied setbacks in Europe and the reports of the enormous number of soldiers who died on the battlefields, the Germano-Indian plot created plenty of unrest in British colonies. France was also not spared the effects of the anti-Allied propaganda. In Madagascar people inspired by 'fallacious literature' tried to poison the officers and non-commissioned officers of the French troops stationed in the island. They failed.[1]

With the Ottoman Empire as its enemy Great Britain had to exercise great prudence in employing Indian and other Asian soldiers abroad. Anti-British propaganda made the task all the more urgent. Revolutionary Indians set out to foment unrest among Indian soldiers specifically and among the Indian population at large. Rebellion was the ultimate aim. In Asia Ghadr agents targeted Indian units in India, Shanghai, Hong Kong, Burma, Penang, and Singapore (Sareen 1995:10). In France and Belgium the British Army had to be on its guard against activities of agitators intent on dissuading Indian soldiers from fighting against Germany.

In India and the Malay peninsula some of the Muslims soldiers were already reluctant to fight the Turkish army. If given a choice, they would have preferred to fight on the side of the sultan, the symbol of their religion. As a consequence the loyalty of a number of Muslim units could not be trusted. The officers commanding the Indian troops were well aware of this. They distributed their own translations of the statement by the British government published in the *Gazette of India*, underlined the British position in speeches to the troops and in private conversations with Indian officers, and gave their troops numerous assurances that the war had nothing to do with religion (Sareen 1995:286, 496, 579).

At a higher level, army command made assiduous efforts to ensure that units known for the strong Islamic disposition of their soldiers were not ordered to battlefields where they might have to fight Turkish troops close to the holy places of Islam (Smurthwaite 1997:165-6). Special care was taken with regiments recruited among the Muslim frontier tribes. The Viceroy of British India, Lord Charles Hardinge, reported to London that these troops were 'so

---

[1] *De Locomotief*, 21-2-1916.

far fanatical' that, in contrast to Muslim soldiers from elsewhere, they did not 'like fighting against the Turks.'[2]

At times marching orders created unrest among Indian soldiers who did not want to fight Turkish troops. In Singapore, the Malay States Guides, made up of Sikhs and Muslim soldiers from India, were stirred up by anti-British propaganda by civilian compatriots in the city (Shennan 2000:89). They initially refused to go to East Africa and fight for Great Britain at the front in December 1914. Army command did not want to utter the word mutiny and spread the word that fear had inspired the soldiers, not Ghadr propaganda (Sareen 1995:11). Despite downplaying the incident army command considered the incident serious enough to send an 'India Agent' to Singapore. His mission was 'to probe the state of native feeling' in the city (Sareen 1995:691). The following month a corporal from the mule battery of the Malay States Guides sent a letter to the Turkish Consul in Rangoon. He vowed that he and other soldiers were ready to fight for Turkey and asked the Turkish government to send a warship to Singapore to fetch them. The letter was intercepted by British intelligence in Burma. The corporal was hanged.[3] In Rangoon, a Ghadr-inspired mutiny could only be prevented at the last moment in January 1915. The incident was frightening enough for the British to institute a new 'citizen-force'. In Basra, in present-day Iraq, soldiers of the 15th Lancers who 'refused to fight fellow Muslims (Turks) in the Holy Land of Islam, although they were prepared to fight them anywhere else' mutinied in February 1916 (Menezes 1997:117).

The most impressive act of disobedience fuelled by a combination of German propaganda and religious feelings took place in Singapore in February 1915. Indian Muslim soldiers of the 5th Light Infantry Battalion rose in rebellion on 15 February. They were among those Indian troops the British were most hesitant to send to the Middle East or even to station in predominantly Muslim surroundings. Earl Kitchener, the British secretary of State for War, had considered the battalion 'too Mohamedan for service in Egypt.'[4] Many of its soldiers, as did those of the Malay States Guides, attended the Kampong Java mosque, which was one of the centres of anti-British and pro-Turkish propaganda; and where the statements of loyalty to British rule had made no impression. Afterwards the British described the imam of the mosque as 'a well-known and most dangerous character' (Sareen 1995:40).

German prisoners of war also did their bit. Until two days before the mutiny, soldiers of the 5th Light Infantry had guarded the Tanglin Camp where the

---

[2] Hardinge to Nicholson, 1-3-1915, PRO FO 800 377.
[3] *Proceedings* 1916:C 169; Ban Kah Choon 2001:28.
[4] Report from Brigadier-General Ridout, General Officer Commanding, Singapore, with remarks on proceedings of Court of Enquiry (Sareen 1995:691).

German prisoners of war and civilians were held. It was clear to the Germans that the loyalty to the British of the soldiers of the 5th Light Infantry and of the Malay States Guides who had initiallly guarded them was questionable. In one of the barracks a picture of Kaiser Wilhelm was displayed prominently which the 'Corporal of the Guard used to salute' (Shennan 2000:93). Lauterbach, the detained *Emden* officer, related how they had called out to him 'Emden officer, Emperor Wilhelm, Enver-Bei, Islam, hurrah!' after Turkey had joined the war (Lauterbach 1918:20). The prisoners did their best to exploit such feelings. Ridout recalled how 'about the middle of January [...] German Prisoners [...] were in the habit of saying prayers at sundown in Mahommedan fashion, and pretended to recite the Koran' (Sareen 1995:699). Such acts had convinced the mutineers that the Germans in the camp were Muslims. Stories that Germans had converted to Islam, and that the Kaiser's daughter would marry the sultan's eldest son circulated (Sareen 1995:122). The Germans also fuelled tales of 'German ascendancy and loss of British prestige' (Sareen 1995:4). There was talk among the soldiers that the days of the British Empire were numbered. Soon there would be 'a German Raj instead of a British Raj' (Sareen 1995:79).

Pro-Turkish propaganda fell in willing ears. For various reasons discipline in the 5th Light Infantry was slack. Discontentment was high. On the top of this after the outbreak of the war rumours 'of the most lurid character' had begun to circulate. The Governor of the Straits Settlements, Sir Arthur Henderson Young, blamed British 'panic-mongers', who had spread tales of 'ruthless warfare', of British failures, and of 'long lists of casualties'. The stories had reached the ears of 'the ignorant and discontented'.[5] Another observation Young made was that discipline 'lax for sometime, had crumbled away completely under the influence of pessimists, alarmists, rumour-mongers, and preachers of fanaticism'.[6] Afterwards the chairman of a Court of Enquiry, E.C. Ellis, concluded that German propaganda had also played a role. He stated that German influences had been at work among the men of the 5th Light Infantry, as they have been throughout the whole of the Far East, including India, with the object of 'stirring up dissension and alienating our native subjects from their true allegiance to His Majesty the KING'.[7]

Events came to a head when the soldiers received orders to be ready to be transported overseas. A pep talk by Ridout had a negative effect on the soldiers. Young explained later that '[c]redulous, pessimistic and suspicious, they misinterpreted everything'.[8] Afraid that they would have to fight Turkish soldiers in the Middle East or would be sent to Europe, where they were sure

---

[5] *Proceedings* 1916:C 169.
[6] *Proceedings* 1916:C 170.
[7] *Proceedings* 1916:B 47-8.
[8] *Proceedings* 1916:C 170; Ban Kah Choon 2001:3.

XII The German menace 321

that he 'who does not fall in battle will die from the cold', part of the 5th Light Infantry rebelled (Lauterbach 1918:21). In actual fact, they were to be transferred on the troop ship *Nore* to Hong Kong out of harm's way. The soldiers had been informed about this, but the news had not quenched the confusion about their destination. It was now of little account. Some of the soldiers had become convinced that while Germany was winning the war, Great Britain no longer had any use for them. The British 'would send them away and sink them' (Sareen 1995:79).

The rebels took control of part of the city. British men, women, and children took refuge on the P&O Lines steamer the *Nile*. Dutch people fled to KPM ships in port. The British found themselves in a precarious position. The 5th Light Infantry, which had transferred to Singapore less than a year before, was the main military force on the island. Those Europeans eligible for military service had left to fight in Europe. For that same reason the number of soldiers stationed in Singapore had been greatly reduced. Law and order was in the hands of Malay and Sikh policemen. They remained loyal.

Twenty-seven British were killed by the mutineers. The rebellion could only be put down three days later, after a Russian, a French, and a Japanese cruiser, alerted by wireless, had come to lend assistance. The sultan of Johore with his own personal army also made his contribution.[9] Forty-seven mutineers were sentenced to death and shot. Some ninety were banished to the British penal colony in the Andaman Islands (Stockwell 1988:46). The trials were conducted in public. Ridout wanted to make sure that everyone realized that 'the men were being tried for mutiny [...] and not, as alleged for refusal to go to Turkey' (Sareen 1995:17). Those soldiers of the 5th Light Infantry, who had remained loyal were given the choice between imprisonment or service at the front. In July 1915 they were sent first to West and then to East Africa to fight the Germans. The Malay States Guides 'renewed' their offer to fight at the front. In September Young could mention that they were 'proceeding gladly on active service'.[10] Later they were sent to the front in Aden. The German prisoners were moved to Sydney. The Muslim community of Singapore pledged its loyalty to the British rule. One of the lasting consequences of the mutiny was that plans were drawn up for the creation of the Special Branch in Singapore (Ban Kah Choon 2001:8).

The inquest into the mutiny indicated that all the British had attempted to assure the loyalty of their subjects in their colonies had had at the most limited effects. The conclusion was that 'Singapore, together with the neighbouring States enjoy[ed] a wide-spread and unenviable notoriety as being a focus for

[9] *Proceedings* 1916:C 170.
[10] *Proceedings* 1916:C 170.

Indian seditionists' and harboured 'many rank seditionists of Indian nationality among its *Residents*' (Sareen 1995:39). The mutiny had weakened British prestige on the Malay Peninsula. Convinced that Great Britain was being defeated in Europe and that all British troops had left for Europe, the scene was considered to be ripe for a rebellion against British rule (Ban Kah Choon 2001:48, 53). Insecurity assailed the British. The Singapore mutiny stirred up older feelings of British insecurity, stretching back the Indian Mutiny. Some of the soldiers of the 5th Light Infantry were 'Hindustani Mohammedans [...] indeed of the same breed exactly that was the worst for cruelties to our women and children during the great mutiny of 1857'.[11] The realization dawned that 'natives [were active] throughout the whole of India, throughout the whole of the Far East, [...] paid by German gold'.[12] The governor of the Straits Settlements, Young, had to admit that feelings in the local Muslim community 'were stirred deeply'. A 'vast majority' remained loyal, but 'there were also a few fanatics who preached extreme doctrines of religious hate'.[13]

The mutiny made a great impression in the Netherlands Indies, where people feared that the rebellion might form a source of inspiration to Muslims on the opposite side of the Straits of Malacca to rise up (Bauduin 1920:84-5). A new foe also had made its appearance: mutinous native soldiers. The composition of the colonial army, with its core of Indonesian soldiers, occasioned some people enormous concern. Others realized that none of the larger cities any longer had fortresses in which the whole European population could take shelter if native troops were to mutiny.[14] The developments in Singapore also were grist to the mill of those Dutch people who opposed the setting up of a native militia. News about the rising disquieted the population of Pulau Tujuh, where food was again boarded.

Initial reports about what had happened in Singapore tended to be confusing. They spoke about riots between Japanese and Chinese, and about Indian soldiers who had risen in mutiny because they had not been sent to the front. The idea that Dutch people might have been killed aroused anxiety. Batavia was blamed for remaining silent and giving no information about the fate of the Dutch community in Singapore.[15] Initially Idenburg and Pinke decided to concentrate the fleet at Tanjung Priok (without the *Tromp*, which was having her periodic overhaul). When the seriousness of the situation in Singapore was realized, the whole squadron was ordered to the Riau Archipelago to be able to act immediately if Dutch lives had to be protected.

[11] R.C.D. Bradley to E.J. Lugard, 28-9-1933 (Sareen 1995:782).
[12] *Proceedings* 1916:B 47-8.
[13] *Proceedings* 1916:C 169.
[14] *De Locomotief*, 16-3-1915.
[15] *De Locomotief*, 19-2-1915, 23-2-1915, 25-2-1915.

Another consequence of the mutiny was the Dutch Navy had to patrol the waters between Singapore and Sumatra in attempts to capture Germans who might be fleeing from Singapore. This, was the 'courteous' way Pinke, sure that there would be no legal reasons to imprison the Germans after questioning, had suggested Idenburg should react to a telegram from the governor of the Straits Settlements asking for their internment of the Germans (Teitler 1986:127). In February, the Germans had already almost completed an escape tunnel in Tanglin Prison, but did not have to use it. The mutiny gave them the opportunity to escape by boat. British ships were also searching for the fugitives. They stopped Dutch merchantmen and inquired whether their crew had spotted a fishing boat manned by Europeans. In their efforts the British also distributed pamphlets promising a reward of $ 1,000 per person for the capture of the escaped Germans in the Malay Peninsula and Netherlands Indies. Anti-climactically the only Europeans briefly arrested were three Dutchmen from Medan on holiday in Penang, whose Dutch was taken for German.[16]

The mutineers had been confident that the German prisoners would join their rising. One of the first acts of the mutinous soldiers had been to march to the prison camp to set the Germans free.[17] Most German prisoners were more scared to death by the mutineers than that they be inclined to sympathize with their action. They hid the British in the camp, tended to the wounded, and preferred to stay where they were. Afterwards the British praised these Germans for their 'correct behaviour' (Sareen 1995:41). One exception was a small group of eleven Germans, formed of crew members of the *Emden* and some leading businessmen. One of them was Lauterbach. According to Lauterbach's own account, the Indian soldiers had asked him to become their leader. Rating the chances of success low, he had refused. The Germans fled to Karimun. In Sumatra the group split. Lauterbach and two other Germans went to Padang, where they were welcomed by the German Consul. Others went to Medan. They also were not arrested. Unarmed, they were not considered a threat. A report of the escape was published in the *Deutsche Wacht*.

Lauterbach, whose name by this time had been mentioned by some of the mutineers as the person who had incited them to rise (the reward for his capture dead or alive had consequently been raised to $ 5,000) and his companions travelled on to Batavia. They boarded a Dutch steamer. To escape arrest should the ship be stopped by the British Navy they assumed Belgian and Danish nationalities. From Batavia Lauterbach went to Surabaya. On one of the German ships in port he met Möller of the *Hörde*. Möller had been moved on to Java as a precaution on one of the warships which returned to there after

---

[16] *Deli Courant*, cited in *De Locomotief*, 15-3-1915.
[17] *Koloniaal verslag* 1915:69-70; Ban Kah Choon 2001:7.

the mutiny in Singapore in early March. He had been interned on parole in Bandung, a city with a large, patriotic German community. Undetected by the Dutch authorities he had made his way to Surabaya.[18] Lauterbach and Möller managed to flee the Netherlands Indies. One of the persons who helped them to escape was an Arab. To the horror of the Dutch, *Oetoesan Hindia* praised the man as a person who wanted to fight for the Caliphate.[19] Möller was killed by Bedouins in the Arabian Peninsula. Lauterbach reached Germany (Lauterbach 1918:51).

The Straits Settlements and the Malay Peninsula were one target for Germano-Indian agitation. India was another and more important one. In India in the early months of the war popular opinion expected that Germany certainly would defeat Russia first, and thereupon also perhaps Great Britain and France. Commenting on the mood among the population of India, Lord Hardinge confessed that this 'is the sort of theory widespread in the bazaars and amongst the uneducated native classes, and [that] it does a lot of harm for it creates a feeling of uncertainty and unrest'.[20]

The plotters aimed at staging an armed uprising in Calcutta on Christmas Day 1915. They expected that the rest of India would follow. A second uprising was planned to take place in Burma. Arms were to reach the rebels in Burma via Thailand (Hopkirk 1994:179). The Netherlands Indies played a central role in these plans. Arms which had been bought in the United States had to be smuggled into India via the Netherlands Indies. To eschew the British censor, the Netherlands Indies was selected as a distribution centre for seditious literature. Inflammatory pamphlets which had been printed in San Francisco, Germany, and the Middle East reached British India and the Malay Peninsula via the Netherlands Indies. Sometimes crews of merchantmen and mail boats were bribed to smuggle such literature to the Netherlands Indies. In other instances, they were asked to mail them in the ports their ships called at along the way. It was also not unheard of for pamphlets to be sent directly from the United States by mail. Initially pamphlets, some of them written by Rifat, actually reached Java and Sumatra by ordinary British and Dutch mails. Pamphlets printed in Germany were sent to the German consulate in Amsterdam or the German Embassy in The Hague. Readdressed to Windels or members of his staff in Batavia, they were thereupon posted at Dutch post offices. Some of these parcel-post packages escaped the attention of the colonial censor. It was quite beyond the bounds of the imagination of postal officials that parcels

---

[18] Bijl de Vroe 1980:44; Pinke to Idenburg, 25-3-1915, Pleyte to Idenburg, 24-4-1915, NA, Kol. Geheim, Vb. 5-5-1915 P7, Vb. 24-4-1915 F7.
[19] Note Schrieke, 30-4-1917, NA, Kol. Openbaar, Vb. 14-2-1918 38.
[20] Hardinge to Nicholson, 8-7-1915, PRO FO 800 378.

from Holland might contain seditious literature and should be checked. Often, pamphlets were deliberately printed on very thin paper so that they could be sent in bulk in innocent looking packages. Yet other pamphlets were sent first to the United States by Dutch mail. From there they were forwarded to the Netherlands Indies.

Such surreptitious activities were carried out under the direction of the General Staff of the German Army in Berlin. The Military Attaché at the German Embassy in Washington, Captain Franz von Papen, also in charge of other acts of German sabotage and espionage in the United States, coordinated the procurement of weapons in the United States. Headquarters in Asia were in Shanghai. Both he and a second Military Attaché were also responsible for planning attempts on British ships in United States and Canadian harbours and on munition factories. The German operations in the Unites States succeeded in generating so much fear that in 1916 policemen had to guard the bridges in New York to prevent bombs being thrown from them.[21] To assist in the planning and running of subversive activities in the British possessions in Asia, three departments were established: one in the Netherlands Indies, one in Siam, and one in Persia. All three were headed by members of German diplomatic or consular staffs who, when necessary could call upon the help of employees of German firms in the region and other German *Residents*.

In Batavia, where the plotters probably had received their latest instructions and information when the *Choising* arrived in Tanjung Priok on 5 August, suspicion focused on Emil and Theodor Helfferich (Shennan 2000:79). The Helfferich brothers were pillars of the German community in the Netherlands Indies. Owing to their position and their jobs, they had contacts all over the Archipelago. Emil Helfferich had started his career in Asia as an employee of Behn, Meyer and Co. in Singapore. A few years later he became Director of the Straits und Sunda Syndikat, a company founded in 1910 with German and Belgian capital which controlled tea, rubber, and coffee estates in Java and Sumatra. The relationship between the syndicate and Behn, Meyer and Co. was 'friendly' (Helfferich 1967:120). At the start of the war Emil Helfferich had been stationed in Singapore. He had been among a group of fifty Germans, men and women, including the German Deputy Consul and the manager of the famous Grand-Hotel de l'Europe, who had boarded the Dutch steamer the *Rumphius* on 6 August. Before the *Rumphius* could set sail, a British army patrol came aboard and forced them to disembark. All German men were declared prisoners-of-war. In the beginning of their captivity they were allowed to resume their pre-war life. If they signed a declaration in which they promised not to take up arms against Great Britain, and would not try to travel

---

[21] *De Locomotief*, 12-2-1916.

to German territory, they would not be interned. Their only obligation was to report once a day. Emil Helfferich was one of the Germans who had signed the declaration. After the actions of the *Emden* had occasioned a vehement anti-German mood in the city, he was again arrested. He had been imprisoned in the Tanglin camp but had managed to escape. In Batavia he soon became one of the leading figures in the German community, which he was to remain till he left the Netherlands Indies in 1928. He is said to have been the person who, after his arrival, had succeeded in forging unity in the divided German community (Mohr 1948:275).

Emil's younger brother, Theodor, was Director of the Batavia branch of Behn, Meyer and Co. To prevent any possibility that the British would seize the Behn, Meyer and Co. assets in the Netherlands Indies through the Singapore head-office, the branch was transformed into an independent limited company after the outbreak of the war (Helfferich 1967:143-4). Theodor Helfferich was also *kaufmännischer Berater* (commercial councillor) of the German Consulate General. In this capacity he was destined to take the place of Windels when something would happen to the Acting Consul General. As commercial councillor, Theodor Helfferich had access to the German code; though he still needed Windels assistance to decode messages. The Helfferich brothers were supposed to have such a prominent role in the German community in the Netherlands Indies that the story went among its members that when war broke out between Germany and the Netherlands one of them would become Governor General of a German Indies (Bijl de Vroe 1980:52).

The Germano-Indian scheme made the Netherlands Indies a hub of anti-British agitation in Asia. All sorts of schemes were hatched by the plotters. One plan, the brainchild of the German Consul General in San Francisco, was to send two British Indians to Batavia to start a newspaper to 'supply false war news to British India' and to set up an illegal radio station to communicate with partisans in the Straits Settlements.[22] Anti-British literature, and occasionally anti-French printed matter such as the one entitled *Les Musulmans de l'Afrique du Nord et le 'Djéhad'*, which was sent to the Netherlands Indies was a more concrete problem to be tackled. The Dutch authorities in Holland and in the Netherlands Indies did all they could to prevent such shipments from reaching their destination; though no action was taken against Malay-language newspaper which published excerpts of seditious pamphlets. Import bans were instituted.

One major reason to take some sort of immediate action was the desire to avoid complications with London. However, there were other reasons for the Dutch authorities not to sit still. Batavia was inspired by a sense of solidarity

---

[22] Pleyte to Idenburg, 28-5-1915, NA, Kol. Geheim, Vb. 28-5-1915 R8.

between the European Colonial Powers which felt they had to help each other if they were confronted with insurrections by the peoples they ruled. The Dutch colonial authorities were also not free of their own concrete fears in this direction. One was the concern that unrest in British India or the Malay peninsula would spread to the Netherlands Indies. Another was that the contents of the pamphlets, usually not of a very subtle nature, was quite shocking to the early twentieth-century European mind. There was no beating about the bush. In calls for the massacre of the British in British India sentences like 'arise in wrath and slay them!' were freely deployed. While most pamphlets directed appeals to Muslims, Hindus had their fair share. One of the documents seized, which had been sent from San Francisco to a member of the German Consulate General in Batavia, was written in Sanskrit and held a picture of Kali, the Goddess of Destruction.[23]

Another disquieting fact was that Arabs and other Muslims in Java and Sumatra were among those to whom such pamphlets were addressed. In March 1916 the *Soerabaiasch Handelsblad* observed that scores of anti-British pamphlets had been distributed among the native population.[24] In next to no time the words Dutch and the Netherlands could be substituted where the text spoke of British and Great Britain. Sometimes the link was made directly, such as when the struggle of the British Indians against Great Britain was equated with the war the Acehnese fought against the Dutch. Some pamphlets were in Arabic, which only some Indonesian Muslims could read. Others were in Malay. One of those in Malay was entitled *Seroean Party Nasional Hindia*, The Appeal of the Indian Nationalist Party, maybe the reason why Arabs called it the 'letter of Douwes Dekker'. The appeal drew attention to the wars Great Britain had waged to acquire new territory, including the Boer War, and announced that the moment to take revenge had arrived. To the alarm of the authorities, it was sent in large quantities to the Netherlands Indies by mail in 1915 and 1916. Among the addressees were local branches of the Sarekat Islam and training institutions for Indonesians. Copies of the appeal had been received by the Colleges for Native Civil Servants in Magelang and Madiun and the School for Native Teachers in Probolinggo. The pamphlet never reached the students. The parcels had been addressed to the school boards. Nevertheless, just in case the students might have read the appeal, the deputy Director of Education and Religion asked the heads of such schools 'to neutralize the undesirable influence which the piece might elicit without making a fuss about the matter through a discussion with the students at a fitting moment.'[25]

---

[23] *San Francisco Examiner*, 10-7-1917.
[24] *Soerabaiasch Handelsblad*, 9-3-1916, cited in *De Indische Gids* 1916, I:786.
[25] Acting Director of Education and Religion to Idenburg, 14-2-1916, NA, Kol. Openbaar, Vb. 12-5-1916 37.

Some of the pamphlets were even penned in Dutch. A shipment to Windels from Holland was confiscated in early 1916. It contained about three hundred booklets originally published by the Indian National Party entitled *Is Indië loyaal?*, Is India loyal? (and a much smaller number of the French edition *La fidélité de l'Inde envers l'Angleterre*).[26]

The colonial authorities acted, fearing both German and Japanese intent, when they could. In July 1916 the rules for entering military buildings and installations were tightened in an effort to combat espionage. Two months earlier an even more important step had been taken. In May 1916 the Politieke Inlichtingendienst (PID, Political Intelligence Service), was established to coordinate the gathering and evaluation of information from various sources about activities dangerous to the state reaching the government. The PID started modestly with a head, a deputy-head, and a clerk (as a suitable candidate for a higher administrative function could not be found). Its first head, Captain (of the General Staff) W. Muurling, revealed two years later that the PID had been founded to collect information about activities which posed a threat to neutrality.[27] Though the service was first and foremost meant to keep track of foreign spies, an additional bonus was that domestic developments could be watched as well. Nevertheless, spokesmen of the government continued to stress that keeping an eye on the foreign enemy was the main object of the PID. Pleyte said this as late as February 1918, while a few months later the Director of the Justice Department stated that the PID did not concern itself with the nationalist movements, as long as these were not set on overthrowing the colonial government.[28]

The British were not impressed by the measures taken to prevent the Netherlands Indies becoming a hotbed of anti-British agitation. In February 1917 a letter from the British Foreign Office to the Dutch Envoy in London stated that it was

> indeed notorious that in spite of the efforts of the Netherlands government, the Dutch East Indies have been a centre of intrigue and propaganda directed by the enemies of this country against British possessions in the Far East, and the object of the transmission of such seditious matter to the Dutch Islands is obviously that stores of such dangerous material may be accumulated at points in the East Asian Archipelago, whence they may be introduced into British possessions themselves by different hands and in quantities small enough to escape detection'.[29]

The plot to use the territory of the Netherlands Indies as the intermediate

---

[26] Chef PTT to Uhlenbeck, 30-3-1916, NA, Kol. Openbaar, Vb. 27-6-1916 4.
[27] *Volksraad* 1918:286.
[28] *Volksraad* 1918:48-9.
[29] British Foreign Office to Dutch Envoy, 10-2-1917, NA, Kol. Openbaar, Vb. 14-3-1917 49.

station for gun-running and the smuggling of pamphlets placed the German community in the Netherlands Indies in the limelight. The then British Consul General in Batavia, W.R.D. Beckett, informed the colonial authorities in October 1915 that the German consuls in Surabaya, Padang, and Celebes, former army officers who had found employment on estates, and members of the mercantile community were implicated.[30] A missionary in Nias, who Pinke was sure was 'technically very skilled' and who had been seen in Padang in the company of officers of the *Kleist*, also attracted the attention of the authorities. Once again Batavia had to consider the prospect of German radio broadcasts.[31]

Though he was the recipient of shipments of seditious pamphlets, Acting Consul General Windels did not play a key role in the department's activities. He attended some meetings, but did not greatly favour the Germano-Indian scheme. He considered the plans developed unrealistic and criticized the plot for its lack of proper organization and planning.[32] Windels's subordinate role was acknowledged by the British. In their evaluation the Helfferich brothers, not Windels, played the leading role in the Germano-Indian complot in the Netherlands Indies. Windels was depicted as weak and spineless.[33] In cooperation with the German Consul in Surabaya, the brothers had also planned Lauterbach's escape. They had arranged for him to be able to flee the Netherlands Indies undetected by British spies. In return for their assistance, they had asked Lauterbach to pass on a message in Shanghai, a port Lauterbach did indeed call at (Lauterbach 1918:80, 87).

Another person accused by the British of playing a leading role in the Ghadr scheme was August Diehn, a German businessman. Before the war Diehn had been manager and chairman of directors of the Singapore branch of Behn, Meyer and Co. In Singapore the British had arrested him on suspicion of having been the mastermind behind the exploits of the *Emden*. Imprisoned in Tanglin Camp Diehn had become one of the ringleaders of the patriotic German prisoners who had planned an escape and used the mutiny of the 5th Light Infantry to seize their opportunity (Ban Kah Choon 2001:18). To tease the governor of the Straits Settlements, he had wired to Young 'arrived safely' when he reached the Netherlands Indies (Harper and Miller 1984:70; Helfferich 1967:139). The British described Diehn as 'a man of ability and influence in Singapore, [who] had money at his command' (Sareen 1995:40). After his escape, the British called Diehn 'one of the principal agents in Sumatra for fomenting trouble among British Indians' who had a leading role

---

[30] Memorandum Beckett, 5-10-1915, NA, Kol. Geheim, Vb. 26-11-1915 C14.
[31] Kindermann to civilian and military authorities of Atjeh, Sumatra's West Coast, Tapanuli, 6-1-1916, NA, Kol. Openbaar, Vb. 9-12-1918 38.
[32] Note Department A1, 15-12-1916, NA, Kol. Geheim, Vb. 18-12-1916 Z16.
[33] Note Department A1, 15-12-1916, NA, Kol. Geheim, Vb. 18-12-1916 Z16.

in the gun-running scheme (Sareen 1995:699). They were sure that Diehn and the Helfferich brothers, with Theodor in the role of the prime conspirator, had drawn up concrete plans to smuggle weapons and literature into British India from the Netherlands Indies. They were also suspected of playing a vital role in providing agents in India with money.[34]

Initially the Dutch colonial authorities found it hard to believe that the Netherlands Indies was being used as a base to subvert British rule in India and the Malay peninsula. The efforts to supply the *Emden* with coal had taught them that Germany had prepared well for war, and that German consuls and other German residents in the Netherlands Indies had played a part in this, which only made Batavia all the more anxious about possible German anti-Dutch activities in the colony. But this was a different matter. Nevertheless, Batavia felt compelled to follow up all the information provided by Great Britain about the plot. One of the persons about whom British intelligence alerted the Dutch authorities was a British Indian, Abdul Salam Rafiqi, or Abdul Selam, the name under which he became known in Java. The Dutch were told that one of his tasks was to act as a contact man between Theodor Helfferich and British Indians visiting Batavia to discuss the sending of arms and money to India. Abdul Selam had arrived in Tanjung Priok from Japan in October 1914. At first he had not attracted the attention of either the Dutch or the British. This changed within weeks of his arrival after Abdul Selam had sent a pamphlet to an Indian in Pahang in the Malay Peninsula by ordinary mail. The pamphlet called for self-government and appealed to Hindus and Muslims to rise up. One of the conditions which Great Britain had to meet to prevent an uprising of its Indian subjects was 'to hand over to Turkey the battleships which if done would end any further trouble between the English and the Turks' (Ban Kah Choon 2001:26). This pamphlet was Abdul Selam's downfall. The British censor intercepted the letter. The postmark launched a British investigation. Abdul Selam was traced. The colonial authorities were informed and had Abdul Selam put under surveillance. A number of times, Abdul Selam was seen entering the German consulate. He was arrested in March after it had been discovered that he ordered the printing of an anti-British pamphlet at the press of *Pantjaran Warta*, a Batavian Sarekat Islam newspaper.

No charges could be brought against Abdul Selam. There was no legislation which dealt with plotting the overthrow of the government of a friendly nation (nor was there any such charge, the staff of the Ministry of the Colonies in The Hague pointed out, in British law). The writing, printing, and distribution of anti-Allied pamphlets could not be tackled judicially as the *haatzaai* articles referred specifically to the domestic situation in the Netherlands

---

[34] Hopkirk 1994:97; Memorandum Beckett, 5-10-1915, NA, Kol. Geheim, Vb. 26-11-1915 C14.

Indies. As long as it could not be proved that words had actually been put into practice and that plotters had concretely helped one of the belligerents, a person also could not be prosecuted for breaching Dutch neutrality.[35] Nor could Abdul Selam be expelled. He had sufficient funds at his disposal. The *Resident* of Batavia, Rijfsnijder, suspected that the money came from German sources, but this was no crime either. Abdul Selam's presence put the authorities in a dilemma. Though Abdul Selam had not broken any law, Idenburg ordered his deportation. The decision was taken after the Attorney-General, G. André de la Porte, had alerted Idenburg to the implicit danger Abdul Selam posed: Great Britain would not stand idly by if people conspired against British rule in Asia on Dutch territory. The consequences could be so serious that Abdul Selam should be considered a danger to public law and order in the Netherlands Indies. Such a line of reasoning provided sufficient grounds to allow the Governor General to use his extraordinary power to ban aliens from the colony.[36]

The verdict threw Abdul Selam into a panic. Being put on a boat to a British colony meant being arrested on arrival, and, he feared, the death sentence. Even should he succeed in boarding a steamer to the United States which stayed clear of any British port – a very unlikely prospect – he would not escape arrest. The British Consulate General would inform the British Navy of his departure. The ship would certainly be stopped after she had left Tanjung Priok. In a last desperate effort to make Idenburg change his mind, Abdul Selam called on the help of Rinkes. When Abdul Selam met Rinkes, he made no secret of the fact that he had been engaged in anti-British activities. In spite of this Rinkes was sensitive to Abdul Selam's predicament. He wrote to Idenburg that European Colonial Powers had to help each other, but that in the case of Abdul Selam 'political detention' could be considered. Rinkes did not overlook the possibility that Abdul Selam might resort to theft, arson, or other crimes to provoke imprisonment and escape deportation. Presenting himself as 'just one of the many proclaimers of progressive ideas in British India', Abdul Selam also personally wrote two petitions to Idenburg. He pledged that if he was interned in the Netherlands Indies, he would cease his agitation against the British and Dutch governments. His appeal was successful. Abdul Selam was transported to Timor in August 1915.[37]

Around the time that Idenburg had to decide on Abdul Selam's fate, the British Consul General, he himself alerted by the British Deputy Consul in Medan, Arthur Law Mathewson, asked the colonial authorities to put an end

---

[35] André de la Porte to Idenburg, 14-7-1915, NA, Kol. Openbaar, Vb. 8-9-1915 22.
[36] André de la Porte to Idenburg, 14-7-1915, NA, Kol. Openbaar, Vb. 8-9-1915 22.
[37] Rinkes to Idenburg 29-7-1915, Selam to Idenburg, 30-7-1915, 9-8-1915, NA, Kol. Openbaar, Vb. 4-10-1915 24.

to agitation among British Indians on Sumatra's East Coast. Copies of inflammatory pamphlets, which called for a holy war and contained sentences like 'Rise Indians rise', had been sent from San Francisco to Sumatra by mail. The same had happened with issues of *Ghadr*, the organ of the Ghadr movement, of which the first number had appeared in November 1913. Printed in San Francisco, it 'aimed at instigating Indians to revolt, [...] to inform public opinion in America about the situation in India and to neutralise British propaganda in the United States and elsewhere' (Sareen 1995:6). At that moment none of the senior Dutch colonial civil servants, not even Rinkes, had any inkling of what Ghadr was. They had never heard of the movement.

Response was swift. On the instructions of Idenburg, the entrance of British Indian migrants and visitors was temporarily restricted. The local authorities were asked to act with prudence when Residence permits came up for renewal. As an additional measure the Dutch *Resident* instructed that British Indians who were returning to Sumatra from abroad had to undergo a body search. Their luggage should be checked carefully and the Indians themselves had to be kept under surveillance.[38] To the delight of the Dutch authorities, it turned out *Ghadr* had been sent to Sumatra by British mail. The Indians who had received the newspaper turned out to be innocent. The investigation concluded that their disposition was strongly anti-British, but that they all were fairly well-to-do, peaceful residents. The Dutch civil servants could not imagine that they had been transformed into agitators.[39]

The investigation into the distribution of *Ghadr* in the territory of Sumatra's East Coast was not completely fruitless. Cotton cloth printed with the portrait of the German Kaiser and pictures of German warships were confiscated. It had been bought in Batavia by an Indian shopkeeper. The Dutch civil servant who reported on the case considered the cloth quite harmless.[40] Two Sikhs were also arrested. They had collected money ostensibly for religious and educational purposes, but there was a strong suspicion that their real intention had been not so innocent. The 'Lieutenant of the Klingalese', that is the head of the local Indian community, had alerted the local Dutch civil servant to the anti-British agitation pursued by the two. One of them, it turned out later, had visited Singapore at the end of 1914, where he had met soldiers of the 5th Light Infantry who had later risen in mutiny. From Singapore he had travelled on to Kedah to incite the population in the Sultanate against British rule. The British

---

[38] André de la Porte to Idenburg, 14-7-1915, Kindermann to Van der Plas, 26-7-1915, Circular Van der Plas 30-8-1915, NA, Kol. Openbaar, Vb. 8-9-1915 22, Vb. 13-11-1915 35.
[39] Obdeyn to Van der Brandhof, 21-8-115, Kindermann to British Consul General, 24-9-1915, NA, Kol. Openbaar, Vb. 13-11-1915 35.
[40] Obdeyn to Van der Brandhof, 23-8-1915, NA, Kol. Openbaar, Vb. 13-11-1915 35.

authorities were informed when the two were put on a ship to Penang.[41]

In the meantime more serious business was brewing. At the end of June 1915 the Navy in the Netherlands Indies was put on full alert after Beckett had informed Batavia about the movement of an oil-tanker, the *Maverick*. The *Maverick* was owned by the Maverick Steamship Co. which used Behn, Meyer and Co. as its agent in Batavia. Beckett revealed that the *Maverick* was on her way to the Netherlands Indies and probably carried 'large quantities of rifles and ammunition' as her cargo. Her destination was Anyer on the Javanese side of the Sunda Strait.[42] Beckett also transmitted the contents of an anonymous letter he had received from Bandung: 'Is a steamer loaded with riffles and ammunitions worth ƒ 500,000 (five hundred thousand) for you to pay me?' Additional information which, as it was suggested, might enable the British to avert a general rising would be provided for free. The sender recommended Beckett place an advertisement in *Het Nieuws van den Dag* for an experienced rubber planter for Perak when he had interest.[43] Beckett did not take up the suggestion. Idenburg was against it. A few days later Beckett alerted the Dutch authorities to a second ship which might have weapons as her cargo: the schooner *Henry S*. She was on her way from Manila to Pontianak.

Beckett urged resolute action. This was indeed taken, not least because Idenburg and his staff did not preclude the chance that the weapons might be used to arm Germans in the Netherlands Indies.[44] This issue had already come up in May 1915 when Beckett had transmitted news that information had reached him from 'official, unofficial and anonymous sources' regarding a scheme of Germans in West Java to arm the *Roon* and other German merchantmen to the colonial authorities. The ringleaders at whom he had pointed a finger were the captain of the *Roon* and two estate managers: Freiherr Hans von Devevere, a former officer in the German infantry, and Curt Opolski, a former German naval officer. Beckett had confessed at that time that the aim was not altogether clear to him. The intention was probably to enable German, Austrian, and Turkish nationals in the Netherlands Indies to escape to a German or Turkish port.[45] The colonial administration had reacted quickly. Within days, an instruction had been sent out to the *Resident* of Banyumas to observe 'the highest possible vigilance'. Other civil servants in whose territories German steamers had sought shelter had also been informed. For a moment, Pinke had toyed with the idea of stationing a warship at Cilacap. He

---

[41]   Obdeyn to Van der Brandhof, 31-8-1915, Obdeyn to Van der Brandhof, 13-9-1915, NA, Kol. Openbaar, Vb. 13-11-1915 35.
[42]   Beckett to Hulshoff Pol, 29-6-1915, NA, Kol. Geheim, Vb. 17-8-1915 F11.
[43]   Beckett to Hulshoff Pol, 29-6-1915, NA, Kol. Geheim, Vb. 17-8-1915 F11.
[44]   Pinke to Idenburg, 18-8-1915, NA, Kol. Geheim, Vb. 4-10-1915 H12.
[45]   Beckett to Kindermann, 31-5-1915, memorandum Beckett, 5-10-1915, NA, Kol. Geheim, Vb. 17-8-1915 F11, Vb. 26-11-1915 C14.

decided not to. Sending a warship might alert the Germans involved that the authorities were on to them.[46]

This time, armed with the information about ships with a cargo of arms sailing in the direction of the Netherlands Indies, the naval squadron put to sea to search for the *Henry S.* and the *Maverick*. The search was hampered somewhat because one of the larger Dutch warships, the *Tromp*, had to remain moored in the roads of Makassar. She had to be ready to be deployed against the 'internal enemy', who kept the Dutch forces in the island busy. As an additional precaution, Dutch civil servants stationed along the route the *Maverick* was supposed to take were alerted. Civil servants in ports where German steamers had anchored were asked to keep a close watch on these ships. Idenburg and Pinke feared that the weapons might be transhipped to these German merchantmen; also not excluding the possibility that the weapons were intended to arm Germans living in the Netherlands Indies in anticipation of a possible declaration of war between the Netherlands and Germany.

The voyages of the *Maverick* and *Henry S.* formed part of the Germano-Indian plan to smuggle weapons into British India. The *Maverick* was supposed to deliver 30,000 rifles and revolvers to Anyer; a destination her captain had imprudently disclosed to a local newspaper in Hawai'i. Fishing boats chartered by German accomplices in Batavia would take the cargo from Anyer to Bengal. The *Henry S.* was to carry 5,000 rifles and 500 revolvers which had been purchased by the German Consul in the Philippines. Her destination was Siam. Two German weapon instructors, and possible also an Indian Hindu agitator, were supposed boarded (Hopkirk 1994:180; Teitler 1986:198-9).

Another way to try to smuggle weapons into the Netherlands Indies was to sent them along as cargo on Dutch ships sailing to the Netherlands Indies from New York and San Francisco. Instrumental in trying this venture was a firm called Schenker and Co., which had submitted 1,000 old Springfield rifles (they dated from 1865) to be sent to Java on Dutch vessels in 1915. The agent of the Dutch shipping line had not been happy about the business. He refused the cargo and alerted the American authorities. This was not an isolated attempt. In view of this, Great Britain urged for a complete ban on the import of arms into the Netherlands Indies, except for those arms consigned to the colonial government. The Dutch government finally complied at the end of 1916. The export and import of private arms was banned.

Theodor Helfferich was informed about the arrival of the *Maverick* by secret German code at the beginning of June 1915. It appears that this intimation of arrival was all and that he had not received detailed instructions about how to

---

[46] Kindermann to Resident Banyumas, 2-6-1915, circular Kindermann, 2-6-1915, 5-6-1915, Pinke to Idenburg, 4-6-1915, NA, Kol. Geheim, Vb. 17-8-1915 F11.

proceed. His brother, Emil, chartered a motor-launch and set out in search for the *Maverick* in an attempt to meet her just outside territorial waters. In spite of the fact that the Batavian police kept a close watch on the brothers, Emil and his party managed to pass undetected. After eight days, Emil Helfferich returned to shore. The others continued the search in the Sunda Straits for another two weeks. They did not see the *Maverick*. Undetected either by the Germans on the lookout and by the Dutch warships patrolling the sea, the *Maverick* reached her destination. The *Maverick* was sighted riding at anchor at Merak on 19 July. The captain sailed on to Tanjung Priok the following day. The *Maverick* was searched but no weapons or seditious literature were found. The journey had been a complete failure. At the outset of her voyage the *Maverick* had failed to rendez-vous along the Mexican Pacific coast with a schooner from which she was supposed to load the rifles and ammunition. The seditious pamphlets she had had on board were burnt near Socorro Island after a British man-of-war had been sighted (Hopkirk 1994:180-4). The Dutch authorities did not know this. To be sure that no weapons had been stacked away on uninhabited islands in the Archipelago, the route which the *Maverick* had taken through the Celebes Sea, the Straits of Makassar and the Java Sea to Merak was retraced by Dutch warships searching for weapons hidden on shore.

The *Henry S.* was sighted near Paleleh on the north coast of Celebes on 7 August. The *Tromp* reached her three days later. The following day a Japanese cruiser, the *Akashi*, appeared on the scene. From a distance her crew observed what was transpiring. The *Henry S.* had two Germans on board. One was Alfred Wehde, an American jeweller from Chicago, who was later to be tried in Chicago for his part in the conspiracy. The other was George Böhm, also an American, the quartermaster. When officers of the *Tromp* had searched the *Henry S.* for the first time, both had been absent. The *Henry S.* had suffered engine trouble and Wehde had gone to Manado by motor sloop in search of a tow. Böhm had had an unlucky fall and had been transported to a government coaling station nearby for treatment. Later Wehde told the Dutch naval officers that he had chartered the ship to collect curiosities for an art gallery in Chicago and to conduct ethnological research.[47]

The voyage of the *Henry S.* had been as great a fiasco as that of the *Maverick*. No weapons were on board. The Dutch authorities were unsurprised. Information had already reached them from Manila that the arms had been removed by the American authorities and that the stated aim of the voyage was to collect ethnographica. The *Henry S.* had still set sail but after she had left Manila her engine had broken down a number of times. Her sailors,

---

[47] Geheim rapport van de verrichtingen van Hr.Ms. *Tromp*, 23-8-1915, NA, Kol. Openbaar, Vb. 13-11-1915 33.

almost all Filipinos, made a sorry impression on the captain of the *Tromp*. He reported that the crew of the engine room was 'absolutely incapable of handling the engine', while the deck-hands 'had little of sailors about them'. It seemed to him as if 'they just had been fetched in from the jungle'.[48] The *Henry S.* was stuck. Wehde's trip to Manado to get a tow had been in vain. Pinke refused to let the *Tromp* tow the *Henry S.* to Manado. In desperation, Wehde turned to the *Akashi* for a tow to the Philippines. The captain of the *Akashi* refused. After he had convinced himself that the *Henry S.* was helpless and formed no threat to Allied interests, the *Akashi* sailed away. Wehde and Böhm were left with no option than to leave the *Henry S.* and to try to return to the Philippines by motor sloop to seek help. With the *Maverick* tied up in Tanjung Priok and the mission of the *Henry S.* foiled the surveillance by the Dutch Navy squadron could be discontinued in September. The *Henry S.* had to be kept under close watch till the end of October when she left the Archipelago. The *Maverick* remained moored in Tanjung Priok. Its owners were afraid that the British might seize her when she sailed. The *Maverick* gained the reputation of 'a mystery ship'. Crew and officers were tight-lipped, but from what little they said it soon became clear that the *Maverick* had been involved in 'one or another secret mission' and that it had failed to rendez-vous with an American schooner.[49] The crew and most of the officers were transported to Manila on another American ship. Dutch, Japanese, and British shipping companies had refused to take them on board. One officer went to Singapore, where he was arrested after a time. His lavish life-style and his requests by telegraph for more money had caught the attention of the Singaporese authorities.

The missions of the *Maverick* and *Henry S.* had failed, but this had not put an end to the Germano-Indian plan. In the remaining months of 1915, a number of people were arrested in Singapore and other British territories in Asia. They confessed to being involved in efforts to provide the rebels in British India with money from Batavia. Among them was Ong Sin Kwie, a Batavian Chinese merchant. Interrogated by the British he admitted that he had travelled to the Malay Peninsula in October to hand over 66,000 guilders to British Indians in Singapore or Penang. If he failed to meet his contacts, he had been instructed to travel on to Rangoon or Calcutta to hand over the money.[50]

To convince the Dutch authorities of the dubious role played by the Helfferich brothers Beckett transmitted the information gathered from the interrogation of Ong Sin Kwie and others to the Governor General. In Holland

---

[48] Geheim rapport van de verrichtingen van Hr.Ms. *Tromp*, NA, Kol. Openbaar, Vb. 13-11-1915 33.
[49] *De Locomotief*, 8-9-1916.
[50] Note Department A1, 15-12-1916, NA, Kol. Geheim, Vb. 18-12-1916 Z16.

Johnstone informed Loudon. He took the opportunity to add the warning that London held 'the Netherlands government responsible for any prejudice caused to British interests by these machinations and reserve[d] the right to claim suitable compensation'.[51]

Notwithstanding British pressure no legal action was taken against Emil and Theodor Helfferich or other Germans. Batavia instigated an inquiry but nothing unlawful was unearthed. The Attorney-General, G.W. Uhlenbeck, interrogated Theodor Helfferich and Windels personally. He had to take their word for what they were. Both refused to hand over their correspondence about the *Maverick* prior to her arrival. Both explained to Uhlenbeck that if they did British agents might be able to break the German code, which the British in fact already had. Theodor Helfferich and Windels persisted that they had done nothing that was in violation of the neutrality of the Netherlands Indies. Both claimed that Emil Helfferich had gone in search of the *Maverick* because they suspected that she carried arms and wanted to order her captain to steer clear of territorial waters.[52] Uhlenbeck also concluded that Ong Sin Kwie was innocent and that he had gone to Singapore for legitimate business purposes. Ong Sin Kwie had been on his way to buy gunny sacks, which had become scarce in Java and of which British India virtually held a monopoly, in Calcutta. His confession in Singapore had been made under duress. Uhlenbecks's conclusions probably suited the Dutch authorities who were hesitant to start a court case against the Germans involved. As no weapons had been found aboard the *Maverick*, there was even less reason to prosecute them.[53]

The German community in the Netherlands Indies caused the authorities plenty of worry, of which their participation in the Germano-Indian plot was only one aspect. Germans and people of German descent were pretty ubiquitous and could be found both in the business and estate sector and in the civil service. To illustrate the potential danger Germans posed, *Het Nieuws van den Dag* pointed out that they were employed in branches of industry which were vital to the defence of Dutch rule: the railways, the naval dockyards, and the post and telegraph service.[54] Even more menacing was that the number of German soldiers in the colonial army was fairly large, and would remain so as German soldiers whose contract had ended could not return home and were left with almost no other choice than resigning. Dutch people entertained grave doubts about the loyalty of the Germans living in the Netherlands

---

[51] Johnstone to Loudon, 17-10-1916, NA, Kol. Geheim, Vb. 18-12-1916 Z16.
[52] Uhlenbeck to Van Limburg Stirum, 3-9-1917, NA, Kol. Geheim, Vb. 10-1-1918 S1.
[53] Van Limburg Stirum to Pleyte, 19-6-1917, Pleyte to Loudon, 24-9-1917, NA, Kol. Geheim, Vb. 22-6-1917 F8, Vb. 24-9-1917 Q11.
[54] *Het Nieuws van den Dag*, cited in *Oetoesan Hindia*, 1-5-1916.

Indies. At least one local civil servant, the *Assistent-Resident* of Kebumen, the son of a German officer, was questioned outright by his superior about how he would act were the Netherlands and Germany to go to war.[55] German soldiers were distrusted even more. Dutch people were convinced that the German soldiers in the colonial army would refuse to fight in a war with Germany, if even worse they did not take the German side.

The question was how should the German soldiers be dealt with. It was a delicate subject, bristling with domestic and international implications. Plans were developed in the course of 1915 about what was dubbed in a rather veiled fashion freedom of movement of foreigners, which in the worst case meant internment. The fate of soldiers of German nationality was a controversial point between Michielsen and the General Secretariat. Michielsen suggested that if war should come, soldiers and civilian employees in the Department of War with an enemy nationality should be stationed in islands outside Java, in Timor or in the Moluccas for instance, where they could do little harm. Another possibility was to concentrate them in parts of Java where they also could not hurt Dutch defence. The civil servants in the General Secretariat disagreed. The Dutch hold over Timor and the Moluccas was not yet so strong that the foreign soldiers could be sent there without a qualm. The General Secretariat also rejected the possibility that German soldiers should all be sent to certain places in Java. Internment was the only feasible course of action. All Germans in government employment and in the army should be dismissed and interned if war with Germany broke out. Michielsen could not agree. He challenged with the proposition that soldiers would never be able to set on the population against Dutch rule. Soldiers were an 'instrument of repression'. For this very reason the population distrusted them and hence would pay them no heed. In Michielsen's opinion civilians were the potential hazard. They could win the trust of the people. They should be interned. Conversely soldiers should be retained in the service; if for no other reason than that otherwise after the war no foreigners would be willing to enlist in the colonial army. The staff of the General Secretariat could not stomach such a suggestion. They considered it a disgrace to accept the services of people whose homeland was at war with the Netherlands.[56]

Nobody had to be interned, but everything was in readiness should that time ever come. In May 1916 Dutch regional civil servants were asked to compile a list of potentially dangerous foreigners in their territory; that was foreign males between sixteen and sixty years of age. One year later, in October 1917, the question of whether persons who were interned and who had been

---

[55] Verwijk to Van Limburg Stirum, 10-7-1916, NA, Kol. Geheim, Vb. 16-11-1916 R14.
[56] General Secretariat to Idenburg, 17-7-1915, Michielsen to Idenburg, 7-9-1915, NA, Kol. Geheim, Vb. 11-2-1916 Y1.

in government employment were entitled to receive their salary came up. Nobody, not even in Holland, could give a clear-cut answer. It was not known how such matters were arranged in the rest of Europe.[57]

Some Dutch people believed the whole colonial army was a bulwark of pro-German sympathies. They suspected that Germans had made good use of the ties of friendship between Germany and Turkey and had managed to win the Indonesian Muslim soldiers onto their side. During a lecture in The Hague in 1918 one Dutch captain even ventured that since the beginning of the century portraits of the German Kaiser (and of the Turkish Sultan) had adorned barracks all over the Archipelago. He warned that sympathy for Germany had been carefully cultivated among the Muslim soldiers.[58]

How much his statement reflected the actual situation is impossible to reconstruct. Certainly portraits of the Kaiser and his wife, of the Sultan of Turkey, and, albeit to a lesser extent, of Emperor Franz Joseph were popular among the civilian population. The Young Turks also had their admirers. In 1918 a shopkeeper used the portrait of Enver Pasha as his trade mark. In the same year Enver Bei watches were for sale. Nevertheless, there was a distinct preponderance of pictures of the German Emperor and the Turkish Sultan on display. When government officials inspected the houses in the villages in Central Java in the course of the campaign to combat the plague at the end of 1914, they discovered to their dismay that this was a very popular form of interior decoration. Concluding that the pictures of the German Emperor and the Turkish Sultan had not been distributed by 'friends of the government' portraits of the Dutch royal couple were at once ordered from Holland. The pictures were to be distributed as an 'antidote' (Bijl de Vroe 1980:71). The Ministry of the Colonies embraced the mission. An order was placed for pictures of the Queen and the royal family with a Dutch printing-firm. They had to be bright and colourful. Pictures of Wilhelmina were available in the colony, (unfortunately not, a civil servant observed, on matchboxes, which carried portraits of almost all monarchs in the world except of the Dutch sovereign) but natives did not buy them because they were too dull. At that time getting top-quality coloured prints was not an easy job. It took almost one-and-a-half years before the first shipment of 500,000 copies of a picture showing three medallions of Queen Wilhelmina, her husband, Prince Hendrik, and her daughter, Princess Juliana, was ready to be sent.[59]

In the minds of the Dutch responsible for planning of the defence of the colony, Germans could pose a much greater danger in times of war than the

---

[57] De Jonge to Pleyte, 3-10-1917, NA, Kol. Geheim, Vb. 10-10-1917 F12.
[58] *De Locomotief*, 15-5-1918.
[59] Pleyte to Van Limburg Stirum, 8-11-1917, NA, Kol. Openbaar, Vb. 8-11-1917 43; *De Locomotief*, 25-3-1916.

Frenchmen and Britons living in the Netherlands Indies. Among the reasons why the Germans especially were distrusted was the suspicion, assiduously fed by the British, that leaders of the German community were actually planning for the moment when war should break out between the Netherlands and Germany. Germans were said to have already tried to incite the Muslim population and the Arab community in the Netherlands Indies to agitate against Dutch rule in the pre-war years. To prepare for a German take-over, they were supposed to have made good use of the cordial relationship between Germany and Turkey. Germans, Arabs, and leaders of the Sarekat Islam were alleged to have held meetings before August 1914 to discuss what to do when war broke out. It was claimed that they had continued to meet after August 1914.

Apprehension about German intentions was one of the main reasons for Idenburg to reject a suggestion by Pleyte in May 1915 to allow foreign consuls in the colony to send and receive telegrams in cipher. Pleyte hoped that by allowing ciphers, London could be persuaded to lift the restriction on telegrams between him and Idenburg, which also had to be sent in plain language. Idenburg rejected the idea. He pointed out that ciphers would only be exchanged between him and The Hague if the Netherlands was a party in an international crisis. At such a moment the British cable companies would certainly not pass messages in cipher. Allowing Germany or Great Britain to use codes would give these two countries a great advantage over the Netherlands if war threatened. Their consuls in the Netherlands Indies might be better informed about the situation in Holland than he would be. Even more dangerous, here Idenburg was referring especially to Germany, was the fact that they might receive instructions freely on how to act after war had been declared. The ban on ciphers had to be accepted. It was an inescapable fate as long as the Netherlands was the weakest party in a conflict and remained dependent on British cables.[60]

Misgivings about a German scheme to undermine the Dutch rule peaked at the end of 1915, early 1916. Rumours about a German conspiracy involving Arabs, Chinese and members of the Sarekat Islam, and about the arrest of Tjokroaminoto because he was one of the plotters, led to all kind of wild speculations in what Emil Helfferich called the anti-German newspapers. One of the stories which circulated was that Javanese Regents and representatives of the courts of Yogyakarta and Surakarta had schemed to establish an Islamic state, protected by Turkey and with the Sunan of Surakarta as head of state. Pieces of red paper would provide the sign that the time had come for blood to flow and that people were to rise up. Such reports were also published abroad.

---

[60] Idenburg to Pleyte, 5-5-1915, NA, Kol. Geheim, Vb. 9-6-1915 G9.

Queen Alexandria on the trade mark of a trading company in Amsterdam (*Javasche Courant* 1916 Trade mark 8166)

Queen Wilhelmina on the trade mark of a trading company in Amsterdam (*Javasche Courant* 1916 Trade mark 8158)

In Tokyo the *Japan Times* maintained that the Germans involved were held largely responsible for disturbances in the Netherlands Indies. In Holland *De Telegraaf* had the same story. Other newspapers in Holland were also sure that there was a 'German complot'.[61]

Almost all the commotion concerned the so-called Buitenzorg affair or Buitenzorg conspiracy. The blame has to be laid at the door of the *Assistent-Resident* of Buitenzorg, who accused five Germans of conspiring against the colonial state in January 1916. He claimed that he acted on information provided by a number of Arabs and Javanese Muslims who had come to him voluntarily and out of their own volition. *Oetoesan Hindia* reacted indignantly to the suggestion that the Sarekat Islam was involved in an attempt to overthrow Dutch rule. True, Indonesian Muslims were pro-German, because it was the ally of Turkey, but it was 'a lie, treason, seditious, wicked' to suggest that they looked to German help to rebel against Dutch rule. In the prevailing critical atmosphere, the Sarekat Islam stood 100 per cent behind the Dutch government. As 'leaders of the people' the editors knew where their duty lay.[62]

Implicated in the Buitenzorg affair were two former employees of the Straits und Sunda Syndikat: Freiherr August von und zu Egloffstein, and Karl Ernst Keil. They were also former officers in the colonial army, who had respectively twenty-five and twenty years service in the course of which they had been awarded medals. Emil Helfferich was said to have been the leader of the complot. Keil was alleged to have chaired meetings in the Arab quarter of Buitenzorg to prepare for an Islamic state. He was supposed to have tried to convince the conspirators that they did not have to worry about arms and medical supplies. The German government had set aside money for this sort of thing. Keil was probably the 'fat European gentleman', who in reports figured as the person who at one of such meetings was pointed to by some of those present as the future king of Java in Dutch-language newspapers. He himself was claimed to have reacted by saying: 'Here is the person who will become king. Germany is the strongest.'[63]

On the initiative of Emil Helfferich the three tried to convince the *Assistent-Resident* that the accusations were unfounded. When this failed, they appealed to the Governor General in a letter in the newspapers to instigate a judicial investigation. They vowed that they were loyal residents of the Netherlands Indies. Other Germans, Austrians, and Hungarians used the celebration of the Kaiser's birthday to express their indignation about the affair in a telegram to

---

61   De Telegraaf, cited in *De Indische Gids* 1916:791; *De Locomotief*, 21-4-1916, 22-4-1916, 19-5-1916, *Oetoesan Hindia*, 9-5-1916; Van Asbeck to Van Limburg Stirum, 26-4-1916, NA, Kol. Geheim, Vb. 13-6-1916 T7.
62   *Oetoesan Hindia*, 9-5-1916.
63   *Het Nieuws van den Dag*, cited in *De Locomotief*, 1-5-1916.

Idenburg. They also asked for an official inquiry.

A similar case evolved in Sumatra. K. Bäumer, editor of the *Sumatra-bode* in Padang asked for an formal investigation into accusations that Germans held secret meetings in Sumatra and incited the local population and Arabs against Dutch rule. Germans were also said to be mapping strategic spots. Especially offensive to Bäumer, a German who lived for thirty years already in the Netherlands Indies, were insinuations about newspaper editors who tried to persuade Indonesian Muslims to side with Germany 'when time had come', because Germany was an ally of Turkey.[64]

The reports about German plots were grist to the mill of the anti-German press. For J.G. Boon, editor-in-chief of the *Soerabaiasch Handelsblad* since April 1915, the affair formed the occasion to launch a campaign calling attention to the stirring by Germans among indigenous Indonesians, Arabs, and Chinese. He claimed that in every large city there was 'great intimacy between the Arabs and our German guests', which could not be attributed to interests of trade or 'les beaux yeux des Arabes' alone. Boon thought the logical explanation was the existence of a German organization spreading anti-Dutch propaganda among Arabs and other Muslims. He appealed to the Dutch in the Netherlands Indies to assist in keeping track of Germans and noting their behaviour. The government should forbid contacts between Germans and Arabs, or Chinese and indigenous Indonesians hostile to Dutch rule. Another suggestion Boon made was to dismiss some of the German soldiers. He generously added that they could retain their pensions. Other German soldiers should be posted to faraway corners of the Archipelago where they could do no harm.[65] The editor-in-chief of *Het Nieuws van den Dag*, W.K.S. van Haastert, hinted that the Sarekat Islam had been able to grow because German support and that its board had a secret 'Young Turks' agenda. The editors of *Oetoesan Hindia* reacted furiously. They denied that there was any truth in the allegations. Van Haastert was called a liar, a falsifier of facts, and a person full of sound and fury signifying nothing. *Oetoesan Hindia* suggested that Van Haastert should be arraigned for his deliberate attempt to sow hatred against the Javanese. By acting as he did, he formed a much greater threat to Dutch rule than either Germany or Japan.[66] Because the colonial administration shared the suspicion that Germans cooperated with the Sarekat Islam no legal action was taken against Van Haastert.[67]

The *Soerabaiasch Handelsblad* and *Het Nieuws van den Dag* were not alone in

---

[64] *De Locomotief*, 2-6-1916.
[65] *Soerabaiasch Handelsblad*, 9-3-1916, 26-4-1916, 27-4-1916, 28-4-1916, cited in *De Indische Gids* 1916:786, 1105-6.
[66] *Oetoesan Hindia*, 29-4-1916, 1-5-1916.
[67] See NA, Kol. Geheim, Mr. 1917/16x.

A conservative view of how the Sarikat Islam should behave seeking guidance from the Dutch Virgin and ignoring the voice of agitators

their condemnation. Abusive anti-German articles in the Dutch-language press now reached a peak. Windels spoke about a *Pressefeldzug* and about the almost daily disgraceful and libellous remarks in which all Germans were depicted as spies and traitors. He claimed that because of such pieces most Dutchmen had started to shun Germans. The argument suited him well. Windels's point was that Germans had become an isolated, distinct group in the Netherlands Indies. This opened the possibility to use the *haatzaai* articles to bring a prosecution against *Het Nieuws van den Dag*, the *Soerabaiasch Handelsblad*, and other anti-German newspapers.[68]

The Buitenzorg Affair proved a hoax. It was an act of revenge against Keil, known as a 'stern landlord' and absolutely no friend of the Sarekat Islam, by Arabs who had been evicted from his estate and who had gained the cooperation of a number of Indonesians who shared their hatred of Keil. In December 1916 the Court of Batavia ruled that there was absolutely no ground for a prosecution. There was no shred of evidence. The Germans had never been near any Sarekat Islam meeting. The Attorney-General decided to appeal. Not because he did not agree with the ruling, but to undo the damage done and to have an opportunity to lecture the press and praise the Germans who had been implicated. In his closing speech before the High Court the Attorney-General concluded that he deemed a ruling by the highest court necessary because the affair had 'produced turmoil throughout the whole country, completely disproportionate to the facts [...] caused by the foolhardy undertaking of a few daily papers, which [...] had no scruples about giving a totally untrue picture [...] on the basis of worthless evidence'.[69] He also accused the press of having published reports on secret meetings of Germans elsewhere in the Netherlands Indies to create the impression that Germans were also plotting there against Dutch rule, 'reports usually so absurd that – would not the mind of many readers have been poisoned by prejudice – nobody would give any credence to them'.[70] The Attorney-General praised the Germans who had been implicated (the name of one Schün had also been mentioned) as decent, quiet persons, whose service and loyalty to colonial society were without doubt. He did not forget to mention that the Arabs in Buitenzorg were equally quiet, decent persons, and that the local Sarekat Islam was unquestionable.

Distrust of German intentions remained. The Governor General and his closest advisors knew about the Germano-Indian complot, other civil servants and the general public who were unaware of it had been confronted with the pamphlets sent from abroad, and had probably also heard some rumours about meetings which would have been held. The *Resident* of Batavia,

---

[68] Windels to 1st Government Secretary, 12-5-1916, NA, Kol. Openbaar, Vb. 9-12-1918 45.
[69] *De Locomotief*, 9-12-1916.
[70] *De Locomotief*, 9-12-1916.

Rijfsnijder, continued to deem it necessary to remain on the alert for such German attempts as late as August 1918.[71] The general public also continued to be suspicious. In its attack on *De Locomotief* in August 1916 *Het Nieuws van den Dag* did not fail to mention that it was strange that a newspaper which followed the ideas of Pleyte, who till he became Minister of the Colonies had been a commissioner of *De Locomotief* so completely had become an instrument of people who wanted the natives to rise in rebellion against Dutch rule.[72]

An additional source of embarrassment to the colonial authorities was that Dutch Indo-Europeans had been recruited as agents by the Germano-Indian conspirators. This was one of the reasons Idenburg distrusted the German community. He was not only sure that was tried to incite the Muslim population and discontented Indo-Europeans against Dutch rule in the Netherlands Indies by Germans in anticipation of war between Germany and the Netherlands, he was convinced that they had especially tried to involve members of the Indische Partij and other Indo-Europeans in the plan to subvert British rule in Asia (Bijl de Vroe 1980:44, 83). In January 1916 he confided to his adjutant in January 1916 that Germans used members of the Indische Partij to smuggle revolutionary pamphlets into India (Bijl de Vroe 1980:83).

One of the reasons for Idenburg to draw this conclusion was that he had learned about the adventures of Douwes Dekker. Douwes Dekker had met leaders of the Ghadr Movement during his trip to Europe in 1910 and 1911. He had kept in touch with them and had asked them to contribute to *Het Tijdschrift*. With the support he still had in the Netherlands Indies Douwes Dekker was an attractive asset to the movement. Within days of the outbreak of the war, Ghadr leaders had made their first move to recruit Douwes Dekker as an agent. His old acquaintance Krishnavarma, who had likewise moved to Geneva, had sent him a postcard and had suggested a meeting. Before Douwes Dekker had made up his mind, Krishnavarma had called at his house. He brought along Har Dayal, who had also been one of the contributors to *Het Tijdschrift*. The three talked about the war. Douwes Dekker later confessed he had liked the initiator of the Germano-Indian scheme to undermine the British position in Asia. Har Dayal had struck him as 'a man with a well-developed intellect'. More meetings with Har Dayal followed. They had long chats, often in Douwes Dekker's house. These were homely meetings during which Har Dayal played with Douwes Dekker's children. At first Har Dayal had held his tongue about the Germano-Indian conspiracy. He had only left no doubt that he would leave no stone unturned to gain independence for India (Van der Veur 2006:314, 322-3).

---

[71] NA, Memorie van Overgave Rijfsnijder, 2-8-1914.
[72] *De Locomotief*, 11-8-1916.

After Turkey had entered the war, efforts to court Douwes Dekker were stepped up. A number of Indians, who all came with letters of introduction from Har Dayal, contacted him. Among them were Chattopadhyaya and Champakaraman Pillai, chairman and secretary of a National Committee of Indians Living in Berlin. They visited Douwes Dekker in December. Pillai, who was an editor of *Pro India*, told Douwes Dekker about the existence of a secret organization in Berlin which had been set up to stir up anti-British feelings in British colonies. He asked Douwes Dekker to join and to become the movement's representative in Zurich, the city to which Douwes Dekker had moved shortly before. Douwes Dekker's task would be to distribute pamphlets from their committee in Zurich. Later, after the British had arrested him, Douwes Dekker claimed that he had refused. Whatever the truth, Douwes Dekker became more deeply involved when he received a telegram from Germany at the end of January 1915 inviting him to Berlin. He asked his wife what he should do. She was unhappy about it, but Douwes Dekker decided to accept.[73] He later told his British interrogators that his main motivation had been his deplorable financial situation: 'At the time I got the wire we were in the last straits of wretchedness. My wife and children were about to leave me, and return to Java, chiefly because of our poverty and the absence of any means of livelihood in Europe.'[74]

Another task Douwes Dekker was asked to perform was to assist in acquiring Dutch passports from the Dutch consulate in Zurich for Indian and other agents of the conspiracy ordered to travel to the Netherlands Indies. Pillai and his friends had found out that the Consul spoke no Dutch or Malay. This would make it the easier for agents sent to the Netherlands Indies to pass as residents of the Netherlands Indies. In May Douwes Dekker helped to arrange the journey to the Netherlands Indies of a Batavia-born man of German origin by the name of C.F. Vincent Kraft. At the request of Pillai he also provided Kraft with a letter of introduction to a friend of his in Java. After his arrest Douwes Dekker claimed that he had added a note of caution in a secret code. He had not trusted Kraft and had not even been sure that Kraft was not a Dutch spy sent to report on him (Van der Veur 2006:323, 325).

Kraft boarded a Dutch mail boat in Genoa in May 1915. After arriving in Batavia he travelled on to Sumatra in the company of Douwes Dekker's friend. Convinced that Kraft was a German secret agent, the latter left Kraft on his own in Medan. Without realizing this, Douwes Dekker had sealed his own

---

[73] After she had returned to Java Douwes Dekker's wife would still be supported by the Tado Fund. In April 1916 she informed Insulinde that she was able to support herself and her children and no longer needed financial assistance (*De Locomotief*, 15-6-1916).
[74] Secret statement, 24-1-1916, NA, Kol. Openbaar, Vb. 27-7-1916 25. See also Van der Veur 2006:314, 322-3.

fate by assisting Kraft to reach the Netherlands Indies. The British suspected Kraft and kept him under surveillance while he was in the Netherlands Indies. Kraft was arrested when he tried to enter Singapore the following month. He made a full confession and revealed all he knew about the Germano-Indian plot. Kraft was turned into a double agent. Under the guidance of British intelligence, he continued to communicate with Berlin. He even returned to the Netherlands Indies as a British spy (Hopkirk 1994:188-9).

Kraft's information would lead to Douwes Dekker's arrest. When he was interrogated by the British authorities, Douwes Dekker remained vague about his involvement in the Germano-Indian plot. At first he admitted that he had discussed the smuggling of 30,000 rifles into British India with Pillai, but claimed that he had only gone along with this to see what financial gain it might bring him. He said that he even had suggested that when he provided with one million German marks he would buy rifles in Japan or the United States and arrange for them to be shipped to British India aboard a Dutch merchantman under a false bill of loading. Douwes Dekker stressed that the plan had never been executed.[75] He also denied ever having played any part in the attempts to smuggle arms into Burma or India. The Berlin committee had only asked him to become an intermediary in the smuggling of seditious literature into India. He explained that the only reason he had agreed was his desperate need of money. He had no qualms about accepting the money. He knew that the schemers were financed by the German state. He claimed that he had had no intention at all of fulfilling his assignment. He had destroyed the pamphlets.[76]

Despite his denials, there can be no denying that Douwes Dekker was thrilled by some of the schemes suggested by the Indians. When they told him that they wanted to send a Javanese Muslim to Turkey to receive a fatwa, a religious ruling, 'calling upon Moslems to remain loyal to their faith, and to do nothing which would act against the "Khalifa"', Douwes Dekker, had been elated.[77] Before his exile in *De Expres* in 1912 there had been a report that some Muslims considered him the reincarnation of Muhammad (Glissenaar 1999:85). A fatwa would raise his standing among members of the Sarekat Islam and other Muslims in the Netherlands Indies even more. Imagining how such a fatwa could boost his 'democratic propaganda', Douwes Dekker had suggested that he himself should go to Istanbul. Pillai had been quick to point out that such a journey would not be of much use. Douwes Dekker was not a Muslim. Unable to perform the mission himself, Douwes Dekker wrote

---

[75] Spakler to Idenburg, 22-12-1915, NA, Kol. Geheim, Vb. 11-2-1916 W1.
[76] Secret statement, 24-1-1916, NA, Kol. Openbaar, Vb. 27-7-1916 25; *Handelingen Tweede Kamer* 1917-18:1447. See also Van der Veur 2006:325, 363-8.
[77] Secret statement, 24-1-1916, NA, Kol. Openbaar, Vb. 27-7-1916 25.

to a Javanese friend. He asked him to come to Holland as soon as possible. He could collect his travelling expenses at Douwes Dekker's father's house. Pillai never seemed to have posted the letter, nor to have remitted any money to Douwes Dekker's father.

Douwes Dekker was arrested at the end of the year, after he had embarked on a journey to the Far East financed by the Germans. Around the time of Kraft's arrest, Pillai and Chattopadhyaya had visited Douwes Dekker in Zurich and had asked him to become their agent in Bangkok (Ban Kah Choon 2001:69). Douwes Dekker had agreed. As by now it was well known even in the Netherlands Indies, he had become fed up with life in Europe and wanted to return to Asia. Insulinde even contemplated sending him the proceeds of cinema shows to allow him to take up residence in Singapore.[78]

Before travelling to Bangkok, Douwes Dekker visited the United States and Japan. In connection with plans for his journey, he went to Berlin once more in July 1915. In Berlin he received his instructions and a code book from the German Foreign Office (Van der Veur 2006:318-9). The code book would allow him to keep in contact with the committee in Berlin by telegrams of which the contents at first glance looked like information about commercial transactions. The Dutch Deputy Consul in Hong Kong, W.J. Quist, was to report a few months later that the code was a very clever one. Simple sentences had a completely different meaning to that which an innocent reader would make of it.[79] The British were not fooled. Kraft had given them the code.

Douwes Dekker, who by now had been studying at the University of Zurich for a year and had passed his exams with flying colours – he was known as a diligent and energetic, albeit somewhat lonely person[80] – left Rotterdam for New York in early September. He travelled in the guise of a commercial traveller. To explain his departure he wrote to his landlord in Zurich that he had tried to be rehabilitated in Holland, that he had failed, and that he was tired of Europe. He wanted to go back to the Netherlands Indies.[81] At the end of the month, Douwes Dekker arrived in San Francisco, still the centre of Indian dissidents. Here he met Rham Chandra Kanta Chakravarti, who was considered by the British to have become the leader of the conspiracy in the United States after Har Dayal had fled the country.[82] From San Francisco Douwes Dekker sailed on to Japan, where he visited one of the leaders of the Indian Revolutionary Party in Japan, Heramba (Hermeba) Lal Gupta. Another of his contacts in Japan was Yusaburo Takekoshi, the author of the fiercely anti-

[78] *De Locomotief,* 21-12-1914.
[79] Quist to Ruempol, 17-12-1915, NA, Kol. Openbaar, Vb. 22-4-1916 5.
[80] Von Claparède-Crola to Van Panhuys, 27-1-1916, NA, Kol. Geheim, Vb. 11-2-1916 W1.
[81] Von Claparède-Crola to Van Panhuys, 27-1-1916, NA, Kol. Geheim, Vb. 11-2-1916 W1.
[82] British memorandum August 1918, NA, Kol. Geheim, Vb. 27-9-1918 F9.

Dutch article which had so shocked the Dutch (Van der Veur 2006:322-3).

From Japan Douwes Dekker travelled on to Shanghai. By now, he was regarded as a highly suspicious character by the Dutch and the British government. Both were aware of his schedule. In Batavia the colonial authorities suspected him of continuing his anti-colonial Indische Partij activities from abroad.[83] To find out more, the Dutch Consul General in Shanghai was instructed to investigate who Douwes Dekker's contacts were. He had to investigate more thoroughly if these persons were Germans, British Indians, Turks, or Arabs. Batavia was also very eager to know to whom Douwes Dekker sent letters in the Netherlands Indies. The British, knowing about Douwes Dekker's part in the Germano-Indian plot, were so eager to arrest him that even a namesake of his was detained when he entered Great Britain.

Douwes Dekker's next stop was Hong Kong. Here he was detained. Douwes Dekker fell ill and had to be admitted to hospital. He had syphilis, but the Dutch authorities were so well-bred they kept this a secret and had not corrected newspaper reports in Java that Douwes Dekker was suffering from dysentery (Van der Veur 2006:319-21). To prevent his escape, the head of the Hong Kong police had Douwes Dekker outer clothing removed. In an interview with a journalist on the *Sumatra Post* who visited him in hospital, Douwes Dekker blamed British reprisals for his pro-German articles in the Dutch press for his arrest. That during his interrogations he had revealed everything about his contacts with the Indian conspirators, he attributed to his poor health. He said he had consumption. The journalist was struck by the 'terribly emaciated face' of 'the father of the Indische Partij'.[84] When he had recovered somewhat, Douwes Dekker was put on a ship to Singapore, where, still weak from his illness, he was arrested by the military authorities on arrival on 21 December 1915. In the Netherlands Indies newspapers reporting on his arrest said that Douwes Dekker's role in the smuggling of inflammatory pamphlets was punishable by British martial law with twenty years' imprisonment.[85]

Batavia welcomed Douwes Dekker's arrest. The Dutch Consul General in Singapore who, had alerted the Singapore authorities to the fact that Douwes Dekker was a 'dangerous agitator' as early as October, made it clear that the Dutch authorities 'had no desire that Douwes Dekker should be released, in fact they hoped that the British authorities would detain him as long as they possibly could'.[86] This they did. Douwes Dekker remained in the Tanglin Prison till 1917 (Van der Veur 2006:334-51), when he was sent to San Francisco

---

[83] Ruempol to Dutch Consul General in Shanghai, 8-11-1915, NA, Kol., Vb. 22-4-1916 5.
[84] *De Locomotief*, 24-1-1916, *Oetoesan Hindia*, 1-2-1916.
[85] *De Locomotief*, 11-1-1916.
[86] Spakler to Colonial Secretary Singapore, 7-10-1915, Beckett to Hulshoff Pol, 10-5-1916, NA, Kol. Geheim, Vb. 11-2-1916 W1, Vb. 27-7-1916 25.

to testify in the 'Hindoo cases', the trials of eight Indian conspirators, including 'his friend' Rham Chandra Kanta Chakravarti, as the latter was described by the *San Francisco Examiner*.[87]

In San Francisco thirty Germans, Americans, and Indians were sentenced for breaching American neutrality. The court case resulted in new embarrassments for the Dutch government. Testimonies implicated Theodor and Emil Helfferich. As far as London was concerned what was disclosed at the trial was reason enough to remind The Hague in August 1918 of the accusations it had made in 1916. It was pointed out that there could no longer be any doubt that Dutch territory had been used as a base for German conspiracies against India.[88] An accompanying memorandum stated that had the Helfferich brothers been brought to trial, they would certainly have been convicted 'for the evidence in the case proved clearly that Batavia was one of the principal scenes of the conspiracy and that Theodor Helfferich was the chief German agent at that place'.[89] Especially Theodor's remark to her supercargo shortly after the arrival of *Maverick* in which 'he expressed regret that the cargo had not come and his disgust that the *Maverick* had arrived without it', was seen by the British authorities (and by the Dutch counterparts when they learned about it) as proof of his complicity. The British government could also point to evidence that Theodor Helfferich had met representatives of the revolutionary movement in India in his house and had discussed the dropping of arms along the coast of India with them. It was also noted that such persons had simply found Helfferich's address by looking it up in a telephone directory. In one case, one of them who should have been introduced to Theodor Helfferich by Abdul Selam (who at that time had been under arrest), had been directed to Helfferich by a 'couple of Java gentlemen'. They had been waiting for a guest from India in the lobby of the hotel where Abdul Selam had been staying.[90] The evidence also showed that Ong Sin Kwie might not have been as innocent as the Attorney-General in Batavia had taken him to be. A telegram exchanged between the United States and Berlin had referred to the arrest of a Chinese friend of Theodor Helfferich.[91]

Likewise unpleasant was that the German plot provided Takekoshi and other expansionist Japanese with yet another argument for the Japanese government to do something about the Netherlands Indies. It became one of the many arguments wielded by Takekoshi to demonstrate that Japan should

---

[87] *San Francisco Examiner*, 10-6-1917; Van der Veur 2006:351-71.
[88] Townley to Loudon, 28-8-1918, NA, Kol. Geheim, Vb. 27-9-1918 F9.
[89] British memorandum August 1918, NA, Kol. Geheim, Vb. 27-9-1918 F9.
[90] British memorandum August 1918, NA, Kol. Geheim, Vb. 27-9-1918 F9.
[91] British memorandum August 1918, Note Department A1, September 1918, NA, Kol. Geheim, Vb. 27-9-1918 F9.

somehow acquire Java and Sumatra. He presented a range of reasons: the failure to maintain neutrality during the Russo-Japanese War; the exploits of the *Emden* and the role of Germans in the Netherlands Indies in stirring up unrest in British India, which showed that the failure to maintain neutrality harmed other nations; the fact that the problems the Allied blockade posed to Germany showed that Japan as an industrialized nation also needed a colony in the tropics to supply the motherland with food and natural resources; and the possibility that after the war the Netherlands Indies could become a base for Japan's enemies.[92]

After the trial, Douwes Dekker returned to Singapore, where on the promise to refrain from political activities he took up residence in a modest hotel, the Hotel Van Wijk.

[92] *De Locomotief,* 6-10-1916.

CHAPTER XIII

The consequences of economic warfare

In the course of time more and more commodities were added to the lists of absolute and conditional contraband drawn up by the Great Britain and France. In September 1914 copper, lead, rubber, and hides became contraband (which as London pointed out in 1917 implied that horses were also contraband, as it was impossible 'to export a live horse without his skin').[1] A month later jute was added. In December rubber and mineral oils were declared absolute contraband. In March, April, and August 1915 the axe fell on raw wool, copra (used for the production of oil and soap), and cotton respectively. The consequences of such announcements were drastic. Immediately prices of cotton and copra dropped sharply in the Netherlands Indies.

Great Britain and France, developing their measures in close concert, aimed at achieving full economic isolation of Germany and Austria-Hungary. In London and Paris depriving the enemy of imports was seen as one of the ways through which Germany and Austria-Hungary might be forced into surrender. Such a strategy had won strong support in the British Navy as early as 1907 (Ferguson 2001:125). Throughout the war the Allied Powers continued to attach great value to the economic blockade of the Central Powers. When Italy entered the war on the side of the Triple Entente in May 1915, the military advantage to the Allied cause was not rated highly at the Foreign Office in London. What counted was that one of the routes along which a considerable amount of commodities had reached Germany in the previous months was now closed.[2]

Great Britain and France controlled the sea, but they did not have control of the land borders of Germany. For diplomatic and economic reasons, they could not put an end to German imports from the northern neutral countries in Europe. Throughout most of the war the German economy remained strong enough to provide the neutral countries with coal, iron, chemical products, medicines, machineries, textiles and other commodities they urgently needed.

---

1   Townley to Cecil, 18-11-1917, PRO FO 800 195.
2   Nicholson to Hardinge, 10-6-1915, PRO FO 800 378.

This made an economic boycott of countries like Holland ineffectual, even counterproductive. Till well into 1917, policy makers in London and Paris had to take into account that an economic blockade of the neutral European states, with the Netherlands because of its location being one of the most likely targets for such a step, might force these countries into the German camp. The fewer the goods the Allied Powers allowed to enter the Netherlands, the more the Dutch had to turn to Germany for essential imports.

To the dismay of politicians and of the general public in Great Britain and France, and later also in the United States, a profitable trade developed between the neutral countries and Germany. A hostile press which attacked the profits Dutch people made from the trade with Germany helped considerably to create an anti-Dutch mood in the Allied countries and in the United States. The Dutch sure in their conviction that they had done nothing wrong and that by showing a fair neutrality they had acted as citizens of a neutral country should, blamed the foreign newspapers, especially the tabloids, almost every time they were confronted by unpleasant reactions from the Allied Powers. A member of the Dutch Senate stated in February 1918 that the 'poisonous gasses of the tabloids' had had a greater effect than 'the poisonous gasses of German bombs in the trenches'.[3]

By November 1914 the heading 'The economic war' appeared above the war telegrams in the Dutch-language newspapers in the Netherlands Indies alongside others like 'War at sea' and 'War in the sky'. Confronted with this special kind of warfare, the Netherlands had to find a way to accommodate both Allied and German demands, and from time to time had to parry severe threats from both sides. Berlin's protests against the way the Netherlands maintained its neutrality were at times, as the British Ambassador in The Hague said, 'guttural and menacing'.[4] London did not eschew 'bullying', a word which after a while began to crop up in the correspondence between London and the British legation in Holland about the way the Netherlands should be treated. With Germany and Great Britain trying to starve each other into surrender, the Netherlands was caught between the devil and the deep blue sea. In its negotiations with Germany and Great Britain, the Dutch government had to make sure that the concessions made to one side did not offend the other. As the war progressed, this became increasingly difficult. The members of the Dutch government, especially the Minister of Foreign Affairs, Loudon, had to tread carefully. Great Britain had the power to make Dutch sea traffic impossible. Germany might well be able, as Loudon explained to London on various occasions, to occupy Holland before Allied forces had

---

[3] *Handelingen Eerste Kamer* 1917-18:191
[4] Townley to Cecil, 17-3-1917, PRO FO 800 195.

had a chance to come to its assistance.[5] In London the Foreign Secretary, Sir Edward Grey, was sensitive to the argument. Unless the Allied Powers were in a position to assure the Netherlands that they could prevent an invasion by Germany, it would not 'be fair in their own interests to suggest that they should cease to be neutral'.[6]

The Netherlands' position in World War One resembled that of Turkey and China in the pre-war years, with Great Britain and Germany competing for control over its economy. Each had allies in the commercial and political elites. Of the two figures who dominated the Dutch business community, Van Aalst, the President of the Nederlandsche Handel-Maatschappij, and therefore with the fate of the colonial estate economy at heart, tended to align himself with the British. His main rival, A.G. Kröller, a Rotterdam shipowner and trader, maintained excellent relations with Germany. In the government Treub, who in concert with Van Aalst determined the bulk of Dutch trade policy, was considered to be not disinclined towards London. His colleague in Agriculture, Industry, and Trade, F.E. Posthuma tended to be pro-German. The same was said about the Prime Minister, Cort van der Linden. In Allied circles he was known as Caught unter den Linden.

Loudon was the first to receive threats and protests from London, Paris, and Berlin. Thrust into the limelight by the war the stature of his Department of Foreign Affairs changed. For a long time it had been a rather insignificant Ministry, greatly overshadowed by that of the Colonies. It was 'a forgotten department'. People considered it to be 'very stuffy' (Colenbrander 1920:102). During the Russo-Japanese War it had even been considered incompetent. World War One changed all this. As Van Kol remarked in the Dutch Senate in 1918 the work of a Minister of Foreign Affairs no longer consisted mainly of 'lunching, dining, having supper, and sauntering'.[7] There was great praise for what Loudon had accomplished. According to the British Ambassador in 1917, Sir Walter Townley, he became 'a sort of national fetish' for keeping Holland out of the war.[8] Loudon, who in the eyes of Townley was 'inspired by a holy terror of Germany' was not considered by the British to be somebody who had ended up in the camp of their enemy because of this.[9] On the contrary. Townley described him as 'undoubtedly pro-Ally at heart, though so intent upon preserving his neutral attitude that it is hard to detect in his public acts much good feeling towards us.'[10]

---

[5] Townley to Cecil 24-3-1917, PRO FO 800 195.
[6] Grey to Johnstone 20-1-1915, PRO FO 800 69.
[7] *Handelingen Eerste Kamer* 1917-8:474.
[8] Townley to Cecil, 29-10-1917, PRO FO 800 195.
[9] Townley to Cecil, 29-10-1917, PRO FO 800 195.
[10] Townley to Cecil, 18-11-1917, PRO FO 800 195.

Unable to control the German land borders, the best London and Paris could do was to prevent neutral merchantmen carrying transit goods to and from Germany. In this way they put an end to the export of colonial wares which had been declared contraband to Germany and Austria-Hungary from the Netherlands Indies. With British warships controlling international seaborne trade, London was virtually in a position to decide which commodities – including goods which before the war had been imported from Germany, but which Germany no longer supplied because of the war – could be transported to the Netherlands by neutral merchantmen. In The Hague, a key role in the supervision of Dutch foreign trade was played by Sir Francis Oppenheimer, the Commercial Attaché at the British Embassy. His job did not make him a popular figure in Holland. Oppenheimer was also disliked by the British, maybe because he was of German descent. His father was a German who had been naturalized. Referring to him in 1917 the British Envoy remarked that he had never 'known a man so universally hated'.[11] Oppenheimer who was tolerated in his function because he was an expert in his field, was 'a horrible difficult question'; 'an unfortunately unsympathetic personality'; a man who had 'deplorable manners'.[12] In Holland for a brief moment in the autumn of 1915, the Allied effort to keep track of Dutch trade was assisted by an 'anti-smuggling bureau' created by H.M.C. Holdert, the majority shareholder of the Dutch newspaper *De Telegraaf*. What its agents discovered about smuggling to Germany and Belgium was reported to the British and French Embassies.

British control of shipping in Asia was as tight as in Europe. All ships which entered and left ports in the Netherlands Indies were stopped. Sometimes they were ordered to sail on to Singapore for a closer inspection of passengers, cargo, and mail. Ships which sailed in the western part of the Archipelago were not exempt from searches. The problem was that the ships sailing between the ports of the Netherlands Indies had to leave the three-mile wide territorial waters. Usually the searches took place on the high seas, but ships sailing in colonial territorial waters were occasionally also arrested so that their cargo, mail, and passengers could be checked. This was usually done by British warships, and occasionally the Australians did the job. Japanese cruisers did their share after May 1916.

The warships had every freedom to act. In the absence of a strong German fleet, they could sail as close to colonial territorial waters as they wanted. A 'distant blockade' as in Europe, where British warships patrolled at a safe distance from German naval bases, was not necessary. Another difference was that in Asia cargo was not the first concern. The Germano-Indian complot

---

[11] Townley to Cecil, 17-3-1917, PRO FO 800 195.
[12] Townley to Cecil, 17-3-1917, PRO FO 800 195.

to foment unrest in India and the Malay Peninsula meant that mail and passengers were the prime target of the searches. One of the first questions asked when a ship was searched was whether there were Germans on board. Other suspect persons – including a German soldier in the colonial army and sailors of German ships stuck in the ports of the Netherlands Indies who had signed off – were also liable to be arrested. Mail was confiscated.

The Netherlands Indies was effectively cordoned off by the British Navy. When Bijl de Vroe accompanied Van Limburg Stirum on a sea voyage from Batavia to Semarang in October 1916, he noted in his diary how they passed 'the wretch of an English cruiser which stops and searches all ships' after they had left port (Bijl de Vroe 1980:98). The ship on which the Governor-General and his adjutant travelled was not stopped. Informed about who was on board, the captain of the cruiser had a twenty-one-salute fired. Bijl de Vroe probably worded the prevailing sentiment amongst Dutchmen. Captains of Dutch ships made the best of it, adding an element of sport to the game. They tried to avoid an encounter with Allied warships and challenged their crews to find them. British captains took up the challenge, pleased with any distraction during what was often a very boring routine patrol.[13]

In the Netherlands Indies the successive British Consuls General were the persons who determined what foreign trade was still allowed and what not in consultation with London. Another of their tasks was to keep track of enemy spies. They were well informed. The Consuls General and the other British authorities in Asia received their information from members of the British community in the Netherlands Indies, from the occasional Dutchman, and from a network of informants and agents. Kraft was one of their spies. Another asset was 'a double agent known by the code name "Oren" born of a Swedish mother and a German father, working under deep cover within the European business community' (Choon 2001:71). Until 1916 yet another good source of information was the British employees of the Eastern Extension at telegraph stations. Occasionally they sent information directly to Allied warships.[14]

One of the results was that when Dutch merchantmen were searched in Asian waters, it was sometimes known in advance that Germans or suspected Indians were on board or that Dutch people living in the Netherlands Indies carried mail for German friends and acquaintances to evade British mail searches carried by neutral ships. They and other Dutch Residents of the Netherlands Indies, who were suspected by the British authorities of being enemy agents, or as it was diplomatically phrased were 'unneutral', were arrested and taken off. One of the persons who fell victim to this was the

---

[13] *Soerabaiasch Nieuwsblad*, cited in *De Locomotief*, 11-1-1917.
[14] *De Locomotief*, 28-3-1916.

Governor General J.P. graaf van Limburg Stirum (Van Gent, Penard and Rinkes 1923: Photo 260)

secretary of the German Consul General, R. Götte. Travelling from Tanjung Priok to Belawan he was taken off in the Straits of Malacca just outside territorial waters in January 1916. The British had been waiting for him. Götte had known that it had not been safe for him to travel, but had taken the risk nevertheless. Another German had more luck. Travelling from Samarinda to Buleleng he was taken off and was interned in British Borneo in July 1916. It was the second time he was interned. He could prove that earlier in Singapore he had been released because of his age, he was fifty-four. The British set him free. They gave him a first class ticket to continue his journey. It was reported that the German in question was 'very satisfied' with the treatment he got.[15] Yet another such incident happened in August 1916. A Dutchman travelling from Padang to Batavia, who British intelligence had been told was carrying mail for 'an enemy official in Batavia', in fact letters from the German Consul in Padang to the German Consul General in Batavia, was taken off. After The Hague had protested, the British government explained that examining the many letters the person in question had in his possession would have delayed the Dutch steamer too long. No incriminating mail was found.[16]

British consular officials also succeeded remarkably well in keeping track of the flow of goods in ports in Holland and the Netherlands Indies; curtailing Dutch commerce accordingly. In September 1917 *The Times* wrote that Great Britain had 'built up an extremely efficient intelligence service to keep watch over the "ins" and "outs" of the "blockade"'. London knew 'pretty nearly everything there was to know about German's war-time methods', including 'the tricks and false scent adopted in ordering goods' in neutral countries.[17]

What lay in store for Dutch seaborne trade had dawned on people's consciousness in September 1914 when the first merchantman from the Netherlands Indies for over a month had reached European waters. It was the *Tambora*. Among her passengers were Idenburg's wife and son, who had left for Europe in anticipation of the Governor General's retirement. The *Tambora* had sailed from Tanjung Priok at the end of July. The voyage to Europe had taken much longer than it would have done under normal circumstances. On 5 September the *Tambora* was detained for one week at Brest, where she had to unload her mail and her cargo of rice, coffee, and tea. The incident was the first of its kind and made a great impression in the Netherlands Indies. Disquieted by the news, the two major Dutch shipping companies – the Rotterdamsche Lloyd and the Nederland – and export houses in the Netherlands Indies decided to

---

[15] *De Locomotief*, 25-7-1916.
[16] *De Locomotief*, 18-8-1916; British Foreign Office to Dutch Legation, 9-2-1917, NA, Kol. Openbaar, Vb. 15-3-1917 3.
[17] *The Times*, 10-9-1917.

ship products such as rice, coffee, tea, and rubber to British and French ports only, and not to Dutch ports. The shipping companies were motivated by the fear that their precious ships might be taken as a prize. The Declaration of London of 1909 (which was never ratified) allowed freighters to be seized as a prize if more than half of the cargo consisted of contraband. Such a proportion could easily be reached after a Dutch ship had unloaded a part of the cargo in British or French ports. At that moment the Dutch business community had no clear notion of what Great Britain and France considered contraband. Neither had the Dutch government in The Hague nor Idenburg and his staff: 'Please wire which colonial products (are) by belligerents considered contraband and if tea and rubber shipped in Dutch steamers and directly consigned to England run any risk', Idenburg asked Pleyte in The Hague by wire in English on 10 September.[18]

Pleyte himself wrote a long letter to Loudon on 11 September 1914. He called attention to the 'grave consequences' for the colonial economy of the detainment of ships. The estates in the Netherlands Indies had survived the August crisis, but it was vital that their products reached their markets. The colonial economy had felt the consequences of war, but these did not have to be as drastic as they were in Europe. It would be a different matter if the export of products became impossible or was seriously hampered. Pleyte wrote gloomily that he agreed with those who predicted a total lay up of the carrying-trade between the Netherlands Indies and Holland. He asked Loudon to explain in London and Paris that French and British investments in the Netherlands Indies would likewise be hurt when this happened. To underline his point, he recalled how he and Idenburg had come to the assistance to the estates in the early days of the war, irrespective of whether these estates were British, French, or Dutch. Pleyte was convinced Great Britain and France should be grateful for this and should appreciate the strict neutrality maintained in the Netherlands Indies.[19]

Loudon did try to persuade London and Paris to relax their supervision of Dutch seaborne trade. It was to no avail. Private initiatives proved more successful. Again Van Aalst played a crucial role. In view of the disastrous consequences the Allied contraband policy might have, a Commissie voor den Nederlandsche Handel (Committee for Dutch Trade) was formed in Holland in September 1914. It was chaired by Van Aalst and Kröller was one of its members. With the approval of Loudon, this Committee for Dutch Trade discussed the consequences of a blockade of the Dutch coast with the British Envoy, Alan Johnstone. To press home their point, the British Envoy was asked

---

[18] Idenburg to Pleyte, 10-9-1914, NA, Kol. Geheim, Vb.11-9-1914 M18.
[19] Pleyte to Loudon, 11-9-1914, NA, Kol. Geheim, Vb. 11-9-1914 M19.

'whether it was necessary or indeed the intention to starve the Netherlands along with Germany' (Houwink ten Cate 1995:26).

This was not the aim of the Allied Powers. The solution was a limited liability company, the Nederlandsche Overzee Trust Maatschappij (NOT, Dutch Overseas Trust Company), founded by the committee on 23 November 1914. The major Dutch banks and shipping companies cooperated in establishing the NOT (Van Dorp 1920:199). Van Aalst became chairman of its five-man-strong executive committee and of its larger executive board. Kröller was a member of the executive board. The goal of the Dutch Overseas Trust Company was to enable goods to be imported from abroad and from the Netherlands Indies into Holland which had been declared absolute and conditional contraband by the Triple Entente and to have the shipment of goods to the Netherlands Indies from Dutch ports proceed as smoothly as possible. Starting modestly with two office rooms in a bank building on the Kneuterdijk in The Hague within the space of little more than one year the NOT developed into a large organization, employing a thousand people, and with offices spread over fifteen houses (Van Dorp 1920:200). The NOT grew into an important institution. It would become, as C.A. van Manen aptly chose to use as the title of her publication about the NOT, the 'centre of foreign traffic of the Netherlands during the World War' (Van Manen 1935). In August 1917 the British Ambassador in Holland concluded that the NOT 'had been able to set up a machinery of government which no real government could have established without legislative acts'.[20]

The British government selected the NOT and not the Dutch government as its trusted partner in regulating Dutch seaborne trade. Being the authority which had the power to grant permission for Dutch imports and exports, the NOT functioned as an extension of British control. The advantage for the British was that Dutch ships with NOT cargo did not have to be searched, with the exception of mail of course, but this was a different matter. The task of the NOT was to ensure that contraband goods shipped to Holland did not end up in Germany; the NOT warned on various occasions after peace might have been reached or after the Dutch government had lifted existing export bans. This gave the trust the responsibility for the distribution of commodities imported from abroad in Holland. The final decision always remained in British hands. Before imported good could leave the warehouses British consent was necessary. Sometimes it could take months before permission was granted. Initially this concerned especially consignments distrusted by the British, which could be released only after the NOT had submitted documents showing that there was nothing wrong with the shipment. Later in the war other shipments had to wait for British consent as well and goods piled

---

[20] Townley to Cecil, 17-8-1917, PRO FO 800 195.

up in warehouses in Holland.

To prevent goods imported under its supervision being smuggled into Germany, the NOT employed an army of inspectors. Their task was to inspect the warehouses and the books of firms engaged in the import and trade of commodities which fell under NOT control. Were the inspectors to find out that goods had been re-exported to Germany, the import firm concerned would be fined and imports might be stopped. One of the instances on which the NOT imposed such sanctions took place in March 1916, when its inspectors discovered that chocolate had been smuggled to Germany. The NOT immediately clamped down on the import of cacao. Hoarding was of no use. By circular the NOT warned about 30,000 Dutch import firms in August 1916 that the bans of re-export to the Continental Powers would remain in force after war had ended.

The NOT decided which goods from overseas could enter Dutch ports, in what quantities, and during which period. Had a shipment not been shipped in the period fixed by the NOT the permission became void. It could be renewed, but the ruling became a problem after some time when shipping opportunities became increasingly scarce. In compliance with the Allied contraband policy, the NOT issued permits for the import of these articles only for domestic use or for transit to other neutral countries. All imports of such goods had to be consigned to the NOT. Originally this only affected a selected number of articles, but gradually Allied bans and in step with this NOT involvement seemed to extend to almost all imports, including such items as rice wine and other spirits, cigarette-holders, rose bushes, calendars, and dog biscuits (Van Dorp 1920:203). With respect to imports from the Netherlands Indies only quinine and cinchona bark did not have to be consigned to the NOT at the beginning of 1917. All other products had.

The presence of the NOT made it possible for colonial wares from the Netherlands Indies which the belligerents had listed as contraband still to reach Holland, providing that they were addressed to the NOT Under the supervision of the NOT, the import of rice from the Netherlands Indies to Holland was resumed in January 1915. When cassava was declared contraband in March 1915, only shipments consigned to the NOT were transported to Holland.[21]

Shipping companies were informed of the import bans and quotas imposed by the NOT. They in turn informed exporters in the Netherlands Indies that they refused to transport the goods concerned if no NOT certificate for import into Holland could be submitted. There must have been some loopholes. The shipping companies warned export firms in the Netherlands Indies that when

---

[21] *Koloniaal verslag* 1916:219-22.

goods were still sent to Holland from the Netherlands Indies which did not comply to NOT regulations the risk was high that these would be returned to the port of shipment in August 1916. Naturally the NOT and the shipping companies would not bear these costs.

When a NOT permit became necessary for goods which had been free from import restrictions up to then, this usually meant that the batches which at that moment had already been ordered or sold but not yet shipped were included. Only when the exporter was blessed by the good fortune to have had his wares already loaded on board ship, was he sure that his wares could still be shipped to Holland. When the quotas fixed by the NOT had been reached, imports had to be stopped. In May 1915 this put a temporary end to the import of tapioca products and in November 1915 to that of maize and rubber from the Netherlands Indies into Holland. The Dutch government had no say in all this. All Pleyte and Idenburg could do was to plead. After the trust had called a halt to the export of maize, all Batavia could manage to do was, to give one example, to ensure that that consignments – in total 6,000 tons – which had already been sold and awaited shipment, could still be exported to Holland.

Initially, a few products which London and Paris still allowed to reach Holland undisturbed were free of NOT supervision. One of these was medicinal wares such as cinchona bark. Another was tobacco (as of mid-1916 restricted to tobacco from the Netherlands Indies, not from elsewhere); a product for which prospects had seemed especially grim at the outbreak of the war because its main market was in Germany and Austria-Hungary. Initially coffee from the Netherlands Indies could also be freely exported to Holland. It fetched 'fabulous prices' in Germany and Austria-Hungary; not least because coffee from South America was listed as contraband. In October 1915 the NOT intervened when a Dutch freighter had hidden Brazilian coffee beans among coffee beans from Java. A special committee was instituted to check coffee arriving in Dutch ports. From that moment on, coffee from the Netherlands Indies had to be consigned to the trust, which inexorably also fixed import quotas. Around the same time, the shipment of tobacco had to be briefly restricted after an Amsterdam firm had literally used tobacco as a cover to smuggle rubber to Holland.

At the end of 1915 it was widely acknowledged that the NOT had become an indispensable adjunct to Dutch international trade. The annual report of the Dutch Kamer van Koophandel (Chamber of Commerce) for 1915 noted that colonial trade had adjusted grudgingly to the shackles of the trust. Unkind criticism had been the result, but gradually it dawned on more and more people that the NOT was 'one of the necessary factors, which would enable the Netherlands as a big Colonial Power to continue to play the role of a buffer state without hurting the traffic between motherland and colonies too much'.[22] Even so the arrangements the NOT made with London were a constant source of criticism. People in Germany, and indeed some in Holland shared this view, saw the NOT as an 'English institution' (Treub 1920:163-4). In their eyes the establishment of the NOT meant that the whole Dutch transit trade had capitulated to Great Britain.

The NOT also played an essential role in the securing of imports from Holland in the Netherlands Indies. From June 1915, British exports to the Netherlands, with a few exceptions, were allowed only for articles consigned to the NOT or for those for which a special licence had been issued. This regulation was also in force for goods which had been ordered from Holland to be transhipped from Dutch ports to the Netherlands Indies.[23] Incontrovertible the power to regulate exports and imports in Holland implied that the NOT had a large say in shipping. Van Aalst boasted that most ships fell under control of the NOT when he was interviewed by the correspondent of *The Times* in Amsterdam at the end of 1915.[24] Pleyte had to admit in March 1917 that all negotiations about calling at British ports were conducted by the Trust.[25]

Even more vital to the colonial economy was that NOT permission was necessary for imports from Germany to the Netherlands Indies. Aware that certain German goods were essential to keeping industries in the Netherlands Indies running, Great Britain permitted the placing of orders from the Netherlands Indies in Germany and Austria-Hungary, but imposed stringent conditions. In March 1915, Great Britain and France announced that they would seize all enemy goods on neutral merchantmen. Immediately the Committee for Dutch Trade contacted the British Embassy to work out a special arrangement for the Dutch colonies. At that moment the Dutch government was still brimming with confidence, at least this is the impression it made on the outside world. Via a message in the *Javasche Courant*, the public was informed that the Committee had begun its negotiations and that the Minister of Foreign Affairs had informed his colleague of the Colonies that the British and French measures would probably not harm the supply of goods 'of enemy origin' to the Dutch colonies.[26] The committee and the British government reached an agreement concerning 'goods of enemy origin required for the factories, industries or public services of Dutch colonies which cannot be procured

---

[22] *Koloniale Studiën* 1916-17:157.
[23] British proclamation relating to the exportation of all articles to the Netherlands during the present war, 25-6-1915, *State Papers* 1915:274.
[24] *De Locomotief*, 3-1-1916.
[25] Pleyte to Koninklijke West-Indische Maildienst, 19-3-1917, NA, Kol. Openbaar, Vb.19-3-1917 13.
[26] *Javasche Courant*, 9-4-1915.

from other sources or the supply of which cannot suffer delay' in July 1915.[27] Armed with what was known as a D-certificate, issued by NOT, such 'licensed goods' could be shipped to the Netherlands Indies without the risk of being confiscated. NOT took its responsibility seriously. The trust refused certificates for shipment if there was a shadow of a doubt about whether the goods met the requirements.

Within months, disagreement arose over the question of whether shipments by the Dutch government were exempt from the obligation to acquire a NOT certificate. The confrontation came at the end of 1915. The villain of the piece was the shipment of chemical dyes. The importation of chemical dyes was highly important to the Netherlands Indies. The dyes were essential to the Javanese batik industry, which was already hard hit by the decreasing purchasing power of the population. Traders and producers had been forced to close up shop. The industry should not have to risk any further decline. Alternatives were unavailable. Germany was the only source of supply of chemical dyes. Shortly after the outbreak of the war Berlin had issued an export ban expressly to hurt Great Britain, who was likewise dependent on German dyes. The consequence had been felt immediately in Java. Firms resold dyes they received for a much higher price. Others held on to their stock in the hope of fetching an even higher price in the future, especially in Great Britain. Prices sky-rocketed. The price of a barrel of one such dyes, alizarin, rose from 63 to 2,000 guilders. Returning to the ways of the past and the use of natural dyes like indigo, sago, *kudu* and *tegerang* bark was not really an option. Production was too small, and domestic and foreign demand sent prices soaring. Another problem was that Javanese craftsmen would again have to learn how to work with natural dyes. The apparently sensible suggestion that bananas could be used as an ingredient to produce all kinds of colours – pink, yellow, brown, green – was only really considered seriously just before the end of the war.[28]

The colonial authorities took the matter very much to heart. Though the production also involved Arabs and Chinese, a decline in the *batik* industry would predominantly harm the prosperity of the Javanese population. After a ban had been issued on the export of artificial dyes from the Netherlands Indies, Berlin permitted the export of dyes to Java in a proportion equal to the export volume of 1913. A second condition was that NOT should not be involved in the purchase, the shipment to Java, or sale in the Netherlands Indies. Following the agreement, the Ministry of the Colonies allowed a number of private companies to buy a large quantity of dyes in Germany in exchange for tin. Batavia set a price limit in Java. To cut out a string of

[27] Oppenheimer to Van Vollenhoven, 6-1-1916, NA, Kol. Geheim, Vb.20-1-1916 U.
[28] *Koloniaal verslag* 1916:231-2; Clarke 1918.

middlemen creaming off their profit, the European import firms agreed to open up the possibility for *batik* producers to buy dyes directly from them. Labelled government goods and addressed to the Governor General the dyes were shipped to Java by the *Kawi* in early November. When he learned of the shipment, the British Ambassador lodged a protest with Van Aalst. Johnstone asked for a copy of the licence issued by the NOT. He also demanded to know why the trust had allowed dyes to be exported. Johnstone stressed that under no circumstances could the goods leave port – which in fact the dyes did the next day – without his consent. He warned that the Dutch government should comply 'in order that complications may not arise in this connection'.[29] In his turn, Van Aalst impressed upon the Ministry of the Colonies that to prevent the arrest of outgoing ships, German goods could be exported when they had a NOT certificate. Van Aalst insisted this was in accordance with the agreement the trust had concluded with the Allied authorities.

Evidently the British government was seriously nettled. It was well aware of the fact that in other instances the label 'government goods' had also been used to circumvent British control over the export of German goods to the Netherlands Indies. In the previous months, the Ministry of the Colonies had been contacted by a number of firms, which had received orders from government departments in the Netherlands Indies, but which the NOT had refused to provide with a certificate. Some of the articles concerned had been transported consigned to the Governor-General as government cargo to the colony.

In unmistakable terms, Oppenheimer warned the NOT that this was untenable. Shipments by the Dutch government fell under the terms of the agreement concluded. In one of his letters he 'kindly' asked the NOT to take 'immediate steps' to provide the 'needful assurance' that in the future the terms of the agreement would be obeyed. Oppenheimer added 'privately' that 'the large quantity of goods of enemy origin shipped under the Netherlands Government contracts' had alarmed the British authorities. For the 'smooth working' of the arrangement, he should 'be able to send home a very early and satisfactory reply' to his letter.[30]

London now had the bit between its teeth. Oppenheimer, who confessed he did not understand why the Ministry of the Colonies had acted the way it had, as dyes could be exported through the intermediation of the NOT, continued to berate the NOT. He asked for copies of the export licence and for 'definite figures' regarding the requirement of the dyes in the Netherlands Indies in the previous years. Had the NOT indeed given permission for the shipment,

---

[29] Johnstone to van Aalst, 5-11-1915, NA, Kol. Openbaar, Vb.16-11-1915 55.
[30] Oppenheimer to Van Vollenhoven, 16-11-1915, NA, Kol. Geheim, Vb. 20-1-1916 U.

the Trust should provide him with guarantees that the dyes were for 'bona-fide use', and that the Dutch government had adopted measures 'to ensure a fair distribution and absolute consumption' in the Netherlands Indies. Once again, he inquired into the measures the NOT had taken 'to control any shipment made by the Netherlands Government to the Governor General or other consignees in the Dutch East Indies'.[31] A few days later Oppenheimer returned to the subject. This time he wanted information about the distribution of the dyes. Did these go to the highest bidder, or to factories according to their known requirements?[32] All this time the Ministry of the Colonies had remained immune to requests for information by the NOT. When it could do so no longer, its Secretary General suggested the NOT reply to Oppenheimer simply telling him that the dyes were destined for firms which had already been using them before the war and sold them to the native batik industry.[33]

The shipment of dyes made London decide to put an end to the export of tin, which had served as a barter for the dyes, to Holland as a punishment. The export of German dyes to the Netherlands Indies was allowed to continue, but the quantities shipped were far from adequate to meet the demand. When the British Consul General in Batavia was not satisfied with the way Dutch firms in Java distributed artificial dyes, shipments were confiscated by the British in mid-1916 but within weeks shipping could be resumed. The colonial government promised to buy the artificial dyes and act as sole distributor, using its civil servants and local banks which had especially been set up to lend money to indigenous business ventures.

The affair had put Pleyte, as he described this in a letter to Idenburg, in an 'extremely painful' situation.[34] It was bad enough his department had to endure embarrassing inquiries by the Trust. In another respect it also found itself in an uncomfortable position. In Java the Batavian branch of the German firm Carl Schlieper had won a tender for the supply of hardware items like nails, screws, and gas pipes issued by the Engineering Corps in the middle of October. It was a large order: in total 1,500 tons. In The Hague its Director Walter Schlieper contacted the Ministry of the Colonies to ask for help. Pleyte decided to lend his assistance. His Ministry would take over the goods and ship them to Java as a government consignment. Oppenheimer nipped the enterprise in the bud. In a letter to the NOT he inquired about the name of the merchantman aboard which the shipment was to be transported to Java in January.[35]

---

[31] Oppenheimer to Van Vollenhoven, 26-11-1915, NA, Kol. Openbaar, Vb. 16-11-1915 55.
[32] Oppenheimer to Van Vollenhoven, 3-12-1915, NA, Kol. Openbaar, Vb. 16-11-1915 55.
[33] Staal to De Beaufort, 8-12-1915, NA, Kol. Openbaar, Vb. 16-11-1915 55.
[34] Pleyte to Idenburg, 11-1-1916, NA, Kol. Geheim, Vb. 11-1-1916 R.
[35] Oppenheimer to Van Vollenhoven, 6-1-1916, NA, Kol., Geheim, Vb. 20-1-1916 U.

Oppenheimer's request could only mean that Great Britain intended to search the ship and seize the cargo. Pleyte was at his wits' end. His Ministry had made a promise but trouble lay ahead if it was honoured. His staff considered buying the goods and storing them at the Colonial Establishment in Amsterdam. This proved impossible. Wares there were already piling up. To rent special storage space was another way out, but Pleyte was against this. He confided to Loudon that such a move would make a strange impression on the Schlieper Firm and on the German government.[36] Thereupon an investigation was mounted as to whether the Engineering Corps in Holland could use the goods. This also offered no way out. Pleyte tried to shelve a decision by asking Loudon to have the Dutch Envoy in London plead that the British Navy should not confiscate the shipment. The plea fell on deaf ears. In the end the Ministry of the Colonies had to go back on its word. Schlieper was informed that he himself had to be responsible for delivery. In order to obtain a D-certificate, Schlieper asked for a statement that goods were destined for the colonial administration. Pleyte did not raise any objections. 'How the man will manage to carry it off is a matter of indifference to us', he penned in a note.[37]

British distrust meant that from the beginning of 1916 German goods ordered by the colonial administration could only be shipped to the Netherlands Indies with a NOT certificate, which was only given after the British Embassy had given its permission. The Trust, which at the height of the conflict callled a temporary halt to the issuing of D-certificates, was only prepared to issue these for government goods if the Ministry of the Colonies submitted a statement that the goods were destined for the public sector. The overall result, compounded by British interference, was extra delays and a less liberal policy. A senior civil servant in the Department of Agriculture, Industry, and Trade in the Netherlands Indies noted in February 1916 that goods in Holland ready for shipment to the colony had been refused a NOT certificate several times.[38] One such instance concerned a shipment of cement ordered for harbour works in Makassar. The argument for refusing to sanction the shipment was that cement was also produced in Great Britain. Another concerned the pipes for the waterworks of Semarang. The Mayor of Semarang warned that without the new pipes contamination of drinking water could not be excluded.[39] The obstruction of shipments of medicines or their ingredients and medical equipment, which the British Embassy claimed, according to the Dutch not always rightfully so, could also be provided (be it against a higher price) by

---

[36] Pleyte to Loudon, 20-1-1916, NA, Kol. Geheim, Vb. 20-1-1916 U.
[37] Note Pleyte, 9-2-1916, NA, Kol. Geheim, Vb. 20-1-1916 T.
[38] De Kruyff to Director Department of Agriculture, Industry, and Trade, 17-2-1916, NA, Kol. Geheim, Mr. 1916/44x.
[39] *De Locomotief,* 14-9-1916.

Great Britain attracted special attention.[40] So it is no surprise, that in October 1916, *De Locomotief* called attention to the novelty that a clinic in Bandung had been equipped with an 'artificial sun lamp' which, it was said, could be used to treat tuberculosis, bone tuberculosis, skin diseases, and rheumatism. It was not only the first such lamp in the Netherlands Indies, it was also of German make and widely used by the German army to treat neglected wounds; 'in case of extensive festering processes the ultra-violet rays have an anti-bactericide effect'. The reader could imagine how much trouble it had been to import the sun lamp under 'the present very abnormal circumstances'.[41]

To spare himself new embarrassments Pleyte instructed Idenburg that no orders for goods to be shipped from Holland should be passed without his Ministry being contacted first. The instruction did not go down well in the European community in Java; sure as people were that the mills of the government ground exceedingly slowly. *De Locomotief* pointed out that experience had shown that goods ordered through the Ministry of the Colonies took a long time to reach Java, even when they were urgently needed. To avoid the treadmill of bureaucracy, in the past orders had been placed directly with private firms in Holland. This had greatly speeded up delivery. Pleyte's instructions would assuredly result in long delays.[42]

On top of the restrictions on contraband trade came export bans to Holland and to the Netherlands Indies instituted in Europe and in Allied colonies. In some cases domestic want was the reason. In late 1914 and early 1915 Australia and British India banned the export of wheat for this reason. As a consequence the price of bread rose all over the Archipelago in March 1915. Complaints were once again heard in Batavia about loaves of bread becoming 'smaller, drabber and more expensive by the day'. The same lament was heard in Medan. Loaves of bread there had become smaller and of poorer quality. Bengalis on the East Coast of Sumatra, who used to eat bread baked with Indian flour and could not afford European bread, had been forced to eat rice and dried fish. In Surabaya, army purchases of flour in August were blamed for the bad quality and high price of bread.[43]

In other instances the ban was motivated by the fear that the goods might end with the enemy. An early example was rice. The French colonial authorities in Saigon decided to ban the export of rice to the Netherlands Indies at the end of January 1915. Exports to other countries were unimpeded. The announcement, an indication that France and Great Britain had stepped up

---

[40] *Nieuwe Rotterdamsche Courant*, cited in *De Locomotief*, 13-9-1916.
[41] *De Locomotief*, 17-10-1916.
[42] *De Locomotief*, 26-1-1916.
[43] *De Locomotief*, 27-8-1914, 19-3-1915, 20-3-1915, 24-3-1915.

their efforts to bring economic ruin upon Germany, came at an inopportune moment, but in the Netherlands Indies this seems to have been the rule rather than the exception. The 1915 rice harvest was expected to be late. Rice stocks were low. Idenburg and his staff were alerted to the ban by telegrams from rice traders. They were perplexed. Batavia had no inkling about the reason why Saigon had prohibited the export of rice, nor had the general public. One thing was sure: there had been no failure of the harvest in Indochina.

Suspecting that re-export to Germany might be the reason H.J. Lovink, head of the Department of Agriculture, Industry, and Trade, suggested to the rice traders that they should tell the authorities in Saigon that Batavia would guarantee that the rice imported would be used for local consumption only. Lovink's suggestion was no full-proof solution. It was difficult to comply with the Allied demand. In the Netherlands Indies there was no institution comparable to the NOT which could keep a check on what happened to the rice imported. Others pointed out that fear about re-export could not be the reason. In Holland an export ban on rice was in force; in the Netherlands Indies a conditional one. They pleaded for an export ban on maize, beans and peas, and cassava. The destination of these secondary crops was not always clear, and they could only be exported in times of plenty when they did not have to serve as a substitute for rice.

Lovink had guessed right. A few days later the French Consul, Fliche, explained that Great Britain and France were concerned that rice grown in their Asian colonies would end up in Germany via the Netherlands Indies. Exports could be resumed when Dutch rice merchants in Indochina could produce a certificate issued by the French consulate in Batavia that the rice they wanted to buy would not be re-exported from the Netherlands Indies. Fliche added that his staff would only issue a certificate if they were presented with a guarantee by the colonial administration that the rice bought would be consumed in the Netherlands Indies. For a moment it appeared that the ban would be lifted before the end of January, but in the middle of February nine Dutch merchantmen still lay idle in the port of Saigon, because the export of rice still had not been resumed. Rice-traders asked Batavia to institute an export ban on Saigon rice.

The solution eventually found was that the colonial government promised dispensation on the ban in the export of rice from the Netherlands Indies would only to be granted for domestic rice, which could easily be distinguished from rice from Indochina by its grain. This decision seemed to do the trick. In March 1915 Paris indicated that it had given Saigon permission to dispense with the consular certificates. Nothing came of this. The screws were really turned as the British colonial authorities started to demand a certificate for the export of Rangoon rice. The French authorities in Indochina tightened the rules on 1 October 1915. They would only allow the export of rice for which a consular certificate had already been wired by the French consulate in Batavia to Saigon. This was tantamount to a complete ban.

The news again came as a shock. Idenburg at once wired Pleyte to 'obtain soonest abrogation exceptional measure'.[44] The trepidations of August 1914 had reappeared. Before the war, between 2 and 3,000 tons of rice had been imported annually for Java alone. Emergency purchases of rice were made in Thailand. Again the local Dutch civil servants were given the authority to fix a maximum rice price. Fearing food shortages, Batavia granted almost no dispensation on its own ban to export rice.

The crisis lasted until April 1916 when Saigon agreed to allow exports of rice to the Netherlands Indies up to a volume equal to that of 1913. A special form had to be filled in by custom officers in the Netherlands Indies and sent to the French consulate acknowledging the import of rice from Indochina. Imports from Burma could be resumed in July, be it also in restricted quantities. The government of British India showed itself lenient. First, when the estates the East Coast of Sumatra complained that the restrictions would endanger their food supply, the region was allowed an extra quotum. Later, in October 1916 any restriction on quantities was lifted. There remained one condition. London was adamant that it considered the stock of rice in Holland sufficient and that it would put a stop to the export of Burma rice the minute Java rice was shipped from the colony to the motherland.[45] The NOT had already refused any imports of rice from the Netherlands Indies in June. In 1915 over 33 million kilograms of rice had still been exported to Holland, but in 1916 the volume fell to about 10 million kilograms, and in 1917 to just 4 million kilograms.[46] Saigon stuck to its policy of limiting exports to the Netherlands Indies to its pre-war level.

Another target of British bans was the coaling station in Sabang. Coal was scarce in the Netherlands Indies. An export ban had been issued in 1915. In October 1915 the colonial administration in British India indicated that it would only allow the export of Bengal coal to the Netherlands Indies on condition that 'no coals of any kind or origin is furnished [...] to any vessel or firm the name of which is specially notified'.[47] Though the Sabang Company complied with this condition, the export of coal from Bengal to Sabang was terminated in January 1916. In an attempt to have the ban lifted, the Sabang Company contacted the British consulate in Batavia. The Consul General suggested that the coaling station should make it clear that it was 'a pure Dutch

---

[44] Pleyte to Loudon, 6-10-1915, NA, Kol. Openbaar, Vb. 6-10-1915 60.
[45] *Handelingen Tweede Kamer* 1917-18:1902-3.
[46] *Rijst* 1919:666; *Volksraad* 1918:37.
[47] Extract from the letter from the Adviser to the Head Administrator, 18-1-1916, NA, Kol. Openbaar, Vb. 14-3-1917 8.

Coaling station Sabang (KITLV 34811)

firm, which had no Germans in its employ'. It should likewise promise that it would not supply coal to German ships.[48] The hint was taken. The Sabang Company promised that it would not furnish coal to ships the British government did not want it to serve on 24 January. Five days later the ban on Bengal coals was lifted.

In Holland the Directors of the Sabang Company had no idea what had transpired in Batavia. They were sure that protests at the British legation in The Hague, at the India Office in London, and at the British Foreign Office had persuaded the British government to lift the ban. They thought that London had been sensitive to the argument that British ships bound for Vladivostok to deliver weapons and ammunition to the Russian army might be among the first ships which could not bunker at Sabang because of a shortage of coal.[49] In actual fact the January promise in Batavia, made by their agent in Netherlands Indies, had caused the British to waver. It was followed by a second pledge

---

[48] Extract from the letter from the Adviser to the Head Administrator, 18-1-1916, NA, Kol. Openbaar, Vb. 14-3-1917 8.
[49] Uittreksel notulen van de vergaderingen van commissarissen der Naamloze Vennootschap 'Zeehaven en Kolenstation Sabang', NA, Kol. Geheim, Vb. 1-2-1917 V2.

in March. The representative of the coaling station in Batavia vowed to the British Consul General that his company would 'decline to fulfil orders to bunker any vessel of whatever nationality if so requested by His Majesty's Consul General at Batavia'.[50]

The supply of coal for and the bunkering of ships of the Netherlands and other neutral countries had been secured. The price was that loading coal by German, Austrian, or Turkish ships and on those owned by companies which the Allies considered to support the enemy had become impossible. They were not only denied Bengal coal, coal mined in the Netherlands Indies were also now out of bounds to them.

Pleyte and Van Limburg Stirum were upset in June when they learned about the pledge the Sabang coaling station had made. They feared serious repercussions if German warships were to call at Sabang.[51] The chance that this would happen was small, but could not be overlooked completely. The last German ship which had entered territorial waters was the *Marie*. She had supplied the German Army in East Africa commanded by Lieutenant-Colonel Paul von Lettow-Vorbeck, which was fighting a guerrilla war against South African, Belgian, and Portuguese troops. Chased by British warships and heavily damaged with parts of the deck shot away and the funnel and masts riddled with bullet holes, the *Marie* entered the port of Tanjung Priok in the night of 14 May 1916. The possibility that German raiders out to capture and sink Allied warships operated in the vicinity of or even in colonial territorial waters could not be excluded, even after the sinking of the *Emden*. In March 1917 British warships suddenly increased their patrols of the entrances to the Straits of Malacca and all lights which could be used by ships to navigate the Straits were extinguished. The *Wolf*, the former Hansa Line *Wachtenfels*, which had left Kiel in November 1916 had reached the Archipelago. The captain carried orders to disrupt British sea traffic by laying mines off Singapore and other British ports and to do his best to hamper Allied commerce by raiding and capturing or sinking Allied merchantmen. On board was a seaplane which flew over Sydney. A few months later, after the United States had joined the war, and in anticipation of this German ships had tried to leave the Philippines, the Rotterdamsche Lloyd received information from Osaka about another German raider operating in the Archipelago. It proved to be false alarm.[52]

Van Limburg Stirum concluded that the vows had placed the Sabang coal-

---

[50] Uittreksel notulen van de vergaderingen van commissarissen der Naamloze Vennootschap 'Zeehaven en Kolenstation Sabang', NA, Kol. Geheim, Vb. 1-2-1917 V2.
[51] Pleyte to Regeringscommissaris b/d NV Zeehaven en Kolenstation Sabang, 1-2-1917, NA, Kol. Geheim, Vb. 1-2-1917 V2.
[52] Halpern 1994:372-3; *De Locomotief*, 8-3-1917; *Neratja*, 22-4-1918, 23-4-1918.

ing station 'under the dictatorship' of the British Consul General. The demands of that gentleman had been excessive.[53] Van Limburg Stirum expressed his 'enormous surprise' about the fact that the company 'had apparently only been considering its own interests and had given no thought to national honour or its duties as a neutral'.[54] Pleyte agreed. The Directors of the Sabang Company were unimpressed. They were convinced that their agent had had no other choice than to yield to British demands. They complimented themselves that pledges had made the bunkering of Dutch vessels with Bengal coal possible without interference from any British authority.[55]

Demanding export bans in the Netherlands Indies as a means of preventing transit trade became a standard procedure of Great Britain and France. Italy joined the van. Batavia had been forced to ban the export of car tyres in May 1915 to assure a supply of imports from Italy. A year later, in July 1916, Batavia even issued an export ban on 'instruments for chemical and other applied science research of not native origin'.[56] In the end, in March 1917, the colonial authorities forbade all exports of products which had been imported from abroad or goods made from such products. The maximum sentence imposed was a three-months' imprisonment or hard labour, or a fine of one hundred guilders. The measure was not well-understood. No explanation had been given why. The editor of *De Locomotief* supposed that the government wanted to prevent that in times of international scarcity the commodities were re-exported to fetch a higher price abroad. Whatever the reason, he considered the ban typical of a 'haughty and silent authority'.[57] Exports bans were no longer issued. The opposite happened. The exceptions were announced, goods which were still allowed to be exported.

Great Britain and France also tightened their control on imports from the Netherlands Indies. Early in March 1915, the Dutch commercial community in the Netherlands Indies had been shocked by the news that France would only allow imports from the Netherlands Indies if a certificate of origin was submitted which made it clear that the goods in question did not originate from the Central Powers. Another document, a certificate of nationality, to be issued by the French consulate in Batavia had to confirm that the companies which exported and transported the goods were not owned by Germans or Austrians. Nor should Germans or Austrians have majority shares in such

[53] Viethoff to Zeehaven en Kolenstation Sabang, 29-12-1916, NA, Kol. Openbaar, Vb. 14-3-1917 8.
[54] Van Limburg Stirum to Pleyte, 26-2-1917, Viethoff to Zeehaven en Kolenstation Sabang, 29-12-1916, NA, Kol. Openbaar, Vb. 14-3-1917 8, NA, Kol. Geheim, Vb. 29-5-1917 K14.
[55] Viethoff to Pleyte, 22-1-197, NA, Kol. Geheim, Vb. 1-2-1917 V2.
[56] *De Locomotief*, 21-7-1916.
[57] *De Locomotief*, 15-3-1917.

companies. The British 'Rules of Trading with the Enemy' also required a certificate of origin.

Great Britain and France announced even stricter rules about trading with enemy companies in neutral countries in February 1916. Firms in neutral countries were warned that they had to sever all ties with enemy companies. The following month it became known that the British War Trade Department had compiled a statutory list, a blacklist containing the names of firms which had not complied. The French and Italians took over the British blacklist. Nevertheless, almost all attention and also all the anger in the Netherlands Indies centred on that compiled by the British. For the Allied warships in Europe and in the Archipelago the black list implied a new task. They were no longer only on the look out for enemy agents and contraband, but also for cargo originating from or shipped to black-listed firms.

Overnight reports appeared in the press in the Netherlands Indies about Dutch companies which had fired German employees because, had he not done so, British firms would no longer do business with them. Newspapers in Holland and in the Netherlands Indies published the first 'black list' at the end of March 1916. At the same time the British Consul General left no stone unturned to ensure that commercial firms and banks were well acquainted with the purport of the Allied economic directives. Beckett himself preferred to speak about providing 'exhaustive explanations'. He provided these 'with pleasure'.[58] Beckett promised that local sensitivities would be spared and that *'bona fide'* Dutch trade would not be hurt. His words did not make the British interference less vexatious. In 1917 the Javasche Bank concluded that the black list, on which the companies which had incurred the wrath of France and Great Britain were noted had 'only aroused bitterness, because it was generally felt that one was being treated unfairly'.[59] Being black-listed meant a boycott by Allied firms, who when they traded with black-listed companies were liable to be fined, and by Dutch companies which feared that otherwise they themselves would suffer the same fate. Dutch shipping companies in the Netherlands Indies refused to transport merchandise, suppliers stopped delivery of goods, and customers stayed away. If a company did not want to run the risk of losing its commercial raison d'être, it had to sever all contacts with a black-listed firm. Cable and mail correspondence should also be terminated. At least one Dutch commercial firm, aware that correspondence with German firms was not allowed, even inquired in London whether it was still permitted to address one last letter to a black-listed company. It wanted to ask its former business partner to stop sending letters or telegrams. Were this not

[58] *De Locomotief*, 15-3-1916.
[59] *De Indische Gids* 1917, II:1430.

permitted, there was no guarantee that the company no longer received mail from the black-listed firm.[60]

It cannot have come as a surprise that Behn, Meyer and Co. and the Straits und Sunda Syndikat were among the first black-listed companies published in the Netherlands Indies. Among the ten firms in Batavia which were mentioned were also the Société Coloniale Indo-Belge, and three Chinese companies. In Medan and Palembang altogether seven firms were blacklisted, in Makassar three. In Semarang one company was on the first list. It was the well-known firm of Carl Schlieper, active in the Netherlands Indies since 1870, and one of the major importers to the colony of machine parts.

The black list was not restricted to fully German- or Austrian-owned companies or companies doing business with them. The same fate befell firms in which Germans or Austrians made up one-third of the Board of Directors, or held one-third of the share capital issued. One of the consequences was that for trade with Great Britain and France a 'certificate of interest' to be issued by the Allied consuls was required as from September 1916. To obtain the certificate, a company had to submit a list of its commissioners, directors, managers, and senior staff, complete with copies of their birth certificates to prove their nationality.

To contain the damage, Behn, Meyer and Co. and the Straits und Sunda Syndikat established their own insurance company, the Javasche Lloyd. They did so in conjunction with 'Chinese friends'. Dutch firms were no longer prepared to insure their goods and property (Helfferich 1967:152). The two companies also founded an estate product bank.

Companies could be removed from the black list, but the opposite happened much more frequently. In the course of time, other companies were added. Even the newspapers the *Java-Bode* and the *Bataviaasch Handelsblad* were black-listed. They no longer received Reuter's telegrams. When mail was searched in British ports copies of the *Bataviaasch Handelsblad*, and probably also of the *Java-Bode*, were confiscated. The mail boats were not allowed to take them along to Holland. It was reported from The Hague as early as August 1916 that neither the Minister of the Colonies nor any private person received the *Bataviaasch Handelsblad* any longer.[61] The Ruygrok Company, the printer of the *Bataviaasch Handelsblad*, was also put on the black list. Among the other victims of the trade boycott was Erdman and Sielcken, a major exporter of Java sugar and active in the Netherlands Indies over fifty years since 1865. Like other firms in the Netherlands Indies, it had a German name. Its senior

---

[60] There was also a Private List B, a so-called grey list. Trading with companies on this list was forbidden, but correspondence was still allowed. The British mail boats would not accept such correspondence, but the British censor let the letters pass, in theory at least.
[61] *De Locomotief*, 7-8-1916, 10-10-1916.

partner, F.A. Warnecke, was a naturalized Dutchman. Of the three junior partners, who were all long-time *Resident* of Java, two were Germans. The third had been deprived of his German nationality. Efforts by the Dutch Envoy in London to annul the listing failed. An additional problem, and the reason for The Hague to take action, was that Erdman and Sielcken acted as the manager of four Dutch-owned mines. Because of the black-listing of Erdman and Sielcken, these mines, with no Germans but only Dutchmen, Britons, and Swedes among their employees, ran into serious problems. They could no longer obtain spare parts for their machinery. Closure threatened, with all the consequences this would have for their employees and the local population. London was unrelenting. The only solution it was prepared to suggest to the Dutch government was that the mines had to find another company to take over their management.[62]

The black list struck terror in the Dutch commercial community in the Netherlands Indies. In some instances 'the mere denunciations of spies' seemed to suffice to be black-listed (Carpentier Alting and De Cock Buning 1928:69). Commercial firms and estates dismissed their German staff. This was repeated at headquarters in Holland. This was not done without some qualms, because of uncertainty about how Germany and the German community would react. British firms and estates which had not yet fired their German employees now did so. They seem to have done so with some reluctance. In the notices to British employees, the companies expressed their regret and wrote that the reason for the dismissal had nothing to do with performance (Helfferich 1948:213). In reaction German-owned firms and estate replaced Dutch, British, and French staff with Germans. Not everywhere did peace reign. The black-list induced an employee of the French consulate in Surabaya to ask the French barbers in town – there were many French barbers in the Netherlands Indies – no longer to serve Germans. He, and the Dutch press did not fail to notice that he was of German descent, could not stand being with 'those awful boches' in one hairdresser's salon. Confused the barbers turned to the French Consulate General in Batavia, wondering whether they would be included on the black-list if they had Germans among their customers.[63] The only sector which seemingly was not affected was the entertainment industry. German male and female light opera singers remained as popular as ever.

Dutch shipping companies refused cargo from black-listed companies. In Surabaya the Droogdok Maatschappij, the company that managed the only large dry-dock in the Archipelago, refused its services to German vessels which were stranded in the Netherlands Indies. As in the case of the Sabang

---

[62] Loudon to Pleyte 15-9-1916, Directors of the mining companies Redjang Lebong, Ketahoen, Simaoe, and Gloemboek to Pleyte, 17-4-1916, NA, Kol. Geheim, Vb. 18-9-1916 K29.
[63] *Bataviaasch Nieuwsblad*, cited in *De Locomotief*, 16-6-1916.

coaling-station, the colonial authorities viewed the decision with apprehension. The decision of the dry-dock company not only gave an indication that it was the British who in the final resort determined the running of colonial trade and industry, but, as had been feared with respect to Sabang coal, the refusal to dock German ships might well be interpreted as a breach of neutrality. Batavia was powerless. The dry-dock company had just recovered from a difficult time. Forcing it to accept German ships might result in a boycott and a halt to the supply of spare parts and equipment.[64]

The black list was grist to the mill of a few rabid Germanophobes. It inspired Boon of the *Soerabaiasch Handelsblad* to suggest that no facility should any longer be lent to the German business community in the Netherlands Indies. Boon wrote that Germans did not deserve any help. In Belgium the 'business scoundrel', the German, has shown himself to be unworthy of any help. In deciding how to act with the prospect of British retaliation and the looming loss of the colony, this had to be given priority. To continue to deal with the German business community was dangerous.[65]

Boon formed an exception. Usually the reaction was one of anger, directed especially towards the British and less so towards the French, or, failing that, of helpless acquiescence. The Dutch government and the Dutch business community had to stand idly by. Washington, among other things enraged over the fact that in the Philippines firms with a German management but with no German capital had been blacklisted could threaten with a ban on loans to the Allied countries, but Batavia lacked any leverage to make London change its mind.[66] The only thing the colonial government could do was to continue to support black-listed firms whenever possible. After the war Emil Helfferich praised the Javasche Bank which had not changed its credit policy for German estate companies, even assisting them when possible (Helfferich 1948:302, 1967:151-2). In an initial reaction *De Locomotief* wrote that though trade might be seriously hurt by the British policy and Dutch feelings were offended, the only reaction could be 'proud resignation'.[67] The newspaper saw the calls in the British press for ever stricter control of neutral trade as merely proof that British newspapers had turned into 'zealots of commercial jingoism'.[68]

Everybody was fully aware that the British and French consuls, especially the British Consul General, had the final say and that it was on their information that London and Paris based their decisions. In Helfferich's words, the British Consul General attained the function of a controller of trade and

[64] Advice General Adviser harbour-works, 7-1-1918, NA, Kol. Geheim, Mr. 1918/42x.
[65] *Soerabaiasch Handelsblad*, cited in *De Indische Gids* 1917, II:1115.
[66] Ferguson 2001:303; *De Locomotief*, 28-9-1916.
[67] *De Locomotief*, cited in *De Indische Gids* 1916, II:998.
[68] *De Locomotief*, 29-3-1916.

export dictator (Helfferich 1921:16). In spite of the feelings of impotence, the British effort to hurt German commercial interests in the Netherlands Indies did result in a protest. In February 1916 a former banker, Jan Dinger, member of the Chamber of Commerce of Batavia and owner of a number of sugar estates, placed an appeal in the Batavian newspapers asking people to attend a 'peaceful meeting' in Batavia to demonstrate against 'the action of foreigners who enjoy the right of being a guest here, of which the purpose is preventing our German co-residents to exercise honest and peaceful professions'.[69] Dinger's initiative was wholeheartedly supported by the pro-German *Bataviaasch Handelsblad*. Its editor, Th. Thomas, used the occasion to lash out at the British. The *Bataviaasch Handelsblad* observed that the consuls increasingly acted as an independent power, as an *imperium in imperio*. The 'British Consul acts in a way which offends and hurts every patriotic Dutchman'. The *Bataviaasch Handelsblad* urged the government to do something and to protect the rights of everybody who lived in the Netherlands Indies. The burning question was, where would it end? Tokyo might demand a Dutch firm fire its Chinese employees. The *Bataviaasch Handelsblad* concluded that a little more deferente to the Dutch government was called for. Great Britain had the right to forbid British companies to trade with the enemy, but should not try to enforce its will in the Netherlands Indies. *Oetoesan Hindia* fully concurred.[70] The *Bataviaasch Handelsblad* suggested prohibiting the export of sugar to Great Britain and have British ships which had come to the Netherlands Indies to transport sugar leave with empty holds a few weeks later. For some this went too far. *De Locomotief* pointed out that this would cost money, and, being more dangerous, might be considered a hostile act by London.[71]

In an effort to forestall complications the authorities forbade nationals of the belligerents to attend the meeting, which took place on 27 February. Sarcastically an inhabitant of Batavia noted in *De Locomotief* that also Bulgarians, Montenegrins, Serbs, and Albanians, were also consequently barred from access.[72] About one hundred and fifty people, or 'independent men' as Dinger called them, attended. Dinger told them that the British black-list meant an infringement of national dignity. The Dutch should remain master in their own house. A letter was sent to Beckett asking him to treat 'our German co-residents' with more clemency, and to take into account the rights of the Dutch in their own country.[73] Beckett was unrelenting. Though he said that he had 'the utmost regard for the feelings and susceptibilities of our good friends the

---

[69] *De Locomotief*, 24-2-1915; *Bataviaasch Handelsblad*, cited in *De Indische Gids* 1916, I:786.
[70] *Bataviaasch Handelsblad*, cited in *De Indische Gids* 1916, I:790; *Oetoesan Hindia* 1-3-1916.
[71] *De Locomotief*, 25-5-1916.
[72] *De Locomotief*, 4-3-1916.
[73] *De Locomotief*, 28-2-1916.

Dutch', he explained that it was his duty to provide his government with information about people and firms 'to whom, owing to their enemy nationality, or their close connection with enemy interests it is advisable that British subjects should not afford any assistance or support by engaging in commercial or other transactions with them'.[74] Enthusiasm to take a common stand against the British measure soon evaporated. A second meeting organized by Dinger on 2 April attracted only forty people. It ended in discord, partly because of the support the *Bataviaasch Handelsblad* had given Dinger's effort.

As had already become evident from the conditions imposed on the Sabang coaling station, British consular agents did not stop at reporting to London which firms had to be black-listed. They began to interfere directly in the business affairs of Dutch companies. In May 1917 the Director of the Dutch company H.N. Smalhout and Co. was summoned to the British Consulate General in Batavia to give a clarification of the trading activities of his firm. Smalhout was sure that the Consul had been alerted by 'a competitor with very little morality and filthy principles'. Smalhout was subjected to what he called 'a complete interrogation, such as that only a examining judge can subject an accused to'. He had not dared to ignore the summons. Had he done so his company would have been entered on the black-list and would 'no longer receive letters or telegrams, while not a single shipping company *and above all the Dutch companies* accepted goods from black-listed firms'.[75] At the consulate Smalhout was questioned about thirteen crates of equipment for the printing industry, most of German make, which he had taken along as his personal luggage and not as freight the previous year. Smalhout was able to explain that he possessed a NOT certificate. Not much later, the British deputy Consul in Medan alerted the local Planters Committee that its representative in Swatow was suspected of 'consorting with the enemy' and that this could have 'unpleasant consequences'. To the annoyance of the authorities, the committee reacted instantly. It concluded that the heart of the problem was the fact that Dutch consular agents had been assigned to represent German interests in China; which was also a source of strained relationships between China and the Netherlands. The Medan Planters Committee asked the Dutch Consul General in Hong Kong to allow its representative to resign as Acting Dutch Consul in Swatow.[76]

---

[74] *De Locomotief*, 15-3-1916.
[75] Smalhout to Attorney-General, 11-5-1917, 6-6-1917, Smalhout to Beckett, 11-5-1917, NA, Kol. Geheim, Mr. 1917/111x.
[76] 1st Government Secretary to Planters-Comité, Planters-Comité to 1st Government Secretary, 11-9-1917, NA, Kol. Geheim, Mr. 1917/229x; Idenburg to Van Limburg Stirum, 9-12-1918, NA, Kol. Geheim, Vb. 9-12-1918 O10.

CHAPTER XIV

Adjusting to economic warfare

In the first days of the war it had been predicted that Dutch shipping would benefit from the disappearance from the seas of German and Austrian freighters. That such ships no longer ventured out was seen as a good opportunity for Dutch shipping to expand its business. A neutral flag could also be an advantage in other respects. To the indignation of the British press, in Europe and in Asia at least one shipping company, a firm in Rotterdam, tried to exploit the situation by sending a circular to British trading firms on both continents in which the message was driven home that because the Netherlands was a neutral country, it could still trade with Germany. As an additional bonus the circular mentioned that mail carried by Dutch ships was free from Allied censorship.[1]

Advertising was not necessary. During the war freight prices rose steeply. A combination of factors was at work: the shortage of tonnage caused by the disappearance of the German and Austrian mercantile fleets; the damage inflicted to the Allied merchant fleet by German U-boats and mines; the requisitioning of part of the Allied merchant fleet for war purposes; and, temporarily, the withdrawal of ships from cargo traffic to repatriate pilgrims. Shipping lines eager to exploit a world-wide shortage of tonnage were not the only reason for rising freight prices. The rising price of coal contributed to the inflation, as did higher premiums for insurance against the risk of war. Extra costs were likewise incurred by longer sailing times if alternative routes had to be sought or if speed was reduced to economize on coal. Yet another cost-increasing factor was the shortage of labourers in Allied ports because of the war. Neutral freighters often had to wait in French and British ports until Allied warships and merchantmen had been taken care of, with all the delays and the running up of harbour dues this entailed.

Nevertheless, the Rotterdamsche Lloyd and Nederland, made good use of the shortage of tonnage, which turned cargo trade into a very profitable business. Between August 1914 and January 1915, freight prices for colonial wares

[1]   *De Locomotief*, 3-11-1914.

increased by fifty per cent. In that same month Lovink, the Director of the Department of Agriculture, Industry, and Trade, noted that 'some of the traders do business with hope in their hearts and consider the trade as a lottery fraught with plenty of bad luck – another group just throws in the towel and dares not undertake anything'.[2] Worse was to come. By August 1916, freight prices were four times as high as at the outbreak of the war. The Nederland and Rotterdamsche Lloyd also upset traders by departing from the custom of concluding shipping contracts with exporters of colonial wares with the freight price being fixed for five months. They reduced this period to two months. The change was a serious setback for exporters. They used to buy up and trade products at the beginning of the harvest, which started in June and ended in October for sugar, shipping the commodities off in portions in the subsequent months.

Throughout the whole of the war people in the Netherlands Indies and in Holland attacked what they were convinced was selfish policy pursued by the Rotterdamsche Lloyd and Nederland. As the two shipping companies (and the Koninklijke Paketvaart Maatschappij (KPM, Royal Packet Company)) worked in close concert under the aegis of their major shareholder, the Nederlandsche Scheepvaart Unie (Netherlands Shipping Union), they were accused by their critics, whose numbers swelled as the freight prices soared, of acting as a trust. There were even accusations after the war that their 'freight usury' had caused more damage than many of the measures imposed by the belligerents.[3] The Nederland and Rotterdamsche Lloyd denied such charges. They defended their price policy by pointing out their critics were unaware of the great difficulties encountered in maintaining sea traffic between Holland and the Netherlands Indies. They also maintained that, compared to non-Dutch shipping companies their prices were still moderate.[4]

Criticism by the colonial trading sector was especially harsh. It was claimed that the shareholders of the Nederland and Rotterdamsche Lloyd were making war profits hand over first at the expense of exporters and producers of colonial wares. The main sin for which the companies were attacked was calculating excessive freight prices. Another accusation levied at them was that they selected sailing routes which produced the highest profits and that by doing so disregarded the interests of colonial trade. The Nederland and the Rotterdamsche Lloyd fuelled indignation still further by cancelling contracts and raising tariffs unilaterally any time when the circumstances of war forced them to change the route of their ships or cancel shipping entirely. It also hap-

---

[2] Lovink to Idenburg, 13-1-1915, NA, Kol. Openbaar, Vb. 15-3-1915 72.
[3] *Bataviaasch Handelsblad*, 3-11-1917 cited in *Koloniale Studiën* 1917:242; Helfferich 1918:480.
[4] Report Chamber of Commerce Rotterdam over 1915, cited in *Koloniale Studiën* 1917-18:157-8.

pened that when for reasons of safety it was decided not to call at Marseille, contracts for goods to be shipped to Marseille were annulled, disregarding the fact that the exporters concerned had their own contractual obligations they had to meet.[5] These were isolated incidents but as they cost the exporters money, not easily forgotten. No one bothered to point out that British lines in Singapore behaved in exactly the same way.

When shipping opportunities grew increasingly scarce, some critics of the Nederland and Rotterdamsche Lloyd even argued that the Dutch government should not leave the vital sea links between the Netherlands Indies and its overseas markets in the hands of private companies which did not have the interests of the colony at heart. Two arguments were especially favoured to demonstrate how 'anti-colonial' the two companies were. One was that they had their head-offices in Holland. The other was that before the war, the Nederland and Rotterdamsche Lloyd had worked in close tandem with British and German shipping companies in the Batavia Vrachten-Conferentie (Batavia Cargo Conference), to regulate cargo and passenger transport between the Netherlands Indies and Europe.[6]

The commercial community in the Netherlands Indies reacted so excessively because colonial trading houses felt trapped. Their managements believed that they had no other choice but to use the services of the Nederland and the Rotterdamsche Lloyd; even when an alternative presented itself, which in fact was few and far between. The bone of contention was the deferred rabat system which had been instituted by the Batavia Cargo Conference in 1900. Export firms which shipped their cargo exclusively with the Rotterdamsche Lloyd and the Nederland were entitled to a discount of ten per cent on the freight costs they had paid in a six-months period. The money, which could amount to a considerable sum, would be restituted afterwards, but only on the condition that during the following six months an exporter would continue to ship his ware on vessels of the two companies. Opponents took every opportunity to drive home that a rabat system had been forbidden by British authorities in Singapore and South Africa.

Exporters staged meetings to end what they called the monopoly of the shipping companies created by the rabat system as early as March 1915. They asked the Ministry of the Colonies in The Hague to mediate. Its civil servants were well aware that there was not much they could do. They lacked the expertise to pass judgement on the arguments advanced by the companies to justify their actions. They had to limit themselves to presenting a 'warm recommendation' the companies would take the interests of colonial exporters to

[5] *De Locomotief,* 6-3-1917.
[6] *Schepenvorderingswet* 1917:86-7.

heart.[7] Probably Pleyte and his staff would have liked to do more. They were not pleased with the policy of the Rotterdamsche Lloyd and the Nederland. Pleyte even hinted that if their directors did not take the interests of colonial trade into account and continued to force prices up, a time could well arrive thoughts would turn to foreign competitors.[8] Pleyte's criticism was shared by the Javasche Bank. In its report for 1916-1917, the bank warned that ultimately the selfish attitude of the shipping companies could force exporters to turn to rival companies, which in the long run might have disastrous consequences for the Dutch lines concerned. The following year, the bank complained about the 'phalanx of the shipping companies', for which exporters were no match.[9] Resentment swelled to such proportions others speculated that traders would turn to Japanese lines after the war had ended because they had become so enraged by the war-time policy of the Dutch shipping companies (Van Heekeren 1919b:140).

In the Netherlands Indies, the commercial community led by the Batavian Director of the Nederlandsche Handel-Maatschappij staged a large protest meeting in the middle of 1917. Among the persons present were H. de Kruyff, the then Head of the Department of Trade and Industry and one of the most important civil servants in the colony, and a representative of the Javasche Bank. Frustrations spilled out freely. One of those present stated that trade was at 'the mercy' of the KPM, the company the Nederland and the Rotterdamsche Lloyd had jointly established in 1891, and of Burns Philp, a Sydney-based company and the agent of the Imperial Japanese and United States Mail Line.[10] A statement read out on behalf of the shipping companies was jeered. There were boos when it was argued that the great demand for cargo place showed that freight prices were not too high, and that even with existing tariffs there still was a market abroad for colonial products. The promise of the Nederland and Rotterdamsche Lloyd that they would foster the interests of colonial exports aroused only disbelief.

A new Dutch government had to be sworn in before at last measures were taken and the colonial administration enlisted a shipping expert to investigate the freight prices demanded by the shipping companies at the end of 1918. By then war was already over.

The estates in Sumatra began to recruit labour in Java again in early 1915. This is a pretty good indication that in the first two years of the war export firms and producers of colonial wares suffered less than the wave of criticism of

[7] *De Locomotief*, 2-3-1915; Note Department A3, NA, Kol. Openbaar, Vb. 15-3-1915 72.
[8] *Koloniaal verslag* 1917:xix-xx.
[9] *De Indische Gids* 1917, II:1428; *Koloniale Studiën* 1918:477.
[10] *De Indische Gids* 1917, II:1189.

the Rotterdamsche Lloyd and the Nederland had suggested. Prices of most export products of the Netherlands Indies remained high. Many benefited from this: the estates, indigenous producers, Chinese and Arab middlemen, and the export houses. In 1912 the value of the export of the private sector had been 533 million guilders, in 1915 the figure had risen to 758 million guilders.[11] The increase coupled with decreasing imports also worked favourably for the colony's balance of trade.

The export of a number of colonial products exceeded that of previous years.[12] The most important of these were sugar and tobacco.[13] Referring to economic performance in 1915 it was stated that also industry had not performed as badly as had been predicted in the closing months of 1914. A notable exception had to be made for the *batik* industry. This cottage industry threatened to disappear and was forced to cede to large-scale industry.[14] Except for the first weeks of the war, import firms also experienced a halcyon period. At the outbreak of the war their warehouses had been packed. With fresh imports diminishing and rising prices they could sell their stock at a good profit. Among the firms which profited was Behn, Meyer and Co. Sales of stocks of imported goods was one of the factors which contributed to its relatively good performance during the war (Helfferich 1967:153).

The war had a number of positive consequences for the colonial economy. As an unexpected bonus the obstacles put in the way of unrestricted export to Europe meant that economically the Netherlands Indies was less dependent on Holland. A number of products were no longer sold on the commodity markets in Holland, but at newly established markets in Batavia. Huge sums in commissions and insurance were saved, and, for trade with countries in the Pacific, freight costs dropped considerably because goods no longer had to be shipped to Europe first. Representatives of foreign trading companies, who had bought the colonial products in London or Amsterdam in the past, now travelled to the Netherlands Indies to buy their commodities. Tea, sugar, rubber, tobacco, and tin were traded in the Netherlands Indies, and no longer, or to a much lesser extent, in Holland.

Boosting to the qualified optimism was the fact that exporters, and to a lesser extent importers, had adjusted themselves to the obstacles they encountered. New export markets were sought and found: first among them in the

---

[11] *Handelingen Tweede Kamer* 1918-19:2061.
[12] See for detailed production and export figures before, during and after World War One *Changing economy* 1975, 1991 and 1992. See for an analysis of trends in imports and exports in the first three decades of the twentieth century Lindblad 1994.
[13] *Koloniaal verslag* 1917:223-6.
[14] *Koloniaal verslag* 1916:233-4; Report Javasche Bank, cited in *De Indische Gids* 1917, II:1432; Helfferich 1917.

Governor General J.P. graaf van Limburg Stirum as trade mark of an export company in Amsterdam (*Javasche Courant* 1916 Trade mark 8088)

United States, and to a lesser extent in Japan, Australia, and South Africa. The report of the Ministry of the Colonies for 1916 noted, that

> under the constraint of circumstances trade departed from the old, long-sailed ways, looked for and found new markets and freed itself from long existing ties. [...] A complete restoration [after the war] of the old links, which mostly passed through the mother country, has to be considered impossible, as the realization gradually dawns that the Netherlands Indies in many instances can do without that link and on its own can and should look after its own interests.[15]

The reallocation of the export markets stimulated the Javasche Bank and commercial firms to establish offices in the United States and Japan. In The Hague the Dutch government reacted by strengthening its consular network in the two countries in an effort to stimulate trade even further. Conversely, American and Japanese companies opened branches in the Netherlands Indies to make the most of new opportunities in foreign trade. Some Dutch firms did the same in the United States. The Bank of Holland was set up in San Francisco in 1917.

The colonial government and the Javasche Bank supported the shifting of the markets for colonial wares to the Netherlands Indies. In the Netherlands Indies, Van Limburg Stirum considered the United States to be vital to the economic future of the colony, and continued to hold the opinion that this would also be true after war had ended (Locher-Scholten 1981:65). In The Hague Pleyte was determined to promote the idea that more and more of the wares produced in the Netherlands Indies were traded in the colony itself. He considered such a development would be highly conducive to the growth of the colonial economy.[16] To stimulate this M. Kolthoff, a former agent of the Handelsvereeniging Amsterdam was sent on a four-month trade mission to Japan in March 1916 to promote the trade of government companies and private firms with Japan. Before Kolthoff left for Japan, he organized meetings in a number of cities on Java to solicit 'orders'.

One of the main arguments of those pleading for a greater say by the colony in economic matters was that centre of colonial trade had shifted from Europe to the Pacific. The United States especially formed a new and valuable market for the constantly growing list of articles which were submitted to NOT control, and export of which to Holland had to be limited or had to stop altogether.[17] Exports to the United States grew more than tenfold between 1914 and 1917, from 16 to 200 million guilders (Carpentier Alting and De Cock Buning 1928:66). As in the case of trade with Japan, the newly found economic

---

[15] *Koloniaal verslag* 1917:xix.
[16] *Koloniaal verslag* 1917:xix.
[17] *Koloniaal verslag* 1917:xviii, 211-2.

relationship was lasting and continued after the war. The United States proved a profitable outlet for rubber, cassava, copra (in the form of coconut oil), and tobacco (from Sumatra, not from Java, where the leaves of the plants grown were not fine enough for the American taste). For some products which had not been shipped to the United States or only in small quantities before the war, such as pepper, tin, and kapok, by 1916 the United States already accounted for more than half of the exports. This removed some of the causes of the worries Pleyte had expressed in September 1914 in his letter to Loudon. The 'fledgling trade with the United States', as it was sometimes referred to, formed the main reason why, as Pleyte in his report to the Dutch Parliament observed, the colonial economy had not been completely dislocated, and all things considered had shown a rather favourable performance. The drop in the export of cassava to Europe was made good by an expanding American market. On the tin market, the United States had replaced Germany as the largest buyer. A remarkable success was also scored by rubber. Forced to take action by the problems encountered with shipping their produce to Europe, rubber planters had opened up a new market in the United States, which previously had obtained most of its rubber from Great Britain. In 1915 the export of estate rubber had swelled almost twofold, increasing from 6,396 to 11,307 tons; doubling again in the case of exports from Java in the following year.[18]

The prices paid for the major export products were excellent. Among the products which fetched higher prices in 1915 than they had done before the war were tobacco, coffee, and tea. The sugar industry was still booming and copra fetched good prices; rubber idem. In short, because of its agricultural sector the Netherlands Indies managed to survive the first two years of the war remarkably well. The prime beneficiaries were the estates. The shadow side was that the consequences for indigenous producers were mixed. Some, especially producers of copra, profited from higher prices, but others who grew other products or products of a lesser quality than those grown on the estates suffered.[19] An additional factor was that export crops grown by the local population had to take the back seat in the competition for scarce cargo space. Exporters gave preference to sought-after, more profitable products, the so-called *fijne lading* (choice cargo). Coupled with the rising prices of daily necessities, this meant that the Indonesian population outside Java producing for the export market suffered a steep decline in purchasing power.[20] Nevertheless, the excellent prospects for tobacco, coffee, and tea stimulated their cultivation by indigenous farmers.

---

[18] *Koloniaal verslag* 1916:223-4, 1917:213-4.
[19] For which export products were grown where by indigenous producers outside Java, see Touwen 2001:167-84.
[20] *Koloniaal verslag* 1916:225-6.

The change in the flow of exports highlighted the different economic aspirations of the motherland and the colony. Those cherishing the interests of the colony stressed greater independence, even from headquarters in Holland. Many Dutch *Residents* in the Netherlands Indies shared this view. Free trade had to replace the monopolies and protectionism, which they suspected the leading businessmen in Holland of wanting to maintain. Directors had to take the place of agents as heads of the colonial branches of the Dutch trading houses, shipping lines, and estate companies (Helfferich 1918:482). In August 1917 the *Java-Bode* wrote that it was a questionable matter to keep the management in Holland simply for the reason that Holland was the source of capital. Changes were in order. Whenever possible, to give the Netherlands Indies real economic resilience jobs should be filled by people living in the colony.[21]

Commercial circles in Holland and those who earned their living from commodity markets there and from the transport of the products traded to Holland watched the development with concern. The 1916 report of the Ministry of the Colonies hinted at the opposition encountered. It noted that not everyone realized the implication of

> the economic awakening that has taken place, and the need to adjust to the new relations, which [...] after the restoration of normal circumstances, demand that due consideration be given to the wishes and the interests of trade and industry in the Indies.[22]

Opponents had to admit that the new markets in the colony were a success, but they expressed their doubts about whether the success would last once war had ended. They were convinced the old situation had to be restored as soon as possible. They feared that a permanent transfer of commodity markets, or even worse a transfer of markets like that of tobacco to the United States, would be a blow to Holland's prosperity.[23] As had been argued in the days of Onze Vloot: too many interests in Holland were at stake, those of the shipping companies transporting the wares to Holland; the firms engaged in loading, unloading and storage: the Dutch railways: Dutch labourers and so on. Another loser might be the NHM, which, because of what had happened in the colony in August 1914, was not held in high esteem by Pleyte and other politicians. The NHM stood a good chance of having to forfeit part of its trading activities. Its most vulnerable aspect was its function as the agent of the colonial government for goods produced by government companies and estates, which had been sold on commodity markets in Europe in the past. In November 1917 members of the Dutch senate decided that the time

---

[21] *Java-Bode,* cited in *Koloniale Studiën* 1917:555.
[22] *Koloniaal verslag* 1917:xix.
[23] *Economisch-Statistische Berichten,* 1-5-1918, p. 368.

had come for the government to sever its ties with the NHM. They preferred open competition and championed the establishment of a special body in the Netherlands Indies to look after the economic interests of the colony.[24]

The focus of discussion was the future location of the tin market. Most tin was now exported to the United States and in 1917 Batavia suggested that the market should not be moved back to Amsterdam after the war. Pleyte was not unfavourably disposed to this idea. He asked the Rotterdam Chamber of Commerce – and not that of Amsterdam, where the interests of colonial business firms was far better represented – for advice. The Rotterdam Chamber of Commerce endorsed the suggestion, taking the side of those who pleaded for a greater independence for the colony. To drive home its advice, the Rotterdam Chamber of Commerce observed that moving the tin market to Batavia had resulted in a large increase in exports. The economic damage to Holland was outweighed by the advantages which had been the result of establishing the tin market in Batavia. The advice occasioned a heated debate. It drew vehement protests from those supporting the economic interests of Holland. *De Telegraaf* called the attitude of the Rotterdam Chamber of Commerce unpatriotic.[25] It goes without saying, the Amsterdam Chamber of Commerce was opposed to the suggestion.

It was a theme that would resurface time and again during the remainder of the war. The business community in Holland was a fervent advocate of markets and bodies regulating trade in the mother country, where the headquarters of the estate companies were located and from where much of the capital came. Before 1914 company headquarters in Holland had resisted with might and main a reallocation of markets, when the matter had come of for the trading of rubber and tea (Ligthart 1923:432). Shifting control to the colony would only scare off Dutch people and other Europeans with disposable capital from investing. People in the colony wanted to have the commodity markets located where the production took place. One of their main arguments was the change in export markets. They were convinced this was a development which would last, even after the war. People in Holland disagreed. They believed the present extraordinary circumstances had to be taken into account. Trade flows would resume their pre-war pattern once peace had been restored.

Another heated discussion raged in August 1918. In this case the founding of a Vereenigde Javasuiker Producenten-Vereeniging (United Java Sugar Producers Associated) in Holland elicited protests in the colony. These very much strengthened as the move aborted an initiative taken by Batavia a few days earlier to regulate the export of sugar in Java and not in Holland. In the

---

[24] *Handelingen Eerste Kamer* 1917-18:67.
[25] *De Telegraaf*, cited in *De Indische Gids* 1917, I:692; Report Chamber of Commerce Rotterdam over 1917, cited in *De Indische Gids* 1918, I:447-8; Gerritzen 1917.

Netherlands Indies the opinion was advanced that even before the outbreak of the war the practice of taking decisions about the selling of sugar in Holland had been an anomaly. Decisions should be taken in Java, even more so in a situation in which many of the buyers were no longer Europeans. Conversely, bodies founded in Java to regulate trade in sugar and coffee had failed because of opposition from Holland.[26] At the end of the war it was maintained that such obstructions had occasioned great harm, had paralysed initiative, and had shown how ignorant people in Holland were about what transpired in the Netherlands Indies. The attitude in Holland was 'petty and ridiculous', and testified to 'bragging and vanity' (Helfferich 1918:479).

Alternatives had also to be found for imports. A major impulse for this was the severed economic links with Austria-Hungary, and especially with Germany, which before the war had been a major, if not the exclusive, source of steel and rails, of machinery and spare parts, of cheap consumer goods bought by the indigenous population, and of surgical equipment. In statistics the volume of trade with Germany was reduced to mere dots. Imports from Germany which had still amounted to 22 million guilders in 1913 dropped almost to zero (Carpentier Alting and De Cock Buning 1928:103). Another reason was the problems experienced in the trade with Holland and the Allied Powers.

The United States, even though its products were considered expensive, emerged as a prime source of steel and iron, which Great Britain and France supplied only in small quantities or not at all. The United States could also supply medical instruments, weapons, and, on a more mundane level, articles of clothing and delicacies for the European community. Orders were placed in America for locomotives and railway carriages. These were urgently needed. Shortages of carriages and locomotives for the transportation of estate products at harvest time to the harbours, the so-called *riettreinen* (cane trains), had already been a problem for years. Fresh orders for rolling stock had been placed in Europe before the outbreak of the war, but it had soon become patently obvious that the goods would not be delivered. American imports of other commodities grew in importance. American imports increased from 9 million guilders in 1913 to 62 million guilders in 1918 (Carpentier Alting and De Cock Buning 1928:103). The growing importance of the United States as a supplier of imports was reason enough for the Ministry of the Colonies to establish a purchasing office in New York, incidentally located in the same building as Schenker and Co., the company which had tried to send a cargo of weapons to the Netherlands Indies on board Dutch ships.

The replacement of Europe, including Holland, as a main source of imports

---

[26] *De Taak*, cited in *De Indische Gids* 1919, I:108.

by the United States provided yet another field in which people saw an opportunity to reduce the supervision by Holland. The colony should have its own purchasing office in the United States. An end had to come to the old system in which Batavia had to submit orders first to the Ministry of the Colonies, which passed them on to New York. Had this suggestion been implemented, it would have meant shifting part of the budgetary responsibilities to the colony. Its proponents saw it as a logical step to take in view of the geographical location of the United States. It would also speed up matters considerably, as the intervention of the Ministry of the Colonies was said to lead to considerable delays (Bryan 1918).

Japan, itself forced to redirect some of its exports and to establish new industries because of the disruption of imports, also figured prominently in Indies trade. The disappearance of German trade from the Netherlands Indies opened the way for Japanese products and Japanese commerce to make their entry on the scene. Japan became a source of cement, coal, sulphur, matches, textiles, beer, rice, cheap paper, and even toys. It could supply the Netherlands Indies with products of which the supply had almost run out. Among these were brass and various chemicals. From a mere 7 million guilders in 1913, the value of Japanese imports reached a value of 114 million guilders in 1918 (Carpentier Alting and De Cock Buning 1928:103). The Japanese were eager to exploit such new export opportunities. Japanese business offices and banks opened up in the larger cities. Japanese trade delegations started to visit the Netherlands Indies.[27] It would be a wild exaggeration to say such Japanese businessmen were trusted people. At times Dutch people could not make up their minds whether the Japanese who visited the Netherlands Indies were bona fide businessmen or spies, and whether information should be withheld from them or not. Suspicions were aroused if Japanese who visited commercial firms or government offices could not give a proper address or if their business cards mentioned a civil servant as their profession and the Japanese Consul could not provide any further information.[28] A highly embarrassing incident was the shadowing and arrest in Surabaya of four Japanese out for a stroll in the spring of 1916. The four were members of a large official eighty-persons-strong delegation of businessmen, government officials, and professors who toured Celebes and Java to celebrate the opening of a Japanese shipping-line to the Netherlands Indies, entertained grandly in all cities they visited. The *Assistent-Resident* offered his apologies. This did not satisfy the

---

[27] Japanese trade delegations were not the only such groups to visit the Netherlands Indies. As the Americans had done before them, the Japanese thought that perhaps they could learn something from the way the Dutch ran their colony. In November 1917, eight Japanese civil servants stationed in Formosa visited Java to study the colonial administrative and legal systems.
[28] *Koloniaal verslag* 1919:259-60; *Neratja*, 19-9-1918.

four, all of whom it was reported were noblemen. They hastened to their Consul to lodge a formal complaint.[29] Nevertheless, something good came out of the visit. One of its members, Inazo Nitobe, a professor in colonial history in Tokyo, wrote after he had returned home that the visit had made him change his mind. Talks with the Governor General and other senior colonial civil servants had convinced Inazo Nitobe that Takekoshi was mistaken when he said that the Dutch were in the Netherlands Indies for economic gains pure and simple and did nothing to try to improve the fate of the natives. His words, the *Japan Advertiser* concluded, were an attack on those in Japan who pleaded for an expansion southwards. Inazo Nitobe's plea for the expansion of trade instead of war did not completely reassure *De Locomotief*. Inazo Nitobe pointed a finger at the Netherlands Indies; Takekoshi raised a fist. Moreover, how much effect would his words have in Japan? Could Inazo Nitobe neutralize 'the untruthful writing' of Takekoshi?[30]

What also made Japan special was that it could provide earthenware, peddlers' wares, and other cheap articles to be sold to the local population. Efforts to find new sources of supply in the United States or Europe for such goods formerly obtained from Germany and Austria-Hungary, had met with failure. Factories in the United States and Europe did not produce for a cheap market. The prices of their products were too high for the population of the Netherlands Indies to afford. In Japan the situation was different. Factories could produce cheaply.

The import of consumer goods from Japan was relatively new. Before August 1914, the European trading houses in the Netherlands Indies had looked down on Japanese products and more often than not had rejected requests from Japanese companies to trade their products. After the outbreak of the war the attitude of the import firms changed drastically. The same companies which had shunted Japanese products in the past now took the initiative to interest Japanese factories in the market in the Netherlands Indies. Often nothing came of it. The commission Japanese exporters were prepared to offer was generally too small to be acceptable to European firms. Trade in Japanese products went almost exclusively to Chinese firms, and in some cities to Japanese shopkeepers, bypassing their Dutch counterparts.

Unfortunately, such new imports did not always meet expectations. Japanese products aroused great disappointment. A much heard complaint was that quality was poor. Confronted with such charges, Tokyo instituted an official inquiry. American imports also do not seem to have always been up to standard. If we may believe contemporary reports, locomotives imported

---

[29] *Oetoesan Hindia*, 24-5-1916.
[30] *De Locomotief*, 25-8-1916, 14-9-1916.

from the United States made a great impression because of their huge size, but tended to break down.[31]

Imports from the United States and Japan gave some relief, but were not varied or in large quantities, enough to bring imports back to their pre-war volume. German products, which could no longer be imported, continued to be in high demand. When the cargo of the *Roon* was finally auctioned in early 1918 European, Chinese, and Arab traders jumped at the opportunity and outbid each other. Bids were made without even knowing what the contents of the crates were. Emil Helfferich recalled how led astray by his eagerness a pious Arab merchant ended up with a sausage machine (Helfferich 1921:15). Scarcity led to acute problems. Since 1916 new telephone connections could no longer be made because of shortage of telephone wire. Railways were another good example. Projects to extend the rail network had to be abandoned, and as early as 1916 the public railways were experiencing a shortage of wagons and locomotives to transport estate products. The reason was that because of the war 3,000 wagons and ninety engines which had been ordered in Europe had not been delivered.[32] Trains began to run at night to cope with the shortage of rolling stock and the transport of non-perishable goods was temporarily stopped. Much to the chagrin of the public, passenger and freight transport were combined in an effort to increase efficient use of material. The hope that any new rolling stock could be imported evaporated in 1917 when the United States entered the war and had to upgrade its own railway system to cope with the problems the increase in freight traffic posed. Seriously hampered by the lack of rolling stock the state railways company at the end of 1918 and the beginning of 1919 contemplated raising the fares in an effort to decrease the number of passengers, though it was seriously doubted whether this would indeed have had the desired effect. Other measures contemplated were reducing the number of passenger trains and even running more combined passenger and freight trains.

Similar problems threw a spanner in the work of mining companies. Throughout the war mining operations were hampered by a lack of machinery. An act had to be promulgated to allow for the extension of the prospecting period after which an exploration claim was still valid. Lack of capital and even more the dearth of equipment caused considerable delays.

After a long and hard look at the problems experienced, the development of an import substitution industry was broached. The efforts gave the colony some additional independence from abroad. The army and police also made their modest contribution. Alternatives had to be found for the production

---

[31] *De Locomotief*, 16-2-1917; *Nieuwe Noordkust,* cited in *De Locomotief,* 17-4-1918.
[32] *Neratja,* 3-12-1918.

of uniforms and the supply of cloth which had been ordered in Holland before the war. Measures had already been taken shortly before August 1914. Expecting that imports could be impeded the army had placed an order for shoes at the prison of Yogyakarta. Later, inmates of a prison in Cirebon were set to weaving the prison garments, which had once been made in Holland. The cotton yarn was imported from Bombay. The uniform of the Armed Police was also produced locally. It was not a great success. Batavia had to admit that the quality of the new uniforms was far from satisfactory.[33] In 1916 the army also considered the establishment of an arms and ammunition factory in Java. After ample thought, the decision was negative. The colonial army was too small to provide a viable market. It would be highly questionable if the products of such a factory could compete with arms factories abroad.[34]

The local metal-working industry profited from the situation. Before the outbreak of the war it had mainly been a subsidiary business of agencies of foreign engineering-works, located mainly in East Java, but there were a few in West Java, to provide the sugar, tea, and rubber estates with their machineries. Confronted with the problems of ordering machinery in Europe and hesitant to place orders in Japan and the United States, an increasing number of orders went to the local metal-working industry.

The colonial government also did its bid. In September 1915 Idenburg installed a special committee for the promotion of the manufacturing industry. The step was later described by Batavia as a 'spontaneous idea' of Idenburg himself.[35] The committee was responsible for investigating which goods could be produced locally, or more precisely in Java, and how the government could assist in this. What Idenburg and other advocates of local industrialization envisaged was not just making the Netherlands Indies more independent of abroad during the war, they were looking far ahead. Two other reasons for them to plead for the encouragement of a manufacturing industry was the rapid growth of the population and the need to improve the standard of living of the people. Additional sources of income had to be created. To continue to rely on agriculture would only result in impoverishment. Consequently, types of industry which were still dependent in imports for the input of raw materials were also considered.

When it was founded the committee was hailed as a step in the direction of the industrial emancipation of the colony. It had to tackle a subject which was close to the heart of many Dutch people in the Netherlands Indies: increasing the independence of the Netherlands Indies from Holland. Initial enthusiasm soon faded. Two years later, Van Hinloopen Labberton criticized the commit-

[33] *Volksraad* 1918:71.
[34] *Volksraad* 1918:578.
[35] *Volksraad* 1918:40.

tee for having accomplished almost nothing at all. Van Hinloopen Labberton was also highly incensed by the fact that the committee was made up of people who never had seen a factory from the inside. The authorities had excluded industrialists from the committee for fear that they would advance their own interests.[36] Lovink thought differently. He wrote that the committee set to work seriously and pointed to the some seven brochures published (Lovink 1919:8). This sounds impressive but most had been written by one man, the government representative on the committee, J.C. van Reigersberg Versluys. He was its only full-time member, and had been especially employed to do such a job. All other members of the committee were pillars of society with busy jobs, who could not devote much time to the work of the committee.

Despite such good intentions and sometimes halting efforts the World War did not mark the take-off of industry in the Netherlands Indies. Nevertheless, a great variety of experiments were tried or suggested. Among the chemicals that were produced in the Netherlands Indies for the first time or in much larger quantities than before were sulphuric acid, sodium bisulphite, used in the sugar industry, and calcium carbide. Anticipating a serious shortage of iron, the prospects for establishing a pig iron foundry were investigated. Research into the construction of blast-furnaces passed in review. The vulcanization of rubber, and the production of pharmaceutical products, sodium carbonate, silk (requiring the planting of mulberry trees), beer, black ink, beeswax, soap, castor oil, cement, pigments and the like were broached. Forced by a shortage of medicines and bandages the Civilian Medical Service started to experiment with the growing of medicinal plants and native fibrous plants, the latter to provide bandages. The service was pleased with the results.[37] A hay committee to study what native grasses were best suited as fodder was instituted. Another committee studied the possibilities of producing fertilizers. This was important because, whether there was a war or not, the growing population and the intensification of agriculture would only increase demand (Van Reigersberg Versluys 1917a:12).

Some were optimistic about the prospects. For a number of new products, immediate profits were high. A prolongation of the war would allow such new industries enough time to develop sufficient expertise to be able to cope with post-war competition. In other cases, the machine industry was one of these, doubts prevailed right from the start about the viability. It was expected that they would not survive peace-time when pre-war international market forces were restored.[38]

A number of the projects suggested gave rise to heated debates. One was

---

[36] *Volksraad* 1918:200.
[37] *Koloniaal verslag* 1918:124.
[38] *Koloniaal verslag* 1917:237-8; *Ontwikkeling* 1917:9.

the production of matches. Enormous effort and a wealth of public discussion went into the question of whether the trees which grew in the colony could supply wood with the necessary smoothness and tensile strength for the production of matches; and if this were so, whether the new industry would be economically sound. In the past experiments had failed. Lack of a sufficient supply of the right kind of timber had made the locally produced matches far inferior to those imported from Europe. They had also been much more expensive than Japanese matches which, though of lower quality, had conquered the cheaper segment of the market (see *Vervaardigen* 1918). The Hague was even asked to send an expert in the field of match production to the Netherlands Indies. By the end of the war no match factory had been founded. A similar story can be told about the production of paper. There were specific problems, such as the absence of a large quantity of rags, a lack of knowledge about the properties of the trees which grew in the colony, and the great diversity in trees in a tropical forest, which had made it difficult to develop commercial woods. Nevertheless, production did not seem out of the question (see Reigersberg Versluys 1917b). No concrete steps were taken. At the end of the war experts were still quarrelling about the feasibility of a paper factory in the colony.

The discussions about the development of an industrial sector in the Netherlands Indies were coloured not only by a conflict of interests between motherland and colony. An issue of equal importance, though the debate had not yet prompted the direct involvement of powerful pressure groups, as that on paper did, was the question of what government support, if any, should be given to the development of an indigenous industry. The colonial government had endorsed recommendations for the development of a big native industry, Van Kol had made after his trips to Japan. Batavia had warmed to the idea that the management of a native industry would be less expensive than industrial projects for which the staff would have had to come from Europe. There was many a slip between the tongue and the lip. Concrete steps had been confined to assisting those industries which existed already, batik, pottery, leather-working, rope-making, and indigenous forges (see also Lovink 1919:9).

In the colony one of the most enthusiastic advocates of a native large-scale industry was the socialist Ch.G. Cramer, an engineer employed by the Department of Public Works. He wanted government support for the establishment of new industries to go primarily – as Van Kol had also suggested – to Indonesian cooperative societies. The government should take the lead. It should select branches of industry in which indigenous big business could develop. It should also stimulate the establishment of cooperative societies eligible for financial support and establish model state factories to teach Indonesians the trade. Cramer was very outspoken in his preference for the development of a native industry. European entrepreneurs should receive

H.H. van Kol, circa 1920 (KITLV 2745)

financial support from the government in exceptional cases only.

Cramer saw good prospects in the textile sector, in the establishment of rice-husking plants, and in the estate sector, especially tea and sugar.[39] He was highly optimistic about the prospects for a colonial textile industry and foresaw that the Netherlands Indies could take over the pre-war role of Holland in providing itself with textiles. Unfortunately, the examples Cramer mentioned to substantiate his view were not the most convincing. He said that in Cirebon there already was 'a more or less primitive textile company'. He meant the local prison. Cramer praised the products made in the prison and argued that the prison experience showed that 'the Javanese quickly understands [the art of] weaving with power looms, which requires attentiveness and skill rather than effort.'[40] To lend extra force to his argument, he pointed out that the Director of the Cirebon prison and the inspector of the prison system were both 'textile experts'.[41] Cramer did not receive much support from his fellow-Europeans. They dismissed his ideas as a utopia. They were convinced that for some time to come industrialization would still have to depend on initiatives from the European community and that native society was not yet ripe for such endeavours. Such a view prompted Cramer to blame the government for having taken no initiatives to develop native industry in the past.[42]

Indië Weerbaar found itself in the spotlight in the discussion about the economic independence of the Netherlands Indies. The war had made people realize that dependency on imports could be a dangerous liability. Abdoel Moeis and Dwidjosewojo and other propagandists of Indië Weerbaar stressed that military force was not the only factor on which a country's defence should rest. Economic strength and the improvement of educational opportunities were essential elements in the colony's ability to withstand a foreign threat. Van Hinloopen Labberton argued that resilience was far more than a matter of soldiers and arms, it embraced economic development and the promotion of science. War created some opportunities towards accomplishing this. In exchange for Indonesian support for the establishment of native militia, the Netherlands Indies was not only to be given a People's Council; it also was granted a technical university.

The appeals for economic development were also voiced by Van Aalst and other businessmen in Holland. In contrast to people in the Netherlands Indies, they only wanted to go a limited way. They did not pay much attention to the implication that the colony should gain a larger degree of economic and political independence from Holland. Criticizing this position, Batavia regularly

[39] *Volksraad* 1918-19:310, 359.
[40] *Volksraad* 1918-19:361.
[41] *Volksraad* 1918-19:361.
[42] *Volksraad* 1918-19:453.

complained that industry in Holland was very hesitant to invest capital in the development of industry in the colony or to share its knowledge for this purpose. Nevertheless, one important initiative was taken in Holland. Van Aalst was convinced of one thing at least: natives should learn how to grow 'good sugar and good coffee' and had to develop technical, agricultural, and commercial expertise.[43] To contribute to this Van Aalst took the initiative of having members of the Dutch business community collect 3 million guilders for the establishment of a technical college in the colony. Van Aalst called the college a token of the sympathy in Holland for the population of the Netherlands Indies.

The good news was announced by Van Aalst during the visit to Holland of the Indië Weerbaar deputation. On this occasion he and Abdoel Moeis had toasted to each other's health. Van Aalst had a glass of champagne in his hand, Abdoel Moeis a glass of mineral water. The words spoken reflected a particular contemporary spirit. Van Aalst had said: 'We want to be brothers to you, Mr Abdoel Moeis'. Abdoel Moeis had replied: 'The Oriental will always grasp the fraternal hand, Mr Van Aalst'.[44]

Van Aalst's 'gift' did occasion some resentment in Java. Nobody in the colony had been consulted in advance. People in Holland had again decided what was good for the colony. What they had in mind could well be unrealistic and not tally with the real needs of the colony. Expansion of a technical middle cadre, of technical schools, might be what was required, not a college for engineers. Businessmen in Holland, who were suffering from an attack of remorse had to realize that the sudden feeding of a seriously undernourished patient who had been neglected for years with toothsome sweets could only lead to indigestion and a waste of money.[45] The government's Director for Education and Religions, K.F. Creutzberg, agreed. Publicly he praised the idea of a technical university as a 'generous plan of a number of interested persons in the Netherlands to make available a substantial sum of money for technical education in the Netherlands Indies'.[46] Whether he was really pleased was a different matter. Still a few months earlier Batavia had rejected the establishment of a technical college and Creutzberg doubted whether it was wise to establish institutions of higher education in the Netherlands Indies. The small number of students who graduated each year from Dutch-style secondary schools did yet not warrant such a step. These views – illustrative of the opinion held by Europeans in the colony that indigenous society was not yet ripe for the establishment of institutions of higher education – did not deter

---

[43] *Koloniaal Tijdschrift* 1917:797.
[44] *Volksraad* 1918-19:346.
[45] *De Indische Gids* 1917, I:61.
[46] *Volksraad* 1918:262.

others from jumping at the opportunity offered. The inhabitants of Bandung took the most decisive action. They formed an Action Committee. In articles in the newspapers and in brochures, they launched a campaign to demonstrate that Bandung was the most suitable place for the school. Bandung had many technical firms within its urban boundaries and was the centre of a plantation belt where the estates applied new technology. They also made much of the fact that Bandung exuded a European atmosphere. The Javanese educated in the city would certainly benefit from this (Rottier 1917). In July 1920 the Indische Technische Hoogeschool opened its doors in Bandung. Among its first students was Soekarno, the future President of Indonesia, who enrolled the following year.

CHAPTER XV

The dangers of war and shipping

Right from the outset British mail checks were a source of embarrassment and bitterness to Dutch people in Holland and in the Netherlands Indies (and in Suriname and the Netherlands Antilles, as Dutch West Indies mail was also checked by the British). In the first months of the war Dutch people were very reluctant to use the British mail. They did not want their letters and parcels checked by a British censor. They quickly had to rid themselves of this idea as British censorship soon became unavoidable. After July 1914, the sending of mail on its first or on its final part of the way between Holland and the Netherlands Indies through Europe by train, as had previously been done, had already become virtually impossible. Passengers and mail could still reach Holland and Germany via Italy, but this route stopped being an alternative to avoid Allied controls, albeit an equally complicated one because of border controls in Europe, after Italy had entered the war. A few persons on their way to or from the Netherlands Indies continued to travel via Italy, Switzerland, and Germany, but mail between the motherland and the colony had to be carried by ships from the ports in Holland to those in the Netherlands Indies and vice versa. Such shipments were carefully checked by the British for seditious pamphlets, letters to and from German and Austrian-Hungarian business firms, and articles of trade sent by parcel post to and from Germany and Austria-Hungary.[1] The stamp 'opened by censor' became a familiar feature of Dutch mail sent to and from the Netherlands Indies. Had the Italian land route remained open, it may not have made much of a difference after fear of Germano-Indian incitement in British colonies motivated London to cordon off the Netherlands Indies and to check all ships entering and leaving its territorial waters carefully. The general public, unaware of the Germano-Indian plot, could only wonder why the British acted in this way. The only conclusion they could draw was that it had something to do with economic warfare.

In the Netherlands Indies itself, British censorship meant that for a few

---

[1] Mail to and from Russia had to be sent via Hong Kong and Shanghai along the Siberian railway.

months in 1916 domestic mail to and from a large part of Sumatra was not longer delivered using the Dutch sub-post offices in Singapore and Penang as a distribution point and was carried only on ships which did not call in there (though here the British naval blockade also meant that the measure was not particularly efficative) on their regular route. Re-routing proved to be very complicated and serious delays were the result. Mail sometimes had to be sent via Batavia. In the case of Jambi, avoiding British ports meant that mail from Batavia was discharged in Riau, transported by another ship to Pulau Sambu, from where it was shipped by yet another steamer which had to make an extra stop for this reason to Jambi. In September 1916 the Postal Service in the Netherlands Indies announced that ordinary letters and money orders (but not registered mail and parcels) could again be sent via the Dutch sub-post offices in Penang and Singapore.

Correspondence between the Minister of the Colonies and the Governor General was not exempt from British searches. To put a stop to this, in March 1916 the Ministry of the Colonies considered having the official letters and reports be shipped in a special red, white, and blue postbag. The bags should be labelled in such a way that it was clear that they contained government mail. In the end the plan was abandoned. Government mail was sent in ordinary postbags on which it was clearly mentioned that they contained government documents. The bags were put in the special charge of the captains of the mailships. They had to try to see that the bags were not searched by the British censor. To give the captains additional status the Ministry of the Colonies provided them with a courier pass. For a time it worked. The Ministry was satisfied with the results.[2]

Searches caused extra delays. When Dutch ships on their way to the Netherlands Indies entered British territorial waters or had no option but to do so the postbags and crates were taken off and inspected by the British censor. This accomplished, the mail was returned, unless of course the censor refused to let it pass. The latter not only included inflammatory pamphlets or mail which was supposed to contribute to the economic well being of the Central Powers or black-listed firms. Neutral newspapers could also not evade censorship. In 1916 when the *Nieuwe Rotterdamsche Courant* published a number of letters to the editor critical of an article by Ronald Donald, editor-in-chief of the *Daily Chronicle*, about the British war effort also published by the newspaper, the British censor removed that section of the paper which contained the letters to the editor from a shipment to the Netherlands Indies.[3]

Because inspection was time-consuming, London changed the system. The

---

[2] Pleyte to Nederland en Rotterdamsche Lloyd, 24-3-1916, Pleyte to Holland Amerika Lijn, NA, Kol. Geheim, Vb. 24-3-1916 S4, 8-11-1916 J14.
[3] *De Locomotief*, 10-10-1916.

mail was no longer put back on board, but was forwarded later on another ship. Mail for the Netherlands Indies was sent on British ships bound for Singapore. The hazard was that the mail could be lost if the ship were torpedoed by German U-boats. A notice in a newspaper in the Netherlands Indies that mail shipped from Holland on a certain date had been lost was not a frequent occurrence but it was certainly not unusual. Initially the mail was checked for a second time in Singapore. The second check was discontinued after a Dutch protest; a decision which may have been facilitated by the fact that expenditure for the censorship of mail and telegrams weighed heavily on the budget of the Straits Settlements.[4] Nevertheless, it could still take two to four months before mail reached its destination.

One of the unintended consequences of this system was that, in spite of the risk that British ships might be torpedoed, Dutchmen started to prefer the British mail to its Dutch counterpart. The reason was simple. Letters and parcels sent by British mail reached their destination much faster. The removal of Dutch mail bags from Dutch ships caused considerable delays, and therefore, people were never tired of pointing out, money.

British fears that goods might end up in the wrong hands could have far-reaching consequences. Early 1917 the management of the Javasche Bank suffered a shock. Three shipments of sovereigns with a total value of 100,000 British pounds had been sent by Dutch mail from Amsterdam. When the Dutch ships arrived in Tanjung Priok, there were no sovereigns on board. Customs officers in Great Britain had told the ships' captains that the British mail would take care of the transport of the coins to the Netherlands Indies. The management of the Javasche Bank wrote to Van Limburg Stirum that it considered such treatment to transgress 'all fairness and justice'.[5] It took six month for the shipment to reach Batavia. The incident was indicative of the growing problems the Javasche Bank encountered in strengthening its stock of gold and silver during the war. After 1916, the dispatch of gold and silver from Holland to Java became impossible. The Javasche Bank had to rely almost completely on the production of domestic mining in the Netherlands Indies. Elsewhere in the world, gold and silver was unobtainable. Because of the disruption of sea traffic, the colony also experienced problems with the circulation of silver and copper coins, which were all minted in Holland. A dearth of copper, silver, and nickel prevented the striking of coins in the Netherlands Indies itself.[6]

There was not much that could be done about the searches of cargo and mail. 'We have to bear and forbear, that we have learned', one author wrote in

[4] *Proceedings* 1916:C 164.
[5] Javasche Bank to Van Limburg Stirum, 30-1-1917, NA, Kol. Geheim, Mr. 1917/28x.
[6] *Volksraad* 1918:112.

1918 (Van Heekeren 1918:191). Some were not so accommodating and protested. The business communities in Batavia and Surabaya did so in January 1917. The colonial government should do something about the delay of the Dutch mail transport. The latest mail that had reached them was from 19 October. *De Locomotief* wrote about *mail-ellende*, mail misery.[7] At that time it was reported with a certain frequency in the colonial press that post bags had been removed from Dutch ships sailing the Archipelago. To add insult to injury, the mail service between motherland and colony had become so irregular that in February 1917 the telegraph service in the Netherlands Indies extended from five to seven months the period in which people could complain about telegrams sent which had not reached their destination abroad. The complainants had to submit a letter from the addressees that they had not received a telegram in order to get their money refunded. The mail service to and from Europe had become too unreliable to limit the period of a refund to five months.

The Batavia Chamber of Commerce condemned the searches as contrary to the obligations of 'good neighbourliness'.[8] It urged the colonial government to do all it could to end the searches. If necessary Batavia should not eschew exerting pressure. It could, for instance, stop British mail sent from the Netherlands Indies to Singapore. Van Limburg Stirum did nothing of this sort. He asked The Hague to protest in London. To demonstrate how serious the situation was, in March 1917 Van Limburg Stirum wired to Pleyte that at the end of December and in the first days of January British warships had systematically searched mailbags on board Dutch steamers in inter-Archipelago service, had seized mail, and had abstracted registered letters. Observing that there was 'no shadow of right nor any acceptable excuse [for] this proceeding', Van Limburg Stirum asked Pleyte to submit a formal protest.[9] Pleyte agreed. He wrote to Loudon that a 'serious protest' was in order.[10]

Protests against what less diplomatic persons called a hostile act against neutral countries had already been submitted in the past few years. Because American mail on Dutch ships including government correspondence, was searched and read, the United States had lodged complaints and other neutral countries had done the same. The Hague had pointed out the Convention Relative à Certaines Restrictions à l'Exercise du Droit de Capture dans la Guerre Maritime of 1907 precluded the searching of mail on board neutral ships in international waters except, in an actual theatre of war. Great Britain had perpetrated a serious infringement of the Freedom of the Sea.[11] Within

---

[7] *De Locomotief*, 22-1-1917, 23-1-1917.
[8] *De Indische Gids* 1917, I:697.
[9] Van Limburg Stirum to Pleyte, 2-3-1917, NA, Kol. Openbaar, Vb. 14-3-1917 49.
[10] Pleyte to Loudon, 14-3-1917, NA, Kol. Openbaar, Vb. 14-3-1917 49.
[11] Loudon to Johnstone, 16-11-1914, *De Locomotief*, 25-3-1915

months after the outbreak of the war The Hague had also been forced to protest about the confiscation of mail in British territorial waters. There was no way neutral ships could escape sailing these waters. After March 1915 all neutral vessels which sailed the Channel had to enter British territorial waters (at the roads of The Downs, off Deal, north of Dover) (Verbeke 2002:223). To enforce the measure, depth charges (aimed to lock German submarines and other warships stationed in Belgium up in port) had been laid in such a way that ships had no other choice. Soon such a measure was no longer necessary. The British government simply ordered neutral ships sailing to and from Europe to call in at a British port for inspection.

Eventually protests took an almost ritualistic guise. In January 1917 alone, the Dutch Envoy in London inquired three times what justification Great Britain had to examine mail on Dutch ships in the Archipelago, which had often been stopped just outside the territorial waters.[12] The protests had always been fruitless. London's reaction was, as one civil servant in the Dutch Ministry of the Colonies chose to describe it, 'laconic'. Sometimes the British government waited for months before replying. It persisted in its opinion that the British Navy had every right to search neutral ships. Making matters even worse London usually also denied the allegation that Dutch ships had been searched in Netherlands Indies territorial waters.

In other instances The Hague was informed that 'enemy goods' had been seized or that seditious pamphlets had been found among the mail which aimed to incite 'His Majesty's Indian subjects to crime and rebellion'.[13] The British Foreign Office made it clear that such 'treasonable matter' fell 'into the category analogues of contraband'.[14] Such arguments – the same Dutch civil servant spoke of a 'fine line of reasoning' – failed to satisfy the Dutch government. Stubbornly The Hague continued to protest, pointing out that mail confiscated, including the materials considered dangerous by the British, was destined for a Dutch and not a British port. Great Britain should only examine post when it reached British India or the Malay Peninsula. It should not do so on board of Dutch merchantmen. In spite of the fact that such protests were futile the feeling of Dutch politicians was that to remain silent would not do if their cause were just. Some Dutch Members of Parliament even criticized Loudon for not remonstrating strongly enough.

Allied control of Dutch mail was stepped up even more after the United States had entered the war in April 1917 (but had refrained from declaring

---

[12] Foreign Office to De Marees van Swinderen, 10-2-1917, NA, Kol. Openbaar, Vb. 14-3-1917 49.
[13] Foreign Office to De Marees van Swinderen, 10-2-1917, NA, Kol. Openbaar, Vb. 14-3-1917 49.
[14] Note Ministry of the Colonies, 14-3-1917, NA, Kol. Openbaar, Vb. 14-3-1917 49.

war on Turkey), and because of Washington's refusal to be called an ally, formally became one of the Associated and Allied Powers fighting the Central Powers (Macmillan 2001:17, Oren 2007:340-50). The British government feared that with the United States in the Allied camp, the Netherlands Indies might become even more important as a base for Germano-Indian subversion in Asia. Beckett told a Dutch intelligence officer that British Indians from the United States and 'fanatical Germans' would be drawn to take up residence in the Netherlands Indies. This would turn the colony into the centre of the Germano-Indian plot.[15]

Such fears inspired London to decree in the middle of 1917 that Dutch ships no longer were allowed to carry ordinary letters and parcel post. Only official and commercial correspondence for which special permissions had been granted was permitted. Mail had to be sent either by British and, as of August 1917, by French mail. This meant that mail from the Netherlands Indies first had to be sent to Singapore on Dutch ships. There it was transferred to British and French ships. Initially the sender in the Netherlands Indies had a choice. He or she could write on the envelope whether letters and parcels should be send by French or British mail. In February 1918 the system was abolished. The mail was sent with whichever French or British ship left port first. The only liberty left was that a correspondent could request that mail be sent via the United States.

The mail service was also affected by the fact that intensified naval warfare made seaborne trade for ships sailing under neutral flags increasingly hazardous. The economic warfare and the war at sea presented neutral fleets with special dangers. Ships ran into mines or were hit by torpedoes or by surface gunfire from German submarines. From August 1914 to October 1916 the tonnage lost in the Dutch merchant fleet amounted to 100,000 tons, one-fifth of the total neutral tonnage lost, and half the damage inflicted on the Norwegian fleet.[16] Passengers travelling between Holland and the Netherlands Indies could take out a special insurance to cover the cost during the voyage if they were forced to stay in a hotel when the ship they sailed on was damaged and had to enter an 'emergency port'.

A spiral had been set in motion. Restrictions on neutral shipping by one side were answered by counter measures by the other, making shipping all the more dangerous. The Dutch viewed the escalation with alarm and indignation. As far as they could see, the efforts of the belligerents to inflict economic ruin upon one another would stop at nothing. One author concluded that during the war 'folios of international law became useless paper'. *De Locomotief*

[15] Report conversation with Beckett on 19 April 1917, NA, Kol. Geheim, Vb. 11-12-1917 A14.
[16] *New York Journal of Commerce*, cited in *Schepenvorderingswet* 1917:74.

spoke about 'the neutrals who are without rights'.[17]

The first indication of what lay in store had come on 8 August 1914 when Germany announced that it would lay mines at the entrance of enemy ports. Great Britain reacted by laying mines in the southern part of the North Sea in October. On 5 November 1914 London declared the North Sea a war zone, a region where mines were placed and neutral ships would be liable to searching. Besides creating a dangerous obstacle course, London tried to force neutral merchantmen to sail the Channel instead of taking the route around the northern part of the British Isles (Halpern 1994:49). Neutral ships also had to make a detour. They had to sail a narrow strip hugging to the British coast between the Straits of Dover and the Farne Islands near Berwick-upon-Tweed, just below the Scottish border. At the Farne Islands they had to sail on to the lighthouse of Landesnaes, from where they could continue southwards or northwards, depending on their destination. Loudon protested that this added a thousand sea miles to the voyage between Dover and Dutch ports.[18] The route made it almost impossible to avoid arrest by British warships and a search of the cargo.

Germany wanted exactly the opposite. Neutral ships should avoid the Channel. They should take the route around Scotland and Ireland. To try to force the issue Germany declared the waters around Great Britain and Ireland, including the Channel, a war zone on 4 February 1915. Berlin warned that all enemy merchantmen in the war zone would 'be destroyed without it always being possible to circumvent the dangers threatening the crew and passengers'.[19] The Dutch government was informed about the German step on 12 February. The letter contained the warning that the German Navy intended to make abundant use of sea mines in the area it had declared a war zone.[20] Such mines were not the only danger which threatened Dutch ships. Berlin left no doubt that neutral ships would not be immune to attacks, not only were there 'the accidents of naval warfare', but neutral flags were 'misused' by the British government.[21] The German Navy made an exception for northward-bound traffic around the Shetland Islands, for the eastern waters of the North Sea, and for a strip of thirty miles along the coast of the Netherlands. When Loudon asked Johnstone about the German claim that neutral flags were being misused, the British Ambassador replied that such a practice was an established stratagem. The British Merchant Shipping Act of 1894 allowed foreign merchantmen to raise the British flag if they were threatened with being

---

[17] Van Reigersberg Versluys 1917:3; *De Locomotief*, 16-3-1915.
[18] Loudon to Johnstone, 16-11-1914, *De Locomotief*, 25-3-1915.
[19] Proclamation, by Pohl, 4-2-1915, *State Papers* 1916:1031.
[20] Oranjeboek, cited in *De Locomotief*, 2-9-1916.
[21] Proclamation by Pohl, 4-2-1915, *State Papers* 1916:1031.

taken as a prize. Great Britain now wanted to adopt a similar means to avoid that British ships being taken as a prize or destroyed. Johnstone wrote that the Admiralty had not ordered British captains to do so, but would without any doubt certainly advise them to hoist a neutral flag to avoid aggression. It emerged that at least two British ships had sailed under Dutch colours. Loudon was not pleased. Van Aalst blamed Great Britain for the German declaration. Insurance companies reacted by raising war risk premiums.[22]

The hazard of falling victim to naval warfare forced the management of the Rotterdamsche Lloyd and Nederland, and of the Oceaan Shipping Line, whose ships only carried freight and no passengers, to keep their newest ships in port. The decision provided colonial export circles with one of the first occasions to grumble about the selfish policy of these shipping lines.

In another respect the Nederland and Rotterdamsche Lloyd also reacted quickly to the changing circumstances. A direct shipping link with New York, the Java-New York Line, was established at the end 1914. To avoid contraband control and searches, which would certainly have taken place if the existing procedure of transhipping cargo for the United States in Holland had been continued, outward-bound merchantmen from the Netherlands Indies sailed via South Africa, another new connection. On their return voyage to the Netherlands Indies, the ships passed through the Suez Canal. As with every other move by the two shipping companies, the opening of the new line was harshly criticized in the Netherlands Indies. It was claimed that the merchantmen which were used on the new line could have been employed to transport products from the Netherlands Indies to Europe.[23] Around the same time plans developed to connect the Netherlands Indies with New York via the Philippines and the Panama Canal were discarded for the time being. Yet another new line, the Java-Pacific Line, was created in December 1915. The first ship to take this route, the *Arakan*, called at Nagasaki and San Francisco in early 1916. In both ports her arrival drew plenty of attention from the local press and the authorities. Lustre was added by festivities to celebrate the new shipping link. In 1918 Idenburg would say in an interview in *De Telegraaf* that the Java-San Francisco Line was one of the few advantages the war had brought the Netherlands Indies.[24]

The sinking of Dutch ships invariably caused an outcry in Dutch society. It also received a fair share of attention in the Malay-language press, in which such incidents occasioned calls to support the Dutch government because neutrality might be in danger. At times the loss of Dutch ships marked the

---

[22] Johnstone to Loudon, 7-2-1915, Loudon to Johnstone, 15-2-1915, *De Locomotief*, 25-3-1915; interview with Van Aalst in *De Nieuwe Rotterdamsche Courant*, 19-2-1915, *De Locomotief*, 25-3-1915.
[23] *De Locomotief*, 12-1-1915.
[24] See for its text *Orgaan der Vereeniging 'Indië Weerbaar'* 1-3:13-4.

start of a mini-propaganda war between Germany and Great Britain. Each put the blame on the other. The German government would deny that a ship had been torpedoed by a German submarine and would attribute the disaster to British mines. The British from their part stressed that no British mines had been placed at the spot concerned. Occasionally when Germany could not disprove that a torpedo was to blame, Berlin suggested that the ship which had been sunk was an enemy ship sailing under Dutch colours. In other instances, after a formal Dutch protest and when it could be proved that a Dutch ship had been torpedoed in the waters the German Navy had reserved for neutral shipping, Berlin paid compensation for the sinking or damaging of Dutch ships.

Fear of a stepping-up of the German submarine campaign prompted shipping companies to decide to change the route of their vessels, or keep them in harbour. Maritime communications were seriously disrupted. What some Dutch people had foretold in August 1914, and had again been speculating about in January 1915 when rumours abounded that the Suez Canal was to be closed by the British, took on a concrete shape in 1916. To avoid the Suez Canal passenger ships of the Nederland and Rotterdamsche Lloyd, which in turn maintained a weekly passenger service between motherland and colony, began to sail around the Cape of Good Hope. The first ship to do so was the *Jan Pieterszoon Coen* of the Nederland which sailed from Amsterdam on 1 January 1916. Again people remonstrated that the decision to redirect the unprofitable passenger traffic had been inspired by purely selfish motives. Throughout 1915 it had been thought likely that the Suez Canal would soon become a theatre of war. Ships were only allowed to go through the Canal in daylight. Passengers had a full view of British soldiers who were there to defend the Canal against Turkish troops. To exacerbate the passengers' anxiety, sandbags were placed on the bridge to protect the captain, helmsman, and pilot against stray bullets. In December 1915 there were additional reasons to avoid the Suez Canal. The cause was not, as had been ventured in 1914, the closing of the Suez Canal by the British. The main reason given, presented by the Rotterdamsche Lloyd and Nederland as the only reason, was that bunkering in the Suez Canal had become too expensive. The operations of German and Austrian submarines in the Mediterranean had disrupted the supply of coal, with a sharp rise in price as the result. On the top of this was the consideration that in the Mediterranean ships might well have to sail through areas full of floating dead bodies of the passengers and crews of torpedoed troopships and merchantmen.

The voyage around the Cape (Van Limburg Stirum on his way to the Netherlands Indies was one of those who was forced to take this route) took almost fifty days, one-and-a-half to two weeks longer than through the Suez Canal route. The detour ineluctably meant extra sailing time. That mail boats and merchantmen, whatever the route they took, sailed at an 'economic rate' to save coal was another reason for the protracted voyage. The price of coal, to cite Abdoel Moeis, made it worth its weight in gold.[25] Further delays were caused because for safety reasons on many ships – even British ones – avoided the Suez Canal, and neutral ships had sometimes to wait for days before they could bunker, especially when Allied warships had arrived. The Dutch shipping companies charged their passengers for the supplementary costs for the extra meals such delays implied: 5 guilders 'per day per first class passenger, children in proportion'.[26]

The longer sea voyage created an uproar among civil servants in the Netherlands Indies. They were entitled to a European furlough of eight months, of which three now had to be spent at sea if they wanted to go home to Holland. Another consequence of the decision to re-route the mail boat was that mail had to be sent on freighters of the Nederland and Rotterdamsche Lloyd which still passed through the Suez Canal. Another option was to put it on ships of the Peninsular and Oriental Steam Navigation Company, which departed from Singapore and continued to go through the Canal. Because of the uncertainty that arose over the duration of the trip, the dates the mails from the Netherlands Indies arrived in Holland were wired to the Netherlands Indies, where they were published in the newspapers.

A total discontinuation of the Dutch mail service and passenger traffic threatened in February and March 1916 when four Dutch vessels were sunk in the North Sea. One was the *Tubantia*, 'the largest neutral ship sunk by submarines during the war' (Halpern 1994:307). She was torpedoed on 16 March. The *Palembang* of the Rotterdamsche Lloyd was sunk two days later. With her the furniture for the new drawing-room suite of the palace of the Governor General in Buitenzorg and the uniforms and livery of its staff which had been specially ordered in Holland by Van Limburg Stirum (as a gesture to his successor, Idenburg had had electric light and European-style bathrooms installed in the Palace) went to the bottom of the sea; which must have come as an extra blow to Van Limburg Stirum as he and his wife detested the way the Palace was furnished (Locher-Scholten 1981:59). Apprehension peaked when Directors of the Holland-Amerika Line visited Hamburg. Albert Ballin, still the Director of the Hamburg-Amerika Linie and a person of influence as adviser to the German government, told them that the time was approaching when German U-boats would no longer spare neutral shipping in the war zone. All ships sailing to and from Great Britain would be liable to attack. The news leaked out. The press in the Netherlands Indies carried Ballin's warning

---

[25] *Neratja*, 24-11-1917.
[26] *De Locomotief*, 17-11-1916.

in large bold type among the war telegrams. The disclaimer that followed was almost worse than useless. Crews in Dutch ports refused to sign on. If they had already done so, they were reluctant for their ship to put to sea. Ship's officers and engineers adopted the same attitude. At least two steamers bound for Great Britain could not sail from Holland. The crew was on board, but the officers had not turned up.

For the Nederland and the Rotterdamsche Lloyd Ballin's words were reason enough to call a temporary halt to all sailings. They delayed the departure of their ships from Dutch ports. Captains of passenger ships and freighters moored in foreign ports were instructed by wire not to sail until further notice. The management of the Rotterdamsche Lloyd and Nederland demanded that the Dutch government should take the measures necessary to guarantee safety at sea. Newspapers in the Netherlands Indies carried the announcement that it was no longer possible to book a passage to Holland. People who had already paid the reservation fee could ask their money back. The companies' attitude aroused disquiet in the Netherlands Indies, not least because it upset the plans of those who still intended to go to Holland for their leave. *De Locomotief* carried the news in extra large bold letters. The headline, again in bold letters, of the war telegram in *Oetoesan Hindia* called the decision a dangerous threat to the survival of the colony.[27] Both companies announced that they contemplated keeping their most precious passenger ships in port for the duration of the war. Their largest freighters would only sail the safe waters between the Netherlands Indies and the United States. The mail service between Holland and the Netherlands Indies could be continued by freighters, which would carry only a limited number of male passengers, with an urgent reason to travel.

The plans of the Nederland and Rotterdamsche Lloyd prompted intense consultation with the government. Representatives of the Nederland and Rotterdamsche Lloyd pointed out that what Ballin had said seemed to reflect the opinion of the political parties in Germany. After all, he was an influential adviser to the German Emperor. They told Pleyte that the passing through the Channel had become too dangerous to continue the mail and passenger services in the usual way. They took good care to mention that both companies had already lost more than one million guilders each maintaining the service. Mailships could perish. Indubitably when this happened this would be a great financial loss. Full insurance against war risk had become unaffordable. There were other, even more important considerations had to be taken into account. The loss of mailships could threaten the future of the Dutch mail service to and from the Netherlands Indies. It would take years before the ships could

---

[27] *Oetoesan Hindia*, 24-3-1916; *De Locomotief*, 15-4-1916.

be replaced. The Dutch shipbuilding yards had orders for the next three years, which meant that it would take five years before new passenger ships to replace the vessels sunk could be launched. The upshot might be that after the war German ships, safely anchored in German and neutral ports, would take over the passenger traffic between Holland and the Netherlands Indies.

Sailing around the northern tip of Scotland instead of through the Channel was an alternative. The representatives of the Nederland and Rotterdamsche Lloyd pointed out that its greatest drawback was in contrast to the Channel, there would be no other vessels nearby to come to the assistance of ships if and when disaster struck. They suggested a passenger service once a month, with the mailships under escort by a Dutch warship. If only male passengers were to be accepted, this would be enough. Mail and soldiers could be transported by freighters. The two companies suggested that the Ministry of the Colonies should issue a circular letter informing prospective government passengers that under the present circumstances it was irresponsible to take their family along.

The Nederland and Rotterdamsche Lloyd demanded two additional conditions. If accepted, they would shift part of the financial risk onto the government. The first was that the government should bear part of the cost of insurance against war risk. The second condition was that the government should promise that after the war because of ship losses the Nederland and Rotterdamsche Lloyd did not have the requisite number of ships to maintain a regular passenger service, the government would not conclude contracts for mail and passenger transport with foreign companies. If such a situation were to eventuate the Dutch government should bear the financial loss which the chartering of passenger ships by the two companies would entail.

The Nederland and Rotterdamsche Lloyd persisted in their demands, even though in a statement published in the Dutch press the German Envoy in The Hague denied that Germany would step up its naval warfare. They demanded that the Dutch government ask Berlin for a guarantee that the German Navy would not attack ships of the Nederland and Rotterdamsche Lloyd. Without such a guarantee none of their ships, not even their freighters, would sail. If an assurance had been given there would also no longer be any need for an armed escort. If sailing could be resumed the Nederland and Rotterdamsche Lloyd now suggested a service every three weeks, using only their older passenger ships. These ships should avoid the Channel and take a route around Scotland. On part of the trip through the North Sea, as far as north of the Dogger Bank, the passenger ships should be escorted by a tugboat, which could come to their assistance should an emergency arise.

Pleyte refused to ask Berlin for a guarantee. He was also not prepared to explore what would happen after the war, or to issue a warning to the passengers not to take their families with them. The only concession he was prepared to make was to contribute to the war risk insurance, but less than the sum the companies had asked for. When the Nederland and the Rotterdamsche Lloyd persisted in their demands, at the end of April Pleyte informed their Boards of Directors that their attitude had 'very much disappointed' him, all the more so because freighters – which were making large profits – had resumed sailings. Pleyte was anxious to keep passenger traffic going. He reminded the two companies of their contract with the Dutch government and threatened that actions could follow.

Respite came in May 1916. The German U-boat campaign was temporarily halted. Berlin wanted to avoid complications with the United States which could follow from American ships being sunk or Americans being killed on Allied ships which were torpedoed. When this news broke, the mail service was resumed, first only once in the three weeks, than once in the two weeks. The route taken was that around the Cape of Good Hope. Passenger ships departed once every ten days. It was a short reprieve. This time the British were the culprit. The end came in September 1916, when the Foreign Office in London announced that Allied interests demanded that neutral ships would only be provided with British coals if 30 per cent of the tonnage was handed over in return. Driving home the message, Great Britain threatened that Dutch ships using German coal would be stopped and that the coal would be confiscated. In fact, the threat was never put into practice (Van Dorp 1920:211). Nevertheless, Dutch ships could no longer bunker in South Africa or in Delagoa Bay. This put an end to trade from Holland and the Netherlands Indies with that region. The consequence was that Dutch ships again had to pass through the Suez Canal from November 1916; which in a sense was not very bad as it saved coal.

Routes and the dangers posed by the war at sea were not the only problems hanging over Dutch shipping. Most Dutch seaborne transport was carried on Dutch ships. The Allied Powers needed their own freighters for transporting their own goods and troops. Lack of tonnage became even more acute because in 1915 and 1916 Dutch ships were needed for the transport of food, fertilizers, and fodder to Holland.

Shortage of tonnage demanded that government control over shipping was essential. Every sinew had to be strained to prevent Holland having to do without essential imports because of a shortage of tonnage. In the course of the war, the Dutch government progressively increased its control over Dutch shipping. The chartering of Dutch ships to foreign ports was forbidden in January 1916. A permit was required for Dutch ships leaving Dutch ports in March 1916. The requisitioning of freighters and of cargo space for the shipment of food from the United States and the Netherlands Indies to Holland and for the import of good from other countries which were deemed essential introduced another factor determining the flow of ships after the middle of 1916. In The Hague the Minister of Agriculture, Industry, and Trade, F.E. Posthuma, rose to prominence in connection with the sailing of Dutch ships. Posthuma, who would earn himself the nickname the 'big ships requisitioner', tried to play down the effects of requisitioning. In January 1917, he told Parliament that in the last six months of 1916, only 7 to 8,000 tons had been requisitioned monthly from the Nederland and Rotterdamsche Lloyd. The drop in tonnage available for colonial trade from between 1.3 and 1.5 million to 895.000 tons, he attributed almost fully to the disappearance of the German freight trade, requisitioning of tonnage of freighters of the Dutch-British Oceaan Shipping Company by the British government, the longer duration of voyages caused by the route around Scotland and the Cape, and delays in ports.[28] Representatives of the shipping and commercial sector took a dim view of his claims. The annual report of the Rotterdamsche Lloyd argued that the commandeering of five freighters to transport grain from the United States to Holland at the end of 1916 had dislocated shipping. It had robbed the Rotterdamsche Lloyd of most of its tonnage for the trade between Holland and the Netherlands Indies. The Rotterdamsche Lloyd could employ only one ship for this purpose in January and February 1917, the period when most colonial crops were exported.[29]

Up to the end of 1916 the requisitioning of tonnage had barely attracted any attention in the Netherlands Indies. The permits to sail which were required in Holland did have their consequences, but these did not affect the colony much. The permission could be coupled with a promise by the owner that the ship in question should return before a specific date to transport food to Holland. It had also obliged the Nederland and Rotterdamsche Lloyd to reserve 75 per cent of the cargo hold of freighters and 25 per cent of that of passenger ships sailing from the Netherlands Indies to Holland for food for Holland. From the point of view of the authorities the weak point of the system was that it only affected ships leaving Dutch ports. The authority of the Dutch government did not extend to Dutch ships sailing between foreign ports or between foreign ports and the Netherlands Indies. This loophole had enabled the shipping companies to redirect freighters from non-Dutch ports to the Netherlands Indies to alleviate the shortage of tonnage there to as late as November 1916.

Anxiety struck in the Netherlands Indies when in the final days of 1916 news reached the colony that the Dutch government was preparing a general ship requisitioning act. *De Locomotief* predicted a 'disastrous situation'

---

[28] *Handelingen Tweede Kamer* 1916-17:1160; *Schepenvorderingswet* 1917:29.
[29] Petition of Handelsvereeniging te Batavia to Van Limburg Stirum, 24-7-1917, NA, Kol. Geheim, Mr. 1917/194x; Voogd 1914:69.

if the tonnage which was still available were to decrease even more.[30] How far the new powers of the government in The Hague would reach was not yet clear. Some reports suggested that the new act would allow the government to requisition 75 per cent of the tonnage, others spoke about 75 per cent of the tonnage of freighters and 25 per cent of that of mail boats. The most pessimistic view was that the government would demand 100 per cent of the tonnage. As always when The Hague took decisions which displeased the Dutch colonial community, there was much grumbling about people living far away in Holland who were ignorant about the situation in the Netherlands Indies but nevertheless took decisions without any effort to consult people in the Netherlands Indies in advance and without taking colonial interests into account. The Governor General and his advisers also did not know what lay in store. They had to wait for news from The Hague.

Trading associations, chambers of commerce, estate organizations, the Nederlandsch-Indisch Landbouwsyndicaat (Netherlands Indies Agricultural Syndicate), and representatives of shipping companies appealed to the Governor General and to Parliament in The Hague not to decrease the tonnage available in the Netherlands Indies even more, and to take the interests of colonial trade into consideration. This was to become a standard phrase, and the negative consequences of a drop in export for the indigenous population. The head-offices of colonial firms in Holland joined the protests. They pointed out that the requisitioning of ships was responsible for the drop in exports from the Netherlands Indies from about 1.5 million tons in 1915 to 900,000 tons in 1916. In a petition to Parliament, they stressed that were requisitioning to be continued the trading houses would not be the only ones to suffer. Estates, with their hundreds of thousands of labourers, would be forced to dismiss part of their workforce. The outcome would be a 'depression among the native population'. It was also noted that the first to suffer would be the native producers of colonial wares. They had no storage facilities and sold their product immediately after harvest. The appeals were met with stony silence. The only reaction was a promise by the Ministry of the Colonies that there was no prospect of the requisition of the total tonnage of the Dutch merchant fleet and that a regular shipping between motherland and colony would be maintained. The assurance was too vaguely worded to appease the commercial community. It was generally considered to be too vague and only resulted in more unease in the Netherlands Indies.[31]

A Schepenvorderingswet (Ships' Requisitioning Act) was promulgated in February. The act gave Posthuma the authority to requisition all Dutch ocean-

---

[30] *De Locomotief,* 31-1-1917.
[31] Report 1917 Vereeniging van Landbouw en Nijverheid in Djember, cited in *De Locomotief,* 16-4-1918; *Schepenvorderingswet* 1917:14-5, 19.

going ships to carry imports to Holland, irrespective of the port at which they were anchored. Responding to his critics, Posthuma pointed out the extraordinary profits being made by ship-owners who refused to take national interests into account. He promised that for the time being mail boats would remain exempt from requisition.[32]

The reason that requisitioning of ships created such an uproar in colonial commercial and estate circles was not that ships were used to transport food to Holland. The need for this was recognized. The fact that, besides grain from the United States, Rangoon rice from Burma had to be shipped to Holland was difficult to swallow in the Netherlands Indies. There, a businessman wrote, 'beautiful Java rice' was rotting in ports, presumably because there was much more money in Burma rice for Dutch rice-mills.[33] The beautiful Java rice lying rotting concerned a shipment bought by the British in November 1916. Most of it could not be shipped, initially because the British government requisitioned part of the tonnage of the ocean freighter destined to transport the rice, and thereupon because Batavia refused to extend the export permit.

The Burma rice was a minor detail. What roused indignation was the suspicion that the Dutch government had requisitioned Dutch freighters for purely financial reasons. People in the Netherlands Indies protested that Scandinavian or American vessels could easily have been chartered, but that the Dutch government had baulked at the cost. By opting for the cheapest solution, The Hague had deprived – robbed was another word used – the Netherlands Indies of valuable tonnage.[34] A newspaper in Semarang spoke about 'the shipping scandal'. Its editor was enraged by the fact that to save the Dutch Treasury money, Posthuma had brought the Netherlands Indies to the brink of a crash. The trading houses in the Netherlands Indies would certainly have voluntarily collected up the money Posthuma had saved had they known in advance that money was the reason. But, 'this is precisely the dreadfulness, the reason for ire in this case, because nobody here knew exactly [...] why the Netherlands Indies had been so cruelly abandoned by the motherland, was therefore heavily damaged, was so shamefully neglected'.[35] Members of the Dutch Senate agreed. Van Kol concluded that the Dutch government had to share responsibility for the tonnage problem because it had requisitioned Dutch freighters at a time when there had still been neutral steamers for charter: 'The Indies, however, had no voice and the guardian decided over the ward and withheld from it ships to which it was entitled'.[36]

---

[32] *Schepenvorderingswet* 1917:11, 13.
[33] *Schepenvorderingswet* 1917:99.
[34] *Algemeen Handelsblad*, cited in *De Indische Gids* 1917, II:1254-5.
[35] *De Nieuwe Courant*, cited in *De Indische Gids* 1917, II:1595.
[36] *Handelingen Eerste Kamer* 1917-18:156

To demonstrate how serious the consequences of requisitioning would be, the newly founded Vereeniging voor de Studie van Koloniaal-Maatschappelijke Vraagstukken (Society for the Study of Colonial Social Questions) set up an inquiry among sixty leading commercial figures in the colony in January 1917. They, Emil Helfferich was one of them, were asked to give their opinion about the consequences for the colonial export and estate sector, for the indigenous producers of export wares, and for the Chinese and Arab middlemen, of the requisitioning of freighters.[37] One of the conclusions was that the indigenous producer for the export market would suffer most. One respondent pointed out that one of the reasons for this was that natives lived from hand to mouth and did not build up financial reserves.[38]

In the Netherlands Indies, the requisitioning of ships was seen as yet another example of the Cinderella treatment of the colony by policy makers in Holland, who were unfamiliar with colonial circumstances. Fears were expressed that the feeding of Holland would be given undue preference to the detriment of international colonial trade, because people in Holland were unacquainted with the needs of the Netherlands Indies. Regular exports of colonial wares were vital. The economy of the Netherlands and of the Netherlands Indies depended on colonial trade.[39] A Member of Parliament in Holland, who shared this view, pointed out that Holland had a population of 6 million people, the Netherlands Indies one of 40 million. Were exports from the Netherlands Indies to grind to a halt, 'want and famine' in the colony would be the inexorable result.[40] This was where the real centre of gravity lay in the weighing up of the pros and cons which had to be made. Not – as the board of the Study Society accused Posthuma to underline his ignorance of colonial economic relations – that between a hungry Holland and a few trading houses in the Netherlands Indies. Many in the colony, first and foremost the indigenous population, would face dire poverty if colonial exports came to a halt.[41]

The commercial communities in Batavia and Semarang protested. Their members suggested to allow for scope for the continuation of exports from the Netherlands Indies, a maximum volume of tonnage that could be requisitioned for the shipping of food to Holland should be fixed.[42] Upset 'interested parties in trade and shipping' met in protest in Batavia at the end of July 1917.

---

[37] *Schepenvorderingswet* 1917:2.
[38] *Schepenvorderingswet* 1917:47.
[39] Handelsvereeniging te Batavia to Van Limburg Stirum, 24-7-1917, NA, Kol. Geheim, Mr. 1917/194x.
[40] *Schepenvorderingswet* 1917:25.
[41] *Schepenvorderingswet* 1917:78, 80.
[42] Report 1917 Handelsvereeniging te Semarang, cited in *De Locomotief*, 10-5-1918.

A six-page petition was drawn up.[43] Arguing that 'Greater Netherlands' interests' should not be sacrificed for those of the motherland, the petition spoke of a 'serious concern about the nearest future', not only regarding the estates but also the colony at large. If the export and production of colonial wares came to a halt, native exporters would suffer and hundreds of thousands of labourers would lose their income. The result would be a 'very difficult domestic situation'. All this meant that the requisitioning of ships in the Netherlands Indies could not be left to the tender mercies of Posthuma, who was said to have little affinity with colonial affairs. The petitioners deemed it necessary that Van Limburg Stirum be consulted in advance. On the same day, the Planters Association of Deli and the Association of Rubber Planters at the East Coast of Sumatra drew up a petition of a similar purport. They asked for more freighters, absolutely not fewer, to sail to San Francisco.[44] Other protests came from the boards of trading firms and estate companies located in Holland: 196 in total. Later, in June, the Rotterdam Chamber of Commerce sent a deputation to Posthuma to convince him of the importance of colonial trade.

Pleyte tried to reassure the business community at the end of August by wiring Van Limburg Stirum that for the time being Posthuma did not consider the requisitioning of ships in Asian waters.[45] Belying these words, The Hague demanded freighters to ship rice and coffee to Holland for Dutch soldiers in the closing months of 1917. These ships were, in the words of the day, 'requisitioned by Posthuma'.

To the great frustration of the trading community in the Netherlands Indies requisitioned Dutch ships awaiting orders often lay idle in Dutch and other ports for a considerable time, for months even. They were not sent from Holland to Asia to assist in the export of colonial wares. It was considered a clear sign of how little thought was expended on the interests of the colony by the decision makers in Holland. In the Netherlands Indies ships also tarried in port for a long time. Batavia was given to understand that these could have sailed to British India, China, or Japan and back. The fact that this had not happened was a tremendous shame in view of the 'emergency in the Netherlands' and the extra financial loss to exporters, who had to spend extra money for storage.[46]

The Hague and Batavia were not the only culprits to be blamed for the delays in the sailing of ships. The British government was a complicating fac-

---

[43] Engels to Van Limburg Stirum, 25-7-1917, NA, Kol. Geheim, Mr. 1917/194x.
[44] Deli Plantersvereeniging to Van Limburg Stirum, 24-7-1917, NA, Kol. Geheim, Mr. 1917/194x.
[45] General secretary to NIPA and Aneta, 20-8-1917, NA, Kol. Geheim, Mr. 1917/194x.
[46] Handelsvereeniging Soerabaja to Van Limburg Stirum, 25-1-1918, NA, Kol. Geheim, Mr. 1918/110x.

tor. In Batavia, the British Consul General made it clear that he had the final say in the sailing of merchantmen to Holland. In January 1918, after learning about the requisitions the new Consul General, W.N. Dunn, assured the agent of the Nederland that he had been authorized by his government to assist 'in a manner which will obviate delays'.[47] But before he gave his consent, he demanded lists of the exporters, of the products shipped, and of the consignees in Holland. He made it plain that only after he had received approval from London would ships be allowed to depart for Europe.[48]

In November 1916 Dutch ships, which could no longer sail around the Cape of Good Hope because of bunkering problems, had started to use the Suez Canal again. It was a nerve wrecking voyage. One of the ships to do so was the *Sindoro*, which had sailed on 3 January 1917. In his travel report Abdoel Moeis relates how nervous the passengers were when the *Sindoro* was in the Mediterranean Sea. At night passengers left the doors of their cabins open or slept with their lifebelt on. Others were afraid to go to their cabins. They tried to sleep on deck but could not because it was too cold.

Any idea of a direct shipping link between Holland and the Netherlands Indies was abandoned after Berlin, deliberately taking the risk that European neutrals including the Netherlands might join the Allied camp, decided to resume an all-out submarine war in January 1917. Convinced such economic isolation would bring Great Britain to its knees, the German Navy declared unrestricted submarine warfare. German submarines would sink all neutral merchantmen bound for enemy territory. Sailing to the United States was confined to a small 'free or safe channel', where neutral merchantmen would not be attacked. In the 'forbidden zone', the *Sperrgebiet*, which was compared with the no man's land between trenches by Berlin, all shipping was at risk of being torpedoed. One Dutch ferry a day was allowed between Flushing and Harwich.[49] Dutch ships bound for the United States were now forced to sail almost due north through a channel to the Norwegian coast. To the left of this lurked German submarines. To the right was an area teeming with German and British mines. Having reached the Norwegian coast, ships turned west in the direction of the United States.

No such safe channel was arranged through the Straits of Gibraltar and the Mediterranean, effectively closing route through the Suez Canal for the rest of the war. At that moment one Dutch ship, the *Prinses Juliana*, had just reached Port Said on her way to Holland. She returned to the Netherlands Indies. Passengers were given the choice of sailing back to the Netherlands Indies or

---

[47] Dunn to Van den Bosch, 30-1-1918, NA, Kol. Geheim, Mr. 1918/59x.
[48] Van den Bosch to General Secretariat, 4-2-1918, NA, Kol. Geheim, Mr. 1918/59x.
[49] Halpern 1994:340; *De Locomotief*, 20-11-1917.

continuing their journey on a non-Dutch ship at their own risk. Freight was unloaded at the ports where it had originally been taken aboard. In retrospect, the Dutch Ministry of the Colonies wrote that the announcement presented a 'great hindrance to shipping'.[50]

The telegram stating that Germany had declared 'a merciless submarine war' was published in bold type in newspapers in the Netherlands Indies.[51] People there thought that the German measure was primarily directed against Dutch shipping.[52] Despite the athmosphere of doom and gloom some could detect one bright side. Great Britain might allow Dutch ships to sail the Atlantic Ocean without obliging them to call in at a British port. When it was erroneously reported that London had indeed done so, *De Locomotief* wrote that Great Britain had saved colonial shipping.[53] From The Hague the Minister of the Colonies sent a telegram to the Governor General issuing a blanket prohibition on the sailing of all ships. The *Kawi*, which was already on her way, was forced to remain in Padang. Freight traffic with Europe was temporarily halted. In the newspapers in the Netherlands Indies it was announced that no cargo for Holland would any longer be accepted. The Nederland and Rotterdamsche Lloyd also announced that for the time being freighters only would sail from Holland to the Netherlands Indies. The route they would take was through the Panama Canal. In Holland the head offices of the Nederland and the Rotterdamsche Lloyd cancelled all contracts and announced an adjustment to passenger and freight prices to cover the extra costs the longer sea voyage entailed. Indignation in the commercial community in the Netherlands Indies was the result (Cramer 1916-17:410; Hogesteeger 1995:71-3). *De Locomotief* wrote that the shipping companies could only get away with such a breach of contract because exporters were completely dependent on them.[54]

It must also have come as a shock when the Nederland and the Rotterdamsche Lloyd announced the discontinuation of passenger service a few days later and ordered their agents in the Netherlands Indies to cancel all bookings and to refund fares already paid. Within days yet another report was published in the newspapers alleging that a system to open a passenger service via the United States in which the passengers would have to travel between New York and San Francisco by rail was under consideration. Civil servants who had resigned in the expectation that they could travel to Holland were promised that wherever possible they could take up their former position

---

[50] *Koloniaal verslag* 1918:203-4.
[51] *De Locomotief*, 2-2-1917.
[52] *De Locomotief*, 3-2-1917.
[53] *De Locomotief*, 15-2-1917.
[54] *De Locomotief*, 6-3-1917.

again. All leaves of absence of civil servants who intended to travel to Europe were initially deferred. A few weeks, later when the possibility for passenger transport via the United States was opened Batavia magnanimously allowed its civil servants who, as an announcement of the Governor General phrased this, still wanted to spend their leave in Europe 'despite the serious drawbacks which encumbered the journey in the present situation journey', to take this route.[55] This was as far as its graciousness extended. It refused to compensate for the extra costs travelling via the United States. Batavia only paid the full fare for civil servants and officers who had retired, whose contract had expired, or who needed medical treatment in Holland. The fare for the rail journey to New York would be paid by the Dutch Consul in San Francisco. Some adventurous persons even tried to reach Europe via China and Siberia.

De Locomotief predicted war. Its editor could understand that Berlin wanted to enforce as complete a blockade of Great Britain as London wanted to cut it off, but feared that, contrary to the British blockade, its German counterpart would only be much more hazardous to neutral ships. When neutral freighters were sunk, the neutral countries might well unite and declare war on the Continental Powers. The newspaper also noted that 'resentment and bitterness [...] knew no bounds'. As on other occasions, when new measures of the belligerents hurt at the interests of the Netherlands and its colony, people clamoured for war. The editor could not understand this. War with Great Britain would mean the end of the Netherlands Indies, war with Germany would bring the 'bloody downfall of the motherland'.[56] Nevertheless, all this was tinged with admiration. Impressed by the accomplishments of this 'guerrilla war at sea,' advocates of a strengthening of the colonial fleet adduced submarines as a major asset for the defence of the Netherlands Indies (Van Heutsz 1917a:19).

Not everyone was brimming with such belligerence. For a moment it seemed that the anxiety which had gripped the colony in August 1914 had reappeared. There was hunger for news. At the end of March the *Bataviaasch Nieuwsblad* announced that it would publish a morning edition for the duration of the war.[57] Shops prepared for a run which did not materialize on a large scale. What did happen was that, calculating that imported goods might rise in prices significantly, Chinese traders tried to buy up the stores of European shops whose owners, expecting the same, usually refused to sell the bulk of their stock. As in other times of heightened political tension, all kinds of scenarios and rumours were banded around. After the United States had severed diplomatic relations with Germany on 3 February, one of these had it that the

[55] *De Locomotief*, 12-3-1917.
[56] *De Locomotief*, 3-2-1917.
[57] *De Locomotief*, 29-3-1917.

two countries were at war and that the Netherlands had joined in on the side of the United Stated. To prepare for the worst ambulance classes were organized again. From Banjermasin in Borneo it was reported with some pride that women attended shooting practices with revolvers and Mauser rifles.[58]

With the prospect of war well and truly in the offing people established branches of Onze Vloot and Indië Weerbaar and launched new membership drives for the volunteer corps. The army decided to contribute to the uniform of the volunteer corps. The handing out of shoes was considered especially important. In the past, poor people had not joined up because they had not wanted to 'wear out their only pair of shoes by marching in terrain befouled with mud and stumbling over stones'.[59] Je Maintiendrai came to the assistance of the Medan volunteer corps. Membership of the corps rose to 400 in 1917. When, still in 1917, indigenous Indonesians were admitted to the Medan volunteer corps (but only to the legally allowed one-quarter of the total strength) membership swelled to 600. At that time it had probably become one of the best trained and best equipped corps. In February 1918 the colonial army allowed it to use three machine-guns.

Batavia also was goaded into action. The authorities had already found out that the *Marie*, which had entered the port of Tanjung Priok in May 1916, was not a German-owned ship but a prize. Nevertheless it had not taken action and had not interned her crew as international law required. Now, suddenly, the Navy confiscated the vessel and its crew was ordered to disembark, but was not interned. *De Locomotief* reported that they were well looked after by the shipping company.[60]

The *Kawi* was the first mail boat which took the route through the Panama Canal. She left Padang in Sumatra in the middle of February 1917 and arrived in Rotterdam on 25 June. The *Kawi* had sailed via Japan to San Francisco. From there she had taken the Panama Canal to Newsport News near Norfolk, Virginia. She remained anchored in Newsport News for seven weeks. After a second delay of a week in Halifax, Nova Scotia, in Canada, the base of the British North American Naval Squadron and the port the British had decided where Europe-bound neutral ships could best be checked on cargo and passengers, the *Kawi* finally crossed the Atlantic Ocean. She in total sailed almost 19,000 English miles, 10,000 more than had she taken the route via the Suez Canal (Hogesteeger 1995:73).

The *Kawi* was also the last passenger ship from the Netherlands Indies to pass through the Panama Canal. The all-out submarine war had made sailing the Atlantic Ocean too hazardous to risk expensive ships. From March 1917

---

[58] *De Locomotief*, 16-2-1917.
[59] *De Locomotief*, 20-2-1917.
[60] *De Locomotief*, 15-2-1917.

mail boats from the Netherlands Indies sailed only to San Francisco. From San Francisco passengers had to travel on to New York by train. There, if lucky, they could board a ship to Holland. Passengers from Holland had to travel overland from New York to San Francisco. Shipping and the mail connection between Holland and the Netherlands Indies had become highly irregular. Nobody could any longer have any inkling how long a voyage would take. In ports in Holland it became an 'event' when a ship from the Netherlands Indies put in.

Dutch shipping had become so disrupted by the war at sea being waged by the British and the Germans that even the crippled link between motherland and colony was presented as an achievement. The report about 1917 given by Pleyte to the Dutch Parliament proudly stated that because of this 'new passenger line', it had been possible to 'maintain the connection between the Netherlands and the Netherlands Indies under the national flag'. The report did not mention that not all had run as smoothly as these words indicated. Once passengers had arrived in New York or San Francisco, all they could do was hope that a ship was available for their onward journey, and that she would indeed sail. After they had taken the train to New York, passengers who had left Java at the end of May on board the *Tjisondari* discovered that there was no onward connection to Holland. In their distress they founded an Association of Stranded Dutch People. In vain they looked for help. They turned to the Dutch Consul, who referred them to the British Consul, who in turn advised them to contact the Dutch Envoy in London. Recalling how in comparable circumstances Dutch shipping had come to the assistance of stranded Americans in Europe after the outbreak of the war made no impression. Most decided that it was best not to try to travel on to Holland but to return to Java.

Likewise, only two Dutch passenger ships were available for the onward voyage to Java for the 1,500 passengers of the *Nieuw-Amsterdam* who had arrived in New York in February 1918. Each could carry only one hundred passengers. Those fortunate enough to travel on reported that the 'rest of the journey was very enjoyable, the weather was good and the food on board was excellent'.[61] The others had to wait patiently. Some took passage to Singapore on American ships, others first boarded a Japanese ship to Hong Kong, where they transferred to a British ship bound for Singapore. For many, including those travelling in the opposite direction, the long delay meant that they had a 'hard time' (Van Heekeren 1918:192). Sea travel had become a source of anxiety for passengers and their families. Passengers were not sure when their ship would finally arrive. Family and friends were left in the dark for weeks about

---

61   *De Locomotief*, 3-4-1918.

where the ship was. They began to worry in earnest when the ship did not reach port at the planned date of arrival. Telegrams sent to New York about the fate of the ship remained unanswered.

The entry of the United States in the war in April 1917 made travelling even more difficult. To prevent German spies or couriers from entering the country, immigration rules were tightened. When rumours spread that Germans had attempted to smuggle in poison to destroy the American harvest, the examination of disembarking passengers became only the more stringent. Drinks, powders, toothpaste, soap, and medicines were confiscated because German poison might be concealed in such goods. Onward passengers had to part temporarily with papers and books, which were bundled and forwarded to San Francisco or New York.

Except with a special permission in May 1917 'natives' from the Netherlands Indies were no longer permitted to enter the country. The American definition of natives included Europeans born in the colony, which must have come as a shock to many of them. When the Ministry of the Colonies in The Hague learned about the strict American immigration rules, it was assailed by fears that on their return journey to Java the members of the Indië Weerbaar deputation could well fall victim to the new American immigration policy. The American government was contacted to ensure that Rhemrev, Abdoel Moeis, and the other members could travel on from New York to San Francisco without encountering any problems. Washington consented. For other people born in the Netherlands Indies, even when they were civil servants, no exception was made. Further careful negotiations were pursued before Washington finally promised to make an exception in the American immigration rules for Dutch civil servants who had not been born in Holland and for first-class passengers.

The lengthy reports and letters sent to and fro by mail between Pleyte and Van Limburg Stirum had to follow the same time-consuming and precarious route. A special courier guarded the mail on the train journey between San Francisco and New York. One of the consequences was that the Ministry of the Colonies in The Hague was deprived of the information which – for legal and bureaucratic reasons – it needed to formulate policy, including the drafting of the colonial budget. Batavia had to do without detailed consultation with The Hague, forcing Van Limburg Stirum to take a more independent course.

CHAPTER XVI

Gloomy prospects

All circumstances considered, the Netherlands fared reasonably well during the first two years of the war. Most pleasing was that the export of agricultural produce proved a gold mine. In Holland shipping and agriculture prospered, while the 'OW'er' or war profiteer made its appearance as an accepted term in Dutch language. In the course of 1916 most of the committees which had been established at the outbreak of the war to support the destitute were disbanded. The stated reason was that unemployment had dropped and was no longer a serious problem. In Batavia, the Central Committee for Relief of the Destitute in Holland and the Netherlands Indies followed the trend in November. The 16,000 guilders it still had in hand went to the Red Cross in the Netherlands Indies.

In the Netherlands Indies too the overall picture in 1915 and 1916 was not as bad as had initially been predicted. Far away from the battlefields, the Netherlands Indies remained 'the most blessed place on God's earth' (Van Heekeren 1919b:139). The gloomy picture many people in Holland and the Netherlands Indies had sketched in August 1914 never eventuated. After the outbreak of the war, estates and other companies had fired staff, or had cut their salary. Nevertheless, the number of Europeans who had lost their job had remained small, and should be counted in the dozens, not in hundreds. In 1915 and 1916 domestic trade in a number of regions in the Netherlands Indies, but not all, recovered from the recession in the closing months in 1914.

The high prices estate products fetched abroad presented a rosy picture. At the Exchange in Batavia, which had partly reopened in April 1915 and had become fully operational again in November of the same year, prices had soon recovered. In early 1916 it was noted with some satisfaction 'how unexpectedly well the stock market, of course following that in the motherland, had overcome the crisis which had looked so threatening.'[1] In its report for 1916-1917 the Javasche Bank remarked that profits were high. With respect to sugar

---

[1] Report Department of Agriculture, Industry and Trade, cited in *De Locomotief*, 28-3-1916.

they were 'even splendid'.[2] The value of exports increased from 614 million guilders in 1913 to 854 million guilders in 1916 (Lovink 1919:13). Overlooked in the jubilation was that the good performance of the colonial export sector could be attributed to one or two products. In Semarang, to give an example, the value of exports rose in 1916 by 25.5 million guilders, but the major reason for this had been an increase in the export of sugar by 20.75 million guilders.[3]

In view of the excellent performance of the sugar industry, a special sugar tax was introduced in the Netherlands Indies in July 1916. The tax never became effective. In October Batavia announced that the sugar tax would not be levied because the government preferred a general war profit tax. As so many other economic and financial decisions the war profit tax triggered off a bitter debate in the colony. A war profit tax of 30 per cent was instituted in both the Netherlands and the Netherlands Indies. People felt that they were being treated unfairly by the mother country. The crux of the matter was that the act on war profits promulgated in 1916 in The Hague stipulated that war profits of companies which were active in the Netherlands Indies (or in Suriname and the Netherlands Antilles) but had their headquarters in Holland would be taxed in the mother country. Consequently, the regulation on war profit tax in the Netherlands Indies of 1917 exempted such companies from paying war profit tax levied in the colony. The war profit tax they paid in Holland had to be divided equally between colony and mother country. People in the Netherlands Indies argued that such a construction was unfair. The colony was entitled to all taxes on war profits made in the Netherlands Indies and not just to half of them. By an overwhelming majority, the People's Council passed a motion to this effect.[4]

In the closing months of 1916 conditions deteriorated. By 1917 the picture had changed completely. In Holland industry was hit by a shortage of coal and raw materials, forcing factories to close down. Committees to support the destitute once again gained prominence. People took to the streets to demonstrate against dearth of food. The reports in the newspapers of the Netherlands Indies about the dire economic conditions in Holland were so alarming that in February 1917 Van Limburg Stirum asked by wire for confirmation of the news carried and he suggested that telegrams to the Netherlands Indies should be censored to avoid any unnecessary commotion there. Pleyte issued instructions to this effect. He hastened to assure Van Limburg Stirum that conditions in Holland were not as bad as they appeared. There had only been

---

[2] Annual report of the Javasche Bank over 1916-1917, cited in Helfferich 1917.
[3] Report 1917 Handelsvereeniging Semarang, cited in *De Locomotief*, 1-5-1918.
[4] *Volksraad* 1918:523.

'insignificant disturbances incited by anarchists'.[5]

In the Netherlands Indies, the estate sector and the trading companies, and not just the Dutch- and German-owned ones, but also their British and French counterparts, were not spared the negative consequences of the war. The same can be said about native producers, usually hit even harder than the European ones. A combination of factors was at work. Trade restrictions imposed by the Allied Powers and the NOT played a role as did differential im- and export duties imposed in Great Britain and its colonies and possessions to discourage neutral trade. The dangers posed by the German submarine war also cannot be excluded from the equation. Most important of all, however, and increasingly so, was the lack of tonnage. The number of ships available was no longer enough to transport all exports from the Netherlands Indies. Stocks piled up. Warehouses in the ports and on the estates could no longer accommodate the growing stocks. At the end of 1916, the volume of products which could not be shipped was estimated to have reached a value of over 100 million guilders.

One of the products to suffer was coffee. Initially, coffee had been one of the few products which could be imported freely into Holland. Re-exports to Germany and Austria-Hungary had guaranteed good prices. The turning point came in the middle of 1916 when the NOT restricted the import of the coffee ready for shipment to Holland to 30 per cent. No alternative markets were found. Prices fell. Robusta coffee, which at the start of 1916 had still fetched 100 guilders per picul, at the end of the year fetched no more than 32.50 guilders per picul. The price of Java coffee displayed a similar pattern. As traders had bought large quantities of coffee against a considerably higher price, the financial losses were great. Inevitably native producers suffered. Though the NOT tried to reserve part of the quotum to what was designated native coffee, preference was given to the import of prime class quality coffee. In 1916 about half a million picul of the coffee harvest could not be shipped.

The export of tea, mainly produced in West Java, was another victim. At the beginning of 1916 the importers of tea in Holland were only allowed to sell to a restricted number of firms in Holland. These had all been selected by a special tea commission which had been forced upon the tea importers by the NOT At the end of the year the tea trade was hurt even more grievously by what the Ministry of the Colonies described as 'orders received from the NOT'. Shipping companies were no longer allowed to transport tea to Holland.

The export of sugar began to decline at the end of 1916. The sugar industry feared the worst. Leaders of the Suikerbond, the union of those employed on sugar estates, told their members in February 1917 that 'they were on the eve

---

[5] Pleyte to Van Limburg Stirum, NA, Kol. Geheim, Vb. 12-2-1917 L3.

of a crisis, so serious as to be only rarely experienced'.[6] One of the reasons for the decline was that Great Britain began to import Cuban sugar. Cuban sugar was more expensive, but fetching Cuban sugar saved Great Britain sailing time and thus tonnage. The consequences in the Netherlands Indies were all the more serious because sugar had become an object of speculation. Because of the excellent price prospects traders, many of them Chinese, had bought millions of piculs of the 1917 sugar harvest in advance. They ran into grave financial difficulties when prices dropped in January 1917. Bankruptcies followed. The larger sugar producers tried to act in concert to prevent a further fall of prices. They established a Javasuiker-Vereeniging (Java Sugar Association). 129 of the 185 sugar factories joined (Lovink 1919:4). The new association could not prevent a further decline, though prices did not drop as much as they might have done. The main fly in the ointment was the way in which business was done. Because consultation with Holland was necessary, it had taken months before the association had been able to take concrete steps. Another reason for the failure was the producers who had not joined and were not bound by its rules, and even some of those who had done so refused to follow the directions issued by the association.

A 'sugar crisis' evolved. One-third of the 1917 sugar harvest remained unsold.[7] The government was forced to build special warehouses in Semarang and Surabaya for the storage of sugar. As nobody had ever had any experience with the storage of large quantities of sugar over a longer period of time all kinds of problems were the result. During the rainy season the high humidity in sheds, which were not equipped with the right type of either roof or floor, affected the quality of the stored sugar.

A similar story can be told about copra. Trade had already suffered after copra had been declared conditionally contraband in April 1915 and the NOT had restricted imports in Holland to 10,000 tons a month. To ease the consequences, oil factories were built in the Netherlands Indies, but this only provided a partial relief. Huge stocks piled up in ports. As in the case of sugar, high humidity took its toll. Hordes of hungry beetles devouring the pulp caused additional damage.

Tobacco growers and exporters likewise experienced storage problems. In the course of 1916 an 'intolerable situation' emerged. Because of diminishing demand abroad tobacco lost its status as choice cargo. Stocks began to pile up because of a lack of shipping opportunities. In January 1917 worried tobacco planters who feared an imminent calamity met in Surabaya. In an address to Batavia, they pointed out that a production stop would be disastrous. Knowing

---

[6]   *De Locomotief*, 16-2-1917.
[7]   *Koloniaal verslag* 1919:255-6.

that it was a problem in which the colonial government took a close interest the planters scrupulously mentioned the consequences for the local population. Hundreds of thousands of Indonesians and hundreds of Europeans would be deprived of their means of livelihood. Financial damage would run into 80 million guilders, more than half of which had to be borne by the local population. In order the convince the government of what was at stake it was – as had been done in August 1914 – stressed that unrest would be a likely outcome. Subversive elements and revolutionaries would certainly exploit the miserable circumstances. Batavia had to come to the rescue to assure continued production through the advance of loans to the estates and the building of warehouses in which to store the crop.[8] The planters also pleaded for government intervention in the shipping of tropical products. If necessary, freighters would have to be requisitioned. Fearing a disaster, Batavia issued an appeal to the Javanese small farmers to limit the planting of tobacco as much as possible. They should concentrate on the growing of rice, maize and other food crops. Doing so would provide them with a smaller, but more stable income. The Javanese tobacco planters who had been lured by the good price for tobacco in the previous years disregarded the government's warning.[9]

At the end of 1916, only one-third of the tobacco harvest had been shipped.[10] It was a disastrous development. The quality of tobacco depreciates rapidly if it is stored in a tropical climate for a longer period. To make matters worse: the carbon disulphide used to combat diseases could no longer be applied because Japan had forbidden its export.

Apart from world-wide lack of tonnage part of the problem was caused by a hardening of the attitude of London and Paris engendered by the growing annoyance in the Allied countries about Dutch policy and the way in which The Hague responded to conflicting pressure from Great Britain and Germany. The Dutch government had irritated London almost from the first day of the war when the refusal to allow armed British freighters to enter Dutch ports as innocent vessels had angered British politicians. A further wave of indignation was created by Dutch exports to Germany. In 1916 the British Foreign Office began to point out that the Netherlands was following a policy which benefited Germany and which was 'anything but friendly' towards Great Britain.[11] From that moment on, forced to do so by London, the Dutch government professed economic neutrality as well. If potatoes or cheese were exported to Germany, an equal amount had to go to Great Britain. At the end

[8]   *De Indische Gids* 1917, II:960-1.
[9]   *Koloniaal verslag* 1917:xx; *Verslag* 1917:1124.
[10] Cramer 1916-17:408; *Schepenvorderingswet* 1917:44.
[11] Cecil to Townley, 24-10-1917, PRO FO 800 195.

of 1917 Cort van der Linden would state in an interview with an American journalist of the United Press Association, that the Netherlands always did its best to divide Dutch exports equally among the belligerents.[12]

This left the problem of transportation, especially after the German Navy resumed its all-out submarine war in January 1917. After Berlin's decision had been made public, Dutch ships in Europe fled to whatever port they could. For a time Dutch – and other neutral – shipping in the Atlantic came to a complete halt. The vacillation of Dutch shipping companies about allowing their freighters to sail added to the indignation in Great Britain aroused by the Dutch attitude in the war. To Viscount Edgar Algernon Robert Gascoyne Cecil of Chelwood, the parliamentary undersecretary for Foreign Affairs and British Minister of Blockade, the behaviour of the Dutch government and that of the Dutch ship-owners was unforgivable. He was adamant that the German submarine campaign should not succeed in preventing neutral merchantmen from sailing to Allied ports. To accomplish this, Cecil was in favour of increasing the pressure exerted on neutral countries; taking for granted the chance that public opinion in neutral countries might turn against the British.[13] He counted it a great achievement that Great Britain had been able to persuade Norwegian and Danish merchantmen to resume sailing. Dutch and Swedish ships should do the same. Dutch merchantmen in British ports, also in Asia and Australia, were not allowed to sail home till trade with Great Britain had been resumed. Dutch people in the Netherlands Indies had no inkling of what was happening when they heard that Dutch ships had been arrested in Singapore and Penang. The intensification of the German submarine war provided one explanation. When the *Melchior Treub* was ordered not to sail on to Singapore but to return to Belawan and when other Dutch freighters were also ordered not to leave that port, people speculated that German submarines had been sighted near Singapore and that Germany had extended its submarine war to Asia. When it dawned on the people that Dutch vessels were forbidden to leave Singapore and Penang, people in the Netherlands Indies could only relate this to a new export ban on rice or on all foodstuffs which they assumed had been instituted by the British colonial authorities.

The arrests were a clear warning. In Asia the Dutch ships were allowed to sail again after some time but London was determined not to lose too much neutral tonnage in Europe. Steamers of the northern neutrals were allowed to sail from ports in Great Britain only if the destination was an Allied port. Were freighters bound for a neutral port, their captains had to promise that afterwards their ships would carry cargo to an Allied port. Merchantmen could sail to a home port if another ship of approximately the same tonnage – in Dutch

---

[12] *De Locomotief*, 3-12-1917.
[13] Cecil to Townley, 7-11-1917, PRO FO 800 195.

called *ruilschepen* (exchange ships) – put to sea to sail to an Allied port.

At the end of February some Dutch freighters finally ventured out. Six of them on their way from Falmouth in Cornwall to Holland were torpedoed when they entered the Channel. The German government had been prepared to allow the ships to sail in safety, but because of a faulty wireless receiver, one German U-boat operating in the waters between Great Britain and the Netherlands had not received the orders countermanding attacks. To compensate for the loss, at the suggestion of the Dutch government Berlin was prepared to open negotiations for the putting of six of the German ships of approximately the same value in mothballs in the Netherlands Indies, among them the *Linden* and *Gernis*, at the disposal of the Netherlands for the duration of the war. Great Britain and France refused to sanction any such compromise. The six German ships remained tied up in the Netherlands Indies (Colenbrander 1920:120).

In early 1917 British politicians seriously considered an outright requisitioning of the Dutch ships anchored in British ports. For the time being, such a measure was rejected. The new British Ambassador in The Hague, Townley, pointed out to Cecil that confiscation would put an end to trade between Holland and Great Britain altogether. He wrote that Great Britain would 'wilfully play Germany's game by removing a considerable amount of neutral tonnage from the seas, whilst we should force Holland to become economically dependent upon Germany, whilst nursing a serious grievance against us which would make itself felt after the war'.[14] The only step of this sort London took was to requisition British-owned ships sailing under a neutral flag in May. Townley explained the decision to Loudon by pointing out that these ships, 'valuable British property', were not armed, and were 'exposed, without defence, to lawless attacks' by the German Navy.[15] The main victim of the requisition was the fleet of the Nederlandsche Stoomvaart-Maatschappij Oceaan, a Dutch shipping company which had its headquarters in Amsterdam. Oceaan, at times also referred to as Ocean, was closely linked to the Blue Funnel Line belonging to the British company Alfred Holt and Co. A majority of the shares were in British hands. The British step still reduced tonnage available in the Netherlands Indies even more drastically. A suggestion by the British government, made after a representative of the Oceaan had travelled from Amsterdam to London, that three requisitioned Oceaan ships should continue to sail between Java and Great Britain on the condition that Dutch colonial authorities would not confiscate them was rejected by The Hague. Two other Oceaan freighters had not yet been confiscated. One was

[14] Townley to Cecil, 24-3-1917, PRO FO 800 195.
[15] Townley to Loudon, 22-5-1917, *State Papers* 1917-18, III:465.

the *Dardanus*, which lay in the port of Amsterdam. The other was the *Tantalus*, on her way to the Netherlands Indies. After much beating about the bush, The Hague agreed to the proposition that *Dardanus* and *Tantalus* would not be confiscated providing they were to confine their future sailing to routes between Java and the United States, Vladivostok, and other Asian ports. The agreement came too late. The *Tantalus* had already been seized by British soldiers who had boarded her in Hong Kong as ordinary passengers. The *Dardanus* remained at anchor in Amsterdam till the end of the war (De Boer 1997:45-6).

The most grievous Dutch sin in British eyes was the so-called sand and gravel question. Bound by international law to allow unrestricted passage of innocent merchandise along the Rhine, the Dutch government had given Germany permission to ship sand and gravel to Belgium. London was completely convinced that the sand and gravel were being used for military purposes and not for the upkeep and repair of Belgian roads as Berlin, and in its wake The Hague, maintained. Impervious to innumerable protests from London, the Netherlands refused to call a halt to the transit before concrete proof had been presented that the sand and gravel were being used for the building of military fortifications.

Cecil took an uncompromising view. In his eyes the Dutch had 'constantly been pro-German in their actions since the outbreak of the war'.[16] They should be punished for this; this was even more necessary as harsh measures and threats appeared to be the only way to force the Dutch government see the error of its ways. One of the options Cecil considered was a British occupation of the Dutch colonies. He wrote to Townley in March 1917 that the Dutch attitude was

> the more provoking because, though it may be true that Holland itself might be successfully attacked by the Germans, there is no doubt that we could if we chose mop up the whole of the Dutch colonies. Java would be indeed an attractive acquisition for us from many points of view, and if we were Germany we should no doubt have threatened the Dutch long ago that we should use our power in that way.[17]

Cecil could not utter such a threat through official diplomatic channels. He toyed with the idea of using the British press to bring it home to the Dutch that if they did not repent the error of their ways their colonies might soon be forfeit. Townley was not a friend to the Dutch. On one occasion he confided to Cecil, that they were 'really a very unsympathetic people'. Nevertheless, he dissuaded Cecil from pursuing his plan to seize the Netherlands Indies.[18] Townley tried to convince Cecil that the Netherlands was not pro-German and

---

[16] Cecil to Townley, 5-3-1917, PRO FO 800 195.
[17] Cecil to Townley, 5-3-1917, PRO FO 800 195.
[18] Townley to Cecil, 15-10-1917, PRO FO 800 195.

that the grievances which Great Britain nurtured against the Dutch were not serious enough to allow for such a drastic step.[19] Cecil was unimpressed, but for the time being no action was taken. The risk that the Netherlands would react by taking the German side was too great. The British General Staff – like its German counterpart – was not looking forward to an extension of the front and the loss of a neutral source of agricultural products. It viewed the entry of the Netherlands into the war on whatever side with 'grave concern'.[20]

For the economy of Holland and the Netherlands Indies the entry of the United States in the war had serious consequences. In the past it had been American protests about the curtailing of neutral shipping which had persuaded London and Paris to make some concessions. This countervailing power had disappeared. To make matters even worse, after April 1917 the United States joined the Allied efforts to accomplish the economic ruin of Germany with fervour. In the process of doing so, the American measures hurt the Netherlands badly. Washington demanded guarantees that the import of American food, fertilizers, and fodder would not facilitate the export of Dutch agricultural products to Germany, not even indirectly.

Dutch shipping was curtailed even further by new steps decided upon in London, Washington, and Berlin. In the middle of 1917 the Allied blockade zone was enlarged, cutting the safe lane from Holland to Norway. The measure stirred up an uproar in the Netherlands. It was said to signal the ruin of Dutch seaborne trade. Pessimism reigned supreme because in reaction Berlin decided to step up its submarine warfare still further and to decrease the width of the free zone along the Dutch coast. Sea-traffic became possible again when, after a personal appeal by Queen Wilhelmina to King George V, Great Britain allowed a certain degree of relaxation.[21] What remained after the British announcement and the German reaction was a very small and dangerous lane through which Dutch and other neutral ships could cautiously make their way. For weeks no freighters left Dutch ports. Ships which did sail and strayed off course, which could very easily happen because of strong winds or adverse tides, ran the risk of striking a mine or when entering the German danger zone of being torpedoed.

As the sinking of the Dutch ships sailing from Falmouth indicates, in the course of 1917 the voyages of Dutch freighters and passenger ships had become dependent not only on the permission of British or American authorities, who decided whether ships were allowed to bunker or to leave port or not; German consent was also indispensable. Before ships sailed a *Geleitschein*,

[19] Townley to Cecil, 24-3-1917, PRO FO 800 195.
[20] Townley to Cecil, 24-3-1917, PRO FO 800 195.
[21] Townley to Cecil, 18-7-1917, PRO FO 800 195.

a safe-conduct had to be requested. This, for instance, was provided in July for ships transporting food from Argentina to Holland. To prevent Dutch tonnage being used for Allied purposes, German authorities demanded proof of innocence of the cargo. When ships sailed from Rotterdam or Amsterdam to the United States, a guarantee had to be presented that after the ships had reached their destination they would return to Holland, and would not be chartered by the Allied Powers. Without a *Geleitschein* the chances of being torpedoed were too great to venture forth.

The new obstacles to Dutch shipping made their presence felt at a moment when a real food and fuel crisis hit Holland. Wheat, bread, potatoes, electricity, gas, and petrol had to be rationed. New words were added to the Dutch vocabulary. Among these were *oorlogsbrood* (poor-quality war-bread, made up of a combination of wheat, rye, grits, and dried potatoes, which prompted some people to say that it made them feel that they had eaten a stone), *eenheidsworst* (standard sausage, a word which in Dutch came to denote all that was dull and uniform), *standaard schoenen* (standard shoes, leather had become scarce as well), and *regeringsvarkens* (government pigs, after the rule, also in force for other products, that when pork was exported a certain amount had to be offered on the domestic market at a moderate price).

Treub and Posthuma had sadly to conclude that Holland was no longer mistress in its own house. All that could be done was to try to limit dependency on the Associated and the Central Powers and see to it that none of the constituent countries of the two gained the upper hand.[22] The United States and Great Britain could block the supply of food, cattle fodder and other products essential to keeping Holland from starving and from a collapse of its economy; but so could Germany. Its government, for instance, could withhold coal.

The dire circumstances in Holland provided yet another opportunity to lash out at the Nederland and Rotterdamsche Lloyd companies. They were accused of not seeing beyond their war profits and of refusing to risk their ships. As a newspaper in Sumatra expostulated: in their 'appalling egoism' the shipping companies ignored national interests. Impeded by their policy, traffic had been disrupted between the destitute Dutch people and the colony which could help them, and, for instance, could supply the fuel for 'the oil can of the Dutch housewife which has already stood empty in the corner for months'.[23]

Confronted with such criticism ranks were closed. Business circles in Holland stood up for the Nederland and Rotterdamsche Lloyd. In its report for 1917, the Rotterdam Chamber of Commerce pointed out that shipping com-

---

[22] *Handelingen Tweede Kamer* 1917-18:2037.
[23] *Sumatra Post*, cited in *De Indische Gids* 1917, II:1113.

panies could not be blamed for the lack of tonnage. People in the Netherlands Indies did not realize what problems had been occasioned for the Nederland and Rotterdamsche Lloyd by the war. Much of the criticism levied at them was baseless, even uncalled for.[24] Pleyte also came to the defence of the Nederland and Rotterdamsche Lloyd. He did so at the end of 1917 when members of the Dutch Senate suggested that a state enterprise should take over the transport of passengers and cargo between Holland and the Netherlands Indies.[25] As was so often the case when points regarding the colony came up, the benefits change would bring to the indigenous population were presented as the main argument. Pleyte could not agree with the suggestion that a state shipping company be established. He said that the shipping companies could not be blamed and even – though he knew better – that they had never shown any reluctance to put their ships to sea.[26] Pleyte flew into a passion when he was criticized by Van Kol, who had dared to speak about the tyranny of the shipping companies: 'Does Mister Van Kol not know that a war is raging in Europe? Or has this great world event completely passed his idealistic mind by?'[27]

The wretched conditions in Holland decreased the amount of tonnage available for Dutch seaborne traffic from the Netherlands Indies. It even limited the freedom to decide which products could be shipped. Dutch freighters had to be sent to the United States to fetch grain, while permission for merchant ships to sail from Holland to the Netherlands Indies, if this were still possible at all, was only given in return for a promise that, after arriving at their destination, these ships would return to Holland along a route stipulated and with a cargo to be determined by the Dutch government.

To add to the predicament of Dutch shipping the amount of tonnage available was cut back even further by Washington's policy. With the exception of one freighter, none of the ships which had been requisitioned by Posthuma to sail to the United States to fetch food was allowed to leave for the return voyage in early 1917. The NOT had no part in this. It was strictly a government affair with the cargo being consigned to the Dutch government (Timmermans 2002:184). Initially no export permits were issued for cargo for the Netherlands. Later bunkering coal were refused without the promise of an exchange ship. Consequently, in August over sixty ships loaded with food and fodder – wheat, flour, oats, barley, maize, linseed-cake, and maize flour – were tied up in ports on the eastern seaboard of the United States.

The political or extraordinary hold-up of Dutch ships, as it came to be

---

[24] Report Chamber of Commerce Rotterdam over 1917, cited in *De Indische Gids* 1918, I:449.
[25] *Handelingen Eerste Kamer* 1917-18:108.
[26] *Handelingen Eerste Kamer* 1917-18:139.
[27] *Handelingen Eerste Kamer* 1917-18:160.

called, saddled Washington with some embarrassing problems. Food was rotting away in ships' holds, causing people in Holland to wonder whether if and when the freighters were finally released the cargo would not have become too rotten to consume. Crews grew restless. Counterproductively, blocking all food transport to Holland would make Holland dependent on Germany, an undesired prospect for the Associated Powers. Consequently, in September Washington decided on another course. Freighters could obtain fuel on the condition that upon completion of their voyage they would return to the United States with cargo.[28]

For Dutch shipping companies the directives of The Hague and Washington were a double bind. They had promised the Dutch government that their freighters which sailed from Dutch ports, would return to Holland after reaching the Netherlands Indies with the cargo the Dutch government wanted them to ship. This made it impossible for them to fulfil American conditions. To find a way out, the shipping companies turned to Loudon, to Posthuma, and to have plead their case with the other ministers, to Pleyte. They asked Loudon to explain to Washington that their ships had already been committed to the Dutch government.[29] Posthuma was appealed to negotiate permission to allow the freighters to make one extra voyage to the United States after they had reached Java, awaiting an agreement between The Hague and Washington on Dutch shipping, which it was believed might take a long time to be rounded off. The extra voyage would be 'highly beneficial' to the export of colonial products. To underline their argument Posthuma was told that one of the freighters on her way to the Netherlands Indies would carry a cargo of fertilizer from Chile, a product which was much needed by the estates in the colony, especially, they did not forget to mention, by those growing sugar.[30] Posthuma refused.

The situation experienced at the outbreak of the war had now returned with a vengeance. Merchandise could not be shipped from the Netherlands Indies to Holland or other countries; nor could goods be sent to the colony from Holland. Although still ninety freighters had reached Holland from Java in 1916, in 1917 only five vessels made the trip. Sixteen ships set out from Holland to the Netherlands Indies in 1917. The cargo space available for exports of the Netherlands Indies to Europe and the East Coast of the United States decreased from 455,200 tons in 1916 to 156,500 tons in 1917. In accordance with the redirection of the exports from the Netherlands Indies only tonnage destined for the west coast of the United States increased: from 56,000

---

[28] Nederland to Pleyte, 12-9-1917, NA, Kol. Openbaar, Vb. 8-11-1917 70.
[29] Nederland to Loudon, 21-9-1917, NA, Kol. Openbaar, Vb. 8-11-1917 70.
[30] Nederland to Posthuma, 10-9-1917, 6-10-1917, NA, Kol. Openbaar, Vb. 8-11-1917 70.

tons in 1916 to 136,000 tons in 1917.[31]

The consequences for the colonial export sector were severe. During 1917 the export of tobacco from Java, which shipping companies were very reluctant anyway to transport because it was more liable to overheating on board ships than tobacco from Sumatra, to Holland amounted to 7,391 tons. In 1916 exports had been tenfold to 71,992 ton. At the end of 1917 550,000 bales of Java tobacco from the 1916 harvest still had not been shipped.[32] In November 1917 *De Locomotief* observed that the chief of tobacco inspection 'has been having a forced holiday for months'.[33] In East Sumatra part of the 1916 harvest – in this case 110,830 bales – could not be shipped in 1917. The only compensation was that top quality tobacco still fetched an excellent price on the American market.[34]

In desperation sailing ships were chartered or bought (a practice also resorted to in Holland and elsewhere in Europe) to transport Javanese tobacco and tea to Europe via the Cape of Good Hope. Such undertakings had the full support of KPM which allowed one of its best Captains, E. Meulemans, 'a natural captain under sail' to advance the leave he was entitled to take charge of one of the ships.[35] As had been realized in advance, such sailing ships setting out on what *De Locomotief* called an 'old-fashioned voyage' were just as vulnerable to attacks as steamers.[36] The voyage of the *Albertine Beatrice* on which Meulemans sailed with a majority Chinese crew, began ill-omened. Having left Tanjung Priok, she collided with a pilot boat in the port of Surabaya. The pilot boat sustained heavy damage. Nevertheless, her sailing on 4 February 1917 was a festive occasion. Guests were invited on board, where they could listen to speeches about the history of Dutch sailing and drink their fill of champagne. Naturally, the national anthem was struck up. The trip of the *Albertine Beatrice* ended in disaster. She was torpedoed in European waters. Another of the sailing ships sustained heavy damage and made it only as far as Durban. Because of what had happened to the *Albertine Beatrice,* her owners did not want to run the risk of having her continue her journey. For the same reason the captain of the third sailing ship, the *John Davis*, was ordered to remain in Gibraltar and not to sail on.

The export of other colonial wares showed a similar pattern. In 1917 only 61,000 kg of Java tea was shipped to the Netherlands, compared to

---

[31] Report Chamber of Commerce Rotterdam over 1917, cited in *De Indische Gids* 1918, I:449; Carpentier Alting and De Cock Buning 1928:66.
[32] *Koloniaal verslag* 1918:217-8.
[33] *De Locomotief,* 6-11-1917.
[34] *Koloniaal verslag* 1918:21-2.
[35] *De Locomotief,* 9-1-1917.
[36] *De Locomotief,* 9-1-1917.

almost fifteen million kilogrammes in 1916, by which time it had already been impossible to export the whole harvest. To make prospects worse, the Russian market, good for about three million killogrammes, was eclipsed after the Russian Revolution. Initially Australia seemed to provide an alternative market, though there was sharp competition from tea from British India and Ceylon, which could no longer be shipped to Great Britain because of lack of tonnage, and likewise had to find a new outlet in Australia. Hopes were dashed when Australia instituted an import ban on foreign tea in June. Before this happened there had already been complaints in Australia about the poor quality of Java tea.

Not all was gloom and doom. Tin, rubber, pepper, and gambir still fetched high prices throughout most of 1917, as did tin. The export of tea from Sumatra increased to about four million killogrammes. Exporting tea to the United States, where, *De Locomotief* noted, tea was still virtually unknown, was also explored in the beginning of 1917.[37] It promised to be a new, but modest market, as Americans were only 'moderate tea-consumers'.[38]

As had happened in August 1914 the Javasche Bank stepped in. The bank financed the new storage facilities that it was essential to build for the colonial products which could no longer be exported. Once again the bank had to shoulder the burden of providing credit to companies, which needed capital to keep their estates running because they could not sell their produce. Care was taken to emphasize that the Javasche Bank acted as it did because the bank considered it 'of paramount importance for the economic life in the Netherlands Indies that work in the export crops is continued with the least possible disturbance'.[39]

Imports also suffered, including those from Holland, which in 1914 had still amounted to 150 million guilders, or one-third of the total value of imports to the Netherlands Indies.[40] In view of the shortages which had arisen in medicines, draperies, certain European foodstuffs, and other goods in the Netherlands Indies and the interruption in commercial sea traffic as early as May 1917 the Ministry of the Colonies had decided to charter a mail boat, the *Tabanan*, from the Rotterdamsche Lloyd. It was proposed the *Tabanan* make an emergency voyage to Java via the Panama Canal. Another argument for chartering the *Tabanan* was the acute shortage of men in the colonial army. The Navy, incidentally, had the opposite problem. The disruption of sea traffic had caused an over-abundance of sailors, who could not be repatriated. These could be taken home on the return journey. More trivial considerations also

[37] *De Locomotief*, 16-2-1917.
[38] *Schepenvorderingswet* 1917:140.
[39] *Koloniaal verslag* 1918:159-60.
[40] Report NHM over 1917, cited in *De Indische Gids* 1918, II:1136.

played a role. With some indignation it was observed that soldiers and non-commissioned officers in the colonial army who were waiting for transport to the Netherlands Indies did get their pay, but passed their days in idleness.

The cost of chartering the *Tabanan* was estimated at 500,000 guilders. The Ministry of the Colonies considered this a considerable sum, but the civil servants had made their calculations. Products bought by the Ministry were stockpiling and renting storage facilities did not come cheap. In view of the uncertainties which plagued neutral shipping, the management of the Rotterdamsche Lloyd stipulated that the passengers should acquiesce in advance to simpler meals than those usually served on mail boats. Passengers also had to promise not to protest about rationing if harbour authorities in ports at which the *Tabanan* was to call limited the supply of provisions.[41]

The question remained how Great Britain, because it was so adamant that no German products should leave Europe, would react. The mediation of the Ministry of Foreign Affairs was sought. Loudon was asked to sound out whether the British government would be prepared to allow the *Tabanan* to sail without stopping her for examination. To impress Loudon of the urgency of the voyage, Pleyte explained that for months it had been impossible to ship people and goods to the Netherlands Indies. The natural outcome had been a whole host of problems, but even more alarmingly under certain circumstances could well form a threat to the safety of the colony.[42] On the advice of Loudon, the Ministry of the Colonies also contacted Van Aalst to solicit him to plead the case with the British Envoy.

The sailing of the *Tabanan* was scheduled to take place at the end of June 1917. The plan was abandoned when a warship, the *Zeeland*, set out for a voyage to the Netherlands Indies via the Panama Canal. It was a drop in the ocean. In November 1917 almost 10,000 m3 and 10,000 tons of government goods were stored in Holland awaiting shipment to the Netherlands Indies.[43] Pleyte told Parliament that the 'impediments of circumstances' increasingly burdened the Netherlands Indies. He said that he had no idea how the colonial government came by some of the goods which were so urgently needed.[44]

The Netherlands was dealt an additional blow in October 1917. As commercial circles had realized in 1914 when they had established their estate committees in Java and Sumatra, the cable link between Holland and the Netherlands Indies was a vulnerable weak spot. Even the Dutch government reluctantly had to admit this. In June 1915 the Dutch *Staatscourant* (Gazette) called atten-

---

[41] Rotterdamsche Lloyd to Pleyte, 16-5-1917, NA, Kol. Geheim, Vb. 16-5-17 C7.
[42] Pleyte to Loudon, 4-5-1917 NA, Kol. Geheim, Vb. 4-5-1917 N6.
[43] Note 8th department NA, Kol. Openbaar, Vb. 19-4-1918 1.
[44] *De Locomotief*, 14-11-1914.

tion to the fact that wires could be rejected or mutilated by the British censor. Great Britain from its part had made no secret of the fact that it controlled Dutch telegraphic communication with the rest of the world and that it could use access to the cable as political leverage. London stressed that the Dutch use of British cables was not a right. It was an act of grace.

The implicit threat was disquieting, but a way out seemed to present itself. Direct wireless communication appeared to be the solution. Radio links would also put an end to the embarrassment of British censorship, which impeded communication, not simply by setting limitations on the text of telegrams, but perhaps even more aggravatingly because of the delays it caused. Telegrams might reach their destination only after eight to twelve days (Lovink 1919:24). Till 1916 the distance between Holland and the Netherlands Indies had been too great to allow for wireless communication. To overcome the problem of geographical distance and create a wireless connection a variety of solutions had been proposed. These ranged from a radio link via the United States to the use of mail boats as intermediate stations. In April 1916 there was a glimmer of hope when a wireless message from the large German Telefunken transmission complex in Nauen was received in Honolulu, some 9,000 miles away. This was not all. In Sabang, transmissions from the Canadian Marconi Radio Station on Cornwallis Island and from Nauen were also received. The latter consisted of war news and of messages to the German Governor of East Africa and to the German Consul in Ispahan. It was a break-through. One month earlier *De Locomotief* had still dismissed a report that the radio station in Sabang had intercepted messages from Nauen as an 'April Fools Day-like' prank. Somewhat prophetically *De Locomotief* had added that were the report true, such long-distance communication would be of incalculable value to the government and to commerce.[45]

Experimental transmissions from Nauen to Java were started in secret. A receiver, a gift from the Gesellschaft für drahtlose Telegraphie (Telefunken), was built on a hill near Bandung at the beginning of 1917. The effort required to build the station and its hundred-metres mast was enormous. Horses had to be used to transport staff, workers, and material to the station. The tests were successful. At the end of March, a few days before the United States entered the war, Van Limburg Stirum cabled Pleyte in cipher via Manila and Washington that seven messages, in total 3,400 words, had been flawlessly received. Pleyte was pleased. A way had been found to transmit secret messages to Java without having to depend on the goodwill of Washington. Nevertheless, he wrote to Van Limburg Stirum, he intended to use the new opportunity to maintain radio communication with Java only in the event of

---

[45] *De Locomotief*, 3-3-1916.

an emergency.[46] Pleyte was a little bit worried that the British would find out. They might be alerted by the frequent use of the codeword 'Webster' announcing the messages sent to Java. They could also, but this escaped the attention of the Dutch authorities, easily find out about the Dutch plans to establish a wireless link between Holland and Java by reading the newspapers and by following Dutch parliamentary debates (though for obvious reasons the Dutch government refused to provide detailed information).

At this moment Le Roy reappeared on the scene. He contacted the Ministry of the Colonies and suggested that Pleyte should allow him to start negotiations with Telefunken to see whether that company was prepared to build a 100 kW transmission station in Java, making two-way wireless traffic possible. Authorization was quickly given. Le Roy was informed that the equipment for such a station could be shipped to Java on board the *Zeeland*. Within days an agreement was reached. Telefunken was more than willing to help out the Netherlands. It promised that private and official messages to Java could be transmitted at all times from the Nauen station. There was one small catch. A German naval officer suggested that in return the Dutch government might allow that 'insignificant' messages be sent occasionally to Germans in the Netherlands Indies.[47] In May the necessary equipment to build a provisional 100 kW radio installation offered for free by Telefunken was transported to Holland. Two Dutchmen were selected to take charge of the building of the radio station. One of them was Karel Moens, an engineer employed by Telefunken. They and the equipment were taken to Java on the *Zeeland*, which also had a new engine on board for the only submarine operating in the Archipelago in June. The *Zeeland* had an ill-fated voyage. In the United States some of her crew – sixty-three people in total – deserted. The equipment reached Java, but was stored for eight months, before the building of a radio station at Cililin near Bandung finally commenced. The delay was caused by a difference of opinion in the Netherlands Indies about what would be the actual use of the Telefunken radio installation.

The plan bristled with pitfalls. The Dutch Minister of Transport and Communications called attention to the fact that a link between Nauen and Bandung could re-institute German communication with the Netherlands Indies, which would heighten the chance of British reprisals. Nevertheless, he realized that Telefunken was the only choice. The Netherlands just did not have the expertise to build a radio station powerful enough to bridge the distance between Holland and the Netherlands Indies. Assistance in building a more powerful station from the British Marconi Wireless Telegraph Company was not likely to be forthcoming. The aim of having a direct wireless link with

---

[46] Pleyte to Van Limburg Stirum, 16-5-1917, NA, Kol. Geheim, Vb. 15-5-1917 C7.
[47] Report Dubois, NA, Kol. Geheim, Vb. 30-4-1917 L6.

the colony was to become independent of British cables, and decrease vulnerability to British sanctions.

The importance of a wireless link was brought home a few months later after the British government had began to suspect that neutrals were misusing the British cable network. The main culprit was Sweden. *The Times* of 9 September reported that Sweden had 'repeatedly placed her diplomatic cable facilities at home and abroad at Germany's disposal' and that the Germans had made use of this to direct their submarine campaign. *The Times* concluded that cable communications was the 'one aspect of our "blockade" which has been insufficiently considered'. The newspaper complained that the policy of allowing neutral countries to use British cables had been 'conducted more with an eye to neutral susceptibilities than with an eye to preventing goods from reaching the enemy'.

The Associated Powers had a mighty weapon to strike at the neutrals. After the United States had entered the war, all cable lines were in the hands of the enemies of the Central Powers. In Europe the cables of the neutral states ran to Great Britain. In Asia Singapore formed a relay station for messages to and from the Netherlands Indies. France and the United States also controlled cable accesses to the Netherlands Indies. In short, as *The Times* concluded: the Associated Powers were 'the absolute masters of the cable communications of Germany, of her allies, and of all the near-by neutral States [...]'.

Great Britain was to use this power against the Netherlands. On 12 October, Pleyte wired Van Limburg Stirum that the Ministry of Foreign Affairs had learned that the British intended to refuse all Dutch commercial telegraph communications. Batavia should prepare for the possibility that official cables might also be rejected or delayed.[48] Whether The Hague was fully aware of the irritation Dutch conduct in their dealings with the belligerents had created in London is doubtful. At the end of June when Van Limburg Stirum had asked Pleyte whether Reuter's reports about a serious difference of opinion between Great Britain and the Netherlands were true, the reply by wire had been brief: 'all humbug'.[49] This was wishful thinking. The Netherlands had squandered almost all the sympathy it had in London. To punish the Dutch government for allowing the transit of sand and gravel, and to force the Netherlands to put an end to such transports, the British government decided to refuse to permit the transmission the non-official wires – especially the commercial ones, private wires would at times still be allowed – between Holland and the rest of the world, including the Netherlands Indies. As explanation of its decision, London pointed out that the use of British cables by the Dutch was a

---

[48] Pleyte to Van Limburg Stirum, 12-10-1917, NA, Kol. Geheim, Vb. 12-10-1917 G12.
[49] Van Limburg Stirum to Pleyte, 26-6-1917, 29-6-1917, Pleyte to Van Limburg Stirum, 29-6-1917, NA, Kol. Geheim, Vb. 2-7-1917 G9.

favour, not a right. This favour had been withdrawn.[50] The Britsche Telegram Onderbreking (BTO, British Telegram Interruption) or, to give it another designation, the telegram blockade was a fact. Loudon called the blockade 'a measure which seriously threatens economic life in the Netherlands and its colonies'. In his view the sanction was out of all proportion to the issue at stake: the transit of sand and gravel.[51] Pleyte was forced to conclude that the matter was 'very serious'.[52]

In Holland and the Netherlands Indies – where the advertisement 'send your telegrams "Via Eastern"' continued to appear in the newspapers – only citizens of the Associated Powers could still send messages along the British lines. An exception was made for Japanese companies in the Netherlands Indies. In the past these had been reluctant to sever their business relations with German firms and, for instance in Medan, had resisted pressure by the British Consul to stop trading with German firms.[53] After protests lodged with the Japanese and British government, Japanese businessmen were allowed to send and receive telegrams, but only with prior permission of the British Consulate General. Another possibility open to them was to send their telegrams by mail to Singapore from where they were forwarded by cable. Likewise, telegrams addressed to them were transported by post from Singapore to the Netherlands Indies.

London had not forgotten its own British interests. The telegraph station in Singapore was allowed to relay wires, even those from Dutch firms, which served Associated interests. These could concern the export of foodstuffs or the transmission of money from the Netherlands Indies to Great Britain. The exceptions hurt Dutch economic interests even more and added to the anger with which the blockade had been greeted. Exacerbating the feeling of isolation telegraph communications with the United States also collapsed. This effectively blocked the only way out for the business community in the Netherlands Indies to circumvent the British blockade. Immediately after the BTO had taken effect, companies had turned to the Exchange in New York instead of that in London for their financial information.[54] The disruption of communications with the United States was seen as additional proof that London had acted in an extremely underhand way and used the ban to promote British commercial interests, to the detriment of American ones as well. In mid-December regulations were tightened even more stringently. Commercial telegrams to and from Great Britain were only accepted if these

---

[50] Townley to Cecil,15-10-1917, PRO FO 800 195.
[51] *De Locomotief*, 3-11-1917.
[52] *Koloniaal verslag* 1918:205-6.
[53] *De Locomotief*, 7-6-1916.
[54] *Indische Financier*, cited in *De Indische Gids* 1918, I:626; Lovink 1919:30-1.

concerned commercial transactions concluded in the past, not any new undertakings. The message from London was that further transactions could be arranged by mail.[55]

Townley called the telegraph blockade a masterstroke. He wrote that it would have been hard 'to find anything that could have hurt the Dutch susceptibilities, for which please read pockets, more than the suspension of the commercial cable facilities'.[56] The only flaw Townley saw was that he had been away from The Hague when the decision had been taken. Had it been up to him, he would have waited a couple of days before communicating London's decision to Loudon. The extra time would have allowed him to contact Van Aalst in order to have the latter put pressure on the Dutch government.[57] Less pleased was the British Secretary of State for India, Edwin Montagu. He had been kept in the dark about the notes exchanged between the Dutch and British governments on the sand and gravel issue, and had to learn about the crisis from the newspapers. Piqued that he had been passed over and believing that in view of the relations between India and the Netherlands Indies he had a right to be informed, he wrote a sarcastic letter to the Foreign Office explaining that it was impossible for his staff to do their job if they had to rely 'not on the cooperation of my colleagues in the Government, but on a careful reading of the newspapers'.[58]

Generally the blockade was received with great wrath. The business communities in Holland and in the Netherlands Indies drew up a variety of petitions to impress upon the government the vital importance to Dutch international trade of cable communications. For the first time during the war public opinion turned against Great Britain. The atmosphere in Holland reminded an Irishman of the days of the Boer War. Friends and acquaintances cold-shouldered him.[59] The coldness was fleeting. As Townley noted, the torpedoing of a number of Dutch fishing boats by German submarines around the same time steered public opinion away from Germany again.[60]

The blockade stimulated a rush of renewed pleas to establish a wireless link. Because of the experiments in Germany, the Netherlands Indies was almost ready. All that was lacking was a station in Holland. Money should not prove to be the stumbling block. As a Member of Parliament remarked: the financial damage caused by the cable blockade was certainly much greater

---

[55] *De Locomotief,* 17-12-1917.
[56] Townley to Cecil, 29-10-1917, PRO FO 800 195.
[57] Townley to Cecil, 29-10-1917, PRO FO 800 195.
[58] Montagu to Drummond, 15-10-1917, PRO FO 800 384.
[59] Townley to Cecil, 28-11-1917, PRO FO 800 195.
[60] Townley to Cecil, 18-11-1917, PRO FO 800 195.

than the cost of the most expensive radio station.[61]

Public opinion about whether The Hague was to be blamed or not was very divided. Some praised the Dutch government for the 'fair' neutrality of the Netherlands, and for avoiding war with Germany by sticking to international conventions in the sand and gravel dispute. Others saw matters differently. They argued that the Dutch government should have steered away from a conflict with London.

The telegram interruption fuelled the fears that the Netherlands could no longer keep out of the war. Especially for those who had always argued that in 1914 the Netherlands had only managed to stay neutral because of Great Britain's benevolence, the cutting of the cable communication was a sign that an appeal could no longer be made to British generosity. This could spell the end of the Netherlands Indies. They and others with them were sure that Japan, the United States and Great Britain, either during the war or when peace had restored would have no qualms about sacrificing the Netherlands Indies in making an adjustment in their power relations in the Pacific. The *Bataviaasch Nieuwsblad* wrote that the Netherlands Indies was completely at the mercy of these three 'itchy-fingered' powers. If the Netherlands entered into conflict with one or more of them in these 'extremely confused times' the colony would certainly be lost.[62] *Kaoem Moeda*, the Sarekat Islam newspaper in Bandung, also ventured to say that the 'teasings' on the part of Great Britain cast a pall of gloom over the future of Holland and the Netherlands Indies. Were the Netherlands forced to cut its relations with Germany, Berlin should realize that this had not been done out of hatred for 'Germania'.[63] To some, and rumours with this purport also circulated elsewhere in Asia, it appeared as if the Netherlands and Great Britain were teetering on the brink of war. In Padang the Captain of the Chinese had some difficulty in persuading anxious Chinese merchants not to leave for the Straits Settlements.[64] Elsewhere, in a place which was described as an isolated post rife with rumours, 'native youths of good family' wanted to learn English as they were convinced that Great Britain would occupy the Netherlands Indies.[65]

Among the persons who feared serious repercussions was Boon of the *Soerabaiasch Handelsblad*. He wrote that the only salvation for the colony would be a defensive pact with Great Britain. A rift with London would usher in 'a disastrous time such as perhaps only a few nations have experienced in this

---

61 *Handelingen Tweede Kamer* 1917-18:1430.
62 Bataviaasch Nieuwsblad, cited in *De Indische Gids* 1918, I:484-5.
63 *Kaoem Moeda*, 15-10-1917, IPO 42/1917.
64 *De Locomotief*, 16-11-1917.
65 *De Locomotief*, 27-5-1918.

war'.[66] Boon went as far as accusing the Dutch government of collaboration with Germany. The colonial authorities reacted furiously. They accused Boon of libel and brought action against him. Once again it was a court case full of sound and fury, signifying nothing. The judge dismissed the claim. Boon's words had also infuriated some of his readers, who wrote a letter to the editor. To let the world know that what Boon had argued did not imply that all Dutchmen considered the British sanction a justified reaction to a wrongful position assumed by the Dutch government the letter was written in English. The indignant readers stressed that Dutch people should support their government in times of trouble and not attack it. They urged subscribers to cancel their subscriptions (which eighty persons did). Advertisers were exhorted to withdraw their advertisements. The attack was partly personal. It was suggested that Boon was inspired by his own frustration about the fact that he had never reached the rank to which he had aspired in the army and had remained a *ritmeester*, a cavalry captain, before he had resigned from the army and had become editor of the *Soerabaiasch Handelsblad* in April 1915.[67]

The cable blockade struck at the heart of the Dutch commercial community. Trade immediately slowed down when telegrams from Holland and more urgently from the major commercial centres in the world, containing orders or listing market prices on commodity markets were not forthcoming. A few telegrams – one congratulating the Escompto Bank with its sixtieth anniversary – did come through, but these remained exceptions, and usually concerned British orders for sugar. The *Bataviaasch Nieuwsblad* observed that commercial life in the colony had come to a standstill: 'The Indies is in a state of resignation. Trade strolls with its hands in its pockets – nothing to do – wait, no wire messages, no telegraphic transactions, no business'.[68]

The sale of export products, already affected by the shortage of tonnage, plunged steeply, if it did not grind to a temporary halt. Among the trade hit was rubber. Rubber prices on the London market had fallen shortly before the telegram ban. Coupled with the isolation from the outside world this meant that rubber fetched such a low price that initially there were almost no transactions at all.

Individuals who were dependent for their income on the transmission of telegraphic transfers found themselves in financial difficulties. Among them was the son of the Susuhunan of Surakarta who lived in Lausanne with his family. Not knowing what was going on, he tried to contact his father by wire, but to no avail. Thereupon he turned to the Ministry of the Colonies in The Hague. It promised to help him, though the staff decided to wait a couple of

---

[66] *Soerabaiasch Handelsblad*, cited in *De Locomotief*, 1-11-1917.
[67] *De Indische Gids* 1918, I:347.
[68] *Bataviaasch Nieuwsblad*, cited in *De Indische Gids* 1918, I:487.

weeks before contacting the colonial authorities. After all, the money might just have been delayed.[69]

On 15 November 1917 the Dutch government called a temporary halt to the transit of sand and gravel. The inevitable upshot was a conflict with Germany. Berlin used the Dutch step to present The Hague with fresh demands. To remain in grace the Netherlands had to allow the restoration of the traffic of merchandise on the railway between Antwerp and Mönchengladbach, part of which ran through Dutch territory. Germany promised that the line would not be used for the transport of war materials or troops, but The Hague refused to listen. The reason was that Berlin had made no exception for foodstuffs (in Parliament Loudon even spoke of army victuals). Because food was contraband, the Netherlands could not permit its transit. The food might be used to feed German troops fighting on the Belgian front.

At the end of November London allowed the sending of private telegrams, but it was February 1918 before Great Britain lifted the telegram blockade completely. New problems soon emerged. On 13 March the telegraph office in San Francisco announced it no longer accepted private Dutch telegrams with trifling messages. The cables were overloaded.

Though London had promised not to obstruct official communications from the Dutch government, a number of wires exchanged between Pleyte and Van Limburg Stirum were not transmitted during the blockade. Official telegrams, and as it turned out in December commercial telegrams as well, could soon be sent again via the American route, but here the complications also reared their ugly head. For weeks it was impossible to send ciphers because of new rules instituted by the United States in the Philippines at the end of October. After the Dutch Envoy in Washington had asked the American government to reconsider the ban at the end of January 1918 ciphers were once more accepted. If we may believe the *Bataviaasch Nieuwsblad*, the disruption of telegram traffic between The Hague and Batavia immediately resulted in inertia in the colonial administration, as Van Limburg Stirum was supposed to be hesitant to act without approval from The Hague. The *Bataviaasch Nieuwsblad* called Van Limburg Stirum's inertia a lost opportunity. The telegram blockade could have given the Netherlands Indies its own independent government had Van Limburg Stirum acted resolutely. Freedom of action had to remain a 'golden fantasy'.[70] Its criticism was rather wide of the mark. In reality the cable blockade confirmed Van Limburg Stirum in his opinion that people in the colony should be allowed a greater say in the decision-making process. The Netherlands Indies could no longer be treated as a mere branch establishment,

---

[69] J. Leyh to the Ministry of the Colonies, 3-1-1918, Pleyte to Leyh, 7-1-1918, NA, Kol. Openbaar, Vb. 5-1-1918 17.
[70] *Bataviaasch Nieuwsblad*, cited in *De Indische Gids* 1918, I:487.

certainly not the economic sector.[71] For others the absence of the possibility to consult Holland, or the long time it took to consult was a reason to plead for the greater economic and political autonomy of the colony.

Loudon took up the matter of government wires with the British Envoy in The Hague, who promised an investigation in Singapore. Initially this had little effect. In January 1918, Van Limburg Stirum felt obliged to inquire in The Hague whether Pleyte had 'reasonable certainty' that if he resent his wires 'at the cost of perhaps three hundred pounds', the messages would come through.[72]

In judging the situation in the Netherlands Indies and Holland respectively, Pleyte and Van Limburg Stirum had become dependent on the telegrams of Reuter, ANETA, and NIPA. This was not always plain sailing. NIPA had been one of the victims of the telegram ban. It had been ANETA, not NIPA which had spread the news on 23 October that London had cut telegraph communications. The blockade – and the disruption of the mail service – only made Spijkman's task more difficult. At the end of 1917 he complained that the circumstances had greatly favoured his rival ANETA, which acted as Reuter's agent. Many NIPA telegrams had not reached Batavia, and those which had, had been held up in London for days. Reuter's telegrams about the same event, which Spijkman claimed had been wired later, appeared in the colonial press days earlier than those of NIPA.[73] Spijkman posed that this hold a real danger to the Netherlands. As an example he mentioned reports by Reuter and ANETA about strikes in Holland, which could be 'neutralized' only days later by NIPA telegrams. After the blockade had been ended, news telegrams about what was happening in Europe again reached the Netherlands Indies, but in a diminishing numbers, and in some instances highly mutilated. At times no Reuter telegrams were received in Java at all. A headline in *Neratja* in February 1918 read 'censorship' when it reported about one such occasion.

Pleyte and Idenburg were pretty much in the same boat. As late as May 1918, Pleyte complained in the Dutch senate about the extraordinary difficulties encountered in consulting with Van Limburg Stirum. It had caused 'some lacunae'. Pleyte explained that telegrams did arrive, but that there was no certainty that they had not been mutilated. He had received the most recent mail from the colony a fortnight ago. It dated from eight months previously.[74] In view of this, after it had discussed Pleyte's policy in April the House had concluded that there was no reason for either praise or criticism. Because of crippled communications, Pleyte was not well informed about the situation

---

[71] *Volksraad* 1918:2.
[72] Van Limburg Stirum to Pleyte, 17-1-1918, NA, Kol. Geheim, Vb. 18-1-1918 C1.
[73] Report Spijkman over the period, 1-10-1917 – 1-1-1918, NA, Kol. Geheim, Vb. 27-9-1918 H9.
[74] *Handelingen Eerste Kamer* 1917-18:568.

in the Netherlands Indies. It was also no use asking questions. The minister would not have been able to answer them.[75]

Because of the complications about the transit of sand and gravel, people in the Netherlands Indies as well, started to fear that a war with Germany was imminent. The prospect became even more likely after Germany had launched an offensive on the Western front on 21 March 1918. A belligerent German press underlined the importance of the Antwerp-Mönchengladbach railway to the battle now raging and stressed that Holland could not avoid war for ever. Holland prepared for a German invasion. The Dutch government got some freedom of manoeuvring when the Associated Powers informed The Hague at the end of April that war between Holland and Germany was not what they wanted (Snapper 2002:299). Berlin also did not want war and backed down the following month. The German government was prepared to limit the quantity of sand and gravel to be transported to a volume well below a Dutch estimate of what was required for the maintenance of Belgian roads. Berlin also promised not to carry foodstuffs on the Mönchengladbach-Antwerp railway. Transit trade of sand and gravel was resumed at the end of May.

The agreement with Berlin created fresh problems with London. On 15 June 1918 *The Times* wrote that it was clear as far as the British were concerned that the agreement formed a German success. It might be true that only innocent goods were transported – 'which is a very large assumption', but the transports would in any case 'greatly relieve the strain on the German railways further south' which ran to the front. These railways could now be reserved for the transport of troops and war materials. The conclusion of *The Times* was as plain as a pike-staff. At a decisive moment in the war the Dutch government 'had rendered their neighbours a very timely service and improved the German position in the matter of rapid communications with an important part of the Western front'. The British government also remained highly suspicious. Repeatedly it asked The Hague for detailed information about the goods transported. Cecil told the House of Commons in the middle of 1918 that the Dutch replies were unsatisfactory.[76]

[75] *Handelingen Eerste Kamer* 1917-18:266.
[76] *De Locomotief,* 26-6-1918.

CHAPTER XVII

Growing domestic unrest

The references in the discussions about tonnage and shipping to the consequences for the indigenous population had not been picked out of thin air. By 1917 the reassuring expressions of solidarity at the outbreak of the Great War had been replaced by vocal attacks on Dutch rule. The Chinese had remained susceptible to nationalist impulses from China, while among the indigenous population the anti-Dutch undercurrent had remained as strong as ever. If anything, the Turkish participation in the war had contributed to a revival of Islam.

It had become almost instantly painfully obvious that the internal foe had not suddenly abandoned its resistance to the expansion of Dutch rule because of feelings of commiseration that the Netherlands was being threatened by war. In Celebes, from where, as Michielsen had requested, Dutch troops had been withdrawn for the defence of Java shortly after July 1914, all kinds of rumours began to circulate about the Dutch leaving the island. Unrest increased when dissatisfied local leaders became convinced that ham-struck by the war the colonial army could not spare sufficient troops to keep the region under control. The same conclusion was drawn in West Seram.

What happened in Sumatra in 1916 made the very greatest impression. In August anti-Dutch violence erupted in Jambi and spread to Palembang.[1] In Tapanuli people also took up arms. In Jambi resistance was fortified by stories about impending Turkish military support and the recognition of the insurrection by Istanbul (Locher-Scholten 1994:297-9). In desperation the colonial authorities sent one of the leaders of the Sarekat Islam, Goenawan, who, as had not passed unnoticed, on a tour to Jambi in early 1916 had been greeted with 'great respect', to Sumatra to calm the population.[2] Armed disturbances

---

[1] Whether it was an act to get even with Batavia or not is not clear but initialy the newspaper *Sumatra Post* refused to publish the statements about the military campaign in Jambi issued by government. The stated reason was that by issuing these statements Batavia broke its own ban on the reporting by the press of movements of Dutch troops and warships in the Archipelago (*De Locomotief*, 4-10-1916).
[2] *Handelingen Tweede Kamer* 1917-18:1498.

of a lesser magnitude, in 1916 and again later took place in Flores, in South and East Borneo, in South Celebes, and on the Tanimbar and Babar Islands. The Dutch senate concluded that such events lent an even more dangerous edge in view of the Great War.[3] The consequence was that throughout the war army and Navy in the colony had to be deployed to enforce Dutch rule, diverting ships and troops from what were two of the main headaches confronting Batavia and The Hague: the guarding of strict neutrality and the defence against a foreign enemy.

The uprising in Jambi especially came as a shock. Reports in the colonial and international press about the insurrection induced the new Governor General, Van Limburg Stirum, to plead for a curtailment of the freedom of the press and of the right of assembly. He did so because the disturbances had done the price of shares on the Exchange no good. Van Limburg Stirum feared that news about such events would discourage foreign investments. Imperatively, outside the colony people should not be encouraged to think that the colonial authorities were unable to maintain law and order.[4] For the wider Dutch community, and Mrs Van Limburg Stirum did her best to stimulate this, the Jambi rebellion was a reason to start collecting money to send cigars and cigarettes, titbits, and 'good books' to the troops in Jambi to cheer the soldiers up.[5]

The developments in Sumatra played into the hands of critics of the leniency shown to political organizations which had begun to emerge in the years just previous to the war. With a few exceptions, the white community in the Netherlands Indies and the press which served it were quick to put most – if not all – of the blame on the Sarekat Islam. In extension of this they condemned the moderate approach to nationalism favoured by Hazeu, Rinkes, and Idenburg. They had allowed the Sarekat Islam to come into existence and to flourish. The colonial government and those politicians in The Hague who were convinced that the Sarekat Islam had a role to play in the gradual emancipation of the Indonesian population argued differently. They put every effort in stressing that when local Sarekat Islam branches were involved in disturbances – as they were – this had been the work of outsiders. Such politicians were greatly relieved when reports indicated that this indeed was the case.[6] In their eyes the disturbances had another discomforting implication. They indicated that in any case outside Java, the colonial administration had failed to accomplish the instigation of the benevolent rule in which so many Dutch politicians sincerely believed. They saw such rule as essential. The cry 'Remember the Philippines'

---

[3] Handelingen Eerste Kamer 1917-18:269.
[4] Note Ministry of the Colonies, 2-2-1917, NA, Kol. Openbaar, Vb. 14-6-1919 26.
[5] De Locomotief, 14-11-1916.
[6] Handelingen Eerste Kamer 1917-18:494, Handelingen Tweede Kamer 1917-18:1498.

had passed into history, but the idea behind it was still very much alive. A benevolent colonial policy should suffice to convince the population, especially its leaders, that Dutch rule was the best, and that its replacement by that of another ruler would only be a change for the worse. Some were more cynical.

An on-the-spot investigation into the causes of popular discontent was set in motion. The task was assigned to one of the members of the Council of the Indies, J.H. Liefrinck, in October 1916. First and foremost he had to investigate what had really happened in Jambi and Palembang, but as it was feared that a more general malaise was at work Liefrinck had to extend his inquiries to Besuki in East Java, Bali, Lombok, Timor, the Minahasa, and Borneo.

Reports by Liefrinck, Snouck Hurgronje and others put the blame on the excessive diligence of the Dutch civil service outside Java. Its officials were said to have been overzealous and been deficient in the necessary tact and expertise. They had put too much pressure on the population in their efforts to achieve reforms and open up their territories to the blessings of civilization; a zeal which as one critic put it, manifested itself especially in the 'construction of many, preferably motor roads'.[7] Pleyte concluded that in their 'desire to introduce radical reforms and some improvement of the backward situations within a short span of time', the civil servants had lacked 'tact, consideration, and moderation'. They had not realized that they had made 'excessive heavy demands on the means and energy of the population'.[8] The civil servants themselves felt that they had been made scapegoats. They claimed that they had tried to convince Batavia of the fatal consequences government policy might have, but that their warnings had been ignored. They averred that they had even been punished for such criticism of government policy.

In Java a new party had taken over the role of the Indische Partij and its successor Insulinde as the mouthpiece of radicalism. Just before Tjipto Mangoenkoesoemo had returned to Java, a new political organization had been born which would exert great influence in the nationalist movement, turning it into a more leftist direction and providing it with a Marxist jargon. Social democrats living in the Netherlands Indies had organized themselves. They had also begun to look for ways to reach the indigenous population.

One of the options by which they might accomplish this was Insulinde. Insulinde confessed to being a socialist organization. As a result, the Semarang congress had accepted a motion to translate socialist literature in Malay. Members started to address each other as comrade. Insulinde's leaders were sure that cooperation with the social democrats was a *fait accompli*. In May

---

[7] *De Indische Gids* 1918:84.
[8] *Handelingen Eerste Kamer* 1917-18:469.

1914 *De Expres* had published a poem by one of its readers hailing Douwes Dekker for accomplishing this:

Kameraden, wilde loten	Comrades, free spirits
Schaart U onder onze vlag	Rally to our banner
Het verbond is thans gesloten	The covenant is now sealed
Kome wat er komen mag	Come what may
Het verbond met de SDAP	The covenant with the SDAP
Danken wij aan onz' DD	For which we have to thank our DD
Onze Tjip, en Soewardi	Our Tjip, and Soewardi
Dat zij leve 'onze Drie'.	Long may the three of them live.[9]

Douwes Dekker may have done much but he was not the most suitable person to reach an understanding with the Dutch social democrats. His own attacks on socialism in the past were in part to blame, whereas social democrats in Holland found it hard to deal with the radical way in which Douwes Dekker and some of his political associates expressed themselves. Social democrats had been highly critical of the decision to exile Douwes Dekker and had used this to castigate colonial relations, but shrank away from the suggestions made by Douwes Dekker and others that violence might be necessary as a means to an end. In spite of the stress on the one Indiër race, some people were convinced the Indische Partij and Insulinde remained unequivocally Indo-European organizations, representing a group many of whose members looked down upon the Indonesian population and were only prepared to fight for their own narrow interests.

Its main antagonist in Holland was Van Kol. Van Kol – the 'anti-revolutionary imperialist', *De Expres* called him – condemned the rash words spoken by members of the Indische Partij. He was convinced that they dreamt of a violent revolution. In the press he called attention to the fact that members of the Indische Partij had imported fire-arms, and during a visit to Java had jokingly told him that they had done so to hunt pigs, but that one day perhaps they might shoot 'other game'.[10] He repeatedly argued that the Indonesians, among them, he thought, the leaders of the Sarekat Islam, did not trust the Indische Partij. Van Kol characterized the majority of the members of the Indische Partij as Indo-Europeans of a certain class. Tjipto Mangoenkoesoemo, whom Van Kol called 'a noble man [...] whose intellectual development I highly esteem', would do better to dedicate himself to the cause of the Sarekat Islam, which was supported by the Javanese intellectuals and commercial middle class.[11] Tjipto Mangoenkoesoemo did not take kindly to Van Kol's words. In his turn,

---

[9] *De Expres*, 14-5-1914.
[10] *Soerabaiasch Handelsblad*, 13-9-1913.
[11] *De Locomotief*, 2-12-1913.

he accused Van Kol of spouting ideas which resembled those of an 'arch reactionary'. Substituting the word proletariat for Van Kol's qualification 'of a certain class ', Tjipto Mangoenkoesoemo expressed surprise about the fact that somebody who professed to be a social democrat could oppose a proletarian organization like the Indische Partij and plead in favour of one supported by the middle class.[12]

Feelings among the Dutch social democrats living in Java were at the best mixed. At first there was an idea that whatever its faults Insulinde was still a valuable vehicle to disseminate socialist ideals to a wider audience. One of the persons who nurtured this view was H.J.F.M. Sneevliet. who had arrived in Java in 1913. Attorney-General Uhlenbeck concluded in 1918 that since his arrival, 'this young man' – he was not yet thirty at that moment – 'considered himself called and entitled to act as a demagogue on the basis of a few half-understood doctrines, in a country which was totally alien to him, with a population whose needs he could not have probed in the short time of his stay here, whose language he hardly understood and spoke'.[13]

Sneevliet was not impressed by Insulinde. He reported home in February 1914 that Insulinde (at that moment still in disarray because of the banishment of the Indische Partij leaders) was a weak party, incapable of even organizing a proper congress.[14] Sneevliet saw a more promising prospect in the Vereeniging van Spoor- en Tramwegpersoneel in Nederlandsch-Indië (VSTP, Union of Rail and Tramway Personnel in the Netherlands Indies). The VSTP was small, but Sneevliet was very optimistic that he could change this. One of the advantages of the VSTP was that like Insulinde it was open to Indonesians. An Indonesian, Moehammad Joesoef, a clerk with a Semarang Railway Company, had become a member of the board as early as October 1913. A second prominent Indonesian socialist, Semaoen, a railway clerk at the station in Surabaya, came on the board in March 1915. Sneevliet was appointed editor of the VSTP periodical *De Volharding* (Perseverance). Moehammad Joesoef edited the Malay version, *Si Tetap*.

Sneevliet was also prominently present when the Vereeniging van Sociaal-Democraten in Nederlandsch-Indië (Union of Social Democrats in the Netherlands Indies) the 'future Indian battalion of the International', as it was expectantly called, was founded on 9 May 1914.[15] After a meal and the singing of lines (adapted) from *The Internationale* like the 'Sterft gij oude vormen en gedachten!' (Die ye old forms and thoughts!) and 'Broeders, laat

[12] *De Indiër* 1-44:37-40.
[13] Demand in appeal of the public prosecution, 27-3-1918, NA, Kol. Openbaar, Vb. 14-6-1919 26.
[14] Sneevliet to Wibaut, 17-2-1914 (Tichelman 1985:171-4).
[15] *De Expres*, 16-5-1914.

ons de kazerne slopen' (Brothers let us demolish the barracks), those present discussed the relationship with Insulinde and the Sarekat Islam. The Sarekat Islam could count on plenty of sympathy. The opinions about Insulinde were not so felicitous. Some accused Insulinde of inciting racial hatred and encouraging a race struggle. Such a policy diverted attention from a correct analysis of colonial society and disregarded the basic tenets of a class struggle. Others saw in an Indo-European bourgeoisie the enemy of 'rising Javanism'. Nevertheless, observing that many Indo-Europeans belonged to the proletariat cooperation was not entirely precluded.[16]

De Expres published the report of the inaugural meeting of the Indische Sociaal-Democratische Vereeniging (ISDV, Indies Social Democratic Union), as it was soon re-christened. It was the only time that its readers, used to excessive praise of Douwes Dekker in the pages of *De Expres*, read less flattery words about their hero in their favourite newspaper. The criticism of Insulinde and the not very complimentary remarks made about Douwes Dekker had not been expurgated. ISDV members had said that Douwes Dekker was not a social democrat at all. He was a nationalist-anarchist.

The uneasy partnership between Insulinde and the ISDV would not last long. Their leaders had completely different political ideals. Sneevliet admired Douwes Dekker's courage and his disregard for racial differences, but the glorification of Douwes Dekker and the veneration with which 'DéDéisme' was presented offended him. Leaving personal considerations aside, Sneevliet rejected almost all the points propagated by Douwes Dekker to improve the lot of the poor Indo-Europeans. Only about one matter Sneevliet had not yet made up his mind. This was the right of landownership for Indo-Europeans. A final evaluation depended on the assessment of the factors required to accomplish a socialist revolution in the colony. If indeed an industrial proletariat was an essential prerequisite for the realization of a socialist society, Sneevliet could accept and even welcome an increase in the number of landless, poor Javanese, if this were the result of allowing Indo-Europeans to own land.[17]

Another reason why relations were strained was that the leaders of the ISDV and Insulinde both looked to the Sarekat Islam (and also to the VSTP) to expand their support among the population and foster their Indonesian activists. In the ISDV Moehammad Joesoef, Semaoen and other future communists were literally indispensable to the translation of the ISDV message to the masses. Most Dutch socialists, many of them teachers at European schools, had little or no command of Malay or Javanese. In Insulinde it was a small group of militant Indonesians from Surakarta operating at the fringe of the Sarekat Islam branch of that city who embarked on a radical nationalist course.

[16] Sneevliet to Wibaut, 26-5-1914 (Tichelman 1985:181-2).
[17] Sneevliet to Wibaut, 17-2-1914 (Tichelman 1985:171-5).

Insulinde also contributed its own efforts towards reaching out to the indigenous population. In August 1914, the Insulinde branch of Semarang had launched *De Goentoer*, The Thunder. It appeared twice a month. It was edited by Darnakoesoemo, one of the Javanese board members of Insulinde, former corrector of *De Expres*, and a close friend of Tjipto Mangoenkoesoemo. Articles were published in Dutch and Malay. *De Goentoer* was in a sense the continuation of *De Expres*. Troubled by financial difficulties, a drop in subscribers and advertisements, the 'Knocker-up of Insulinde, the Scourge of Evil', as *De Expres* describes in the last issue, had ceased publication at the end of July 1914. In the same issue Darnakoesoemo announced the birth of *De Goentoer*: 'In the cradle at the side of the bier lies the baby, De Goentoer. The dark bright eyes look around terrified, the cry is a sign of the longing for mother's milk. Alas the breast has dried up! The milk supplier asks cash on the nail, think about that comrades!'[18]

In this race to win the hearts and minds of the population, Tjipto Mangoenkoesoemo was assigned a significant role. The sea voyage and the return to his fatherland in August 1914 had done Tjipto Mangoenkoesoemo good. He made a speedy recovery. Idenburg had not expected this. As far as he was concerned, a return to health was a reason to worry. Idenburg was afraid that when people were confronted with a healthy Tjipto Mangoenkoesoemo they might not understand the real reason for the decision to revoke his banishment. They might interpret the permission he had given Tjipto Mangoenkoesoemo to return a sign of weakness on his, Idenburg's, part.[19]

Tjipto Mangoenkoesoemo had first taken up residence in Semarang, the centre of Insulinde activities. Before the end of the year he moved to Surakarta, where he lived with Kebo Panatas. Together with a small number of radical Javanese journalists Kebo Panatas had founded the Inlandsche Journalisten Bond (IJB, Native Journalists' Union) in December 1913. They had done so at the office of the local branch of the Sarekat Islam. President of the union was Marco Kartodikromo, born in Cepu in Central Java around 1890. Mas Marco, as he was usually called, was editor of *Sarotomo*, published by the Surakarta Sarekat Islam, and appearing twice a week. The colonial authorities considered Mas Marco 'extremely dangerous'.[20]

The goal of the IJB was to establish a fund to pay for legal aid for members who were prosecuted by the authorities and for the financial support of their families if journalists ended up in jail. Such financial guarantees were one of the reasons why the union's leaders stressed that journalists should not hesitate to speak out. Courage became their password. The IJB motto reflected this: *Berani*

---

[18] *De Expres*, 31-7-1914.
[19] Kindermann to Rinkes, 4-1-1915, NA, Kol. Openbaar, Vb. 6-1-1916 1.
[20] *De Expres*, 8-1-1914, citing *Soerabaiasch Handelsblad*.

Mas Marco Kartodikromo and his wife in better days (KITLV 4451)

karena benar, takoet karena salah, Courageous because of right, afraid because of wrong. The nationalist were right and had nothing to fear, the Dutch were in the wrong and because of this were afraid. In February 1914 the IJB launched *Doenia Bergerak* (The World on the Move), a bi-weekly. *Doenia Bergerak* wanted to become 'the trumpet of the truly suppressed and deceived'.

The founding of the IJB and the publication of *Doenia Bergerak* was hailed in Insulinde circles. 'Do not slumber', *De Expres* had exhorted its readers, 'we are now in the period of *Doenia Bergerak* says the Native Journalists' Union. Rise, Indiërs and close ranks and join together, because unity gives strength.'[21] *De Indiër* wrote that the IJB had Sarekat Islam leaders as its organizers and 'IP tendencies in its expressions'.[22] *Sarotomo* and *Doenia Bergerak* had no formal link with Insulinde, but both were printed on the presses of *De Expres* in Bandung.

De Goentoer, *Sarotomo*, and *Doenia Bergerak* were militant in tone. They could not count on any sympathy in government circles. Rinkes called them scurrilous rags and disqualified their editors as a 'pathetic scolding club'.

---

[21] *De Expres*, 16-2-1914.
[22] *De Indiër* 1-2.

Nevertheless, in the same breath Rinkes had to admit that they were widely read by the 'pious but backward' community of Central Java and by 'semi-intellectuals', that is Indonesians employed in the lower ranks in government enterprises and the bureaucracy.[23]

The content of the three papers worried the colonial authorities. Batavia feared that it could set people in Central Java against Dutch rule. The authorities ignored that the persons behind *De Goentoer, Sarotomo,* and *Doenia Bergerak* expressed their ideals in radical words and fierce sounding slogans, but beneath this brimstone were truly concerned about the plight of the Javanese; those half-humans, as the nationalist leaders liked to call them.[24]

Restoring the dignity of their fellow-countrymen meant more to them than political and economic emancipation or a better education. A moral awakening – the renaissance Tjipto Mangoenkoesoemo had referred to when he left Holland – also had to be achieved. The Javanese should cast off their servile attitude and their gestures of submission in front of superiors. Social abuses had to be combated. Darnakoesoemo, for instance, and for such campaigns the Sarekat Islam had set the tone in Java, was chairman of the Madjoe Kamoeljan (Progress of Honour) founded to fight prostitution in March 1915. When he learned of a girl of about fifteen years of age, who was lured by a Briton to become his housekeeper by the promise of a high salary, he visited the girl in the company of the female treasurer of Madjoe Kamoeljan to urge her not to accept the offer. The girl was told that her future was bleak, all the more so because her prospective employer was British. It was well known that might there be a child, how much the British despised half-castes. She would end up in the kampong, where she would be treated with disdain because of her past.[25]

Much of what people like Darnakoesoemo strove for did actually correspond to the stated intentions of the colonial administration to elevate the Indonesian population. Their main fault was that they rejected the guidance by the authorities. They defied established etiquette and in their writings paid no heed to the limitations set by the authorities. This earned them a reputation of being ill-mannered at best and subversive at worst. Upset by their words, the colonial authorities ordered action to be taken against the inflammatory articles written by them. These were plentiful. The authorities were at their wit's end. It was a hopeless task to take legal action against all the articles which were considered seditious. The problem was compounded because many of

---

[23] Rinkes to General Secretary, NA, Kol. Openbaar, Vb. 17-9-1915 46.
[24] A similar notion was presented outside Java. In *Pewarta Deli*, for instance, it was noted that the native was sliding down to the status of a buffalo, an ox, a monkey and other animals (*Koloniaal Tijdschrift* 1917:396).
[25] *De Expres,* 14-7-1914.

the contested articles were written in such a way that a court could never pin down a charge on the author. Mas Marco, Tjipto Mangoenkoesoemo, Darnakoesoemo and other authors of malicious articles also were not the sort of men to be discouraged by a jail sentence or banishment to remote places. On the contrary, they would wilfully exploit every attempt to prosecute them to draw public attention to their cause. The only way to stop them was to close down their printing-works or to impose direct censorship. Since 1906, when the press law had been reviewed, this sort of intervention had become impossible, but action had to be taken. If not, the authors would only become increasingly audacious and in the end their writings could not but have a baleful effect on the mind of the population.[26]

Batavia blamed Tjipto Mangoenkoesoemo for this upsurge in radicalism in the vernacular press.[27] Tjipto Mangoenkoesoemo did indeed enthusiastically support the union of native journalists. He became a contributor to *Doenia Bergerak* and came out in support of Mas Marco when an investigation against the latter was started in January 1915. One of Mas Marco's sins was that he had used Soewardi's slogan *Rawé-rawé rantas malang malang poetoeng*. Another was that he refused to disclose the name of the authors of a number of letters to the editor which had appeared in *Doenia Bergerak* in July and August 1914, to which the authorities had taken offence; among them one entitled 'Oh, Javanese are very stupid', written by M. Juist (M. Right).

What Tjipto Mangoenkoesoemo wrote about Mas Marco's prosecution occasioned his first collision with the colonial authorities since his return. Rinkes even went as far as to conclude that Tjipto Mangoenkoesoemo had gone mad and might need psychiatric treatment.[28] The bone of contention was a pamphlet – *Persdelict* – written in January 1915 in support of Mas Marco and Darnakoesoemo, who also had to stand trial around the same time. Written in Malay and Javanese it ended with the sentence 'The members of the judiciary will confront our brothers Marco, Darnakoesoemo or Diponegara, even though they will find themselves in troubled waters with the IJB'.[29] These words were considered shocking. Reading them the head of the Insulinde printing-works in Bandung went to the *Assistent-Resident* of the city to inquire whether publishing the pamphlet would still be within the confines of law. He also asked the authorities' opinion about another pamphlet *'Justitie ngamoeg'*, Justice runs amok, written by one Mintarogo, which, he disclosed, was a pseudonym used by Tjipto Mangoenkoesoemo.[30] 'Why', it began, 'is action

---

[26] André de la Porte to Idenburg, 30-3-1915, NA, Kol. Openbaar, Vb. 17-9-1915 46.
[27] Note Rinkes, 7-6-1915, NA, Kol. Openbaar, Vb. 17-9-1915 46.
[28] Rinkes to Idenburg, 13-2-1915, NA, Kol. Openbaar, Vb. 6-1-1916 1.
[29] NA, Kol. Openbaar, Vb. 6-1-1916 1.
[30] Janssen to Idenburg, 20-2-1915, NA, Kol. Openbaar, Vb. 6-1-1916 1.

taken against the article in *Persdelict* by brother Tjip. The piece is unimportant. [...]. In point of fact, the brother in question is completely debilitated [a reference to the medical report of Dr Winkler] and prefers to eat saté or soto on the aloen-aloen [the town-square].' Other parts of the text fell more alarming on Dutch ears: *'Rawe rantas, malang malang poetoeng* I cry in chorus with Tjip en Soewardi. We want to declare war on all those people, who do not join forces [with us] in our country, and woe to them who dare to take up arms against us.' 'If', it ended, 'my brothers and fellow-countrymen would just show themselves to be "daring", if we have the "right", then the power of the Javanese will return and a Kingdom of Majapait will rise again.'[31]

Sneevliet and the ISDV were not behind-hand in springing to the defence of Mas Marco. The ISDV and Insulinde staged a joint public meeting in Semarang to protest about the sentence of two years' imprisonment the prosecution had demanded on 7 July 1915. The speakers included Tjipto Mangoenkoesoemo (who later attacked Tjokroaminoto for not joining in the protests), Sneevliet, and Mas Marco himself. Mas Marco stressed the familiar theme: 'as long as you, people of the Netherlands Indies, do not have courage, you will always certainly be trampled on and be said to be quarter human beings'. The Dutch public was shocked; not only by the fierce speeches of Tjipto Mangoenkoesoemo and Sneevliet, but also because of the prominent presence of 'a Marxist like Mr Sneevliet' who was set on exploiting the harshness of the public prosecutor to propagate his own revolutionary ideas.[32]

The protest meeting did not achieve much. The following day Mas Marco was sentenced to nine-months' imprisonment. He appealed. The sentence was reduced to seven months in October. A Committee for the Freedom of the Press, constituted in August and supported by the ISDV, Insulinde, the IJB, and the VSTP, gave Mas Marco's wife financial support. After Mas Marco had been sentenced, *Sarotomo* mentioned between brackets in its colophon that Mas Marco was in the *boei*, the jail of Semarang; maybe the initiation of the habit of radical papers of the Netherlands Indies of mentioning a special type of staff member: the editor in jail (Soebagijo 1981:5).

The authorities' anger had repercussions on Tjipto Mangoenkoesoemo's personal life. When he had moved to Surakarta, Tjipto Mangoenkoesoemo had hoped to resume his practice as a 'private native doctor', as he chose to call himself. The local Islamic press had welcomed the prospect. At last there would be a doctor in town who would take care of poor patients.[33] Tjipto Mangoenkoesoemo had a hard time. Because of his reputation he did not attract many moneyed patients. He tried in vain to become the per-

---

[31] NA, Kol. Openbaar, Vb. 6-1-1916 1.
[32] *De Nieuwe Soerabaia Courant,* cited in Baars and Sneevliet 1991:54; *Oetoesan Hindia,* 1-4-1916.
[33] *Sarotomo,* cited in *De Locomotief,* 18-12-1914.

sonal physician of the Mangkunegara, one of the two rulers in Surakarta in February 1915. Tjipto Mangoenkoesoemo stood no chance, not least because the *Resident*, S.P. Sollewijn Gelpke, refused to write a recommendation. Tjipto Mangoenkoesoemo had never made a secret of the fact that he did not care a fig for Javanese noble titles and steadfastly refused to use his own title of Mas. The prime minister of the Mangkunegara disqualified Tjipto Mangoenkoesoemo as somebody 'who did not like the Javanese'.[34] The following month Sollewijn Gelpke again refused to help Tjipto who had asked Idenburg to appoint him to the medical staff to combat an outbreak of plague in Surakarta. Sollewijn Gelpke would not hear a word of it. He wrote to Idenburg that Tjipto Mangoenkoesoemo was an arrogant, conceited person and did not enjoy a good name among the Javanese notables in Surakarta, who valued good manners. Tjipto Mangoenkoesoemo could be given a job as a plague doctor, but not in Surakarta.[35] On hearing that his request had been turned down Tjipto Mangoenkoesoemo angrily returned his decoration. 'Poor Javanese', the newspaper *Djawa Tengah* commented, contrasting Tjipto Mangoenkoesoemo's willingness to combat the plague, even if it had to be without pay, with the egoism of Dutch doctors.[36]

Another person to suffer was Soewardi. Mr. J.H. Abendanon, an influential former colonial civil servant, informed Pleyte in March 1915 that Soewardi's wife was expecting a baby and that she was apprehensive about having a delivery in Europe far away from her relatives.[37] Batavia was unrelenting. Two months earlier Idenburg had asked the opinion of his advisers about allowing Soewardi, who had made no radical remarks for almost a year, to return to Java. On the advice of Rinkes, who was sure that Soewardi had not changed his political views, and the Council of the Indies Idenburg decided against clemency. Mas Marco and Tjipto Mangoenkoesoemo had already caused enough trouble. Idenburg wired Pleyte that Soewardi would only be allowed to return to the Netherlands Indies if he took up residence in Bangka and 'if he himself requests this in writing'.[38] Pleyte was prepared to pay a third class ticket if Soewardi agreed to the conditions. Soewardi refused. He wanted to return to the Netherlands Indies only if he were allowed to take up residence in Java. The refusal to allow him back was the end of Soewardi in his role as a quiet exile. He castigated Indië Weerbaar as Dutch imperialist propaganda,

---

[34] Sollewijn Gelpke to Idenburg, 26-2-1915, Rinkes to Idenburg, 15-10-1915, note about Tjipto, NA, Kol. Openbaar, Vb. 17-9-1915 46, Vb. 26-1-1916 32.
[35] Tjipto to Idenburg, 1-4-1915, Sollewijn Gelpke to Idenburg, 6-4-1915, NA, Kol. Openbaar, Vb. 12-10-1915 31.
[36] *Djawa Tengah*, cited in *Koloniaal Tijdschrift* 1917:404.
[37] Abendanon to Pleyte, 9-3-1915, NA, Kol. Openbaar, Vb. 16-1-1916 1.
[38] Idenburg to Pleyte, 3-9-1915, NA, Kol. Openbaar, Vb. 6-1-1916 1.

and contributed articles to *Het Volk*, *De Groene*, *De Nieuwe Amsterdammer* and other leftist periodicals in Holland.

Afterwards Tjipto Mangoenkoesoemo tried to convince the colonial authorities that they had only themselves to blame for the turn his life had taken by refusing him the opportunity to practise as a plague doctor. He explained to Van Limburg Stirum that it had forced him to take up journalism to find an additional source of income.[39] Admittedly Tjipto Mangoenkoesoemo did not exactly make a fortune as a journalist. One of the problems was that he, as Darnakoesoemo observed in a letter to Sneevliet, was 'a champion of his people', but definitely not a businessman.[40] At the end of September 1915, when Mas Marco had to enter the 'journalists' hotel', as the prison was ironically known, and Darnakoesoemo moved to Semarang to become the book-keeper of the VSTP, Tjipto Mangoenkoesoemo took over leadership of the financially not very viable weekly *Goentoer Bergerak* (Thunder on the Move). Published partly in Dutch and partly in Malay *Goentoer Bergerak* had appeared for the first time in February 1915 after the merger of *De Goentoer* and *Doenia Bergerak*.

From its inception Tjipto Mangoenkoesoemo had played a key role in *Goentoer Bergerak*. In the first issue, using the pen-name Djajabaja – a Javanese king supposed to have prophesied the coming of a Just King who would replace Dutch rule – he had outlined its editorial policy. *Goentoer Bergerak* would follow 'the old IP orientation, guided by the spirit of DD'.[41] These were no idle words. In one of the next issues Tjipto Mangoenkoesoemo proposed extenuating circumstances for the assassination of Franz Ferdinand in Sarajevo: 'it has been a political murder and in us oppressed it strikes a cord of sympathy when we think about this'.[42] As editor-in-chief Tjipto Mangoenkoesoemo decided to rename *Goentoer Bergerak Modjopait*. In revealing this he made no secret of the fact that he wanted the initially bi-lingual *Modjopait* to be a Malay *De Expres*. His wishes were fulfilled. People were quick to liken *Modjopait*, defending the interests of Javanese and Indo-Europeans alike, to the former *De Expres*. To the additional dismay of the authorities in the first issue he announced that *Modjopait*'s aim was to strive for an independent Netherlands Indies, free of foreign tyranny. In the eyes of the authorities, *Modjopait* qualified as a dangerous periodical, through which the 'well-known agitator' Tjipto Mangoenkoesoemo could conduct a vicious Insulinde and Indische Partij campaign.[43]

After Mas Marco had served half his sentence, in February 1916 Idenburg

---

[39] Tjipto to Van Limburg Stirum, 19-7-1916, NA, Kol. Openbaar, Vb. 22-11-1916 6.
[40] Darnakoesoemo to Sneevliet, 16-9-1915 (Tichelman 1985:274).
[41] Note about Tjipto, NA, Kol. Openbaar, Vb. 26-1-1916 32.
[42] Note about Tjipto, NA, Kol. Openbaar, Vb. 26-1-1916 32.
[43] Attorney-General to Idenburg, 5-10-1915, *Assistent-Resident* Surabaya to *Resident* Surabaya, 12-4-1916, NA, Kol. Openbaar, Vb. 14-6-1919 26, Vb. 1-8-1916 15.

ordered his release from prison. The difference between the sentences pronounced against Mas Marco and Darnakoesoemo and against Dutchmen prosecuted for a similar offence had become too blatant. In a comparable court case in October a Dutch officer had been sentenced to one day's military detention. After he had appealed he was acquitted in December.[44]

A few months after his release Mas Marco went to Holland. He was impressed by the political freedom in Holland and by the activities of radical Dutch socialists. In The Hague he discussed the publication of a political journal in Malay with Soewardi. To avoid censorship it should be printed in Holland. High printing costs and the uncertainties of sea traffic prevented the realization of the plan. Instead, Mas Marco had a pamphlet printed in Holland: *No 1 November 1916, Boekoe Sebaran jang pertama oleh Mas Marco* (The first brochure by Mas Marco). A glance at the first page left no doubt about Mas Marco's intentions. It stated that to prevent people contemplating rising against Dutch rule in increasing numbers (it were the days of the troubles in Jambi and other parts of Sumatra), the colonial government should acquiesce in the requests made by the Javanese. On other pages the word *pemberontakan*, rebellion, figured prominently.

Mas Marco stayed in Holland for five months. His intention had been to stay longer but he decided to leave earlier. The winter cold had made him ill.[45] Upon his return in Java in February 1917, Mas Marco took over leadership of *Pantjaran Warta* (News Broadcast), a Sarekat Islam newspaper published in Batavia, from Goenawan, who did not feel physically fit enough to continue as editor-in-chief. For months *Pantjaran Warta* had earned itself the displeasure of the authorities for its attacks on the colonial government and its civil servants.[46] Mas Marco continued along this line. In Holland he had made no secret of the fact that he sympathized with the Jambi rebels and that a rebellion might be the right way to react to injustice and ill-treatment.[47] Back in Java Mas Marco called for action with renewed vigour. He told his readers that his time in Holland had fortified him in his conviction that courage was a prerequisite for success.[48] To bring home his ideas, Mas Marco started a series of articles in *Pantjaran Warta* entitled 'Sama rasa sama rata' (Fraternity and equality) published from 14 to 19 February. Soewardi, who, as Mas Marco wrote, 'lived in distressing circumstances' in Holland, was held up as an example. By exemplifying Soewardi, Mas Marco wanted to impress upon his readers

---

[44] Idenburg to Pleyte, 27-1-1916, NA, Kol. Openbaar, Vb. 13-4-1916 26.
[45] *De Indische Gids* 1917, I:520.
[46] Van Vuuren to Lulofs, 7-9-1916, Hazeu to Van Limburg Stirum, 15-10-1916, NA, Kol. Openbaar, Vb. 14-6-1919 26.
[47] *Sinar Djawa*, cited in *Koloniaal Tijdschrift* 1917:544.
[48] *Pantjaran Warta*, 13-2-1917, cited in *De Indische Gids* 1917, II:1080.

that sacrifices were essential on the road to emancipation. People who were afraid of 'convict labour, hunger, defamation, and death' would never attain their ideals.[49]

Mas Marco clearly did not believe that the Dutch government would grant the indigenous population status equal to that of the Europeans of its own free will: 'Brothers [...] the Government does not want this because it is afraid that then we the children of the Indies could no longer be extorted'.[50] He hinted that Indonesians would rise in rebellion if the demands for emancipation were not met: 'Government, we ask for equal rights! We the children of the country are dissatisfied. Agree to our request and avert a general uprising in the Indies, our fatherland!'[51] Mas Marco stressed, and he could hardly have done otherwise in the hope of escaping prosecution, that his words should be seen as a warning. He valued good relations with the 'elder brother', but if emancipation did not come, other ways would have to be resorted to reach this ideal.

Dutch people were shocked. They wanted the blood of this 'notorious native loudmouth', this 'demagogue in the worst sense of the word', whose short stay in Holland had turned his head. What he had written was worse than the 'Marxist bombast of Tjipto and Sneevliet'. Freedom of the press was one thing, allowing boorish improprieties of juveniles and loutish protests against the authorities by 'so-called intellectuals' was another.[52]

The public prosecutor of Batavia, Ch.Ph. du Cloux, decided to act. Mas Marco was taken into preventive custody on 21 February 1917. He was charged with sowing hatred and inciting the population to change or bring down the colonial government. Within days pamphlets in Malay and in Arab script were discovered, in which 'friends of Mas Marco' urged the members of the Sarekat Islam to rise on the first day of the Fasting Month against 'the unjust government, which had assailed Mas Marco who had only spoken the truth – and how well he had done so! – by putting him in jail'.[53] On the initiative of Insulinde, a committee was founded, the Sedyo Tama Fund, to support Mas Marco, his family, and 'others who will suffer in their struggle for the own people'.[54]

One side effect of Mas Marco's arrest was a change in the prison system. When they were interrogated, European prisoners were transported from the

---

[49] *Pantjaran Warta,* cited in *De Indische Gids* 1917, II:1079.
[50] *Pantjaran Warta,* cited in *De Indische Gids* 1917, I:793.
[51] *Pantjaran Warta,* cited in *De Indische Gids* 1917, II:1080.
[52] *De Preanger-bode, Bataviaasch Nieuwsblad, Bataviaasch Handelsblad,* and *Sumatra Post,* cited in *De Indische Gids* 1917, II:959, 1079-80, 1219, 1529.
[53] Hazeu to Van Limburg Stirum, 21-3-1917, NA, Kol. Openbaar, Vb. 8-11-1917 36.
[54] De Roo de la Faille to Van Limburg Stirum, 5-4-1917, NA, Kol. Openbaar, Vb. 8-11-1917 36.

prison to the courts by carriage. Indonesian prisoners were handcuffed and forced to walk escorted by a native policeman. Mas Marco felt humiliated by this treatment and protested. Du Cloux and Uhlenbeck had not given the way Mas Marco was treated a second thought. Handcuffing was standard procedure for native prisoners to prevent them trying to make their escape in the busy streets of Batavia. They had never heard a prisoner complain before. Nevertheless, swayed by Mas Marco's protest, Uhlenbeck instructed Du Cloux to discontinue this custom, but only in certain cases. Natives accused of offences against the press code and those who had to stand trial with European accomplices should in future be transported by carriage.[55] Du Cloux had to consent, but suggested that ordinary thieves and robbers should remain handcuffed. An exception might be made for 'prominent natives [...] and civilized and more educated natives, and all women'.[56] While making these concessions Du Cloux defended the old custom. He wrote to Uhlenbeck that it was common knowledge that native police officers were 'lazy, indolent, and corrupt, furthermore brazen and arrogant towards their inferiors and equals, and submissive and servile towards those who because of their previous post or previous social position, even though they were prisoners, were still seen by their guards as superiors, which explains why those guards in most instances would not act if such prisoners were to walk away during the transport'. Du Cloux gave the impression that Mas Marco had been done a great honour. Guards should be seen as escorts of honour to prisoners of high status. To explain this Du Cloux related how one important prisoner had 'strolled at his ease' from prison to the courthouse with the native police officer three steps behind him, carrying a dinner pail in one hand and in the other a bunch of bananas.

This time Mas Marco was sentenced to two years' imprisonment. The pretext of legal equality was abandoned. Later a representative of the colonial administration would state that the heavy sentence had nothing to do with class justice. Mas Marco simply had to be punished much more severely than Dutch journalists.[57] After Mas Marco appealed, the sentence was reduced to one year. By now he had become so popular that a Chinese firm in Kudus announced that it would sell cigarettes with the brand name Marco.[58] While serving his sentence in the civilian and military prison in Batavia, Mas Marco was not allowed to write for newspapers. He used his time to write *Student Hidjo* (Green Student) and other novels (Kartodikromo 2000:ix).

[55] Uhlenbeck to Du Cloux, 20-6-1917, Uhlenbeck to Van Limburg Stirum, 17-7-1917, NA, Kol. Openbaar, Vb. 8-11-1917 36.
[56] Du Cloux to Uhlenbeck, 7-7-1917, NA, Kol. Openbaar, Vb. 8-11-1917 36.
[57] *Volksraad* 1918:47.
[58] *Pantjaran Warta*, 6-7-1917, IPO 27/1917.

Tjipto Mangoenkoesoemo and Mas Marco were both avowed opponents of Indië Weerbaar. Tjipto Mangoenkoesoemo even had to deny the rumour that he would organize a protest meeting on 31 August 1916. Tjipto Mangoenkoesoemo of whom it was said at that time that he would again be banned to a far-away island, was too ill to do anything.[59] Mas Marco appealed to the readers of *Pantjaran Warta* to disobey the law and become conscientious objectors if a militia were to be created at the expense of the Javanese. He made this point crystal clear in a poem, 'Comité Indië Weerbaar', published in *Pantjaran Warta*, in which he observed that Indonesians refused to be used as soldiers by those who sucked their blood:

> Children of the Indies beware of the savages
> Because they are robbers of our vast lands
> Children of the Indies rely on God the Almighty
> The cheat cheats you.
> Children of the Indies beat them within an inch of their lives
> If necessary kill them
> Courage that is our weapon
> To live and to die truly.[60]

The same issue contained a drawing by the cartoonist of the Dutch monthly *De Wapens Neder* (Lay Down Your Arms) who Mas Marco had met in Holland. It showed a well-fed, fat Dutchman who held a skinny Javanese to the ground in a virtual stranglehold, exclaiming: 'O Lord! Please have this damned native defend my precious Insulinde!'[61]

The attacks by Tjipto Mangoenkoesoemo and Mas Marco were indicative of the fact that inadvertently the Indië Weerbaar drive had created a new and more intense debate about Dutch rule. Indonesian protagonists and opponents of Indië Weerbaar alike used a native militia as political leverage to win political reforms. As usual Tjipto Mangoenkoesoemo had been among the first who had seen the opportunity. Shortly after the outbreak of the war, *De Indiër* had carried an article written by Madjapaïtatma, who was almost certainly Tjipto Mangoenkoesoemo. Madjapaïtatma observed the war showed that in the West conflicts could only be solved by violence. It was a malicious delight to 'rejoice in the débâcle of that most superior of all races: the white one', but the readers should realize that the war could be used to force the oppressor into making concessions. Aware of their helplessness, the Dutch would realize that they had to appease the Indiërs by making allowances. The time had come to resist.[62]

---

[59] *De Locomotief*, 18-8-1916.
[60] *Pantjaran Warta*, 14-2-1917.
[61] *Pantjaran Warta*, cited in *De Indische Gids* 1917, II:1080.
[62] *De Indiër* 1-43:204.

In efforts to gain political concessions, good use was made of the fear the Japanese threat had elicited among the Dutch. Abdoel Moeis, for instance, capitalized on such trepidations during the dinner in the Zoological Gardens in Amsterdam when he spoke about a Foreign Power which threatened to become increasingly popular in the Netherlands Indies.[63] In an effort to demonstrate that a militia should be financed by those who had a vested interests in the Netherlands Indies remaining Dutch: the Dutch government and the rich, not the small people Dwidjosewojo said that ordinary people did not mind whether the foreign ruler was the Netherlands or Japan.

They tried to exploit Dutch fears just at a moment when Dutch people really became apprehensive about the consequences of a struggle for hegemony in the Pacific Ocean. Some were ready to accept the possibility that what they considered to be a contest between the white and yellow races would start with an invasion of the Netherlands Indies. Among the more prominent persons who held this view was the new naval commander, J.A.M. Bron, who had succeeded Pinke in 1916.[64] Others dreaded a situation in which the Allied Powers would sacrifice the Netherlands Indies to their own interests and Japan would have a free hand. The British would be too busy fighting a war in Europe. The United States would not dare to enter into a war which would give Tokyo the excuse to invade either the west coast of the United States or the Philippines.[65]

Opponents of Indië Weerbaar especially succeeded in touching a raw Dutch nerve. Dutch people felt it very difficult to swallow, after Tjipto Mangoenkoesoemo had resumed his political activities, what he said about Dutch fears of Japan. Hazeu noted that he did so with a certain degree of pleasure.[66] The cry 'banzai' could be read in issues of *De Voorpost* (The Advanced Position), a weekly started by Tjipto Mangoenkoesoemo in December 1915 as the Dutch-language equivalent of *Modjopait*. When Tjipto Mangoenkoesoemo ventured to suggest that Batavia would not dare to act against Insulinde if Insulinde had the support of Tokyo, this provoked howls of outrage in the Dutch community. *De Locomotief* called Tjipto Mangoenkoesoemo's remark below the belt. Other Dutch-language newspapers speculated about the likelihood of Tjipto Mangoenkoesoemo's arrest. Indignation reached a peak when *Modjopait* wrote in the middle of 1916 that Insulinde would accept Japanese as members. Tjipto Mangoenkoesoemo ventured to speculate how strong eight to ten thousand Japanese members would be making Insulinde. The PID was

---

[63] *De Indische Gids* 1917, I:802.
[64] Bron to Van Limburg Stirum, 15-5-1917, NA, Kol. Geheim, Vb. 3-5-1918 O4.
[65] Note retired officer P. van der Haas, NA, Kol. Openbaar, Vb. 8-12-1916 ????.
[66] Advice Hazeu 21-8-1916, NA, Kol. Openbaar, Vb. 22-11-1916 6.

goaded into action, searching assiduously for information about the relationship between Insulinde and Japanese living in the Netherlands Indies. In Muurling's eyes *De Voorpost* was 'unquestionably revolutionary'. It showed the same tendencies as the Indische Partij. What was written in *De Voorpost* coupled with the 'prophet's mantle of the former Indische Partij' which Insulinde now wore warranted the surveillance of Insulinde by the PID.[67] The distrust of Insulinde, strengthened by the information about Douwes Dekker's exploits in Japan transformed Insulinde into a dangerous party. It also was an extra reason to distrust Minami, the editor of *Pertimbangan*. After his arrest, a police investigation revealed Minami's contacts with Insulinde members. All was a hoax, which happened at a rather unfortunate moment, just when renewed speculations about an alliance between Germany and Japan began to be bandied about. Only one Japanese in Batavia had asked whether he could join Insulinde. There had been no objections. Britons, Germans, Frenchmen and other foreigners were also welcome if they supported the policy of Insulinde.[68] Tjipto Mangoenkoesoemo and other party leaders had deliberately spread the word about the prospective Japanese members to tease the PID and to irritate the Dutch community.

Mas Marco also made good use of the spectre of a Japanese threat to the Netherlands Indies:

> I think that the Government knows very well, that we natives, children of the Indies, will reach out our hands to the Japanese as gesture of fraternization. [...] Would the government be strong enough to ward off the [combined] force of the danger that is already present domestically and the one that threatens from abroad?[69]

Japan was more than a bogeyman to frighten the Dutch government into concessions. Japan was also a symbol to Indonesians. It may even be that, in contrast to the many public statements to the contrary, some Indonesians would have actually preferred Japanese rule over that of the Dutch. In the past, *al-Imam*, which was published in Singapore between 1906 and 1908, had already in some of its articles expressed the hope that Japan might liberate the Javanese (Laffan 2006:12). Such hopes probably had not disappeared. In 1917 the Malay-Chinese newspaper *Perniagaan* wondered whether those who favoured a change in overlordship were really convinced that Japan would honour their aspirations, and under such circumstances what the fate of 'the Chinese and other races' would be.[70]

As a modern nation ranking among the world Powers, Japan provided an

---

[67] *Volksraad* 1918:288.
[68] *De Locomotief,* 7-6-1916, 10-6-1916.
[69] *Pantjaran Warta,* cited in *De Indische Gids* 1917, I:794.
[70] *Perniagaan,* 7-7-1917, IPO 27/1917.

alternative to the option of assimilation to Western culture. Some Javanese – the *Nieuwe Rotterdamsche Courant* called them discontented natives – contemplated sending their children to Japan for their education.[71] Hearing about such plans radical Muslims prayed that these children would succeed and become examples for their fellow-countrymen in their struggle to gain their rights as human beings.[72] Even leaving aside the consequences of the war, going to Japanese schools made good sense. Japan was much closer by than Holland. Education in Japan was cheaper. As in the case of Arab children who went to school in Turkey, the matter was blown up out of proportion. Figures of over a hundred children who wanted to go to Japan to study were mentioned. Probably not many more than five actually went. Certainly a certain degree of alarm was felt. Dutch people nurtured some apprehension that the discontent the desire for schooling in Japan reflected could provide Japan with the pretext to intervene and invade the Netherlands Indies to liberate its population.[73]

In the eyes of Indonesian nationalists, the reports about boys leaving for Japan provided an excellent occasion to attack the lack of educational facilities for the indigenous population. Soewardi said that it may come as an unpleasant surprise to the Dutchmen to learn about such cases, but they should realize that parents wanted to send their children to Japan because of the very limited educational opportunities on offer in the Netherlands Indies. As long as the Dutch tried to keep Indonesians 'quiet by ethical promises and bureaucratic intentions without any visible deeds and tangible results', it was in the interests of Indonesians to send their children to schools in Japan.[74]

In the second half of 1916 and the beginning of 1917, opposition to Indië Weerbaar became increasingly articulate. The founding of the Indië Weerbaar committees formed a kind of fault line. Nationalists were forced to make up their minds. Illustrative of this choice is how Moehammad Joesoef, a future leader of the Indonesian left, reacted. As chairman of the Semarang branch of the Sarekat Islam he had become a member of the local Indië Weerbaar committee. He was forced to resign after a meeting of the Semarang Sarekat Islam had spoken out against the movement.[75] Other leaders of the Sarekat Islam and Boedi Oetomo, but not all of them, continued to support the Indië Weerbaar ideas. Sometimes they turned the meetings of these organizations into manifestations of loyalty. Audiences stood to attention when the Dutch national anthem was sung and cheered speakers who praised the

---

[71] *Nieuwe Rotterdamsche Courant*, cited in *De Indische Gids* 1918, I:483.
[72] *Islam Bergerak*, 20-5-1917.
[73] *Indische Gids* 1917, II:1110; *Koloniaal Tijdschrift* 1917:1089-90.
[74] *Indische Gids* 1917, II:1110.
[75] *De Locomotief*, 12-8-1916, 14-8-1916.

achievements of Dutch rule. On other occasions, praise was greeted with hoots. Opposition to a militia was growing. Proponents who observed that, if anything, the ordinary people who were anti-militia began to waver.[76] Branches which had initially spoken out in favour now turned against. This happened not only in Java, but also in Sumatra, where the *Sinar Sumatra* (Ray of Sumatra) and the Chinese-Malay newspaper *Andalas* now proved extremely hostile. Anti-Indië Weerbaar pamphlets were distributed, some of which were in Malay, and at times confiscated by the authorities. The word conscript was translated as *soldadoe paksaan*, coerced soldier. Militia members would be *oempan meriam*, cannon fodder. A much used argument was that soldiers were supposed to defend house and homeland; but did the Javanese have a house and homeland of their own? The trend was unmistakable. ISDV members did their best to stir opposition. Sneevliet made the slogan *geen man en geen cent* (no man and no penny) for defence purposes a popular one. Another prominent ISDV leader who put his oar in was A. Baars, an engineer from the Technical University of Delft, who had found work as a teacher at the Koningin Emmaschool, a technical high school in Surabaya. Baars was one of the few Dutch ISDV members fluent in Malay. *De Locomotief* reported on 28 August that 'Mr Baars especially distinguished himself by going around the kampongs, advising non cooperation'.

On 31 August 1916, when the pro-Indië Weerbaar movement climaxed, a protest meeting was held in Semarang in the theatre (and not in the City Gardens; its board had refused to host the meeting). The protest meeting was organized by local leaders of the Sarekat Islam, Insulinde, and the ISDV; perhaps the reason why Insulinde and the Semarang branch of the ISDV were described at that time in *De Locomotief* as 'the anti-Netherlands groups'.[77] The leftist Sarekat Islam newspaper, *Sinar Djawa*, estimated that the protest meeting was attended by 4,000 people. Most were Javanese.[78] *De Locomotief*, writing that about 3,000 people had been present, was impressed. Never had the theatre been so chock-full. *De Locomotief* was also a little awed. Most of those attending were natives, who were certainly not drawn from 'intellectual circles'.[79] Posters were distributed by Ch. Razoux Kühr, one of the nestors of the Indo-European and nationalist press. It showed a column of Indonesians being drilled by Van Hinloopen Labberton. Sneevliet was one of the speakers. Initially the *Resident* had forbidden the meeting. His colleague in Surabaya had done the same. In Semarang, the *Resident* finally capitulated when J.J.E. Teeuwen of Insulinde and others told him that if he persisted trouble might

---

[76] See, for instance, Dwidjo Soemarto in *Neratja*, 18-9-1918.
[77] *De Locomotief*, 6-9-1916.
[78] *Sinar Djawa*, cited in *Koloniaal Tijdschrift* 1917:100.
[79] *De Locomotief*, 31-8-1916.

be in store. There was a great chance that the opponents of a militia would attend the pro-Indië Weerbaar manifestation in town. Even though allowed to go ahead, the freedom of the meeting was strictly curbed. The organizers had had to submit an anti-Indië Weerbaar resolution to the authorities in advance for approval. When they read out another one at the meeting – mentioning colonial capitalist interest as the main motivation for the Indië Weerbaar movement and speaking about the population being without rights and politically kept under tutelage – they were called to order. The organizers had to settle with the original resolution, which merely stated that the founding of a militia should be decided upon by an elected parliament in the Netherlands Indies. In Surabaya protesters, not allowed to have their own meeting, had succeeded in putting leaflets on the chairs and tables in the City Park where the pro-Indië Weerbaar meeting was to take place. The leaflets with the texts 'Against Indië Weerbaar' and 'Demand debate!' were removed by the police before the meeting opened.

The report to Parliament by Pleyte about 1916 noted that the campaign for a militia had unintentionally contributed to 'the growth of the slumbering political life'.[80] The editor of *De Locomotief* agreed. Though he absolutely could not bring himself to agree with the anti-Indië Weerbaar manifestations – Stokvis called these politically dirty and inferior and seemingly blamed a number of Europeans and Indo-Europeans for this – he wrote that 31 August had been a 'beautiful day'. For the first time a political issue had been raised in the Netherlands Indies in which Europeans and Indonesian groups showed an almost general interest. It also, pleased him that Indonesians had made their own judgement, based on their own interests.[81]

The Semarang meeting was an unequivocal indication that leaders had emerged who would give substance to an Anti-Weerbaarheids movement. They rejected a militia out of hand, at least as long as political and social emancipation had not been attained, or, as some stressed, as long as compulsory education had not yet become a fact. Fuelling the doubts about a native militia was the fact that also outside the Dutch community defeatism about the outcome of a war which might have to be fought ran riot. In July 1917 *Oetoesan Hindia* wrote that it was useless to defend the Netherlands Indies against Japan. Better it was to promote the spiritual and material development of the Netherlands Indies. The best course would be to pray to God that one might be spared an invasion.'[82]

Among all non-European population groups, the militia debate was a means to call attention to the discrimination their members experienced.

---

[80] *Koloniaal verslag* 1917:1.
[81] *De Locomotief*, 1-9-1916.
[82] *Oetoesan Hindia*, 28-7-1917, cited in *De Indische Gids* 1918, I:225.

Opposition to a militia among the Chinese was widespread. They had been conspicuously absent at Indië Weerbaar manifestations. The government did not intend to include Foreign Orientals in a militia but this did not prevent Chinese-Malay newspapers and Chinese organizations rejecting conscription with a passion. They seized upon the militia debate to bring home their demands for emancipation. Why should they become cannon-fodder as long as the colonial government treated Chinese as Foreign Orientals, as long as nothing had been done to make the Chinese feel that the Netherlands Indies was their home?[83] Or, as one of them put this in an article in the *Soerabaiasch Handelsblad* why should the Chinese care about the defence of the Netherlands Indies when they were clearly treated as foreigners and not as Indonesians. The government viewed them as Foreign Orientals. It discriminated against them in many ways including the field of education. The schools open to Chinese were few and of a lower quality than the elementary schools for Europeans. Worse, other foreigners, including the Japanese, 'who are not on a higher level in civilization than the average Chinese', were treated better. Almost all Dutch-language newspapers contained offensive remarks about Chinese. In a nutshell the message was the Chinese could not feel any love for the Netherlands Indies as their homeland. Supporting Indië Weerbaar meant treason against their real homeland, China.[84] Dutch officials tried to neutralize such voices by pointing out that Chinese should be aware that they would be much worse off under Japanese rule. Reaction was prompt. The Chinese suffered from legal discrimination and the lack of educational opportunities.[85] It did not take long for those Chinese who had acquired European status to realize that a militia might well imply, as it indeed did, that their sons would be called up for military service.

One of the specific objections the Chinese raised was equally relevant to many Javanese, at least to the devout Muslims among them. In a letter to *De Locomotief* it was explained that conscription posed insurmountable problems for the Chinese community. The wives of Chinese conscripts could not join their husbands in the barracks. Inescapable part of an unyielding patriarchal society for them to live on their own was out of the question. Another problem adduced was that Chinese did not pray in a church or mosque. They did so at home in front of a family altar. This made compulsory military service even more problematic. In short: the militia was 'a terrible blow to Chinese prosperity'.[86]

In the Arab community there was likewise much opposition to compulsory

---

[83] *Warna Warta,* cited in *Koloniaal Tijdschrift* 1917:1360.
[84] *Soerabaiasch Handelsblad,* cited in *De Locomotief,* 7-9-1916.
[85] *Warna Warta,* cited in *Koloniaal Tijdschrift* 1917:113.
[86] *De Locomotief,* 19-11-1917.

Abdoel Moeis, circa 1916 (KITLV 7814)

military service. At protest meetings rejection was coupled with demands that the immigration rules be relaxed. Yet another group which used the discussion about a native militia to protest about discrimination was the Ambonese. Their major complaint was that in the army they were treated as inferiors to Europeans. Spokesmen in the Ambonese community despised the idea that only when the very existence of the Netherlands Indies was in danger was assistance asked of people who had not even been considered to be human beings in the past.[87]

In Java the Indië Weerbaar movement became a serious bone of contention within the Sarekat Islam. It split the party into two camps, if indeed it did not threaten to break it up completely. Dissenting voices reached a crescendo when the Indië Weerbaar deputation visited Holland. In Surakarta, the local Sarekat Islam branch sent a wire to the Queen, stating that Abdoel Moeis did not have the support of the native population or that of the Sarekat Islam.[88] In Semarang a massive protest meeting organized by both the Sarekat Islam and Insulinde and attended by two thousand people demanded that a representative body be formed first before the constitution of a militia could be contemplated. In Batavia speakers at a Sarekat Islam meeting warned that a native militia might well turn against the Dutch.[89] In the same city Goenawan, an avowed opponent of Indië Weerbaar, sent a telegram to Soewardi in The Hague, who forwarded it to the Dutch socialist leader, P.J. Troelstra. It claimed that 90 per cent of the Sarekat Islam supporters did not give a damn about a militia.[90]

Singled out for attack was Abdoel Moeis. He would suffer greatly for his participation in the deputation. In *Sinar Djawa* and its successor, *Sinar Hindia*, he was castigated for his role in Indië Weerbaar and for the alleged anti-Chinese speeches he had made in Europe. From then on, relations between Abdoel Moeis and the radical nationalist left would only deteriorate. His moderate, independent views constantly drew the scorn of the left wing of the Sarekat Islam. In the political struggle Abdoel Moeis had to fight with radical ISDV and Sarekat Islam leaders he could count on the support of the non-Javanese members among the Sarekat Islam leaders and in Java on that of a still large section in the Islamic community who could not stomach ISDV propaganda. Some of them presented Abdoel Moeis's trip to Europe as a great contribution to the nationalist cause. Abdoel Moeis's achievement had been to inform the public in Holland about the miserable fate of the indigenous people in the colony. What Abdoel Moeis had said about the Chinese did not bother such people. He had merely put their thoughts into words.

Abdoel Moeis became an easy prey after his return from Holland when he resigned his position as editor-in chief in *Kaoem Moeda* to become editor-in-chief of the daily *Neratja* (Balance), in which he would strike back at his ISDV critics in September 1917. *Neratja* was founded, Spijkman had played a role in this, with the financial support of the colonial administration. The formal reason for the support given *Neratja* was that Batavia needed a Malay-language

---

[87] *De Voorpost*, cited in *Koloniaal Tijdschrift* 1917, I:112.
[88] *De Locomotief*, 12-2-1917.
[89] *Koloniaal Tijdschrift* 1917:239, 1109.
[90] *Indische Gids* 1917, I:799, II:1080.

newspaper if only to allow the government to keep track of what its inhabitants thought. *Pantjaran Warta* had run into financial troubles and was tottering on its last legs.[91] It were good intentions, weren't it that as early as January 1913 Rinkes had suggested to Idenburg that were a Malay version of *De Expres* to be published, it might be worthwhile considering support for 'good native papers'.[92] As its name indicates *Neratja* wanted to present a balanced view of developments in the Netherlands Indies. To make matters worse for Abdoel Moeis he also became an editor of *Inlandsche Stemmen* (Native Voices), a few months later baptized *Indische Stemmen*, a weekly dedicated to 'the association idea', of which the purpose was to provide Europeans who were 'well-disposed towards the natives' with information about developments in the indigenous society.[93] Contrary to what his critics said, Abdoel Moeis had not forfeited his nationalist views. *Neratja* remained critical of colonial conditions. Abdoel Moeis was in favour of association and gradual emancipation. This ideal was likewise expressed in the name of the firm which printed *Neratja*: Evolutie.

The attacks on Abdoel Moeis formed part of the efforts of the ISDV to expand its influence. Leftist Indonesians took control of the VSTP. They also made considerable headway in the Sarekat Islam. In Central and East Java especially the influence of the ISDV in the Sarekat Islam and among the indigenous population at large was growing fast. The social democrats had succeeded in forming a strong leftist faction in the Sarekat Islam. This success had largely been because of a number of prominent Indonesian members of the ISDV: Semaoen, Moehammad Joesoef (Deputy Chairman of the Semarang Sarekat Islam branch), Alimin (who had been raised by Hazeu), and Darsono. The advance to prominence of ISDV members who had also succeeded in taking control of the VSTP, in the Sarekat Islam was grist to the mill of those pleading for resolute action against a radical vernacular press and against inflammatory speeches. The *Resident* of Surabaya went as far as to suggest that the enrolment of Indonesians in secondary schools should be restricted. Too many teachers were Dutch social democrats.[94] The ISDV also gained some influence in the Chinese community, but this received much less attention in the reports and comments on the actions of the ISDV than its efforts to win over the Javanese.

To step up propaganda amongst the population, the ISDV founded an

---

[91] *Volksraad* 1918:550.
[92] Rinkes to Idenburg, 16-1-1913 (*Bescheiden 'Indische Partij'* 1913:159).
[93] *De Locomotief*, 6-11-1917.
[94] Creutzberg to Van Limburg Stirum, 24-11-1916, Hazeu to Van Limburg Stirum, 23-3-1917, NA, Kol. Openbaar, Vb. 14-6-1919 26.

organization especially for Javanese in April 1917. The initiative was taken by Baars. The movement founded was the Inlandsche Sociaal-Democratische Vereeniging Hindia Bergerak (Native Social Democrat Union Hindia Bergerak). Sometime later the organization was rechristened Sama Rata Hindia Bergerak (Equality in the Indies [Nationalist] Movement). It had about two hundred members.[95] President was Darsoeki. Darnakoesoemo (who also had been editor of *Pertimbangan*) was one of the board members. The first issue of its weekly, *Soeara Merdika*, the Voice of Freedom, was published in Semarang at the end of April 1917. Among its editors were Semaoen and Baars. The Perhimpoenan Kaoem Boeroeh dan Tani (PKBT, Labourers' and Farmers' Union), was also said to be a 'native ISDV'. Most of its leaders were members of the ISDV.[96]

One of the consequences of the growing influence of the ISDV in the Sarekat Islam and the VSTP was the worsening relationship between Tjipto Mangoenkoesoemo and Sneevliet. One reason for the deterioration was that international socialist ideals and Insulinde's nationalism were out of kilter with each other. Tjipto Mangoenkoesoemo stressed that in the Netherlands Indies nationalism was more important than the attainment of socialist ideals. Sneevliet wanted to run before he could walk. Nationalism and a gradual evolution was what the Netherlands Indies needed. His flirtation with Japanese support aggravated the divide. The sarcasm and teasing tone with which Tjipto Mangoenkoesoemo played on the Dutch fear of Japan completely passed Sneevliet. To Sneevliet, who had also fallen to the hoax about Japanese membership of Insulinde, any praise of Japan was an abhorrence. When rumours circulated about groups in Japan which claimed Java and Sumatra as a reward for Japan's involvement in the war in May 1916, the ISDV put a number of questions to the central board of Insulinde. One concerned information about Douwes Dekker's trip to Japan and China. The Insulinde leaders likewise had to explain what they thought about the slogan 'Asia for the Asians', a possible Germano-Japanese coalition, and the threat Japan posed to the Netherlands Indies. When Sneevliet failed to get a satisfactory reply, he attacked Tjipto Mangoenkoesoemo and Douwes Dekker for their sympathy for Japan, the imperialist enemy. Referring to Douwes Dekker's role in the Germano-Indian plot, at its annual meeting in June 1916 Sneevliet also succeeded in having the ISDV accept a motion ending any cooperation with Insulinde at its annual meeting. The motion was received with 'lively applause' and carried unanimously.

The Insulinde leaders denied any knowledge of Douwes Dekker's exploits. In their turn they attacked Sneevliet's denunciations of Douwes Dekker, the

---

[95] Annual report ISDV, cited in *Neratja* 16-5-1918. In total the ISDV was said to have 740 members.
[96] *Assistent-Resident* Kudus to *Resident* Semarang, 25-8-1919 (*Sarekat Islam* 1975:182).

Indische Partij, and Insulinde and countered by asking whether the ISDV supported the statement of the Dutch social democrat, W.H. Vliegen, asserting that were the Netherlands to become involved in the war it would have to side with the Allies, if only not to lose the Netherlands Indies.[97]

On its side, Insulinde indicated that it would only be prepared to cooperate with the ISDV if Sneevliet (and the chairman of the VSTP, H.W. Dekker) resigned as members.[98] The writing was on the wall. After the ISDV motion Insulinde announced in *De Voorpost* that it had ended all cooperation with the ISDV.[99] The two parties still fielded a joint candidate for the election to fill a vacancy in the municipal Coucil of Semarang in August 1916, but after this they grew only further apart. In August 1917 Insulinde once more declared it had broken with the ISDV. Its leaders accused 'a few' ISDV members, namely Sneevliet and his associates, of trying to drive a wedge between the Indo-Europeans and the indigenous population and of sowing discord within and between organizations.[100] *De Indiër*, a new Insulinde daily newspaper which had replaced *De Voorpost*, deplored the uncompromising criticism with which the ISDV greeted 'the nationalism which we have taken as the motor of our movement'.[101] Later, in March 1918, during the annual Insulinde congress where the stage was brightened up by life-sized portraits of Douwes Dekker and Diponegoro, Tjipto Mangoenkoesoemo, who by now styled himself the most irreconcilable enemy of Sneevliet complained about the destructive criticism uttered by 'a certain group of fellow-citizens, who pretend all the time they have a monopoly on wisdom'.[102] With 'sweet but cunning' words these 'political adventurers' had come in as guests, had enjoyed the hospitality of Insulinde, but after a while had begun to try to sow discord.[103]

In Holland Soewardi took the side of his long-time friend and of Insulinde. In favour of continuing the cooperation with the ISDV, he put the blame for the rift on a small faction in the ISDV, which 'bluntly loathes the nationalism of the Indiërs and because of this fiercely fights the members of Insulinde'. The main culprit was the 'Marxist Sneevliet'. Soewardi's conclusion was that because of 'his fierce fight against our nationalism' Sneevliet had done 'a great deal to discredit the whole socialist movement'.[104] Others used the nationalist argument to explain why they sought cooperation with Insulinde and not with ISDV. Among them were leaders of a newly established Chinese labour

[97] *De Locomotief*, 7-6-1916.
[98] *De Locomotief*, 20-5-1916.
[99] *De Locomotief*, 21-6-1916.
[100] Tichelman 1985:630; *De Indische Gids* 1918, I:333.
[101] *De Indische Gids* 1918, I:334; *Volksraad* 1918:288.
[102] *De Locomotief*, 1-4-1918.
[103] *De Locomotief*, 1-4-1918.
[104] *De Indische Gids* 1917, II:1221.

organization in Semarang, the Tiong Hoa Ieng Giap Hwe.[105]

The position of Sneevliet and his close political friends was not uncontested even in the ISDV. The opposition was led by R.A. Schotman and other members of the Batavian branch. They wanted the ISDV to follow a more moderate course. Eschewing militancy they stressed evolution and the parliamentary way of tackling matters. What the Dutch government was doing in the colony was not all wrong. Schotman and his friends, much more akin to the rest of the Dutch community in the colony than Sneevliet and Baars were, were convinced Indonesian society was not yet ripe for radical action or independence. The 'naive and by inclination quickly inflammable population' should be taught discipline and had to be shown how to organize themselves.[106] Sneevliet's mistake was that he did not differentiate between the conditions in Holland and those in the Netherlands Indies. He treated the people of the Netherlands Indies 'as if they had already reached the same level as most peoples in Europe in political and economic respect'. The great majority of them were still peasants. They were not yet ripe for real social-democratic propaganda, which a proletariat was. Industrialization had to proceed before a strategy like that advocated by Sneevliet could be implemented.[107] A suggestion by Baars that the Indonesians be given universal suffrage did not go down well with them either.[108] Schotman had a low opinion of Indonesians. At most they could manage a *warung*. Were they to become independent their leader would become 'a tyrant, such as Holland has never known and never again will know' (Tichelman 1985:517). He and his friends also feared that the agitation by Sneevliet and Baars might in the end only result in another country taking over. Such a new overlord would behave in such a way that Dutch rule would seem to have been 'mere child's play' (Tichelman 1985:534).

The ideological differences came to a head at the fourth general meeting of the ISDV held in Surabaya in May 1917. It was attended by a little over twenty members and about an equal number of Indonesians. The content of *Het Vrije Woord* (The Free Word), the organ of the ISDV established in October 1915 and edited by Sneevliet, Baars, and D.J.A. Westerveld, was one of the issues. The Batavian branch protested about the way in which *Het Vrije Woord* made propaganda for 'a sectarian school of thought in the International'.[109] Schotman blamed Sneevliet's continued exhortion of European dogmas in a colonial society without having provided the most elementary social demo-

---

[105] *Neratja*, 6-8-1918.
[106] *De Indische Gids* 1917, II:1073.
[107] *De Indische Gids* 1917, II: 1223.
[108] *Handelingen Tweede Kamer* 1918-19:2079; Tichelman 1985: 662.
[109] *De Indische Gids* 1917, II:1217.

cratic schooling for the fact that the ISDV had remained such a small group (Tichelman 1985:516). A breach had become unavoidable. The tone at times was harsh. Schotman said that Sneevliet suffered from 'auto-sadism'; later at the request of an angry Sneevliet toned this down to *zelfpijniging,* self-torment, that is denigrating himself as a Dutchmen, as a *totok*. Baars was a 'revolutionary romanticist'. Another ISDV radical, J.C. Stam (or Aroen), was *daverend krankzinnig* (completely and utterly mad). Mas Marco was a *fantast* (dreamer) (Tichelman 1985:517, 520, 534-5).

The war had exacerbated the conflict among the socialists. Sneevliet and his friends were avowed opponents of the support the socialist parties, including the Sociaal-Democratische Arbeiderspartij gave their government during the war. They wanted to continue to fight colonialism and capitalism, preferably in fact to intensify the struggle (Baars and Sneevliet 1991:100-1).

The moderate members – ten in total – parted company with the ISDV on 1 September 1917. The following week they formed the Department of the SDAP in the Netherlands Indies. Ch.G. Cramer was appointed chairman. He averred that the SDAP in the Netherlands Indies was prepared for an 'enduring struggle by a resolute, well-organized mass'. It detested the anarchistic action of which it accused the ISDV, which would only result in 'disturbances and slaughter, by which the people's movement will be seriously harmed and which will set the movement back for years'. A revolution had to wait till a 'well-educated, excellently organized working class was ready to take over the government from the ruling class'.[110] These were fine words but they did not butter any parsnips. Cramer and his political friends were apparently among those leftist Dutchmen whose contacts with ordinary Indonesians were minimal. Tjokroaminoto at least asked them to show that they were prepared to assist in organizing the masses and 'to descent down from their high position to [join] the mass, the people'.[111] The breach was later singled out by Idenburg as the moment from which the ISDV and the influence it exerted on the Sarekat Islam had gone from bad to worse.[112]

The ISDV propaganda did not fail to leave its mark. Some newspapers began to be replete with socialist jargon. One of these was *Sinar Djawa*. In October 1917 it came under the control of the ISDV. Alimin, Semaoen, and Moehammad Joesoef took on the job of unpaid editors and announced that *Sinar Djawa* was of 'a radical persuasion'.[113] In April 1918 their friend, Darsono, started a campaign against the 'money devils' in *Sinar Djawa* in April 1918. His articles

---

[110] *Volksraad* 1918-19:210.
[111] *Volksraad* 1918-19:544.
[112] *Handelingen Tweede Kamer* 1918-19:2079.
[113] Press report Rinkes, NA, Kol. Openbaar, Vb. 17-9-1915 46; *De Locomotief,* 26-11-1917.

made a great impression. The pejorative 'money devils' was soon copied by others. Darsono stressed that once the money devils had disappeared, an 'equitable government (*pemerintah sama rasa sama rata*)' would be achieved. He gave his words an extra dimension by adding that such a government was what had been called the coming of the Just King in ancient prophecies.[114] Though Attorney-General Uhlenbeck rated the articles by Darsono 'boyish' and 'inexperienced', and therefore not worth a prosecution, he still considered it necessary to keep a weather eye on *Sinar Djawa*.[115] Other Indonesian nationalists and their press began to attack the 'capitalists'. At times they included the Chinese in their assessment.

Socialist ideas and socialist jargon spread in broad layers of the nationalist movement, never again to lose their popularity. Tjokroaminoto blamed capitalism for the war in Europe.[116] The nineteenth-century Javanese rebel and hero Diponegoro was introduced to readers of *Oetoesan Hindia* as an anti-capitalist.[117] In another issue the commemoration of the martyrdom of Muhammad's grandsons, Husein and Hasan, was taken up to demonstrate that the price of the advancement of Islam and the protection of the people against oppression was 'a flood of blood'. 'Life... or death! should become the banners of the leaders of the People.'[118] Muhammad, it had already been stated at the first national congress of the Sarekat Islam in June 1916, was 'the father of Socialism and the pioneer of democracy'. He was the 'Socialist *par excellence*'.[119] Villagers in Cilacap were told that *sama rata* was the aim of Islam.[120] In *Islam Bergerak* contributors did their utmost to explain that the ideals of social democracy, social justice, and *sama rasa sama rata* had been an integral part of Islam since the time of Muhammad. In its pages it was stressed that a proper interpretation of Islam and the courage to resist the whims of an arbitrary government were essential to instil in the *kromo*, the people, in order they might recover their dignity and become full human beings. Islam demanded that an unjust government be opposed.[121] 'Si Rakjat' (The People) pointed out that China and Russia had shown what the fate of an oppressive regime which sided with the capitalists and was insensitive to the suffering of the people could be.[122] Illustrative of the mood among some Javanese was the plan to publish a bi-weekly in Purbalingga named *Anti Willekeur*, Anti-Arbitrariness.[123]

[114] *Sinar Djawa*, 4-4-1918, NA, Kol. Openbaar, Vb. 14-6-1919 26.
[115] Uhlenbeck to Van Limburg Stirum, 20-4-1918, NA, Kol. Openbaar, Vb. 14-6-1919 26.
[116] *Volksraad* 1918:150.
[117] *Oetoesan Hindia*, 17-9-1918.
[118] *Oetoesan Hindia*, 15-10-1918.
[119] *Sarekat-Islam Congres* 1916:27.
[120] *Oetoesan Hindia*, 1-8-1918.
[121] *Islam Bergerak*, 10-6-1918, 20-8-1918.
[122] *Islam Bergerak*, 20-7-1918.
[123] *Neratja*, 21-8-1918.

Suppression became a catchword to explain all evil. In August 1918 Uhlenbeck observed that suppression was invariably mentioned in the native press in the evaluations of events, whether this was relevant or not. The trend was reason enough for him to urge a closer supervision of this press, and to advise the colonial government not to hesitate to take legal action.[124]

Echoing what had happened to Douwes Dekker a few years earlier Sneevliet and Baars had become an example to all groups demanding radical change. They had earned themselves a reputation as unselfish champions of the oppressed. In a Chinese newspaper Sneevliet was compared to Sun Yat Sen. A parallel was drawn between the Netherlands Indies and the overthrow of the Emperor by social democrats in China. The author wrote that Sneevliet had shown both natives and the Chinese how to force white people to respect them as human beings and finally to realize that they too were members of humankind.[125]

Tjipto Mangoenkoesoemo and Insulinde were less successful. Using slogans such as *Rawé-rawé rantas malang malang poetoeng, Berani karena benar takoet karena salah* (maybe the most popular of them all and also adopted as its motto by the Chinese/Malay newspaper *Djawa Tengah*), *Semoea boeat satoe, satoe boeat semoea* (All for one, one for all), and *Sama rasa dan sama rata*, Tjipto Mangoenkoesoemo had tried to expand his influence. Incontrovertibly he did succeed in winning a following, especially in Surakarta and surrounding areas. Elsewhere he and Insulinde lost out to the ISDV. As early as February 1915, Rinkes concluded that the Indische Party or Insulinde was no longer very *lakoe*, very popular.[126] In August 1916 Hazeu stated that Tjipto Mangoenkoesoemo had become isolated. Other nationalists had surpassed him.[127] In spite of his political demise, Tjipto Mangoenkoesoemo continued to be widely revered as a person who had made great personal sacrifices for his people. Only very conservative groups thought otherwise.[128]

The apparent success of the ISDV propaganda, for contemporaries, as well as for later generations, has clouded the importance of people like Douwes Dekker and Tjipto Mangoenkoesoemo to the development of radical nationalism. The irritation and anxiety they had caused seemed to have been forgotten. They were not held responsible for what was considered a turn to the left in the nationalist movement. Still viewing moderate nationalism as the way in which a gradual emancipation of the population could be accomplished

---

[124] Circular letter Uhlenbeck, 26-8-1918, NA, Kol. Geheim, Mr. 1918/371x.
[125] *Tjhoen Tjhoei*, cited in *De Locomotief*, 4-6-1918.
[126] Rinkes to Idenburg, 13-2-1915, 15-10-1915, NA, Kol. Openbaar, Vb. 6-1-1916 1, Vb. 26-1-1916 32.
[127] Advice Hazeu, 21-8-1916, NA, Kol. Openbaar, Vb. 22-11-1916 6.
[128] Advice Hazeu, 21-8-1916, NA, Kol. Openbaar, Vb. 22-11-1916 6.

and prepared to put up with the occasional 'excesses', Batavia and The Hague acted as stern fathers who were prepared to forgive their sons much. Van Limburg Stirum appointed Tjipto Mangoenkoesoemo a member of the People's Council. Soewardi was allowed to return to Java as early as August 1917, but because of the disruption of sea traffic had been forced to remain in Holland. Van Limburg Stirum revoked the decision to intern Douwes Dekker in Timor in July 1918. Douwes Dekker returned to Java at once. Even before the end of the month he had travelled on to Semarang. Here at the end of July he met Tjipto Mangoenkoesoemo for the first time in years. The reunion was 'touching'.[129]

In the Netherlands Indies there was not much opposition to Douwes Dekker's return. The reason for this, and maybe such considerations had also inspired Pleyte and Van Limburg Stirum, was the hope that he could act as a counterpoise to ISDV propaganda. Suddenly editors of the Dutch-language newspapers concluded that what Insulinde and Douwes Dekker were striving for, independence of the Netherlands Indies, was a moderate course. It was greatly to be preferred to what Sneevliet and his comrades wanted to accomplish.[130] After all, the European community was also steering for greater independence from Holland.

---

[129] *Neratja*, 1-8-1918.
[130] *Nieuwe Courant, Bataviaasch Handelsblad*, and *Java-Bode*, cited in *De Indische Gids* 1918, II:1474-5.

CHAPTER XVIII

The end of Dutch international shipping and trade

In the course of 1917 people in the Netherlands Indies became increasingly alarmed about what the future would bring. 'Imagine', the Director of the Colonial Civil Service had posed in January 1917

> what will happen when all imports and exports come to a halt because of the isolation from the outside world, [...] the repercussions for the centres of trade and industry, the population compelled to stay alive by planting all available land with foodcrops only, the almost complete unemployment of the European and Chinese populations, and the increasing multitude of Natives who no longer make a living from handicrafts, precisely the so-called intellectuals whose influence on the population is great.[1]

He gloomily predicted that Java would survive only for a few months. The collapse would be accelerated by social unrest. The same scenario was envisaged for the north of Sumatra. Isolated and deprived of rice from Java, the estate region could not hold its own for long.

Though the possibility that the Netherlands would be drawn into the Great War was on everybody's mind at the beginning of 1918, it would not need war to bring about the ruination of the colony. The disappearance of foreign markets and the disruption of sea transport could achieve the same miserable outcome. The Jember Association of Agriculture and Industry noted that 1918 had 'started so sombrely that – it could be said – it can bring no disappointments'[2]. A report about the sugar industry for 1917 predicted that if the war did not end soon 'unprecedented misery' would be in store.[3]

Others calculated the financial consequences of a collapse of the agricultural export market. Huge amounts of money would be withheld from colo-

---

[1] Quoted in Bron to Van Limburg Stirum, 15-5-1917, NA, Kol. Geheim, Vb. 3-5-1918 O4.
[2] Report 1917 Vereeniging van Landbouw en Nijverheid te Djember, cited in *De Locomotief*, 16-4-1918.
[3] *De Locomotief*, 25-6-1918.

The KPM freighter *Van Cloon* (Rinkes, Van Zalinge en De Roever 1925:107)

nial society if wages and taxes could not be paid by the estates, or had to be expended without being compensated by income. Sixty-five million guilders were paid out in wages in the sugar industry each year.[4] Annual expenditure for wages in coffee, tea, and tobacco amounted to 43 million guilders (Cramer 1917:407-8). The only bright side was that 'neither education of children nor position [to keep up] nor fashion' would make it extra difficult for the indigenous population to make ends meet if they became unemployed or had to cope with a drop in income.[5]

The entry into the war of the United States had added to the gloom. It meant that the alternative trading links established by the commercial world in the Netherlands Indies to compensate for dwindling trade with Europe came under threat. The consequences could be severe. The United States and Japan were the only remaining export partners of any significance. Not taking sugar into account, the United States was good for more that half of the market of the Netherlands Indies. Almost the entire rubber export went to the United States.

In early 1918 the capital tied up in stocks of colonial products stored in the Netherlands Indies because they could not be shipped had reached an

---

[4] *Regeering* 1919:10, citing a report by C. Lulofs and L. van Vuuren about the food situation in the Netherlands Indies; *Bezwaren* 1919:673.
[5] *Sumatra Post*, cited in *De Indische Gids* 1918, I:492.

estimated value of 287 million guilders.[6] In the rare cases that goods could be shipped transport costs had risen to unprecedented heights. Freight costs to the United States tripled. In 1918 for some products they exceeded market price. For a picul of copra bringing in about ten guilders (in 1913 this had been seventeen guilders) the freight price was forty-four guilders.[7] Most of the goods stockpiling were perishable. With this in mind the unrealistic suggestion was made in Holland to ship them all to there. In the more temperate climate, decay would proceed more slowly. The Allied Powers might object, but the NOT, it was hoped, could play a decisive role in making the British and American governments change their minds.

Until the end of 1917 the American hinderance of Dutch shipping had been confined to transatlantic shipping. Sea traffic between the Netherlands Indies and the United States had been left unhindered. In January 1918 this changed. A KPM freighter of the Java-Pacific Line, the *Van Cloon*, was given only enough coal to sail to Java on the condition that she would return to San Francisco with cargo for the United States. On hearing the news, the KPM management forebode shipping to the United States. The complete isolation of Holland and the Netherlands Indies loomed. One author concluded that the Dutch flag had as good as disappeared from the seas. The 'free seas' had become 'the most blocked territory on God's earth's surface' (Van Heekeren 1918:191). Worse was to come. Desperate to free their own merchant fleets for the shipping of American troops and equipment to the front in France, the Associated Powers tried to force neutral countries to hire out tonnage. They wanted the Netherlands to surrender its merchant fleet for charter with the exception of the tonnage needed for colonial trade and for the transport of food and fodder to Holland which they would graciously allow in return. Indications were strong that draconic sanctions would be in store if the Dutch government did not comply. In that case all Dutch ships in Allied ports might be impounded.[8]

The Hague could hardly refuse. Various people remarked in 1918 that the Netherlands was caught between three fires: the Associated Powers, the Central Powers, and hunger.[9] Wheat was needed to avert a famine in Holland. A 'basis of agreement' was reached in London on 18 January 1918. Under this, Holland would receive 400,000 tons of food. In return, the Associated Powers were promised the use of 500,000 tonnage for a period of ninety days. This left about 350,000 tons for the transport of colonial wares to non-European ports, and about 300,000 tons for the transport of food to Holland and for shipping

---

[6] *Handelingen Eerste Kamer* 1917-18:156.
[7] *Handelingen Eerste Kamer* 1917-18:157.
[8] *Morning Post*, 28-12-1917, cited in *De Locomotief*, 9-5-1918.
[9] *Handelingen Eerste Kamer* 1917-18:194, *Handelingen Tweede Kamer* 1917-18:2045.

between the Netherlands and the Netherlands Indies.[10]

In the end, when the Dutch government inquired whether the Associated Powers would allow an initial shipment of 100,000 tons of wheat to Holland before the final agreement had been signed, the Asssociated Powers had no objections. The condition was that simultaneously the total amount of Dutch tonnage that had been promised by the Dutch government in January would be placed at their disposal. Initially Washington demanded that freighters would have to sail from Holland to the United States to fetch the wheat. Later Washington permitted that three Dutch merchantmen already in the United States could transport the wheat to Holland. Simultaneously three Dutch ships had to sail from Holland to the United States. Germany would not object. The only sticking point for Berlin was the increase of Dutch tonnage in American ports and so it demanded that in exchange for every ship that left a Dutch port for the United States, a ship of comparable tonnage should sail from the United States to Holland. In Holland desperation had so threatened to engulf the country, that the German position was considered a friendly gesture by Berlin.

Just when everything seemed to have been arranged, a new condition was imposed by the Associated Powers and caused additional delay. Initially the Dutch government had been given the assurance that the chartered Dutch ships would not have to sail the 'danger zone'; the area where German submarines were active. Before any ship could sail, the hawk Cecil on behalf of the Associated Governments informed The Hague that no exception with regard to the danger zone would be made for the Dutch ships they wanted to employ. The Dutch government had considered the non-sailing of the danger zone a matter of principle. The Hague reacted by stating that the new condition was of a 'very onerous nature'. In a final and desperate attempt to find a way out, The Hague inquired with Germany whether it could deliver 100,000 tons of wheat within two months. The answer was no. The Dutch government was informed that Germany's ally, Austria, was suffering a severe food shortage and that any surplus food it might have had to be sent there.

Forced by what Loudon called the stress in Holland and the Netherlands Indies the Dutch government had to accept that the Dutch ships chartered by the Associated Powers would have to sail the danger zone.[11] It posed some counter-conditions: the Dutch ships would remain unarmed; they would transport no soldiers or war materials; and crews would be free to decide whether to sign on or not. The Hague realized that these conditions were unacceptable, but it had to avoid any chance that Germany could accuse the Netherlands of

---

[10] *Handelingen Tweede Kamer* 1917-18, II:1081; Colenbrander 1920:128.
[11] *Handelingen Tweede Kamer* 1917-18:2016, 2043.

a serious breach of neutrality which allowing Dutch ships to transport soldiers and arms to the front would imply (Timmermans 2002:190).

In explaining Dutch policy in Holland, Loudon took great pains to avoid any impression that the interests of Holland and not those of the Netherlands Indies had been decisive in bowing to the Allied Powers' demands. He explained in Parliament that it was the duty of the government to assure that the Dutch fleet would 'not be banned from the seas, especially from the Eastern seas, to ensure that for as long as possible that we are not completely cut off from our Colonies'.[12] Loudon added that the alternative, requisition, would mean that 'our ships will not be Dutch ships, our colonial trade will disappear, our colonial commercial interest will become totally dependent on the good will of the Associated Governments'.[13] The crisis in Holland and in the Netherlands Indies had become so acute that the interests of motherland and colony could no longer be reconciled. Loudon's words had been intended to soothe sentiments in the colony, but they really stirred up opposition in Holland. Troelstra had the impression that in yielding to Associated demands the government first and formost had had colonial interests at heart. He could not agree. Troelstra said that it should not be forgotten that 'our interest lies in the colonies, but that our heart beats here, that the colonies are important to our wealth, [but that] our history, our soul lie where we live, on the estuary of the Rhine'.[14] These words did not go down well with Loudon. He riposted that the future of the Netherlands was to a high degree dependent on the way the Dutch fulfilled their colonial task: 'Exactly in the hour of tribulation we have to show millions of Dutch subjects in the colonies that our policy is not tainted by self-interest, that our and their ideals are one, that the loosening of the historical tie would cut us to the quick, that we are prepared to make a sacrifice to maintain it'.[15]

The Associated Powers, suspecting that the Dutch government was dragging out on negotiations only because Dutch shipowners did not want to risk their precious freighters, announced that they had rejected the Dutch conditions. They acted accordingly. On 20 March the United States, Great Britain, France, and Italy requisitioned all the Dutch ships in their ports. In one blow the Dutch merchant fleet had lost a total tonnage of almost 700,000 tons.[16] At least one Indonesian crew of an impounded ship showed that they sided with the Dutch. When the *Rochussen* was seized 'the native crew which was lined up suddenly without any order being given to that effect, on their own initia-

---

[12] *Handelingen Tweede Kamer* 1917-18:2042.
[13] *Handelingen Tweede Kamer* 1917-18:2042.
[14] *Handelingen Tweede Kamer* 1917-18:2049.
[15] *Handelingen Tweede Kamer* 1917-18:2082.
[16] *Economisch-Statistische Berichten* 24-4-1918, p. 344-5.

The KPM passengership *Melchior Treub* (Rinkes, Van Zalinge en De Roever 1925:109)

tive squatted and made the *sembah* as final homage to our tricolour, while it was lowered'.[17]

Loudon learned about the Allied Powers' step in the evening of the following day; Van Limburg Stirum only on 28 March. To justify the requisition London explained that the Associated Powers had exercised their right of angary. The Dutch objected that this right of belligerents to confiscate neutral vessels for their own use when they were hard-pressed for shipping facilities was an obsolete, obscure relic of international law, which the United States and Great Britain had not recognized in the past.[18]

In Asia, Dutch freighters in British and American colonial ports had been refused permission to put to sea as early as 8 March. At that moment twenty Dutch ships were anchored in Singapore alone. Other Dutch freighters were stuck in Rangoon, Manila, Hong Kong, Colombo, Bombay, and Brisbane. The price of rice in the Netherlands Indies had risen immediately. When the actual seizure became a fact, prices of shares dropped in Holland and the Netherlands Indies. From Semarang it was reported that there were 'panic-

[17] *De Locomotief*, 3-4-1918.
[18] De Boer 1997:44-5; *Economisch-Statistische Berichten* 16-1-1918, p. 46.

stricken quotations' on the local exchange.[19] Most heavily affected were sugar, shipping, and industry. Some prices of stocks dropped to their 1914 level.

Indignation in the Netherlands Indies was great. Bijl de Vroe wrote in his diary that the whole of the Netherlands Indies was in turmoil:

> they are wretches n.b. the peoples who claim to fight for the right of the small nations! [...] Still people here remained rather calm about the affair, resigning themselves to what appears inevitable. For the export crops which will miss even more of the necessary tonnage prospects look grim' (Bijl de Vroe 1980:140).

In a telegram to the Dutch Ministry of Foreign Affairs the Batavia Chamber of Commerce also noted that 'Batavia [was] seething with indignation and disgust'.[20] Such feelings were shared in Holland. Queen Wilhelmina spoke of robbery of ships (Timmermans 2002:177). Senator J.Th. Cremer lamented that the merchant fleet in the Netherland Indies 'which is one of the most beautiful fleets in the East and the life-blood of our Archipelago, has been subjected to the indignity of confiscation'.[21] He was especially shocked by the confiscation of the *Melchior Treub*, which sailed the route Medan-Singapore-Batavia-Semarang-Surabaya. Cremer called the *Melchior Treub* the 'most beautiful of our passengerships out there'.[22] Her passengers were transported by steam-launches to an adjacent Dutch island from where a Dutch ship transported them to Batavia.

National pride was hurt most. The requisitioning was less galling than it seemed. From the outset, it was clear that profitable times might be in store for the shipping companies. Their ships could sail and the Associated Powers offered the owners fair compensation.[23] In view of the freight prices offered by the Associated Powers and the high compensation paid for ships that were lost, it was in retrospect indeed concluded that the requisitioning was 'the largest fixture ever recorded in the annals of shipping' (Van Dorp 1920:216).

The confiscation of the merchant vessels – the words theft and robbery tended to be used by Dutch and Indonesian residents alike in the Netherlands Indies – ushered in a new period of anxiety. In the Netherlands Indies the fleet was put on the alert. The sailing times of freighters under Dutch flag became a state secret. On 3 April newspapers were forbidden to report on ship movements. To ensure that the editors complied, the regulation dating from the Russo-Japanese War was reinstated. The anouncement aggravated the nervous mood prevailing in the Dutch community, already upset by reports

---

[19] *De Locomotief,* 6-4-1918.
[20] *De Locomotief,* 3-4-1918.
[21] *Handelingen Eerste Kamer* 1917-18:190.
[22] *Handelingen Eerste Kamer* 1917-18:190.
[23] *Economisch-Statistische Berichten,* 27-3-1918, p. 275.

about the dire food situation in Holland, the German offensive launched on the Western front on 21 March, and the sand and gravel conflict. People began to fear that the Netherlands might no longer be able to escape being dragged into the war. From Surabaya it was reported that these were 'days of enormous tension' in which there was no room for 'drinking-table or tango-dinner Patriotism'.[24] After the United States had entered the war, one of the conclusions drawn was that the American presence in the Philippines no longer formed any protection against a Japanese advance. In the mind of some the requisitioning of the Dutch ships turned the United States into a real enemy. Speculation was rife that one of the first hostile steps the United States, said to lust after the annexation of the Central American islands, might take would be the occupation of Curaçao to give Washington a Caribbean base to act if ever Venezuela and its oil reserves were lost to the United States. *De Standaard* concluded that as a Colonial Power the Netherlands found itself 'in a very threatened position'. Meek acquiescence was the only course of action open. One false move in Holland would have repercussions in the Netherlands Indies, and vice versa.[25]

The tenseness of the situation and the possibility of a clash with the Allied Powers did not escape the Indonesian population. In July *Neratja* commented that the Dutch government was really in trouble. *Neratja* made this remark after it had become known that a lieutenant in the colonial army had been put on the black list. *Neratja* was sure that London would place the colonial government on the black list if the soldier in question was not cashiered from the army.[26]

Pressure likewise mounted because the confiscation of the Dutch ships gave rise to the fear that Great Britain might try to seize the German and Austrian merchantmen stranded in the Netherlands Indies. What should be done? There had been no request from the German Consul General, but Commander Bron of the colonial Navy decided that two freighters should be moved to a safer location: the *Anhalt* away from Telukbetung and the *Wismar* away from Banyuwangi. The merchantmen anchored in Sabang, Emmahaven, Tanjung Priok, Cilacap, and Surabaya were or, in the case of Emmahaven soon would be, protected by artillery. The four German ships in the roadsteads of Makassar also had a relatively safe anchorage. Other ships were too small to be employed for ocean-going trade, or, as in Ambon, could be and were moved from the roadstead to the safety of an enclosed bay. The plan was to sail the *Anhalt* to the Bay of Bantam and the *Wismar* to the roadstead of Pasuruan, voyages of respectively thirteen and twenty-two hours. From there

---

[24] *De Locomotief,* 2-5-1918.
[25] *De Standaard,* cited in *De Indische Gids* 1918, I:721.
[26] *Neratja,* 18-7-1918.

it would take only a few hours under way to reach Tanjung Priok or Surabaya if war were to threaten. It was not plain sailing. There were two problems. A minor one was that the hulls of the *Anhalt* and *Wismar* had not been careened for four years and were covered with barnacles. There was a good chance they would have to be towed. A more serious problem was that the two German freighters would have to traverse international waters. Van Limburg Stirum was against granting protection by Dutch warships outside territorial waters, and did not disallow the possibility that the *Anhalt* especially, which had to sail some ten miles through international waters, might be intercepted by a British or a Japanese cruiser. Though Bron had estimated the risk low, Van Limburg Stirum decided that the dangers were too great.[27]

Assurances by the Associated Powers that no more ships were to be confiscated and that bunkering would be allowed in their ports failed to win the trust of either the shipping companies or the Dutch authorities. In Holland and the Netherlands Indies Dutch ships simply did not venture out to Associated ports. For the crews a period of boredom lay in store. As people were aware of what this might portend initiatives were taken to entertain them. In Surabaya a society was formed, De Nederlandsche Handelsvloot, The Dutch Merchant Fleet, to ensure that the spirit among the European officers remained high. One of the events organized was a dinner in the local theatre. It lasted from 11:30 in the evening till 7:00 in the morning. The three hundred guests ate, sang, recited, danced, and drank toasts. A local newspaper reported that it was 'a smashing do'.[28]

Some of the resulting gaps in shipping in the Netherlands Indies were filled by Chinese traders. They chartered small steamers in Singapore to sail between there and Jambi. Such initiatives were just a drop in the ocean. In most ports warehouses, if this was not already the case, were crammed to capacity, forcing some of the companies which owned them to announce they would no longer accept additional goods for storage. In Belawan, near Medan, this even affected imports, including rice. In Padang copra was stored in houses all over the town, even a cinema was pressed into service. The townspeople suffered. The stench became unbearable and innumerable small, black copra beetles invaded their houses. Nothing could be done to prevent the practice. Copra fell outside the scope of the Nuisance Act.[29]

In the Netherlands Indies, the decision not to sail to an Associated port resulted in fresh complications with the British. Van Limburg Stirum had discussed the fact that goods transported by KPM freighters to Sumatra were

---

[27] Bron to Van Limburg Stirum, 8-4-1918, 1st Government Secretary to Bron, 22-4-1918, NA, Kol. Openbaar, Vb. 9-12-1918 73.
[28] *Nieuwe Soerabaia Courant*, cited in *De Locomotief*, 16-4-1918.
[29] *De Locomotief*, 18-5-1918.

forwarded by non-Dutch freighters to Singapore and ports in the Malay Peninsula with the KPM management. At his suggestion, the KPM decided to ask for a guarantee from its clients affirming that the cargo KPM ships transported from Java to ports near Singapore would not have a British or American port as its final destination. In this way the company hoped to protect its future interests and to prevent making it too easy for foreign competitors to exploit the 'forced unemployment' of its ships. Without hesitating a second, the British Consul General, Dunn, called the KPM to account. He suspected that the KPM had taken this step in retaliation for the requisitioning of KPM freighters. Consequently, Dunn left no doubt that the guarantee requested by the KPM was a 'most serious' matter; important enough for him to have informed London about it. Ominously he told one of KPM representatives that the KPM was playing for too high stakes. Retaliatory measures might lead to a declaration of war and were the prerogative of governments. Private individuals should never take such steps.[30] Batavia drew in its horns and accused the KPM of having acted foolishly. The KPM should have made it clear that its only objective had been to combat unfair competition. The company should have explained that it was impossible to prevent a direct cargo trade from the Netherlands Indies by foreign freighters, but that it was in no way to assist competitors by shipping cargo from Java to other ports in the Archipelago, from where it might be easier for a non-Dutch freighter to transport the goods abroad.[31]

This was not the only clash between the KPM and Dunn. Initially the local management of the KPM believed that refusing to sail to British ports would lead to the release of some of its freighters. It was able to entertain such hopes because the requisitioning of Dutch ships had not had the result the British had hoped for. Crews could not be forced to sail. In both American and British ports it was almost impossible to replace the Dutch officers by experienced American or British counterparts. Finding competent British or American captains, navigation officers, and engineers to replace their Dutch counterparts proved more difficult than had been expected. The result was that in Asia as well requisitioned Dutch freighters remained idle, moored in ports, decreasing and not increasing the tonnage available to the British in Asia. Trade in Burma and the Straits Settlements suffered. In Australia exporters complained about the inconvenience the requisitioning had caused.[32]

The KPM racked its brains about how to exploit the situation. In February the colonial authorities in British India had forced the KPM to conclude a contract in which the latter promised to deploy a number of its freighters for

---

[30] Koning to Van Limburg Stirum, 25-4-1918, NA, Kol. Geheim, Mr. 1918/161x.
[31] Hulshoff Pol to President Director KPM, 23-4-1918, NA, Kol. Geheim, Mr. 1918/161x.
[32] *De Locomotief*, 4-6-1918.

the transport of coal between ports in British India. As compensation these ships were allowed to take on board a fixed amount of Burma rice – in total 400,000 tons – on their return journey to the Netherlands Indies. The KPM had assented after consulting the Nederland and Rotterdamsche Lloyd, and after it had received the assurance that none of the ships of the three companies would be requisitioned; a clause, the Dutch never tired of pointing out, the British had violated in March when they seized possession of the Dutch freighters in their ports.

By keeping its steamers in port, the KPM gambled that a moment would come when the British would be so desperate for extra tonnage to transport coal from British India or rice from Burma that they would release the requisitioned Dutch ships in an effort to enlist the service of Dutch freighters held back in the Archipelago. Van Limburg Stirum let it be known he did not share this opinion. Nevertheless, he gave the plan the benefit of the doubt; warning that might he be forced to order freighters to Rangoon to fetch rice, the stubborn attitude of the KPM could have dire consequences for the company.[33]

At the end of April Dunn inquired on what date sailing to British India would be resumed. A representative of the KPM explained to him that to execute the contract between the KPM and the government of British India, six freighters were needed. Dunn was also told that thirteen ships of the KPM, Rotterdamsche Lloyd, and Nederland had been requisitioned, which left the shipping companies with insufficient tonnage to fulfil even the contracts concluded with the government and exporters in the Netherlands Indies. Dunn appeared impressed. He promised to inquire by wire in London how the British government imagined that the KPM could honour the contract. The following day Dunn demanded a specification of the tonnage needed to fulfil the obligation of the three companies to the Dutch government, to exporters, and to the government of British India. Dunn suggested that if these figures showed that there was a shortage of tonnage, the British government would certainly release some of the requisitioned freighters. The KPM refused to provide the information. It was not prepared to go so far in its efforts to get its ships back.[34]

In early May headquarters in Holland realized that the KPM management in Java was cherishing false hopes and that shipping to British India and the Straits Settlements had to be resumed to avoid 'unpleasant reprisals' on the part of the British.[35] Shipping seemed safe. London and Washington had given the assurance – by now on paper – that no more Dutch vessels would

---

[33] Van Limburg Stirum to Pleyte, 17-5-1918, NA, Kol. Geheim, Vb. 13-9-1918 S8.
[34] Koning to Van Limburg Stirum, 25-4-1918, 27-4-1918, NA, Kol. Geheim, Mr. 1918/166x.
[35] Pleyte to Van Limburg Stirum, 6-5-1918, Koning to General Secretary, 10-5-1918, NA, Kol. Geheim, Vb. 6-5-1918 Q4, NA, Kol. Geheim, Mr. 1918/161x.

be requisitioned. The condition was that nowhere, also not in the territory of the Netherlands Indies, would there be any transport of German, Austrian, or Turkish goods and passengers, or of cargo of black-listed firms.[36]

The first Dutch steamers left for British ports in Asia on 15 May. The colonial government, responsible for the regulation of Dutch sea traffic in the Netherlands Indies, allowed ships to sail on the principle, as Pleyte put this, that 'they can get from us all what we still have to give, providing that we can also get those articles which we so badly need'.[37] Grudgingly the trade with British India and the Straits Settlements was resumed. The Dutch shipping companies explained that there were 'practical reasons' for taking this step, but that they still considered the requisitioning of their ships a breach of contract.[38] Two days later the ban on the reporting on the movement of merchant vessels was lifted.

By that time some of the ships seized had already been released. A few had been allowed to sail within a few days of their having been requisitioned. One of them was the *Melchior Treub* which, as a passenger ship and not a freighter, was not of great value to the Associated Powers in Asia. The last vessels confiscated in Asian waters were handed back in June. Optimistically Dutch people assumed that the importance of colonial wares for the world market was the reason for this act of grace

For the passenger transport between Holland and the Netherlands Indies the seizure of Dutch ships had no consequences. Simply because passenger traffic had come to a standstill. As a consequence the shortage of trained personnel in the private and public sector, already palpable at the outbreak of the war in the Netherlands Indies, had become more acute. The civil service, for which even under normal circumstances it was difficult to interest suitable candidates in Holland, was understaffed. There was also a shortage of professionals, schoolteachers, and trained technical staff. The recruitment of doctors was out of the question. All over Europe they had been mobilized.

The other side of the coin was that Europeans could no longer send their sons to Holland for higher education. Both factors combined to push people to take initiatives to improve the educational system in the Netherlands Indies. As late as 1915 the colonial administration had still rejected plans to establish technical secondary schools in the Netherlands Indies. In 1917 Batavia was forced to revise its position. Various projects, most serious among them water management schemes to increase food production, had been delayed because of a shortage of skilled technicians. In 1918 a special engineering course was

---

[36] *Koloniaal verslag* 1919:247-8; *De Locomotief,* 7-5-1918, 14-5-1918.
[37] *Handelingen Eerste Kamer* 1917-18:568.
[38] *De Locomotief,* 11-5-1918.

set up in Batavia for students who had completed their secondary education but could not travel to Delft to study at the Technical University. The breakdown in the shipping link between colony and motherland also brought a certain emancipation in its wake. European and Chinese children who could not travel to Europe for higher education were allowed to follow classes at the NIAS medical training college, initially intended only for indigenous students.

The army experienced problems similar to those of the civil service. Most crucially the army was short of officers who had been trained in Holland. Indirectly the civil service also suffered. Forced by circumstances, in 1915 Batavia had taken the much criticized decision of having eight army officers fill some of the vacancies in the civil service outside Java, paying them 150 guilders on top of their military pay. Army command refused to supply any more officers for the civil service in 1917.

The modest size of the army had already been a cause for concern at the outbreak of the war. This had been qualified as 'downright alarming' in 1915.[39] The shortage of European soldiers had risen to 3,478 on a supposed strength of 11,960, or 30 per cent, at the end of June 1917. To make matters worse: almost one-fifth of the some 8,000 Europeans serving in the army was for one reason or another not available for active service. Sixty-three per cent of the European soldiers suffered from a venereal disease. (For the whole army including the Indonesian soldiers the percentage was 30 per cent.)[40] As in 1914 part of the answer to diminish the shortage was sought in stepping up the recruitment of indigenous soldiers in the Archipelago and in easing the rules for promotion. The shortage of European soldiers was also the reason why such a haste was made with the creation of a European militia, which it was calculated would soon be 10,000 men strong.[41]

Officers in the colonial army could no longer be sent to Holland for supplementary training. Special courses had to be organized in Java; in this respect again giving the colony some degree of independence. Though delayed by the cable troubles which made consultation with The Hague a difficult and time-consuming process, plans to establish a Higher Military Academy and a Cadet Training bore fruit in 1918.

The manpower problem was compounded by a lack of munitions, armaments, and other military paraphernalia the colonial army needed, shortages

---

[39] Note Department 8, NA, Kol. Openbaar, Vb. 19-4-1918 1.
[40] The percentage had increased over the years. One explanation advanced was the introduction of the Decency Act of 1911 in the Netherlands Indies. It had meant an end to the medical examination of prostitutes and (because of this) to an increase in the number of prostitutes in the Netherlands Indies (*De Locomotief*, 6-6-1916).
[41] *Volksraad* 1918:577.

which had been felt almost right from the outbreak of the war; and which would have been felt almost as badly had a regular shipping been maintained because the army in Holland did not fare much better. A circular issued by the Indië Weerbaar movement in May 1917 noted: 'In times like these, now that we live constantly in danger [...] it has to be realized that we are unable to make one gun, not one machine-gun, not one torpedo, not one aircraft'.[42] What the circular did not mention was that the commander of the colonial army had given the order in December 1916 to start as soon as possible training in the digging of trenches 'in a way the modern war demands this'.[43] On 9 April 1918, Bijl de Vroe wrote down with dismay in his diary that in the almost four years of war no economic and military precautionary measures had been taken: 'The army still consists in all of about 35,000 man as good as without munitions, artillery, dressings, aeroplanes and so forth. Nothing is in order' (Bijl de Vroe 1980:140). Pistols, field-glasses, cloth to make uniforms, and horses (for which Australia was a main source of supply) can be added to his list of items the army was in need of. An export ban on horses had been instituted as early as March 1915. The lack of horses forced the cancellation of annual cavalry manoeuvres in 1918.

The shipment of goods from Holland had also grounded to a halt. The value of imports from Holland dropped from 124 million guilders in 1914 and 48 million guilders in 1917 to 11 million guilders in 1918. Not even government goods could be shipped. In mid-February 1918 the man-of-war *Hertog Hendrik* had set out on a voyage to the Netherlands Indies through the Panama Canal to replace the *Tromp*, which had sailed to Holland in August 1917. The *Hertog Hendrik* carried the equipment for a 400 kW radio installation on board. Her total cargo amounted to 20 m^3; a fraction of the 10,000 m^3; of government goods that had been piling up. The Minister of the Navy had informed Pleyte that a limited number of goods could be transported on the *Hertog Hendrik* 'which would be impossible to ship on a private steamer because of the origin of those goods'.[44] The *Hertog Hendrik* made it as far as the Faroer Islands. There she ran into a heavy storm and sustained engine damage. The *Hertog Hendrik* had to be towed to Bergen in Norway, from where she returned to Holland.

To relieve the shortage of military and civilian personnel, and of urgently needed goods in the Netherlands Indies, an emergency plan was developed. The idea was to have a convoy protected by two warships sail to the Netherlands Indies in June. During the whole journey, the convoy should remain independent of any goodwill or services from the side the Associated Powers. This meant that it had to sail the route around the Cape of Good

---

[42] *De Indische Gids* 1917, II:1186-7.
[43] *De Locomotief*, 11-12-1916.
[44] Rambonnet to Pleyte, 3-1-1918, NA, Kol. Geheim, Vb. 9-1-1918 P1.

Hope and that it had to take along its own coal. The Ships' Requisition Act was amended to allow requisitioning for the purpose of sending ships to the Netherlands Indies. Initially the Dutch government may have had something grander in mind. There was talk of a large convoy of merchantmen. Soon the intelligence dawned that the convoy could only be a small one. Because coal was scarce, it would have been out of the question to arrange a larger convoy. Dutch industry could not sustain a large drain on its resources, especially not in a time when the import of coal from Germany and Great Britain had stopped. Additional limits on the size of the convoy were set by the fact that coaling from colliers on the high seas, as it had been during the Russo-Japanese War, was still a difficult undertaking.

On the return voyage the convoy could bring colonial products which Holland badly needed. Posthuma reminded 'the consumers' in Holland that the 'fat problem' which had arisen could only be solved with fats from the Netherlands Indies.[45] Naturally, national prestige was also at stake. Civil servants in the Ministry of the Colonies were afraid that it would only make an unfavourable impression on the population of the Netherlands Indies if the motherland found itself unable to maintain communication with its colonies, even though it was not at war.[46]

Opinion in Holland about the convoy vacillated between extreme caution and stubborn intent to restore the sea link with the Netherlands Indies. Some pointed out the possibility that warships of the Associated Powers might want to search the convoy. One member of the Lower House feared that such an incident would 'simply be war'.[47] Others were furious at the hesitation shown. They stressed that the Netherlands should not abandon the right to send Dutch ships wherever it wanted. Representing this view, a Member of Parliament said that Dutch shipping had been crippled because the Dutch ships had always needed something from other countries. Was such help – coal – not needed then the interference by a third country would amount to a grave injustice: 'We abide therefore by the proper view, when we try to find the way to the Netherlands Indies under our own steam'.[48]

Plans had to be adjusted. Repairs to the *Hertog Hendrik*, one of the two warships which was to protect the convoy, took longer than expected. The boiler of another warship, the *Gelderland*, exploded. To prevent the number of seaworthy Dutch ships in the fleet shrinking to an unacceptable level, a passenger ship, the *Tabanan*, was transformed into an auxiliary cruiser.

By far the greatest delay was caused by the Associated Powers. Initially the

---

[45] *Handelingen Tweede Kamer* 1917-18:2649.
[46] Note Department 8, NA, Kol. Openbaar, Vb. 19-4-1918 1.
[47] *Handelingen Tweede Kamer* 1917-18:2649.
[48] *Handelingen Tweede Kamer* 1917-18:2650.

Dutch government does not seem to have given much thought to British objections. In the middle of May Loudon assured Parliament that he did not expect problems with London.[49] If he was sincere, Loudon had completely misjudged the situation. British opposition was vehement. In 1909 the British government had consented to a right of convoy, but only on the condition that the captain of the accompanying warships could present cargo manifests and that should doubts arise about the accuracy of the manifests, the merchantmen in the convoy could be searched. Some civil servants in the Ministry of the Colonies believed that such an eventuality could be avoided if the Netherlands sent out warships, not merchantmen. They proposed to charter a mailship and have her sail under a naval ensign. The crew was to enter the voluntary *landstorm*, home guard, for the duration of the voyage.[50] Other civil servants in the Ministry considered such a decoy a folly. They warned Pleyte that the 'comedy of transformation' would not deter the British, or for that matter the Germans, who, they pointed out, did not shun from violating every tenet of international law when their interests demanded them to do so.[51]

London's reaction was prompt and unequivocal. The British Foreign Secretary, A.J. Balfour, lost no time in instructing the British Ambassador in The Hague to impress upon the Dutch government that Great Britain 'of course' did not recognize a 'right of convoy'. British warships would exercise 'the belligerent right of visit and search'.[52] The Dutch government tried to prevent the perpetrating of such an act and the loss of face such a search would have implied. The Dutch Envoy in London, R. de Marees van Swinderen, was asked to explain to the British government that the voyage was purely a government undertaking and was in no way intended to circumvent the Associated blockade. Van Swinderen wrote to Balfour that the purpose of the convoy was to relieve military men and to send out civil servants with their families. Dutch officials would supervise the loading of goods. They would also ensure that only passengers to whom the Associated Powers could have no objections sailed. No private correspondence would be allowed on board, nor would ordinary mail be sent along. The government goods transported would all have a certificate of origin. The British could inspect the certificates before the convoy set sail.[53]

This was not the reply Balfour had been waiting for. He had expected a

---

[49] *Handelingen Tweede Kamer* 1917-18:2649.
[50] Note Department 8, 21-2-1918, NA, Kol. Openbaar, Vb. 19-4-1918 1.
[51] Addendum to note of Department 8, 21-2-1918, NA, Kol. Openbaar, Vb. 19-4-1918 1.
[52] Balfour to Townley, 25-4-1918, Balfour to De Marees van Swinderen, 7-6-1918, *State Papers* 1917-18, III:533, 539.
[53] De Marees van Swinderen to Balfour, 29-4-1918, Balfour to Townley, 7-6-1918, *State Papers* 1917-18, III:534, 540.

prompt reaction to the message Townley had conveyed. The 'friendly warning' Townley had presented to Loudon on his behalf, which had been in a 'courteous form suited to such a communication to a friendly neutral Government', had been ignored.[54] To Balfour's 'considerable surprise' the Dutch Minister of the Navy, Rambonnet, had made matters worse by blazoning abroad that the commander of the convoy would not tolerate a search of the merchantmen. An admonition was in order. It was conveyed in 'the most formal manner'. Balfour refused to let pass what he considered a Dutch demand that Great Britain abdicated 'her belligerent right to stop contraband trade by the regulated exercise of naval force, and, in the middle of a great war, abandon the Allied blockade'.[55]

Balfour made it perfectly plain that he was of the opinion that the Dutch government had blundered. An 'international complication of the utmost gravity' could be the result.[56] He had Lord Cecil inquire of Van Swinderen why the protection by warships was needed. The escort of a warship was 'hardly capable of explanation', except if the convoyed vessels were 'to be protected in some transaction which the belligerents do not recognize as legitimate'.[57] The conclusion was that the Dutch authorities might in 'good faith' have expected that the guarantees as conveyed by Van Swinderen would suffice, but the course taken by The Hague, was 'lacking both in courtesy and in prudence'.[58] The Netherlands should be under 'no misapprehension' that the British Navy would not exercise its rights. Nevertheless, the British government wanted to 'maintain their relations with the Netherlands Government on the most amicable footing'. They were prepared 'to go out of their way in order to save the susceptibilities which the Dutch official announcement was calculated to arouse', but only 'to prevent the action of the Netherlands Government from definitely creating a situation gravely imperilling the friendly relations between the two countries'.[59]

London would allow the convoy to sail undisturbed, providing that The Hague did not take this as a precedent. There were a number of conditions. A list of names of passengers, all of whom had to be government officials, had to be handed over, as had full particulars of the cargo. The Dutch government had to guarantee that none of the goods shipped were wholly or in

---

[54] Balfour to De Marees van Swinderen, 7-6-1918, *State Papers* 1917-18, III:539.
[55] Balfour to De Marees van Swinderen, 7-6-1918, *State Papers* 1917-18, III:540.
[56] Memorandum recording confidential statement Lord R. Cecil to Dutch Envoy, *State Papers* 1917-18, III:541.
[57] Memorandum recording confidential statement Lord R. Cecil to Dutch Envoy, *State Papers* 1917-18, III:541.
[58] Memorandum recording confidential statement Lord R. Cecil to Dutch Envoy, *State Papers* 1917-18, III:541.
[59] Memorandum recording confidential statement Lord R. Cecil to Dutch Envoy, *State Papers* 1917-18, III:541.

Noordam

part of enemy origin. The escorting warships should not transport civilian passengers or civilian goods. They could carry only articles for the colonial army and Navy, a list of which had to be submitted for examination. Finally, 'no mails, correspondence, private papers, printed matter, or parcels [were] to be carried by any ship in the convoy (except official dispatches of the Dutch Government)'.[60] The Hague accepted, trying to save as much face as possible. Van Swinderen wrote to Balfour that the British conditions were almost identical to what the Dutch government had asked him to convey from the outset. Information about passengers and cargo would be sent to 'all foreign legations, as the Netherlands Government wished to avoid any possible impression that anything is being concealed'.[61]

Impeded by what Cort van der Linden described as objections by the British government to the transport of 'a small part of the cargo' and other points of 'minor importance' which had to be investigated, sailing was delayed still further.[62] There were even rumours that a British squadron had taken up position just outside Dutch territorial waters to await the convoy. In actual fact the objections raised by the British were far from trivial. There was the usual dispute over chemical dyes. British suspicion also thwarted the plans to build a more powerful radio station in Java. Equipment for a Telefunken 400 kW installation had been loaded on the *Hertog Hendrik*. Much to the dismay of Pleyte it never left port. Together with other government goods, the radio equipment had to be unloaded. Pleyte wired in cipher to Van Limburg Stirum

---

[60] Statement of conditions handed to De Marees van Swinderen, 7-6-1918, *State Papers* 1917-18, III:542-3.
[61] De Marees van Swinderen to Balfour, 15-6-1918, *State Papers* 1917-18, III:543.
[62] *Handelingen* 1917-18, Aanhangsel: 251, 257.

via Washington that the 'circumstances' under which the *Hertog Hendrik* had to sail made its shipment impossible.[63] Disillusioned by the delay, Rambonnet resigned. He did so shortly before a new Dutch cabinet was to be formed. Nevertheless, his 'firm' attitude reaped Rambonnet much applause.

To underline the national importance of the voyage, the commander of the convoy and the captain of the auxiliary cruiser, the *Tabanan*, were received in audience by Queen Wilhelmina. Thereupon the *Noordam*, with 1,200 passengers, the *Hertog Hendrik*, and the *Tabanan* set out for the Netherlands Indies on 5 July 1918. Taking part in the convoy was a freighter of the Netherlands, the *Bengkalis*, from which coal had to be transhipped at a number of points along the route of the voyage which took the ships around Scotland and the Cape of Good Hope. Great Britain did not allow coaling in South Africa. Among the passengers were fifty army officers and 155 non-commissioned officers and their families. They and the other passengers did not have a very pleasant trip. The *Noordam* was not suitable for the voyage to the Netherlands Indies as she had been built to sail the Atlantic Ocean. Because of the high temperatures on board caused by lack of ventilation ten babies died during the passage (De Haas 2002:175).

The arrival of the convoy was announced in the press in the Netherlands Indies when the Sabang radio station succeeded in contacting the *Hertog Hendrik*. At that moment the convoy was still seven days' sailing away. A warship was sent out to welcome the convoy. On board was the journalist Berretty, keen to report on the last leg of the voyage. The convoy finally reached Tanjung Priok on 27 September 1918. The arrival had been intended to be a big occasion. Van Limburg Stirum boarded a ship to meet the convoy on the last miles of its trip. To the disappointment of the Governor General, the occasion did not turn into a grand ceremony. His adjutant, Bijl de Vroe, agreed: 'It was a failed entrance. The Allied Powers again refused to permit the convoy to return without being inspected. Fine freedom of the seas.' (Bijl de Vroe 1980:162-3.) This meant that the *Tabanan* and *Noordam* were constrained to remain in the Netherlands Indies till the end of the war. After the war the *Noordam* was to provide the first opportunity to sail to Holland for the many people in the Netherlands Indies waiting to return to the mother country.

Export prospects alarmingly in 1918. When there was a choice between buying colonial wares from the Netherlands Indies or from British and French colonies, the Associated Powers gave preference to the latter. Trade with the United States slackened. For almost all imports, the United States had introduced a licensing system before shipment. Because the telegraphic communi-

---

[63] Pleyte to Van Limburg Stirum, 11-7-1918, NA, Kol. Geheim, Vb. 11-7-1918 L6.

cation between the Netherlands Indies and the United States was poor, a great deal of time had elapsed before consent to import reached the Netherlands Indies (Idenburg en De Graeff 1920:391). The value of exports to the United States dropped from 200 to 111 million guilders in 1918 (Carpentier Alting and De Cock Buning 1928:102).

The fate of the export of colonial wares during 1918 presented a sorry picture. The market for tapioca (a cassava product) almost disappeared when the United States, which had been a valuable expanding market for this product in recent years, instituted a full import ban in April. Coffee suffered greatly after Washington demanded a licence for its import in May. As a result, the export of coffee from Java dropped from 13,400 tons in 1917 to 5,400 tons in 1918.[64] In the same month the United States banned the import of tobacco. Consequently the export of tobacco from the East Coast of Sumatra declined even further: from 20.75 million kilos in 1916, via 4.75 million kilos in 1917, to 3.5 million kilos in 1918. From Java there was almost no export at all.[65] In May a licensing system for rubber was also instituted. The impression made by the ban in the Netherlands Indies was great. Rubber was considered to be one of the products of which the export would surely continue unobstructed because of the great demand abroad. The export of cocoa in 1918 was half of what it had been in 1917. The culprit was an American import ban brought in August. In July Washington demanded a licence for the import of tea. Batavia tried to support local tea producers by banning the import of tea. The Chinese business community protested. The ban hit the import of tea from China and Japan the most. In retrospect it had to be admitted that the import ban in the Netherlands Indies had made no difference.[66]

It was the same story with sugar. In 1917 people still cherished the hope that in view of high demand abroad, American and British freighters would certainly continue to call in Java to fetch sugar. It was not to be. In early 1918 the *Washington Post* observed that Java sugar had become 'as useless to the world as unmined gold, because no nation can spare the ships to carry it'.[67] 'Sugar circles in Amsterdam' were sure that a debâcle was in the making.[68] The price of sugar which in May 1917, when the crisis began, had still been 13 guilders per picul, dropped to 5.50 guilders in July 1918. Afraid of being saddled up with large stocks, producers sold sugar at a great loss.[69] The realization that

[64] *Koloniaal verslag* 1919:253-4.
[65] *Koloniaal verslag* 1919:61-2, 257-8.
[66] *Koloniaal verslag* 1919:257-8.
[67] NA, Kol., Vb. 22-4-1918 89.
[68] *De Locomotief*, 6-5-1918.
[69] Report of the Javasche Bank over 1917-18, cited in *Koloniale Studiën* 1918:474, 477; *Koloniaal verslag* 1919:255-6.

this erstwhile major export earner, the 'motor' of trade as it was called, was caught up in a crisis brought home to Europeans and non-Europeans alike the inexorably growing seriousness of the situation. In April 1918 the Sarekat Islam concluded that the whole population was suffering. The consequences would be grave if the government did not act quickly.[70]

Plans again had to be thrashed out to come to the rescue of estates which had run into financial problems. The situation appeared more alarming than it had been in August 1914. With the falling away of markets, the collapse of the estate sector loomed. Continued operation would mean an accumulation of debts. Closure would imply the annihilation of capital, and many were sure, domestic disturbances. In 1914 people had expected the disruption of export trade not to last long. In 1918 nobody had an inkling of how long the import restrictions and bans abroad would be in operation (Helfferich 1921:18-9). In the previous year, some plantations had only been able to continue to function thanks to soft loans provided by the Javasche Bank; the 'most powerful moral back-up of agriculture and products trade' as the institution was lauded in 1918.[71] Other estates, which had made huge profits from the sale of colonial wares in the first years of the war, still had enough financial reserves to cope with the crisis that emerged in 1917, but if the war were not to end soon – it was feared – a catastrophe was just waiting to happen. For their working capital an increasing number of estates would become dependent on the Javasche Bank, which could not come to their assistance forever. The annual report of the Ministry of the Colonies stated in retrospect that '[t]he situation threatened to become fatal in the second half of 1918'. Elsewhere in the same section, the phrases 'a desperate situation' and the Netherlands Indies having escaped a 'serious disaster' were used.[72]

This time the Javasche Bank did not intend to lend money directly to the plantations. It opted instead for a special institution that would be responsible for managing the bank's aid to the estate industry. A Cultuur-Hulpbank (Estate Relief Bank) was instituted in the middle of September. From the Estate Relief Bank estates could borrow money on their produce against production costs and at a moderate rate of interest. The Javasche Bank would provide most of the money needed. The colonial government would act as guarantor for the repayment of the loans. The Estate Relief Bank was also envisaged as a mechanism to prevent a steep decline in export prices. Estates were only eligible to borrow if they promised not to sell their produce below a minimum price. Praiseworthy though it was, the rescue operation did not bring instant relief. Some estates had to be closed, or because 'times were not good' had to

---

[70] *De Locomotief*, 25-4-1918.
[71] *Bataviaasch Handelsblad*, cited in *De Indische Gids* 1918, II:1376.
[72] *Koloniaal verslag* 1919:201-2

refuse demands for a cost-of-living allowance, at most willing to supply their labour force with cheap rice.

The only export market which did not suffer was that in Japan. Japan had not issued import restrictions or bans and Japanese companies deployed enough freighters to keep trade going. Japan even opened new shipping lines between Japan and the Netherlands Indies and between the Netherlands Indies and Calcutta. The only time the apple-cart seemed upset was in August 1918 after Japanese forces had landed in Siberia. It was feared that Japanese trading companies would stop buying produce from the Netherlands Indies because all Japanese freighters would be needed to transport troops to Vladivostok for the Japanese war effort against Russia in Siberia.

In the course of the war various non-food products had become scarce. Iron, steel, concrete, and coal were among the more important items. The import of coal to Java had dropped from 244,092 tons in 1916 to 94,716 tons in 1917.[73] One of the consequences was that the Dutch squadron in the Archipelago had stopped using Cardiff coal in order to 'maintain an adequate war stock'. The Navy stoked with domestic and Japanese coal. Cardiff coal was held in reserve.[74] The government impressed on foresters in Java that 'every pile metre produced above the normal amount does its part in relieving the fuel need'.[75] Relief was also provided by the intensification of domestic coal production in South and East Borneo. This had the additional advantage that it 'was a Godsend to the population of a large part of the region'.[76]

The import of iron had dried up completely. This meant that plans to replace obsolete ships employed by the colonial government with new ones could not be implemented. The building of wooden ships (as was done in Europe and in British India) was considered. It did not prove a viable alternative. Besides the fact that there were doubts about whether shipyards in the Netherlands Indies had the capacity to build larger wooden ships, the expertise had disappeared. Lack of know-how was compounded by the fact that iron was not available in sufficient quantities for the machines and boilers required.[77] Iron had become so scarce that in the draft colonial budget of 1919 money was set aside to send an engineer to Australia. He was to study whether the wooden pipes used there, could also be used in the waterworks in the Netherlands Indies. An export ban for products like barbed wire and nails had been instituted as early as 1916. In 1918 there was even a shortage of oil can. Oil companies published advertisements in the newspapers stating that if

---

[73] *Koloniaal verslag* 1919:262-3.
[74] *Koloniaal verslag* 1918:53-4.
[75] Circular Wehlburg 6-3-1917, NA, Kol. Geheim, Mr. 1917/92x.
[76] *Koloniaal verslag* 1918:27-8.
[77] *De Locomotief*, 3-6-1918; *De Indische Gids* 1919, I:113; *Koloniale Studiën* 1918:104.

the old cans were not returned no oil would be supplied.[78]

With the exception of so-called 'European writing and printing-paper', paper was still available from Japan, but as the war staggered on this had become highly expensive. This included the price of newsprint. Scarcity had threatened from the outbreak of the war and had forced printers to increase their prices sharply. Consequently, Dutch-language and vernacular newspapers and periodicals had to put up subscription rates; a measure sometimes described as a 'high cost allowance'. Some publications closed never to re-open, in an exceptional case as happened with the *De Noordkust* (The North Coast) published in Cirebon, because the editor's health was failing and the high price of paper made it impossible to employ a replacement; and weeklies only appeared only once a fortnight. Some editors had to resign and take on a job that offered them a better income. The severe consequences for the vernacular press prompted Abdoel Moeis to plead in the People's Council for the establishment of a paper industry in the Netherlands Indies. Mentioning the Dutch paper producer Van Gelder by name he accused those who maintained that a paper industry was not viable of having their own particular reasons for saying so.[79] Other Indonesians worried about the high price of paper, slates, slate pencils, penholders, writing pens, and pencils. That these school necessities could no longer be bought at an affordable price formed 'an obstacle in the way of progress of the natives'.[80]

The government and private firms were both equally plagued by the shortage of paper. Private firms had started to economize on the use of paper as early as the end of 1916. In 1917 the colonial government urged its officials to be thrifty with paper. Army Command followed suit in May 1918. It suggested that instead of using envelopes, sheets of paper could be folded up, and the address written on the back. Even the planned first national census had to be postponed because of lack of paper.[81]

In early 1918 the economic problems the war caused in the Netherlands and in the Netherlands Indies prompted representatives of the business community in Holland to plead for central control of colonial foreign trade. Exports should be banned except if special permission had been given. One major reason for advancing this idea was that a section of international trade had begun to resemble barter. Imports to Holland were only possible in return for promises to supply the Associated Powers and Germany with specific goods, loans, or tonnage. Those in favour of the centralization of colonial trade stressed that

---

[78] *Neratja*, 28-2-1918; *De Locomotief*, 3-6-1918.
[79] *Volksraad* 1918:299.
[80] *Neratja*, 8-1-1918.
[81] *Handelingen Tweede Kamer* 1917-18:1443.

the motherland and colony were one, and that the Netherlands Indies had to assist in alleviating the misery experienced in Holland. The Netherlands Indies had much to offer in this respect. Wheat for Holland might be obtained in exchange for rubber or sugar from the Netherlands Indies. Another reason to stress the unity between motherland and colony was that politicians and businessmen in the Netherlands believed that the Netherlands Indies should also shoulder its share in the raising of money for loans the belligerents wanted to conclude and which could hardly be refused. Such credit had to be financed by banks and by the shipping and trading companies. It was only fair that colonial companies should share part of the burden.

Some of the arguments advanced to convince the decision makers in Java that centralization of colonial foreign trade was necessary were impeccable. By giving priority to the export of products urgently needed abroad, Batavia would be in the position to demand a supply of goods urgently needed in the colony such as iron and rice. An additional bonus, and according to some the most important reason to intervene, was that by supervising foreign trade the colonial government could control the shipment of goods and ensure a fair allocation of scarce tonnage. By taking control Batavia would be able to prevent companies with special influence or connections thrusting themselves forward. As with almost all debates about what economic measures should be taken the fate of the indigenous population entered the picture. Control would allow Batavia to assure the shipment of colonial wares specifically produced by them.[82]

The idea of regulating colonial foreign trade appealed to Pleyte. Within days of the proposal being suggested to him, he sent a telegram to Van Limburg Stirum in which he mentioned three reasons in favour of the centralization of colonial foreign trade. The first was that it would thwart efforts, especially in the United States, to wrest a lower price for colonial products. He mentioned this point because his staff shared the suspicion of the Dutch business community that traders in the United States were trying to take advantage of the circumstances to buy colonial wares for a low price with the intention of re-exporting them to Europe for a higher price. Secondly, it would enable the colonial government to assure the import of essential goods. His staff had suggested that sugar could be used to guarantee the import of rice from British India. The third reason was the 'threatening danger' of the credit demanded by Foreign Powers.[83]

Van Limburg Stirum was not eager to comply. The topic again brought to the fore the distrust felt in the Netherlands Indies for suggestions emanating

---

[82] *Economisch-Statistische Berichten*, 1-5-1918, p. 366-7; *Handelingen Eerste Kamer* 1917-18:269.
[83] N.U.M. to Pleyte 4-2-1918, NA, Kol. Openbaar, Vb. 14-2-1918 59; Pleyte to Van Limburg Stirum, 14-2-1918 in *Economisch-Statistische Berichten*, 15-5-1918, p. 415.

from Holland. The plea for central control was seen as an effort on the part of the commercial community in Holland to regain some of the control it had lost over the running of the colonial economy.[84] Van Limburg Stirum replied that he lacked the staff with the necessary expertise to execute a licence system. In the back of his mind lurked a fear of retaliation from abroad and the imposition of additional export obstacles and he was afraid that for products such as tin and rubber a loss of markets to foreign competitors would be the outcome. In contrast to the people in Holland, Van Limburg Stirum advanced the fate of the indigenous population as an argument against export restrictions. He foresaw that export bans on copra, tapioca, tea, kapok, and pepper would have adverse consequences for them. The colonial government lacked the funds to buy up their produce.

This was not all. In view of the large amounts of foreign capital invested in the colony, and the unremitting efforts to attract even more (that is money from Europe and the United States to block Japanese investments), Van Limburg Stirum considered it 'very risky' to abandon the colony's open door policy.[85] In short, the interests of the Netherlands Indies demanded freedom of foreign trade. Seemingly unaware that the colony was expected to share some of Holland's burdens, Van Limburg Stirum was not impressed by the reasons put forward by Pleyte. He wired Pleyte that he had consulted leading figures in the commercial community in the Netherlands Indies and that he had learned of no indications that their customers abroad had exploited the situation to demand lower prices or that governments demanded special credit. In no way should anything comparable to the NOT be created in the Netherlands Indies. Were centralization to be inevitable this should take the form of a special government bureau, not of a private organization like the NOT.[86] Van Limburg Stirum and his advisers made one concession. They were prepared to contribute to the credit demanded from Holland but this should only happen on a voluntary basis and on the condition that 'the present freedom of trade' was maintained.[87]

When export prices continued to plummet, Van Limburg Stirum and his advisers changed their minds. In April and May the export of a number of products was forbidden. Among these were tin, timber, tobacco, sugar, tea, coffee, pepper, copra, petroleum, kapok, and quinine, to mention the most

---

[84] See the discussion between H.H.A. van Gybland Oosterhoff, J.T. Cremer en H. Colijn in *Economisch-Statistische Berichten* 1918:366-9, 415-8, 443-4, 466-7, 500-1.

[85] Van Limburg Stirum to Pleyte, 20-2-1918 (*Handelingen* 1917-18, Aanhangsel: 196); De Kat Angelino to Van Limburg Stirum, 27-2-1918, NA, Kol. Geheim, Mr. 1918/99x.

[86] Van Limburg Stirum to Pleyte, 2-3-1918 in *Economisch-Statistische Berichten*, 15-5-1918, p. 415.

[87] Van Limburg Stirum to Pleyte, 2-3-1918 in *Economisch-Statistische Berichten*, 15-5-1918, p. 415.

important ones. Later other products such as rubber were added to the list. In an attempt to forestall sanctions abroad, Batavia announced its new policy in newspapers in the Straits Settlements and in British India. Batavia tried to argue that the government of the Netherlands Indies had been forced to act as it did because of export bans abroad and conditions which were impossible to meet imposed on exports. As example, the agreement between the KPM and the government of British India was mentioned. The Netherlands Indies was no longer able to honour the arrangement (and hence could no longer import Burma rice) after the requisitioning of Dutch freighters.[88]

Export permits would be granted, but only when essential commodities were imported in exchange. A firm, as did happen, which wanted to export kapok to the United States was only allowed to do so on the promise that it import iron and steel of equal value. In this case the condition was difficult to meet. Washington had instituted an export ban for iron and steel.

Now it was the turn of the business community in Holland to be angry. Two hundred trading companies impressed upon Pleyte that the Netherlands Indies needed free trade, not export restrictions. It was pointed out that even firms which were engaged in both import and export lacked the necessary expertise and contacts to fulfil the conditions set. This made the exchange of commodities demanded by the government a graver financial risk. The only result of the regulation would be that export would come to a complete standstill. Adding to the discontent was the conviction that decisions about colonial trade had to be taken in Holland, where the headquarters of the Dutch estate companies were located, and from where most of their capital came, not in Java. *De Telegraaf* even blamed Van Limburg Stirum for having declared economic war on the Associate Powers, offending the United States especially by prohibiting the export of a number of products the Americans needed in great quantities for their war efforts.[89]

The commercial world in Java also reacted sceptically. The only advantage some saw in the licensing system was that government supervision of colonial export might curtail what they considered the power of the shipping companies and lower freight prices. The Netherlands Indies was in too weak a position to lift restrictions on imports imposed by the belligerents. Foreign suppliers would simply not deliver, which meant that colonial exports would be hurt even more. In a petition to Van Limburg Stirum, the Trade Association of Semarang dismissed the licensing system as 'absolutely impracticable'.[90]

In practice the licensing system was applied with leniency. One of the reasons for this was probably fear. The Dutch government shrank from

---

[88] *Economisch-Statistische Berichten*, 15-5-1918, p. 427.
[89] *De Telegraaf*, cited in *De Indische Gids* 1918, I:730.
[90] *De Locomotief*, 10-5-1918, 5-6-1918; *De Indische Gids* 1918, II:1369.

the consequences a ban especially on petroleum, the only real means of putting pressure on the Associated Powers the Netherlands had, could have (Helfferich 1921:19). At the end of May Van Limburg Stirum reported to Pleyte that licences for exports to the United States, France, Hong Kong, and the Straits Settlements were freely being handed out, and that trade with Japan had encountered no difficulties. Only with respect to Australia was the licence system in force.[91] The sentence in the report of the Ministry of the Colonies for 1918 that in October the export of rubber was forbidden 'except when permission had been obtained in advance, which was never refused' was pregnant with significance.[92] Nevertheless, in retrospect it could not be denied that the system had caused 'unavoidable impediment' to exports.[93] Partly this could be attributed to procedure. The Department of Agriculture, Trade and Industry, which had to issue the permits, did not inform the applicants about its decisions. When an export permit was granted it informed the Custom House, which in turn had to contact the company concerned.[94]

In spite of all its trials and tribulations, the licensing system bore one result: it gave Van Limburg Stirum the leverage to force the sugar producers to act in concert. In June, Batavia faced as it was with the plummeting of the price of sugar decided to intervene in the sugar trade. Where the Java Sugar Association had failed to make producers act in concert and headquarters in Holland could not agree on what course should be followed, Van Limburg Stirum succeeded in bringing about the almost impossible. He called together a 'sugar meeting' attended by planters and exporters and forced them to cooperate to prevent a further drop in price at the end of July. Export permits would only be granted by a Regeerings Commissie van Advies voor de Suiker (Government Committee of Advice on Sugar) founded on 30 July 1918. The committee only issued a permit when sugar was sold above a certain price (7.35 guilders per picul), thus preventing sales at extremely low prices, even below the cost of production as had been happened. Another condition was that the firm or estate in question would be prepared to enter an Association of Java Sugar Producers and Exporters. One conclusion was, that Holland had only become a complicating factor in international economic relations. The Netherlands Indies had to look after itself.[95] The committee was a great success. It accomplished 'a complete turn around in the situation'.[96] Aided by a returning demand, and by the news that the Continental Powers had sug-

---

[91] *Handelingen Eerste Kamer* 1917-18:568.
[92] *Koloniaal verslag* 1919:250.
[93] *Koloniaal verslag* 1919:249-50.
[94] *De Locomotief,* 3-6-1918.
[95] *Bataviasch Handelsblad,* 21-9-1918, cited in *Koloniale Studiën* 1918:371.
[96] *Koloniaal verslag* 1919:255-6.

gested an armistice in early October, prices recovered. In October the price of sugar reached 13 guilders per picul.

Much to the displeasure of the Governor-General and the Minister of the Colonies the Advisory Committee on Sugar and the Association of Java Sugar Producers and Exporters were dissolved at the end of October. The headquarters of the sugar companies in Holland, united in the Bond van Eigenaren in Nederlandsch-Indische Suikerondernemingen (BENISO, Union of Owners of Netherlands Indies' Sugar Estates), which had been founded in November 1917 at the height of the sugar crisis, rejected any government interference in the sugar trade (Taselaar 1998:106). The headquarters also refused to allow their estates in Java any freedom of action. To counter the steps taken in Batavia, the sugar companies in Holland founded their own organization to regulate trade, the Vereenigde Java Suiker Producenten (United Java Sugar Producers Association), in August 1918. When he left the Netherlands Indies in July 1928, Emil Helfferich was still complaining about the negative consequences of this and similar organizations in Holland for the spirit of enterprise in the estate sector in the Netherlands Indies (Taselaar 1998:1-2).

Nevertheless, producers had been made to see the benefit of cooperation and 'voluntary was continued, what had been established by pressure from the government'.[97] Batavia and the business community in the Netherlands Indies had discovered the proper instrument to regulate trade and fix prices. A Rubber Producers Association, with a special branch in Medan, and a Coffee Producers Association were established in November. A Tea Producers Association and a Cocoa Producers Association were not far behind.

---

[97] *Koloniaal verslag* 1919:255-6.

CHAPTER XIX

Rice and sugar

To Dutch people who had travelled on the *Noordam* it appeared as if the consequences of the Great War had almost passed by the Netherlands Indies. People in the Netherlands Indies thought differently. They were aware that they were better off than the people in Europe, but as a woman wrote to *De Locomotief* in March 1917 'is it not beginning to become alarming expensive. The price of everything is rising: food, clothing, building materials (and as a consequence more expensive rents) and earnings remain the same'.[1]

War had made life only more expensive for all population groups. *Duurte*, dearness, was on everybody's mind. Europeans complained about high prices and grumbled because they had to forego with luxuries like Eau-de-Cologne and some of the foodstuffs and drinks which pleased their palate most. Initially there had been substitutes. Europeans could buy 'Edammer' cheese and 'Rheinwein' from Australia and 'Bordeaux wines' from California. They could eat delicatessen products imported from the United States and drink beer from Japan, which people by now had started to appreciate.[2] Maintaining eating and drinking habits only became a problem in the later years of the war, when imports from Australia, an important source of ham, flour, cheese, and butter, and from the United States were disrupted.

The Netherlands Indies were not completely dependent on imports, a modest effort was made to set up an import substitution industry. Beer was produced locally. In Java jenever distilleries were established; in Sumatra cigar factories. Erdman and Sielcken experimented with the production of margarine from coconut oil. Another novelty was the First Medan Tea Factory, a Chinese initiative, where tea was blended and packed. A Dutch rusk factory and a vermicelli factory were opened. A special treat was guaranteed when a company succeeded in producing Haagse hopjes (coffee-flavoured butterscotch sweats). Such efforts were a drop in the ocean. Their European bias irritated nationalist leaders. In February 1918, when a chocolate and cacao fac-

---

[1] *De Locomotief*, 14-3-1917.
[2] *De Locomotief*, 14-1-1915; *Koloniaal verslag* 1919:261-2; Helfferich 1921:14.

tory commenced production, *Neratja* wondered when finally a factory which catered for the needs of Indonesians would be built. The same newspaper reacted differently when Australia issued a ban on the export of butter and cheese. This time *Neratja* expressed the hope that the ban would be a stimulus to start the production of these products in the Netherlands Indies.[3]

Europeans began to worry that because of a shortage of wheat soon bread could no longer be baked. Once again it was observed that loaves of bread had become smaller.[4] Fortunately, in Bandung an experiment to make 'flour' suitable for the production of bread from cassava was successful. For some time the army had already been trying to develop such a product, but in vain. Now someone had succeeded. A local reporter noted that mixed with real flour, the bread, biscuits, and cakes made from it were rather tasty.[5] Others disagreed. There were plenty of complaints about its taste when the tapioca flour bread reached the shops. Earlier, in the middle of 1917, experiments to grow wheat in the Archipelago had been successful.

The relief afforded by all such experiments and initiatives was pretty small. In early 1918 the price of butter rose by 50 per cent within two months after Australia had imposed an export ban. The shortage that followed forced the colonial Navy to institute 'butterless days'. No butter was served if there was jam, meat, or sardines on the table.[6] The price of bread and tinned milk had doubled since 1914. That of other foodstuffs had also mounted: 'Who', an angry speaker in Ambon demanded, 'remembers what the inside of a tin of sardines looks like?'[7] The prices of medicines, clothing, and textiles followed exactly the same pattern. Shoes, those markers of European status and of modernity, had become too expensive to buy for people with a modest income.[8] Rents had risen. In some instances they had doubled by 1917.

The time was ripe for the European community to complain. In *De Locomotief* a reader from Blitar indignantly asked why the colonial government did not intervene? When matters affected 'the brown brother,' Batavia was quick to act. If the daily lives of the Europeans were put under pressure, and if the colonial government was confronted with the might of the large import companies, Batavia hesitated to take appropriate action. He posed that it was the 'pur-sang' Europeans who were hurt most. They could not do without European foodstuffs, or, we may conclude from the way he went on, their drinks (a bottle of Dutch gin had become four to five times more expensive).

---

[3] *Neratja*, 18-2-1918, 13-3-1918.
[4] *De Locomotief*, 21-5-1918.
[5] *De Preangerbode*, cited in *De Locomotief*, 8-4-1918.
[6] *Nieuwe Soerabaia Courant*, cited in *De Locomotief*, 3-6-1918.
[7] *De Locomotief*, 21-5-1918, 25-5-1918.
[8] *De Locomotief*, 12-4-1918, 13-4-1918.

The reader angrily suggested that everybody should become a teetotaller. This would teach the import companies not to stock their warehouses full of jenever in expectation of higher prices.[9]

Indonesians did not lay behind in lamentations. As early as May 1916, in a fierce editorial *Oetoesan Hindia* had observed that since the outbreak of the war not only had prices of imported goods risen steeply but it was the same story for products made and grown in Java. *Oetoesan Hindia* urged the government to act against the 'capitalists', the leeches, who were making money hand over fist from huge war profits and who were responsible for the rise in the price of domestic products. Batavia had to wake up to just how serious the situation was. If they could not buy enough food, the Javanese might not support the Dutch if the Japanese invaded the island.[10] People's welfare was hard hit. In February 1917, a contributor to *Islam Bergerak* put the consequences of the war on a par with other disasters such as the plague, floods, and earthquakes.[11] A few months later *Oetoesan Hindia* wrote that natives did not worry about the telegraphic blockade. For them there was only one question: *mati atau roti*, dead or bread.

Indicative of the growing poverty outside Java was the drop in government income from commutation of statute labour outside Java. It fell from 632,121 guilders in 1914 to 191,500 guilders in 1918.[12] The increasing profits at government pawnshops mirrored the steep economic decline of the indigenous population of Java. Receipts increased from 10 million guilders in 1914, to 12 million guilders in 1916 and 14 million guilders in 1917.[13]

Prickled into action by the *duurte*, a variety of European and Indonesian organizations staged meetings to protest about the consequent high cost of living, in 1917 and early 1918. They asked the government to intervene and to fix prices. If we may believe a statement by the central board of the Sarekat Islam of March 1918, almost all its branches had organized protest meetings, which had drawn hundreds, thousands, and even tens of thousand people.[14] On the principles the organizations were all agreed. The difference lay in the way the message should be conveyed. The ISDV and the Sarekat Islam wanted to present demands directly to the government. Boedi Oetomo and other more moderate organizations did not want to go further than to draw up urgent requests. Usually the resolutions accepted at such protest meetings were brought to the attention of Van Limburg Stirum by wire. A reader of

---

[9] *De Locomotief,* 17-4-1918.
[10] *Oetoesan Hindia,* 9-5-1916.
[11] *Islam Bergerak,* 10-2-1917.
[12] *Volksraad* 1918:529.
[13] *Volksraad* 1918:528.
[14] *Neratja,* 30-3-1918.

A sugar cane estate in Java (Van Gent, Penard and
Rinkes 1923: Photo 173)

Oetoesan Hindia protested about this practice. It was a waste and a shameful fashion, a mania, at a time when entrenchments were being propagated from all sides. Each word cost 10 cents. Some telegrams held hundreds even over a thousand words. This was typical capitalist behaviour. It would be better to send a registered letter to the Governor General. The editors of *Oetoesan Hindia* begged to disagree. They claimed that it was a well-known fact that Batavia paid attention only to telegrams, registered letters got short shrift.[15]

To compensate for the higher cost of living, European firms, the NHM in the forefront, had already increased the salaries of their European staff by adding a special allowance in 1916. At first no more than a few per cent, the allowance could rise as high as 15 per cent at the beginning of 1917. Some companies restricted this to Europeans who earned less than 500 guilders per month. Other companies gave their European staff an allowance depending on the composition of their family. Sometimes Indonesian and Chinese employees and labourers were also compensated, but often, not always – Internatio was one of the exceptions – at a lesser rate than the European staff. *Neratja* reacted

[15] *Oetoesan Hindia*, 23-4-1918.

indignantly. Indonesians also worked hard and could not be treated as 'mere natives'.[16] The labour force usually had to do without. They were precisely the people leaders of the Sarekat Islam sagely pointed out without whom the estate owners would not have been able to grow rich.

Judging from a report in *Djawa Tengah*, which urged its readers to demand a similar measure from Chinese employers, Chinese firms did not follow suit, at least not immediately.[17] Among those Chinese who did not pay their employees compensation, or perhaps not enough, were Chinese owners of sugar estates. The trade union of people employed in the sugar industry in Java and Madura, De Suikerbond (Sugar Union) called for action.[18] Initially Batavia had also refused to pay a cost-of-living supplement, a *duurtetoeslag*, a word which was to enter the Malay vocabulary. The colonial government admitted that life had become expensive, but refused to follow the example of the private sector. A cost-of-living supplement would cost too much. Van Limburg Stirum's staff had calculated that it would require expenditure of 8.7 million guilders annually. This calculation did not yet take into account a similar allowance for the soldiers in the colonial army.

Van Limburg Stirum tried to convince the civil servants that in the Netherlands Indies people had 'more reason for gratitude than for complaint'.[19] They should not demand a special allowance. People in Holland were far worse off. The colonial government could not 'neutralize every consequence of war for civil servants'.[20] As an additional argument, in the closing months of 1917 Batavia pointed out that it was no great burden for private firms to pay a cost-of-living supplement. They could well afford it. They only had few Europeans with a permanent appointment and in 'the present circumstances' they were doing 'good, many even very good business'.[21] The state was in a different position. It was suffering the financial consequences of the war, had to cope with an ever increasing expenditure, and had a much larger number of people with a permanent appointment.

The VSTP which had made a cost-of-living allowance a centre piece of agitation since January 1917, dismissed Batavia's decision as a gross neglect of the interests of the civil servants.[22] It did so at the end of the year in an appeal to other unions of public servants to make a united stand to force a fair cost-of-living supplement out of the government. Earlier attempts to make a

---

[16] *Neratja*, 10-4-1918.
[17] *Djawa Tengah*, cited in *Koloniaal Tijdschrift* 1917:687.
[18] *De Locomotief*, 19-2-1917.
[19] Van Limburg Stirum to Pleyte, 17-12-1917, NA, Kol. Geheim, Vb. 31-12-1917 A15.
[20] Van Limburg Stirum to Pleyte, 17-12-1917, NA, Kol. Geheim, Vb. 31-12-1917 A15.
[21] Circular, cited in *De Locomotief*, 5-11-1917.
[22] *De Locomotief*, 27-12-1917.

common stand had failed. This time the VSTP appeal was successful. Twelve trade unions and other organizations met in Yogyakarta on 2 February 1918. They claimed to have 17,464 members.[23] A telegram was sent to the Parliament in The Hague to ask for support. Among its signatories were Dwidjosewojo of Boedi Oetomo and Sneevliet of the ISDV. The telegram had at least one unexpected result. It made members of Parliament aware that Great Britain had ended its wire blockade.

The government gave in in April 1918. Batavia announced that it would compensate civil servants and soldiers who earned less than 315 guilders per month for the high cost-of-living. It was a progressive allowance. Those with a salary of less than 50 guilders received an increase of 20 per cent; those earning between 200 and 315 guilders 5 per cent. It was calculated that these allowances would cost the government 7.5 million guilders annually.

The compensation was immediately attacked as being too low. Throughout 1918 trade unions and other organizations continued to plead with the People's Council, in petitions and in letters, for higher wages. To show that the government measures were inadequate some argued that the cost of living had risen by 30 per cent.[24] To illustrate the desperate living conditions of Indonesian civil servants, Malay newspapers published surveys of how much money ordinary Indonesian civil servants had to spend on daily necessities and how inadequate their salaries were. The discrepancy between low pay and high expenditure was also presented as a reason – besides the rigid labour relations and the marks of homage superiors still demanded from their underlings – why, as Europeans did not fail to notice, fewer and fewer Indonesians entered the civil service. It was also claimed that only uneducated civil servants were forced to remain in government employment because they could find no job elsewhere.[25]

Critics also stigmatized the compensation as inadequate. One of the reasons for them to argue in such a vein was that a cost-of-living allowance was only given to those who had a permanent appointment; not the people, some pointed out, who needed it most.[26] Initially even retired people were excluded, but this mistake was redressed at the end of October 1918. Widows and orphans, many struggling with a very small pension, did not receive an allowance either. Batavia said that it had forgotten to include them.[27] Yet another point of criticism was that the compensation did not take into account regional differences in the cost of living. One of the complaints claimed that

[23] *Handelingen Tweede Kamer* 1917-18:1493.
[24] *Volksraad* 1918:135.
[25] *Neratja*, 2-11-1918.
[26] *De Locomotief,* 5-4-1918.
[27] *Volksraad* 1918:206.

life in Ambon was much more expensive than in Java. A teacher in Ambon who earned 300 guilders was still reduced to poverty and had experienced great difficulty in making ends meet. Consequently the local branch of the Nederlandsch-Indisch Onderwijzers Genootschap (NIOG, Netherlands Indies' Teachers' Association) asked for a special cost of living allowance of 25 per cent for salaries below 600 guilders. Those who earned less than 100 guilders should get even more.[28]

The criticism failed to make an impression on Batavia. The representative of the government for general affairs in the People's Council, the lawyer D. Talma, explained that it never had been the intention to compensate in full for the rise in the price level. It would be unfair were only civil servants to be fully compensated and the rest of the population still continued to suffer from the high prices.[29]

Another specific point of complaint was rent. There was a housing shortage in almost all the larger cities. Housing had not kept pace with the increasing number of Europeans who had come to the colony before the war. It had also not been able to accommodate the growing number of employees on modest pay. During the war rents rose steeply, one reason lay the blame at the door of Arabs and Chinese especially, often the owners of houses rented by Europeans, even in the richer neighbourhoods. Relaxing the restrictions on residence of the Chinese and Arab population had also contributed its mite. Rich Chinese and Arabs took up residence in the quarters of town where the Europeans lived.

Projects to build cheaper houses had been started or were planned by municipalities and public companies before 1914. During the war such plans were still contemplated by Insulinde, the Sarekat Islam, and the NIOG. Suggestions that civil servants be given a special rent-allowance could be heard as early as January 1915. In the course of the war matters only became worse. In view of this, government services gave their employees a special supplement to cover rising rents, or paid them as travel allowance, to give them the opportunity to rent a cheaper house outside the city. In Surabaya, said to be a city where rents were especially high, civil servants who earned less than 60 guilders a month received a rent allowance of 5 guilders. Javanese assistant-teachers were excluded from the rent allowance. They complained bitterly about this; the more so because Batavia intended to deny them the rises in salary it gave to the better-educated ordinary teachers.[30]

Housing and rent affected people of all population groups, but the protests against rising rents focused on the problems it created for Europeans.

---

[28] *De Locomotief,* 10-4-1918, 17-4-1918, 27-5-1918, 5-6-1918.
[29] *Volksraad* 1918:557.
[30] *Oetoesan Hindia,* 24-5-1918, 29-8-1918.

At times the issue drove Europeans and Indonesians apart. The Sarekat Islam withdrew as co-organizer of a well-organized protest meeting held at the City Gardens of Surabaya on 30 April 1918, attended by over 5,000 people. It did so after a conflict with the NIOG, an exclusive European organization, about what the aim of the meeting should be. The NIOG leaders wanted to highlight high rents. The representatives of the Sarekat Islam protested that rent was mainly a problem affecting the European population. Food prices and hunger should take centre stage.[31]

Measures were taken in June 1918. The first step was an ordinance which protected house-owners against eviction by the owner of the land on which their houses were built. An 'ordinance against the unreasonable forcing up of rents' was issued a few days later. It pegged the rent level at that of 1 January 1916. Higher house rents were allowed only when local rent commissions gave permission. The Sarekat Islam organized information meetings to assist Indonesians tenants. The stated aim was to prevent that people were evicted or were tricked into paying a higher rent than that allowed.

Though hailed as a welcome step the rent ordinance did not bear full fruit. Not everywhere was it easy to appoint a rent commission. In Cirebon, in an effort to guarantee impartiality, the municipal Coucil looked for somebody as a chairman who was neither a tenant nor a landlord. As most Europeans in the city rented their houses from Arabs or Chinese, such a person was difficult to find.[32] In Semarang the mayor was reluctant to institute a rent commission. In his opinion rents had not increased too sharply. Ways were also found to circumvent the ordinance. From Batavia it was reported that Arabs did precisely this by upgrading the value of the furniture in the houses they rented out. Yet other owners tried to evict their tenants under the pretext that they needed the house for themselves to live in.

The adverse circumstances forced the colonial government to announce, as leaders of the Sarekat Islam and others in Java and West Sumatra had already asked, that it would be lenient with the collection of tax.[33] As in 1914 Dutch colonial civil servants also hastened to urge the population to be thrifty. Leaders of the nationalist movement made similar appeals. The central board of Boedi Oetomo issued a manifesto, in Javanese and in Latin script, about the shortage of food and clothing amid ever-rising prices in May 1918. It urged the people to be careful how they spent their money. They should avoid all extravagant activities and purchases. The measures taken by the government to guard the welfare of everybody had to be obeyed to the letter. They should

---

[31] *Oetoesan Hindia*, 27-4-1918, 29-4-1918, 2-5-1918.
[32] *De Locomotief*, 19-6-1918.
[33] *Oetoesan Hindia*, 18-5-1918.

not be misunderstood. It was the duty of all who read the manifesto, the statement ended, to explain the message to others, especially to those who could not read.[34] Within the devout Islamic community, similar pleas were coupled at times with admonitions not to spend money on watching traditional performances of dance, gamelan, wayang, and other un-Islamic activities.[35]

The dilemma was that food and clothing had gone up in price, and the economic consequences of the war had made it more difficult to find employment. A picul of rice which had cost 6 guilders in 1916 cost 11 guilders in February 1918, in Batavia as much as 12. Cassava had become more expensive. The price of eggs and chickens had doubled since the outbreak of the war. That of fresh fish had tripled. *Kain* had become twice as costly.[36] Equally burdensome was that the price of petroleum used in lamps had mounted. It was claimed that some Indonesians could no longer afford to light their houses at night because of this.[37] On top of this, the tariffs on public transport had gone up. Decreasing purchasing power also affected the demand for luxury goods, which had still been bought by the indigenous population in the past. Among these were the better quality draperies, household utensils, and tinned food. More than under normal circumstances, people who were trying to cope with adverse circumstances pawned their possessions; not only bracelets, rings, necklaces, and other items of jewellery but also clothes. There were some who maintained that matters were even worse. People had become too poor. They had nothing left to pawn.[38]

The consequence of rising prices for domestic retail trade were twofold. Increased unemployment in the estate sector and diminishing purchasing power in various regions – Semarang, Pasuruan, Kediri, Malang, Yogyakarta, Surakarta were examples – forced many *warung*, small shops, to close down. Elsewhere people who had been forced out of a job or had experienced a drop in income had undertaken new economic activities. In West Java and in Madiun and Pacitan an increase in petty trade and in the number of food stalls was noticeable.[39] In Madiun these activities were initiatives taken by women who had formerly worked in the *batik* industry.

Especially hard hit were indigenous producers of export wares. The decreasing markets abroad for coffee, tea, rubber, copra, and forest products, and the necessity to keep local selling-prices low to compensate for high

---

[34] *Oetoesan Hindia*, 13-5-1918.
[35] *Oetoesan Hindia*, 18-5-1918, 21-8-1918.
[36] *Schepenvorderingswet* 1917:59; *Handelingen Tweede Kamer* 1918-19:2065; *Soerabaiasch Handelsblad*, cited in *De Indische Gids* 1918, II:889; *Koloniaal verslag* 1919:261-2; *De Locomotief*, 1-5-1918.
[37] *Neratja*, 31-1-1918.
[38] *Neratja*, 15-8-1918.
[39] *Koloniaal verslag* 1919:265-6; *Oetoesan Hindia*, 30-10-1918.

Transport of sugar cane (Van Gent, Penard and
Rinkes 1923: Photo 172)

freight prices, had taken their toll. The consequences were glaringly visible. People in Tapanuli neglected their coffee plants. In Jambi, also hit by a decreasing market for rattan, the price for rubber grown by the population more than halved in the last three months of 1917. Rubber trees went untapped.[40] From Bali it was reported that the customary sight of women carrying the coffee harvest down from the hills had become rare. In this case the NOT directives were blamed. Pleas by the Dutch government to the NOT to reconsider fell on deaf ears.[41]

In North Celebes, a major copra-producing area, people were confronted with a lack of shipping opportunities, exacerbated by a low copra price. The situation looked alarming. There was little planting of rice, and with the disappearance of the copra market, no money to buy it.[42] As a representative from the Minahassa in the People's Council said: 'As in Java and many other places in Insulinde, the economic conditions of the native population in the Minahassa are deteriorating fast, very fast'.[43]

There were only a few products which still did well – pepper was one

---

[40] *De Locomotief*, 12-12-1917; *Koloniaal verslag* 1919:55-6, 59-60; Locher-Scholten 1994:296.
[41] *Koloniaal verslag* 1917:217-8.
[42] *Schepenvorderingswet* 1917:49; *Koloniaal verslag* 1918:31-2.
[43] *Volksraad* 1918:206.

of them, pinang another – from which local producers in Aceh, Lampung, Bangka, West Borneo profited greatly. In the Riau Archipelago export of people's rubber increased considerably.[44]

In Java one of the sources of concern was the native tea producers. 1918 was a bad year for them. It was estimated that their income dropped to a quarter of what they had earned in normal times.[45] In April some tea factories in West Java which used to buy their tea leaves stopped production. Other factories still accepted leaves from the population, but only when these were of top quality, while the price they offered was almost not a paying proposition. Driven into a corner by economic circumstances, indigenous producers had to sell their land. A report about one such case in West Java claimed that the owner received between 50 and 75 guilders per bau (7096.5 m^2). Before the war the equivalent price had been between 400 and 500 guilders.

In April 1918 the colonial government decided to act. Batavia hired a tea factory in Cicurug, a region where indigenous production was high and factories had stopped buying leaves from the Indonesian producers. To defend the step Batavia pointed out that the local population could not do without its income from tea, and that if the government were not to act as a wholesale buyer, gardens would be neglected.[46] Though in reaction to the government move, neighbouring tea factories increased the price they were prepared to pay to indigenous producers for their tea leaves, the government intervention had only a modest effect. A few months later *Neratja* observed that Indonesian producers of tea who had once been rich had been forced to become labourers on the land they had once owned. *Neratja* contrasted their fate with that of the European owners of the sugar estates which had recovered with the help of government assistance. In one and the same breath *Neratja* complained that sugar now had become too expensive. Poor people could no longer afford it.[47]

In Java the consequences of the war for the population at large had been somewhat hidden by the export of sugar which had continued unhampered for such a long time. Nevertheless, income had not kept pace with rising prices, and admittedly the number of Javanese and others employed in the sugar industry was small. There were about 51,000 people with a permanent appointment, about 600,000 in seasonal appointment (Carpentier Alting and De Cock Buning 1928:98). Those Javanese, and they were the majority, who only produced just enough rice for their own consumption, were badly stricken by the mounting prices, the more so when they had no secondary crops to sell.

[44] *Koloniaal verslag* 1919:63-4.
[45] *Koloniaal verslag* 1919:51-2; *De Locomotief*, 12-4-1918.
[46] *Volksraad* 1918:59.
[47] *Neratja*, 5-11-1918, 6-11-1918.

Europeans and their press seemed to have had little regard for the fate of the indigenous population. How the economic consequences of war affected them scarcely ever rated a mention in the European-language press. When it did the discontinuation of the haj was often used to demonstrate that it was not necessary to worry too much about a drop in the purchasing power of the population. Some Europeans completely ignored the consequences of the war for the indigenous society. In 1917 the President of the Javasche Bank still maintained that the situation of the population was very favourable. He claimed that native prosperity was permanently entrenched and would not be affected by the war. The following year he made the same observation.[48] Others used the familiar colonial argument reiterating that natives were used to bad times:

> Do not assume Reader that *kromo* can eat rice as he pleases throughout the year. He is not acquainted with such a luxury, he has never been acquainted with it. There are, even in the most favourable circumstances, always a few months in the year when he does not eat any rice at all. Then he eats secondary crops namely tuberous plants and root vegetables, like sweet potatoes, tubers, maize, peas, and the like. Then he seems equally happy and contented, at least he does not grumble and complain.[49]

The Nederlandsche Handel-Maatschappij was more realistic. About 1916 it noted that because of the rising prices of foodstuffs and imports life had become more expensive for the population and that as a consequence prosperity was declining.[50] The same can be said of the *Bataviaasch Handelsblad*. It concluded in early 1918 that conditions for the few thousand members of the European community were better than those for the people in Holland, but that millions of Indonesians were really suffering.[51] A reader of *De Locomotief* made a similar observation. At the end of December 1917 he wrote that bad times had arrived for many families. How would the population for whom many essential goods had become too expensive to buy react? It 'would be all too sad' if food were to be among these items.[52]

The Malay-language press generally sketched a gloomier picture. Its journalists claimed that the high price of food had forced people to cut down meals to only once or twice a day; that some could no longer afford any rice and had turned to maize, when this was available, and cassava; and that side

---

[48] *De Indische Gids* 1917:1432; *Eenige* n.d.:9.
[49] *De Locomotief*, 6-11-1917.
[50] *Verslag* 1917:1123.
[51] *Bataviaasch Handelsblad*, cited in *De Indische Gids* 1918, I:747.
[52] *De Locomotief*, 22-12-1917.

dishes were skipped. *Oetoesan Hindia* concluded that the Netherlands Indies had entered a 'season in which everything was expensive'.[53] In another issue *Oetoesan Hindia* wrote that it was the Takdir Toehan, the Divine Decree of the Lord, that almost all over Java people were confronted with hunger and expensive foodstuffs.[54] Leaders of the nationalist movement made the same observation. They stressed – at times overstressed – the misery war had brought upon the ordinary people. Tjokroaminoto pointed out that all goods, especially those which were counted among the necessities of life for the population, had become expensive.[55] He spoke about 'the poverty which had become chronic and the economic breakdown of a very large part of the native population in Java'.[56]

The blame for the alleged decrease in rice consumption again went to the Chinese. They were accused of hoarding and were consequently called capitalists and egoists.[57] At various places members of the Sarekat Islam went into the countryside to investigate how bad circumstances were and to advise the farmers on how to cope. In Jombang they were pleased with the result: almost no farmer any longer sold his rice to 'the leech alias the middleman of the Chinese race'.[58] Sometimes there were rather ugly incidents. In Leuwiliang Javanese women looted the shop of a Chinese because he refused to lower the price of the rice he sold.[59]

The colonial administration denied that the situation was as alarming as the nationalist press and leaders depicted.[60] Nevertheless, how a continued supply of rice could be assured had remained one of its top priorities; especially, as a Dutch man wrote, 'because of the spirit of the population' (Van Heekeren 1919b:139). Javanese agreed. During a meeting in Surabaya in April 1918, when a member of the Minahassa Union drew attention to the high price of butter he was jeered: 'Rice, rice! We do not need butter! The stomach of a son of the soil demands rice!'[61]

In spite of restrictions and obstacles, the import of rice had only increased in the course of the war: from 443,307 tons in 1913 to 741,576 tons in 1917. In

---

[53] *Oetoesan Hindia*, 20-8-1918, 21-8-1918.
[54] *Oetoesan Hindia*, 8-5-1918.
[55] *Volksraad* 1918-19:550.
[56] *Volksraad* 1918-19:543.
[57] Significantly, one of the few press reports about the arrests tells of an indigenous Indonesian apprehended at the Batavia railway station of Meester Cornelis for carrying thirty kilos of rice (*Neratja* 31-1-1918). Chinese on their part organized relief actions for regions where a famine threatened.
[58] *Oetoesan Hindia*, 8-5-1918.
[59] *Neratja*, 31-1-1918, 2-2-1918, 12-2-1918.
[60] *Volksraad* 1918:38.
[61] *Oetoesan Hindia*, 2-5-1918.

Java it had even doubled (Lulofs 1919:7). The entry into the war of Siam on the side of the Associated Powers in 1917 created an additional reason for people to ponder about cutting off of imports. All rice-producing regions in Southeast Asia had entered the Associated camp, and thus, as it was said, would follow economic directions from London. The 'Entente circle' around the Netherlands Indies had been closed.[62]

The colonial authorities began to worry in earnest when Burma instituted a ban on the export of rice in October 1917. More expensive rice had to be bought in Siam, and this was reflected in an increase in rice prices on the domestic market. High prices affected not only the city dwellers. Other victims were the many farmers who could hardly make ends meet, or who were in the habit of selling their crop before harvest for a low price because of dire financial circumstances. Nevertheless, Batavia still refused to fix a maximum price for rice on the domestic market. It considered this would not be in the interests of the population.[63] What was done was to instruct the civil servants in Java to make an inventory of the food supplies and to prepare for the day rice could no longer be imported in the Netherlands Indies.

To keep the food situation under control, the export of rice from Palembang and Sumatra's West Coast to other parts of the Archipelago was forbidden on New Year's Eve of 1917. Bans for other regions and for maize and cassava products followed. The contract between the KPM and the colonial government of British India in February gave some relief. It also permitted the KPM to strike back at its critics. Pointing out in an influential economic magazine that it asked a low freight price for the shipping of rice, importers and traders were blamed for the high prices of rice in the Netherlands Indies.[64] Private organizations also tried to do their bit. Early March 1918, when rice imports from Burma had once more become possible, Insulinde, the Indische Bond, the SDAP, and a number of other European organizations announced that they had succeeded in buying rice in Rangoon and that they would sell this rice at a low price.[65]

The seizure of Dutch ships quashed all optimism there still might have been. In some places, like Manado, people panicked when they realized that the requisitioning had put a halt to the import of rice.[66] The crisis that threatened laid the colonial government open to attacks that it had failed to act with competence and resolution. Action should have already been taken in the wake of August 1914, when it had become clear how vulnerable the colony

---

[62] *Bataviaasch Handelsblad,* cited in *De Indische Gids* 1918, I:80.
[63] *Volksraad* 1918:330.
[64] *De Indische Financier,* cited in *De Indische Gids* 1918, II:874.
[65] *Neratja,* 7-3-1918.
[66] *Volksraad* 1918:207.

would be if rice imports were to fall away.[67]

To prevent a sky-rocketing of prices, the colonial government instituted a maximum price for rice and wheat on the very day news of the seizure of Dutch freighters reached the Netherlands Indies; this time showing no hesitation about doing so. A week later the stock of tinned milk was confiscated in Batavia and other cities to assure the supply to hospitals, children, and the sick. The decision to confiscate milk had been taken in a panic. Within days, the measure was abrogated when it was realized that there was still a supply large enough to last for five months.

To be able to enforce a maximum ceiling price of rice, Batavia earmarked special funds to allow central and regional authorities to buy up rice through the intermediary of village heads. *Oetoesan Hindia* endorsed the government policy. It appealed to farmers to sell their rice to the government, and not to the (Chinese) capitalists, who, the newspaper claimed, were the reason why food was so expensive.[68] As an additional precaution, legislation to combat the forcing-up of prices was tightened.

Impressed by the seriousness of the situation, Van Limburg Stirum called together an emergency meeting with the *Residents* in Java in early April. He revealed that without imports the annual shortage of rice would amount to 400,000 tons for Java and Madura, and 300,000 tons for the rest of the Netherlands Indies. There was still some stock, which meant that shortage in 1918 would be 550,000 tons if rice could no longer be imported. The situation looked 'very alarming'.[69] The general public was told a different story. It was assured that not all was as bad as it looked. There were still sufficient stocks of food.

Leaders of the nationalist movement were also concerned. Abdoel Moeis wrote in *Neratja* that the season of famine was just around the corner.[70] After a meeting with representatives of local boards, the central board of the Sarekat Islam concluded that with the requisitioning of the Dutch freighters it 'absolutely no longer had any faith that rice could still be obtained from abroad as it used to be'.[71] The Sarekat Islam suggested that the government should be given a monopoly in the rice trade. It should buy up rice stocks and the crop in the fields, and sell the rice to the population at an affordable price. Batavia refused to acquiesce in this. It feared that such a drastic step would create too much unrest; a prospect it was not willing and probably would not be able to handle. The suggestion was also said to be impracticable. Most Javanese

---

[67] *De Taak* and *De Locomotief*, cited in *De Indische Gids* 1918, II:1003.
[68] *Oetoesan Hindia*, 21-6-1918.
[69] *Handelingen Tweede Kamer* 1918-19:2077.
[70] *Neratja*, 4-4-1918.
[71] *Neratja*, 30-3-1918.

farmers were small peasants who harvested only a small amount of rice, just sufficient for their own family. If the government were to buy up their rice, it would almost immediately have to be resold to them.[72]

As with almost every measure taken by the colonial administration, the fixing of a maximum price met with criticism. Some considered intervention in the free market an infringement of personal freedom.[73] Others were sure that price control would not work. The small retailers from whom the poor bought their rice would ignore it. Larger traders would simply sell second-grade rice as a more expensive variety.[74] Yet others claimed that because of the maximum ceiling price traders would be hesitant to buy rice from the Javanese peasants. Even worse, a fixed price would deprive the small farmer of the opportunity to make a nice profit at last. European traders with their lawyers and connections could continue to make war profits; the Javanese peasant had nobody to defend his interests.[75]

Things did indeed go wrong. Batavia had to admit that enforcing a maximum price was 'a matter that was completely new' and that it had 'no experience whatsoever' in this field.[76] In Batavia the price fixed was lower than the existing market price, which put the retail traders in a difficult position. The price was even lower than the market price outside Batavia. Traders bought rice in Batavia and sold it for a higher price outside the city. To make such a trade impossible, the transport of rice from one regency to another was forbidden. Even in Batavia itself it was difficult to enforce the maximum price. State companies and the army bought up rice at a higher price. This had been done, it was explained, because of the 'extraordinary circumstances'.[77] Traders also ignored the price limit set. One of the reasons for them to do so was that they themselves had bought rice at a price higher than which they were allowed to sell. If rice was not sold openly at a higher price, one of the tricks to circumvent the maximum price indeed was to sell cheaper rice as a more expensive variety. In other cases local authorities acted too hastily. In Semarang the municipality sold rice at a price lower than that on the market. It turned out to be a fiasco. There was no shortage of rice in the town, while people considered the rice offered to be too poor a quality for the price asked.[78]

The main goal Batavia set itself was to increase the production of rice and other food crops. Van Limburg Stirum personally impressed upon the

---

[72] *De Locomotief,* 2-4-1918, 6-4-1918; *Volksraad* 1918:58.
[73] *De Locomotief,* 13-4-1918.
[74] *De Locomotief,* 17-4-1918.
[75] *De Locomotief,* 10-5-1918.
[76] *Volksraad* 1918:330.
[77] *De Indische Gids* 1919, II:883.
[78] *De Locomotief,* 16-5-1918.

Residents of Java that they had to convince their staffs of the utmost importance of food production. All other interests had to bow before this.[79] Javanese farmers were advised not to grow tobacco or other export products which no longer yielded a profit. They should concentrate on the planting of food crops. Rewards were held out to Javanese civil servants who really flung themselves into increasing food production.

In their effort to circumvent the imminent food crisis the authorities also tried to change the diet of the Indonesian population. If all else failed, substitute staples would have to do the trick. A campaign was started to have people eat less rice and more cassava (which they liked less than maize). Civil servants outside Java were informed that if the local population was not yet familiar with cassava as a staple, Batavia was more than happy to send a trial packet.[80] The sooner people changed their eating habits the better. The Director of Agriculture wrote to the *Residents* in Java that care had to be taken to see that people should not start eating alternative foodstuffs only after rice had become unavailable. Rice was a product that could be stored for a long time. Its major substitute, dried cassava roots, could not. After a while dried cassava roots tended to 'disintegrate into powder'.[81] It can be deduced from the words of his successor that it was hoped that cooking instructions would help. He had come to Java on the *Noordam* and was of the opinion that there was no reason to complain in the Netherlands Indies. War bread in Holland tasted more like putty than real bread. With this in mind, he tried to convince the People's Council that there was nothing wrong people ate cassava or maize in times of shortage of rice, providing that 'there is enough food and they learn to prepare it in a tasty way'.[82]

There was no lack of suggestions. A reader of the *Bataviaasch Nieuwsblad* wrote that sago formed a good alternative to rice. In Java 'Ambonese soldiers could teach the population how to eat the eat sago'.[83] Others were dubious. Sago was a blessing as well as a curse. It was a curse because it was easy to produce and had made those who had sago as their staple lazy and lacking in initiative. Consequently, people living in sago-producing regions could not be counted upon to increase their harvest. They could not be tempted by money to work extra hours. Perhaps, a solution would be to involve prisoners in the production.[84]

The suggestions that eating habits be changed did not have much effect as

---

[79] *De Locomotief*, 5-4-1918.
[80] *De Locomotief*, 16-4-1918, 2-5-1918; *Oetoesan Hindia*, 3-5-1918.
[81] *De Locomotief*, 2-5-1918.
[82] *De Indische Gids* 1919, II:881.
[83] *Bataviaasch Nieuwsblad*, cited in *De Locomotief*, 5-4-1918.
[84] *De Locomotief*, 30-5-1918.

long as the necessity to do so was not clearly felt. In the cities people refused to part with their rice. With 'some amazement' it was also observed that Chinese in Sumatra refused to eat maize instead of rice.[85]

At times the appeals completely misfired. In Surakarta where the food situation looked particularly alarming in the hinterland, the Sunan issued a proclamation drafted by the Dutch *Resident*. Rich and poor were asked to have only one meal a day (in the evening) with rice, maize, or cassava and eat other foodstuffs at other meal times. The statement was read at markets and the *Resident's* request was also brought to the attention of the workers on the estates in view of the 'present, extremely abnormal times'.[86]

To issue such an appeal was not a prudent step, especially not at a time when Javanese rulers, civil servants, and notables had become an object of criticism in nationalist circles, and not only there. Even Dutch-language newspapers made fun of the 'fatherly proclamation'. *De Locomotief* suggested that the rulers should also address their advisors, the Dutch authorities. They should ensure that such Dutchmen and their servants and pets no longer ate rice, bread, or potatoes. They should also stop consuming large quantities of biscuits, macaroni, vermicelli, or other rich people's foods. It was these Dutchmen who could afford a slimming, not the ordinary Javanese. They were already undernourished because of the present difficult circumstances. To ensure that Europeans heeded the food restrictions, they should be weighed once a month. After a few months, if their well-fed corporations did not shrunk, this was proof of the fact they still had a hidden supply of food.[87]

Part of the Malay-language press seized upon the proclamation to attack the Javanese rulers. Intentionally or not, the proclamation was sometimes presented as an order to eat only one meal a day. It was also subtly insinuated that the police would enforce the order. Malay newspapers used the proclamation to point out how much the Javanese suffered from taxation and other demands imposed on them by the colonial government. The blame for their tribulations was set squarely on the shoulders of the own rulers and civil servants who condoned and shared in this.[88] The weekly *Medan Boediman* explained that once upon a time the rulers had cared for their people. They had supported them in bad times with goods and prayers. This was no longer the case: 'the rulers do not care about the people and consequently the people do not care about the rulers'.[89] Instead of handing over land to their subjects to be planted with food crops as they should, the rulers of Yogyakarta and Surakarta had

---

[85] *Nieuwe Financier en Kapitaal*, cited in *De Indische Gids* 1919, I:377; Bezwaren 1919:670.
[86] *De Locomotief*, 2-5-1918.
[87] *De Locomotief*, 10-5-1918.
[88] *Islam Bergerak*, 20-5-1918.
[89] *Medan Boediman*, 30-10-1918.

rented out land to the capitalists for their estates. Because they blocked any improvement in the lot of the people in other ways as well, it would be best if the rulers were pensioned off. It was a view which was also voiced in the Sarekat Islam. *Oetoesan Hindia* attacked the Regents Association for remaining silent at a time when the people suffered.[90] Even worse, by pretending that all was well and by not informing others about shortages of food, it was the Javanese civil servants who were to blame if the people were starving. Dutch civil servants acted differently. The *Resident* of Kediri was cited as an example. He had admitted to representatives of the Sarekat Islam that there was a shortage of food in his territory.[91]

The phrase about rulers who cooperated with the capitalists was one of the ways in which the growing hatred towards the European estates manifested itself. Discussions in early 1918 about stepping up the production of rice focused on the need to reduce the acreage planted by the sugar factories. Such a solution had already been suggested as early as August 1914. Speculating then about a blockade of the ports of Java, *Oetoesan Hindia* had suggested that Idenburg should prepare for such an eventuality by ordering the estates to grow food crops.[92] The idea resurfaced in public debate in 1918. The suggestion that estates be turned into *sawah* was highly controversial. Because of this, the food situation was a topic which, as was observed, was written and spoken about almost more than the war itself.[93] 'The people cannot live from sugar', became a popular expressions, also in the Dutch-language press.

The reputation of the sugar estates was bad. The Javanese and progressive Europeans put the way in which estates hired land from the population and arranged the irrigation of their fields to the detriment of local farmers on a par with outright exploitation. It was common knowledge that the war had brought the sugar estates great profits; profits in which the population did not share. In order not to alienate the more moderate members and those who propagated the growth of Indonesian trade and industry, during its second national congress in October 1917 the Sarekat Islam announced a battle against what was called *kapitalisme jang berdosa*, sinful capitalism, by which in the first place the sugar estates were meant.[94] Abdoel Moeis described the sugar industry as the 'goldmine of the big capitalists'.[95] For the Malay press the estates formed an easy butt of propaganda. *Oetoesan Hindia* called the estate owners

---

[90] *Oetoesan Hindia*, 8-5-1918.
[91] *Oetoesan Hindia*, 22-4-1918.
[92] *Oetoesan Hindia*, 11-8-1914, 19-8-1914, 12-8-1914.
[93] *De Indische Gids* 1919:743.
[94] *Sarekat-Islam Congres* 1919a:83, 1919b:78.
[95] *Volksraad* 1918:298.

the cruellest people on earth.[96] *Djawa Tengah* blamed the expanding acreage of the sugar estates for the fact that the population had to eat expensive imported rice.[97] In *Oetoesan Hindia* it was argued a few months later that this sort of rice not only cost over the odds, the quality was also nothing to write home about. The rice was said to be extremely poor, to have lost most of its vitamin value because it was too old, making it a health hazard, and when cooked exuded a nasty smell.[98] The way in which the sugar industry was castigated even in the People's Council shocked the public in Holland. The words used did in a sense backfire. Not all criticism was taken seriously, people were suspicious that it was inspired by a general desire to lash out against the 'big capitalists'.[99]

Even an organization so loyal to Dutch rule as the Regents Association criticized the way the estates operated. At its meeting in November 1914, after the association had testified to its loyalty, attention had been drawn to the unrest created by the sugar estates. The warning had not been without reason. It was by no means a rare occurrence for angry villagers to set fire to sugar-cane fields or for labour unrest to erupt. Some estates even reserved a special sum of money to buy off potential trouble-makers. The estates were not unaffected by the mood of the population. By the autumn of 1916 the anxiety of August 1913 when European newspapers speculated about the prospect of a St Bartholomew's Night reared its ugly head again. The President of the General Syndicate of Sugar Producers informed the government that, on the basis of information gathered by its informers, he was sure that a violent attack on Europeans was planned in Central and East Java. The object was nothing less than 'a general massacre'. On behalf of the sugar estates, he asked Batavia to provide the European employees with extra weapons and ammunition. Batavia refused as it wanted to avoid a panic. No Europeans were murdered at that time. The only variation in the general pattern to be observed was an increase in visits to the mosque.[100]

Undeniably unrest had reappeared in the countryside in its pre-war intensity. As in the past, members of the Sarekat Islam intimidated or boycotted outsiders, including the Chinese. A 'social democrat and member of the SI' wrote in October 1918 in *Oetoesan Hindia* that the people 'felt *so* oppressed, *so* bled white, *so* humiliated, *so* discriminated against, *so* unprotected, *so* irritated, *so* enraged', that they no longer cared a straw for the law and had started 'to

---

[96] *Oetoesan Hindia*, 24-4-1918.
[97] *Nieuwe Soerabaia Courant*, cited in *De Locomotief*, 2-4-1918; *Djawa Tengah*, cited in *Koloniaal Tijdschrift* 1917:1111.
[98] *Oetoesan Hindia*, 20-8-1918.
[99] *Handelingen Eerste Kamer* 1918-19:461.
[100] Note by vd. H.v.O. [Van der Houven van Oordt], 2-11-1916, *Resident* Rembang to Van Limburg Stirum, 6-11-1916, NA, Kol. Geheim, Vb. 26-7-1917.

burn the forest, to burn sugar cane, to murder Europeans, to steal, etc.'.[101] It was the 'season of fire' and of thefts and strikes on estates. Many were the instances of the burning of crops in the field and in sheds. Figures presented were horrendous. In 1917 the total number of sugar-cane fires had been 900. In 1918 1,326 fires were lit between January and the end of August.[102] One sugar-cane estate had been struck by 75 cane fires in eight months.[103] Theft of sugar cane, sometimes committed by large gangs of Javanese operating in broad daylight, showed a similar upward trend. One estate claimed that of some of its field 35 to 50 per cent of the crop had been stolen. The damage was estimated at 88,000 guilders.[104] Railways sleepers, rails, and parts of the lorries of sugar trains were also stolen.

Elsewhere people stole tobacco from the estates and set fire to tobacco sheds. Organized theft of cassava from the fields was also rampant. One estate was reported to have had 2,600,000 cassava plants, representing a value of 200,000 guilders, stolen. At times groups of people took away tens of thousands of plants at night. Sometimes, as happened in Blitar, they even ventured this in broad daylight. Kediri, which had a reputation as being a 'difficult region', suffered especially badly. Such thefts had started here in December 1917. Some Dutchmen blamed the local Sarekat Islam. They accused its leaders of having hinted that should people be unable to buy cheap food, they could always steal cassava. Extra guards did not help. Troops had to be sent to Kediri to guard the cassava planted on estates.[105]

Managers began to complain that estates might be forced to close if thefts continued on such a large scale.[106] Leftist Europeans and the leftist and moderate nationalists blamed hunger, high food prices, capitalism, and economic exploitation for the increase in thefts of agricultural produce and for the fires on sugar and other estates. Indubitably another reason for the thefts was the money thieves could make from selling sugar cane and cassava. Hatred of the sugar estates was also said to lurk in the background. In the People's Council Tjokroaminoto pointed out that cane-fields were supplied with water in abundance. While cane flourished rice withered in adjacent fields because of lack of water. He said that cane was burnt because of anger about such injustice or in an attempt to obtain water for the rice fields.[107]

Perhaps not surprisingly many Europeans had other ideas. They blamed the colonial government for its failure to maintain law and order. In the

---

[101] *Oetoesan Hindia*, 22-10-1918.
[102] *Volksraad* 1918-19:225.
[103] *Oetoesan Hindia*, 20-8-1918.
[104] *Volksraad* 1918:225.
[105] *Koloniaal verslag* 1919:45-6; *Neratja*, 12-11-1918.
[106] *Volksraad* 1918-19:226-7.
[107] *Volksraad* 1918-19:549.

Trade mark of an Italian export company. Social unrest led to in increase in weapon purchases by Europeans and Chinese (*Javasche Courant* 1916. Trade mark 7942).

Soerabaiasch Handelsblad Boon went as far as to suggest that if the Dutch authorities could no longer protect the estates, other countries with large investments in the plantation sector should be invited to intervene.[108] Europeans interpreted what was happening as an increased threat to their person and goods. They pointed to the many burglaries of houses of European staff on estates, and to the occasional murder of Europeans. On plantations which had run into financial difficulties, staff were sometimes attacked by coolies who had not been paid. Again wild stories ran riot recounting threats to life and property. The European community demanded a strengthening of the police force, especially in Central Java and the Eastern Salient of East Java. Estate employees armed themselves with a pistol when they went out into the fields. Their companies once more turned to the government for extra protection. Such appeals were greeted with some malicious delight in *Oetoesan Hindia*. The rich who had so far only profited from the war, had now begun snivelling to their father to ask for protection.[109]

To be fair, estates also took their own precautions. Private security guards had there also been in the past. In 1896 the colonial government had given them the power to arrest people, but only on the land of the estate itself. By 1918 such bodies were considered to be ineffective. The Vorstenlandsche Landbouwvereeniging (Agricultural Association of the Principalities) founded a *cultuurpolitie*, estate police, or *cultuurbrigades*, estate brigades in October 1918. *Neratja* claimed that the aim was to act upon villagers who had enough of the way the estates operated and burnt and destroyed crops and property. It was estimated that each estate needed a brigade of about thirty guards. Local

[108] *Soerabajaasch Handelsblad*, 2-11-1918, cited in *Volksraad* 1918-19:207.
[109] *Oetoesan Hindia*, 3-10-1918, 17-10-1918, 26-10-1918.

colonial civil servants supported the initiative. The guards should be Javanese, but as they might be on friendly terms with local villagers, each unit should be commanded by three or four policemen from North Sulawesi or Ambon.[110] At the end of the same month, during a meeting in the Concordia Club in Malang, the Java Sugar Association suggested that European staff on the estates should always go around armed with a Browning and a revolver (which most already did). In order to be able to hit the mark, they also had to learn to shoot well. It was no use waiting till the government acted. That might be too late. 'Before that time you might already be dead and buried, and your family reduced to extreme misery. No rot! Act! Self Help!' Malay newspapers copied the report about Dutch fears and brave words.[111]

Shivers of alarm spread through the Sugar Union. Its board sent out a circular. To convince the government of the necessity of additional security measures, the members were asked to report all the information they had about violent incidents. The Sugar Union was especially interested in attacks on employees 'whether or not committed under a certain provocation', thefts of produce from the fields, and 'incidents of laxness or unwillingness on the part of the police'. 'Blatantly deliberate rudeness to Europeans', and acts of instigation by natives and Europeans should also be reported. The information was needed to prove that

> in the interior respect for the authorities is declining, that the native no longer spares the life and property of Europeans, that there are incontrovertible indications of a definite rebellious spirit among the population and of an increase in explosions, in magnitude as well as in number.

No less important was the need to convince the government that 'orally and in writing the population is incited to commit acts of violence'. The circular advised the members to act 'dispassionately'. Restraint was necessary in view of the 'irritability of the population which unarguably does have its natural causes, but which, because of the systematic, artificial feeding by demagogues represents a very large danger to the employees'. In short, the population 'suffered from severe overstrain'. Only the government had the power to 'cure' this.[112] In the magazine of the union the '(criminal) slackness' of the colonial administration was blamed for the circumstances that had arisen. South Africa was held out as an example. There 'no Kaffir will dare to walk on the pavement'. In Java, a Javanese would rather collide with a European than step aside.[113]

---

[110] *Neratja*, 19-10-1918; *Volksraad* 1918-19:228.
[111] *Soerabaiasch Nieuwsblad*, cited in *Oetoesan Hindia*, 4-11-1918 and *Neratja*, 11-11-1918.
[112] *Volksraad* 1918-19:160.
[113] *De Suikerbond*, cited in *De Indische Gids* 1919, I:248.

As uncultivated land in Java was scarce, there was no other option but to turn for an increase in food production to the estates. As early as 1916, building on earlier experiments, the colonial government had taken steps to develop an irrigation system which would allow for better irrigation of the fields planted by the Javanese farmers, without damaging the growing of sugar cane. It had tried to convince the estates companies to build large water reservoirs on their land which would allow the land planted with food crops to be irrigated during daytime, and not only, as was the practice, at night. Because the estates had to bear the costs, the reaction had been negative. Now the time had come to contemplate more drastic measures. The estates could provide the land for additional rice fields should food production have to be stepped up. The food situation appeared so alarming in early 1918, Van Limburg Stirum seriously contemplated using the option to force sugar and tobacco estates to reserve one-quarter of their acreage for the production of rice. It was borne in mind that other estates might have to follow. Indigenous producers of export crops should be left untouched as long as possible. Should circumstances require that land of indigenous producers of export crops had to be planted with rice, the measure should be confined to those crops which no longer yielded a profit.

The scheme to reserve part of the land of the sugar estates for the production of food won the wholehearted support of the nationalist movement. During meetings of Boedi Oetomo and Sarekat Islam motions with this intent were carried, loudly applauded by those present. The Sarekat Islam wanted to go further than Van Limburg Stirum did. In April 1918 the Sarekat Islam presented Van Limburg Stirum by wire with a motion carried at a meeting of its central board with local branches and with representatives of the ISDV and Insulinde. The Governor General was asked to convert half of the sugar acreage into rice fields. This was presented as a minimum requirement. The meeting had only taken the food situation in Java into account. The rice shortages elsewhere – which the Sarekat Islam leaders said they were not in a position to calculate – might well imply that a larger acreage would have to be reserved for food production. The meeting did not confine itself to demands to do with the sugar industry. The land of tobacco, tea and coffee estates producing for the foreign market should also be turned into rice fields. The government should take the responsibility for the rice production on these additional fields, or should give financial assistance to the 'people' to plant them. In no way should the estates themselves be allowed to arrange the planting of food crops on their land, and profit from this at the expense of the Javanese farmers.

The scheme was opposed by the owners in Holland, who had united themselves in the BENISO. According to the BENISO reduction would disrupt the industry and would vitiate the expansion, which had cost so much effort and money to attain in previous years.[114] The BENISO and those who agreed with the union stressed that the volume of extra rice produced – usually putting forward much lower figures than those mentioned in the estimate of the government – bore no relation to the financial consequences for the industry, and, a point such people never failed to mention, the Javanese labour force. To demonstrate the wickedness of the scheme it was also suggested that a reduction in production could well lead to the mass slaughter of the buffaloes used for the transportation of sugar.[115]

Dutch colonial civil servants also were not without reservations. They had calculated that a reduction by one-fifth would mean a loss in wages of 11.5 million guilders. The additional rice planted might bring in six million guilders for the Javanese.[116] They also had started to realize that having labourers return to their villages would not solve all problems, as had been suggested it would do in the past. Even Javanese needed money; if only to buy clothes and household utensils. How much money the redundant labourers would need and to what extent fellow-villagers would support them when they returned to their village remained an ideological issue, an argument to be used when it suited a person's own position. In 1918 leaders of the Sarekat Islam argued that the estate labourers could well be embraced by the village community. The following year it was the communists in Dutch Parliament who echoed the same sentiment.

When Pleyte informed him that the 'general feeling' in Holland was that only in an extreme emergency should sugar fields be turned into rice fields, Van Limburg Stirum changed his mind.[117] On 29 April 1918, he told a deputation of the Sarekat Islam that for the time being it was not necessary to issue a directive forcing the sugar estates to plant part of their acreage with rice. The deputation had come to try to convince Van Limburg Stirum of the urgency of the food situation. Van Limburg Stirum assured them that they did not have to worry. Rice imports had been resumed. No famine loomed. There was only a shortage of food.

Tjokroaminoto did not agree. A statement issued by the Sarekat Islam in March 1918 had claimed that Indonesians were suffering from lack of food and had been forced to eat inferior food (such as *gadung*, a kind of yam) which endangered their health and was in fact only fit for animals. It was claimed that in some places, Indonesians had died of starvation.[118] At the meeting

---

[114] *Economisch-Statistische Berichten*, 24-4-1918, p. 343.
[115] *De Locomotief*, 18-6-1918; *Bezwaren* 1919:673; *Volksraad* 1918:57.
[116] *Volksraad* 1918:38.
[117] Van Limburg Stirum to Pleyte, 14-2-1918, Pleyte to Parliament, 17-5-1918 (*Handelingen* 1917-18, Aanhangsel: 152, 197); *Handelingen Tweede Kamer* 1918-19:2077.
[118] *Neratja*, 30-3-1918.

Tjokroaminoto presented Van Limburg Stirum with proof. He showed him pictures of starving people in one especially hard-hit area: Trenggalek in the south-west corner of East Java; a region which by now had become the symbol for the Sarekat Islam of the suffering of the ordinary Javanese and of what might be in store if the food situation deteriorated any further. Tjokroaminoto explained that these were photos of people who were best situated, people who could still walk to a relief centre established by Sarekat Islam members and a number of Chinese. *Oetoesan Hindia* reported that on seeing the photos Van Limburg Stirum's face had become grave. Tjokroaminoto also told Van Limburg Stirum that the Sarekat Islam not only blamed the war for the food crisis, the 'capitalists', hoarding food, were equally culpable. The government should interfere and take the distribution and trade in rice into its own hands.[119]

What had happened during the meeting was part of a recurrent phenomenon. Spokesmen of the colonial administration downplayed the effects of the war on the living conditions of the Indonesian population. They also denied that hunger had struck on a unprecedented scale. At most they were prepared to speak about food shortages, or the threat of these in the near future. Nationalist leaders told a different story. They talked about famine and highlighted the miserable conditions of the population. Members of the ISDV and the Socialists in the Netherlands Indies shared their view. In the People's Council Cramer observed that '[h]unger uprisings are not rare and are often counted among the most vicious ones!'[120]

No directive about a decrease in the sugar acreage was issued, but Van Limburg Stirum had created the impression that when forced to choose between sugar and rice, he would opt for the latter. He also had made no secret of the fact that when circumstances necessitated this he would give preference to the irrigation of rice fields above those of sugar cane. This was much to the dismay of the Sugar Syndicate which protested about such an idea to Van Limburg Stirum and Pleyte.[121]

Van Limburg Stirum had not completely discarded the idea of a reduction in sugar production. He and his staff pondered about the possibility that, even if ships were available for transport, bad harvests in the rest of Asia could put an end to the import of rice. Another thought that haunted them was that after the war the Allied Powers would reserve all surplus rice in their colonies and in Siam to feed people in Europe.[122] The sugar companies were made

---

[119] *Oetoesan Hindia*, 4-5-1918, 13-5-1918, 14-5-1918, 15-5-1918.
[120] *Volksraad* 1918:168.
[121] *Economisch-Statistiche Berichten*, 24-4-1918, p. 343, 1-5-1918, p. 367; *Java-Bode*, cited in *Oetoesan Hindia*, 24-4-1918.
[122] *Volksraad* 1918:37.

to understand that the government would welcome a reduction in acreage. Management was asked to consider such a step. The Javasche Bank exerted extra pressure. The bank pointed to the difficulties experienced in exporting sugar and indicated that it might be less forthcoming with loans to estates which did not reduce their sugar-cane fields.[123]

In some cases such gentle pressure was unnecessary. The poor export prospects did the government's work for it. Sugar and tobacco estates reduced their acreage and started to grow rice. The sugar estates did so by 15 per cent on the average (Carpentier Alting and De Cock Buning 1928:70). As had been predicted during the discussions about a forced limitation of their fields, they often only let go of their less productive fields.[124] The reduction in sugar production was welcomed by members of the Sarekat Islam. For them it was proof that their agitation had worked. It was even claimed that the local population had revived and had become prosperous.[125] In Sumatra the rubber estates were ordered by their head offices to reduced production by one-third. No labourer was sacked because the managements of these estates were anxious to avert lack of manpower when peace had been restored and exports could resume their normal course. Surplus capital and labour were employed to improve drainage, and to build or improve factory buildings, warehouses and living-quarters.

The panic seemed to have subsided at the end of May 1918. Batavia concluded that the danger of a food shortage in Java had been averted. Large quantities of rice had been imported. In spite of temporary export bans abroad and in spite of the requisitioning of Dutch ships, Batavia had succeeded in importing even more rice than in the same period in 1917. A small amount of rice, 13,200 picul, taken from the government stock of imported rice, had even been sent to Suriname, to alleviate the food shortage over there.

Outside Java, the food situation had also remained under control. Nevertheless, additional measures had to be taken in Sumatra because private estates and mines had not heeded the earlier suggestion to build up a stock of food sufficient to last a couple of months. East Sumatra was an exception, but in Lampung, Biliton, and Bangka stocks were small. Estates and mining companies asking for rice from Java were urged to take measures to cut down on the consumption of rice. The Biliton Company complied by forbidding the feeding of rice to pigs and poultry and by restricting the production of rice wine. It also decided to employ between 5 and 10 per cent of its labour force in the growing of maize and cassava instead of in tin-mining. Another 500 of

---

[123] *Economisch-Statistische Berichten*, 24-4-1918, p. 343.
[124] *De Locomotief*, 3-4-1918, 3-6-1918; *Volksraad* 1918:298.
[125] *Sarekat-Islam Congres* 1919:24.

its Chinese labourers were employed in dry-rice cultivation.[126] In Biliton the results were disappointing, but in Bangka the rice harvest of 1918 was one-and-a-half time larger that in the previous year.[127]

---

[126] *Distribution report* 5 (5-22 April 1918), NA, Kol. Geheim, Mr. 1918/144x.
[127] *Koloniaal verslag* 1919:63-6.

CHAPTER XX

Restlessness

The problems experienced by the estates all fitted into a broader pattern. Deteriorating living conditions had again made crime a cause of concern, as it had been in 1914. In the Volksraad the Director of Justice complained that prisons were full because of the war.[1] One of the Dutch members, J. Schmutzer, spoke about *verwildering*, lawlessness, in certain parts of Java.[2] In some regions of the Archipelago – Java (especially Kediri), Sumatra's West Coast, Palembang, and Borneo – crime increased to a greater or lesser extent in 1918. The colonial government attributed this at least in part to worsening economic conditions.[3] Crime was also said to have become rampant in Celebes. In this case the authorities did not blame deteriorating economic conditions, but 'the quarrelsome and rapacious nature of the population, [...] its gaming fever, its scattered pattern of residence and its reckless carelessness, and to round it off the lack of sense of responsibility of its heads'.[4] On Bangka special measures had to be taken to prevent an increase in crimes committed by Chinese labourers, who could not be sent home because of a lack of shipping.[5] In Java it was observed that more beggars had appeared in the street. A correspondent of *Neratja* in Surakarta spoke about a 'rain of beggars'. Walking around town for one hour he had counted fifty of them.[6]

Coinciding with this general turbulence the Sarekat Islam had taken a more radical direction. Comparing the atmosphere at successive national conferences of the Sarekat Islam, the Ministry of the Colonies referred to what had happened in 1917 as remarkable. In 1916 the general mood had still been in favour of cooperation with the government. In October 1917 the tone had been 'more intemperate, from time to time on the rude side [...] and there appeared to be very little room for appreciation of the intentions of

---

[1] *Volksraad* 1918-19:500.
[2] *Volksraad* 1918-19:540.
[3] *Koloniaal verslag* 1919:47-50.
[4] *Koloniaal verslag* 1919:69-70.
[5] *Koloniaal verslag* 1919:63-4.
[6] *Neratja*, 14-3-1918.

the government'.[7] Criticism had become 'often one-sided destructive, rarely constructive'.[8] In line with this, after he had become Minister of the Colonies in September 1918 Idenburg observed in Parliament that even the editorials in *Oetoesan Hindia* had become unequivocally inflammatory.[9] Senior colonial civil servants spoke about 'nihilistic' tendencies.[10] A similar trend, though less general and less radical, was observed in the Boedi Oetomo. At its meetings capitalism was identified as the enemy.[11] In its newspaper, *Darmo Kondo*, that is in its Javanese not in its Malay edition, readers who were not familiar with Latin script were instructed in the principles of Socialism.[12]

What Dutch people thought had happened was expressed in the People's Council by one of them, Z. Stokvis. Stokvis deplored the fact that the leaders of the Sarekat Islam should come

> under the influence of a few persons [...] who with a dogma cultivated in Europe, with all the obstinacy of zealots want to force the leadership in a direction which they consider the only one which leads to the only goal acknowledged by them as right and desirable, irrespective of the circumstances here.

Stokvis clearly could not stand 'young men who only recently had left school and with a curious facility for assimilation and an even more curious memory gave speeches about the most difficult subjects which required long study'.[13] Idenburg concluded that through

> the press, through the propaganda meetings, where leaders of the ISDV spoke, the public which reads newspapers and that part of the population organized in associations (not only in the SI) have gradually learned to denote he complex of political, social, and economic factors, which in the course of time has affected the indigenous population and brought it to its present position as capitalism.

They had 'learned to see this as one big, all-dominating power, as if it were an enormous, many-armed monster'.[14]

The turn matters had taken in the Sarekat Islam was a great personal disappointment to Idenburg, who in the early years of its existence had been fiercely criticized for the leniency he had shown towards the association. In April 1919 he recalled with fondness how, when he had left for Holland, a Sarekat Islam deputation had seen him off at Tanjung Priok. Idenburg told the

---

[7] *Koloniaal verslag* 1919:1-2.
[8] *Koloniaal verslag* 1919:3-4.
[9] *Handelingen Tweede Kamer* 1918-19:2080.
[10] *Volksraad* 1918-19:244.
[11] *Koloniaal verslag* 1919:7-8.
[12] *Bataviaasch Handelsblad*, cited in *De Indische Gids* 1917, II:1365.
[13] *Volksraad* 1918-19:217.
[14] *Koloniaal verslag* 1919:3-4.

Dutch Parliament that at that time the Sarekat Islam and Boedi Oetomo were still 'completely loyal'. There had been 'excesses', but these had not been supported by the chief Sarekat Islam leaders. They had testified of their loyalty in the 'most unambiguous' way.[15]

Colonial civil servants were especially piqued that the population did not value the good intentions of the government. As early as February 1915, Rinkes had had to admit that his visits all over Java had made him realize that because of Douwes Dekker and the Indische Partij 'even the most sedate persons, sometimes without being aware of this', expressed ideas and misconceptions about what he called the good measures taken by the government. Such ideas had become an *idée fixe* and were difficult to erase.[16]

A case in point, which contributed hugely to the unruly mood among the population, was the measures taken to combat the plague. These measures interfered deeply in the lives of Javanese and crystallized into a focus of passionate opposition. A protest meeting in Yogyakarta in May 1918 attracted an audience of 2,000 persons. *De Locomotief* saw this as proof of how deeply the matter touched the 'otherwise calm native from Djokja'.[17] There was a variety of complaints. Some were minor. The regulation that houses had to have single plaited bamboo walls instead of double plaited ones caused villagers to fear that break-ins would become easier. This worry was exacerbated by the idea that in the evening, when the lamps were lit, potential thieves could easily select valuable possessions in advance. Others blamed the single walls for their having caught a cold. One or two unfortunate people fell victim to compatriots who posed as housing inspectors and threatened to draw up unfavourable reports if no money were handed over to them. More important were religious objections to the compulsory puncture of the spleen of corpses, the indignation raised by the medical examination of females by male doctors, and the anger about the ban on burying a deceased before a doctor had established the cause of death, which disregarded the Islamic rule that a corpse had to be buried on the day death occurs. Such sentiments were whipped up at times by local religious leaders. Occasionally they found expression in attacks specifically on plague doctors and their staff and on civil servants who tried to impose government regulations, and more generally in 'plague riots'.

A point stressed by leftist, nationalist Muslims was the financial burden the housing improvement scheme implied. Houses constructed in accordance with government regulations, which, as it was said at times had to be 'completely rat free', cost 150 guilders, and according to some Indonesian sources, stressing how much the common people – the *bangsa kromo* – suffered from

---

[15] *Handelingen Tweede Kamer* 1918-19:2079.
[16] Rinkes to Idenburg, 13-2-1915, NA, Kol. Openbaar, Vb. 6-1-1916 1.
[17] *De Locomotief,* 28-5-1918.

the scheme, even more than 200 guilders. This was three to five times as much as the costs of the construction of the houses in the past.[18] The government provided loans which had to be repaid in four years, but during the war it was claimed that the rising prices of daily necessities and of building materials made the monthly instalments too high. Assurances issued by Batavia that, in view of the economically averse times the government would be lenient in collecting the advances, made little impression.[19] A great deal of fuss was made of people who had ran in financial trouble because of such loans and whose houses had to be auctioned.[20] Referring to the fact that once a week improved houses were inspected, during which time the occupants had to empty and clean their houses to prevent rats being able to take refuge behind cupboards and other furniture, Steeds Lijder (Eternal Sufferer) wrote that for Javanese all the housing improvement not only meant that houses and yards looked clean. It also meant that houses looked empty because possessions had to be pawned or sold. Steeds Lijder concluded that fear of the plague had evaporated but that it had been superseded by the prospect of hunger or at best a want of food.[21]

During the closing months of the war grievances about the ill-fated efforts to combat an epidemic of cholera were added to the flow of these complaints. The measures taken created a storm of protest in Batavia and Surabaya in August 1918. Families of sufferers were moved to barracks. Here males and females had to sleep in the same dormitory. Meals had to be eaten with the hand. It was stressed indignantly that such treatment resembled life in prison. To make the comparison even more fitting, people had to keep quiet after six o'clock in the evening. The rules set by the authorities for the way the dead had to be buried in this case again added to the indignation. One point in question was that when a person died in the barracks, only people who had been vaccinated were allowed in to attend the burial. One positive side was that Indonesians became so afraid of what could happen to them and their families that they by the thousands volunteered to be vaccinated. Nevertheless, the vaccinations led to grumbling. People complained that the places where this was done were inadequate, that the treatment was rough, and that the rules of decency for Muslim women were not observed. Racial discrimination raised its ugly head. It was observed that white people were not subjected to such humiliations and that they also were not forced to enter the barracks.[22]

---

[18] *De Locomotief*, 3-4-1916; *Islam Bergerak*, 20-5-1917.
[19] *Oetoesan Hindia*, 18-5-1918.
[20] *Islam Bergerak*, 1-5-1917, 20-5-1917; Van Reigersberg Versluys 1917:17.
[21] *Islam Bergerak*, 1-8-1918.
[22] *Oetoesan Hindia* 31-7-1918, 9-8-1918, 10-8-1918, 13-8-1918, 16-8-1918, 20-8-1918, 21-8-1918, 22-8-1918, 26-8-1918, 27-8-1918.

If this was not enough, a world-wide epidemic of Spanish influenza reached a climax in the Netherlands Indies in November 1918.[23] The Spanish influenza truly made the second half of 1918 'the season of illness (and the season of expensive foodstuffs)'.[24] Even coffins became scarce and expensive. Muslims were not bothered by this, but the Eurasians, Christian Indonesians, and Chinese were. This *penjakit baroe* or 'new disease' had made its appearance in the middle of 1917. Eventually it would cost the lives over 1 million people in the Netherlands Indies.[25] A less moderate estimate spoke of a death toll of 2 million.[26] The enormous dimensions of the epidemic threw a spanner in economic life. Land remained untilled, schools and offices had to close. The disease gave the Sarekat Islam a new *nom de plume*. Its leaders began to refer to it as the S(panish) I(nfluenza); an epidemic that could seriously weaken the colonial system.

The Spanish influenza affected all population groups. *Neratja* called it the *sama rasa sama rata* illness.[27] Europeans living in the colony were disturbed by the thought that the Spanish influenza did not bypass the army and police, (even the commander-in-chief of the army was not immune). This significantly weakened the operational force of the army and police at a time when unrest among the Indonesian population had mounted. Nevertheless, the Spanish influenza struck especially at the native society, taking a large toll among people whose health conditions were poor and who, unlike Europeans, could not count on an adequate medical service. The epidemic provided yet another opportunity to remonstrate about how subordinated and neglected the Indonesian population was. It was pointed out that poor people could not afford to remain in bed for as long a time to recover as others could. *Oetoesan Hindia* also observed that few European doctors were prepared to make house-calls in Javanese neighbourhoods.[28] The epidemic even provided an opportunity to lash out at the housing improvement programme. *Neratja* published a plea that houses without a masonry wall should again be allowed to have double windows and attics. Such adaptations would mean that influenza would not endanger the health of the population even more by their having to be in a draught.[29]

Developments in Europe had resounding echoes in the colony. When news about the February Revolution in Russia reached Java on 18 March 1917,

[23] In the Malay Peninsula the Spanish influenza was also called the Russian disease (*The Singapore Free Press*, cited in *Neratja*, 19-10-1918).
[24] *Oetoesan Hindia*, 20-8-1918; *Neratja*, 5-12-1918.
[25] Information of the Burgerlijke Geneeskundige Dienst, cited in *Neratja*, 15-1-1919.
[26] *Neratja*, 5-12-1918.
[27] *Neratja*, 20-2-1919.
[28] *Oetoesan Hindia*, 12-11-1918.
[29] *Neratja*, 28-11-1918.

Sneevliet had been jubilant. He immediately had put pen to paper and had written an article, 'Zegepraal' (Victory). It was published in *De Indiër* the following day. In his enthusiasm Sneevliet had chosen *De Indiër* and not *Het Vrije Woord* because he did not want to delay publication for six days. That it was an Insulinde newspaper did not matter. *De Indiër* was, as 'oppositional, nationalist paper', the only Dutch-language newspaper that he considered eligible to publish his article. It was his only choice. Because he lacked the necessary skill to write the article in Malay, he depended on a Dutch-language newspaper which all, with the exception of *De Indiër*, were against him. *De Indiër*, moreover, was read by the 'followers of Douwes Dekker therefore in a political sense the dissatisfied' (Baars and Sneevliet 1991:296-7). Darnakoesoemo, still a loyal Insulinde leader, made a Malay translation. It was published in *Pertimbangan*. Cautiously Darnakoesoema had added a postscript: the article did not aim to set the population against the government (Baars and Sneevliet 1991:315).

In 'Zegepraal' Sneevliet applauded the deposing of the Czar, and wondered whether this would also mean revolution in Germany and Austria. Sneevliet had a message for 'the people that endure and suffer' and who since Diponegoro had had no leaders who 'galvanized the masses into action to take their destiny in their own hands'. The Russian Revolution held a lesson for them: 'The Russian people had also endured oppression for centuries, were poor and for the greater part illiterate as you are'. Sneevliet ended by stating that the Javanese would certainly attain what the Russian people had accomplished: Victory (Tichelman 1985:464-7).

Sneevliet was not the only one who had made the obvious link. Others had done the same. Tjipto Mangoenkoesoemo had presented the Russian Revolution as proof of what the fate would be of a government which expected its subjects to bear everything, however much they were bleed white and exploited.[30] In Semarang and Surabaya the ISDV and Insulinde had asked permission for joint meetings to discuss the developments in Russia (Baars and Sneevliet 1991:xxv). In both cities permission was refused. The authorities too were alarmed by Sneevliet's reaction to the dethronement of the Czar. In Semarang the organizers appealed to the Attorney-General. He refused to intercede. He explained that the reports about the revolution in Russia were still too incomplete to serve as a basis for 'an objective historical discussion'.[31]

Public indignation centred on Sneevliet. 'Zegepraal' created an uproar, assiduously fanned up by the Dutch-language press. Retribution was quick in coming. In April 1917 Sneevliet was sacked by his employer, the Semarangsche Handelsvereeniging (Semarang Trade Society) though he himself maintained

[30] *Warna Warta*, cited in *Koloniaal Tijdschrift* 1917:969.
[31] *De Locomotief*, 26-3-1917.

that he had resigned of his own free will. Sneevliet was also prosecuted. The outcome was a victory for Sneevliet. The Court of Justice in Semarang ruled that 'Zegepraal' had been no more than a sharp attack on colonial conditions and had not incited feelings of hatred against the government. The verdict greatly disappointed the Attorney-General. G.W. Uhlenbeck called it an example of racial justice. He was sure that were a non-European to have been charged with the same offence, a heavy sentence would have ensued. Heavy sentencing of 'insignificant' Indonesians, whose articles were only an imitation of the words of Sneevliet and his European political friends, and letting Sneevliet go free could not but give the impression that judges did decide differently when a European stood trial. It was best to avoid such an impression in such turbulent times as these.[32] Uhlenbeck appealed at the High Court in Batavia. The High Court ruled that the Semarang court had rightly acquitted Sneevliet and in March 1918 threw the case out of court.

It was easier to act against Baars, a civil servant. Batavia seized upon a request by Baars to have his temporary assignment as a teacher transformed into a permanent appointment in August 1917. Baars had been warned that he risked his job if he continued with his agitation against Dutch rule. The immediate cause of government wrath was an article by Baars about education in the Netherlands Indies which had been published in *Het Vrije Woord* in March 1917. The contents had piqued his highest superior, the Director of Education and Religion, who took the initiative to issue the warning. K.F. Creutzberg had been especially offended by one sentence in which it was postulated that Dutch rule formed the greatest obstacle to the development of the Netherlands Indies. In Creutzberg's eyes such an observation was the strongest stand anyone could take against legal authority. He was all in favour of strong measures. He detected growing opposition to the Indië Weerbaar campaign and feared a confrontation between the colonial authorities and dissatisfied Indonesians. In his mind violent oppression could only be avoided if the European community and most Indonesians remained loyal to Dutch rule. Referring to a similar measure in British India, as early as November 1916, he had written, that the time might be fast approaching when a ban would have to be issued that forbade civil servants to engage in anti-government activities.[33] In The Hague Pleyte agreed with Creutzberg. He singled out the same sentence as Creutzberg had done as his main argument to defend the action taken against Baars in Parliament. Pleyte called the warning a *standje*, a friendly rebuke.[34]

---

[32] Appeal 27-3-1918; Van Limburg Stirum to Pleyte, 20-4-1918, 29-5-1918, NA, Kol. Openbaar, Vb. 14-6-1919 26, Vb. 17-6-1918 62.
[33] Creutzberg to Van Limburg Stirum, 24-11-1916, NA, Kol. Openbaar, Vb. 14-6-1919 26.
[34] Director Department of Education and Religion to Van Limburg Stirum 28-6-1917, NA, Kol. Openbaar, Vb. 20-4-1918 28; *Handelingen Tweede Kamer* 1917-18:1509.

ISDV leader A. Baars, circa 1917 (KITLV 12545)

A chance to suit the action to the word presented itself the following month. The occasion was a debate between Baars and Abdoel Moeis in the Indonesian club, Panti Harsojo, in Surabaya on 12 September 1917. The core issue was the familiar question which had dogged the Indië Weerbaar discussions from the start: would a different foreign ruler be a change for the worse? It is not clear what Baars's exact words at the meeting were. The Dutch-language press reported that speaking of the insurrections in Sumatra, Baars had said that there was no government more *boesoek*, more rotten, than that of the Dutch in the Netherlands Indies.[35] Baars denied this. He had wanted to counter Abdoel Moeis's argument in favour of Indië Weerbaar that the population would be worse off under the rule of another power, and had only stated, first in Dutch and then again in Malay, that it was not a foregone conclusion that the rule of other powers would be more rotten than that of the Dutch.[36] Claiming to base itself on reports of officials present Batavia turned a deaf ear to Baars's explanation. Baars had to be fired. His command of Malay made him an especially dangerous person in the eyes of the colonial authorities. As the banishment of Douwes Dekker and his friends had patently shown, the language used in communicating political ideas mattered very much to them. In The Hague when a Member of Parliament pointed out that Dutch people were allowed to write that they thought the British or American colonial system was better, Pleyte reacted by stating they should not venture such opinions in 'native company' and in 'ugly Malay words'.[37]

Baars was granted 'an honourable discharge' at the end of October 1917. Creutzberg objected to the qualification.[38] The Department of Education and Religion was instructed to reclaim the money Baars had received for his journey from Holland to Java and for the tropical outfit he had had to buy at that time. A socialist member of Dutch Parliament observed that for a 'boy without means' the sum, 3,000 guilders, was a large amount of money.[39] Later the court acquitted Baars. The judge ruled that Malay had no word for 'bad' that was less strong than *boesoek* and that to convict somebody for using such a word would leave little over of the freedom of speech. Baars's acquittal was no reason for the government to re-instate him as a teacher. His agitation had convinced Van Limburg Stirum and his advisers most adamantly not to do so. Talma explained in the People's Council that a judge used the penal code as the

---

[35] Secret report Political Intelligence Service, 6-10-1917; Creutzberg to Van Limburg Stirum, 18-10-1917, NA, Kol. Openbaar, Vb. 20-4-1918 28.
[36] *De Locomotief*, 10-12-1917, 13-12-1917.
[37] *Handelingen Tweede Kamer* 1917-18:1513.
[38] Creutzberg to Van Limburg Stirum, 18-10-1917, NA, Kol. Openbaar, Vb. 20-4-1918 28.
[39] Besluit Gouverneur-Generaal, 23-10-1917, NA, Kol. Openbaar, Vb. 20-4-1918 28; *Handelingen Tweede Kamer* 1917-18:1441.

yardstick to determine what was still permissible and what not. A government had to bear in mind other considerations. It demanded a 'minimum of reserve in its civil servants in their political behaviour'. Baars had disregarded this, 'however low the minimum had been set'. Batavia could not tolerate propaganda among the population aimed at bringing the government down.[40]

Set virtually beyond the pale by the government, their fate enhanced the status of Sneevliet and Baars among their Indonesian supporters. In *Islam Bergerak* it was pointed out that some Indonesian nationalists professed their love of their nation with no more than just a pen and some speeches. They refused to fraternize with the common, poor people. Sneevliet and Baars were different. They did not 'love a nation' nor did they care for nationality. They 'loved the oppressed human being' and suffered personally for this.[41]

Sneevliet was given a great welcome when he returned from Batavia to Semarang after his trial at the High Court on 5 April 1918. The *blijde incomste*, the joyful entrance, the headline of *De Locomotief* read the following day. *Sinar Djawa* claimed that 6,000 members of the Semarang Sarekat Islam and 200 soldiers had come to the railway station to welcome him. A police report spoke about 2,000 Sarekat Islam members and 20 European soldiers. *Neratja* put the crowd at 3,000. Van Limburg Stirum steered a middle course in a telegram to Pleyte: 3 to 4,000 natives and some European soldiers. When the 'once-a-day' from Batavia arrived in the early evening, the crowd shouted its acclamation and cheered. Among them was Mas Marco, who had become one of the editors of *Sinar Djawa* after his release. The mood was clearly anti-Dutch. Observing the 'impudent' way in which the assembled Indonesians treated Europeans, the *Resident* of Semarang, who happened to be on the same train, did not dare to leave his carriage.[42] *De Locomotief* reported that Sneevliet 'surrounded by many private soldiers and crowded around by thousands of small natives, who often cheered loudly', was lifted onto their shoulders and carried across the platform to the exit.[43] European soldiers waved red banners and shouted 'Long Live Sneevliet! Long Live Sneevliet!'

From the railway station Sneevliet and his supporters marched in procession into town.[44] Skirmishes followed. The chief of police of Semarang, C.A. Ruempol, was hit on the head when he tried to disperse the crowd. The police had to use clubs and called for the assistance of the fire brigade, which dispersed the crowd with spurts of water. Van Limburg Stirum had to admit that the police was taken by surprise. Its officers were unable to calm the

---

[40] *Volksraad* 1918:33, 169, 552.
[41] *Islam Bergerak*, 1-5-1918.
[42] *Neratja*, 9-4-1918; *De Indische Gids* 1918, I:718.
[43] *De Locomotief*, 6-4-1918.
[44] *Handelingen* 1917-18, Aanhangsel: 237.

demonstrators down. After reinforcements had arrived, the authorities asked Sneevliet to disband the demonstration. Sneevliet complied. He climbed up a lamp-post and thanked 'the brothers and sisters' who had come to celebrate his 'victory'. He concluded his brief speech with the words 'Long live the SI, long live the fraternity, the Indies will be independent'.[45] *Sinar Djawa* warned the government and the money devils that the demonstration was a clear indication that Sneevliet was loved by the people. If the government saw him as an enemy, this meant that 'we all from the bottom of our hearts HATE HATE the government and the capitalists, who never cease to oppress us'.[46]

A similar scene evolved the following day when Semaoen, chairman of the Semarang branch of the Sarekat Islam, returned to town. Again a large crowd – according to police estimates 2,000 men strong – assembled at the railway station in the early evening. It was a manifestation of solidarity. There was no specific reason to demonstrate. In view of what had happened the previous day, the police allowed only Europeans and members of the Semarang Sarekat Islam board to enter the station. The authorities gave the Sarekat Islam leaders to understand that the police would not allow 'shouting along the road, therefore the disturbance of public order and the hindering of traffic'.[47] The warning went unheeded. Again the assistance of the fire brigade had to be called in. It was reported that telling blows were dealt out by the police. Among those who made good use of his baton was the Superintendent of Police, who kept his end up. Disquieted about the 'troublesome spirit among a part of the native population', a public viewing of the film 'Rasputin' in the town square was forbidden after one showing the following day.[48]

In 1918 Semarang had definitely acquired fame as a revolutionary city. In view of this, the authorities had decided to station a special officer of the PID in Semarang as early as the beginning of 1917. The decision had been taken that Semarang needed the presence of such a person more than Surabaya, the only other city which then had already a local PID official. Semarang was politically much more stormy.[49] The city's fame had reached such heights that in May 1918 the Native Pawnshop Union decided to make Semarang the venue of its meeting. The chairman explained that in Semarang 'the actions of the proletariat were most strongly visible'.[50] In Semarang and its hinterland Semaoen could also count on a large, loyal, and militant following. One cogent example of this took place in December 1917 at the commencement of a mass meeting

---

[45] *De Locomotief,* 6-4-1918.
[46] *Sinar Djawa,* 6-4-1918, NA, Kol. Openbaar, Vb. 14-6-1919 26.
[47] *De Locomotief,* 8-4-1918.
[48] *De Locomotief,* 8-4-1918.
[49] Attorney-General to Van Limburg Stirum, 28-12-1916, NA, Kol. Openbaar, Vb. 7-1-1918 57.
[50] *De Locomotief,* 13-5-1918.

in the City Gardens of Semarang. According to a report in *De Locomotief*, it was attended by 5,000 members and a few thousand other people. When Semaoen was summoned by the *Assistent-Resident* to discuss the removal of protest signs, the rumour spread that he had been arrested. Reaction was immediate and among the crowd there was talk about launching a riot and that blood would flow if Semaoen had indeed be apprehended.[51]

The events are indicative of the fact that, since the latter part of 1917, discontent with Dutch rule had manifested itself in an increasingly militant way. The ISDV and the Sarekat Islam both actively sought to organize labourers and farmers, including those in the sugar-producing areas. Strikes, which were a relatively new phenomenon in the Netherlands Indies, became more frequent in the cities and on the estates. The reasons for such strikes were manifold. Equal pay irrespective of race was one reason. Other strikes could be occasioned by derogatory remarks about the Sarekat Islam or Tjokroaminoto by the staff and by dissatisfaction with the distribution of land and water to the sugar estates. Other strikes started when demands for a cost-of-living compensation were not met, when the customary advances during the Fasting Month were not paid, or when wages were not paid in time. The high costs-of-living which it was said had made people touchy and 'hunger' were also put forward as reasons. Java had entered upon what *Neratja* called a season of strikes.[52]

In view of the wave of strikes, estate managers decided to cooperate in July 1918. They pledged to help each other out. They would provide labour for those estates where the workforce was on strike and refuse to employ persons who had played a leading role in strikes elsewhere.

In the countryside of Java unrest seemed to reign, especially in the second half of 1918. The European press began to bandy the word 'terror' about.[53] In Kediri to the fright of Europeans it turned out that the local police was inadequate to repress unrest on a somewhat larger scale quickly. In Semarang, in reaction to the disturbances in its hinterland, fully armed policemen were put on patrol. In Majalaya the relationship between Chinese and Javanese was tense. Some Chinese had fled to Bandung. In the same region it was rumoured that a large uprising was nigh and that Tjokroaminoto would soon be crowned King of Java.[54] The government decided to send three hundred soldiers to the area at the end of September. In Bantul, a region where attacks on estates were especially frequent, houses of Javanese went up in flames. In Kudus racial riots

---

[51] *De Locomotief*, 24-12-1917, cited in *De Indische Gids* 1918, I:562-3.
[52] *Neratja*, 4-4-1918.
[53] *Soerabaiasch Handelsblad*, cited in *Neratja*, 19-10-1918.
[54] *Assistent-Resident* Bandung to *Resident* Preanger, 21-9-1918, NA, Kol. Geheim, Mr. 1918/365x.

Veldpolitie in Rembang (Van Gent, Penard and Rinkes 1923: Photo 56)

erupted in October 1918.[55] In Demak angry Sarekat Islam villagers armed with clubs, spears, sickles, and machetes besieged the house of a village headman. When troops had to be sent to restore order, it were white European soldiers who were deemed suitable to perform this task, added occasionally by the odd soldier from the Moluccas and the Minahassa. Restlessness seemed on the rise. Commenting on the Kudus riots, Idenburg spoke about 'the irritability of the mind, which originated from Semarang'.[56] Abdoel Moeis's *Neratja* blamed the war. *Neratja* claimed that all over the world the war had made people hot-tempered and susceptible to agitation. This mood had also taken hold of the Javanese, who now could easily be provoked to quarrel among themselves and fight one another.[57]

The authorities and the public put the blame for the upsurge in rural

---

[55] The Kudus riots were also an embarrassment to Batavia. In another way, Chinese protested about Batavia's failure to protect the Chinese population and demanded that the government should cover the damage. To underline the claim *Sin Po* drew a comparison with the compensation the Dutch government had received after the Boxer Rebellion. The Chinese Consul General in Batavia agreed. He called to mind that after anti-Chinese riots in Mexico, the Mexican government had promised that it would pay indemnity to the Chinese government.
[56] *Handelingen Tweede Kamer* 1918-19:2080; McVey 1965:36.
[57] *Neratja*, 27-4-1918.

unrest and the defiance Javanese showed towards the Dutch on Sarekat Islam agitation and by extension on people like Sneevliet and Baars. From their side activists of the ISDV and Sarekat Islam stressed that one of the reasons for the strikes and other militant actions was the fact that the high cost-of-living had touched people on a raw nerve. Semaoen used a similar argument to deny that the Sarekat Islam leaders were the puppets of Sneevliet. In April 1918 in a letter to the editor of *De Locomotief* he explained that the European community had convinced themselves so thoroughly that Sneevliet was behind all the unrest that there was almost no point in denying it. Yet he had to do so. By blaming all on Sneevliet people underestimated the intelligence of the ordinary people and could disregard all the abuses to which they were subjected. Semaoen stressed that all Sarekat Islam actions originated among the people themselves 'BECAUSE THE PEOPLE HARDLY CAN ANY LONGER BEAR THE PRESSURE OF TIME'. There was the *duurte*. This was the root and branch of the unrest. People had become irritable, and it was no longer possible to convince them that they should protest in an orderly manner (as the Dutch community stressed they should) and not resort to strikes and other undisciplined actions.[58]

To deny the accusations Tjokroaminoto, Semaoen, Sneevliet, Tjipto Mangoenkoesoemo and others would travel to trouble spots to investigate the causes of the unrest. When they arrived in such regions, the local authorities treated them with distrust. Occasionally, as happened to Tjipto Mangoenkoesoemo when he visited Majalaya and to Tjokroaminoto when he went to Kudus, they were met by a detachment of soldiers or policemen.[59] In their reports about what had transpired Tjokroaminoto and the others stated that Europeans, civil servants and ordinary citizens alike, had misrepresented the causes of the unrest. They had exaggerated the reports which highlighted unruly activities of Sarekat Islam members, or had credulously taken incredible stories at face value. Enemies of leftist or Islamic agitation remained unmoved. They saw what took place as a clear demonstration of how damaging Sneevliet's agitation was. Another reason they ventured, although less frequently, was religious fanaticism. As a consequence, indigenous civil servants were asked to keep an eye on the activities of zealous Islamic religious leaders.[60]

The pupil clearly was no longer behaving in the way the mentor wanted. Malay newspapers assumed an increasingly belligerent tone. The Sarekat Islam had made, what Idenburg later called, a 'strong shift towards the left'. It had begun to side with the enemies of the state. Idenburg blamed Semaoen,

---

[58] *De Locomotief*, 13-4-1918.
[59] *Volksraad* 1918-19:163-4.
[60] *Neratja*, 26-10-1918, 29-10-1918.

'that *pur-sang* disciple of Mr. Sneevliet'.[61] The 'Semarang extremists', that is the Indonesian ISDV members, were propagating hatred and distrust of the government. They did so without taking into account – as Idenburg and other Dutch people were not tired of stressing – the 'immaturity' of the population.[62]

One of the ways in which the authorities in the Netherlands Indies reacted to the apparent revolutionary spirit that seemed to have gripped many was by tightening their control over the nationalist movement. At times, although there does not seem to have been a general pattern in this respect, local Dutch civil servants refused permission to hold meetings protesting about the high cost of living or against the Indië Weerbaar movement. Others delayed the start of meetings, or decided that public meetings held by certain organizations such as the ISDV were not allowed. The consequence of such harassment was that at some meetings the chairman not only thanked the audience for attending, but also the local authorities for allowing the meeting to take place.

Were such and other gatherings grudgingly allowed there was a second, more frequently used mechanism to assure that the harm done was minimal: setting limits on who were allowed to attend and on what was said. Only those persons who could show their membership card were allowed in, or only two or three representatives of other organizations invited were allowed to attend. Once a public meeting had started a variety of Dutch authorities – the local Dutch civil servants, representatives of the police, and members of the PID – would be present.[63] They did not hesitate to intervene and to forbid speakers to continue if Dutch rule (or the belligerents) were criticized in what they considered to be an unwarranted way. Sneevliet was to remark during his trial that police commissioners had 'an epidemic inclination' to call meetings to order and to interrupt (Baars and Sneevliet 1991:245).

Such actions also baffled members of the Dutch Parliament. Speaking about the presence of three superintendents of police, the local head of the PID, and an agent of the PID at a VSTP meeting in Surabaya where the cost-of-living allowance was discussed, one of them, SDAP MP M. Mendels, remarked that when 'at every sentence which does not please these gentlemen it is said you are not allowed to speak about this, then I thank heaven for the fact that I do not live in the Netherlands Indies, because I would not possess as

---

61   *Handelingen Tweede Kamer* 1918-19:2080.
62   *Handelingen Tweede Kamer* 1918-19:2080.
63   In June 1918 Muurling denied in the People's Council that the PID kept track of nationalist organizations. The fact that PID members were present at their meetings he explained by pointing out that, in the early days of the PID's existence, its staff had had to make itself familiar with the political climate in the colony. They had done so by visiting meetings and reading periodicals (*Volksraad* 1918:308).

much self-control as these speakers to be able to speak under such a Russian supervision'.[64] The number of authorities present at the VSTP meeting was actually rather modest. The record in this respect perhaps goes to the mass meeting organized by the Sarekat Islam in December 1917. It was attended by the *Assistent-Resident*, the public prosecutor, the local head of the PID, the chief superintendent of police, six chief constables, and a score of police officers. It also does not seem to have been an exception that armed policemen attended meetings of nationalist organizations. Abdoel Moeis complained in the People's Council about the presence of members of the armed police or ordinary policemen armed with Beaumont rifles when he addressed public meetings.[65]

There was one specific development which made everything appear even more threatening in the eyes of the Dutch authorities and those of the general public. As Sneevliet's triumphant entry into Semarang indicated, the ISDV had succeeded in catching the ear of soldiers and sailors. There was much to worry about. The army and police were undermanned; and at that moment seriously affected by the Spanish influenza. In Kudus 22 out of a total of 30 policemen had been ill at the time of the riots. Even more serious, discontent in the army, Navy, and probably also the police, was rife. The spirit affected both officers and lower ranks, and Europeans and non-Europeans.

For European policemen in Batavia, we can read, the war could not end soon enough. They wanted to return to Europe.[66] In the army, even before the outbreak of the war, officers had been displeased – according to some very displeased – with the fact that plans to improve their financial position had been shelved for years. They earned less than people in the business sector and people with a comparable education or rank in the colonial civil service. War had blocked any possibility of a significant increase in salary, and this at a time when in their daily lives they had to cope with increasingly high living costs. Officers had started to study in their spare time to prepare for a civilian career, it was reported in 1918.[67]

Non-commissioned officers also had their complaints. A report from Surakarta in July 1916 spoke about discontent on all sides among the three thousand non-commissioned officers. One of the reasons was said to be the privileges given to married non-commissioned officers in an effort to combat

---

[64] *Handelingen Tweede Kamer* 1917-18:1437-8.
[65] *Volksraad* 1918:147.
[66] *De Locomotief*, 23-1-1917.
[67] *De Locomotief*, 2-1-1915, 4-1-1915; Van Heekeren 1919b:146; *Nieuwe Soerabaia Courant*, cited in *De Indische Gids* 1919: 251.

concubinage.[68] It were not just privileges, such as better housing (also for married non-European soldiers) and an extra crossing's premium (when the wife indeed travelled along). Concubinage was forbidden in the barracks.

Civilians were well aware that resentment ran deep in the army. Desertion among European soldiers had, in the words of a military journal, taken on 'really serious dimensions' in 1917.[69] One reason adduced for this was the presence of recruitment agents of the belligerents in the Archipelago. But even if such persons really existed – there was no actual proof of this – they were not the major cause. Many other reasons were not difficult to find. The food was bad, the housing in the barracks was a cause of complaint, the medical service was inadequate, and pay had not kept pace with rising prices.

Discipline in the army was strict and brutal. Punishments included caning with rattan (there was a special rank of *korporaal stokkenknecht*, corporal lathy), having to carry a heavy metal ball weighing twenty-six kilogrammes, and being bound with barbed wire. Most notorious of all was the so-called *kromsluiten*, shackling a person tightly in such a way that he was forced to remain in a bent position for hours at a stretch. Though the regime had become more humane over the years, the most extreme forms of punishment were only abolished after the war. That they were no longer meted out was partly in response to the agitation by members of the ISDV, Insulinde, and the Sarekat Islam. In part the reform was brought about by what was described as the urge for action on the part of Van Limburg Stirum who ignored protests by the army command.[70] Before the punishments were abolished army authorities stressed that some had only rarely been administered, and others were obsolete. To illustrate that conditions had improved, it was mentioned that the chain to which metal ball was attached had been lengthened, which allowed the miscreant to carry the ball over his shoulder.[71] Civil critics were not convinced that the army officers spoke the truth or suggested that they did not know how their underlings, the prison guards, acted in actual practice.

The sorry state of affairs in the army led to the demise of its commander, General W.R. de Greve. In May 1916 De Greve had succeeded Michielsen, who had died two months earlier during one of the first trials in the Netherlands Indies of a military aeroplane when the plane he had boarded crashed. De Greve was held responsible for the troubles in the colonial army. His successor was Lieutenant General C.H. van Rietschoten. Van Rietschoten had been sent to Java by Pleyte in June 1917. Officially he was to assist in the reorganization

---

[68] *De Locomotief*, 13-7-1916.
[69] *Algemeen Militair Weekblad*, cited in *De Locomotief*, 24-11-1917.
[70] *Sumatra Post*, cited in *De Indische Gids* 1919, I:634.
[71] The ball had been made heavier. It now weighed thirty-six pounds. The chain weighed six pounds (*Volksraad* 1918-19:473).

of the colonial army and the preparations for the setting up of a militia. In reality he was to be prepared to take over from De Greve as commander of the colonial army.[72] De Greve was given to understand by Van Limburg Stirum that he had to go in January 1918 and was honourably discharged at his own request in May 1918.

By this time Dutch-language and Malay newspapers had started to report on incidents in the army and the Navy in which soldiers and sailors disobeyed orders or testified to their leftist sympathies. Even more frequent were reports about arrests of European and Indonesian soldiers who had deserted. Dissatisfaction in the colonial army and Navy had reached an unprecedented level. What a discontented army and Navy might mean had been shown by developments in Russia, as what was happened in Germany and Austria. In the *Sumatra Post* it was pointed out that Russia had learned that people eager for a revolution could best begin by trying to get the army on their side. Though the newspaper considered the chance that soldiers in the Netherlands Indies would refuse to obey orders slight, the conclusion was that 'an army, made up of sections constantly sulking and grumbling and embracing passive resistance' was not a force to be relied upon. The situation was all the more alarming as the army and Navy might have to act 'any moment'.[73] In the spring of 1918 other Dutch-language newspapers – *De Locomotief,* the *Preangerbode,* and the *Bataviaasch Handelsblad* – called for extraordinary government measures to prevent strikes by soldiers and labourers.[74] All laid the blame at the door of Sneevliet and his friends. It had not escaped their attention that Sneevliet had called it the duty of the ISDV to convince soldiers not to take up arms against the population and 'to make these mercenaries unreliable for Her Majesty, unreliable for the propertied class'.[75] As a consequence he asked soldiers and sailors to display a spirit of resistance.

One of the outcomes of the discontent in the army was that, as in many other places in the world, soldiers' Coucils and unions were formed in the cities on Java which had a military garrison. Again Sneevliet was the alleged culprit. In fact, the motor behind the movement to radicalize the soldiers was another ISDV member, J.A. Brandsteder, a major champion in the campaign to improve the living conditions for the soldiers in the colonial army. Brandsteder, a former sailor, was the administrator and leader of the Bond van Minder Marine-Personeel (Union of Lower-Ranking Naval Personnel) in the Netherlands Indies, the organization which had been so patriotic at the outbreak of the war. The union had taken the lead in giving expression to the

---

[72] Pleyte to Wilhelmina, 23-6-1917, NA, Kol. Geheim, Vb. 23-6-1917 V8.
[73] *Sumatra Post,* cited in *De Indische Gids* 1918, II:895.
[74] *Neratja,* 18-4-1918, 23-4-1918.
[75] *Handelingen Tweede Kamer* 1918-19:2080.

feelings of frustration of sailors in an organized way and its members wanted the soldiers to follow suit. At the end of 1917 and in 1918 the Union of Lower-Ranking Naval Personnel often now referred to as the Matrozenbond (Sailors' Union) started to try to win soldiers over to join in their agitation. At the end of January 1918 when sailors marched through Surabaya after they had attended a meeting addressed by Sneevliet, one of the slogans they carried read: 'Soldiers join us!'[76] On the instigation of the Union of Lower-Ranking Naval Personnel, a Soldiers' Union was founded in the garrison city of Malang in March. Soldiers in almost every barrack flocked to join in. Within three months the union claimed a membership of 3,000 (Perthus 1953:58). In many garrisons vocal local soldiers' unions began to stir.

The propaganda spread among soldiers by Sneevliet, Brandsteder and others and the blatant manifestations of discontent turned public attention to conditions in the army. In the closing months of 1917 Dutch-language newspapers published numerous pleas to improve the lot of the ordinary soldiers. An additional incentive to do so was the knowledge that soon the first recruits for the European militia would be called up. The new recruits, already unhappy with their fate and hence thought to be extra susceptible, should not be infected by the immoral habits of the professional soldiers and should not be influenced by ISDV agitation. Various solutions were contemplated to improve the atmosphere in the army. The most impressive initiative was the establishment of a Vereeniging ter Verbetering van den Maatschappelijke Staat van den Militair (Society for the Improvement of the Social Status of the Soldier) at the end of 1917. Patron was Van Limburg Stirum. The board consisted of thirty-eight members, many of whom were pillars of society. Besides a clergyman, a priest, a district nurse, and the obligatory army officers, it had among its illustrious members J.H. Carpentier Alting, President of the High Court; his wife (*née* Deibel, in her capacity as President of the Women's Council, an umbrella organization for women's organizations in the Netherlands Indies founded after the example of its Dutch counterpart in the middle of 1916); L. Engel, President of the NHM; s'Jacob of the Batavia Chamber of Commerce; Koning of the KPM; and Muurling of the PID. Van Rietschoten, soon to become the commander of the colonial army, also joined. The society observed that soldiers were in fact outcasts and that their life had been reduced to the 'greatest possible frugality'. The result had been 'bitter resentment' which manifested itself in 'acts in violation of order and discipline', and in a despairing flight to liquor and in the 'dark hideaways of society'. Faced with this conclusion a plan of action was hammered out. Concubinage and dipsomania were the evils to be combated. Housing should be improved. In their spare time soldiers should

---

[76] *Neratja*, 2-2-1918.

be presented with opportunities for 'sound work and decent repose'.[77]

The Dutch-language press commented that the founding of the society was a futile gesture which had come far too late. Agitation by the ISDV and by the Union of Lower-Ranking Naval Personnel struck a much more favourable chord. It was not difficult to reach this conclusion. Soldiers had started to vent their anger against the rich, white Europeans, who had made no secret of the fact that they despised the lower ranks in the past. In Bandung a fusilier threw his food into the car of a European. It was remarked in Parliament in The Hague by a sympathizer of the ISDV that this of course was a pity for the dress of the lady in the car who caught the full blast. In Semarang a soldier shouted to a lady in a car that she and those of her kind would soon be thrown out of the colony and that then he and his friends would be driving around in motor cars. In Semarang the mood among the soldiers in the local garrison had become so implacable that the commander decided to set up secret patrols in the city on a regular basis in May 1918.[78]

At first Van Limburg Stirum did not give the impression that he was particularly upset. He wired Pleyte at the end of May that the social democratic movement among soldiers should not be seen as too great a tragedy. It was 'symptomatic of the present world circumstances'.[79] Army staff also pretended that there was not much amiss. Its members spoke about 'a few regrettable facts' and claimed that the 'bad spirit' was confined to a small section of the European soldiers.[80] Belying these words army command did all it could to prevent the proper functioning of soldiers' unions. It was made clear that unions 'which go into or make propaganda for a purely anarchistic goal' were unacceptable.[81] The colonial authorities also left no room to doubt that they were set to combat 'the brewing of propaganda for revolutionary principles in the barracks'.[82]

As a consequence, soldiers were not allowed to attend public meetings addressed by radical leftist orators. Initially no names were mentioned. It was left to the discretion of the local army commanders to identify the leftist trouble-makers. In March 1918 the army commander in Surabaya forbade soldiers to attend meetings of the Union of Lower-Ranking Naval Personnel, or any other meetings whatsoever at which Brandsteder, Sneevliet and others who called themselves 'friends and defenders' of the ordinary soldiers were among the speakers.[83] In early April a general order went out forbidding European

[77] *De Indische Gids* 1918, II:848-52.
[78] *Handelingen Tweede Kamer* 1918-19:2068; *De Locomotief*, 11-4-1918; *Neratja*, 15-5-1918.
[79] Van Limburg Stirum to Pleyte, 29-5-1918, NA, Kol. Openbaar, Vb. 17-6-1918 62.
[80] *Volksraad* 1918:579, 544.
[81] *Volksraad* 1918:581.
[82] *Volksraad* 1918:545.
[83] *Neratja*, 11-3-1918.

and native soldiers to attend ISDV meetings. SDAP meetings, whose members in actual fact tried to counter ISDV propaganda by promoting a soldiers' association with a less radical course of action, were also declared out of bounds. Occasionally Sarekat Islam meetings and even celebrations were also off limits to soldiers. When contested events took place, patrols were sent out to assure that no soldiers or sailors attended. Meetings at which Sneevliet and other ISDV members were among the speakers were raided by the police if soldiers attended. It was not unknown, as happened at a meeting in the City Theatre of Batavia on 5 November 1918 where Sneevliet was one of the speakers, for the premises to be cordoned off by soldiers.

In the People's Council Van Rietschoten stressed that such measures were not taken out of fear that soldiers would be influenced by the wrong ideas. The reason for the directive had been his 'sincere efforts to protect people from thoughtless acts'.[84] He added that he did not fear the influence of anarchistic soldiers' unions. He had another reason for not tolerating them. Soldiers' unions did not 'serve the well-being of the simple soldier'.[85] Even the Protestant Church came to the assistance of the authorities. In Surabaya during a service in June for soldiers from the Moluccas and the Minahassa the minister appealed to his congregation not to join the soldiers' union.

Van Rietschoten's words obfuscated the whole truth. The authorities appear to have been scared to death of soldiers criticizing conditions in the army in public. They made a distinction between public meetings and closed meetings. Batavia claimed that soldiers were free to speak their minds at closed meetings which no outsiders were allowed to attend.[86] With public meetings it was different. These were off limits when it was suspected that they were intended to stir up agitation or were held preliminary to establishing soldiers' unions. If the ban was ignored such meetings were disbanded. Following their own agenda, sailors and soldiers met in restaurants, houses of ISDV members and elsewhere to discuss plans to organize soldiers and to coordinate action. When army command were able to learn about such intentions in advance, patrols were sent out to prevent the meeting, especially if Brandsteder or Sneevliet were to be present. Soldiers who played a role in the founding of unions were arrested, as were those who attacked conditions in the army at public meetings. At times the officers' corps had to act to keep soldiers who had been angered by such acts in check.

In Surabaya the building of the Union of Lower-Ranking Naval Personnel, which had also been frequented by soldiers in search for recreation in the past, was now forbidden territory for soldiers. In the eyes of the authorities

---

[84] *Volksraad* 1918-19:482.
[85] *Volksraad* 1918-19:490.
[86] *Volksraad* 1918:580-1.

the building had become a centre of agitation and a place where soldiers hatched subversive plans. Soldiers who tried to enter the building by disguising themselves as sailors were sentenced to detention if they were caught. In Surabaya three members of the board of a Corporals' and Other Ranks' Union got two weeks' close arrest for dodging the ban at the end of April. Two weeks' detention seems to have been the normal punishment for such offences, often repeated in the months to come. In what amounted to paternalistic censorship action was taken to prevent the reading of leftist literature. The authorities tried to ban *Het Vrije Woord*, the *Soldaten- en Matrozenkrant*, Soldiers' and Sailors' Paper, of which Brandsteder was the editor, and other socialist periodicals and pamphlets from places frequented by soldiers and sailors. Such publications were strictly forbidden on board warships. Inexorably reading these journals could result in detention.[87]

Another, perhaps cleverer, way to keep soldiers and sailors away from revolutionary meetings was by organizing alternative events. On 2 May a naval review was held in Surabaya to make it impossible for the sailors to attend an ISDV meeting in the building of the Union of Lower-Ranking Naval Personnel. The stratagem failed. Sailors informed the union leaders who saw to it that the date of the meeting was put forward by one day. About four hundred people, sailors and others, were present. The local police commissioner had to abandon his plan to dissolve the gathering when angry sailors who were present insisted that the meeting should proceed. Sneevliet addressed his audience with the words 'Fellow party members, friends, red guard of the Indies fleet'.[88] The authorities tried to repeat the same trick more often, seemingly without any success. To take the wind out of the local soldiers' union sails, the army commander in Semarang convened a meeting in the Club for Soldiers and Corporals to discuss their 'improvement of position'. Nobody came.

Impeded by the repressive measures taken by the military authorities, the soldiers' movement remained fragmented, without much coordination. It was more difficult for army command to put a stop to the blatant discontent in the army. Not without a certain degree of pleasure the editors of *Oetoesan Hindia* concluded in the middle of May that the seeds of danger were growing into something big.[89] There were problems in the barracks, soldiers took part in anti-Indië Weerbaar manifestations, and expressed their support for strikes. One such latter incident which attracted plenty of public attention happened in Semarang in April 1918. During a strike at the local gas-works the authorities decided that soldiers should replace the striking workers. A

---

[87] Tichelman 1985:282; *De Indische Gids* 1918:997; *Neratja*, 20-6-1918, 4-12-1918.
[88] *Neratja*, 6-5-1918; Perthus 1953:58.
[89] *Oetoesan Hindia*, 16-5-1918.

Dutch private called upon his fellow-soldiers not to act as blacklegs. When he was punished, the Semarang Sarekat Islam wanted to reward him with a watch for his courage, paid for by the members of the board. This gave rise to a dilemma. The Dutch authorities summoned Semaoen and Darsono (a person who had become an avowed socialist after he had attended Sneevliet's court case) and told them that presenting the private with a watch would be considered an attempt to undermine order and discipline among the soldiers. They also threatened the soldier in question with severe punishment if he were to accept the gift. Implacably Semaoen realized that giving in would make a bad impression. It was decided to let the Sarekat Islam members settle the matter. They voted overwhelmingly in favour of presenting the watch. The words of one person who argued against were greeted with shout of *takoet, takoet*, afraid, afraid.[90] Unfortunately history does not tell us what followed next, but probably a watch was never presented.

With relief the Ministry of the Colonies had concluded from the reports it had received from Batavia about Sneevliet's return to Semarang that native soldiers had not joined in the demonstrations.[91] There may have been relief in The Hague but this did not mean that native soldiers were immune to the spirit of the day. Semaoen even claimed a large following for the Sarekat Islam among the Indonesian soldiers.[92] Differences in payment, pension, and treatment added to the resentment of Indonesian soldiers. This was especially so among Javanese soldiers, who stood on the lowest rung of the ladder, and received less pay than the soldiers from the Minahassa and the Moluccas. Minahassans and Moluccans were not without their complaints. One was that they were paid less than their European equals. Another had to do with the conditions in the barracks. They had increasingly come to detest the degradation caused by the fact that a group of soldiers, each with his wife and children, had to live in one *chambrée*, one common room, in the barracks, virtually without any privacy.

In the course of 1918 the Indonesian soldiers started to organize themselves too. In Batavia a union of native soldiers, Djawa-Setia (Faithful Java), was formed in April. The initiative had been taken by a gunner, Raden Soedarsono. Within days Djawa-Setia boasted a membership of over 800. Djawa-Setia demanded higher pay, equal status with European soldiers (Javanese were not allowed a hammock), and better education for themselves and their children. Other demands were a shorter time in military service and a better pension. Djawa-Setia also aimed at improving the moral standards and health of the

---

[90] *De Locomotief,* 25-4-1918, 1-5-1918, 6-5-1918; Morriën 1984:79.
[91] Van Limburg Stirum to Pleyte, 29-5-1918; note Department A, 17-6-1918, NA, Kol. Openbaar, Vb. 17-6-1918 62.
[92] *Sinar Hindia,* cited in *De Indische Gids* 1919:643.

Javanese soldiers. They should be prevented from taking to the bottle as Europeans soldiers did. Their marriage partners were also a point of discussion. Javanese soldiers should not 'marry as they wish, because the offspring of such marriages are very bad and when the native offspring are bad then the name of the Javanese is also dragged through the mud'.[93]

In reporting about the activities of Djawa-Setia, *Neratja* stressed that a native soldiers' union was very different from its European counterpart. It did not undermine army discipline and morale.[94] Nevertheless, among Indonesian soldiers desertion was also frequent. To collect the enlistment premium was one thing, to remain in the army another. It frequently happened that soldiers ran away to become estate labourers. To prevent Indonesians deserting immediately after they had cashed in their recruitment premium, the suggestion was made that new recruits be finger printed. To catch such culprits the fingerprints plus a photo of the person in question in his 'native dress' had to be sent to the recruitment offices of the estates.[95] Others deserted and enlisted again to cash in a second or third premium. To prevent this, around the same time it was suggested that fresh recruits be vaccinated in such a way that the scar left no doubt that they were soldiers.[96] When deserting was made impossible more drastic action was resorted to. At the end of 1917 a warning had to be issued against dripping gonorrhoea fluid into the eyes in an attempt to be declared medically unfit for military service.[97] The fluid inflamed the eyes. The results could be disastrous. The warning was issued after it had come to the attention of army headquarters that many Indonesian soldiers in Malang had been discharged because they had gone blind.

In spite of all the indications to the contrary, in public Van Rietschoten vehemently denied that the civilian assessment that there was 'general unrest' in the army was true. He admitted that living conditions in barracks were deplorable, and that the food soldiers had to eat left much to desire. This was as far as he was prepared to go. Grousing was second nature to soldiers. He attributed the increase in manifestations of discontent to trouble-makers who tried to impress upon the soldiers that they were being treated unfairly. Van Rietschoten claimed that their propaganda had not exerted an influence on the 'experienced soldier'. Only the 'many inexperienced men and weaklings, and not least the bad elements' were infected.[98]

While this may have been its public face, army command made some

---

[93] *Neratja*, 1-6-1918.
[94] *Oetoesan Hindia*, 24-4-1918; *De Locomotief* 11-5-1918; *Neratja*, 15-5-1918, 1-6-1918, 19-6-1918.
[95] *Soerabaiasch Handelsblad*, cited in *De Indische Gids* 1917, II:1248.
[96] *De Locomotief*, 23-5-1916.
[97] *Nieuwe Soerabaia Courant*, cited in *De Locomotief* 14-12-1917.
[98] *Volksraad* 1918-19:463, 481-2.

efforts to remove the causes of discontent. Recreation rooms were set up in barracks. Initially only European soldiers profited. By the end of 1918 no such facility had yet been offered to Indonesian soldiers. European soldiers were even moved *en bloc* to garrisons outside Java. It was hoped that a change in environment would make the men less discontented.[99] Material circumstances were also improved. In July 1918 Van Rietschoten instructed the local commanders to announce that it had been suggested to the government the pay of soldiers and corporals be increased by five cents per day. The pay increase was intended to kill two birds with one stone. It should diminish the unrest in the army and should stimulate recruitment of new soldiers. Simultaneously vague promises were made to abolish the difference in treatment between the European soldiers and their Manadonese and Ambonese counterparts. This had to be done gradually. Otherwise it would have cost too much money.[100] Javanese, earning twelve cents a day less than the Ambonese, were not yet considered to deserve the same advance in status. They were still written off as too poor a soldier. Yet another measure was to open up the opportunity for Indonesian soldiers to learn Dutch.[101]

In the Navy discontent, at times finding its expression in acts of sabotage on board of Dutch warships, was even greater. European sailors were perhaps even more despised by the civilian European society than soldiers were (Tichelman 1985:15). They were definitely better organized and displayed a strong sense of solidarity. Their union, the Bond van Minder Marine-Personeel, was also far more radical than its mother organization in Holland. By the end of the war Brandsteder and the union had earned the deep distrust of the authorities. According to the Minister of the Colonies the union showed 'very anarchical' tendencies.[102] In Batavia the commander of the Navy, J.A.M. Bron, by now promoted from rear admiral to vice admiral, agreed.[103]

What the European sailors were capable of had already become evident when they had staged a protest about the bad conditions in the military hospital in Surabaya in May 1916. It was a wild-cat action. Brandsteder had not endorsed it because he had had no time to consult with other members of the union board. Four hundred sailors – rumour had it that half of them carried arms – staged a march in Surabaya on Sunday morning 7 May. As they marched the sailors sang socialists songs and carried banners with texts like 'To the hospital', 'We protest about the filth', 'We protest about the bad food',

---

[99] Van Heekeren 1919b:137; *Neratja,* 10-10-1918.
[100] *Volksraad* 1918:585.
[101] *Volksraad* 1918:541; *Neratja,* 27-7-1918, 26-6-1918.
[102] *Handelingen Tweede Kamer* 1918-19:2153.
[103] *Neratja,* 4-12-1918.

and 'We protest about the bedbugs'.[104] Another banner showed money-bags with the text 'War profits' written below them. The police reacted resolutely. Pistol shots were fired and policemen charged brandishing naked klewangs. The following day warships could not sail because 300 sailors had refused to board. They roamed through the city in small groups.[105] Among the sailors who did report were seven, among them one who had been hurt the previous day, who had discharged themselves from the military hospital 'because they were tormented there by hunger and wanted a chance to eat'. The seven sailors, still in their hospital clothes and bare-foot, were cheered by the other sailors.[106] The incident, in The Hague the newspaper the *Nieuwe Courant* spoke of the 'Navy rebellion', formed the occasion to draw attention to the 'recalcitrant feelings' of the sailors and the ease with which these had been aired in acts of vulgar protest and sabotage.[107]

In The Hague, the government, already somewhat apprehensive about morale in the Navy, decided to close a loophole in naval legislation, but it did not yet go as far as forbidding gatherings of naval ratings. Pinke was alarmed. He concluded that there was a malaise prevalent in the Navy which was 'absolutely incompatible with the objectives of a military naval force'. The malaise had resulted in 'gross unmilitary conduct, yea even in some instances in the foulest acts of sabotage'.[108] There could only be one response. Rigid disciplinary measures had to be taken. All shore leaves were cancelled. Within days 59 sailors were told that they were no longer welcome in the Navy in the Netherlands Indies. They were shipped to Holland where the Ministry of the Navy had to decide whether they would be dishonourably discharged or not. To replace them fifty conscript sailors from Holland were shipped to the Netherlands Indies, an indication of how dire the shortage of professional sailors had become. The decision elicited a protest from the conscript sailors' union. Those who went loudly protested their fate when they left Holland in July. Of these fifty conscript sailors nineteen deserted. Nor was this the end of the story. On their return to Holland the sailors from the Netherlands Indies created a small riot. Without seeking any permission a dozen of them marched

---

[104] Afterwards the Dutch government disclosed that an earlier investigation into the conditions in the hospital had revealed that the sailor's complaints were exaggerated. The commander of the colonial army blamed much of the excitement on the fact that sailors were not used to paillasses. The Governor General pointed out that the majority of the 'naval patients suffer from venereal diseases, does not feel ill, and is bored' (*De Locomotief,* 13-9-1916).
[105] *De Locomotief,* 8-5-1916, 9-5-1916.
[106] *De Locomotief,* 10-5-1916.
[107] *Nieuwe Courant,* cited in *De Locomotief,* 19-5-1916, *Soerabaiasch Handelsblad,* cited in *De Locomotief,* 13-5-1916.
[108] *De Locomotief,* 21-9-1916.

into the small town of Hellevoetsluis, singing songs and resisting arrest.[109] Pinke himself was one of the victims. In The Hague, J.J. Rambonnet, no friend of Pinke, disapproved of the way in which he had handled the protests. He should have been even more resolute and have instituted criminal proceedings against the ringleaders.[110] Pinke was replaced as commander of the Dutch fleet in the Netherlands Indies. Van Limburg Stirum accepted the change in command *'à contrecœur'*.[111]

Dissatisfaction in the Navy came sharply to the fore once again in the middle of 1918. The crew of the *Koningin Regentes* – who had sent a telegram to the annual meeting of the ISDV wishing it success a few days earlier – went on strike on 5 June 1918. They refused to report for duty after the captain had disregarded protests about having to eat brown instead of white rice at breakfast. Officers had to draw their revolvers to push the sailors back into line again. Food that was not the only gripe. Socialists condemned the 'Prussian behaviour' of the captain and depicted him as a person who loathed the sailors' union.[112] It was also pointed out that he had commanded the *Zeeland* on her trip from Holland to the Netherlands Indies and that it was his rigid command which had induced so many sailors to desert in the United States. The Navy presented a different picture. Bron depicted him as a wise, almost ideal commander.

Eighty-five crew members were sentenced to between three and twelve months' imprisonment. Because such a large number of prisoners could not be accommodated elsewhere, they were interned on the island of Onrust. This led to a scandal when one of the internees, J. Bezema, had to be taken into hospital in Surabaya where he died of dysentery two weeks after his release. It was alleged that his death had been caused by the inferior food on Onrust, which contained less fat than the food sailors were used to on board. Idenburg was not impressed. He told Parliament that sailors were 'difficult about their food'.[113] Bezema's death also occasioned a debate about the climate of Onrust. In the past the island, where Jambi insurgents had also been brought, had earned itself a reputation as an extremely unhealthy place. In those days Onrust had been described as a graveyard for the labourers in its shipyard. After Bezema's death stories about the bad physical conditions on Onrust abounded. In the People's Council Bron and the Director of Justice denied the stories. Praising the fresh sea breeze the Director of Justice called the imprisonment of the sailors on Onrust *'a trouvaille'*. The island was influenza- and

---

109   Thirteen did later report and were sent to the Netherlands Indies at a later date.
110   *Handelingen Tweede Kamer* 1915-16:224.
111   Teitler 1986:xvii; *De Locomotief*, 4-12-1916, citing the *Java-Bode*.
112   *Volksraad* 1918-19:492.
113   *Handelingen Tweede Kamer* 1918-19:2152.

malaria-free and a transfer to Onrust had cured prisoners of pneumonia. His conclusion was that Onrust was a much healthier place than Batavia.[114] Such remarks prompted Cramer to suggest that Onrust could become a sanatorium for TB patients. He wondered why he and many other inhabitants of Batavia had not known that they lived so close to 'such a convalescent haven'. Otherwise, 'plans would have been made for the building of a large hotel; maybe a new Scheveningen might have arisen'.[115] In The Hague, Idenburg also put his oar in. He pointed out that Onrust was a quarantine station for returning hajis and that a few years earlier large sums of money had been invested in improving its hygienic conditions. To underline this, he cited from a telegram he had received from Bron. Onrust must have been paradise: 'Island very healthy, no malaria, no mosquitoes, good water, cool climate, is used as a health resort for prisoners'.[116]

Those interned there were inclined to think differently. Thirty-four of them were discharged from the Navy after they had served their sentence. Unable to show that they had found employment in civilian society or owned at least 500 guilders, they were classified as destitute persons, and consequently were not allowed to remain in the Netherlands Indies. They were forced to spend an extra month on Onrust before they were shipped back to Holland on board the *Noordam*, the first shipping opportunity to Holland that presented itself. The Navy had refused to allow them to take up temporary residence in the building of the sailors' union in Surabaya, which had also offered to pay for their upkeep. Permission had been withheld because the union was not a legal association. In a letter to the *Bataviaasch Nieuwsblad* the sailors complained about this and about the conditions on Onrust. They wrote that their health had been undermined by dirt and undernourishment and that many of them had suffered from abdominal illnesses.[117] An additional reason for the sailors to be angry was that their treatment stood in sharp contrast to that of German sailors who the colonial authorities had been forced to intern on nearby Kuyper Island. The Dutch sailors could not leave Onrust to travel to Batavia to look for work. The German sailors were allowed a three days' trip to Batavia once a month to look for a job.

The affair had a sting in its tail. Brandsteder and Baars let it be known that they wanted to attend Bezema's funeral. The announcement fortified naval command's fear that 'revolutionary elements' would seize upon the occasion to demonstrate. Only seventy sailors received permission to attend. They were marched to and from the ceremony in tight formation. All the other sailors in

[114] *Volksraad* 1918-19:500-2.
[115] *Volksraad* 1918-19:493, 502.
[116] *Handelingen Tweede Kamer* 1918-19, Aanhangsel: 145, 175.
[117] *Bataviaasch Nieuwsblad*, 25-10-1918, cited in *Volksraad* 1918-19:493-4.

Surabaya were refused leave. No wreaths with red ribbons were allowed to be carried in the procession, but this instruction was ignored. Speeches were also inappropriate. In defiance of the ban, one of Bezema's comrades, D. Kraan, stepped forward, coming within one step of the officer-in-charge after the order to march off had been given. Facing the grave and with his back to the officer – which was considered a grave insult – he held a speech. Kraan mentioned the word graveyard in relation to Onrust and said that Bezema was a victim of the conditions on the island. He added: 'This is the way in which the government treats you men!'[118] Kraan was silenced at once by the duty officer. The Director of Justice, Kraan's superiors, and Idenburg all agreed that what Kraan had done had been 'most grievous and insulting'.[119] Kraan should be punished. This was not simply because of what he had done, the mood in the Navy weighted in very heavily. Bron pointed out that it should not be forgotten what kind of persons were being dealt with. This consideration forced him to nip any manifestation of revolutionary fervour in the bud.[120]

Sailors protested. On the evening of Bezema's funeral, 400 of them attended a meeting in Surabaya. They lamented the fact that Kraan had not been allowed to continue with his speech and called the internment of sailors on Onrust after they had served their sentence 'in violation of the most elementary feelings of humanity'. They pleaded that the sailors who were still held on the island should be given better food and should be allowed to read what they wanted.[121]

Indonesian sailors also had their grudges. Differences in racial and ethnic background created animosities. Some Dutch officers had a low opinion of the seamanship of the Javanese. Crew from the Minahassa certainly looked down on the Javanese. They protested when the differences in treatment (and food) between Minahassan and Javanese sailors were abolished in October 1914 because of the Great War. There was no justice in the Navy one Javanese sailor wrote in May 1916, complaining about the treatment of Javanese sailors.[122] Among Indonesian sailors propaganda put about by the Union and by the Sarekat Islam had left an indelible mark. The same Indonesian sailor revealed that he had been punished for having in his possession *Het Anker*, the journal of the Bond van Minder Marine-Personeel, the rules of the Sarekat Islam, and other seditious literature, but this he could endure. He knew that those who were right dared and those who were wrong feared.[123] Indonesian

---

[118] *Handelingen Tweede Kamer* 1918-19:2152; see also *Volksraad* 1918-19:494-6.
[119] *Handelingen Tweede Kamer* 1918-19:2152.
[120] *Handelingen Tweede Kamer* 1918-19:2149.
[121] *Volksraad* 1918-19:495-6.
[122] *Oetoesan Hindia*, 1-2-1916, 18-2-1916, 20-3-1916, 29-5-1916.
[123] *Oetoesan Hindia*, 29-5-1916.

sailors could not join the Union of Lower-Ranking Naval Personnel, this was an exclusively European association, but they had their own organization, the Sinar Laoetan (Light of the Seas). Sinar Laoetan had been founded by an able Javanese seaman, M. Argawidjaja. Its leaders had wanted Sinar Laoetan to become part of the Sarekat Islam, but naval command had made it clear that it wanted nothing of the sort. Instead, Tjokroaminoto was its adviser.

In 1918 red had already been in fashion as a favourite colour for more than a year. 'We live in the red century', it was proclaimed at a meeting in Kudus. In Rampah in the north of Sumatra, the authorities forbade a new design for the Sarekat Islam flag: the crescent and stars on a red (and not a green) background. Similarly, at the mass meeting of the Semarang branch of the Sarekat Islam in the City Gardens at the end of December 1917, all members had donned hats adorned with a red piece of paper on which were written the initials S.I. The podium was decorated with red draperies, protest signs were coloured red.

The radicalization also manifested itself in the language used. There were two developments. One was that Indonesians began to loathe the use of Dutch in organizations with a mixed European-Indonesian membership. It had started innocently. About sixty Javanese members of Insulinde (the *Javaantjes*, those little Javanese, *De Expres* called them, a qualification not infrequently used by the newspaper) had held a separate meeting in Surabaya and elected their own board in June 1914. The move was welcomed in *De Expres*. At ordinary meetings it was difficult to have to speak in both Dutch and Malay. In The Hague Tjipto Mangoenkoesoemo attacked the decision. It was not in the spirit of Douwes Dekker. The gap between the races had to be bridged, not be re-instituted.[124]

Tjipto Mangoenkoesoemo fought a losing battle. The editors of *Goentoer Bergerak* were criticized by readers who wanted to get rid of its Dutch section the following year. Opposition to bilingual publications assumed such proportions that Tjipto Mangoenkoesoemo had to make concessions. He published *De Voorpost* in December 1915 and transformed *Modjopait* from a bilingual magazine into a Malay one. In the VSTP leftist Indonesians took control. It became an almost exclusively Indonesian organization. The Indo-European members, many supporters of Insulinde, had become a liability. So had the Dutch language. True to the multi-racial membership, Dutch and Malay were the languages of communication. Irrespective of the composition of the audience at all meetings each point on the agenda had to be discussed in both languages. Each speech was translated into the other language. The long-

---

[124] *De Expres*, 5-6-1914; *De Indiër* 1-39.

drawn-out practice had begun to irritate Indonesian members, who wanted to do away with it. The Semarang branch, by far the most radical one, was split in two in June 1918: one VSTP for Indonesian members with Malay as the medium of communication; and one for Indo-European members with Dutch as the language.[125]

The language battle reached its zenith in 1918 when the Djowo Dipo movement gathered momentum. In an advertisement in *Oetoesan Hindia*, its founder announced his intention. In future he would address everybody in *ngoko*. Djowo Dipo members, recognizable by a triangle insignia with in Javanese the words Djowo Dipo written on it, stressed that *kromo*, the refined variant of Javanese in which superiors had to be addressed, was a language of 'cowards, slimers, mock-humble people, and those spoiling the race'.[126] *Kromo* was 'poison'. All signs of deference had to be abolished. *Kromo* was rejected by 'the non arrogant (The Egalitarians or Democrats) and the rebels'.[127] *Djowo dipo*, that is *ngoko*, the language used to address a person of lower or equal rank, should be used in private conversations and at public meetings. Some even had the nerve to address Europeans in *ngoko*. Egalitarianism was the aim. Javanese titles should no longer be mentioned. Those who came out in defence of *kromo*, and who had founded special organizations to combat the Djowo Dipo movement in reaction, were represented as persons who blocked the advancement of the Javanese and supported their exploitation.

The movement gained great popularity. In the pages of *Oetoesan Hindia* its activities received plenty of attention and much was made of the fact that at Sarekat Islam and even at VSTP meetings Djowo Dipo was used. It was explained on one such occasion Djowo Dipo was used to assure that everybody could understand what was being discussed. A great many branches of the Sarekat Islam established Djowo Dipo committees. Speaking *ngoko* was presented as the duty of a Muslim. Speaking *kromo*, thereby humbling oneself, implied a humiliation of Islam. Calls to speak only *ngoko* went hand in hand with pleas to provide children with a sound religious education and not as was the wont of the members of the Javanese civil service, to train them in sinfulness.[128]

Race had definitely become a mark of distinction in the nationalist movement. In February 1916 Tjipto had already complained that the Javanese distrusted him because of his contacts with people of mixed race.[129] In 1918 even Dutch ISDV members were forced to take the rap. In a weekly, described by the

---

[125] *De Locomotief*, 13-6-1918.
[126] *Oetoesan Hindia*, 28-10-1918, 1-11-1918.
[127] *Sarekat-Islam Congres* 1919:33; *Oetoesan Hindia*, 23-10-1918.
[128] *Oetoesan Hindia*, 1-8-1918.
[129] *De Locomotief*, 3-2-1916.

Dutch authorities as extremist, it was postulated that Baars was a European, a foreigner, and that he could well be motivated by the desire to make himself indispensable as a leader of and adviser to the natives. Everybody was intent on seeking his own advantage. Baars claimed that he lived and fought for the small man, but he had proved this? Could he live as the small man lived, could he eat what the small man ate?[130]

The rebuke to Baars was an exception. The prime victim of the radicalization in the Indonesian nationalist movement was Insulinde. The unity of all *Indiërs* it championed was attacked as amounting to dreams of Indo-European rule and nothing else. The fact that *De Indiër*, the newspaper of Insulinde was written in Dutch did not help. Taking this tack Insulinde could never reach out to Kromo.[131] The divide had become greater because Insulinde had achieved more than a modicum of moderation and because of the perceived threat from abroad was more appreciative of the government than before. Insulinde leaders pleaded for moderation in the present difficult circumstances (and were also a little bit afraid that Douwes Dekker might try to radicalize Insulinde again after his return). They condemned the rash strikes which sometimes ended in disaster. Calling strikes the last resort, when every other means had failed, Insulinde lashed out at people who 'drove the workman-minimum wage-earner to desperation' only to gain an image of courage and compassion for the people.[132] Even a militia was no longer a taboo, though Tjipto Mangoenkoesoemo hastened to explain that what Insulinde had in mind was different from what was being propagated by the Indië Weerbaar movement. Van Hinloopen Labberton and his friends wanted a militia to defend the interests of the rulers, of the 'sugar lords'; Insulinde wanted a militia to defend the Netherlands Indies in the interests of its population (Tjipto Mangoenkoesoemo 1917:60). The colonial authorities for their part no longer distrusted Insulinde. Muurling even went so far as to praise it in June 1918.[133]

Tjipto Mangoenkoesoemo exacerbated the estrangement with the radical nationalist movement by rejecting the Djowo Dipo ideals. In October 1918 he enraged the audience at Djowo Dipo meetings in Surabaya by addressing them in *kromo*. He was laughed at and had scorn heaped on his head. The conclusion was that people like him were no longer the real leaders of the nationalist movement and of the people.[134] Douwes Dekker, full of plans to start a new weekly and then a Malay daily newspaper, was also to blame.

---

[130] *Medan Boediman*, 30-10-1918.
[131] *Sri Diponegoro*, 28-10-1918.
[132] *De Locomotief*, 13-5-1918.
[133] *Volksraad* 1918:288-9.
[134] *Oetoesan Hindia*, 3-10-1918, 10-10-1918, 11-10-1918, 14-10-1918.

He was unprepared for the turn the nationalist movement had taken during his absence. Douwes Dekker reverted to his old habit and embarked upon a propaganda tour, this time by car, throughout Java. Accompanied by European and Indonesian party leaders he visited about twenty cities in Java between 6 October and 1 November. Speeches were delivered in Dutch and Malay. In expounding his political ideas, Douwes Dekker followed the line Tjipto Mangoenkoesoemo and Soewardi had already stressed. He said he gave priority to a national revolution, not to the class struggle. This also caused him to remark that Insulinde welcomed national capitalists, who belonged to the oppressed in a colonial society. A class struggle should not be fought before the Netherlands Indies had gained independence, especially not if it stressed race differences and distracted people from the ideal of reaching an independent state for the Indiër.[135]

By airing such opinions Douwes Dekker only succeeded in alienating the Indonesians who had fallen under the spell of the ISDV. His debating style contributed to this. Indonesians complained that Douwes Dekker treated them condescendingly during debates, and that he acted 'coarsely and roughly'. As an example *Djawa Kondo* reported that Darsono, who only had a primary school education, had been called not mature enough for a debate by Douwes Dekker because of this. Insulinde should ensure that in future Douwes Dekker spoke about *'Nasi in de maag'* (Rice in the stomach), and no longer about *'Natie in de maak'* (Nation in the making).[136] Darsono for his part wondered what revolution Douwes Dekker aspired to. Was it one by Kromo, the little man, or by the middle classes? Douwes Dekker was a talker. He should understand that when revolution came it would be stomach-driven. It would not come about as the result of Douwes Dekker's political theories. It would be better were Douwes Dekker to explain to Kromo how much he was being exploited by taxes, compulsory labour, factories, banks, pawnshops and the like, and how some of his richer compatriots assisted in his exploitation.[137] Douwes Dekker also succeeded in insulting Semaoen. When Semaoen asked Douwes Dekker, for whom Western attire was a sign of emancipation of the Indo-Europeans, whether his nationalism went so far that he was prepared to dress in a *sarong* and head-cloth, Douwes Dekker dismissed this as a childish question.[138]

Exclusiveness seemed unavoidable. Movements sprang up which aimed at preventing people from taking a spouse from another race. According to their proponents, such a stand was justified by Islam.[139] Indonesian members of

---

[135] *Volksraad* 1918-19:219, 243.
[136] *Darma Kondo*, 28-10-1918, 20-10-1918, 2-11-1918.
[137] *Soeara Ra'jat*, 1-11-1918.
[138] *Oetoesan Hindia*, 17-10-1918.
[139] *Oetoesan Hindia*, 18-11-1918.

the ISDV also stressed the racial divide. Discussing the racial riots in Kudus, Semaoen, who must have been aware of growing anxiety in the European and Chinese communities, warned the Chinese and Europeans that they had come to Java only in small numbers and that they should stop trampling on the feelings of the Javanese.[140] Fortunately, a Chinese-Malay newspaper responded, there was still the Dutch army to quell unrest.[141] Semaoen's assessment of the Kudus riots provided Abdoel Moeis with the moment to get even. What Semaoen had written was exactly what he had said in Zurich and Holland. He, too, wanted to 'free Kromo from the leeches of Capitalism'.[142] Angrily Dutch members of the VSTP also reacted to an article by Semaoen in *Si Tetap* in which he had argued that with only one or two exceptions Indo-Europeans despised the Javanese. Semaoen was steadfast. At a VSTP meeting he stated that Indo-Europeans only considered their own interests. He saw proof of this in a cost-of-living allowance for railway personnel of only 8 per cent, which was all right for the Indo-European employees, but not for their poorly-paid Javanese fellow-workers. His words were greeted with rapturous applause.[143]

At meetings and in the press Mas Marco, Darsono and others suggested that Insulinde was an Indo-European organization which strove for a kind of self-government in which the natives would be assigned only a subordinate position.[144] Bluntly Darsono, who on another occasion took great pains to underline that he did not agree with Semaoen's racialist remarks about the Kudus riots and that socialists did not think in terms of either race or creed, told Douwes Dekker that unity of the races was impossible. Natives and Indo-Europeans had conflicting interests.[145] Elsewhere Douwes Dekker was given to understand that fraternity between Indo-Europeans and the natives was a chimera. It was unlikely to be accomplished as long as most Indo-Europeans continued to consider themselves superior (or as it was put on another occasion were equalized to Europeans).[146] Douwes Dekker could only counter this by stressing that Indo-Europeans who behaved in this way did not belong to Insulinde, and that various of its branches were headed by Indonesians.[147] Occasionally he could score a better point. At one meeting an Indonesian member of the ISDV, Soegono, pointed out that what Douwes Dekker wanted was excellent, but that, as not many of his race shared his ideals, it would be better were he to become a native. The remark was greeted with loud applause

---

[140] *Oetoesan Hindia*, 18-11-1918.
[141] *Pewarta Soerabaja*, cited in *Oetoesan Hindia*, 18-11-1918.
[142] *Neratja*, 9-11-1918.
[143] *Oetoesan Hindia*, 15-8-1918.
[144] *Wasisir-Oetama*, 2-11-1918.
[145] *Darma Kondo*, 2-11-1918; *Oetoesan Hindia*, 18-11-1918.
[146] *Darma Kondo*, 30-10-1918; *Kaoem Moeda*, 4-11-1918.
[147] *Kaoem Moeda*, 4-11-1918.

by the audience. Douwes Dekker reaped a similar applause when he replied that Insulinde was a party of *Indiërs*, and that in Zurich he had enrolled as a Javanese student.[148]

[148] *Kaoem Moeda*, 4-11-1918.

CHAPTER XXI

November 1918

Revolutionary fervour reached an unprecedented intensity in the Netherlands Indies in 1918. In Holland in retrospect the Ministry of the Colonies spoke in its annual report for 1918 about 'a certain restlessness' in the colony as a result of the activities of Sneevliet and others. This was an understatement. Unrest had been widespread.[1] Again taking a backward glance the editor of *De Indische Gids*, E.A.A. van Heekeren, noted 'serious happenings'. One was 'a progressive spirit of resistance in native society, which manifested itself in a mounting insecurity of persons and goods, in attempts made on Europeans'. The other was that the army was 'affected by a spirit of disobedience' (Van Heekeren 1919b:13). In the Netherlands Indies the question of whether or not the indigenous population, and the other population groups perhaps as well, had lost faith in the government had emerged as an earnest subject of debate. In the People's Council various members – J.J.E. Teeuwen, Achmad Djajadiningrat, Sastrowidjono, and Abdoel Rivai – repeatedly pointed out that large segments of the population from the highest level to the lowest echelon distrusted the government. A 'spirit of discontent' reigned. They argued that the anti-Dutch mood had been exacerbated by the poor economic conditions and by the high-handed and conservative way in which Dutch people, civil servants, and staff of the estate in the vanguard, continued to treat Indonesians.[2] Spokesmen for the colonial government denied that this was indeed the case.

The mood thus discerned coupled with doubts about the capability or even willingness of the colonial army to suppress large-scale popular unrest engendered renewed reservations about the creation of a native militia among Europeans. Arming natives under such circumstances might be dangerous (Van Heekeren 1919b:142). Cogently, many of the nationalist leaders continued to oppose a militia. Attacking Indië Weerbaar had become one of the ways for the ISDV activists to wrest control of the Sarekat Islam from Tjokroaminoto, Abdoel Moeis and other moderate leaders. To achieve their

---

[1] *Koloniaal verslag* 1919:47-8.
[2] *Volksraad* 1918:176, 186, 1918-19:235.

purpose they hammered away at the argument that a militia was only of benefit to no one but the capitalists, and that the Javanese population did not have much to fear if the Netherlands Indies were conquered by a foreign nation. Only the Dutch would lose their jobs, one of the ISDV members, B. Coster, a schoolteacher in Malang, for instance, stated at an ISDV meeting in Semarang in early September.[3]

Indië Weerbaar assumed the shape of the catalyst for a confrontation between the left and the right, which also set people in the European community at odds. Indië Weerbaar was intensely promoted by the colonial government and part of the white establishment. They did so with a certain urgency, afraid that it might not be long before war would be declared on the Netherlands because of the complications about the Dutch position which had arisen in Europe. A new Indië Weerbaar Association had been formed on 31 August 1917. It united local Indië Weerbaar branches which were still extant or had been newly formed. A telegram was sent to Queen Wilhelmina to congratulate her on her birthday and to inform her about the founding of the new association. The chairman was K.A.R. Bosscha. Among the other members of the board were G.J.C.A. Pop, one of the driving forces behind the new association, Koning of the KPM, and Muurling.[4] A number of Indonesians also joined the board: R.A.A. Achmad Djajadiningrat, J.A. Soselisa, Pangeran Raden Soerio Atmodjo, Raden Temenggoeng Sosrowerdojo, and Raden A.A. Tirtokoesoemo. Lieutenant General H.N.A. Swart, adjutant to the Queen and Civil and Military Governor of Aceh, became honorary chairman. An *Orgaan der Vereeniging 'Indië Weerbaar'* (Organ of the Association The Resistant Indies) began to be published in February 1918. Initially Malay and Javanese translations of some of the articles were included. Later it would become a fully bilingual Malay-Dutch journal. A few months later a march, the *Indië Weerbaar Marsch* was composed by F.H. Belloni. A postage stamp was designed as well.

Initially the aim of the founders had been 'military defence'. When this caused opposition – a few people wanted to do away with the term completely – the goal was changed to 'economic and military defence'. Branches took the non-military part of the drive seriously, linking it with the development of the indigenous population. One example was the Banyuwangi branch. It funded a 'domestic science school for native girls' and a seedling farm for rice and 'native crops'. The human body was not forgotten. As Bosscha said: 'the labourer and the soldier should be physically strong and possessed of the

---

[3] IPO 1917 no. 36, citing *Kaoem Moeda*, 6-9-1917.
[4] When a general meeting was held in August 1918, the KPM promised a reduction in the fare for people who wanted to attend.

stamina to be able to maintain our nationality'.[5] Physical education should be promoted. True to this spirit, one of the many committees the board founded was a hygiene or health committee. What 'use is the battle cry of the last few years "Indië Weerbaar" if it is not proceeded by "*Indië gezond*"' (the Indies healthy), it was stated in an article about hookworm disease in 1919.[6]

The association claimed to have twenty-seven branches spread over the Archipelago in early 1918, with the promise of the founding of twenty-eight other branches. Not much later it was said that the association had 14,000 members. A great deal of emphasis was placed on the fact that Indonesians had also joined and that in many places it had been they who had taken the initiative to found branches. It was too rosy a picture. An Indië Weerbaar meeting held in Yogyakarta in July 1918 was a failure. Almost nobody turned up and none of those who did come wanted to sit on the board of the local branch.[7]

The main objective of the new association was fund-raising. One of the suggestions made at the foundation meeting was to raise money especially for 'a submarine for the Indies'. Opponents were of the opinion that the aim was unrealistic. The coastline of the Netherlands Indies was vast. One submarine would cost at least two million guilders. Presenting only one was a mere trifle, as good as admitting the level of incapacity. If a gesture were to be made at least six or twelve submarines should be given. This would require an enormous amount of money. 'Machine guns, for instance, would only cost a few thousand guilders' or 'aeroplanes which cost about Dfl. 40,000 a machine' would be a much better proposition.[8] Twenty-five aeroplanes would be a nice gift. Others suggested raising money for the defence of ports or for wireless communication with Holland. Money should also go to 'volunteer motorbike- or bicycle-riders, and defence corps, shooting clubs, etc.' and to the organization of first-aid courses. The men who had founded the association seemed to have thought about almost everything, even about 'the planning of factories and industries, which are suitable to be turned into munition factories within a short space of time in the event of war'.[9]

One of the achievements the new association did make was the organization of an Indië Weerbaar Week in September 1918. The idea had come from the Batavia branch. This time there was no talk of buying armaments. The national board had rejected this option. It also had come to the conclusion that armaments were difficult to purchase. Instead, money should be raised to

[5] *Orgaan der Vereeniging 'Indië Weerbaar'* 1-2:5.
[6] *Orgaan der Vereeniging 'Indië Weerbaar'* 2-1:5.
[7] *Neratja*, 27-7-1918.
[8] *Orgaan der Vereeniging 'Indië Weerbaar'* 1-1:6.
[9] *Orgaan der Vereeniging 'Indië Weerbaar'* 1-1:2-4.

> **20, 21, 22 MEI 1920**
> **INDIE-WEERBAAR-DAGEN TE BANDOENG**
> **ALGEMEENE VERGADERING**
> in te leiden
> ONDERWERPEN:
>
> a. de economische weerbaarmaking van Nederlandsch-Indië;
> b. hoe Nederlandsch-Indië militair weerbaar te maken.

Announcement of Indië-Weerbaar days in Bandung stressing the new goal of the movement: economic resilience (*Orgaan der Vereeniging 'Indië Weerbaar'* 1-6:23)

improve the social position of the ordinary soldier and to build up a 'central cash point' to support the activities of local branches and other organizations with similar aims. The disruption of sea traffic had left its mark. In presenting the plans special emphasis was put on the fact that the present circumstances had shown how important it was that the Netherlands Indies made itself less dependent on imports, especially food. Economic development should be the catchword. True to this conviction, the *Orgaan* held articles about improving stock and other economic subjects. Industry, agriculture, and animal husbandry should be promoted to increase the self-sufficiency of the Netherlands Indies. One of the offshoots of the stress on economic development was the founding of a Nederlandsch-Indische Tentoonstelling Vereeniging (Netherlands Indies Fair Association).

The association had done its utmost to make the week a grand manifestation. Planning had started in April. In May a special committee had been formed to organize the festivities. Among its members were Koning, Muurling, J.A. Soselisa, and the *patih* of Batavia. Honorary chairman was A.C.D. de Graeff, the Deputy Chairman of the Council of the Indies. Other honorary members were Bron, Van Rietschoten, J.C. Koningsberger (chairman of the People's Council), and Swart.

For one reason or another festivities started in Sumedang. Here the Indië Weerbaar week was held as early as the middle of July. In Sumedang Rhemrev, 'the father' of the Indië Weerbaar movement, as the local *Assistant-Resident* chose to address him, played an active role. Rhemrev seemed to have undergone a *volte-face*. In the speech he gave he said that the new movement was different to the one first founded. It was no longer 'purely militaristic' but aimed especially at building up the economic resilience of the colony. Consequently an exhibition arranged in Sumedang stressed industry, agriculture, and stockbreeding. The military aspect was confined to a demonstration with a military carrier pigeon.[10]

In the first week of September other cities followed Sumedang's example. All kinds of economic fairs were organized which highlighted agriculture, animal husbandry, and domestic production. Among the items prominently featured were such dire necessities as tinned food, cigars, soap, and products of the indigenous industry such as *wajang* puppets, textiles, and pottery. To add to the festive atmosphere, houses and vehicles were adorned with Dutch flags. During the festivities no population group was forgotten. There were attractions for everybody. In a great many cities in Java and elsewhere, the Indië Weerbaar week was the occasion for the usual festive events which had also coloured the independence celebrations: parades; military tattoos; early morning musical interludes by schoolchildren; all kinds of balls, open-air film showings; and European, Javanese and Sundanese theatre. The Javanese were entertained by wayang shows, and *ronggeng* and *serimpi* performances. People could also watch egg-and-spoon races on bicycles, soccer games for natives and Europeans, sack races, and fireworks. As in 1913, members of all population groups flocked to the events. In Saparua, the Indië Weerbaar Week even turned out to be an almost exclusively indigenous feast. Only five Europeans lived on the island, and two of them did not participate. One of the events on Saparua contemporaries deemed worth mentioning was the singing of an Indië Weerbaar song composed by a 'native schoolteacher'.[11] In Java the Regents' houses were a favourite venue to organize festivities for the indigenous Indonesians. Barracks held open days. Near Bandung soldiers acted out a mock battle. Before battle commenced, the audience could have a look at the weapons used, the mobile canteen, the wireless system, and the trenches that had been dug. Money was raised by asking entrance fees to events and by selling flags and cockades. The proceeds went to Indië Weerbaar, and also to charity. Patriotic speeches were held, the national anthem was sung, and telegrams were drafted to be sent to the Governor General or to Holland.

The festivities in Batavia formed the climax. They lasted for eleven days. During the Indië Weerbaar week in Batavia 'the sweetest of young ladies', as *De Locomotief* described them, sold Dutch pea soup, which also was a favourite

---

[10] *Orgaan der Vereeniging 'Indië Weerbaar'* 1-3:19.
[11] *Orgaan der Vereeniging 'Indië Weerbaar'* 1-4/6:12.

treat in other cities, and, again according to *De Locomotief*, expensive little Indië Weerbaar flags.[12] How many were sold is not mentioned. The number may not have been staggering. To commemorate the Indië Weerbaar week, 44,040 poster-stamps had been distributed, but of these only 5,527 were sold, bringing in 276.34 guilders.[13]

There were many activities in Batavia. People could admire a gymnastic display by soldiers, figure cycling, and a *gymkhana*, and attend all kinds of martial demonstrations. Among the latter were a military tattoo, flying shows, and demonstrations of the assembling of a mountain cannon and a mortar, and in loading machine guns. Van Limburg Stirum attended all these martial events. The public cheered. For the colonial elite there was a formal ball in the military club Concordia, a rare occasion because Van Limburg Stirum had continued the policy of his predecessor, Idenburg, of not holding such festive events at his palaces. It would only be on 4 March 1919 that the first ball was held at the Governor General's palace in Buitenzorg, though this would still be a chaste occasion as 'Steps' were considered slightly immoral and thus were not allowed (Bijl de Vroe 1980:166). Ordinary soldiers were placated with leave or a Sunday duty roster.

Opponents of Indië Weerbaar were equally passionately busy. Among them were the members of the Batavia SDAP. Cramer called the Indië Weerbaar movement the 'Indies Junker Party'.[14] He and other antagonists had likewise done their best to make the Indië Weerbaar week a memorable occasion. Everywhere in the city posters formulating the demands of the soldiers had been pasted up: better food, a better legal position, no more corporal punishments, and leave in Europe. Pamphlets were distributed and demonstrations planned. The reaction of the military authorities was uncompromising. One of the victims was the chairman of the Batavia Branch of the Soldaten Bond (Soldiers' Union). He was held responsible for one of the pamphlets which drew attention to the soldiers' demands. His punishment was demotion from bombardier to ordinary gunman. He was also transferred from his relatively comfortable job at the warehouses of the Department of Defence to active military service. To make the punishment more provoking he was not allowed to leave the barracks, which made it impossible for him to continue his job on the side (many soldiers had such an additional source of income) as a cobbler. Cramer pointed out in the People's Council that this punishment was made even more callous as the person in question suffered from 'severe chronic rheumatism' which made it impos-

---

[12] *De Indische Gids* 1918, I:93.
[13] *Koloniaal verslag* 1919:276.
[14] *Volksraad* 1918-19:210.

sible for him to participate in military exercises.[15]

Another pamphlet which attracted plenty attention was a call in Malay by the Batavia SDAP to attend a protest meeting organized in conjunction with Insulinde and the Sarekat Islam in the Deca Park on 1 September, the first day of the Indië Weerbaar Week. The pamphlet began by reminding Indonesians of earlier occasions on which the government had made them part with their money: Princess Juliana's birth, the celebration of the Netherlands' Independence, and the Onze Vloot drive. It was pointed out that people had obeyed a *perintah haloes*, a gentle order, not to mention less gentle hints, had 'stifled their curses', and had donated. This time once again they were asked to sweat cash. Indië Weerbaar wanted the people's money to finance the training of soldiers and to buy rifles. In the pamphlet it was suggested that it was the Indonesians who had to pay for these soldiers and rifles and that it was these very same Indonesians against whom the weapons would be used:

> Will it strike you that the projectile, bought with your money, hit you or your brother in the body? Make your wife a widow, your children orphans? But what more do you black wretches want to have than the honour of being a loyal subject. The people of Indië Weerbaar will toast your loyalty with champagne.[16]

The message was clear. Not a farthing should be given. The fine talk of Indië Weerbaar advocates about the development of the colony would only serve to ensure the continuation of Dutch rule. They did not bother themselves about the real needs of the population. The small Dutch flags which could be bought were but symbols of bondage. During the meeting itself the ISDV was conspicuously absent, though Alimin addressed the crowd. The soldiers were also absent. They had been forbidden to attend. Those who had disregarded the order were ejected by the police. In spite of these precautions European soldiers, the authorities estimated about one hundred, staged protest marches on 1 and 2 September. Fearing more protests the military authorities decided to act. Instead of enjoying leave or a Sunday duty roster soldiers and NCOs were confined to the barracks. Dutch officers kept watch to prevent any mischief. Armed patrols were out on the street.

Much went wrong in Batavia during the Indië Weerbaar Week. Cavalrymen, machine-gunners and other soldiers had trained for two days for a military tattoo on 2 September. *De Locomotief* described the parade which passed the palace of the Governor General as 'marvellous'. Nevertheless, it was not 'the buglers, drummers, staff music, battalion music, fife players' who were the cynosure of all eyes and excited colonial society.[17] Demonstrating soldiers

---

15 *Volksraad* 1918-19:464.
16 *De Indische Gids* 1919, I:89-90.
17 *De Indische Gids* 1918, I:93.

Cakalele dance at the Indië Weerbaar exhibition in Bandung in 1918 (*Orgaan der Vereeniging 'Indië Weerbaar'* 1-4/6:15)

singing the *Internationale* who preceded the tattoo stole the show. The cavalry had to disperse them.

Not everything that happened could be ascribed to the machinations of the anarchists and *ellendelingen*, wretches, to borrow the words Bijl de Vroe used to describe people like Baars, Sneevliet, Brandsteder, and Schotman (one of the organizers of the meeting in the Deca Park), whom he held responsible for the protests. Two flying shows were held in the mornings of 1 and 2 September at the Koningsplein, the present Medan Merdeka, on the northern side of which the palace of the Governor General was located. During the second, the engine of one of the aircraft failed. The plane crashed. The pilot was seriously wounded and died a few days later. The accident had consequences for the defence of the colony. As Bijl de Vroe noted: with one more plane down, half the colonial air-force of four planes was out of action (Bijl de Vroe 1980:162).[18] *Neratja* drew a different lesson from the incident: it was a clear indication that 'Nature' did not want the Indië Weerbaar movement in the Netherlands Indies

---

[18] Little more than a week later yet another plane crashed.

to continue in its present militaristic form. Economic development and education should come first.[19] Among the restless soldiers, the accident almost led to a fight between Moluccan or Manadonese soldiers (the source was unable to make up its mind which of the two groups was involved) and the police. It started when policemen stopped the soldiers who were running into the direction of the plane wreck. One of the soldiers protested. This was followed by an exchange of abuse and him being hit on the head by a mounted policeman. His friends joined a verbal 'attack'. Policemen had to draw their pistols to keep the soldiers at a distance. The soldiers vented their anger by pelting the policemen with stones.[20]

The establishment of the People's Council with twenty-one European, fifteen Indonesian, two Chinese and one Arab member had not made the opposition to Indië Weerbaar less vehement among Indonesians. Batavia and The Hague were well pleased with the quasi-parliament they had bestowed on the colony and never ceased speaking about the new political relationship that had taken shape. In a telegram to Van Limburg Stirum Pleyte called the opening of the People's Council on 18 May 1918 'the most memorable day' of his ministerial life.[21] Van Limburg Stirum had sent an equally jubilant telegram to The Hague. Nationalist leaders likewise welcomed the creation of the People's Council. *Neratja* even launched a campaign for a People's Council Monument.[22] Tjipto Mangoenkoesoemo, critical as ever, concluded that by establishing the People's Council 'the government got so many feathers in its cap' that it resembled an Indian with his cock's feathers as head-dress'.[23] Tjipto Mangoenkoesoemo was exaggerating. From the start, and this for a variety of reasons, the People's Council met with fierce opposition from within all population groups. One of the major points of criticism, also shared by its members, was that the powers of the People's Council were limited, even too limited for some Dutch people who wanted greater independence for the colony. Consequently it had garnered all kind of nicknames. *Volksraad palsoe*, False People's Council, Barnum and Bailey People's Council, *couveusekindje*, premature baby, are just of few of these (Van Heutsz 1917b:23). It was a real representative parliament with real powers, which even the more moderate faction in the Sarekat Islam argued, whose task it was to decide on the institution of a militia.[24]

If anything, Abdoel Moeis and others who had initially supported Indië

---

[19] *Neratja*, 1-9-1918.
[20] *Neratja*, 3-9-1918.
[21] *De Locomotief*, 29-5-1918.
[22] *Neratja*, 8-12-1917.
[23] *Volksraad* 1918-19:159.
[24] *Oetoesan Hindia*, 2-10-1918.

Weerbaar had sharpened their critical faculties. Probably they were also disillusioned by the fact that their earlier campaign to obtain concessions from The Hague in return for a militia had borne no fruits. Though less radically than the opponents from the left, Abdoel Moeis began to stress that he could not consent as long as the Indonesians had nothing worthwhile to defend, in short had no 'fatherland'. To show how little was done for the development of the Indonesian population, he pointed out that expenditures on defence accounted for between 20 and 30 per cent of the colonial budget, that for education only between 2.5 and 5 per cent.[25]

Diminishing support for Indië Weerbaar went hand in hand with deteriorating relations in the Sarekat Islam between its Islamic and leftist wings. In October 1917 Sneevliet had stated that the members of the central board of the Sarekat Islam had turned away from the masses and had destroyed the 'fresh, young movement' the Sarekat Islam once had been. They should forsake their policy of 'no action, no agitation', a course of action Rinkes had asked them to follow, and should no longer rely only on consultation with colonial government and the submission of requests.[26] In their turn in *Oetoesan Hindia* Sneevliet and the other Dutch radical propagandists of the ISDV were accused of having sown discord in the Sarekat Islam by their relentless agitation against the Indië Weerbaar movement. They were said to have succeeded in convincing the 'stupid and less educated element among the Natives' that their leaders were 'traitors to the people'; a qualification Baars denied as ever having used.[27] *Neratja* spoke about the rotten influence – *boesoek* was the word that was used – of Sneevliet and Baars on the Sarekat Islam.[28] Aversion in the Boedi Oetomo was perhaps even stronger. During a debate in Surakarta with Dwidjosewojo in September 1918 Baars accused the Boedi Oetomo of being supported by the capitalists so that they could continue to exploit the people in September 1918. One of the members of Boedi Oetomo responded to this insult in *Darmo Kondo*. He ended his article with the Dutch words: 'Leave us alone! Leave all that concerns our land and people completely to us, we ourselves will carry the ups and downs of our own future in the name of God.'[29]

Since then the antagonism in the Sarekat Islam had only increased. The moderate leaders refused to let control slip from their hands. They could still count on plenty of support. Members made it clear where their loyalty lay by shouting 'Follow the Sarekat Islam! Follow the Sarekat Islam!' when presented with the choice between the Sarekat Islam and ISDV. Briefly it appeared that

---

[25] *Volksraad* 1918:148, 543.
[26] *Het Vrije Woord*, 20-10-1917 (Tichelman 1985:672).
[27] *Oetoesan Hindia*, 14-9-1917, 15-9-1917, 17-9-1917 (Tichelman 1985:636, 642).
[28] *Neratja*, 13-11-1918.
[29] *Neratja*, 26-10-1918.

unity had been restored. This happened at the third national Sarekat-Islam Congress which was held in Surabaya at the end of September and the beginning of October 1918. It was deliberately convened just in advance of the next session of the People's Council, so as to be prepared if the native militia were to come up for discussion. Behind closed doors a truce was reached between Abdoel Moeis, who had been attacked even more vehemently by the European and Indonesian members of the ISDV after his debate with Baars in September 1917. Even the fact that Abdoel Moeis owned a motor car was used as a powerful argument against him. Abdoel Moeis's *Neratja*, in turn, questioned Sneevliet's, using his past employment by the *Soerabaiasch Handelsblad* and the Semarangsche Handelsvereeniging to argue that Sneevliet had always been a tool of the capitalists.[30] The immediate cause to talk matters over had been that *Neratja* had called Sneevliet and Baars divisive elements in the indigenous movement. In reaction the Semarang branch of the Sarekat Islam called for Abdoel Moeis's resignation. After Abdoel Moeis had defended himself spiritly, a compromise was reached. Abdoel Moeis, Darsono, and Semaoen, all three pledged to uphold the principles of the Sarekat Islam. They also promised not to fight out their differences in the press but to try to talk it out in the board of the Sarekat Islam. They would refrain from personal attacks and would criticize only one anothers' deeds.

It was the congress which afterwards was so much hated by Idenburg for its radicalism. The leftist members as usual lashed out against the Indië Weerbaar movement. They gained some success. As late as October 1917 Tjokroaminoto had still threatened to step down if the Sarekat Islam would condemn the Indië Weerbaar movement. A year later a motion rejecting a militia was accepted by the congress. Abdoel Moeis supported it.[31] Tjokroaminoto assumed a more radical tone. Provoked by Semaoen, he indicated that if the government was not prepared to carry out political reforms, the Sarekat Islam itself would institute representative bodies. Not much later, in a speech in the People's Council, he would accuse the government of having misunderstood the pro-Indië Weerbaar motion of the Sarekat Islam of August 1916 and of having started preparations for a militia without granting the population more rights.[32] On top of all this, Semaoen gained a seat in the central board of the Sarekat Islam. He became commissioner for the northern part of Central Java.

Baars was jubilant about the congress's outcomes. He concluded in *Het Vrije Woord*, predicting turbulent times when hunger or a 'sugar debacle' would come about, that Tjokroaminoto's words meant that Tjokroaminoto, though he might not have realised this, had threatened with a Soviet government.

---

[30] *Neratja*, 28-3-1918.
[31] *Neratja*, 8-10-1918.
[32] *Volksraad* 1918-19:546.

Indië Weerbaar festivities in Tapanuli in 1918 (*Orgaan der Vereeniging 'Indië Weerbaar'* 1-4/6:18)

According to Baars what had transpired at the congress showed that the Sarekat Islam had become a revolutionary organization, prepared to act, and much more revolutionary than its counterparts in British India. Proudly he claimed that all this had been brought about by the Indonesian members of the ISDV. Baars concluded that the Sarekat Islam had made an important step forward in becoming a 'class-organization of labourers and farmers'.[33] Less radical Europeans drew a similar conclusion: Tjokroaminoto had come under the spell of the ISDV leaders and the Sarekat Islam would in future follow the course of action propagated in *Het Vrije Woord* and in the radical indigenous press.

Semaoen was also pleased. He concluded that his inclusion in the board and the other decisions taken were proof that his revolutionary socialist opinions prevailed in the Sarekat Islam and were highly appreciated by the board.[34] Indeed, the central board announced at the end of the month that strikes which aimed at improving the circumstances of labourers, or started to

---

[33] *Sarekat-Islam Congres* 1919:71.
[34] *Oetoesan Hindia*, 18-10-1918.

fight for their rights or to combat arbitrary treatment should be endorsed.[35]

Within days the unity achieved at the congress broke up. Trouble started when *Neratja* published an editorial 'To Canossa' on 2 October. The author probably was the newspaper's other editor R. Djojosoediro. It certainly was not Abdoel Moeis, who was still in Surabaya. Later Abdoel Moeis apologized for what had been written and pledged that all articles in *Neratja* about the Sarekat Islam in future would be signed.[36] In 'To Canossa' Semaoen was called a *splijtzwam*, a divisive element, and a person influenced by Sneevliet and Baars. Triumphantly it was observed that by accepting the agreement with Abdoel Moeis Semaoen had backed down. Semaoen reacted by writing 'Tidak berobah' (Unchanged) published in *Soeara Ra'jat* on 12 October. In it Semaoen wrote that his ideas were *lakoe*, popular, while *Neratja* was not. He asserted that the course of the Sarekat Islam was much closer to his own one than that of Abdoel Moeis and that it was easy for revolutionary socialists to strive for the principles of the Sarekat Islam. Again he stressed that he was not under the influence of Sneevliet and Baars. Such an assessment was an insult to the Javanese. It suggested that they were more stupid than Europeans.

In an atmosphere of unrest and agitation, news about the socialist revolutions in Europe sent a shockwave through the Dutch community in the Netherlands Indies. Rumours did the rounds about 'the proclamation of a republic of Holland' and about Troelstra proclaiming that 'the socialists would have no scruples about resorting to violence'. In their news telegrams, newspapers frequently reported about the activities of Republican movements in Holland, Germany and the rest of Europe, and about the many strikes which were taking place all over Europe. One of these reports stated that in Holland the population wanted to stage large-scale disturbances.[37]

Some feared that something similar could happen in Java. There was plenty to worry about. Rice prices on the international market had risen steeply since September. One of the reasons for this was that Japan, itself threatened by a food shortage, had been forced to make emergency purchases abroad. Siam had to ban the export of rice in October because of a disappointing harvest. Rice imports from French Indochina and Burma also dried up. In the Straits Settlements the transport of rice to the Netherlands Indies was no longer allowed.

The export bans came at an unfortunate moment. In the Netherlands Indies the prospect of a shortage of food had re-emerged. The production of rice and maize was threatened by an exceptionally long drought. In June in the People's

---

[35] *Sarekat-Islam Congres* 1919:64.
[36] *Neratja*, 2-10-1918, 15-10-1918.
[37] Bijl de Vroe 1980:164; *Neratja*, 16-11-1918, 18-11-1918.

Council Tjipto Mangoenkoesoemo and Tjokroaminoto had spoken about hunger in Central and East Java, West Borneo, and Sumbawa.[38] The colonial administration prepared for the worst. The export of sago, sago products, peas and beans, and chickens from the Netherlands Indies was forbidden. In the Priangan the cassava acreage was expanded.

In retrospect the annual report of the Ministry of the Colonies concluded that the future had looked worrisome.[39] It also noted an extraordinary rise in the price of rice in certain parts of the colony.[40] Idenburg himself described the food situation as 'very sad and gloomy'.[41] Large parts of Java, as Talma was to say in the Volksraad on 2 December, had become 'completely dependent' on government hand-outs of rice, edible roots, and maize on the market.[42] From 15 October part of the Priangan cassava harvest had been distributed in other parts of Java to alleviate food shortages. With the same aim in mind the government had to distribute lentils in villages near Surabaya. In Yogyakarta measures had to be taken to assure the supply of food for the workers on the estates. In Madura rice was rationed. Yet another measure taken was to change the diet of soldiers. They were expected to eat less rice and more bread and potatoes.[43] Ambonese soldiers complained that they were no longer served bread but sago at breakfast.[44] In order to have distribution proceed smoothly Batavia informed the railways that it intended to transport large quantities of food by rail in early November. The transportation of other commodities would have to cede priority. The advance warning could not prevent the shortage of engines and wagons delaying the distribution of food.

The trade in a number of foodstuffs was again subjected to government control. The most important of these were rice, maize, cassava, and sago. The transportation of rice was forbidden from between *Residencies*, except under special licence. In November 1918 the *Residents* in Java once again were given the authority to fix a maximum price for food, not only for staples but also for such products as tinned milk. Rice also had to be shipped to regions outside Java. In the East Coast of Sumatra the government created a special Office for Foodstuffs with branches in the subdistricts, which acted as the buyers of rice and sago and sold cheap 'government rice'. An ordinance to force estate-owners outside Java to grow food-crops for their labourers was issued in September 1918.

Malay and European newspapers in the Netherlands Indies speculated

[38] *Volksraad* 1918:125, 318.
[39] *Koloniaal verslag* 1919:261-2.
[40] *Koloniaal verslag* 1919:61-2.
[41] *Handelingen Tweede Kamer* 1918-19:2077.
[42] *Volksraad* 1918-19:365.
[43] *Neratja*, 7-1-1919.
[44] *Volksraad* 1918-19:437-8.

about a pending food crisis. One of them, the *Bataviaasch Nieuwsblad*, suggested a novel solution: the 'native associations' should promote the growing of rice outside Java, that is should encourage Javanese to migrate to other islands.[45] Malay-language newspapers were full of reports about how expensive rice had become and about hunger. Sections with headings like' Perkara makanan', Food cases, and 'Lapar Hindia', Hunger in the Indies, at times covered a page or more. When it became known that Rangoon had stopped the export of rice, *Neratja* announced the news under the headline 'Moelai lagi', It is starting again.[46] At the end of October *Kaoem Moeda* wrote that 'Kromo shouts, Kromo cries, because his stomach is empty and he is on the brink of death, but the money devils do not worry about this'.[47] Again there was also some good news about new foodstuffs having been invented. In Buitenzorg a teacher at the secondary agricultural college invented what he called *kwak*, dollop, made from cassava. It could be eaten raw, could be stored for months, and was said to taste like a biscuit.[48]

There was one difference with earlier food scares: the Spanish influenza. It climaxed in November 1918 and claimed an unprecedented toll of victims in that month. The Spanish influenza was mentioned as an additional reason for the food shortage. The rice-fields of peasants with influenza remained untilled. Others who had just recovered from the illness were still too weak to work the fields. People were disturbed by the fact that malnutrition made everybody more vulnerable to the epidemic and exacerbated the effects. People who had caught influenza were unable to work, and therefore to earn an income for themselves and their families large enough to buy adequate amounts of healthy food. A plethora of committees was formed to provide financial and food aid to influenza sufferers and to distribute medicines among them. They operated alongside others which aimed to help the poor and the hungry. The link was also perceived by the Civilian Medical Service. In a circular letter published in December 1918, the service stressed that medical treatment by itself was not enough. On its own it was not enough to combat the illness if the patients were weak or undernourished. Poor families had to be provided with food. The service suggested that Batavia should set up a network which reached down to the villages to provide care and food for the needy.

Though some peasants profited from the increasing price of food, worsening living conditions set the stage for growing agitation. In sugar-producing areas the farmers began to complain about the rent they received for their land, which, they argued, was too low in view of the high prices of almost

---

[45] *Volksraad* 1918-19:365.
[46] *Neratja*, 19-10-1918.
[47] *Kaum Moeda*, 28-10-1918.
[48] *Neratja*, 4-11-1918.

Opening of the Volksraad by Governor General Van Limburg Stirum, 18 May 1918
(KITLV 4513)

all the goods and foodstuff they had to buy.[49] The rural unrest fortified some Dutchmen in their long-standing suspicion that members of the Sarekat Islam were out to kill the Europeans and Chinese.[50] In the cities leftist soldiers and sailors, under the impression of the revolutionary developments in Europe joined in demonstrations and held meetings to voice their demands and protests. In Surabaya, Batavia, and Semarang especially the leftist movement among soldiers and sailors made its mark. Troops had to be confined to barracks. In naval circles there was talking about a mutiny.[51] The editor of *De Indische Gids*, Van Heekeren, drew the right conclusion when he wrote that the Dutch means of exercising power were weak (Van Heekeren 1919b:140).

Because of their anti-Indië Weerbaar agitation coupled with what was happening in Europe, no socialist, even not those who had deplored the revolutionary agitation of Sneevliet in the past, was any longer trusted. Discussing

---

[49] *Oetoesan Hindia*, 6-6-1918.
[50] *Neratja*, 26-11-1918.
[51] Bijl de Vroe 1980:26; McVey 1965:32; *De Indische Gids* 1919:89-91.

the revolutions in Europe was a taboo subject at public meetings of leftist organizations.[52] Upset by stories that socialists in the Netherlands Indies would ineluctably follow the European example, the authorities even put a close watch on their leader, Cramer. His only fault was that he was a social democrat and that he did not hide the fact that he was pleased with the turn political developments had taken in Europe. Rumours were rife that Cramer would lead a march to the palace of the Governor General to demand a transfer of power.[53]

The political developments in Europe gave a boost to the revolutionary élan of the leaders of the Indonesian nationalist movement. Semaoen was impressed. In *Sinar Hindia*, the new name of *Sinar Djawa*, he published an article about what would happen if Batavia were to refuse to recognize the socialist government in Holland and he ventured into the possibility of a socialist government in the colony. Semaoen remarked that because the number of Indonesian socialists was small, the assistance of Sneevliet, Baars, Brandsteder and other Dutch ISDV members would still be essential. European socialist soldiers and sailors were also indispensable to the new socialist country. Their role would be to protect it against an assault by capitalist states such as Great Britain and Japan.[54] A Dutch translation appeared in *De Indiër*. In *Soeara Ra'jat* (Voice of the People, which had superseded *Soeara Merdika* as the Malay-language newspaper of the ISDV, and called *Soeara Baars*, the Voice of Baars, by its enemies) Darsono urged his fellow-countrymen to rise up in rebellion. 'What can stop the common man once he rebels? Let the red flag wave!' (McVey 1965:32.) Elsewhere, in a letter to *De Locomotief*, Darsono wrote that he and other revolutionary socialists wanted 'action, resistance' and that they would fan up 'the glowing hatred, which is beginning to be kindled in the hearts of Kromo, so that our fight against capitalism, against economic oppression, grows even more bitter and the day of victory will soon be there'.[55] Even Tjokroaminoto warned that if the 'enemy did not change its course large-scale disturbances' would be the result. He stressed that hurt feelings and hunger were weapons in the hands of the Sarekat Islam.[56] W. van Ravesteijn, a Communist member of the Dutch Parliament, concluded that the Netherlands Indies were living through 'eventful times'. He observed among 'the native population tremendous unrest and commotion which are the consequence of the social developments which have taken place and still are taking place all over the world'.[57]

---

[52] *Volksraad* 1918-19:219.
[53] *Volksraad* 1918-19:223; McVey 1965:31.
[54] *Sinar Hindia*, cited in *De Indische Gids* 1919:643.
[55] *De Locomotief*, 9-11-1918, cited in *Volksraad* 1918-19:222.
[56] *Oetoesan Hindia*, 17-11-1918, 18-11-1918.
[57] *Handelingen Tweede Kamer* 1918-19:2021.

In the People's Council Cramer tried to impress upon the government the need for change and far-reaching reforms, including the transformation of the People's Council into a true parliament. He and like-minded spirits in the People's Council argued that the revolutions in Austria, Germany, Hungary and elsewhere in Europe had demonstrated that repression did not work and in the end would only begin a revolution. Reforms were all the more necessary because the Netherlands Indies might be teetering on the threshold of a food crisis. Cramer warned that the government should not think that matter would not come to this pass:

> We live in a time of great events, in which all the thrones in Europe are tottering, in which militarism, we hope, is finished, in which nobody can say in advance whether we are standing on the threshold of a social revolution. [...] It is certain that among soldiers as well as among the general population the revolutionary spirit is not lacking.[58]

These were 'stirring times'. Asia would not remain unscathed by the political developments in Europe.[59]

Speaking in the People's Council on 16 November, Cramer announced that the present circumstances necessitated a 'concentration of the pronounced democratic Native and European elements' to strive for reforms which were 'necessitated by the events which had taken place in Europe'.[60] Five members of the People's Council – Cramer, who had taken the initiative, Tjokroaminoto of the Sarekat Islam, A. Sastrowidjono of Boedi Oetomo, and Tjipto Mangoenkoesoemo and J.E.E. Teeuwen of Insulinde – met to discuss how to use the occasion to press for political reforms. Promising that they would do all they could to keep their followers under control, they urged for the establishment of a real parliament.

Van Limburg Stirum was among those Dutch people in the Netherlands Indies who thought it very likely that Holland might go the way of Germany and Russia. He had even discussed about how to proceed should a socialist revolution succeed in Holland with his advisers. It would mean a break with the fatherland. The Netherlands Indies would continue on its own (Locher-Scholten 1981:87). Van Limburg Stirum could relax somewhat after he was informed about developments in Holland by Idenburg in a wire of 15 November. The telegram contained some alarming news. It spoke about '[w]idespread nervousness caused by Troelstra's speeches [...] urging immediate transfer government to socialists following German example'. The telegram also explained that the new Dutch Prime Minister, C.J.M. Ruijs de

---

[58] Volksraad 1918-19:210.
[59] Volksraad 1918-19:216.
[60] Volksraad 1918-19:211.

Beerenbrouck, had declared that the government 'will resist all violence and attempts overthrow constitutional powers' and that 'this declaration was followed by general movement [in] all quarters to resolutely resist revolutionary movement'. Fortunately, the telegram ended on a reassuring note: 'Yesterday nervousness considerably allayed Troelstra declared no intention use violence'.[61] The telegram was received in Batavia on 17 November with much relief. Its contents were published immediately. Nevertheless, newspapers still contained reports about Troelstra's demand that as in Germany a socialist government should be formed in Holland (and that women's suffrage should be introduced) on 18 November.[62]

No revolution took place in Holland and Queen Wilhelmina had not abdicated as was rumoured in Batavia (Locher Scholten 1981:87-8). This reality did nothing to dissuade Cramer, Stokvis, and Teeuwen from pleading for fundamental changes. Teeuwen expressed the hope that Batavia and The Hague would learn a lesson from the collapse of governments in Europe which 'relied on the power of the military, relied on censorship, on the restriction of associations, on the imprisonment and banishment of political enemies and so on. Mr Chairman! Where are these governments now? Does one want to go the same way here?'[63] Oppression was dangerous. Only a policy based on justice and cooperation with all population groups could save colonial rule. Tjipto Mangoenkoesoemo, other Indonesian nationalists, and the vernacular newspapers also continued to give dissertations about a revolution and what changes were needed to prevent this.

The news from Holland was, of course with some exceptions, greeted with delight by the Dutch community. When Koningsberger opened the new session of the People's Council at nine o'clock in the morning of the 18 November, he started by expressing his gratitude that 'no turn about of affairs has taken place of such an abrupt nature as would make it difficult to reconcile with the well-understood, permanent and true interest of the Mother Country'.[64]

Talma made a surprise appearance in the same session. His words mirrored the relief with which the authorities had received Idenburg's first telegram. Talma began by saying that the reports received from the Netherlands were a source of gratitude, especially so because they clearly showed that the people in Holland did not intend 'to be robbed by violence of their national treasure of constitutional institutions by a minority'.[65] He also called it gratifying that the government in The Hague wanted to 'implement with full speed

---

[61] *Handelingen Tweede Kamer* 1918-19:2086.
[62] *Neratja*, 18-11-1918.
[63] *Volksraad* 1918-19:239.
[64] *Volksraad* 1918-19:235.
[65] *Volksraad* 1918-19:251.

social reforms, following the legal road, and maintaining order'.

Evidently international developments and the domestic threats of a severe food shortage, an unruly labour force and mutinous soldiers and sailors, and growing discontent among the population had upset the Governor General and his advisers. They showed themselves prepared to make far-reaching concessions to gain broadly based support in society in an effort to avert the danger of a break-down in law and order. After his opening remarks Talma added that the 'new direction which the most recent world-shattering affairs have prescribed also laid down the course which also has to be followed here'. Having said this, he added the qualification that what Batavia had in mind was 'less a change of course than an acceleration of tempo'. Nevertheless, he mentioned new relationships and shifts in powers between the colonial government and the People's Council. Talma announced that 'in these tense days' the government desired closer contacts with the People's Council, and intended to discuss with its members how this could be achieved; all this to secure 'domestic peace' and to 'keep the spectre of a bitter food shortage outside the door'.

Another reason Talma adduced to explain why Batavia strove for 'hearty cooperation' with the People's Council was its effort 'to raise the general level of prosperity'. Because this implied the removal of 'abuses' in the sugar industry, Talma announced the establishment of a committee of inquiry into such evils. Tjokroaminoto had been invited to sit on it. (Among its members would also be J. Schmutzer, who had spoken out in defence of the estate industry in the People's Council.) While denying that there was 'general discontent' in the army, Talma also promised improvements in the living conditions of the soldiers and in the military criminal code. And he had more good news: Van Limburg Stirum had asked The Hague for a Royal Decree to specify the existing general ban on associations and meetings of a political nature.

On the day Talma made his speech in the People's Council, Idenburg could wire still more reassuring news from Holland: 'Today enormous crowd demonstrating against revolution cheered queen royal family Malieveld Hague'.[66] The telegram referred to a huge manifestation in the afternoon of the same day on the Malieveld in The Hague. At the entrance to the park soldiers had unharnessed the horses from the royal carriage in which Queen Wilhelmina, her husband, and Princess Juliana were seated. Amidst the cheers of a large crowd they had pulled the carriage along. Idenburg's telegram was received in Batavia on 20 November (Van Miert 1995:144). Following the news from Holland, reports quoting from Dutch appeared in newspapers in the Netherlands Indies recounting the failure of any revolutionary plan the socialists in Holland might have had. They stated that 'the danger of a revolution

---

[66] *Handelingen Tweede Kamer* 1918-19:2086.

had passed', that 'Holland was safe again', and informed their readers about massive demonstrations of loyalty to the Queen in Holland.[67]

Talma had not voiced a totally new opinion about the future of the People's Council on 18 November. In May, at the opening of the People's Council, Van Limburg Stirum had already alluded to a semi-independent colony governed by his administration in cooperation with the People's Council. At that time Van Limburg Stirum had spoken about an 'unwritten constitutional law' which would develop and about the shifting of competence from the motherland to the colony.[68] The crux of the matter was how long it would take before the population was considered mature enough to take such a step in his eyes and in those of the policy-makers in Holland. A second indication that Van Limburg Stirum was in favour of at least some political reform had come in June 1918. Talma had noted that the discussion of the colonial budget had given the government the strong impression that the 'development process' of the People's Council had gone faster than expected. He indicated that political concessions, albeit modest ones, might be made, though he refused to state what form these would take. He had said that the government deemed a 'development process' desirable, and had coupled this with the caution that matters should not be rushed. Efforts should be concentrated on developing the People's Council within the legal boundaries set.[69]

In his 18 November speech Talma elaborated on the same theme. He did not promise the People's Council full parliamentary powers in the near future, but this did not matter. From all sides this was how his words were interpreted. What Talma had said was grist to the mill of Indonesians and Europeans dreaming of the greater independence of the colony. *Neratja*, of which Abdoel Moeis was no longer an editor since 14 November, even wrote that Van Limburg Stirum had promised self-government. It concluded that developments in Europe had induced a turn to a more democratic political structure all over the world and that the colonial government did not want to lag behind and therefore intended to follow the same course.[70]

European and Indonesian members of the People's Council jumped at Talma's suggestions, and asked for significant reforms in the near future. In the morning of 20 November, members of the People's Council met in a closed session to discuss Talma's speech. The answer they formulated was accepted on 25 November. The People's Council promised to cooperate in the efforts to avert the 'spectre of bitter food shortage'. The members of the People's Council clearly also wanted to seize the opportunity presented. They asked to be

---

[67] *Neratja*, 19-11-1918, 21-11-1918, 28-11-1918, 25-1-1918.
[68] *Volksraad* 1918:1.
[69] *Volksraad* 1918:550.
[70] *Neratja*, 21-11-1918.

informed as quickly as possible about the reforms Van Limburg Stirum would suggest to The Hague and inquired whether these reforms also concerned the relationship between the colonial administration and the People's Council. To make it all the more clear what they had in mind, at the end of the reply it was observed that Batavia should be given the power to decide on measures taken to improve the political and economic situation in the Netherlands Indies independently of The Hague.

Members of the People's Council wanted to move fast. Tjokroaminoto, Sastrowidjono, Dwidjosewojo, Radjiman, Cramer, Tjipto Mangoenkoesoemo, Abdoel Moeis, Teeuwen, and Thajeb proposed a motion urging for a 'parliament elected from and by the People, with full, legislative power and the establishment of a government accountable to this parliament' on 25 November.[71] The new constellation should be realized before the mandate of the People's Council expired in 1921. When the motion was submitted Koningsberger revealed that he knew that Batavia was 'spontaneously' preparing measures which were in concert with the motion, and that a special committee would be formed headed by J.H. Carpentier Alting, President of the Supreme Court.[72]

Batavia's answer came on 2 December. Talma, clearly satisfied with what he was to say and with the impression his November speech had made, reaffirmed Van Limburg Stirum's intention. Once again Talma drew attention to the impact of the political developments in Holland and the rest of Europe: 'Everywhere radical reforms of Public Institutions on the basis of new principles are deemed essential, or – when these had already been accepted – in a faster tempo'.[73] This time Talma recalled how the People's Council, envisaged as a 'mere advisory body [...] with a very limited task', had grown in importance 'at very vast tempo' in the previous six months. 'Unwritten constitutional law' had developed much faster than expected. Talma agreed that this achievement could partly be attributed to the People's Council itself, but Batavia also took some credit. It had consciously tried to stimulate this development. Talma used this observation to deny the opinion that Batavia had watched the growing influence of the People's Council with alarm. He also said that Batavia regretted the doubts voiced about its sincerity when it spoke about reforms. Mutual trust and cooperation was what the Netherlands Indies needed, and this applied to the government and the People's Council. To stimulate this, a special government commissioner would be appointed to serve as a liaison officer between the colonial administration and the People's Council. From Talma's speech it became clear that Batavia considered the tone of part of the European and Malay press a threat to the unity of all groups; a

---

[71] *Volksraad* 1918-19:300.
[72] *Volksraad* 1918-19:300.
[73] *Volksraad* 1918-19:429.

condition it deemed essential to be able to weather the difficult times ahead. Talma even called what he said about the press a warning. He revealed that a number of times Batavia had considered sterner regulations to act upon stirrings of agitation in the press. In the end, it had decided against pursuing these. The reasons Talma gave were that Batavia did not want to impede the development of the indigenous society and that the remedy would be worse than the disease, and would only result in bitterness.

Talma promised that more reforms were in store. These would be realized soon, 'now that the general political current is running in a direction which places in the vanguard, as the number one demand, a greater say of those ruled in the government of the country'. The ultimate goal was 'a central government with participation by and accountability to the native population'. Observing that reforms were impossible without a 'substantial extension of the competence of the People's Council', Talma announced the formation of a Commissie tot Herziening van de Grondslagen van den Staatsinrichting van Nederlandsch-Indië (Commission of Inquiry into the Form of Government of the Netherlands Indies). It would be chaired by Carpentier Alting. Among the persons invited to sit on the Herzieningscommissie were s'Jacob, H.H. Kan, R.M.T.A. Koesoemo Oetoyo, W.M.G. Schumann, Teeuwen, and A.L. Waworoentoe. The commission was installed on 20 December. This time it was Van Limburg Stirum himself who spoke about the changed relationship between the People's Council and the colonial administration, and the need for legal reform (Van Helsdingen 1926:6).

There were even more goodies in store. Talma's speech was laden with promises. Local Coucils would be given more responsibilities. The relationship between mother country and colony would have to change 'possibly with a shift in centre of gravity'. When the People's Council wanted to use the right of inquiry, Batavia would do all it could to assist. All legal or administrative discrimination based on religion and race would be abolished. Only on rare occasions in future would the government resort to detention on remanding in future. Batavia also intended to mitigate the ban on political organizations and meetings, and considered it a 'painful deficiency' that because of difficulty in communicating with Holland, no new rules had yet been promulgated. Talma also announced a committee, headed by Schumann, which would have to study working conditions and labour relations in the Netherlands Indies. Refining on this, Talma said that it was the duty of the government to draft labour legislation to protect the economically weak.

As a word of caution Talma took up the familiar theme that the population was not yet mature enough for a true democracy. The political reform Batavia had in mind could only be realized if there was 'a broad population group with sufficient development and moral strength to call its own leaders to account for the policy they pursued as representatives of the population'. To reach this stage, a schooling in 'the responsible exercise of authority' would be necessary. The government was prepared to provide this through *ontvoogding*, decreasing the role of the Dutch as the *voogd*, guardian, of Indonesian society, giving the Indonesians a greater share in regulating their own lives and society. Another way would be through the creation of provincial Coucils to act as bodies of indigenous authority.

The following day Achmad Djajadiningrat and five others submitted a new motion. One of their points was that there should be a Rijksraad (Empire Council) in which all parts of the empire, each with its own government should be fairly represented. All members of the People's Council had to be elected. The People's Council itself should be given legislative power and should decide on the budget of the Netherlands Indies, and no longer have merely an advisory function.

Van Limburg Stirum had yet even more surprises in store. On 28 November Koningsberger had adjourned the debate in the People's Council to allow R. de Kat, Director of the Department of Government Enterprises, to make a statement. De Kat announced that the government intended to establish a 'Bureau for Social Affairs in State Enterprises'. It would be headed by someone with practical experience in the field, 'who has sympathized with the social progress in Western countries'. To attract such a person, the government was prepared to pay a high salary. The task of the bureau was to promote good industrial relations, especially in such vital government enterprises as the public railways and the post, telephone, and telegraph services. It should formulate proposals about working hours, pensions, health services, and other financial support for people in temporary appointment. De Kat also announced that by improving conditions of employment in the state mines Batavia hoped that the labour force of contract labourers and convicts could be replaced by one consisting of professional miners in permanent employment.[74]

Soldiers were not forgotten in this orgy of promises. In November Batavia established a committee of advice to look into their pay. Van Rietschoten, while still stressing that there was nothing wrong with the morale in the colonial army was suddenly prepared to make some concessions when he addressed the People's Council on 3 December. He promised better food, better housing, and an amendment of the military penal code. Teeuwen saw this not only as an opportunity to stress once again that the Netherlands Indies did not need soldiers from Europe. He hammered home that Indonesians and Indo-Europeans could do the job perfectly well, providing that they had something to defend.[75]

The aversion of the socialist danger was also the moment to stage a show of

---

[74] *Volksraad* 1918-19:387-8.
[75] *Volksraad* 1918-19:470-1.

loyalty in the Netherlands Indies. Impressed by the massive display of royalism in Holland, influential figures in the Dutch community organized a petition among Dutch citizens in the Netherlands Indies and the Straits Settlements to express their loyalty to and love for the Queen at the end of November. The initiative for what the Malay press called the Comite Memoeliakan Radja (Committee for the Glorification of the Queen) had been taken by J. Schaap, editor-in-chief of the *Java-Bode*. Koning, Berretty of ANETA, Zaalberg (who had left the *Bataviaasch Nieuwsblad* in June), E.A. Zeilinga (President of the Javasche Bank), and J. Houtsma of the NHM were among the persons who backed the initiative. Support was also pledged by R.A.A. Achmad Djajadiningrat, S. Ismail bin Abdoellah Alatas (an Arab), J.A. Soselisa (an Ambonese), Waworoentoe (from the Minahassa), and O.H. Kouw (a Chinese).

The movement was well planned. Agents of the NHM, KPM, and the Javasche Bank were instructed to assist in the drive to collect signatures. The cooperation of European and Indonesian civil servants was also enlisted. Newspapers were asked to promote the drive for signatures. Lists circulated in government offices, European schools, cinemas, and restaurants. Even in the Zoological Garden of Batavia people could sign a list to testify to their loyalty to the Queen. Within days the committee could wire to Van Limburg Stirum that the number of people who had signed was 'enormous'.[76] The European Dutch reacted with enthusiasm. The will to sign tapered off among the indigenous population and could not be compared with the wave of the declaration of loyalty in the closing months of 1914. The Minahassa, parts of North Sumatra and other Christian regions formed an exception.[77] At times – in East Sumatra and in Penang in the Malay Peninsula – the expression of loyalty was coupled with the demand that Troelstra should be banished from Holland.

Batavia was not fated to bathe in total, uncritical glory. Some Indonesian nationalists received the November promise with scepticism. Indonesian members of the People's Council were upset that Van Limburg Stirum had extended his hand to them individually, but had not made any gesture of goodwill towards the organizations they headed, which were still treated with distrust. People were also aware that politicians and the business community in Holland would never agree to fundamental reforms. The Indonesian members would not refrain from expressing their surprise about the reforms suggested. They rightly surmised the reasons for the sudden change in policy. Abdoel Moeis concluded that fear had once again been effective.[78] Nevertheless, he observed that if he read the intentions of the colonial government correctly,

[76] *Neratja*, 3-12-1918.
[77] *Neratja*, 3-12-1918; *De Indische Gids* 1919, I:387.
[78] *Volksraad* 1918-19:530.

independence might only be gained in 'the far, far distant future'.[79] He also expressed the worry that what Van Limburg Stirum might have in mind was the independence of the colony and not independence of the autochthonous population. Abdoel Moeis and others were fully conscious of the fact that the colonial authorities suddenly no longer considered them too 'unripe' to have a share in the governing of the colony. Batavia even gave the impression that it appreciated their nationalist activities, which not so long before it had roundly condemned.

Many Dutch people were outraged. Talma's suggestions occasioned a storm of protests in the Netherlands Indies, where the Dutch-language press in its usual savage style lashed out against Van Limburg Stirum, and this action was repeated in Holland after the news had reached Europe. The Dutch people in the Netherlands Indies were usually not averse to greater political independence. Some even dreamed of a dominion status. Van Limburg Stirum (or his principal advisers, who according to some were most to blame), however, had gone too far, even in the eyes of some who viewed the nationalist movement with some degree of sympathy. *De Locomotief* commented that the population was not yet mature enough for political change. Motivated by the 'revolutionary epidemic' in Europe, Batavia had embarked on an 'abnormal passion for reform'.[80]

In Holland there was yet a second reason to tear a strip off Van Limburg Stirum. Talma had also announced the intention to decrease the acreage planted with sugar and tobacco on European estates in 1919. Talma said that Batavia was prepared to go as far in this as the food situation demanded.[81] Van Limburg Stirum, who earlier in 1918 when he had issued the exports bans had been praised for his determination, came under attack for the way he handled the situation. His critics accused him of having bowed to the pressure exerted by the nationalist movement. In Holland, the Netherlands Indies, and abroad the opinion was voiced that Van Limburg Stirum had panicked. Especially the promise to reduce the production of sugar in 1919 – if necessary by 30 per cent – in anticipation of a possible shortage of food did not go down well. The conclusion was that Van Limburg Stirum had succumbed to 'a few hot-headed members of the People's Council', to the 'wild demands of a revolutionary party'. He had shown excessive lenience towards 'a few Native fanatics'.[82]

D. Fock, the chairman of Parliament, and from 1905 to 1908 Minister of the Colonies described Van Limburg Stirum's stand as very peculiar, inexplicable,

---

[79] *Volksraad* 1918-19:520.
[80] *De Locomotief*, 23-11-1918.
[81] *Volksraad* 1918-19:440.
[82] *Regeering* 1919:3, 8; *De Indische Gids* 1919, I:393.

and incomprehensible.[83] He was angry. Van Limburg Stirum had acted on his own initiative without informing Idenburg in advance about his intention to set political reforms in motion. Discussing the powers of People's Council was a prerogative of Parliament in Holland. A Governor General should never on his own initiative publicly air his personal opinions on the subject. The time had not yet come for fundamental changes. Idenburg reassured Fock. The Dutch government might consider some minor changes in the functioning of the People's Council, but no significant extensions of its powers were foreseen. Later, the announcement about a possible reduction in the sugar acreage was enough reason for Fock to take an almost unprecedented step. In April 1919, when it had finally become clear what had transpired in Batavia in November, he addressed Parliament about Van Limburg Stirum's mistakes and the blessings brought by the sugar industry to Java and attacked the crude political campaign against the estates. It was the first time in forty years that a chairman of Parliament had taken the floor to speak. Fock's criticism and the way he expressed 'deeply wounded' Van Limburg Stirum's feelings (Van Anrooij 2001:16).

In Holland the independence the Netherlands Indies had raised some heckles. The *Algemeen Handelsblad* commented that the expectations Van Limburg Stirum had created with his headstrong and weak policy could lead only to bitter disillusionment. It would make Holland's heavy task even more burdensome.[84] Van Limburg Stirum had lost his head, even the communist D.J. Wijnkoop concurred.[85] Yet others depicted Van Limburg Stirum as spineless. Both in Holland and in the Netherlands Indies people called for Van Limburg Stirum's resignation. Advanced as a good candidate to replace him was Colijn, who had made no secret of the fact that he thought the People's Council with its 'tribunes of the people' could best be abolished, and that no time should be wasted in reacting to 'hyper-criticism'.[86] The harsh judgements passed on Van Limburg Stirum annoyed Idenburg. He explained that Van Limburg Stirum had acted for economic reasons, not because he had felt pressured by demonstrations and protests: 'This Governor General is not a man to be cowed. He is not under the thumb of the capitalists, nor is he under the thumb of the leaders of the people.'[87]

The political developments in Holland allowed the authorities in the colony to breathe more easily. With the wind out of the sails, the fine words and the promises of reform did not bring about any lasting changes. It was

---

[83] *Handelingen Tweede Kamer* 1918-19:2014.
[84] *Algemeen Handelsblad*, cited in *De Indische Gids* 1919, I:607.
[85] *Handelingen Tweede Kamer* 1918-19:2070.
[86] *De Indische Gids* 1919, I:632-3.
[87] *Handelingen Tweede Kamer* 1918-19:2078.

even denied that there had ever been any such intention. Repression now set in. The first victims were the ISDV activists. Up to then the authorities had done no more than keep Sneevliet and Baars under close surveillance. As late as the middle of November Cramer had still praised the government because it had informed the People's Council that it did not intend to banish Sneevliet and Baars. The reason, Batavia had explained on 16 November, was that it 'did not want to hamper the exposure of abuses, nor the organizing of actions to obtain better living conditions'.[88] Two days later, in his 18 November speech Talma announced the decision to ban Sneevliet; though he did not mention him by name, simply referring to a person who 'in spite of serious warnings even in such days as these tries to paralyse the organs of public authority'.[89] Talma said that the colonial government had acted with regret.[90] His words may well have been mere window-dressing. The decision to banish Sneevliet probably would have been taken earlier had shipping between Holland and the Netherlands Indies not come to a standstill. The arrival of the *Noordam* and *Tabanan* had now opened the opportunity to get rid of Sneevliet. In Augustus 1918 Sneevliet's friend, J.C. Stam, one of the ISDV members who had been active in organizing soldiers and sailors, had already reported from Java to *De Tribune* in Holland that such a step was being prepared by the colonial authorities (Morriën 1984:77-8).

On 18 November, in one and the same breath, Talma suggested that similar measures might well be taken against 'persons stepping into the limelight who are playing with fire by flirting with extreme elements'.[91] A few days later Brandsteder was detained in the military prison in Batavia. In *Het Vrije Woord* he had exposed the cruelty and arbitrariness of military punishments and had urged soldiers to refuse to administer corporal punishment, or, as *Neratja* chose to phrase this, to beat up their fellow-soldiers. Brandsteder was accused of inciting wilful disobedience.[92] The Court of Surabaya had sentenced him to three months' imprisonment, nine months fewer than had been demanded. At the hearing Brandsteder had brought along the heavy metal ball prisoners had to carry and the iron fetters and manacles used for *kromsluiten*. When his appeal was turned down Brandsteder was arrested without any advance warning, when he happened to be in Batavia to advise the local Soldiers' Union. Soldiers and sailors protested. One of their actions drew tremendous public attention. Enraged about the arrest of Brandsteder, probably no more than twenty-five soldiers and sailors met in the building of the Bond

---

[88] *Handelingen Volksraad* 1918-19:213.
[89] *Volksraad* 1918-19:251.
[90] *Volksraad* 1918-19:433.
[91] *Volksraad* 1918-19:251.
[92] *Neratja*, 21-5-1918.

van Minder Marine-Personeel on the evening of 20 November. They decided to strike in protest of Brandsteder's arrest. The participants in the meeting were arrested, but the following day a small group of soldiers did indeed go on strike. They walked out of the gate of the barracks and roamed through the city. Some returned to the barracks in the course of the day. The diehards assembled in the union building. Carried away by revolutionary fervour they discussed taking the city by force. Eighteen soldiers were arrested and immediately transported to the punishment detachment in Ngawi.[93]

Once again it was one of his articles which ultimately prompted Batavia to take action against Sneevliet. *Het Vrije Woord* published 'Honger en machtsvertoon' (Hunger and displays of power) on 16 November. In it Sneevliet addressed himself to the soldiers of the colonial army. Recalling the display of force used to suppress unrest in Java, he wondered whose power the soldiers were representing. His conclusion could be foreseen. It was that of the government which was acting in the interests of the ruling class, the owners of banks, factories, and estates; persons who were strangers to hunger and lived a life of luxury; people, who

> using all kinds of subterfuges seized control of the land for their sugar factories, diverted the irrigation water that makes the land fertile to it, who even in times of imminent food shortage preferred to grow sugar instead of returning the sawahs to the people for the planting of rice.

Sneevliet urged European soldiers, who themselves came from urban working class and poor farmers' families, to show the same understanding for the Javanese they were ordered to suppress as soldiers in Holland had displayed towards the riots by the members of their own class. Referring to the Indonesian soldiers, Sneevliet noted that they were extremely capable of understanding why Kromo refused to take it any longer. Soldiers from Ambon and the Minahassa should understand that 'Kromo does not ask for bullets and death, but that he has every right to stand up for his life'. Soldiers who were aware of the conditions in the Netherlands Indies – 'hunger, disease, deprivation, the burden of taxation, unfathomable misery, luxury, flashiness, making a profit at all costs' – should execrate the task they were ordered to perform. In Europe soldiers showed their solidarity with the people. This should guide them when orders were given which could make them the murderers of their own brothers, whose only crime it was that they did not want to die silently of starvation, that they longed for a little more freedom, a little more happiness in life. In conclusion Sneevliet suggested the soldiers turn to the Soldiers' Union, the Sarekat Islam, and the ISDV to contrive the means to

---

[93] *Neratja*, 23-11-1918; *Soerabaiasch Handelsblad*, cited in *De Indische Gids* 1919, I:258.

ensure themselves a decent existence.[94]

The authorities considered 'Honger en machtsvertoon' a blatant appeal to refuse to undertake military duties. They saw it as an outright attempt to sow hatred. Sneevliet's appeals to join soldiers and sailors unions, or soviets as these were sometimes also referred to in the vernacular press, were considered subversive. As could be expected the announcement that Sneevliet was to be banned was highly acclaimed in European circles. For months people in Holland and the Netherlands Indies had been demanding Sneevliet's expulsion. Among those who made such a plea was the editor of *De Locomotief* who was alarmed by the strikes and the unruly behaviour of the soldiers. Vowing to respect human rights, he argued that the rights of an individual were constrained by public interest. This was all the more true under present conditions. Only a 'strong regime' could safely guide the Netherlands Indies 'through a period in world history of which not many realize the tremendous gravity'.[95] Sneevliet and other agitators should not be allowed to sow disorder. It did not matter that no crimes had been committed. What counted was that they resorted to dangerous methods to incite 'a primitive population'.[96] Some went even further. Recalling the fate of Karl Liebknecht and Rosa Luxemburg, it was hinted in *Jahns Advertentieblad*, published in Malang, that if the government did not act 'the citizens will be ready to give the instigator to murder, arson and rape what is coming to him'.[97]

Abdoel Moeis and other Indonesians had voiced the same demand. Some leaders of the Sarekat Islam condemned the actions of Sneevliet and Baars as detrimental to the interests of the Indonesian population. They wondered why the colonial authorities had not yet taken any action. There was even more reason to banish Sneevliet and Baars than there had been in the case of Douwes Dekker. In the same breath they accused not only a number of European newspapers, which still wrote in the same insulting tone as they always had done about the natives and the nationalist movement, but also *Het Vrije Woord*, *Soeara Ra'jat*, and *Sinar Hindia* of sowing hatred. Some added the Chinese newspaper *Djawa Tengah*, and curiously enough also *Oetoesan Hindia* to the list.[98] The compromise that had been reached between the Islamic and leftist factions at the party congress had temporarily put an end to the calls within the Sarekat Islam to banish Sneevliet. True to this spirit, in the People's Council in November Tjokroaminoto stated categorically that the Sarekat

---

[94] *Het Vrije Woord*, 16-11-1918.
[95] *De Locomotief*, 12-4-1918.
[96] *De Locomotief*, 13-4-1918.
[97] *Handelingen Tweede Kamer* 1918-19:2070.
[98] *Neratja*, 5-11-1918, 13-11-1918.

Islam was against the expulsion of Sneevliet and Baars.[99]

Nevertheless, after the decision to ban Sneevliet had been announced, some Indonesians could not conceal their delight. *Neratja* welcomed the news. In an editorial printed in larger type *Neratja* stigmatized Sneevliet as an anarchist who had set up Indonesian organizations against one another to serve the interests of his own small group, and who had planted the seeds of discord and mutual resentment in the nationalist movement. Praising him for his ability to expose abuses, *Neratja* pointed out that of late Sneevliet had done so without taking the interests of the indigenous population into account and without accomplishing a change for the better.[100]

Support for Sneevliet from within the nationalist movement seems to have been more widespread. There were letters to the editor of European newspapers and other forms of protest. The secretary of the Sarekat Islam sent an address to Parliament in The Hague to protest about the decision to banish Sneevliet. A number of local branches of the Sarekat Islam – Semarang, Salatiga, Surabaya, Gondong, Demak, Babat, Cirebon, and Tegal – sent telegrams to the People's Council. The Union of Rail- and Tramway Personnel in Semarang, Pekalongan, and Surakarta did the same. The Sarekat Islam branch in Surabaya set up a fund for organizing financial assistance to victims of government repression. Sneevliet was to be the first recipient of its benefactions (Van Heekeren 1919b:138). The Semarang branch sent Van Limburg Stirum a telegram informing him that Sneevliet's banishment had caused so much frustration, the word used was *sakit hati*, that people had been poised on the brink of a riot, but that the board had succeeded in calming down emotions, thereby preventing disturbances. Such words caused perturbations in the European community. A number of European newspapers perceived the telegram as a threat. Leaders who could calm people down could also incite them.[101] Naturally ISDV branches protested.

Some Dutchmen also disagreed. In the People's Council Teeuwen said that the government 'should allow this man to stay in the Indies. He makes a good living here and he is not dangerous enough to ruin.'[102] Yet another argument was advanced in the *Nieuwe Courant* in Semarang. What Sneevliet really wanted was a revolution in Europe. Banning him from the Netherlands Indies meant that he could return to Holland on the first available shipping opportunity, and would not have to wait for months like others.[103] Another daily, the *Sumatra Post*, suggested Sneevliet's banishment was a sign of weak-

---

[99] *Volksraad* 1918-19:184-5.
[100] *Neratja*, 18-11-1918.
[101] *Bataviaasch Handelsblad,* cited in *Neratja,* 27-11-1918.
[102] *Volksraad* 1918-19:246.
[103] *Nieuwe Courant* and *Sumatra Post,* cited in *De Indische Gids* 1919, I:381.

ness. Sneevliet should be allowed to continue with his rash actions and wildcat strikes. In the end 'the masses' would realize that such a course only hurt them. Van Heekeren, the editor of *De Indische Gids*, was appalled by such reactions. He himself applauded the banishment and mildly criticized Batavia for waiting too long. In a colony with a still largely uneducated population, Van Heekeren argued, actions against Sneevliet and other demagogues were a matter of self-preservation. From Van Heekeren's perspective, Sneevliet and his political associates had shown sure aim. They had targeted 'the pillar of our rule in those extensive territories: the army' (Van Heekeren 1919a:67).

The authorities were determined to put an end to the ISDV agitation once and for all. ISDV branches were so frequently refused permission to hold meetings, that even a political adversary like Teeuwen protested. Teeuwen had an additional point to make. He wondered why the ISDV meekly submitted to the government's power to forbid meetings. It made the ISDV 'a placid, legal association, in its acts completely non-revolutionary'.[104] Such an attitude contrasted sharply with what the Indische Party had done in the past. European members of the ISDV and soldiers who distributed 'Honger en machtsvertoon' and other pamphlets among soldiers and sailors were apprehended. Those who were found guilty were sentenced to three months' imprisonment instead of the six months demanded. Semaoen, who had made a Malay translation, was given two weeks. Repression seemed to work. A lecture by Baars on 22 November on 'Bolshevikisme' had to be cancelled because almost nobody turned up.[105]

Investigations were also started against authors of both recent and older articles in *Sinar Hindia*, *Soeara Ra'jat* and other leftist publications. In the eyes of both Dutch people and Indonesians these investigations were clearly linked to the 'Sneevliet press offence'. Quizzed were Semaoen, Mas Marco, Darsono and other Indonesians. Semaoen was sentenced to four months' imprisonment in 1919. He used the opportunity to write a novel: *Hikayat Kadiroen* (Semaoen 2000:ix). Another victim of the harsher mood among the Europeans was Tirtodanoedjo, an editor of *Oetoesan Hindia*. He was accused of having incited its readers to resist the police; that is policemen who acted incorrectly. He was sentenced to six months' imprisonment.[106]

Sneevliet, Brandsteder, and Baars all were externed and left the Netherlands Indies. Sneevliet demanded to be brought before the court instead of being expelled. It was to no avail. He was questioned by the *Resident* of Semarang, who was especially interested in his appeals to establish soldiers' and sailors' unions. After the court had allowed this, Sneevliet was arrested, put on the

---

[104] *Volksraad* 1918-19:248.
[105] *Neratja*, 23-11-1918.
[106] *Neratja*, 9-12-1918.

train to Batavia, and shut in the military prison. Sneevliet was served with the decision of the Governor General to exile him on 5 December 1918. He left the Netherlands Indies aboard the *Noordam* on 20 December. In the early 1920s he acquired fame as a member of the Executive Committee of the Communist International and founder of the Chinese Communist Party. In April 1942 he was executed by a German firing-squad in Amsterdam (see Tichelman 1974). Baars was determined to leave the Netherlands Indies. The Mayor of Semarang had offered him a job as municipal engineer, but he refused. Baars left for Holland in the spring of 1919. The following year he returned to the Netherlands Indies and was employed as an engineer by the municipality of Semarang, only to be banished in May 1921 (Tichelman 1985:228). Brandsteder served his three month's prison sentence. Remembering Sneevliet's reception in April the previous year, the authorities had a military guard at the railway station when he returned to Surabaya after he had been released in February 1919. As it was only a few sailors turned up to meet him. A welcoming party was organized in the building of the Sailors' Union. Brandsteder was banned from the Netherlands Indies in September 1919. The main stated reason to expel him was his articles in the *Soldaten- en Matrozenkrant*. He left the Netherlands Indies the following month and moved to Russia. In 1927 Baars returned to Holland. He died in Auschwitz in 1944.[107] Brandsteder, who was also sacked by the headquarters of the Union of Lower-Ranking Naval Personnel in 1919, went to live in Holland. He died in 1986.[108]

Members of the ISDV who were in government service were transferred to outposts. Van Limburg Stirum had concluded a few months earlier that expelling all the social democrat teachers, some of whom had made no secret of the fact that they sympathized with the protesting soldiers and sailors, would have been impossible.[109] One of the first victims had been G. van Burink, a teacher at the Dutch-Chinese School in Semarang. To punish him for his agitation among the soldiers he was transferred in June 1918. The government had planned to post him in Gorontalo. When Van Burink protested Batavia decided on the small island of Banda Neira in the Moluccas. Van Burink resigned to become a private teacher.[110]

---

[107] Tichelman 1985:282, http://www.iisg.nl/archives/nl/files/b/10729033full.php.
[108] http://www.iisg.nl/bwsa/bios/brandsteder.html.
[109] Morriën 1984:80; Van Heekeren 1919b:146; Van Limburg Stirum to Pleyte, 29-5-1918, NA, Kol. Openbaar, Vb. 17-6-1918 62.
[110] *Neratja*, 5-6-1918, 15-6-1918.

CHAPTER XXII

Peace
Missed opportunities

The armistice on the Western front on 11 November 1918 rendered some of the measures the colonial government superfluous. The ban on reporting on troop movements was lifted before the end of the month. Foreign consuls were again allowed to send telegrams in code after February 1919. Muurling's PID, formally created to gather information about activities which might endanger neutrality, was disbanded in April 1919. During its brief existence it had acquired such notoriety that the abbreviation continued to be used in popular speech for years after to refer to the gathering of political intelligence by the colonial authorities (Poeze 1994:231).

A native militia never saw the light of day. Batavia and The Hague refused to take the final step which would have permitted it to be raised. To arm a large section of the population was too dangerous. Perhaps the only Indonesians ever called to arms were the son of the Regent of Semarang and another Javanese pupil of the HBS in Utrecht, about whose fate Soewardi reported in *Het Volk*. They contacted the Minister of the Colonies in their efforts to escape conscription. The only advice the latter could give was that the best course for them to take would be to arrange their passage back to Java.[1]

In the Sarekat Islam the different factions continued to quarrel. During its national congress in October 1918 no decision had been taken about the question of whether the party should concentrate on its religious aims or should give preference to the economic and political emancipation of the Indonesian population. It had also not decided which tactics should be adopted: the 'revolutionary' road propagated by Semaoen and Darsono, or the parliamentary route advocated by Tjokroaminoto and Abdoel Moeis. When these points came up again, the contention sounded the death knell of the already troubled cooperation between the leftist and the Islamic leaders of the Sarekat Islam.

---

[1] *Neratja*, 16-11-1918.

The leftist members founded the Indonesian Communist Party in 1920 and they were gradually forced out of the Sarekat Islam between 1921 and 1923.

The sugar estates remained a major source of agitation. Events in the closing months of 1918 and early 1919 were a repeat of those at the beginning of 1918. Sugar and rice dominated the news in the press in the Netherlands Indies. Between February and December the government had still been able to import 2 million piculs of rice worth 17 million guilders, but the stock of government rice would suffice only till March, and this only if imports from abroad were not to dry up completely. Batavia did not preclude the eventuality that the moment might come at which rationing would be required. In its efforts to avert a serious food crisis, it even arranged for the import of soya beans from Manchuria in early 1919.

The upshot of the new food crisis was that the sugar estates once again became the target of an intense campaign propagated by both the radical and the more moderate wings of the nationalist movement. The Sarekat Islam wanted to 'wage a war fought in a way which was legally permissible' against the sugar factories.[2] Much to the horror of the Dutch authorities, a reduction in the sugar acreage had become a subject about which leaders of the nationalist movement among them Tjokroaminoto were contemplating calling a strike. In the People's Council, he stigmatized private sugar estates as obsolete.[3]

As in the previous years, again there were pleas by the government to intensify the growing of alternative food crops. Estates were asked to expand their food crop acreage. Initially the response had been positive. The chairman of the Landbouw Syndicaat (Agriculture Syndicate), T. Ottolander, travelled round Java in the first weeks of November 1918, appealing to estate managers to comply. Some decided to plant rice on their land as a secondary crop. Such initiatives did not prevent the outbreak of a bitter war of words about whether or not the estates had been doing enough to assist in preventing the onset of a food crisis. In regions where water was scarce, it was intimated that estates refused to relinquish the part of the irrigation water they depended on for the growing of sugar cane, thereby preventing the growing of secondary crops on a large scale. The suspicion was also rife that rice and other secondary crops were planted only on waste land and not on the fields of farmers on their estates, who consequently also did not profit. A more serious outcome was that farmers who had listened to the exhortations of the government and had planted rice as a secondary crop saw their harvest fail through lack of irrigation water. In some places this was an additional reason why the harvest though not totally ruined was so poor. The government blamed the farmers.

---

[2] *Neratja*, 13-11-1918.
[3] *Oetoesan Hindia*, 15-7-1918.

They had disregarded the voice of cautious warning that a shortage of irrigation water set limits on the acreage which could be planted.[4]

In early 1919, when the export of sugar was resumed, the sugar companies were less enthusiastic about lending a willing ear. They condemned the plan to reduce the sugar acreage as unrealistic and dangerous. Agitators who had campaigned against the sugar industry for years would reap the fruits. Batavia and the estates would be blamed for the loss of income. Theft and unrest would be rife. Some were quick to point out that experiences in 1918 had shown that not much could be expected of any efforts to turn sugar fields into rice-fields. In various places people had even asked the estates to quash the reduction of the cane acreage. Among the 'defenders of capitalism', as *Neratja* chose to describe them, who spoke out against a reduction in the sugar acreage was Rhemrev supported by his nationalist Orange Union of Law and Order.[5] The 'sugar newspaper', the *Soerabaiasch Handelsblad*, calculated that Batavia's plan would cost the state 18 million guilders in taxes. The sugar estates would forfeit 42 million guilders.[6] To the indignation of politicians in The Hague, the management of the sugar companies in Holland, angry that they had not been consulted in advance, hinted that they might ignore instructions of the Governor General to reduce the area under cultivation. Simultaneously, estate managers prepared for unrest and strikes, which they feared would be organized by the Sarekat Islam if the area of production was not cut back. Apprehension even extended abroad. Sugar from the Netherlands Indies was again in great demand. Great Britain was so eager to buy it negotiations were launched to see whether, in spite of a bad harvest in British India, Rangoon rice could be supplied to Java in an amount equal to the extra harvest the authorities hoped to reap if there were a decrease in sugar production.[7]

In a reaction, in an article headed 'A refined, intellectual pack of murderers', the editors of *Sinar Hindia* had no compunction in calling the sugar planters 'cold blooded murderers' because they refused to decrease the sugar acreage in January 1919.[8] In February 1919 such articles prompted the Sugar Syndicate to ask the colonial administration to check the inflammatory rhetoric in the Malay press.[9] Inevitably, the recalcitrant attitude of the sugar industry resulted in protests from the nationalist movement. The issue was important enough to unite Sarekat Islam, Boedi Oetomo, and ISDV, which staged joint mass meetings. Confidence among Indonesian nationalists and

---

[4] *Volksraad* 1918-19:439.
[5] *Neratja*, 20-2-1919.
[6] *Regeering* 1919:4-5.
[7] *De Indische Gids* 1919, I:759.
[8] *Sinar Hindia*, 25-1-1919 (*Handelingen Tweede Kamer* 1918-19:2017).
[9] *De Locomotief*, 25-2-1919, 26-2-1919.

leftist Dutchmen that Batavia was in earnest its intention to have estates reduce their cane acreage was not boosted by the appointment of J. Sibinga Mulder as Director of Agriculture in December 1918. He replaced Lovink who had not been averse to a reduction in the sugar acreage or to the promotion of an indigenous industry. Sibinga Mulder was cut from different cloth. He was generally known as a *toean goela*, a sugar lord, a 'sugar fanatic', as *De Locomotief* called him, or, as Cramer expressed it a protagonist *à tort en à travers* of the sugar industry. He was, a speaker at the Sarekat-Islam Congress concluded, an unvarnished capitalist.[10] Tjipto Mangoenkoesoemo predicted that as far as Sibinga Mulder was concerned the native could be no more than a 'rough worker destined to produce a dividend for the shareholders in Holland'.[11] Talma let it indirectly be known that Van Limburg Stirum was far from happy with the choice, taking pains to stress that Sibinga Mulder's appointment was solely the responsibility of The Hague.[12]

By March it had become clear Batavia would not enforce a reduction in the sugar acreage. The harvest of maize and other of secondary crops had been excellent and a normal rice harvest was expected.

Initially, after the uncertainty of the first months of the World War, the colonial export economy had done well. The export of a number of colonial products exceeded that of previous years and excellent prices were fetched. Sugar especially was in great demand. Contributing to the success was the accident in disguise that wartime conditions had forced exporters to find new export markets and that the war had also opened these up when long-established international trading relations between the warring powers and other countries were cut off. New-found trade with the United States and Japan more than compensated for a drop in trade with Europe. In the closing months of 1916 conditions deteriorated. By 1917 the picture had changed drastically. The economic war fought by the Allied Powers, the perils of the sea in wartime, the decrease in shipping opportunities, aggravated by the Allied and later the Associated Powers' demand for tonnage, brought the colony to the brink of economic disaster. A concomitant factor was that in South Asia Allied colonies were also confronted with the Associated Powers hunger for ships to sustain the war effort in Europe. In British India the lack of shipping opportunities, compounded by the danger U-boats and mines posed, affected sea trade and sea traffic with the motherland. Life was affected in a similar way to that in the Netherlands Indies. The well-off colonial élite, for instance, could no longer send their sons home for education at prestigious schools in Great Britain as

---

[10] *Sarekat-Islam Congres* 1919:7; *De Indische Gids* 1918, II:1493; *Volksraad* 1918-19:212.
[11] *Volksraad* 1918-19:160.
[12] *Volksraad* 1918-19:442.

its members had been used to doing, but had to enrol them at 'war schools' in India (Buettner 2004:105-6). The British Indian need of ships threw weight behind the demands to put Dutch tonnage at the disposal of the Associated Powers.

Disruption of international sea traffic hurt not only the colonial export and import sector in the Netherlands Indies. Throughout the war, but especially towards the end, the colonial authorities were greatly worried by the fact that the Netherlands Indies was not self-sufficient in the production of rice. For adequate supplies of its staple, it needed imports from Burma, Indochina and Thailand. Disruption of sea traffic and export bans abroad raised the spectre of food shortages, famine, and social unrest, forcing the Governor General and his staff to contemplate a reduction in the acreage planted by the sugar factories to allow a concomitant increase in the production of food crops.

By the autumn of 1918, confidence in the economic future of the Netherlands Indies had been somewhat restored. One reason for hope had first been perceptible in September when the prospect of peace was in the air. This was indeed followed by the armistice, and then the peace talks. Each of these events had stimulated trade and speculation in rubber, copra and a few other commodities produced in the Netherlands Indies. Thanks to this recovery in prices, the Cultuur-Hulpbank did not have to come to the assistance of any estate.[13]

What the economic future would bring nobody knew in 1918. Some were optimistic. They expected old markets to be restored and foreign trade to accelerate to satisfy pent-up demand. Others were pessimistic. Peace might also mean that a belligerent mentality might come to dominate international economic relations. The prospect of trade-blocks loomed. As 1918 wore on, many had predicted an intensification in the economic war once the military battle had been won by the Associated Powers. In the People's Council in June 1918 D. Birnie warned that the Netherlands Indies was especially vulnerable to this because it was so heavily dependent on foreign trade.[14] The greatest cause for apprehension was uncertainty about how the United States and Great Britain would enforce their economic interests. Germany was also left out of the equation. The German economic threat was considered even more real because the German merchant Navy was thought to have survived the war almost undamaged, safely sheltered in German and neutral ports. Early in 1918 Loudon had confided to Parliament that, during negotiations with Germany, it had emerged that Berlin was highly interested in the economic state of affairs in the Netherlands Indies. Loudon had gained the impression Germany wanted to make Dutch shipping subservient to post-war German

---

[13] *Koloniaal verslag* 1919:201-2.
[14] *Volksraad* 1918:323.

interests.[15] The defeat of Germany banished all such fears. To compensate for the damage German U-boats had inflicted, Germany was forced to surrender all German merchant ships of 1,600 tons and more, half of its ships of between 1,000 and 1,600 tons, and a quarter of all other ships to the Allies (Van der Mandere n.d.:85).

As of the beginning of February 1919, the Dutch ships held in British and American ports were gradually released. London and Washington even promised to assist in their return to sea by facilitating their intake of coal and provisions. In the same month, Nederland, Rotterdamsche Lloyd, and Oceaan decided to lower their freight tariffs by 30 per cent. In May the first ship to sail the usual route through the Suez Canal left Tanjung Priok. Shipping restrictions imposed by the Associated Powers were not lifted immediately. The mail service to Europe was restored, but initially letters and parcels still had to be sent by British Mail. The first Dutch ships which sailed from the Netherlands Indies to Europe in December 1918 – the *Noordam* and the *Tabanan* – still had no Dutch mail on board. In July 1919 the censorship Great Britain had imposed on telegraphic communications was ended. A transmission station for wireless messages to replace the provisional one was sent to Java in 1919. The station became operational in 1922.[16]

Trade with the motherland was not liberalized immediately. The sea blockade had remained in force after the armistice. In an economic agreement concluded with the Associated Powers by The Hague, a new quota system was proposed, which limited the volume of exports from the Netherlands Indies to Holland between October 1918 and October 1919. In return, The Hague promised to lend the United States 120 million guilders (including the proceeds of confiscated and sold freight), Great Britain 75 million guilders, France 30 million guilders, and Italy 11 million guilders. The shipments of colonial wares to the Netherlands had to be addressed to the NOT, which had lost much of its influence when shipping to and from the Netherlands had dwindled. The trust had to decide which portion was allowed to be exported to the motherland in the first half of the period and which in the second one. The agreement covered about twenty-five products including tea, coffee, tobacco, rice, sago, maize (including maize for fodder), kapok, cotton, oil, and tin. Once more the NOT appeared all powerful. In the Netherlands Indies a Ladies Aid Committee, made up of women who were worried by reports about hunger in Holland, collected food to be shipped to the motherland. Idenburg was grateful for the gesture, but pointed out that the NOT had to be consulted before the aid could be shipped.[17] The NOT was disbanded before the end of the year.

---

[15] *De Locomotief*, 13-6-1918.
[16] Gerdus Oosterbeek 1927:340.
[17] *Neratja*, 22-1-1919.

Bringing to an end what the Ministry of the Colonies reporting on the event chose to call the NOT 'tutelage'.[18]

The black list was abolished in April 1919. The Associated Powers also gradually began to lift their import restrictions. In the Netherlands Indies itself export bans were lifted in 1919: those on kapok, wood, tobacco, sugar, and rubber in June, those on tin, tea, coffee, and copra in August, that on pepper in September, and that on synthetic dyes in October. Export products would fetch spectacular prices in the course of 1919, the only exception being tobacco. Prospects seemed bright. In its annual report over 1919 the Ministry of the Colonies wrote about 'relief and recovery' and of a 'lively demand for almost all colonial products in Europe and elsewhere which made prices jump and reach a level never known before.'[19] The assessment was too optimistic. Also 1920 started well but by the middle of the year an economic crisis loomed. It turned out that it took the Netherlands Indies and the world longer to recover than people had foreseen. Poverty in Europe, a depression in Japan, and Washington fighting inflation caused prices and demand drop. Stocks were piling up again. The high prices fetched earlier had been mainly attributable to speculation. Worst affected were rubber, sugar and tea.[20] It was not before the end of 1922 that the situation changed for the better for colonial export trade.

The effect of the imminent peace on consumer behaviour had been the opposite to what trade in export products initially experienced. In the expectation that retail prices would soon drop, consumers postponed purchases. In January 1919 the Associated Powers benevolently promised that they would not hinder the import of goods of which they themselves had enough into the Netherlands Indies, providing that the latter did not restrict the export of goods needed by the Associated Powers. Despite such promises imports remained expensive, not least because cargo space was still at a premium. At first shortages appeared to have become more acute. As at other times of economic depression and high prices, people noted the increase in beggars and vagrants. The economic decline experienced by the population, which had already caused the authorities alarm before the war, would continue well into the 1920s (Carpentier Alting and De Cock Buning 1928:96-8).

After the armistice one cause for anxiety was that the Dutch had the impression that elsewhere in Associated countries a misconception about the Dutch role during the war reigned. The Netherlands might have to pay for its neutrality. The new Dutch Minister of Foreign Affairs, H.A. van Karnebeek, tried to make a confident impression at the end of 1918. Addressing Parliament,

[18] *Koloniaal verslag* 1920:291.
[19] *Koloniaal verslag* 1920:291.
[20] *Koloniaal verslag* 1921:251.

he said that the behaviour of the Netherlands between 1914 and 1918 had been so impeccable that the Dutch could be confident about the outcome of the negotiations with the Associates.[21] Privately Van Karnebeek must have had misgivings. He requested Idenburg to ask Van Limburg Stirum for an assessment of the damage caused by the war and about the measures the colonial government had been forced to take. The picture entertained of the Netherlands by the Associates should be put right. Van Karnebeek wrote that abroad it was 'generally not sufficiently realized what great sacrifices the war has demanded' from the Netherlands. It was 'even not infrequently thought that the Netherlands had profited economically from the war'.[22] He need not have bothered. In Paris, the leaders of the Associated Powers had too much on their minds, worrying about the rampant unrest in Europe, trying to create new states, redrawing boundaries, and dividing up German colonies and part of the Ottoman Empire, under heavy fire from all the protests and violent reactions this elicited, to worry about the Netherlands.

When the Peace Conference, to which the Netherlands was not a party, commenced in Paris in January 1919, new fears loomed. For a long time, at least since 1916, there had already been talk that Belgium would claim part of Dutch Limburg and Zeeland Flanders at the peace conferences. Some rumours went even further and stated that Belgium would also demand parts of the Netherlands Indies. As it happened, the Dutch did not have any reason to worry. The leaders of the Associated Powers were not greatly concerned with a small and powerless country like Belgium. Belgian interests and wishes, including those with regard to the border with the Netherlands, were paid so little attention that at one point the Belgian delegation in Paris even threatened that it would not sign the peace treaty (Macmillan 2001:285-6).

Another rumour was somewhat embarrassing. Some anxiety had been caused by the vague references the American President, Woodrow Wilson, had made about the right to self-determination of nations and the development of backward regions under colonial rule for the good of the international community. Wilson might well want to press such issues at the peace conference. Fearing that this might indeed be so, and that a Colonial Power might be forced to develop certain regions, and even worse, to accept the participation of the contemporary World Powers in the People's Council, s'Jacob pressed for the development of the non-Javanese part of the Netherlands Indies, in order to forestall foreign countries using yet another excuse for interference in Dutch colonial affairs.[23]

An additional cause for discomfort was the prospect, that as the rumour

---

[21] *Handelingen Tweede Kamer* 1918-19:786.
[22] Van Karnebeek to Idenburg 4-2-1919, NA, Kol. Geheim, Vb. 21-2-1919 G1.
[23] *Volksraad* 1918:314.

had it, Chinese in the Netherlands Indies wanted to seize the opportunity of the peace talks to have the representative of the Chinese government draw attention to the discrimination against Chinese in the Netherlands Indies. It was hinted he had been given the task of achieving a decision by which Chinese who had settled in the Netherlands Indies would be treated as subjects of China and no longer as Dutch subjects. Since 1911 restrictions on travel and residence had gradually been lifted, only to be abolished completely in November 1918, but since 1910 a new source of discontent had presented itself. A new act on citizenship made Chinese born in the Netherlands Indies of parents who had settled there Dutch subjects. The Chinese government had protested in 1910. It had recalled its Ambassador from The Hague (Han Tiauw Tjong 1919:952). In the Netherlands Indies the new act had not been well accepted. Protests peaked at the time of the peace talks in Paris. Instrumental in mobilizing Chinese discontent was *Sin Po*. This newspaper launched a campaign coupling a rejection of compulsory service with a rejection of Dutch nationality. The *Sumatra Post* claimed that 28,789 Chinese families and 300 Chinese associations had rejected the idea of becoming Dutch subjects (Oei Kiauw Pik 1919:960). In the end it was not the Chinese but the Japanese who were to raise the point of racial discrimination. The Japanese delegation gained wide support for insisting on the inclusion of a clause on racial equality in the Preamble to the Covenant of the League of Nations, but it ran up against a brick wall of opposition erected by the Americans and British, afraid of losing political support at home and, in the British case, especially in Australia and New Zealand which like the United States wanted to bar Japanese immigrants (MacMillan 2001:329).

When the Treaty of Versailles was signed on 28 June 1919, on the same date in the same palace Wilhelm I had been crowned Emperor of Germany, Germany lost all its telegraph cables. Its Navy and a good part of its commercial fleet had to be handed over to Great Britain. Germany also had to part with its colonies and protectorates. Brutal German colonial rule was the justification given for such a decision. The argument was the umpteenth reason for some Dutchmen to torment themselves. Associated propaganda had contributed to this bad image of German rule, and passionate speeches in the People's Council making the most of abuses in the Netherlands Indies might well create the impression abroad that the Dutch did not behave much better in their colony than the Germans had done in their Asian and African colonies (Van Renesse 1920:316-7).

Although the Netherlands Indies emerged intact from the Great War and the Peace Conference, it was a different colony from what it had been in 1914. In pre-war years there were signs that the mood among the population had already been changing. The Ethical Policy introduced after the turn of the century facilitated the calls for emancipation, but the internal dynamics in the Indonesian, Indo-European, Arab, and Chinese communities also had contributed. The emergence of a popular nationalist movement in the early 1910s had prompted Dutch people to question the loyalty of the indigenous population were the Netherlands become involved in the Great War. To their relief Indonesians shouted 'Long live the Queen' and not 'Down with the Dutch' during meetings organized in the months following August 1914. What remained was a certain unease about the pro-German sympathies of Indonesians who clearly sided with their fellow-Muslims in the Ottoman Empire, Germany's ally, and later in the war, about a radicalization of the nationalist movement. Stimulated by the native militia discussion, the nationalist movement grew increasingly vocal and self-confident (and according to some extremists) in tone between 1914 and 1918. Nationalist and Islamic leaders called for political concessions in exchange for Indonesian conscripts to assist the Dutch in defending the colony, demanding equal treatment, a truly representative body in the colony, and better education.

Increasingly communist leaders also made their voices heard and Marxist jargon became fashionable among nationalist of all denominations. The advance of Indonesian communist leaders spelled the demise of the leaders of the pre-war Indische Partij and their disregard for racial differences. Understandably in a society in which race was one of the real and also perceived markers of social status and occupational group, racial antagonisms influenced the course of the nationalist movement. The VSTP became an almost exclusively Indonesian organization; an indication that Indo-Europeans and the Dutch language had become a liability in the nationalist movement. Indonesian members of the ISDV stressed the racial divide. The Chinese who seemed to arouse negative feelings among colonial administrators, part of the European community, and the indigenous population also suffered. Abdoel Moeis's remarks in Europe about Chinese middlemen who exploited the small man, Semaoen's lashing out against the Chinese after the Kudus riots and his attack on Indo-Europeans in *Si Tetap* testify to the significance of racial sentiments. In a sense the failure of Douwes Dekker, Tjipto Mangoenkoesoemo, and Soewardi Soerjaningrat to win support for their 'Indiër nationalism' can be considered a missed opportunity, though now it is only possible to speculate about what the consequences for racial relations would have been had they been able to win over at least part of the nationalist leaders, especially those of the Sarekat Islam.

Taking post-war development into account, it is easier to speak about prospects which were not realized in the field of political and economic relations. In the course of the Great War, it had become increasingly difficult to communicate between motherland and colony. The regular mail and passenger services of pre-war years proved impossible to maintain. Commercial sea traffic to and from Rotterdam and Amsterdam broke down when the dangers of war at sea intensified or when Allied pressure on tonnage became too great. Even any idea of a direct shipping link between Holland and the Netherlands Indies had to be abandoned after Berlin decided to resume an all-out submarine war in January 1917, while the requisitioning of all the Dutch ships in the ports of the Associated Powers put an end to all Dutch international sea traffic in March 1918. Such a decline in Dutch sea traffic was first and foremost an economic disaster. It also hampered communications between Holland and the Netherlands Indies, but what had been of even greater influence was that right from the outbreak of the war the Allied Powers had aimed to control the flow of mail and goods between motherland and colony. Incontrovertibly this was part of the Allied endeavour to bring down the German economy and to isolate German commercial interests in the rest of the world. Another reason for the tight control kept on Dutch mail was the fear for what might be accomplished by a Germano-Indian conspiracy to undermine British rule in Asia by inciting unrest among indigenous soldiers from the British colonies and fomenting a rebellion in India. In the schemings of the plotters, the Netherlands Indies had a vital role to play as a transit station for arms and seditious pamphlets; inevitably such suspicions necessitated close British supervision of all shipping to and from the Netherlands Indies. Telegraphic communications had also been at the mercy of the British who had even temporarily denied the Dutch access to a cable system when London instituted the British Telegram Interruption to punish the Netherlands for the way its government interpreted its duties as a neutral country in October 1917.

The break-down in communications between colony and motherland which had been the result of the problems encountered in keeping shipping, the mail service, and telegraphic connections functioning smoothly had given the colonial administration and the business community the chance to act with some independence (and at certain moments with complete independence) from directives from the Netherlands. Pessimism that the end of the war might see the restoration of the pre-war economic relations and make the mother country all powerful once again had persisted throughout the war. This would halt the modest steps the colony had set on the road to industrialization. After the war company headquarters in Europe and politicians in The Hague indeed again took control. Company headquarters tried to regain lost ground. The 'old battle' between the economic interests and status considerations of those in Holland and those in the Netherlands Indies was resumed (Ligthart 1923:432). The first indication of this had already emerged to the full light of day in August 1918 when the sugar companies in Holland had founded their own organization to regulate trade, the United Java Sugar Producers Association, and the Advisory Committee on Sugar and consequently the Association of Java Sugar Producers and Exporters had to be dissolved a few months later.

Some companies even succeeded in having Holland once again become the place where the colonial export products were traded and have such wares shipped to Holland on consignment (Ligthart 1923:432). It was an outcome much deplored in the colony and one which even made Emil Helfferich conclude that the Netherlands Indies had more freedom in the political than in the economic field (Taselaar 1998:1-2). Companies based in Holland even regarded with distrust trade missions abroad sent by the government to stimulate the sale of colonial products, afraid that such missions could result in direct trade relations with the Netherlands Indies bypassing the Netherlands.[24] Despite being assailed by such threats, the new system which had taken shape during the war was too practical and too cost-effective to be abolished completely. The sugar market remained located in Java (but the United Java Sugar Producers Association was firmly in control) and the sale of Bangka tin still took place in Batavia. Tea was sold in Amsterdam and Batavia (and in London).[25]

Any thought about the political autonomy of the Netherlands Indies or a certain degree of self-rule remained a dream. The prospect of a famine in 1919 had been one of the motives for Van Limburg Stirum to have Talma call for unity and cooperation in his speeches to the People's Council. Talma had addressed himself specifically to the 'native associations' in his speech of 2 December 1918. He had asked for the assistance of their leaders in attempts to explain the measures taken by the government to avert a food crisis to the population. Significantly, he also asked them to help in 'urging the population to spare the crops, already in the ground, so that they could be used to benefit society'.[26] On the same occasion and true to the spirit of the day, Talma had announced the establishment of local advisory Coucils on food production. The members were to be drawn from all population groups, but not from the civil service. By adopting this course Batavia hoped to make good use of the expertise of the population. Talma promised that the members of such committees could turn to the Head of the Department of Agriculture, Trade and Industry if they had the impression that their suggestions were being ignored or were not being properly implemented. It all fizzled out.

In May 1919, when he opened a new year of sessions of the People's Council Van Limburg Stirum spoke of 'the transfer of powers to representative bodies' but left no doubt he was talking about a long-term project: 'Where an abrupt transformation from a bureaucratic form of government to its antipode, the modern Western one, would only give a semblance of reality, what is called for is to pave the way for a gradual transfer'.[27] His speech made it clear that

---

[24] *De Indische Gids* 1922, I:160.
[25] Ligthart 1923:432; *Koloniaal verslag* 1920:296-7.
[26] *Volksraad* 1918-19:441.
[27] *De Indische Gids* 1919, II:993.

the development of local representative bodies was what the government had in mind, not a change in the political relationship between colony and motherland. Consequently, the motions submitted in the People's Council on 25 November and 3 December calling for far-reaching political reform came to nought. First, discussion was postponed till the Herzieningscommissie (Commission of Inquiry) had submitted its report, which it did in June 1920. One of its proposals was to change the name the Netherlands Indies to the Indies. This was suggested to do justice to the fact that the colony was 'a separate, as much autonomous as possible part of the Kingdom of the Netherlands' (Carpentier Alting 1920:144). Another was to give the People's Council (for which it invented the awful name *Landsstaten*, National Council) the status of a real co-legislative body, and virtually to remove the authority of Parliament in The Hague in matters concerning the Netherlands Indies. The Committee also suggested that in The Hague when important decisions concerning the Indies were to be made a deputation of Members of the People's Council and of the colonial administration could travel to Holland where its members would have 'a consultative voice' in the deliberations in the States General (Carpentier Alting 1920:73). Yet another suggestion was that Queen Wilhelmina should visit the Indies: 'no other personal deed of Her Majesty could so strengthen the tie between the Indies and the Netherlands as a visit to these territories' (Carpentier Alting 1920:286).

Such recommendations were too outlandish for Dutch politicians to accept them. In the Netherlands Indies no discussion of the 25 November and 3 December motions in the People's Council followed the publication of the Commission's bulky, over 600 page-thick report. The deadline set by the Members of the People's Council who had proposed the November motion, 1921, passed. The appointment of a new Governor General, D. Fock, in September 1920 did not inspire hope either. As Chairman of Parliament he had reacted angrily to the November promises and had praised the sugar industry in the same breath. Moreover, before being appointed Governor General he had left no doubt that 'retention of the Dutch authority in the Indies would be the basis of his policy' (Van Anrooij 2001:135). It is no surprise that at the end of 1921 *De Locomotief* concluded that Fock was less a proponent of political reform than Van Limburg Stirum had been.[28]

The reluctance of Batavia and The Hague to act prompted the founding of a Comité voor de Autonomie voor Indië (Committee for Autonomy for the Indies).[29] Its aim was, to quote its secretary A.F. Folkersma, to create 'an

---

[28] *De Locomotief*, 31-12-1921.
[29] Chairman of the committee was H.C. Kerkkamp, a member of the People's Council. Among the other members of the People's Council who sat on the committee were M.Ng. Dwidjosewojo and A.L. Waworoentoe.

autonomous Indies, in accordance with the principles of the Commission of Inquiry'.[30] The Sarekat Islam, Boedi Oetomo, the Regents' Union, the Indische Sociaal-Democratische Partij, and the National Indische Partij (National Indies Party, the new name borne by the Indische Partij since 1919) were among the organizations the Committee could count on for support. In the opinion of some, the Committee did not go far enough. It did not, as communists were inclined to do, champion the more radical Los van Holland (Separated from Holland) demand. Another not satisfied with mere autonomy was Tjipto Mangoenkoesoemo. At an Autonomy Meeting in Bandung he demanded that the colony should become *lepas dari Nederland*.[31] In all probability taking the militia campaign as an example, the Committee organized meetings all over the Netherlands Indies on 29 January 1922. It also considered the sending to Holland of a deputation to be chaired by Achmad Djajadiningrat, Regent of Serang. There was one big stumbling block. In contrast to the militia campaign the aims of the Committee could not count on any sympathy from the colonial administration. It was intimated to the Regents that Fock did not want them to support the campaign. This spelled the end of any idea of Achmad Djajadiningrat heading the deputation. The Regentenbond distanced itself from the Committee, while the three Regents who had been members of the Committee resigned (Stokvis 1922).

The political participation of Indonesians in the running of the colony and even the freedom to manoeuvre of the nationalist movement suffered a commensurate if not worse fate. November 1918 had made the difference. There had been no revolution in Holland or the Netherlands Indies, and the matter of involvement of Indonesians in the defence of the colony had lost its urgency. In Parliament in April 1919 Wijnkoop stated that after November 1918 'the most rampant reaction' reigned supreme in the Netherlands Indies.[32] Yet other Dutch people showed themselves pleased with the harsher policy embarked upon by the colonial authorities. In his survey of developments in the Netherlands Indies in 1919, the editor of *De Indische Gids*, Van Heekeren, exclaimed that '[f]inally the government of the Netherlands Indies has discarded its lenient attitude and has taken very rigorous action against the zealots who tried to set the population against the legal authorities with their wild theories' (Van Heekeren 1920:96). Grossly misjudging the actual situation, another Dutch person observed in the *Bataviaasch Nieuwsblad* that the indigenous movement was quiet. He attributed this to the fact that 'the iron had entered the soul' of its leaders'.[33] The implication of the actions taken by

---

[30] *De Indische Gids* 1922, I:355.
[31] *De Indische Gids* 1922, I:433.
[32] *Handelingen Tweede Kamer* 1918-19:2069.
[33] *De Indische Gids* 1922, I:48.

Batavia was that the thriving political climate of the 1910s gradually faded away. In keeping with the new policy the Malay-language press also was brought under control. With the Press Ordinance of 1931, popular known as the Press Curb Ordinance, Batavia appropriated the power to deal directly with newspapers which had displeased it, bypassing the judiciary. The ordinance was issued, as is stated in its text, to safeguard public order against undesirable periodicals.

It was not just political repression. The opinions and advice of Indonesians, which Batavia not so long before had explicitly said it welcomed, seemed no longer to count. This new course of action assumed a firmer outline during the term in office of Governor General Fock from March 1921 until September 1926. Fock was well aware of the aversion his policy had aroused in nationalist circles. At the end of his term, he observed that some of the Indonesian intelligentsia had gained the impression that they were no longer taken seriously, that their contribution to the development of the Netherlands Indies was rejected, and that consequently they distrusted the colonial administration (Van Anrooij 2001:1). The final straw which broke the camel's back presented itself just after Fock's term had ended: the ill-fated communist rebellions of November 1926 in West Java and January 1927 in West Sumatra. In spite of the name under which they have gone down in history, they were inspired as much by religious as by communist sympathies. These ushered in the end of what M.C. Ricklefs has called the 'first stage of national revival' (Ricklefs 1981:170). In reaction to the rebellions, the notorious prison camp Boven-Digul was constructed in an inaccessible and insalubrious part of Papua. Any tendency to emerge as a key figure in the nationalist movement became dangerous. Douwes Dekker, Tjipto Mangoenkoesoemo, and Soewardi Soerjaningrat had been banned and 'irresponsible' journalists had been punished, but at times the colonial authorities – the senior ones at least – had regretted that such steps had to be taken and, at least till the middle of 1917, had looked upon the emancipation movement growing among the indigenous population with a certain degree of sympathy. The Governors General and their staff may well have agreed with what Sir Edward Grey, the then British Foreign Secretary, wrote in 1908 to his Envoy in Istanbul, Sir Gerard Lowther: 'Hitherto, wherever we have had Mahometan subjects, we have been able to tell them that the subjects in the countries ruled by the head of their religion were under a despotism which was not a benevolent one; while our Mahometan subjects were under a despotism that was benevolent'.[34] After the Great War, the tolerance and understanding had evaporated. The new leader of the nationalist movement who entered the stage in the 1920s, Soekarno, was arrested in 1929.

---

[34] Grey to Lowther, 31-8-1908, PRO FO 800 79.

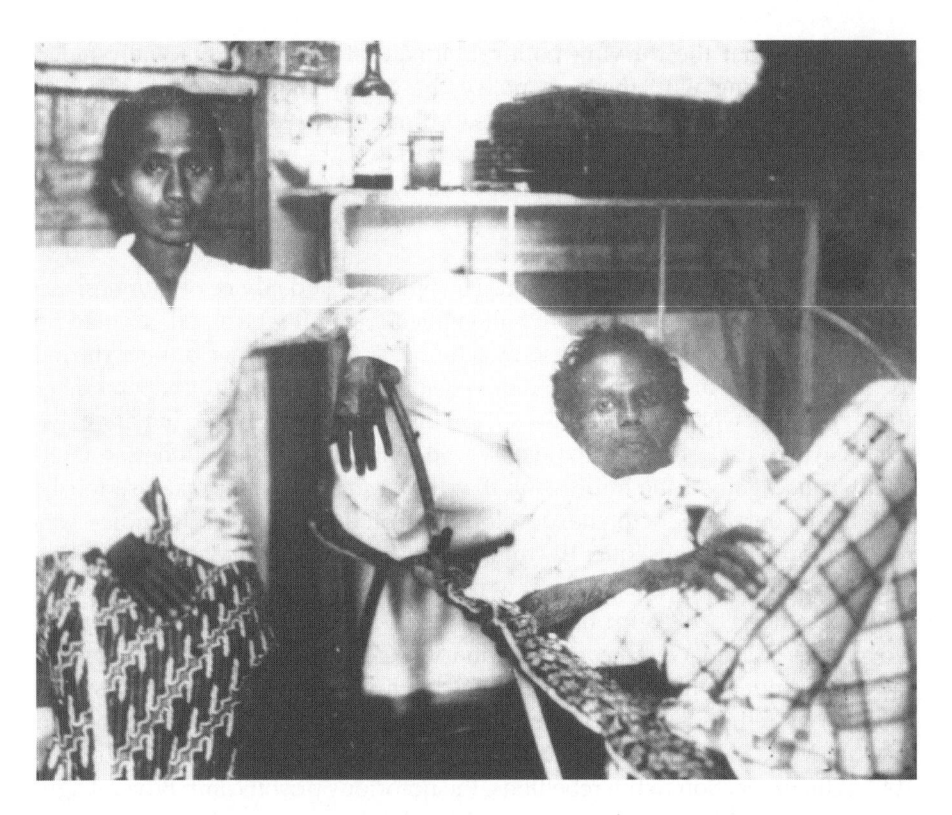

Mas Marco and his wife in the prison camp Boven-Digul, 1932 (KITLV 4452)

He was sentenced to four years' imprisonment in 1930. In December 1931 he was released, only to be re-arrested again in August 1933 and exiled first to Flores and then to Bengkulu. Two other important leaders, Mohammad Hatta and Soetan Sjahrir, were banned to Boven-Digul in February 1934, from where they were moved to Banda in 1936.

Sarekat Islam leaders also found to their cost that the wind was changing. At the end of 1918 Abdoel Moeis was prosecuted. The crux of the charge against him was a speech he had given during a Sarekat Islam meeting in Ciawi earlier in the year. The *Bataviaasch Nieuwsblad*, quoting from a report said to have been made by the Sundanese District Chief of Ciawi, claimed that Abdoel Moeis had made an appeal for civil disobedience. He is alleged to have urged people not to appear when summoned to court. Abdoel Moeis was furious. He called the district chief 'one of those stupid *priyayi* who think that he serves the government by libel'. Abdoel Moeis apologized in *Neratja* after the district chief had written to him saying that his report had differed from the version published in the *Bataviaasch Nieuwsblad*.[35] Nevertheless, the district chief took Abdoel Moeis to court for slander. The result was that Abdoel Moeis was arrested in December. He was accused of contempt of court for refusing to answer a summons. Abdoel Moeis blamed his failure to appear on a misunderstanding. He had asked for the postponement of the court session because he had to address the People's Council. Abdoel Moeis had been sure that his request had been granted, but it turned out that the session had not been adjourned. The court in Buitenzorg sentenced Abdoel Moeis to two months' imprisonment. As so often happened, the Indonesian nationalists had a good case to show how racially biased the administration of justice in the Netherlands Indies was. They contrasted the judicial sentences in the cases against Semaoen, Abdoel Moeis and others against that of one Van Metz van Enghuizen, a planter, who had ordered the binding with barbed wire and the flogging with the same material of a female employee. Van Metz van Enghuizen was sentenced to a mere one month's imprisonment.

Soon Abdoel Moeis got in trouble again. He was once more arrested after a Dutch civil servant was murdered in Toli-Toli in North Sulawesi shortly after Abdoel Moeis had visited the region on a propaganda tour in May 1919 (Ricklefs 1981:165). In 1923 he abandoned national politics and moved to West Sumatra, his native region, where he continued his nationalist campaign. The colonial administration acted promptly and displayed its unforgiving memory. In January 1924 Abdoel Moeis was banned from Sumatra and was not allowed to live anywhere other than in Java and Madura. His 'agitation' in Toli-Toli was one of the reasons adduced by Batavia for taking this decision (Petrus Blumberger 1931:79-80). Abdoel Moeis chose Garut as his residence. He died in 1959.

The other key Sarekat Islam leader, Tjokroaminoto, found himself into trouble a few weeks after the Toli-Toli disturbances when violence erupted in Garut and rumours flew thick and fast that a secret B department of the Sarekat Islam was planning a rebellion. He was arrested for perjury when being cross-examined as a witness in the Garut court cases in August 1921, preventing him from attending an important Sarekat-Islam Congress in Surabaya in October. Tjokroaminoto was released in April 1922 and acquitted in May of that same year. In 1927 he refused an appointment to the People's Council; an indication of the growing rift between the colonial government and the nationalist movement (Petrus Blumberger 1931:75, 312). Tjokroaminoto remained the most important leader of the Sarekat Islam till his death in 1934.

Of the three Indische Partij leaders, Tjipto Mangoenkoesoemo was banned from living in Central and East Java in 1919. Worse was to come for him. After

[35] *Neratja*, 20-12-1918.

the Communist rebellion in Java he was arrested and subsequently was exiled to Banda in 1927, and from there, just before World War Two, to Makassar. In 1940 he was allowed to move to Sukabumi in West Java for health reasons. Tjipto Mangoenkoesoemo died in 1943. Soewardi Soerjaningrat was finally given permission to return to Java in 1919. In 1922 he acquired new fame as the founder of a nationalist school system, Taman Siswa or Garden of Pupils. He also changed his name in Ki Hadjar Dewantara. He died in April 1959, after having served among other functions as the first Indonesian Minister of Education. Douwes Dekker assumed the Indonesian name of Danudirdjo Setiabudhi. Shortly before the Japanese invasion he was arrested on suspicion of being a Japanese spy and was transported to Suriname. He returned to Indonesia in 1946 and died in 1950.

Of the other persons who played such an important role in nationalist movement in the Netherlands Indies during World War One, Semaoen was exiled in mid-1923. He went first to Holland and thereafter moved to Russia. He was active in the Executive Committee of the Communist International. Semaoen returned to Indonesia in 1956, where he died in 1971. Darsono was exiled from the Netherlands Indies in 1926, after which he went to live in Russia, where he became an alternate member of the Executive Committee of the Communist International. In 1935 he moved to Holland. Darsono returned in Indonesia in 1950, He died in 1975.[36] Mas Marco Kartodikromo was arrested again in 1926. He was sent to Boven-Digul where he died in 1932 (Chambert-Loir 1974:205).

The whirligig of time has taken its revenge. The Dutch persons who figure in this book have largely faded like thin air from the consciousness of Indonesia but the merits of the once unsung heroes have been recognized in Indonesia. Abdoel Moeis, Soewardi Soerjaningrat, Tjokroaminoto, Tjipto Mangoenkoesoemo, and Douwes Dekker have been declared national heroes by the Indonesian government. For various reasons communists have never made it to National Heroes in Indonesia.

[36] http:/www.iisg.nl/archives/nl/files/d/10886432.php.

Bibliography

Arkib Negara Malaysia, Kuala Lumpur

Nationaal Archief, The Hague
Ministerie van Koloniën, 1850-1900 (1932), nummer toegang 2.10.02
Ministerie van Koloniën, Openbaar Verbaal, 1901-1953, nummer toegang 2.10.36.04
Ministerie van Koloniën, Geheim Archief, 1901-1940, nummer toegang 2.10.36.051
Ministerie van Koloniën, Memories van overgave, 1852-1962 (1963), nummer toegang 2.10.39

The National Archives, London
Public Record Office

Adam, Ahmat B.
1995 *The vernacular press and the emergence of modern Indonesian consciousness (1855-1913)*. Ithaca, NY: Southeast Asia Program, Cornell University. [Studies on Southeast Asia 17.]

Adviezen
1913 *Adviezen van den Adviseur voor Inlandsche Zaken betreffende de vereeniging 'Sarekat Islam'*. Batavia: Landsdrukkerij.

Anrooij, Francina van
2001 *Groeiend wantrouwen; Onderwijsbeleid in Nederlands-Indië onder gouverneur-generaal D. Fock (1921-1926)*. Amsterdam: Thela Thesis. [PhD thesis, Utrecht University.]

Baal, J. van
1976 'Tussen kolonie en nationale staat; De koloniale staat', in: H.J.M. Claessen, J. Kaayk and R.J.A. Lambregts (eds), *Dekolonisatie en vrijheid; Een sociaal-wetenschappelijke discussie over emancipatieprocessen in de Derde Wereld*, pp. 92-108. Assen: Van Gorcum.

Baars, A. and H. Sneevliet
1991 *Het proces Sneevliet 1917*. Ingeleid en bewerkt door Emile Schwidder en Fritjof Tichelman. Leiden: KITLV Uitgeverij. [Socialisme in Indonesië 2.]

Ban Kah Choon
2001 *Absent history; The untold story of Special Branch operations in Singapore 1915-1942*. Singapore: Horizon Books.

Bauduin, F.
1920   *Het Nederlandsch eskader in Oost-Indië 1914-1916; Benevens eenige beschouwingen over onze marine.* 's-Gravenhage: Nijhoff.

Berghahn, V.R.
1993   *Germany and the approach of war in 1914.* Second edition. Houndmills/ Basingstoke: Macmillan. [The Making of the 20th Century.] [First edition 1973.]

Bescheiden
1913   *Bescheiden betreffende de vereeniging 'De Indische Partij'.* Batavia: Landsdrukkerij.

Beunders, Henri J.G.
1984   *'Weg met de vlootwet!'; De maritieme bewapeningspolitiek van het kabinet-Ruys de Beerenbrouck en het succesvolle verzet daartegen in 1923.* Bergen: Octavo.

Bezwaren
1919   'De bezwaren van het suikersyndicaat tegen de inkrimping', *De Indische Gids* 41, I:668-76.

Boer, G.J. de
1997   *De Nederlandse Blauwpijpers.* Alkmaar: De Alk.

Boeka [pseud. P.C.C. Hansen Jr]
1903   *Zijn wij in staat Oost-Indië te verdedigen?; Leekenbeschouwing over een vraag van algemeen Nederlandsch belang.* Amsterdam: Van Rossen.
1909   'Indie Weerbaar', *De Indische Gids* 31, I:1441-7.

Bootsma, N.A.
1986   *Buren in de koloniale tijd; De Philippijnen onder Amerikaans bewind en de Nederlandse, Indische en Indonesische reacties daarop, 1898-1942.* Dordrecht/Riverton: Foris. [KITLV, Verhandelingen 119.]

Bosma, Ulbe
1995   *Karel Zaalberg, het Bataviaasch Nieuwsblad en de Indo-europese emancipatie (1880-1930).* [PhD thesis, Leiden University.]

Bossenbroek, Martin
1996   *Holland op zijn breedst; Indië en Zuid-Afrika in de Nederlandse cultuur omstreeks 1900.* Amsterdam: Bert Bakker.

Browne E.G.
1904   'Pan-Islamism', in: Frederick Alexander Kirkpatrick (ed.), *Lectures on the history of the nineteenth century; Delivered at the Cambridge Extension Summer Meeting August 1902.* Cambridge: Cambridge University Press.

Buettner, Elizabeth
2004   *Empire families; Britons and late imperial India.* Oxford: Oxford University Press.

Burger, D.H.
1975   *Sociologisch-economische geschiedenis van Indonesia.* Historiografische introductie door J.S. Wigboldus. 's-Gravenhage: Nijhoff. Two vols.

Bryan, A.
1918   'Over de wenschelijkheid van oprichting in Ned.-Indië van een centraal bureau voor aanschaffing van alle artikelen benoodigd voor het

Gouvernement van Ned.-Indië en zoo nodig ook voor Gewesten en Gemeenten', *De Indische Gids* 40, II:917-31.

Bijl de Vroe, C.L.M.
1980   *Rondom de Buitenzorgse troon; Indisch dagboek van C.L.M. Bijl de Vroe*. Ingeleid en bewerkt door Marian Schouten. Met een woord vooraf door A. Alberts. Haarlem: Fibula Van Dishoeck.

Carpentier Alting, J.H. (ed.)
1920   *Verslag van de commissie tot herziening van de staatsinrichting van Nederlandsch-Indië, ingesteld bij gouvernementsbesluit van den 17en December 1918 no. 1*. Weltevreden: Landsdrukkerij.

Carpentier Alting, J.H. and W. de Cock Buning
1928   *The Netherlands and the World War*. New Haven: Yale University Press.

Casserly, Gordon
1903   *The land of the Boxers or China under the allies*. London: Longmans, Green.

Chambert-Loir, Henri
1974   'Mas Marco Kartodikromo (c. 1890-1932) ou l'éducation politique', in: *Littératures contemporaines de l'Asie du Sud-Est; Colloque du XXIXe Congrès International des Orientalistes; Organisé par P.-B. Lafont et D. Lombard*, pp. 203-14. Paris: l'Asiathèque. [Congrès International des Orientalistes 29.]

Changing economy
1975   *Changing economy in Indonesia; A selection of statistical source material from the early 19th century up to 1940. Vol.1: Indonesia's export crops 1816-1940*. The Hague: Nijhoff.
1991   *Changing economy in Indonesia; A selection of statistical source material from the early 19th century up to 1940. Vol. 12a: General tarde statistics 1822-1940*. W.L. Korthals Altes. Amsterdam: Royal Tropical Institute (KIT).
1992   *Changing economy in Indonesia; A selection of statistical source material from the early 19th century up to 1940. Vol. 12b: Regional patterns in foreign trade 1911-1940*. Adrian Clemens, J. Thomas Lindblad and Jeroen Touwen. Amsterdam: Royal Tropical Institute (KIT).

Clarke, E.M.
1918   'Bereiding van kleurstoffen; Een belangrijke kwestie voor Oost- en West-Indië', *De Indische Gids* 40, I:528-32.

Clemens, Adrian, J. Thomas Lindblad and Jeroen Touwen *see Changing economy* 1992

Colenbrander, H.T.
1920   'De internationale positie van Nederland tijdens, vóór en na den Wereldoorlog', in: H. Brugmans (ed.), *Nederland in den oorlogstijd; De geschiedenis van Nederland en van Nederlandsch- Indië tijdens den oorlog van 1914 tot 1919, voor zoover zij met dien oorlog verband houdt*, pp. 103-33. Amsterdam: Elsevier.

Cramer, P.J.S.
1916-17   'Onze landbouw en het gebrek aan scheepsruimte', *Koloniale Studiën* 1-1:402-11.

Dorp, E.C. van
1920 'Handel en nijverheid', in: H. Brugmans (ed.), *Nederland in den oorlogstijd; De geschiedenis van Nederland en van Nederlandsch- Indië tijdens den oorlog van 1914 tot 1919, voor zoover zij met dien oorlog verband houdt*, pp. 191-248. Amsterdam: Elsevier.

Douwes Dekker, E.F.E.
1911a 'Parool', *Het Tijdschrift* 1-6(15-11-1911):165-72.
1911b 'Brownings', *Het Tijdschrift* 1-8(15-12-1911):237-42.
1912a 'Verschuivingen', *Het Tijdschrift* 1-13(1-3-1912):409-14.
1912b 'Jezus', *Het Tijdschrift* 1-14(15-3-1912):437-43.
1912c 'Probleem', *Het Tijdschrift* 1-15(1-4-1912):469-74.
1912d 'Oogst', *Het Tijdschrift* 2-1(1-9-1912):2-8.
1912e 'Nationalisme', *Het Tijdschrift* 2-8(15-12-1912):247-54.
1912f 'Daadpolitiek', *Het Tijdschrift* 2-24(15-8-1912):745-52.

Douwes Dekker, E.F.E., Tjipto Mangoenkoesoemo and Soewardi Soerjaningrat
1913a *Onze verbanning; Publicatie der officiëele bescheiden, toegelicht met verslagen en commentaren, betrekking hebbende op de Gouvernements-Besluiten van den 18en Augustus 1913, nos. 1a en 2a, regelende de toepassing van artikel 47 R.R. (interneering) op E.F.E. Douwes Dekker, Tjipto Mangoenkoesoemo en R.M. Soewardi Soerjaningrat*. Schiedam: De Indiër.
1913b *Mijmeringen van Indiërs over Hollands feestvierderij in de kolonie*. N.p.: Comité Boemi Poetra. [Vlugschriften van het Comité Boemi Poetra 2.]

Drooglever, P.J.
1980 *De Vaderlandse Club, 1929-1942; Totoks en de Indische politiek*. Franeker: Wever.

Duitschers
1885 'De Duitschers op Nieuw-Guinea', *Tijdschrift voor Nederlandsch Indië* 14, II:42-7.

Dijk, Kees van
1997 'Sarong, jubbah and trousers; Appearances as a means of distinction and discrimination', in: Henk Schulte Nordholt (ed.), *Outward appearances; Dressing state and society in Indonesia*, pp. 39-83. Leiden: KITLV Press. [Proceedings 4.]

Eenige
n.d. *Eenige groepen van cijfers welke een aanduiding geven omtrent den economischen toestand van de inlandsche bevolking in de laatste jaren*. N.p.: n.n.

Egbert
1902 *Het in verdedigbaren staat brengen van Nederl. Oost-Indië*. 's-Gravenhage: Couvée.

Elout, C.K.
1920 'De Nederlandsche oorlogspsyche', in: H. Brugmans (ed.), *Nederland in den oorlogstijd; De geschiedenis van Nederland en van Nederlandsch- Indië tijdens den oorlog van 1914 tot 1919, voor zoover zij met dien oorlog verband houdt*, pp. 353-69. Amsterdam: Elsevier.

Evans, D.H.
1987 'The "meanings" of Pan-Islamism; The growth of international con-

sciousness among the Muslims of India and Indonesia in the late nineteenth and early twentieth century', *Itinerario* 11-1:15-35.

Feiten
1916   *Feiten en maatregelen in verband met den Europeeschen oorlog welke voor het economisch leven van Nederlandsch-Indië van belang waren.* Batavia: Papyrus. [Publicaties van de Afdeeling Nijverheid en Handel.]

Ferguson, Niall
2001   *Der falsche Krieg; Der Erste Weltkrieg und das 20. Jahrhundert.* Münster: Deutscher Taschenbuch Verlag.

Fokkens, F
[1916]   *De pensioenbond van Indische ambtenaren en de gevraagde waarborg voor de uitbetaling onder alle omstandigheden van de pensioenen der Indische landsdienaren.* N.p.: Korthuis.

Fromberg, P.H.
1918   *Het geval Soewardi.* 's-Gravenhage: Indonesische Persbureau.

Galli, Gottfried
1915   *Dschihad; Der Heilige Krieg des Islams und seine Bedeutung im Weltkriege unter besonderer Berücksichtigung der Interessen Deutschlands.* Freiburg im Breisgau: Troemer.

Gedenkboek
1924   *Gedenkboek der Nederlandsche Handel-Maatschappij, 1824-1924.* Amsterdam: De Maatschappij. [Door de directie uitgegeven op den 29sten Maart 1924 ter gelegenheid van het honderd-jarig bestaan der Maatschappij.]

Gerdus Oosterbeek, W.F.
1927   'Post-, telegraaf- en telefoondienst', in: *Encyclopædie van Nederlandsch-Indië.* Vijfde deel, pp. 330-44. 's-Gravenhage: Nijhoff, Leiden: Brill.

Gerritzen, J.
1917   'Verouderde opvattingen', *Koloniale Studiën* 1-2:410-4.

Gestel, Magda van
1987   'Japanse spionage in Nederlands-Indië; De oprichting van de politieke inlichtingendienst (PID) in 1916', in: Elsbeth Locher-Scholten (ed.), *Beelden van Japan in het vooroorlogse Nederlands Indie; Resultaten van een doctoraal-werkcollege*, pp. 89-114. Leiden: Werkgroep Europese Expansie.

Geuns, M. van
1918   'Een diep-onrechtvaardige straf', *De Indische Gids* 40, I:211-3.

Glissenaar, Frans
1999   *D.D.; Het leven van E.F.E. Douwes Dekker.* Hilversum: Verloren.

Gobée, E and C. Adriaanse
1957-1965   *Ambtelijke adviezen van C. Snouck Hurgronje 1889-1936.* 's-Gravenhage: Nijhoff. Three vols. [Rijks Geschiedkundige Publicatiën, Kleine Serie 33, 34, 35.]

Greve, W.R. de
1913   *Het rapport van de Staatscommissie voor de Verdediging van Nederlandsch Indië.* 's-Gravenhage: Nijhoff.

Gründer, Horst
1999 '... da und dort ein junges Duetschland gründen'; Rassismus, Kolonien und kolonialer Gedanke vom 16. bis zum 20. Jahrhundert. Eingeleitet und herausgegeben von Horst Gründer. München: Deutscher Taschenbuch Verlag.

Haas, K. de
2002 'Het stoomschip Noordam liep twee keer op een mijn', in: Hans Andriessen, Martin Ros en Perry Pierik (eds), De grote oorlog; Kroniek 1914-1918, pp. 162-76. Soesterberg: Aspekt.

Haastert, W.K.S.
1916 De Sarikat Islam. Weltevreden: Albrecht.

Halpern, Paul G.
1994 A naval history of World War I. London: UCL Press.

Han Tiauw Tjong
1919 'De Chineezen op Java en het Nederlandsch onderdaanschap', De Indische Gids 41, II:937-58.

Handelingen
 Verslag der handelingen van de Staten Generaal gedurende de zitting van [...]. 's-Gravenhage: Algemeene Landsdrukkerij.

Harper, R.W.E. and Harry Miller
1984 Singapore mutiny. Singapore/Oxford/New York: Oxford University Press.

Haushofer, Karl
1913 Dai Nihon; Betrachtungen über Groß-Japans Wehrkraft, Welststellung und Zukunft. Berlin: Mittler.

Heekeren, E.A.A. van
1914 'Heeft Engeland aan Japan de Nederlandsche koloniën beloofd?', De Indische Gids 36, II:1660-3.
1918a 'Nederlandsch Oost-Indië in 1917', De Indische Gids 40, I:191-203.
1918b 'Nederland en Japan', De Indische Gids 40, I:513-6.
1919a 'Sneevliet verbannen', De Indische Gids 41, I:65-9.
1919b 'Nederlandsch Oost-Indië in 1918', De Indische Gids 41, I:137-47.
1920 'Nederlandsch Oost-Indië in 1919', De Indische Gids 42, I:97-108.

Helfferich, Emil
1917 'Het jaarverslag van de Javasche Bank over 1916-1917', Koloniale Studiën 12:506-16.
1918 'Het jaarverslag der Javasche Bank over 1917-1918', Koloniale Studiën 2-2:465-86.
1921 Die Wirtschaft Niederländisch Indiens im Weltkriege und heute. Hamburg: Friederichsen. [Vortrag gehalten in der Geographischen Gesellschaft in Hamburg am 7. Oktober 1920.]
1948 Ein Leben. Hamburg: Dulk.
1967 Zur Geschichte der Firmen Behn, Meyer & Co. gegründet in Singapore am 1. November 1840 und Arnold Otto Meyer gegründet in Hamburg am 1. Juni 1857. Band 2: [1863-1933]. Hamburg: Christians.

Helsdingen, W.H. van
1926 De Volksraad en de Indische staatsregeling. Weltevreden: Visser.

Heutsz Jr., J.B. van
1917a   *Indië Weerbaar; Wien de goden verderven willen slaan zij met blindheid*. Rotterdam: Brusse.
1917b   *De invloed van den oorlog op onze koloniën*. Purmerend: Muusses.

Hogesteeger, G. (ed.)
1995   *Naar de Gordel van Smaragd; De postverbindingen tussen Nederland en Nederlands-Indië, 1602-1940*. Den Haag: Sea Press and Het Nederlands PTT Museum.

Hopkirk, Peter
1994   *Like hidden fire; The plot to bring down the British empire*. New York, Tokyo, London: Kodansha International.

Houwink ten Cate, J.
1995   *De mannen van de daad en Duitsland, 1919-1939; Het Hollandse zakenleven en de vooroorlogse buitenlandse politiek*. Den Haag: SDU.

Idenburg, A.W.F and A.C.D. de Graeff
1920   'Nederlandsch-Indië onder den invloed van den oorlog', in: H. Brugmans (ed.), *Nederland in den oorlogstijd; De geschiedenis van Nederland en van Nederlandsch- Indië tijdens den oorlog van 1914 tot 1919, voor zoover zij met dien oorlog verband houdt*, pp. 370-400. Amsterdam: Elsevier.

Jong, C. de
1979   'Lotgevallen van drie broers Douwes Dekker en de Anglo-Boerenoorlog 1899-1902. I: Ernest Francois Eugène Douwes Dekker', *Historia; Amptelike orgaan van die Historiese Genootskap van Suid-Afrika* 24:32-43.

Kartodikromo, Mas Marco
[2000]   *Student Hidjo; Sebuah novel*. Yogyakarta: Yayasan Benteng Budaya. [First published 1919.]

Kol, H.H. van
1916   *De ontwikkeling der groot-industrie in Japan; Rapport samengesteld ingevolge opdracht van den minister van kolonien. Deel. 1*. 's-Gravenhage: Bootsma.

Koch, D.M.G.
1960   *Batig slot; Figuren uit het oude Indië*. Amsterdam: De Brug-Djambatan.

Korthals Altes, W.L. see *Changing economy* 1991

Koschitzky, Max von
1887-88   *Deutsche Colonialgeschichte*. Leipzig: Frohberg. Two vols.

Krishnavarma, Shyamaji
1911   'Indië, tweede fase van het despotisme', *Het Tijdschrift* 1-4(15-10-1911):106-9.

Kuitenbrouwer, M.
1985   *Nederland en de opkomst van het moderne imperialisme; Koloniën en buitenlandse politiek: 1870-1902*. Amsterdam: De Bataafsche Leeuw.

Laffan, Michael
2006   'The prince has not asked what Sayyid Abdallah does .... Rethinking al-Imam's critique of *tariqa* Sufism, Singapore 1908'. [Manuscript.]

's-Lands welvaart
1913   *'s-Lands welvaart in gevaar! Een ernstig woord tot het Nederlandsche volk: Beschouwingen naar aanleiding van het rapport van de Staatscommissie voor*

de Verdediging van Nederlandsch-Indië. Bussum: Märkelbach. [Nederlandsche Vereeniging Onze Vloot.]

Larson, George D.
1987 *Prelude to revolution; Palaces and politics in Surakarta, 1912-1942*. Dordrecht/Cinnaminson: Foris. [KITLV, Verhandelingen 124.]

Later, J.F.H.A.
'De Inlandsche en Chinesche pers', in: L.F. van Gent, W.A.Penard and D.A. Rinkes (eds), *Gedenkboek voor Nederlandsch-Indië; Ter gelegenheid van het regeeringsjubileum van H.M. de Koningin, 1898-1923*, pp. 58-60. Batavia-Leiden: Kolff.

Lauterbach, Julius
1918 *1000 £ belooning dood of levend; Avontuurlijke vlucht door de Hollandsche koloniën van den voormaligen prijsofficier van de 'Emden'*. Amsterdam, Rotterdam: Van Langenhuysen. [Originally published as *1000 £ Kopfpreis tot oder lebendig*, Berlin: Scherl, 1917.]

Ligthart, Th.
1923 'De import en exporthandel', in: L.F. van Gent, W.A.Penard and D.A. Rinkes (eds),
Gedenkboek voor Nederlandsch-Indië; Ter gelegenheid van het regeeringsjubileum van H.M. de Koningin, 1898-1923, pp. 428-36. Batavia-Leiden: Kolff.

Lindblad, J. Thomas
1994 'The contribution of foreign trade to colonial state formation in Indonesia 1900-1930', in: Robert Cribb (ed.), *The late colonial state in Indonesia; Political and economic foundations of the Netherlands Indies, 1880-1942*, pp. 93-116. Leiden: KITLV Press. [Verhandelingen 163.]

Locher-Scholten, E.B.
1981 *Ethiek in fragmenten; Vijf studies over koloniaal denken en doen van Nederlanders in de Indonesische archipel, 1877-1942*. Utrecht: HES. [PhD thesis, University Leiden.]
1994 *Sumatraans sultanaat en koloniale staat; De relatie Djambi-Batavia (1830-1907) en het Nederlands imperialisme*. Leiden: KITLV Press. [Verhandelingen 161.]

Loon, F.H. van
1919 *Pest en pestbestrijding*. Amsterdam: Koloniaal Instituut. [Mededeeling Afdeeling Tropische Hygiëne 7.]

Lovink, H.J.
1919 *Les Indes Néerlandaises pendant la Guerre Mondiale*. La Haye: Nijhoff. [Réimprimé de *Grotius; Annuaire international* pour 1919.]

Lulofs, C.
1919 *De voedselvoorziening van Nederlandsch-Indië*. Prae-advies van C. Lulofs met medewerking van L. van Vuuren. Batavia: Kolff. [Vereeniging voor Studie van Koloniaal Maatschappelijke Vraagstukken 6.]

M.
1922 'Hr. Ms. Pantserschip "Koningin Regentes", 1900-1922', *Ons Element* 1-52(30-12-1922):842-6.

MacMillan, Margaret
2001	*Peacemakers; The Paris Conference of 1919 and its attempts to end war*. London: John Murray.

McVey, Ruth T.
1965	*The rise of Indonesian Communism*. Ithaca, NY: Cornell University Press.

Mandere, H.Ch.C.J. van der
[1922]	*Het vredesverdrag van Versailles en de daarmede verbandhoudende verdragen van St. Germain, Trianon, Sèvres en Neuilly; Korte schets van den inhoud dezer verdragen; Bijgewerkt met de dienaangaande gegeven beslissingen en uitvoerings-maatregelen*. Hillegom: Editio.

Mandal, Sumit K.
1997	'Arab organizations and society in early twentieth century Java; The tacit socialization of leadership roles'. Paper, The Arabs in South-East Asia (1870-1990), International Workshop on South-East Asian Studies 12, Leiden, 8-12 December.

Manen, C.A. van
1935	*De Nederlandsche Overzee Trustmaatschappij; Middelpunt van het verkeer van onzijdig Nederland met het buitenland tijdens den Wereldoorlog*. 's-Gravenhage: Nijhoff.

Mangoenkoesoemo, Tjipto
1915	*Ik beschuldig, ...* N.p.: n.n.
1917	'Insulinde's politiek programma', *Koloniale Studiën* 1(Extra politiek nummer):43-66.

Mees, A.C.
1915	'Verbod van rijstuitvoer uit Nederlandsch-Indië', *De Indische Gids* 37, I:457-66.

Menezes, S.L.
1997	'Race, caste, mutiny and discipline in the Indian army from its origins to 1947', in: A.J. Guy and P.B. Boyden (eds), *Soldiers of the Raj; The Indian army 1600-1947*, pp. 100-17. London: National Army Museum.

Miert, Hans van
1995	*Een koel hoofd en een warm hart; Nationalisme, javanisme en jeugdbeweging in Nederlands-Indië, 1918-1930*. Amsterdam: De Bataafsche Leeuw.

Mohr, F.W.
1948	'Emil Helfferichs Abschied von Niederländisch-Indien', in: Emil Helfferich, *Ein Leben*, pp. 274-8. [Originally published in *Hamburger Nachrichten*, 21-9-1928.]

Morriën, Joop
1984	*'Aroen'; Jan Stam, rebel in Indonesie en Nederland*. Amsterdam: Pegasus.

Mücke, H. von
1916	*Ayesha*. Berlin: Scherl.

Mulders, J.
1987	'De ambitie van Japan; Nederlands-Indië en Japan tijdens de Eerste Wereldoorlog, een bronnenonderzoek', in: Elsbeth Locher-Scholten (ed.), *Beelden van Japan in het vooroorlogse Nederlands Indie; Resultaten*

van een doctoraal-werkcollege, pp. 114-40. Leiden: Werkgroep Europese Expansie.

Nagazumi, Akira
1989 Bangkitnya nasionalisme Indonesia; Budi Utomo 1908-1918. Jakarta: Grafitipers. [Seri Terjemahan KITLV-LIPI.; Originally published as *The dawn of Indonesian nationalism; The early years of Budi Utomo 1908-1918*, Tokyo: Institute of Developing Economies, 1972.]

Neerland's ondergang
1914 *Neerland's ondergang kan en moet voorkomen worden; Een toelichting en een vervolg op de brochure 's Lands welvaart in gevaar!'*. N.p.: n.n. [Nederlandsche Vereeniging Onze Vloot.]

Niemeijer, A.C.
1972 *The Khilafat movement in India, 1919-1924*. The Hague: Nijhoff. [KITLV, Verhandelingen 62.]

Nierop, F.S. van
1914 'De financiëele crisis', *De Gids* 78-4:348-68.

Nota Douwes Dekker
1913 *Nota betreffende de geschriften van Douwes Dekker*. Batavia: Landsdrukkerij.

Oei Kiauw Pik
1919 'De Chineezen en het Nederlandsch onderdaanschap', *De Indische Gids* 41, II:959-67.

Ontwikkeling
1917 *De ontwikkeling van de Ned. Indische nijverheid gedurende den oorlog*. Batavia: Mercurius. [Departement van Landbouw, Nijverheid en Handel, Nederlandsch-Indië, Publicaties van de Afdeeling Nijverheid en Handel 4.]

Opkomst
1967 *De opkomst van de nationalistische beweging in Nederlands-Indië; Een bronnenpublikatie*. Bewerkt door S.L. van der Wal. Groningen: Wolters. [Uitgaven van de Commissie voor Bronnenpublicatie betreffende de Geschiedenis van Nederlandsch-Indië 1900-1942 van het Historisch Genootschap (gevestigd te Utrecht) 4.]

Othman, Muhammad Redzuan
1997 'Arab political activities and colonial reactions in Malaya before World War II'. Paper, The Arabs in South-East Asia (1870-1990), International Workshop on South-East Asian Studies 12, Leiden, 8-12 December.

Pakenham, Thomas
1994 *The Boer War*. London: Abacus.

Palmer, Alan
1993 *The decline and fall of the Ottoman empire*. London: John Murray.

Palte, J.G.L. and G.J. Tempelman
1978 *Indonesië; Een sociaal-geografisch overzicht*. Tweede herziene druk. Bussen: Romen. [Panorama van de Wereld.] [First edition 1975.]

Perthus, Max (ed)
1953   *Voor vrijheid en socialisme; Gedenkboek van het Sneevliet Herdenkingscomité.*
            N.p.: n.n.
Petrus Blumberger, J.Th.
1931   *De nationalistische beweging in Nederlandsch-Indië.* Haarlem: Tjeenk
            Willink.
Poeze, Harry A.
1986   *In het land van de overheerser; Deel 1: Indonesiërs in Nederland 1600-1950.*
            Met bijdragen van Cees van Dijk en Inge van der Meulen. Dordrecht/
            Cinnaminson: Foris. [KITLV, Verhandelingen 100.]
1994   'Political intelligence in the Netherlands Indies', in: Robert Cribb (ed.),
            *The late colonial state in Indonesia; Political and economic foundations of the
            Netherlands Indies, 1880-1942*, pp. 229-47. Leiden: KITLV Press. [Verhandelingen 163.]
Proceedings
            Proceedings of the Legislative Council of the Straits Settlements. Singapore:
            Government Printing Office.
Raadt, O.L.E. de
1919   'Pestbestrijding', in: *Encyclopædie van Nederlandsch-Indië.* Derde deel, pp.
            391-3. 's-Gravenhage: Nijhoff, Leiden: Brill.
Radjiman
1917   'De vertegenwoordiging der Inlanders', *Koloniale Studiën* 1-3:147-55.
Rapport
1913   *Rapport van de staatscommissie voor de verdediging van Nederlandsch-Indië.*
            's Gravenhage: Bootsma.
Ratu Langie
1917   'Uit de Minahassa', *Koloniaal Tijdschrift* 6-2:1329-47.
Regeering
[1919]   *De regeering en de suiker.* [Soerabaja]: n.n. [Overdruk uit het *Soerabaiasch
            Handelsblad* van Dinsdag 31 december 1918 en *De Indische Financier* van
            Vrijdag 10 Januari 1919.]
Reigersberg Versluys, J.C. van
1917a   *Fabrieksnijverheid in Nederlandsch-Indië.* Batavia: Ruygrok.
1917b   *Fabricage van kunstmest in Nederlandsch-Indië.* Batavia: Landsdrukkerij.
            [Mededeelingen van de Commissie tot Ontwikkeling van de Fabrieksnijverheid in Nederlandsch-Indië 3.]
1917c   *Fabricage van papier en aanverwante halfstoffen in Nederlandsch-Indië.*
            Batavia: Landsdrukkerij. [Mededeelingen van de Commissie tot
            Ontwikkeling van de Fabrieksnijverheid in Nederlandsch-Indië 2.]
Renesse, A.M.W. van
1920   'Nederlandsch-Indië en het buitenland', *De Indische Gids* 42, I:315-20.
Rhemrev, W.V.
1917   *Indië Weerbaar; Rede uitgesproken door den Kapitein der Inf. van het O.I.L.*
            N.p.: n.n.

Ricklefs, M.C.
1981 A history of modern Indonesië, c.1300 to the present. London, Basingstoke: Macmillan.

Rinkes, D.A., N van Zalinge and J.W. de Roever (eds)
1925 Het Indische boek der zee. Met medewerking van vele deskundigen. Weltevreden: Volkslectuur.

Rottier, J.
1917 Waar moet het koninklijk instituut voor hooger technisch onderwijs komen? [Bandoeng]: Comité van Actie.

Rijst
1919 'Rijst', in: Encyclopædie van Nederlandsch-Indië. Derde deel, pp. 648-66. 's-Gravenhage: Nijhoff, Leiden: Brill

Sandberg, C.G..S.
1914 Indië verloren, rampspoed geboren. 's-Gravenhage: Daamen.

Sareen, T.R.
1995 Secret documents on Singapore mutiny 1915. New Delhi: Mounto.

Sarekat Islam
1975 Sarekat Islam lokal. Dihimpun oleh Sartono Kartodirdjo. Jakarta: [Arsip Nasional Republik Indonesia; Penerbitan Sumber-Sumber Sejarah 7.]

Sarekat-Islam Congres
1916 Sarekat-Islam Congres (1e Nationaal Congres) 17-24 Juni 1916 te Bandoeng. Uitgebracht door G.A.J. Hazeu. Batavia: Landsdrukkerij. [Behoort bij de geheime missive van den wd Adviseur voor Inlandsche Zaken dd. 29 September 1916 no 226.]

1919 Sarekat-Islam Congres; (3e Nationaal Congres) 29 Sept.-6 Oct. 1918 te Soerabaja. Uitgebracht door G.A.J. Hazeu. Batavia: Landsdrukkerij. [Behoort bij de geheime missive van den Regeeringscommissaris voor Inlandsche en Arabische Zaken van 9 December 1918 no 599.]

Schepenvorderingswet
1917 De schepenvorderingswet en het belang van de scheepvaart voor de economische toestand van Nederlandsch-Indië. Weltevreden: Albrecht. [Vereeniging voor Studie van Koloniaal-Maatschappelijke Vraagstukken 1.]

Semaoen
1918 'Anti-Indië Weerbaar, anti-militie en 't 3e nationaal congres van de Sarekat-Islam', in: Sarekat-Islam Congres; (3e Nationaal Congres) 29 Sept.-6 Oct. 1918 te Soerabaja. Uitgebracht door G.A.J. Hazeu, pp. 81-95. Batavia: Landsdrukkerij.

2000 Hikayat Kadiroen. Sebuah novel. Yogyakarta: Yayasan Bentang Budaya. [Originally published in 1920.]

Setiabuddhi, D.
1950 70 jaar konsekwent. Bandung: Nix.

Shennan, Margaret
2000 Out in the midday sun; The British in Malaya, 1880-1960. London: John Murray.

Shiraishi, Takashi
1990   *An age in motion; Popular radicalism in Java, 1912-1926*. Ithaca/London: Cornell University Press.
Smurthwaite, D.
1997   'The Indian army in the era of two world wars', in: A.J. Guy and P.B. Boyden (eds), *Soldiers of the Raj; The Indian army 1600-1947*, pp. 162-79. London: National Army Museum.
Snapper, F.
2002   'De bedreiging door Duitsland van Nederland in de Eerste Wereldoorlog', in: Hans Andriessen, Martin Ros en Perry Pierik (eds), *De grote oorlog; Kroniek 1914-1918; Essays over de Eerste Wereldoorlog*, pp. 284-302. Soesterberg: Aspekt.
Snouck Hurgronje, C
1915   *Nederland en de Islâm*. Tweede vermeerderde druk. Leiden: Brill. [First edition 1911.]
1917   'Een belangrijk document betreffende den Heilige Oorlog van den Islam (1914) en eene officiele correctie', *Bijdragen tot de Taal-, Land- en Volkenkunde* 73:255-85.
Soebagijo I.N.
1981   *Jagat wartawan Indonesia*. Jakarta: Gunung Agung.
Soeratman, Darsiti
1981   *Ki Hajar Dewantara*. Jakarta: Proyek Inventarisasi dan Dokumentasi Sejarah Indonesia, Direktorat Sejarah dan Nilai Tradisional, Departemen Pendidikan dan Kebudayaan,
Stockwell, A.J.
1988   'The war and the British Empire', in: John Turner (ed.), *Britain and the First World War*, pp. 36-53. London: Unwin Hayman.
Stokvis, J.E.
1922   'Autonomie voor Indië', *De Socialistische Gids* 7:397-404.
Storss, Ronald
1937   *Orientations*. London: Nicholson and Watson
Taselaar, Arjen
1998   *De Nederlandse koloniale lobby; Ondernemers en de Indische politiek, 1914-1940*. Leiden: Research School CNWS. [CNWS Publications 62.]
Teitler, G..
1986   *Dagboekaantekeningen van vice-admiraal F. Pinke, commandant zeemacht in Nederlands-Indië, 1914-1916*. Bewerkt door G. Teitler. 's-Gravenhage: Nijhoff. [Rijksgeschiedkundige Publicatiën, Kleine Serie 60.]
1988   *Anatomie van de Indische defensie; Scenario's, plannen, beleid, 1892-1920*. PhD thesis, Leiden University.
Thijs, J.D.
1965   *De invloed van de opkomst van Japan en van de Japanse overwinning op Rusland in Azië*. Kampen: Kok.
Tichelman, Fritjof
1974   *Henk Sneevliet, 1888-1942; Een politieke biografie*. Amsterdam: Van Gennep. [Kritiese Bibliotheek.]

1985   *Socialisme in Indonesië; Bronnenpublicatie; De Indische Sociaal-Democratische Vereeniging; Deel 1 1897-1917*. Dordrecht/Cinnaminson: Foris. [KITLV.]

Timmermans, M.M.H.
2002   'De inbeslagname van de Nederlandse koopvaardijvloot door de geallieerden in 1918', in: Hans Andriessen, Martin Ros en Perry Pierik (eds), *De grote oorlog; Kroniek 1914-1918; Essays over de Eerste Wereldoorlog*, pp. 177-97. Soesterberg: Aspekt.

Touwen, Jeroen
2001   *Extremes in the Archipelago; Trade and economic development in the Outer Islands of Indonesia, 1900-1942*. Leiden: KITLV Press. [Verhandelingen 190.]

Treub, M.W.F.
1920   'De economische toestand van Nederland gedurende den oorlog', in: H. Brugmans (ed.), *Nederland in den oorlogstijd; De geschiedenis van Nederland en van Nederlandsch-Indië tijdens den oorlog van 1914 tot 1919, voor zoover zij met dien oorlog verband houdt*, pp. 134-90. Amsterdam: Elsevier.

Van Niel, Robert
1984   *The emergence of the modern Indonesian elite*. Dordrecht/Cinnaminson: Foris. [KITLV, Reprints on Indonesia.]

Verbeke, P.
2002   'De terechtstelling van Captain Fryatt in 1916', in: Hans Andriessen, Martin Ros en Perry Pierik (eds), *De grote oorlog; Kroniek 1914-1918; Essays over de Eerste Wereldoorlog*, pp. 220-51. Soesterberg: Aspekt.

Verboom, J.J.
1987   'Het Japanse gevaar in opkomst; Beelden van Japan in de politiek en de pers van Nederlands-Indië in de priode 1904 tot en met 1914', in: Elsbeth Locher-Scholten (ed.), *Beelden van Japan in het vooroorlogse Nederlands Indie; Resultaten van een doctoraal-werkcollege*, pp. 51-89. Leiden: Werkgroep Europese Expansie.

Verslag
1917   'Verslag omtrent den toestand der Nederlandsche Handel-Maatschappij en haar handelingen in het boekjaar 1916', *De Indische Gids* 39, II:1119-27.
1920   *Verslag van de commissie tot herziening van de staatsinrichting van Nederlandsch-Indië; Ingesteld bij Gouvernementsbesluit van den 17en December 1918 no 1*. Weltevreden: Landsdrukkerij.

Vervolg
1913   *Vervolg der nota betreffende de geschriften van Douwes Dekker*. Batavia: Landsdrukkerij.

Veur, Paul W. van der
1955   *Introduction to a socio-political study of the Eurasians of Indonesia*. PhD thesis, Cornell University, Ithaca, NY
2006   *The lion and the gadfly; Dutch colonialism and the spirit of E.F.E. Douwes Dekker*. Leiden: KITLV Press. [Verhandelingen 228.]

Visser, C.W. de
1913   *De verdediging van Ned.-Indië tegen het Oost-Aziatisch gevaar; Eene aanvulling op en eene beoordeling van het verslag der staatscommissie.* Haarlem: Tjeenk Willink.

Vissering, G.
1920   'Geld- en credietwezen', in: H. Brugmans (ed.), *Nederland in den oorlogstijd; De geschiedenis van Nederland en van Nederlandsch-Indië tijdens den oorlog van 1914 tot 1919, voor zoover zij met dien oorlog verband houdt,* pp. 251-78. Amsterdam: Elsevier.

Volksraad
               Handelingen van den Volksraad. Batavia: Volksraad van Nederlandsch-Indië.

Voogd, A.
1924   *De scheepvaart op Indië en de Rotterdamsche Lloyd.* Rotterdam: Schueler.

Watson Andaya, Barbara
1977   'From Rūm to Tokyo; The search for anticolonial allies by the rulers of Riau, 1899-1914', *Indonesia* 24:123-56.

Weijden, J. van der
1916   *Weerplicht voor inlanders en samenstelling van de weermacht in Nederlandsch-Indië.* Amsterdam: Van Holkema en Warendorf.

X.
1900   'De groote oorlog', *Indisch Militair Tijdschrift* 31:293-6.

Zwitzer, H.L. and C.A. Heshusius
1977   *Het Koninklijk Nederlands-Indisch leger 1830-1950; Een terugblik.* 's-Gravenhage: Staatsuitgeverij.

General index

Action Committee 401
Advisory Committee on Sugar 514, 623
Agricultural Association of the
 Principalities *see* Vorstenlandsche
 Landbouwvereeniging
Agriculture Syndicate *see* Landbouw
 Syndicaat
Akashi 335-6
Al Arabijjah 214
Al-Azhar 294
Al-Imam 471
Al-Liwa 293
Albertine Beatrice 439
Alfred Holt and Co. 433
Algemeen Handelsblad 74, 258, 605
Algemeen Nederlandsch Verbond
 voor de Bestrijding van Onjuiste
 Beoordelingen en Berichten in
 de Buitenlandsche Pers (General
 Netherlands League to Counter
 Incorrect Judgements and Reports
 in the Foreign Press) 228
Algemeen Nieuws en Telegraaf
 Agentschap (ANETA, General
 News and Telegraph Agency) 229,
 450
Algemeen Syndicaat van
 Suikerfabrikanten (General
 Syndicate of Sugar Producers) 269
Alhilal Alahmar 295-6, 315, *see also* Red
 Crescent
Ambonsch Studie-Fonds (Ambonese
 Study Foundation) 239
Ambulance Committee Central Java 268
American Revolution 49

Andalas 89, 473
ANETA *see* Algemeen Nieuws en
 Telegraaf Agentschap
Anglo-Japanese Treaty 74
Anhalt 494-5
Anker, Het 96, 571
Anti-Weerbaarheids movement 474
Anti Willekeur 483
Arakan 410
Argus 42
Association for the Penetration of the
 Pacific 206
Association for the Study of Military
 Science *see* Vereeniging ter
 Beoefening van de Krijgs
 wetenschap
Association for Women's Suffrage 61,
 214
Association of Rubber Planters 420
Association of Stranded Dutch People
 425
Association of Java Sugar Producers and
 Exporters 513-4, 623
Ayesha 197-8

Balkan Wars 82, 94, 117, 295-6
Baltic Fleet 15-6, 86
Bank of Holland 387
Bank of Taiwan 262
Batavia Cargo Conference *see* Batavia
 Vrachten-Conferentie
Batavia Vrachten-Conferentie (Batavia
 Cargo Conference) 383
Bataviaasch Handelsblad 185, 222, 376,
 379-80, 531, 560, 570

Bataviaasch Nieuwsblad 47, 266, 310, 423, 447-9, 526, 593, 603, 626, 628-9
Behn, Meyer and Co. 138, 190, 199, 325-6, 329, 333, 376, 385
Belgen-dagen (Belgians Days) 216
Belgium Committees 214
Belgium Red Cross 214, 314
Bendor 89
Bengkalis 505
BENISO *see* Bond van Eigenaren in Nederlandsch-Indische Suikerondernemingen
Berlin to Baghdad Railway 288
Bestuursschool 275
Biliton Company 541
Blue Funnel Line 433
Boedi Oetomo 46, 50, 52, 61, 238-40, 244, 250-2, 256-7, 263-4, 268, 270, 275, 280-1, 472, 517, 520, 522, 538, 544-5, 588, 596, 615, 626
Boer 10-2, 51, 61, 209, 228
Boer Republic 10, 119, 243
Boer War 10-3, 74, 78, 120, 173, 176, 210, 218, 221, 228, 293, 327, 446
Bond van Eigenaren in Nederlandsch-Indische Suikerondernemingen (BENISO, Union of Owners of Netherlands Indies' Sugar Estates) 514, 538-9
Bond van Indische Ambtenaren (Union of Indies Civil Servants) 89, *see also* Pension Union of Indies Civil Servants
Bond van Minder Marine-Personeel (Union of Lower-Ranking Naval Personnel) 96, 130, 560-4, 567, 571-2, 606-7, 611
Borneo Affair 1
Boxer Rebellion 78, 555
Breslau 289, 304
British Colonial Secretary 184
British Foreign Secretary 627
British Marconi Wireless Telegraph Company 443
British Merchant Shipping Act of 1894 409
British North American Naval Squadron 424

British Prince of Wales National Relief Fund 314
Britsche Telegram Onderbreking (BTO, British Telegram Interruption) 445, 623
British Telegram Interruption *see* Britsche Telegram Onderbreking
BTO *see* Britsche Telegram Onderbreking
Buitenzorg Affair 345
Bureau for Social Affairs in State Enterprises 602
Burns Philp 384

Cadet Training 499
Caliph, Caliph of Islam, Caliphate 294, 297, 308, 312, 314, 316, 324
Canadian Marconi Radio Station 442
Carl Schlieper Firm 3678, 376
Central Bank 131, 284
Central Committee for Relief *see* Centrale Comité voor Hulpverschaffing
Central Committee for Relief of the Destitute 427
Centrale Comité voor Hulpverschaffing (Central Committee for Relief) 214, 217
Central Council of Roman Catholic Social Unions 285
China Press 312
Chinese Communist Party 611
Chinese Revolution 31, 49
Choising 187, 198, 325
Civilian Medical Service 396, 593
Club of Egyptian Patriots 317
Cocoa Producers Association 514
Coffee Producers Association 514
Colleges for Native Civil Servants 327
Colonial Council *see* Koloniale Raad
Colonial Exhibition 178, 180, 212
Comité voor de Autonomie voor Indië (Committee for Autonomy for the Indies) 625
Comité Boemi Poetra *see* Native Committee for the Commemoration of the Netherlands Centenary of Freedom

Comité Indië Weerbaar *see* Indië Weerbaar
Comite Memoeliakan Radja (Committee for the Glorification of the Queen) 603
Comité Menoeloeng Hadji2 Bermoekim di Mekah (Committee to Help Hajjis Living in Mecca) 300-1, 304
Commissie tot Herziening van de Grondslagen van den Staatsinrichting van Nederlandsch-Indië, Herzieningscommissie (Commission of Inquiry, Commission of Inquiry into the Form of Government of the Netherlands Indies) 601, 625-6
Commissie voor den Nederlandsche Handel (Committee for Dutch Trade) 360-1, 364
Commissie voor Volkslectuur (Committee for the Spread of Popular Literature) 260
Commission *see* Staatscommissie voor de Verdediging van Nederlandsch-Indië
Commission of Inquiry *see* Commissie tot Herziening van de Grondslagen van den Staatsinrichting van Nederlandsch-Indië
Commission of Inquiry into the Form of Government of the Netherlands Indies *see* Commissie tot Herziening van de Grondslagen van den Staatsinrichting van Nederlandsch-Indië
Committee *see* Native Committee for the Commemoration of the Netherlands Centenary of Freedom
Committee for Autonomy for the Indies *see* Comité voor de Autonomie voor Indië
Committee for Dutch Trade *see* Commissie voor den Nederlandsche Handel
Committee for the Freedom of the Press 463
Committee for the Glorification of the Queen *see* Comite Memoeliakan Radja
Committee for Seized Exports 135
Committee for the Spread of Popular Literature *see* Commissie voor Volkslectuur
Committee Pro India 66
Committee to Help Hajjis Living in Mecca *see* Comité Menoeloeng Hadji2 Bermoekim di Mekah
Committees for Relief 244
Communist International 611, 630
Communist Party 281, *see also* Sociaal-Democratische Partij
Concordia 267, 584
Convention Relative à Certaines Restrictions à l'Exercise du Droit de Capture dans la Guerre Maritime of 1907 406
Corporals' and Other Ranks' Union 564
Cultuur-Hulpbank (Estate Relief Bank) 507, 617
Curaçao Relief Committee *see* Netherlands Indies Relief Committee for the Destitute on Curaçao

Daily Chronicle 404
Daily Mail 128
Dardanus 434
Darmo Kondo 544, 588
Decency Act of 1911 499
Declaration of London of 1909 360
Defence Association *see* Weerbaarheidsvereeniging
Deli Automobile Club 214
Deli Planters' Association 285
Deli Spoorweg Maatschappij 155
Deutsch-Australische Dampfschiff Gesellschaft 187
Deutsche Levant Linie 288
Deutsch-Niederländische Telegraphengesellschaft 14
Deutsche Wacht, Die 223, 323
Deutscher Bund in Niederländisch-Indien 223
Djaja-baja 248
Djawa Kondo 575
Djawa-Setia 565-6

Djawa Tengah 241, 464, 484, 519, 534, 608
Djowo Dipo movement 573-4
Doenia Bergerak 460-2, 465
Droogdok Maatschappij 377
Dutch-British Oceaan Shipping Company 416
Dutch-Chinese School 611
Dutch Correspondence Bureau for Newspapers *see* Nederlandsch Correspondentiebureau voor Dagbladen
Dutch East Indies Company *see* Vereenigde Oostindiesche Compagnie
Dutch Overseas Trust Company *see* Nederlandsche Overzee Trust Maatschappij
Dutch Royal Military Academy 13
Dutch Squadron in the East Indies 95

Eastern Extension *see* Eastern Extension Australasia and China Telegraph Company
Eastern Extension Australasia and China Telegraph Company 139, 141, 357
Eeuwige Juliana Instituut voor de Eenheid en Vooruitgang van Grooter Nederland, Het (The Eternal Juliana Institute for the Unity and Progress of the Greater Netherlands) 249
Emden (Flying German, Kapal Setan, Devil Ship) 174, 182-7, 189, 193, 195, 197-8, 320, 323, 326, 329-30, 352, 373
Empress of Japan 198
Engineering Corps 367-8
Erdman and Sielcken 376-7, 515
Escompto Bank 448
Estate Relief Bank *see* Cultuur-Hulpbank
Ethical Policy 19, 57, 109, 238, 265, 621
Exford 198
Expres, De 32, 39, 41, 47, 51, 53-4, 58-9, 61, 65-7, 94, 96, 107-9, 113, 117, 119, 121, 242-3, 261, 348, 456, 458-60, 465, 478, 572

February Revolution (Russia) 547
First Battle of Ypres 222

First Medan Tea Factory 515
Flottenverein 111
Flying German *see* Emden
Franco-German (Prussian) War 1, 131 287
Freiberg 194-5

Gazette of India 304, 318
Geier 182, 185-6, 193, 204
Gelder, Van (paper producer) 509
Gelderland 501
General Syndicate of Sugar Producers 534
German-Dutch Telegraph Company 14
German Emperor 288, 294, 413
German Union 175
Gernis 189, 433
Gesellschaft für drahtlose Telegraphie (Telefunken) 442
Ghadr (Mutiny) Movement 317-8, 329, 332, 346
Goeben 289, 304
Goentoer, De 459, 461, 465
Goentoer Bergerak 465, 572
Goentoer Bergerak Modjopait 465
Government Committee of Advice on Sugar *see* Regeerings Commissie van Advies voor de Suiker
Groene Amsterdammer, De, De Groene 99, 109, 465

Hagen 195
Hamburg-Amerika Linie 187, 190, 196, 288, 412
Hamburger Nachrichten 223
Handelsvereeniging Amsterdam 387
Hansa Line 373
HBS *see* Hoogere Burgerschool
Hertog Hendrik 180, 500-1, 504-5
Hejaz Railway 293, 297
Henry S. 333-6
Heramba (Hermeba) Lal Gupta (Indian Revolutionary Party) 349
Herzieningscommissie *see* Commissie tot Herziening van de Grondslagen van den Staatsinrichting van Nederlandsch-Indië
Higher Military Academy 499

Hindia Serikat (The United Indies) 57
Hörde 187, 189-90, 323
Holland-Amerika Line 412
Holland American Plantation Company
    see Hollandsch-Amerikaansche
    Plantage Maatschappij
Hollandsch-Amerikaansche Plantage
    Maatschappij (Holland American
    Plantation Company) 270
Hoogere Burgerschool (HBS, Dutch
    secondary school) 45, 613
Houtman 182

Imam, al- 76
Imperial Japanese and United States
    Mail Line 384
India-Japanese League 81
Indian Committee 303
Indian Military Association *see* Indische
    Krijgskundige Vereeniging
Indian National Pary 328
Indian Revolutionary Party *see* Heramba
    (Hermeba) Lal Gupta
Indian Sociologist, The 47-8
Indian Mutiny 317, 322
Indië Weerbaar 255, 260-1, 264, 267-71,
    273-8, 280, 282-5, 399-400, 424, 426,
    464, 469-70, 472-5, 477, 500, 549, 551,
    557, 564, 574, 579-90, 594
Indië Weerbaar Week 581, 583, 585
Indiër, De 65-7, 71, 109, 113, 243, 460, 469,
    480, 548, 574, 595
Indies Military Navy 7, 99
Indies Party *see* Indische Partij
Indies Social Democratic Union *see*
    Indische Sociaal-Democratische
    Vereeniging
Indische Bond 528
Indische Financier 143
Indische Gids, De 255, 579, 594, 610, 626
Indische Lloyd 268
Indische Krijgskundige Vereeniging
    (Indian Military Association) 267
Indische Partij (IP, Indies Party) 50-3, 55,
    57-8, 60-1, 64-5, 67, 69, 94-5, 97, 109,
    208, 219, 235, 242, 346, 350, 455-7, 465,
    471, 480, 484, 545, 610, 622, 626, 629
Indische Sociaal-Democratische
    Vereeniging (ISDV, Indies Social
    Democratic Union) 458, 463, 473,
    477-82, 484-5, 517, 520, 538, 540, 544,
    548, 550, 554, 556-64, 569, 575-6, 579-
    80, 585, 588-90, 595, 606-7, 609-1, 615
Indische Sociaal-Democratische Partij
    626
Indische Stemmen 478
Indische Technische Hoogeschool 401
Indische Vereeniging 281
Indonesian Communist Party 614
Inlandsche Journalisten Bond (IJB,
    Native Journalists' Union) 459-60,
    462-3
Inlandsch Sociaal-Democratische
    Vereeniging Hindia Bergerak
    (Native Social Democrat Union
    Hindia Bergerak) 479, *see also* Sama
    Rata Hindia Bergerak
Indologen-Vereeniging 281
Insulinde 61, 257, 268, 455-10, 463, 465,
    470-1, 473, 477, 479-80, 484, 521, 528,
    548, 559, 572, 574, 576-7, 596
Insulinde Red Cross 216
Internatio *see* Internationale Crediet- en
    Handelsvereeniging Rotterdam
International Club 183
International Credit and Trading
    Association Rotterdam *see*
    Internationale Crediet- en
    Handelsvereeniging Rotterdam
Internationale Crediet- en
    Handelsvereeniging Rotterdam
    (Internatio, International Credit and
    Trading Association Rotterdam)
    150, 181
IP *see* Indische Partij
IP Day 61
ISDV *see* Indische Sociaal-Democratische
    Vereeniging
Islam Bergerak 483, 517, 552
Islamic Fraternity, The 32
Iswestia 83
Italo-Turkish War 117
IJB *see* Inlandsche Journalisten Bond

Jahns Advertentieblad 608
Jan Pieterszoon Coen 411

Japan Advertiser 393
Japan Times 342
Java-Bode 98, 125, 174, 255, 315-6, 376, 389, 603
Java-China-Japan Line 87
Java-New York Line 410
Java-Pacific Line 410, 489
Java-San Francisco Line 410
Java Sugar Association *see* Javasuiker-Vereeniging
Java War 258
Javasche Bank 134, 144-50, 156-7, 163-4, 276, 375, 378, 384, 387, 405, 427, 440, 507, 526, 541, 603
Javasche Courant 30, 135, 162, 173-4, 185, 205, 211, 341, 364
Javasche Lloyd 376
Javasuiker-Vereeniging (Java Sugar Association) 430, 513, 5637
Je Mainteindrai 270-1, 285, 424
Jember Association of Agriculture and Industry 487
Jihad Document *see* Universal Proclamation to All Peoples of Islam
John Davis 439
Juliana Club 270

Kabar Perniagan (Trade News) 75
Kaoem Moeda 57, 252, 282, 310, 447, 477, 593
Kawi 366, 422, 424
Kleist 178, 180, 198, 329
Kolff and Co., G. 223
Koloniale Raad (Colonial Council) 55
Koningin Regentes 172, 180-1, 186, 188, 569
Koninklijk Nationaal Hulp Comité (Royal National Relief Committee) 128
Koninklijke Paketvaart Maatschappij (KPM, Royal Packet Company) 125, 148, 268, 277, 321, 384, 439, 489, 492, 495-7, 512, 528, 561, 580, 603
KPM *see* Koninklijke Paketvaart Maatschappij
Krupp 111, 288

Labourers' and Farmers' Union *see* Perhimpoenan Kaoem Boeroeh dan Tani
Ladies Aid Committee 618
Landbouw Syndicaat (Agriculture Syndicate) 614
Law and Order Leagues 235
Law College 28
Le Petit Hindoestani 308
Leagues of Law and Order *see* Ordebonden
League of Nations 621
Legislative Council of the Straits Settlements 183
Linden 187, 433
Lloyd Othman 312
Locomotief, De 39, 63-4, 74, 83-4, 88, 92-5, 99, 102, 109, 113, 121, 125, 128, 134, 142-3, 145, 152, 156, 162, 175-6, 179-80, 197, 202-4, 207-8, 211, 213-5, 218, 220, 222-4, 234, 244-5, 250, 258, 266, 268, 270-2, 274, 281-2, 346, 369, 374, 378-9, 393, 406, 408, 413, 416, 422-4, 439-40, 442, 470, 473-5, 515-6, 526, 532, 545, 552, 554, 556, 560, 584-5, 595, 604, 608, 616
Lübeck 196
Luneberg 193, 196

Madjoe Kamoeljan (Progress of Honour) 461
Makassaarsche Courant 214
Malay States Guides 319-21
Manchu dynasty 29
Marie 373, 424
Markomannia 187, 197-8
Matrozenbond (Sailors' Union) 561
Maverick 333-5, 337, 351
Maverick Steamship Co. 333
Medan Boediman 532
Medan Moeslimin 311
Medan Planters Committee (Planters Committee) 380
Melchior Treub 432, 492-3, 498
Middelbaar Uitgebreid Lager Onderwijs (MULO, Dutch lower secondary school) 64
Minahassa Union 527
Modjopait 465, 470, 572

Moehammadijah 39
Monroe Doctrine 1
Morning Post 221
MULO *see* Middelbaar Uitgebreid Lager Onderwijs

Narpo Wandowo (Union of Princes) 268, 276
Nationaal Indische Partij (National Indies Party) 626
National Committee of Indians Living in Berlin 347
National Indies Party *see* Nationaal Indische Partij
Native Committee *see* Native Committee for the Commemoration of the Netherlands Centenary of Freedom
Native Committee for the Commemoration of the Netherlands Centenary of Freedom (Native Committee, Comité Boemi Poetra) 55, 57, 59, 248, 285
Native Journalists' Union *see* Inlandsche Journalisten Bond
Native Pawnshop Union 553
Native Social Democrat Union Hindia Bergerak *see* Inlandsch Sociaal-Democratische Vereeniging Hindia Bergerak
Nederland (steam-shipping company) 87, 298, 381-5, 410-6, 421-2, 436-7, 497, 618
Nederlandsch Correspondentiebureau voor Dagbladen (Dutch Correspondence Bureau for Newspapers) 117
Nederlandsch-Indische Fascisten Organisatie (Netherlands Indies Fascists Organization) 283
Nederlandsch-Indische Gas-Maatschappij (Netherlands Indies Gas Company) 148
Nederlandsch-Indische Landbouwsyndicaat (Netherlands Indies Agricultural Syndicate) 417
Nederlandsch-Indische Officiers Vereeniging (Netherlands Indies Officers Association) 267

Nederlandsch-Indisch Onderwijzers Genootschap (NIOG, Netherlands Indies 'Teachers' Association) 521-2
Nederlandsch-Indisch Pers Agentschap (NIPA, Netherlands Indies Press Agency) 229, 450
Nederlandsch-Indische Tentoonstelling Vereeniging (Netherlands Indies Fair Association) 582
Nederlandsche Handel-Maatschappij (NHM, Netherlands Trade Company) 121, 133, 135, 144, 148-50, 154-6, 164, 281, 355, 384, 389-90, 518, 526, 561, 603
Nederlandsche Handelsvloot, De (The Dutch Merchant Fleet) 495
Nederlandsche Scheepvaart Unie (Netherlands Shipping Union) 382
Nederlandsche Stoomvaart-Maatschappij Oceaan, Oceaan 298, 433, 618
Nederlandsche Overzee Trust Maatschappij (NOT, Dutch Overseas Trust Company) 361-8, 370-1, 380, 387, 429-30, 437, 489, 511, 524, 618-9
Neratja 450, 477-8, 494, 516, 518, 524, 529, 537, 543, 547, 552, 554-5, 566, 586-9, 591, 593, 599, 606, 609, 615, 629
Netherlands Indies Agricultural Syndicate *see* Nederlandsch-Indische Landbouwsyndicaat
Netherlands Indies Fair Association *see* Nederlandsch-Indische Tentoonstelling Vereeniging
Netherlands Indies Fascists Organization *see* Nederlandsch-Indische Fascisten Organisatie
Netherlands Indies Gas Company *see* Nederlandsch-Indische Gas-Maatschappij
Netherlands Indies 'Teachers' Association *see* Nederlandsch-Indisch Onderwijzers Genootschap
Netherlands Indies Officers Association *see* Nederlandsch-Indische Officiers Vereeniging
Netherlands Indies Relief Committee for

the Destitute on Curaçao, Curaçao Relief Committee 216-8
Netherlands Shipping Union *see* Nederlandsche Scheepvaart Unie
Netherlands Trade Company *see* Nederlandsche Handel-Maatschappij
Neu-Guinea Compagnie 2
Newsport News 424
NHM *see* Nederlandsche Handel-Maatschappij
NIAS (Nederlandsch-Indische Artsen School) 499
Niederländisch-Indische Monatschrift für Kolonialpolitik 223
Nieuw-Amsterdam 424
Nieuw Soerabajasch-Handelsblad 113
Nieuwe Amsterdammer, De 465
Nieuwe Courant 89, 568, 609
Nieuwe Rotterdamsche Courant 31, 112, 209, 266, 294-5, 298-9, 404, 472
Nieuwe Soerabaia Courant 112, 173
Nieuws van den Dag 277
Nieuws van den Dag voor Nederlandsch Indië, Het 221-3, 225-7, 259, 333, 337, 343, 345-6
Nile 321
NIOG *see* Nederlandsch-Indisch Onderwijzers Genootschap
NIPA *see* Nederlandsch-Indische Pers Agentschap
Noordam 504-5, 515, 531, 570, 606, 611, 618
Noordkust, De 509
Norddeutsche-Seekabelwerke 14
Norddeutscher Lloyd and Hamburg-Amerika-Linie 190
Nore 321
NOT *see* Nederlandsche Overzee Trust Maatschappij
Nuisance Act 495

Ocean *see* Nederlandsche Stoomvaart-Maatschappij Oceaan
Oceaan *see* Nederlandsche Stoomvaart-Maatschappij Oceaan
Ocean Shipping Line 410
Ocean Steamship Line 300
Oetoesan Hindia 63, 134, 233, 235-9, 246,
248, 250, 252-3, 262, 307-12, 314, 324, 342-3, 379, 413, 474, 483, 517-8, 527, 529, 533-4, 536, 540, 544, 547, 564, 573, 588, 608, 610
Offenbach 181-2, 186
Ons Belang (Our Interest) 213
Onze Vloot 8, 110-4, 114, 116-20, 242, 255, 260, 273, 281, 289, 389, 424, 585
Oorlogs-commentaar 202
Oorlogsberichten uit Duitsche Bladen (War Reports from German Papers) 224
Opium War 309
Orange Union of Law and Order *see* Oranjebond van Orde
Oranjebond van Orde (Orange Union of Law and Order) 283, 615
Order of Orange-Nassau 53
Ordebonden (Leagues of Law and Order) 209-10
Orgaan see Orgaan der Vereeniging 'Indie Weerbaar'
Orgaan der Vereeniging 'Indie Weerbaar' (Organ of the Association The Resistant Indies) 580
Osmanischer Lloyd 288
Ostasiatische Lloyd 224
OSVIA (Opleidingsschool voor Inlandsche Ambtenaren) 64, 245, 257
Ottoman Empire 2, 21, 33, 137, 287, 290-1, 293-5, 304, 311, 313, 318, 620, 622

Pahang 306
Palembang 412
Pantjaran Warta 330, 466, 469, 478
Pasar Gambir Fair 217
Patrie Egyptienne 309
Peace Conference 182, 620-1
Penal Code 224, 226
Peninsular and Oriental Steam Navigation Company 412
Pension Union of Indies Civil Servants *see* Bond van Indische Ambtenaren
People's Council *see* Volksraad
People's Credit Banks 232
Perhimpoenan Kaoem Boeroeh dan Tani (PKBT, Labourers' and Farmers' Union) 479
Perniagaan 471

Perserikatan Minahasa, Minahasa Union 111, 277
Pertimbangan 260-2, 471, 479, 548
Pewarta Deli 461
Pewarta Wolanda 294
PKBT *see* Perhimpoenan Kaoem Boeroeh dan Tani
Pinang Gazette 42
P&O Lines 321
PID *see* Politieke Inlichtingendienst
Planters Association of Deli 420
Politieke Inlichtingendienst (PID, Political Intelligence Service) 328, 470-1, 553, 557-8, 561, 613
Political Intelligence Service *see* Politieke Inlichtingendienst
Pontoporos 187, 197
Postal Service 404
Preanger-bode 125, 201, 209, 264, 560
Press Curb Ordinance *see* Press Ordinance of 1931
Press Ordinance of 1931 (Press Curb Ordinance) 627
Preussen 189, 196
Prinses Juliana 421
Pro India 347

Red Crescent 246-7, *see also* Alhilal Alahmar
Red Cross 209, 218, 247, 268, 427
Regentenbond (Regents' Union) 239, 245, 268, 276, 626
Regents' Union *see* Regentenbond
Regeerings Commissie van Advies voor de Suiker (Government Committee of Advice on Sugar) 513
Reshadieh 289
Reuter 222, 229, 289, 307, 312, 444, 450
Rio Päsig 187
Rochussen 491
Roon 175, 178-80, 192-3, 196, 199, 333, 394
Rotterdamsche Lloyd 87, 135, 192, 298, 373, 381-5, 410-4, 416, 422, 436-7, 440-1, 497, 618
Royal National Relief Committee *see* Koninklijk Nationaal Hulp Comité
Royal Packet Company *see* Koninklijke Paketvaart Maatschappij
Rubber Producers Association 514
Rumphius 325
Russian fleet 14-5, 85, 103-4, 112, 440, 548
Russo-Japanese War 10, 14-7, 73, 76, 86, 92, 95, 103, 126, 166, 168-9, 171, 173-4, 199, 207, 218, 317, 352, 355, 493, 501
Russo-Turkish War 290
Ruygrok Company 376
Rijkspostspaarbank (State Postal Savings Bank) 131
Rijksraad (Empire Council) 602
Rijndam 284

Sabang Company 189, 371-2, 374
Sabang Setia (Loyal Sabang) 278
Sailors' Union *see* Matrozenbond
Salvation Army 213
Sama Rata Hindia Bergerak (Equality in the Indies [Nationalist] Movement) 479, *see also* Inlandsch Sociaal-Democratische Vereeniging Hindia Bergerak
San Francisco Examiner 351
Sarekat Islam (SI) 37, 39-44, 50-3, 60-3, 106, 109, 121, 231, 233, 235, 238-41, 245, 248-9, 251-3, 256, 264-6, 268, 270-1, 275, 278-81, 296, 301, 307, 311, 315-6, 327, 330, 340, 342-5, 348, 447, 453-4, 456, 458-61, 466-7, 472-3, 477-9, 482-3, 507, 517, 519, 521-2, 527, 529, 533-5, 538-41, 543-5, 547, 552-6, 558-9, 563, 565, 571-3, 579, 585, 588-91, 595-6, 607-9, 613-6, 622, 626, 628-9
Sarotomo 459-61, 463
Scandia 195
Scheepsagentuur, De 180
Schelde, De (shipbuilding yard) 119
Schenker and Co. 334, 391
Schepenvorderingswet (Ships' Requisitioning Act) 417, 501
Schlesische Zeitung 73
School for Native Teachers 327
School for the Training of Native Docters *see* School tot Opleiding van

Inlandsche Artsen School tot Opleiding van Inlandsche Artsen (STOVIA, School for the Training of Native Docters) 28, 46, 53, 64
Schwäbische Merkur 73
SDAP *see* Sociaal-Democratische Arbeiders Partij
SDP *see* Sociaal-Decmocratische Partij
Sea War Conference 127
Second Peace Conference 126, 169
Sedyo Tama Fund 467
Semarang Railway Company 457
Semarang Savings Bank *see* Semarangsche Hulpspaarbank
Semarang Trade Society *see* Semarangsche Handelsvereeniging
Semarangsche Handelsvereeniging (Semarang Trade Society) 548, 589
Semarangsche Hulpspaarbank (Semarang Savings Bank) 150
Ships' Requisitioning Act *see* Schepenvorderingswet
SI *see* Sarekat Islam
Si Tetap 457, 576, 622
Sin Po 247, 262, 555, 621
Sinar Djawa 252, 307, 311, 473, 477, 482, 552-3, 595
Sinar Hindia 477, 482, 595, 608, 610, 615
Sinar Laoetan 572
Sinar Sumatra 473
Sindoro 278, 421
Singapore Munity 322
Sino-Japanese War 241
Smalhout and Co., H.N. 380
Sociaal-Democratische Arbeiders Partij (SDAP, Social Democratic Labour Party) 25, 61, 281, 456, 482, 528, 563, 584-5
Sociaal-Democratische Partij (SDP, Social Democratic Party) 281, *see also* Communist Party
Social Democratic Labour Party *see* Sociaal-Democratische Arbeiders Partij
Social Democratic Party *see* Sociaal-Democratische Partij
Société Coloniale Indo-Belge 376

Society for the Improvement of the Social Status of the Soldier *see* Vereeniging ter Verbetering van den Maatschappelijke Staat van den Militair
Soeara Merdika 479, 595
Soeara Ra'jat 591, 595, 608, 610
Soeloeh Kemadjoean (Torch of Progress) 21
Soerabaiasch Handelsblad 84, 88, 173-4, 221, 224, 269, 304, 327, 343, 345, 378, 447-8, 475, 537, 589, 615
Soldaten Bond (Soldiers' Union) 584, 606-7
Soldaten- en Matrozenkrant (Soldiers' and Sailors' Paper) 564
Soldiers' Union *see* Soldaten Bond
South Manchuria Railway Company 87
Special Branch (Singapore) 321
Staatscommissie voor de Verdediging van Nederlandsch-Indië, Commissie 100-2, 104, 106
Staatscourant 441
Standaard, De 494
State Commission of 1912 283
State Postal Savings Bank *see* Rijkspostspaarbank
State Railways and the Postal and Telegraph Service 27
Stollberg 193-4
Stoomvaart Maatschappij Nederland 135
STOVIA *see* School tot Opleiding van Inlandsche Artsen
Straits Times, The 42
Straits und Sunda Syndikat 325, 342, 376
Study Society *see* Vereeniging voor de Studie van Koloniaal-Maatschappelijke Vraagstukken
Society for the Study of Colonial Social Questions *see* Vereeniging voor de Studie van Koloniaal-Maatschappelijke Vraagstukken
Sugar Union *see* Suikerbond
Sugar Syndicat 540, 615
Suikerbond (Sugar Union) 429, 519, 537
Sultan Osman 289
Sumatra News 242

Sumatra Post 88, 308, 350, 453, 560, 609, 621
Sumatrabode 343
Sydney 196-7

Tabanan 440-1, 501, 505, 606, 618
Tado Fund (Tot aan de Onafhankelijkheid, Till Independence) 61, 65, 68
Taman Siswa 630
Tambora 359
Tanglin Camp 319, 323, 326, 329, 350
Tantalus 434
Tea Producers Association 514
Teachers' Training College 239
Telefunken 191-2, 442-3
Telegraaf, De 81, 113, 174, 221, 342, 356, 390, 410, 512
Times, The 127, 290, 359, 364, 444, 450
Times of India 128
Tiong Hoa Ieng Giap Hwe 481
Tjahaja Selatan 262
Tjisondari 425
Trade Association of Semarang 512
Treaty of Versailles 621
Tribune, The 606
Triple Alliance 18
Triple Entente 18, 127, 290, 304, 309, 353, 361
Tromp 180, 182, 186-7, 322, 334-6, 500
Trust *see* Nederlandsche Overzee Trust Maatschappij
Tubantia 412
Turco-Italian War 295
Turkish Red Crescent 314-5
Tijdschrift, Het 47-50, 53-4, 66-7, 275, 346
Twenty-One Demands 242

Ulm 187
Unfederated Malay States 306
Union of Indies Civil Servants *see* Bond van Indische Ambtenaren
Union of Lower-Ranking Naval Personnel *see* Bond van Minder Marine-Personeel
Union of Non-Commissioned Officers 210
Union of Owners of Netherlands Indies' Sugar Estates *see* Bond van Eigenaren in Nederlandsch-Indische Suikerondernemingen
Union of Princes *see* Narpo Wandowo
Union of Rail and Tramway Personnel in the Netherlands Indies *see* Vereeniging van Spoor- en Tramwegpersoneel in Nederlandsch-Indië
Union of Social Democrats in the Netherlands Indies *see* Vereeniging van Sociaal-Democraten in Nederlandsch-Indië
United Java Sugar Producers Associated *see* Vereenigde Javasuiker Producenten-Vereeniging
United Java Sugar Producers Association *see* Vereenigde Java Suiker Producenten
United Press Association 432
Universal Proclamation to All Peoples of Islam, Jihad Document 290, 296

Vaderland, Het 266
Van Cloon 488-9
Vereenigde Javasuiker Producenten-Vereeniging (United Java Sugar Producers Associated) 390
Vereenigde Java Suiker Producenten (United Java Sugar Producers Association) 514, 623-4
Vereenigde Oostindische Compagnie (Dutch East Indies Company) (VOC) 23, 250
Vereeniging ter Beoefening van de Krijgswetenschap (Association for the Study of Military Science) 284
Vereeniging van Sociaal-Democraten in Nederlandsch-Indië (Union of Social Democrats in the Netherlands Indies) 457
Vereeniging van Spoor- en Tramweg-personeel in Nederlandsch-Indië (VSTP, Union of Rail and Tramway Personnel in the Netherlands Indies) 457-8, 463, 465, 478-80, 519-20, 557-8, 572-3, 576, 622
Vereeniging voor de Studie van

Koloniaal-Maatschappelijke Vraagstukken (Society for the Study of Colonial Social Questions) 419
Vereeniging ter Verbetering van den Maatschappelijke Staat van den Militair (Society for the Improvement of the Social Status of the Soldier) 561
VOC *see* Vereenigde Oostindische Compagnie
Volk, Het 120, 465, 613
Volksraad (People's Council) 286, 294, 399, 428, 485, 509, 520-1, 531, 534-5, 540, 543-4, 551, 557-8, 563, 569, 579, 582, 584, 587, 589, 591-2, 594, 596-606, 608-9, 614, 617, 620-1, 624-5, 629
Volharding, De 457
Volkswirtschaft und Völkerrecht 223
Voluntary Automobile Corps *see* Vrijwillige Automobiel Korps
Von Podbielski 14
Voorpost, De 470-1, 480, 572
Vorstenlandsche Landbouwvereeniging (Agricultural Association of the Principalities) 536
Vriendenkring, De (Circle of Friends) 213
Vrije Woord, Het 481, 548-9, 564, 589-90, 606-8

Vrijwillige Automobiel Korps (Voluntary Automobile Corps) 209
VSTP *see* Vereeniging van Spoor- en Tramwegpersoneel in Nederlandsch-Indië

Wachtenfels 373
Wapens Neder, De 469
Warna Warta 208, 241
Washington Post 506
Weerbaarheids-vereeniging (Defence Association) 271
Weerbaarheidsdag (Defence Day) 268
Weltpolitik 287
Wismar 494-5
Wolf 373
Wolff News Agency 224, 312
Women's Council 561

Yarmouth 197
Young China Movement 29
Young Egyptian League 48
Young Turks 295-6, 339, 343

Zeeland 441, 443, 569
Zeven Provinciën, De 180, 187

Index of geographical names

Aceh, Acehnese 5, 62, 76, 103, 167, 187, 196, 213, 252, 269, 273, 278, 290, 295, 327, 525, 580
Aden 13, 321
Afghanistan 290
Africa, Africans 2, 4, 9, 75, 138, 167, 305, 309, 621
   East - 179, 309, 319, 321, 373, 442
   North - 117, 309
   Portuguese East - 13
   Southwest - 3
   West - 321
Albania, Albanians 22, 134, 379
Alexandria 309
Alfur, Alfurese 213
Algeria, Algerian 222
Algiers 47
Alsace 7, 9
Ambarawa 63-4
Ambon, Ambonese 22, 42, 93, 167, 178, 187, 213, 269, 278, 476, 494, 516, 521, 531, 537, 567, 592, 603, 607
Ambon Bay 178
Ameland 202
America, Americas, American *see* United States of America
America
   North - 135
   South - 135, 363
Amsterdam 117, 119, 127, 131, 143, 161, 181, 294, 324, 341, 363-4, 368, 385-6, 390, 405, 411, 433-4, 436, 470, 506, 611, 623-4
Andaman Islands 321
Andaman Sea 183

Antwerp 195, 202-4, 449, 451
Anyer 333-4
Arab, Arabic, Arabs 22-3, 27, 29, 40, 62, 64, 87, 144, 149-50, 157, 176, 214-5, 245-7, 249, 256, 269-70, 290-1, 293, 296-7, 306-8, 312-5, 324, 327, 340, 342-3, 345, 350, 365, 385, 394, 419, 467, 472, 476, 521-2, 587, 603, 622
Arabian Peninsula 179, 298-301, 324
Argentina 436
Armenia, Armenian 225, 310
Asia, Asian, Asians 5, 7, 12, 15-6, 19, 22, 32, 45, 68, 73-8, 83, 85, 87, 89, 91-2, 97, 100, 105, 119, 135, 137-9, 142, 158, 178-9, 206-8, 237, 260, 266, 288, 296, 309, 318, 325-6, 331, 336, 346, 349, 356-7, 370, 381, 408, 420, 432, 434, 444, 447, 492, 496, 498, 596, 621, 623
   East - 2, 14, 65-6, 73, 117, 186, 191, 310, 328
   - Minor 305
   North - 14, 73
   South - 177, 616
   Southeast - 1, 73, 81, 169, 177, 182, 184-5, 192, 235, 304, 307, 528
Atlantic Ocean, Atlantic 422, 424, 432, 505
Austria, Austrian 1, 126-7, 135, 142, 162, 177-8, 199, 223-6, 246-7, 305, 309, 333, 342, 373-4, 376, 381, 411, 490, 494, 498, 548, 560, 596
Australia, Australian 1, 3, 42, 82, 99-100, 112, 175, 177, 183, 192-3, 197, 356, 369, 387, 440, 496, 500, 508, 513, 515-6, 621

Austria-Hungary, Austro-Hungarian 17-8, 256, 353, 356, 363-4, 391, 393, 403, 429, 432
Auschwitz 611

Babar Islands 454
Babat 609
Baghdad 288
Baku 311
Balearic Islands 47
Bali 76, 154, 180, 228, 232, 455, 524
Balikpapan 111, 176
Balkan, Balkans 201, 296, 309
Banda, Banda Neira 60, 70, 611, 628, 630
Banda Aceh 213, 270
Bandung 50-1, 53, 57, 64, 152, 158, 167, 201-2, 209-10, 218, 239, 247-8, 264, 269, 273, 276, 278, 286, 301, 324, 333, 369, 401, 442-3, 447, 460, 462, 516, 554, 562, 582-3, 586, 626
Bangka, Bangka Island 60, 117, 154, 163, 464, 525, 541-2, 543, 624
Bangkok 349
Banjarmasin 269, 424
Bantam 52
Banten Bay, Bay of Bantam 166, 494
Bantul 554
Banyumas 333
Banyuwangi 494, 580
Basra 319
Batak 278
Batavia, Batavian 5, 14-5, 19, 23, 30-2, 41, 45-6, 50, 55, 57-8, 60, 64, 70, 77, 82, 85-6, 111, 121-2, 125, 129, 135, 141, 143-4, 146, 148-9, 151-2, 154-5, 158, 161, 163, 167, 169-70, 174-6, 178, 181-2, 184-5, 190-1, 194-6, 203, 206, 208, 210, 212, 214-9, 225, 228-9, 231-2, 241-2, 247, 249, 251-2, 255, 259-60, 262, 264, 267-8, 271-4, 276-8, 286, 291, 297-8, 301, 304, 307-8, 311, 313-6, 322-3, 325-7, 329-35, 337, 345, 347, 350-1, 357, 359, 363, 365, 367, 369-74, 376-80, 384-5, 390, 392, 395, 397, 399-400, 404-6, 418-24, 426-8, 430-1, 444, 449-50, 453-5, 461-2, 464, 466-8, 470-1, 477, 481, 485, 493, 496, 498-9, 506, 510, 512-4, 516-23, 525, 528-31, 534, 541, 546, 549, 551-2, 555, 558, 561, 563, 565, 567, 570, 581-5, 587, 592-5, 597-8, 600-7, 610-1, 613-6, 624-5, 627, 629
Batavian Chinese 336
Bavaria, Bavarian 47, 82
Bay of Bengal 183, 189, 193
Bedouins 324
Belawan 359, 432, 495
Belgian Congo 7
Belgium, Belgians 17, 47, 177, 179, 202-4, 214-8, 220-1, 225, 238, 247, 309, 312, 318, 323, 356, 373, 378, 407, 434, 449, 451, 620
Bengali, Bengalis 62, 215, 334, 369, 371-4
Bengkulu 628
Bergen 500
Berlin 3-4, 7, 15, 25, 82, 131, 178, 202, 204, 228, 287, 305, 317, 325, 347-9, 354-5, 365, 409, 411, 414-5, 421, 423, 432-5, 447, 449, 451, 490, 623
Berwick-upon-Tweed 409
Besuki 455
Billiton 153, 541-2
Bismarck Archipelago 3, *see also* New Britain Archipelago
Bizerta 135
Black Sea 289
Blitar 241, 516, 535
Blora 113
Boer republics 10
Bojong 64
Bombay 303, 395, 492
Bone 278
Borneo 2-7, 24, 74, 83, 167, 173, 176, 201, 295, 424, 455, 543
  East - 166, 454, 508
  East Coast of - 310
  North - 4, 74
  South - 153, 454, 508
  West - 166, 525, 592
Bosnia 305, 308
Boven-Digul 627-8, 630
Brazil, Brazilian 363
Brest 359
Brisbane 492
British *see* Great Britain
British Borneo 359

Index of geographical names

British India 66, 77, 81, 128, 169, 183, 246, 291, 298, 308, 317, 324, 326-7, 329-30, 332, 334, 336-7, 348, 350, 352, 369, 371, 407-8, 420, 440, 496-8, 508, 510, 512, 528, 549, 590, 615-7
Briton *see* Great Britain
Brunei 306
Brussels 74, 217
Bugis 23
Buitenzorg 7, 14, 209-10, 213, 248, 286, 342, 412, 584, 593, 629
Bulan 191
Buleleng 359
Bulgaria, Bulgarians 379
Burma 153, 163, 318-9, 324, 348, 371, 418, 496-7, 512, 528, 591, 617

Cairo 73, 229, 294
Calcutta 184, 191-2, 324, 336-7, 508
California 515
Canada, Canadian 325, 424
Cape *see* Cape of Good Hope
Cape of Good Hope 16, 411, 415-6, 421, 439, 500-1, 505
Cardiff 508
Caribbean 494
Caroline Islands, Carolines 5, 9
Celebes 5, 7, 74, 77, 83, 106, 117, 122, 139, 182, 186, 205, 214, 295, 311, 329, 392, 543
- North 14, 98, 147, 168, 232, 278, 453, 524
North Coast of - 335
- South 153, 454
Celebes Sea 335
Cepu 459
Ceylon 183, 440
Channel 110, 407, 409, 413-4, 433
Cherbourg 135
Chicago 317, 335
Chile 438
China, Chinese 2, 7, 15, 17, 20, 22-3, 27-33, 35-7, 39-43, 46, 49, 51-2, 60, 62-4, 67, 73-5, 77-8, 81, 87-9, 93, 96, 100, 117, 119, 121, 134, 143-4, 147-50, 152-4, 157, 160-1, 179, 184, 189, 201, 208, 214-5, 217, 219, 225, 234-6, 238, 241-2, 244, 247, 250, 256, 261-2, 268-72, 274, 279, 299, 305, 309, 313-4, 322, 336, 340, 343, 355, 365, 376, 379-80, 385, 393-4, 419-20, 423, 430, 439, 447, 453, 468, 471, 475, 477-80, 483-4, 487, 495, 499, 506, 515, 518-9, 521-2, 527, 529, 532, 534, 536, 540-1, 543, 547, 554-5, 576, 587, 594, 603, 621-2
Ch'ing-tao 242
Ciawi 628
Cibadak 125
Cicurug 525
Cilacap 175, 179, 191-2, 196, 199, 333, 483, 494
Cililin 443
Cirebon 63, 176, 212, 215, 235, 395, 399, 509, 522
Cocos Islands 197
Colombo 142, 177, 183, 197, 305, 492
Cornwall 433
Cornwallis Island 442
Crimea 222
Cuba 117, 119, 228
Curaçao 141, 494
Cyprus 307
Czechs 134

Damascus 293-4
Danes *see* Denmark
Dardanelles 289
Dar-es-Salaam 189
Delagoa Bay 415
Delft 473, 499
Deli 155
Demak 239, 555, 609
Denmark, Danes, Danish 13, 323, 432
Dinant 225
Dixmude 222
Dogger Bank 414
Dordrecht 228
Dover 126, 135, 407, 409
Duke of York Islands 3, *see also* Neu-Lauenburg Group
Durban 185, 439
Dutch, Dutchmen *see* Netherlands
Dutch New Guinea 247
Dutch Timor 150

East, Eastern 293, 493

Egypt, Egyptian 48, 66, 75, 232-3, 293, 303-4, 309, 317, 319
Emmahaven 197-8, 494
Ems 6
English *see* Great Britain
Enschede 119
Europe, European 1-2, 5-7, 11-2, 14-5, 17-8, 19-24, 26-9, 31-2, 35, 41-2, 48, 51, 59-60, 62-3, 66, 73-6, 81, 83-4, 91-4, 96-7, 99, 101-2, 106-7, 120, 125, 129-31, 134-5, 137, 139, 142-5, 147-8, 150, 152-7, 159, 162-3, 165-8, 174, 177, 179-80, 186, 197, 199, 201-29, 231-4, 235-7, 241, 243, 244, 247-8, 255-6, 262-3, 265, 267-9, 271, 274, 278, 281-3, 285-6, 289, 291, 298, 308, 310, 318, 320-3, 327, 331, 339, 342, 346-7, 349, 354, 356-7, 360, 366, 369, 375, 381, 383, 385, 387-94, 397, 399, 403, 406-7, 410, 412, 421-6, 427, 429, 431-2, 437, 439-41, 444, 450, 464, 467-8, 474-8, 481, 483, 487-9, 495, 498-9, 507-11, 515-6, 518-22, 525-6, 528, 530, 532-7, 540, 544, 547, 549, 552-6, 558-62, 565-7, 572-7, 579-80, 583-5, 587, 589-92, 594-7, 599-600, 602-4, 607-10, 616, 618-20, 622-3
Central - 288

Falmouth 433, 435
Far East 15-6, 74, 112, 115, 165, 320, 328, 349
Farne Islands 409
Faroer Islands 500
Fiji Islands 2
Finland 134
Flanders, Flemish 215, 620
Flores 454, 628
Flushing (Vlissingen) 119, 137, 204, 421
Formosa 2, 7, 73, 275
Fort de Kock 249
France, French 1-2, 6-7, 12-4, 17-8, 47, 55, 62, 68, 75, 83, 107-8, 111, 126, 128, 133, 135, 137, 141-2, 162, 175-9, 182-4, 201-4, 212, 214, 231-2, 279, 287, 289, 304, 308-9, 318, 321, 324, 326, 328, 340, 353-4, 356, 360, 364, 369-71, 374-8, 381, 391, 408, 429, 433, 444, 471, 489, 491, 505, 513
French Indochina 153, 177, 222, 591

Gallipoli 312
Garut 629
Geneva 66, 68, 243, 279, 309, 317, 346
Genoa 137, 142, 347
Germany, German 1-4, 6-7, 9-15, 17-8, 25, 67-8, 78, 82-3, 93-5, 99-101, 107, 110-1, 121, 126-8, 133-5, 137-8, 141-3, 145, 157, 162, 165-6, 170-1, 173-9, 181-7, 189-99, 201-8, 213-5, 218, 220-9, 231-2, 238, 240, 242, 246-7, 262, 279, 287-9, 296, 304-10, 313-4, 317-52, 353-7, 359, 361-70, 372-81, 383, 388, 391-4, 403, 407-16, 422-6, 429, 431-6, 438, 441-9, 451, 471, 490, 494-5, 498, 501-2, 509, 548, 560, 570, 591, 596-7, 611, 617-8, 620-3
Gibraltar 135, 278, 439
Gondong 609
Gorontalo 147, 159, 205, 611
Gowa 268
Gravesend 137
Great Britain, Britain, British, Briton 1-4, 6-7, 10-4, 17-8, 25, 47-9, 60, 65, 67, 74-5, 78, 82-3, 93-5, 99, 101, 108, 111-2, 120, 126-8, 133, 135, 137-9, 141-2, 145, 155, 161-3, 169-71, 175-87, 189-98, 201-6, 214, 219, 222-3, 225, 227-8, 231-2, 237, 240, 243, 287-90, 295, 298, 299, 301-12, 314, 317-37, 340, 346-51, 353, 355-7, 359-61, 364-81, 383, 388, 391, 403-13, 415-6, 418, 420-3, 425, 429-36, 440-51, 461, 470-1, 489, 491-2, 494-8, 501-6, 520, 551, 595, 615, 617-8, 621, 623
Greek 187
Guam 14, 100, 141, 187, 202

Haarlem 112-3, 119
Hadhramaut 313-4
Hague, The 5, 7, 10, 12, 14-6, 19, 32, 36, 48, 55, 58, 60, 66, 68, 70, 73, 79, 85, 89, 94, 108, 122, 126, 128-9, 134, 139, 146, 150, 164-5, 169, 172-3, 185, 191, 195-6, 199, 203-5, 214, 219, 227-8, 243, 255, 259-60, 273, 283-4, 299, 302-3,

Index of geographical names

314, 324, 330, 339-40, 351, 354, 356, 359-61, 367, 372, 376-7, 383, 387, 397, 406-7, 414, 416--8, 420, 426, 428, 431, 433-4, 438, 444, 446-51, 454, 466, 477, 485, 489-90, 499, 502-4, 520, 549, 562, 565, 568-70, 572, 587-, 597-8, 600, 609, 613, 615-6, 618, 621, 623, 625
Halifax 424
Halmahera 187
Hamburg 138, 412
Hanoi 185
Harwich 421
Hawai'i 9, 83, 334
Hellevoetsluis 569
Herzegovina 308
Hokkaido 2
Holland *see* Netherlands
Hollandia 177
Hong Kong 177, 305, 318, 321, 349-50, 380, 425, 434, 492, 513
Honolulu 193, 442
Hungary, Hungarians 1, 162, 223, 231, 342, 596

India, Indian, Indiërs 45-71, 74, 174, 192, 198, 288, 295, 305-6, 308-9, 317-9, 322-4, 330, 332, 334, 346-8, 351, 357, 372, 446, 587, 617, 623
Indian Ocean 182, 190
Indo-European 26-8, 35-7, 45-6, 51-2, 64-5, 94, 219, 225, 229, 245, 257, 456, 458, 465, 622
Indochina, Indo-Chinese 2, 185, 222, 370-1, 617
Iraq 319
Ireland 409
Ispahan 442
Istanbul 287, 289, 293-6, 307, 311-2, 348, 453, 627
Italy, Italian 1, 6, 18, 47, 74, 137, 142, 216, 231, 304, 374, 403, 491, 536

Jambi 153, 278, 404, 453-5, 466, 495, 524, 569
Jampea 182
Japan, Japanese 1-2, 7, 9-10, 12, 14-6, 18, 22, 28-9, 73-89, 93-5, 97, 99-101, 104, 108-9, 112, 117, 119, 121-2, 125, 134, 138, 152, 165, 174, 183-4, 197, 205-8, 228, 237, 240, 242-3, 249, 260-3, 266, 275, 299, 313, 321-2, 328, 330, 335-6, 343, 350, 351-2, 356, 384, 387, 392-5, 397, 420, 424-5, 431, 445, 447, 470-1, 472, 475, 479, 488, 494-5, 506, 508-9, 511, 513, 515, 517, 591, 595, 616, 619, 621, 630
Java, Javanese 5, 10-2, 14, 19, 23-4, 26, 32-3, 35-7, 39-42, 46, 49-52, 54, 57-9, 62, 64-5, 67-71, 75-7, 79, 83, 86-7, 91-4, 99, 101, 103-7, 109, 113, 115, 120, 122, 127, 129-30, 134, 139, 141-3, 145, 147, 151, 153, 156-7, 159, 161, 163, 166-7, 173, 175, 178, 180, 192-3, 205, 207, 208, 214, 216-7, 224, 229, 233-40, 242-5, 250-1, 247-8, 255-60, 263-5, 267-9, 271, 275, 277, 279-86, 291, 293, 302-3, 307-1, 314, 323-5, 327, 330, 333-4, 337-8, 340, 342-3, 347, 349-52, 363, 365-7, 369, 371, 376-7, 384, 387-8, 390-2, 395, 399-401, 405, 418, 425-6, 429, 431, 433-4, 438-43, 450, 453-9, 461-6, 469, 472-3, 477-8, 483, 485, 487, 489, 496-7, 499, 504, 506, 508, 510, 512, 514-5, 517-9, 521-2, 524-5, 527-33, 535, 537-41, 543-8, 551, 554-6, 559-60, 565-7, 571-3, 575-7, 580, 583, 591-3, 605, 607, 613-5, 618, 620, 624, 629-30
- Central 53, 339, 459, 461, 478, 534, 536, 589, 592, 629
- East 41, 45, 53, 111, 174, 202, 395, 455, 478, 534, 536, 540, 592, 630
- West 125, 152, 231, 234, 264, 269, 333, 395, 429, 523, 525, 627, 630
Java Sea 134, 166, 335
Jeddah 137, 297-304
Jepara 53, 244
Johore 306, 321
Jombang 527

Kaatsheuvel 119
Kaiser-Wilhelms-Land 3
Kangean Islands 166
Karimun 323
Karimun Jawa Islands 166
Kebumen 338

Kedah 303, 332
Kediri 304, 523, 533, 535, 543
Kedu 248, 257
Kelantan 306
Kiaochow 177
Kiel 373
Klingalese 332
Korea 260, 275
Kuala Lumpur 83
Kudus 20, 468, 554-6, 558, 572, 576
Kupang 60, 62, 150
Kutaraja 189
Kuyper Island 570

Lampung 153, 541
Landesnaes 409
Latin America 2
Le Hâvre 135
Leiden 296
Lembang 209
Leuwiliang 527
Libya 117, 295, 309
Limburg 128, 204, 620
Lombok 154, 180, 187, 278, 455
London 3, 10, 12-3, 15, 74, 126-7, 131, 135, 141, 162, 170-1, 202-4, 288-9, 295, 302-3, 308, 318, 326, 328, 337, 340, 351, 353-7, 359-60, 363-4, 366-8, 371-2, 375, 377-9, 385, 403-4, 406-9, 415, 421-3, 425, 431-5, 442, 444-51, 492, 494, 496-7, 502, 528, 618, 623-4
Lorraine 7, 9
Los Angeles 317
Lourenço Marques 187
Louvain 225, 251

Madagascar 318
Madiun 50, 64, 327, 523
Madrid 279
Madura 23, 89, 166, 186, 233, 263, 519, 529, 592, 629
Magelang 64, 213, 239, 241, 245, 247, 249, 269, 276, 327
Majalaya 554, 556
Majapahit 463
Makassar, Makassarese 77, 117, 165, 178, 181-2, 191, 193-4, 250, 269, 334, 368, 376, 494, 630

Malacca 181
Malang 50, 55, 155, 209-10, 286, 523, 537, 561, 566, 580, 608
Malaya, Malay 29, 36, 52, 54, 56, 58-9, 75, 117, 183, 197, 207-8, 228, 232, 236, 241, 252, 261-2, 274, 279, 294, 301, 306-7, 310-1, 318, 321, 326-7, 330, 347, 410, 455, 457-9, 462, 465-7, 477-8, 484, 519-20, 526, 532-3, 537, 544, 548, 551, 556, 560, 572-5, 580, 585, 592-3, 600, 603, 610, 615, 627
Malay-Chinese 247, 471
Malay-Dutch 580
Malay Peninsula 174, 177, 183, 302-3, 305, 314, 318, 322-4, 327, 330, 336, 357, 407, 496, 547, 603
Malay States 305
Malta 135
Manado, Manadonese 14, 93, 117, 139, 141, 165, 168, 258, 335, 336, 528, 567, 587
Manchuria 242, 614
Manila 100, 187, 189-90, 206, 333, 335-6, 442, 492
Marseilles 135, 137, 142, 383
Mecca 137, 291-4, 297, 299, 301-4, 308, 314
Medan 62, 88, 137, 156, 161, 175, 196, 201, 207, 210-1, 214, 242, 249-50, 270-1, 308, 323, 331, 347, 369, 376, 424, 445, 493, 495, 514
Medina 301
Mediterranean Sea, Mediterranean 278, 288, 411, 421
Melbourne 4, 42
Merak 335
Mesopotamia 305
Mexico, Mexican 82, 335, 555
Micronesia 100
Middle East 33, 76, 232, 291, 298, 300-1, 312-3, 319-20, 324
Minahasa 85, 98, 252, 256, 277-8, 282, 455, 524, 555, 563, 565, 571, 603, 607
Mindoro Sea 9
Mönchengladbach 449, 451
Moluccas 180, 239, 245, 252, 277-8, 338, 555, 563, 565, 587, 611
Montenegro, Montenegrins 379

Morocco, Moroccan 17, 117, 222, 309
Moscow 82
Munich 48

Nagasaki 410
Nauen 442-3
Near East 317
Negeri Sembilan 306
Netherlands, Dutch, Dutchman, Holland 1-7, 11-2, 15, 17, 19-27, 29, 31-3, 35-7, 40-5, 47, 49-53, 55-7, 59, 63-5, 67-70, 73-9, 81, 85-6, 88-9, 91-2, 96, 125-6, 128-31, 133-5, 137-9, 142-8, 154, 156, 159-67, 169-77, 180, 182, 184-7, 189-90, 192-3, 196-9, 201-5, 207-8, 210-5, 214-5, 217-29, 231-34, 236-46, 248-53, 255-84, 286-7, 289-90, 293-304, 307, 312-5, 323-8, 330-6, 338-40, 342-3, 345-51, 354-7, 359-65, 367-71, 373-80, 381-2, 384-5, 387, 389-93, 395, 399-400, 403, 405-8, 410-7, 419-20, 422-6, 427-51, 453-61, 463-73, 475, 477, 480-2, 485, 487-515, 517, 522, 524, 527-9, 531-9, 541, 543-5, 548-9, 551-2, 554-8, 560-2, 565, 567-76, 579-81, 583, 585, 587-8, 591, 594-605, 607-11, 615-26, 629-30
Netherlands Antilles 403, 428
Neu-Lauenburg Group 3, see also Duke of York Islands
Neu-Mecklenburg 3, see also New Ireland
Neu-Pommern 3, see also New Britain
New Britain 3, see also Neu-Pommern
New Britain Archipelago 3, see also Bismarck Archipelago
New Guinea 1-4, 24, 182
    Dutch - 247
    East - 3-4
    West - 4
New Ireland 3, see also Neu-Mecklenburg
New York 288, 317, 334, 349, 391-2, 410, 422-3, 425-6, 445
New Zealand 82, 621
Ngawi 607
Nias 329
Nile 9

Nordenham 14
Norfolk 424
North Sea 93, 107, 126, 134, 137, 202, 204, 409, 412, 414
Norway, Norwegian 408, 421, 432, 435, 500
Nova Scotia 424

Odessa 289
Oldenzaal 119
Onrust 178, 569-71
Orange Free State 10
Osaka 373
Oxford 317

Pacangakan 53
Pacific 2-4, 9, 73-4, 82-3, 100, 112, 141, 182, 208, 335, 385, 387, 447
    - Islands 28
    - Ocean 9, 112, 470
Pacitan 523
Padang 23, 85, 88, 91, 165, 180, 189, 210, 278, 323, 329, 343, 359, 422, 424, 447, 495
Pahang 330
Paleleh 335
Palembang 294, 313, 376, 453, 455, 528, 543
Panama Canal 81-2, 100, 410, 422, 424, 440-1, 500
Pangkalan Brandan 247
Papua 627
    - New Guinea 177
Paris 10, 47-8, 128, 131, 185, 202-4, 353-6, 360, 363, 378, 431, 435, 620-1
Pasir 310
Pasuruan 45, 494, 523
Pathans 306
Pekalongan 50, 247, 609
Peking 32, 78, 206
Pelabuhan Ratu 125
Penang 137, 183, 299, 318, 323, 333, 336, 404, 432, 603
Perak 306, 333
Persia 117, 309, 325
Persian Gulf 288
Philippines, Filipino 2, 5, 7, 9-10, 19, 49, 76-7, 83-4, 100, 119, 266, 334, 336,

373, 378, 410, 449, 454, 470, 494
Poland 134
Pontianak 76, 141, 166, 201, 333
Port Arthur 14, 81, 104
Port Said 302, 421
Portugal, Portuguese 7, 373
Preange, Priangan 57, 592
Probolinggo 202, 327
Prussia, Prussian 2, 14-5, 47, 222, 569
Puerto Rico 141
Pulau Sambu 404
Pulau Tujuh 153, 322
Punjabis 306
Purbalingga 483
Purwakarta 269
Purworejo 63, 269

Rampah 572
Rangoon 153-4, 163, 184, 319, 336, 370, 418, 492, 497, 528, 593, 615
Red Sea 198, 278, 288
Rembang 40, 63, 555
Rhine 6, 434, 491
Riau Archipelago 77, 85, 153, 178, 191, 322, 404, 525
Rotterdam 119, 127, 181, 192, 349, 355, 381, 390, 424, 436, 623
Russia, Russian, Russo, Soviet 1, 6, 12, 16, 18, 73-8, 93, 117, 119, 126, 183, 231, 290, 299, 304-5, 309, 311, 318, 321, 324, 372, 440, 483, 508, 547-8, 558, 560, 589, 596, 611, 630

Sabah 2
Sabang 88, 103, 165, 171, 174, 178, 180, 189, 191-2, 195-6, 199, 278, 371-3, 377-8, 380, 442, 494, 505
Saigon 141, 163, 184-5, 369-71
Salatiga 151, 213, 269, 609
Samarinda 359
Samoa 2, 5, 9, 134
San Francisco 202, 284, 317, 324, 326-7, 332, 334, 349-51, 387, 410, 420, 422-6, 449, 489
Santo Domingo 141
Saparua 245, 583
Sarajevo 465
Saudi Arabia 307

Saxony 47
Scandinavia 47, 418
Scheldt 174, 184, 202, 204-5
Scheveningen 570
Scotland, Scottish 126, 409, 414, 416, 505
Sebastopol 289
Selangor 306
Semarang 9, 23, 50, 61-4, 121, 147-9, 151-2, 161, 166, 176, 178-80, 196, 212-5, 222, 234, 239, 241, 244, 247, 250-1, 260, 268-9, 307, 357, 368, 376, 418-9, 428, 430, 455, 459, 463, 465, 472-4, 477-81, 485, 492-3, 522, 523, 530, 548-9, 552-5, 557-8, 562, 564-5, 572-3, 580, 594, 609-1, 613
Senen 272
Serang 301, 626
Seram 187, 453
Serbia, Serbs 125, 238, 257, 379
Shanghai 14, 139, 206, 224, 318, 325, 329, 349-50
Shantung 242
Shetland Islands 409
Siam 153, 235, 325, 334, 528, 540, 591
Siberia 423, 508
Sidoarjo 248
Sierra Leone 307
Sikhs 306
Simalur 187, 192
Simeulue 187
Singapore 1, 13, 31, 40, 42, 60, 75, 84, 137, 158, 164, 169, 177, 181, 183-5, 187, 191, 204, 262, 299-300, 306, 318-9, 321-6, 329, 332, 336-7, 348-50, 352, 356, 359, 373, 383, 404-6, 408, 412, 425, 432, 444-5, 450, 471, 492-3, 495-6
Situbondo 192, 235
Socorro Island 335
Soesterberg 281
Somalis 309
South Africa *see* South African Republic
South African Republic, South Africa 10-2, 209, 228, 373, 383, 387, 410, 415, 505, 537
Soviet *see* Russia
Spain, Spanish 9, 15, 19, 47, 547, 558, 593
Straits *see* Straits Settlements
Straits of Dover 409

Straits of Gibraltar 421
Straits of Makassar 335
Straits of Malacca 15, 322, 359, 373
Straits Settlements 11, 29, 42, 60, 135,
    137, 147, 183, 191, 207, 225, 296, 299,
    305, 312, 320, 322-4, 326, 329, 333,
    335, 405, 447, 496-8, 512-3, 591, 603
Stuttgart 73
Suez Canal 110, 278, 309, 410-2, 415, 421,
    424, 618
Sukabumi 125, 152, 155, 209-10, 269, 630
Sulawesi 85
    North - 537, 629
Sulu Archipelago 4, 15
Sumatra 1-2, 5, 15, 42, 82, 84, 99, 104-6,
    130, 142-3, 153, 155-6, 159, 178, 186-
    7, 198, 207, 215, 236, 249, 286, 294-5,
    323-5, 327, 329, 332, 343, 347, 351,
    383, 388, 404, 424, 436, 439-41, 453-4,
    466, 473, 479, 487, 495, 515, 532, 541,
    551, 572, 629
    East - 249, 270, 439, 541, 603
    East Coast of - 26, 153, 160, 271, 332,
    369, 371, 420, 506, 592
    North - 159, 198, 209, 247, 603
    West - 76, 105, 270, 522, 627, 629
    West Coast of - 85, 241, 528, 543
Sumedang 582-3
Sumenep 186
Sunda, Sundanese 235, 239, 583
Surabaya 11, 21, 23, 30-2, 42, 50, 63-4, 88,
    96, 111, 113, 123, 130, 149-51, 161,
    165-6, 171, 173, 176-7, 181-4, 209,
    212-5, 217, 223-4, 245-6, 269, 301,
    315, 323-4, 329, 377, 392, 406, 430,
    439, 457, 473-4, 478, 481, 493-5, 521-
    2, 527, 546, 548, 551, 553, 557, 561-4,
    567, 569-72, 574, 589, 591-2, 594, 606,
    609, 611, 629
Surakarta 37, 40, 152, 207, 241, 257, 269,
    276, 340, 448, 458-9, 463-4, 477, 484,
    523, 532, 543, 558, 588, 609
Suriname 403, 428, 541, 630
Swatow 380
Sweden, Swedish 357, 377, 432, 444
Switzerland, Swiss 17, 47, 68, 142, 243,
    279, 317, 403
Sydney 321, 373, 383

Syria 222

Taiwan 260
Tamils 306
Tangerang 53
Tangling Barracks 198
Tanimbar 454
Tanjung Priok 87, 165-6, 177, 187, 194-5,
    199, 208, 322, 325, 330, 335-6, 359,
    373, 405, 424, 439, 494-5, 505, 544,
    618
Tanjungpandan 153
Tapanuli 453, 524, 590
Tarakan 166
Tegal 50, 609
Telok Dalem Bay 187, 190
Telukbetung 494
Thailand 324, 371, 617
Thursday Island 169
Tibet 78
Timor 2, 60, 62, 258, 331, 338, 455, 485
    Dutch - 150
    Portuguese - 4
Tokyo 73, 76, 82, 84-6, 89, 141, 165, 174,
    205-6, 228, 237, 242, 260, 342, 379,
    393, 470
Toli-Toli 629
Transvaal 10-2, 115, 117
Trenggalek 540
Trengganu 306
Tripolitania 117
Tunisia, Tunisians 222
Turkey, Turkish, Turks 22, 117, 121, 137,
    176, 198, 237-8, 246-7, 249, 287-321,
    330, 333, 339-40, 342-3, 347, 350, 355,
    373, 408, 411, 453, 472

United States *see* United States of
    America
United States of America, United States
    1, 9-10, 13, 18, 19, 22, 76, 81-2, 93,
    99-100, 112, 134, 138, 187, 201, 284,
    309, 317, 324-5, 331-2, 334-6, 348-9,
    351, 354, 373, 387-95, 406-8, 410, 413,
    415-6, 418, 421-4, 425-6, 432, 434-6,
    438-40, 442-5, 447, 449, 470, 488-92,
    494, 496, 505-6, 510-3, 515, 551, 569,
    616, 618, 620-1

Utrecht 213, 613

Venezuela, Venezuelan 210, 494
Vesoix 68
Vienna 125, 131, 166, 226, 290, 305
Vladivostok 81, 372, 434, 508
Vlissingen 119, *see also* Flushing

Wageningen 119
Washington 9-10, 83, 141, 317, 325, 378, 408, 426, 435, 437-8, 442, 449, 490, 494, 497, 505-6, 512, 618-9
West, Western 32, 207, 237, 258, 293, 297, 313, 451, 469, 472, 494, 575, 602, 613, 624
West Indies 133

Wijnkoopsbaai 125

Yap 14, 139, 141, 206
Yemen 313
Yogyakarta 50, 53, 129-30, 136, 151, 212, 214-6, 240, 244, 247, 340, 395, 520, 523, 532, 545, 581, 592
Ypres 222

Zanzibar 13
Zeeland 620
Zurich 66, 68, 317, 347, 349, 576-7

Index of personal names

Aalst, C.J.K. van 121-3, 132-3, 149, 161, 164, 280-1, 355, 360-1, 364, 366, 399-400, 410, 441, 446
Abdoel Moeis *see* Moeis, Abdoel
Abdulaziz 290
Abdulhamid II 287, 289-90, 294
Abendanon, J.H. 464
Adiningrat, Pangeran Ario 239
Aguinaldo, Emilio 49, 76
Ahmad bin Abdoellah Bobsaid 214
Aken, W.A. van 112
Albarda, J.W. 279
Alexandria, Queen 341
Alimin 478, 482, 585
André de la Porte, G. 331
Argawisjaja, M. 572
Arisugawa, Prince 16
Asbeck, D. van 205, 260
Atkins, Thomas 62

Baars, A. 473, 479, 481-2, 484, 549-52, 556, 570, 574, 586, 588-91, 595, 608-1
Balfour, A.J. 126, 502-4
Ballin, Albert 412-3
Bauduin, F. 204
Bäumer, K. 343
Beaufort, W.H. de 291
Beckett, W.R.D. 329, 333, 336, 375, 379, 408
Belloni, F.H. 580
Berding, Frans 66
Berretty, D.W. 229, 505, 603
Bethmann Hollweg, Th. von 7
Bezema, J. 569-71
Birnie, D. 617

Bismarck, Prince Otto von 2-3, 5
Bobsaid, Ahmad bin Abdoellah *see* Ahmad bin Abdoellah Bobsaid
Boeka *see* P.C.C. Hansen
Böhm, George 335-6
Bogaardt, W.H. 296
Boon, G.J. 221, 269, 343, 378, 448, 536
Boon, A. van der 111, 273
Borel, Henri 81
Bosscha, K.A.R. 273, 580
Brandon, H.G. 268, 274
Brandsteder, J.A. 560-4, 567, 570, 586, 595, 606-7, 610-1
Bron, J.A.M. 470, 494-5, 567, 569-71, 582
Brooshooft, P. 128
Burink, G. van 611
Bijl de Vroe, C.L.M. 111, 357, 493, 500, 505, 586

Campbell-Bannerman, Henry 126
Carlisle, T.F. 169-70, 184, 193-4
Carpentier Alting, E.H. 273
Carpentier Alting, J.H. 561, 600-1
Casajangan Soripada 249
Cecil *see* Gascoyne Cecil of Chelwood, Edgar Algernon Robert
Chakravarti, Rham Chandra Kanta 349-50
Chattopadhyaya, Virendranath 347, 349
Churchill, W.S. 202
Clockener Brousson, H.C.C. 94, 97
Cloux, Ch.Ph. de 467-8
Colijn, H. 111, 605
Cort van der Linden, P.W.A. 130, 355, 432, 504

Coster, B. 580
Cramer, Ch.G. 397, 399, 482, 540, 570, 584, 595-7, 600, 606, 616
Cremer, J.Th. 281, 291, 493
Creutzberg, K.F. 400, 549, 551
Crowe, E. 127
Cunow, Heinrich 68

Daalen, G.C.E. van 87, 106
Danudirdjo Setiabudhi *see* Douwes Dekker, Ernest François Eugène
Danoeredjo, Ario Adipati Pangeran 214
Danoesoegondo, Temenggoeng 276, 280
Darnakoesoemo 261, 459, 461-2, 466, 479, 548
Darsoeki 479
Darsono 478, 483, 565, 575-6, 589, 595, 610, 613, 630
DD *see* Douwes Dekker, Ernest François Eugène
Dédéism *see* Douwes Dekker, Ernest François Eugène
Dekker, H.W. 480
Deromps, Mathilde 48, 67
Deventer, C.Th. van 57, 252, 281
Devevere, Hans von 333
Dewantara *see* Soewardi Soerjaningrat
Dhingra, Madan Lal 47, 67
Diehn, August 329-30
Dinger, Jan 379-80
Diponogoro 258, 480, 483, 548
Djajabaja (pen-name) *see* Tjipto Mangoenkoesoema
Djajadiningrat, R.A.A. Achmad 273, 301, 579-80, 602-3, 626
Djam, Mohamad 270
Djojosoediro, R. 591
Does de Willebois, P.J.J.S.M. van der 228, 289
Donald, Ronald 404
Douwes Dekker, Ernest François Eugène, Danudirdjo Setiabudhi, DD, Dédéism, Nes 28, 45-55, 58-61, 65-9, 243-4, 247, 261, 317, 327, 346-50, 352, 456, 458, 465, 471, 479-80, 484, 545, 548, 551, 572, 574-7, 608, 622, 627, 630
Dunn, W.N. 420, 496-7

Duymaer van Twist, L.F. 93
Dwidjosewojo, Ngahebi 239-40, 250-1, 263, 275, 279-83, 285-6, 399, 470, 520, 588, 626

Egloffstein, August von und zu 342
Ellis, E.C. 320
Emma, Queen Mother 280
Engel, L. 561
Enver Bei 339
Enver Pasha 339

Ferdinand, Franz 67, 311, 465
Feydeau, Georges 213
Fliche, H. 176, 370
Fock, D. 604-5, 625-7
Fokkens, F. 89
Folkersma, A.F. 625
Franz Joseph, Emperor 339
Fukuda 626

Gascoyne Cecil of Chelwood, Edgar Algernon Robert 432-5, 451, 490, 503
George V, King 307, 435
Gerlings, J.Th. 281
Geuns, M. van 174-5, 221, 224
Ghert, E. van 173
Goenawan 453, 466
Götte, R. 359
Graeff, A.C.D. de 87-8, 582
Greve, W.R. de 104-5, 109, 125, 267, 313-4, 559-60
Grey, Edward 126, 169, 191, 203, 355, 627
Gijn, A. van 102, 108

Haastert, W.K.S. van 212, 343
Haig, Douglas 310
Ham, J.G. van 51, 61
Hamengkubuwono VII 136
Haminsar 248
Han Tjiong King 214
Hansen, P.C.C. (Boeka) 255
Har Dayal 48, 317, 346-7, 349
Hardinge, Charles 198, 318, 324
Hartmann, E. von 6
Hatta, Mohammad 628
Haushofer, Karl 82
Hazeu, G.A.J. 21, 57, 69, 236-7, 295, 315,

454, 478, 484
Heekeren, E.A.A. van 579, 594, 610, 626
Helfferich, Emil 157, 203, 222-3, 325-6, 329-30, 335-7, 340, 342, 351, 378, 394, 419, 514, 624
Helfferich, Theodor 325-6, 329-30, 334-7, 351
Hendrik, Prince 208, 280, 339
Henken, J. 189
Hensen, R.O. 189-90
Hertlein, Lydia 48
Heutsz Jr., J.B. van 120, 284
Hinloopen Labberton, D. van 271, 274, 277, 279-81, 283-6, 395, 399, 473
Hirsch, S.J. 269
Holdert, H.M.C. 356
Horst-den Boer, Mrs Ter 213
Houtsma, J. 603
Houven van Oordt, J.B. van der 214
Howard, Henry 10

Idenburg, A.W.F. 36, 41-2, 46, 57-8, 60-1, 65, 68-9, 81, 87-8, 95, 106, 108, 111, 121-2, 129, 139-40, 145, 147-50, 156-7, 161-5, 167, 169, 172-5, 177, 182, 185, 189, 191-3, 196, 199, 204-6, 211, 213-4, 219-20, 224, 226, 228, 238, 241, 252, 258-9, 266, 274-5, 279-81, 296, 322-3, 331-4, 340, 343, 346, 359-60, 363, 367, 370-1, 394, 412, 450, 454, 459, 464-5, 478, 533, 544, 555-7, 570-1, 584, 589, 592, 596-8, 605, 618, 620
Ismail bin Abdoellah Alatas, S. 603

s'Jacob, H. 267, 271-5, 278, 285-6, 561, 601, 620
James, Edward Holten 48
Janssen, T.J. 57-8
Jerram, Thomas Henry Martyn 186, 191, 194
Joesoef, Moehammad 457-8, 472, 478, 482
Johnstone, Alan 191-3, 203, 337, 360, 366, 410
Juist, M. 462
Juliana, Princess 339, 585, 598
Jumbo 214

Kan, Hok Hoey 601

Karnebeek, H.A. van 619-20
Kat, R. de 602
Kautsky, Karl 68
Khan, Aga 305, 307-8
Keil, Karl Ernst 342, 345
Kerkkamp, H.C. 625
Ketner, H. 270, 273
Kiewiet de Jonge, H.J. 228-9
Kitchener, Horatio Herbert Earl 319
Koch, D.M.G. 45-6, 53
Koesoemo Oetojo, R.M.T.A. 601
Koesoemodiningrat, Ario 276, 280
Kol, H.H. van 1, 5, 9, 25, 32, 45, 79, 83, 103, 106, 108, 296, 355, 397-8, 418, 437, 456-7
Kolthoff, M. 387
Koning, M.C. 268, 561, 580, 582, 603
Koningsberger, J.C. 582, 597, 600, 602
Kouw, O.H. 603
Kraan, D. 571
Kraft, C.F. Vincent 323, 325, 347-9, 357
Krishnavarma, Shiyamaji 48, 66, 68, 317, 346
Kröller, A.G. 355, 360-1
Kropveld, D.G.J.H. 123
Kruyff, H. de 384
Kuchlin, E.A. 195
Kuijper, A. 74

Laoh, F. 277, 282, 285-6
Lauterbach, Julius 198, 320, 323-4, 329
Lelyveld, Th.B. van 212
Lettow-Vorbeck, Paul von 373
Liebknecht, Karl 608
Liefrinck, J.H. 455
Lievegoed, A.J. 134
Limburg Stirum, J.P. van 158, 180, 199, 226-9, 273-4, 276, 357-8, 371, 373-4, 386-7, 405-6, 411-2, 420, 426, 428, 442, 444, 449-50, 454, 465, 485, 492, 495, 497, 505, 510-3, 517, 519, 529-30, 538-40, 551-2, 559-62, 569, 584, 587, 594, 596, 598-605, 609, 611, 616, 620, 624-5
Limburg Stirum, Mrs C.M.R. van 454
Locher-Scholten, E.B. 19, 25
Loon, G. van 225
Loudon, J. 85, 169, 191, 193, 196, 337,

354-5, 360, 368, 388, 406-7, 433, 438, 441, 445-6, 449-50, 490-2, 502-3, 617
Lovink, H.J. 370, 382, 396, 616
Lowther, Gerald 288, 627
Lübcke, H.H.V.F.A. 189
Luxemburg, Rosa 608

Madjapaïtatma *see* Tjipto Mangoenkoesoemo
Manchu 31, 40
Manen, C.A. van 361
Mangoenkoesoemo, Tjipto (pseudonym Mintarogo, pen-name Djajabaja, Madjapaïtatma) 53-5, 57, 59, 64-6, 68-70, 76, 227, 248, 250, 455-7, 459, 461-5, 467, 469-71, 479-80, 484-5, 548, 556, 572, 574-5, 587, 592, 596-7, 600, 616, 622, 626-7, 629
Marco Kartodikromo, Mas 459-60, 462-9, 471, 482, 552, 576, 610, 628, 630
Marees van Swinderen, R. de 502-4
Marmelstein, A.F. 148-50, 164
Marx, Karl, Marxism, Marxist 33-4, 455, 463, 467, 480, 622
Mas Marco *see* Marco Kartodikromo
Mathewson, Arthur Law 331
Matsumoto 261
Mechmed V 289
Meester, Th.A. de 123
Melvil van Lynden, R. 16
Mendels, M. 557
Metz van Enghuizen, Van 629
Meulemans, E. 439
Michielsen, J.P. 106, 151, 165, 167-8, 173, 205, 210, 213-4, 236-7, 338, 453, 559
Minami, Yoroshi 260-2, 275
Mintarogo *see* Tjipto Mangoenkoesoemo
Moeis, Abdoel 57, 180, 248, 264-5, 275-6, 278-86, 311, 399-400, 412, 421, 426, 470, 476-8, 509, 529, 533, 555, 558, 576, 579, 587-9, 591, 599-600, 603-4, 608, 613, 622, 628-30
Möller, Erwin 189-90, 323-4
Moens, Karel 443
Moestapa, Hassan H. 301
Mohamed Saleh *see* Saleh, Mohamed
Moltke, H.J.L. von 317
Monsanto, H.V. 227

Montagu, Edwin 446
Mother, Queen *see* Queen Emma
Mücke, Hellmuth von 197-8
Muhammad 483
Müller, A.H. 149
Muller, W. 224
Multatuli 45
Muurling, W. 267, 273, 275, 328, 471, 557, 561, 574, 580, 582, 613

Napoleon 2, 55, 104, 218
Nes *see* Douwes Dekker, Ernest François Eugène
Neuman 277
Niti Adiningrat, R.T.A. 214
Nitobe, Inazo 393
Notodirodjo, Prince 50

Ong Sin Kwie 336-7, 351
Oppenheimer, Francis 356, 366-8
Ottolander, T. 614

Pabst, J.C. 82, 228, 252, 286
Paku Alam III 53
Paku Alam V 50
Panatas, Kebo 459
Papen, Franz von 325
Pasha, Enver 310
Pillai, Champakaraman 347-9
Pinke, F. 105, 107, 151, 165-6, 169, 172-4, 180-1, 184-6, 189-91, 193-4, 198-9, 205-6, 214, 322, 329, 333-4, 336, 470, 568-9
Pleyte, Th.B. 18, 20, 40-1, 68-70, 97-8, 122-3, 135, 139, 141, 145-7, 149, 156, 161-3, 169-70, 174, 181, 189, 192-3, 196, 205-6, 211, 226-8, 243-4, 252, 273, 279, 281-2, 285, 297, 328, 340, 346, 360, 363-4, 367-9, 371, 373-4, 384, 387-9, 406, 413-5, 420, 425-6, 437-8, 441-5, 449-50, 455, 464, 474, 498, 500, 502, 504-5, 510-3, 539-40, 549, 551-2, 559, 562
Posthuma, F.E. 355, 416-20, 436, 438, 501
Princip, Gavrilo 67, 311

Quist, W.J. 349
Raalte, J. van 119

Radjiman 600
Rafiqi, Abdul Salam 330-1, 351
Rambonnet, J.J. 93, 95-7, 99, 171, 173, 197, 503, 505, 569
Ravesteijn, W. van 595
Razoux Kühr, Ch. 473
Reigersberg Versluys, J.C. van 396
Rhemrev, W.V. 268, 273, 277-8, 280-1, 283-5, 426, 582-3, 615
Ricklefs, M.C. 627
Ridout, Dudley Howard 306, 320-1
Rietschoten, C.H. van 559, 561, 563, 566-7, 582, 602
Rifat, M.M. 309, 317, 324
Rinkes, D.A. 36-7, 39-40, 43, 50, 53, 57, 93, 229, 246, 252, 259, 296, 301-2, 304, 315-6, 331-2, 454, 460-2, 464, 478, 484-5, 588
Rinze, Jac. 117
Rivai, Abdoel 286, 294, 579
Roosevelt, Theodore 270
Roy, J.J. le 13, 139, 443
Ruempol, C.A. 552
Ruijs de Beerenbrouck, C.J.M. 596-7
Rijfsnijder, H. 195, 231, 331, 346

Saladin 287
Saleh, Mohamed 249
Sandberg, C.G.S. 113, 115, 117
Sastrowidjono, A. 596, 600
Satiman 267
Schaap, J. 603
Schlieper, Carl 367, 376
Schlieper, Walter 367
Schmutzer, J. 543, 598
Schotman, R.A. 481-2, 586
Schrieke, B.J.O. 221
Schumann, W.M.G. 601
Selam, Abdul see Abdul Salam Rafiqi
Semaoen 457-8, 478-9, 482, 553-4, 556, 565, 575, 589, 591, 595, 610, 613, 622, 629-30
Sibinga Mulder, J. 616
Singa Mangaradja 278
Sjahrir, Soetan 628
Smalhout, H.N. 380
Sneevliet, H.J.F.M. 457-8, 463, 465, 467, 473, 479-80, 482, 484, 520, 548-9, 552-3, 556-8, 560-6, 579, 586, 588-9, 591, 594-5, 606-1
Snouck Hurgronje, Christiaan 291-8, 312, 315, 455
Soedarsono, Raden 565
Soegono 576
Soekarno 46, 401, 627
Soemarsono 251
Soemataram 243
Soerio Atmodjo 580
Soerjaningrat, Soewardi (Ki Hadjar Dewantara) 46, 53-5, 57-60, 65-71, 227, 282-3, 456, 462-4, 466, 472, 477, 480, 485, 575, 613, 622, 627, 630
Soeropati 76
Soewardi see Soerjaningrat, Soewardi
Sollewijn Gelpke, S.P. 464
Soselisa, J.A. 273, 580, 603
Sosrowerdojo, Temenggoeng 580
Spijkman, N. 229, 252, 250, 477
Stam. J.C. 482
Stokvis, J.E. 220, 222-3, 474, 597
Stokvis, Z. 544
Strickland, Walter W. 48, 66, 317
Sun Yat Sen 484
Swart, H.N.A. 270, 580, 582
Swinderen, R. de Marees van see Marees van Swinderen, R. de

Tafel, Albert 78
Tafsir Anom, R. Pengoeloe 301
Takekoshi, Yosaburo 206-7, 237, 349, 351, 393, 471
Talma, D. 521, 551, 592, 597-601, 604, 606, 616, 624
Teeuwen, J.J.E. 473, 579, 596-7, 600-2, 609-10
Tersteeg, H. 173-4
Thajeb 600
Thomas, Th. 379
Tirpitz, Alfred von 7
Tirtodanoedjo 610
Tirtokoesoemo, A.A. 580
Tjipto see Mangoenkoesoemo, Tjipto
Tjokroaminoto, H.O.S. 22, 39, 233, 251, 276-7, 286, 301, 316, 340, 463, 482-3, 527, 535, 539-40, 554, 556, 572, 579, 589-90, 592, 595-6, 598, 600, 608, 613-

4, 629-30
Toemenggoeng, Soetan 272
Townley, Walter 355, 433-4, 446, 503
Treub, M.W.F. 133, 281, 436
Troelstra, P.J. 25, 120, 130, 477, 491, 591, 596-7, 603

Uhlenbeck, G.W. 337, 457, 468, 483-4, 549
Utika, S. 87-8

Veen, Jos van 48
Verkade, Eduard 130
Visser, C.W. de 117
Vissering, G. 119, 284
Vliegen, W.H. 480

Waal Malefijt, J.H. de 36, 69, 228
Ward, Reverend 201
Warnecke, F.A. 377
Waworoentoe, A.L. 601, 603, 626
Weckherlin, W.F.H. von 287-8
Wehde, Alfred 335-6
Welter, Ch.J.I.M. 79
Westerveld, D.J.A. 481
Weijden, J. van der 255-6, 258
Wignjadisastra 57, 248

Wilhelm I, Emperor 3, 621
Wilhelm II, Emperor 3-4, 287-8, 294, 320
Wilhelmina, Queen 16, 57, 63-5, 102, 110, 121, 128, 147, 176, 208, 214, 239, 241, 245, 252, 270, 272-4, 276, 279-80, 284, 294, 315-6, 339, 341, 435, 477, 493, 505, 580, 597-9, 603, 625
Wilm, A. 195
Wilson, Woodrow 620
Windels, E. 178, 220, 225-6, 324, 326, 328-9, 337, 345
Winkler, C. 69-70, 463
Wolff, J. 299-300, 302-3, 312
Wijbrands, Karel 221
Wijck, C.H.A. van der 111
Wyllie, Curzon 47
Wijnkoop, D.J. 605

Yap Hong Sing 214
Young, Arthur Henderson 320-2

Zaalberg, Karel 221, 603
Zain, Muhammad 248
Zeilinga, E.A. 273, 603
Zimmermann, Theodor Victor 223